THE TRAINING AND DEVELOPMENT SOURCEBOOK

THE TRAINING AND DEVELOPMENT SOURCEBOOK

Edited by

- **Lloyd Baird**
  Boston University

- **Craig Eric Schneier**
  University of Maryland

- **Dugan Laird**
  Consultant

Human Resource Development Press
Amherst, Massachusetts

ISBN Number: 0-914234-64-1

First printing: October 1983
Second printing: February 1985
Third printing: November 1985

Manufactured in the United States of America

CONTENTS

PREFACE

This book deals with designing, implementing, and evaluating training and development to improve individual and organizational performance. Its purpose is the same as our first book in the "Sourcebook" series, "The Performance Appraisal Sourcebook," to provide a unique combination of materials that are above all useful for managing personnel programs and practices. We have included readings, checklists, questionnaires, models, and methods for analysis that we and others have found valuable in our consulting and teaching.

The materials included are the best we could find on training and development programs, their design, methods of teaching, management support, implementation, transfer of skills, and evaluation. We have selected and organized the materials so they can be used by both professionals well established in the training and development field and those learning.

Following the format of the "Sourcebook" series, our checklists, questionnaires, models, and analyses can be duplicated, converted to overhead transparencies, or modified in any way that makes them useful to you. Of course, materials referenced from other publications are copyrighted by those publishers and appropriate permission should be sought from them.

We would like to acknowledge the organizations and practitioners that have given us the opportunity to be involved in their training and development. From them we have learned what works. We are also indebted to the authors and publishers who have given us permission to include their materials. Finally we are grateful to Fern Lazarus, Ray Mariani, and Michelle Poirier. They were relentless in their search for that one perfect article or example. Without them this book would have lacked many of the unique materials included.

Realizing the field of training and development is changing at an ever increasing pace, we will be updating these materials as more advanced and insightful ones become available. Your suggestions and contributions are always welcome. Feel free to send them to any of us.

Lloyd Baird
School of Management
Boston University
621 Commonwealth Avenue
Boston, MA 02215

Craig Eric Schneier
College of Business
  and Management
University of Maryland
College Park, MD 20740

Dugan Laird
9 Willow Drive
Decatur, GA 30038

INTRODUCTION: PURPOSE AND USE OF THE TRAINING AND DEVELOPMENT SOURCEBOOK

The field of training and development is growing now faster than ever before. As organizations become more complex and we move more and more toward an information- and service-based economy, people truly become organization's most important resource—a resource that must be managed and developed. For a long period organizations too often regarded training and development as an expendable part of personnel administration that could be cut any time the budget needed balancing. Now we are entering an era in which effective training and development mark the difference between successful and unsuccessful organizations.

Managing training and development so that they contribute the maximum to organizations and people follows a logical sequence that we use to organize this book: identify the need, gain commitment, develop training and development objectives, choose a training method, implement the program, and evaluate the results. From this list it should be obvious we believe training and development are much more than facilitating programs.

A training and development program is successful if it fulfills an organizational or personal need. Logically then, managing training and development should start with identifying the need and using it as the basis for the program. Once a need is identified, management support to commit the time and resources necessary to address the need is sought. With that support, objectives for the training and development program can be set, the program designed, and the teaching techniques chosen. When the training and development program is completed, the work is not ended—the program must be evaluated. Did it accomplish its objectives? Did it meet the needs of the organization and the people involved? How should it be modified and improved? Following this sequence from needs analysis to evaluation will help you manage training and development to have a major impact on your organization and on the lives of those with whom you work.

HOW TO USE THIS BOOK

To help you manage training and development we include in this sourcebook different types of materials: readings, training roles, and instruments for determining needs, selecting a physical facility, selecting visual aids, structuring methods, dealing with special students, evaluating the program, and designing a budget.

PART ONE: SOURCES

Source readings were selected in 11 different areas: introduction to training and development, identifying needs, gaining commitment, understanding the learning and training process, developing objectives, choosing methods, techniques for implementation, transferring learning, evaluating the program, training and development for targeted audiences, and strategic uses. In the "Sourcebook" series, readings are selected which met the following set of criteria:

1. Views training and development as a critical part of personnel management and human resource development;
2. Up-to-date with current legal and professional guidelines;
3. Applicable for those creating a new training and development program as well as those improving upon an existing one;
4. Readable and clearly presented; and
5. Consistent with current research results.

If you are using this book to set up a new training and development program, we suggest you follow the sequence in which the articles are presented. This will help you better understand how a program is developed based on the needs of the organization and a thorough study of the learning process before attempting to select methods and implement the program.

If you are using this book to improve upon an already existing program, we suggest you still review the earlier sections to find out if your organization has correctly analyzed performance problems and needs. You may, however, wish to proceed immediately to a section that you consider most important. To help you understand what is presented in each part we present here a brief summary:

Section 1:   Introduction

Topics
An introduction to the field of training and development and its role within personnel management and human resource development. Relates training to other management activities and suggests it as a cure for performance problems. Guides for the overall development of the training and development program are included.

Questions Addressed
1. Where do training and development fit into the overall management process?
2. How can performance problems be analyzed?

3. What is the procedure for designing a training and development program?

Section 2:   Identifying Training and Development Needs

Topics
Means of determining managerial training and development needs. Assessing needs of a geographically diverse organization.

Questions Addressed
1. What are the objectives of the assessment process?
2. What different methods of needs analysis are available?

Section 3:   Gaining Commitment

Topics
Methods of gaining management support for training and development programs. How to present a program proposal to management.

Questions Addressed
1. What does management look for in a training program?
2. Which approaches work best when the proposal is made?

Section 4:   Understanding the Learning and Training Process

Topics
How learning theories form the basis of training and development programs. Where learning theory principles are included in various phases of training.

Questions Addressed
1. Why must we understand the learning process to build a successful training program?
2. How does adult learning differ from that of children and what implications does the variance have?
3. What are the most important aspects of learning?

Section 5:   Establishing Training and Development Objectives

Topics
Methods of establishing instructional goals. Enabling objectives and their importance. How to individualize the training process.

Questions Addressed
1. How are program objectives set?
2. Should the training program be more individualized?
3. Why are enabling objectives a priority?

Section 6: Choosing Training and Development Methods

Topics
The variable that will help determine the training method. Critiques of the most common methods of teaching. Computer-based learning and some common terminology.

Questions Addressed
1. How is a desired learning situation matched with a proper training technique?
2. What can be inferred from a prior demonstration of job ability before training?
3. How does behavior modeling fit into training programs?

Section 7: Techniques for Implementing Training and Development Programs

Topics
How to establish the proper climate for training. Guidelines for choosing a physical environment. The usefulness of questions and techniques to effectively use them.

Questions Addressed
1. How can managers prepare people for maximum use of a development program?
2. What is the most productive type of physical surroundings for the training program?
3. How can the supervisor become involved in training?

Section 8: Transferring Learning

Topics
How to complete the carry-over of acquired skills from the training and development program to the job. What factors encourage continuation of a specific desired behavior. How to decrease role conflicts among the trainer, supervisor, and the trainee.

Questions Addressed
1. How can one maximize the effects of training?
2. Why do some trainees tend to continue specific behavior but others do not?

Section 9: Evaluating Program Results

Topics
Assessing evaluation alternatives. Approaches and effects of evaluation. The importance of daily evaluation of the training process. Analyzing training as an investment.

Questions Addressed
1. What are the legal requirements of training?
2. How can the cost-effectiveness of the training program be determined?

Section 10: Training and Development for Targeted Audiences

Topics
Methods of training low-tech workers for high-tech jobs. Successful in-house management training programs. Vocational and technical educational resources available to training professionals. Sales training.

Questions Addressed
1. How do some specialized training programs differ from others?
2. Should training be focused on individual career development?

Section 11: Strategic Uses: Fitting Training and Development into the Organizations

Topics
Training as organizational development. The role of training in the long run. Ways of developing, implementing, and managing change in the organization. How trainers can prepare themselves for the future.

Questions Addressed
1. What is organization development?
2. How will training be used in the future?
3. How do training and development fit in with other personnel systems?

PART TWO: TRAINING AIDS

Section I: Training Roles, Competencies, and Vocabulary

In the early 1980s, the American Society for Training and Development launched a study to identify the tasks performed by and the skills needed by training and development specialists. They eventually determined that there are 15 distinct roles which involve a total of 38 competencies. Of course, proper and complete performance of any role involves the use of more than just one competency. Three exhibits represent summary findings of that study.

Section II: Training Aids and Tips on Determining Training Needs

Training needs are determined through some form of communication between a training person and the client, or user in other parts of the organization.

Interviews and questionnaires are the common media for gathering the data upon which to base decisions about what training to offer.

This raises questions such as "Which medium is better?" and "What questions should one ask?" Four exhibits deal with these questions.

Section III: Training Aids Involving Physical Facilities

The learning environment is both a psychological and a physical reality. The physical conditions of the classroom can have enormous impact on the psychological atmosphere. Checklists are presented to help you determine if a room is ready for use.

Section IV: Instruments for Gathering Data About Students

Instructors need to know a great deal about their students. The instruments exhibited are designed to obtain that information.

Section V: Training Aids Related to Visual Aids

It is difficult to overestimate the importance of visual aids in training programs! Some studies indicate that 75% of an adult's knowledge is acquired through the sense of sight. With this in mind, materials are presented to help you choose proper visual aids and use them effectively.

Section VI: Training Aids and Tips in Training Methods

The design of training programs should permit learners to reach desired behavioral objectives. This section includes instruments to help you select the proper methods.

Section VII: Training Aid for Dealing with Special Students

When people gather to learn, a number of interpersonal dynamics inevitably develop. Sometimes these dynamics involve behavior that proves troublesome to the instructor. In other words, the student participation seems inappropriate.

A guide sheet is presented identifying some of these behaviors and suggesting their causes and some things to do when the instructor feels it necessary to take corrective action.

Section VIII: Evaluation Instruments

Evaluation forms represent an extremely wide range of format and content, depending upon what aspect of the training one wants to measure and analyze. Included are several options.

Section IX: Training Aids Involving Training Budgets

Training budgets vary considerably in size and policy. The instruments present in this section are designed to help determine the share of total budget that should be allocated to training ("Some Budgeting Policies for Training Functions") and what costs should be attributed to training ("The Cost of Doing Training").

Section X: Miscellaneous Training Aids and Instruments

The remaining instruments cover a wide array of applications. Each is labeled to reflect its intent.

THE TRAINING AND DEVELOPMENT SOURCEBOOK

PART ONE
SOURCES

SOURCES SECTION I
INTRODUCTION

A. Training and Development and Personnel Management
by Albert C. Hyde and Jay M. Shafritz
- Explains how training and development fits objectives of personnel management
- Identifies areas where improvements are needed

B. Human Performance Problems and their Solutions
by Geary A. Rummler
- Develops a questionnaire for analyzing human performance problems
- Shows how training relates to other management activities

C. Analyzing Performance Problems: Quick-Reference Checklist
by Robert F. Mager and Peter Pipe
- Provides a brief checklist of common performance problems

D. Guide for Designing Training Programs
- Provides a guide for a training staff in designing and implementing training programs.

Training and Development and Personnel Management

by Albert C. Hyde and Jay M. Shafritz

During this last decade, organizations seem to have re-discovered training and development. Everyone has always known about training, but the increasing commitment to training and development programs by many private and public sector organizations comes as somewhat of a surprise to many observers, especially in the public sector.

Proof that such a trend or increase in effort exists can be seen in the establishment of larger and more sophisticated training programs, greater numbers of staff being hired as training specialists, increasing support for external educational programs, and a somewhat more tenuous factor—the coming of age of a distinct literature in Training and Development, marked by a number of major books, symposiums, journals, technical reports, and newsletters that cover training.

Training has always been viewed as the step-child of the personnel and human resource management functions. Consequently, it has usually been the first area to be sacrificed in a budget crunch. That training is coping more successfully with the era of resource scarcity is a further indication that the function has matured. While it still gets pushed around, it no longer simply quits the playing field.

Training has always had an especially tough time with budgeting. Since so many jurisdictions meet budget shortages *via* meat-axe approaches (for example, often they will first cut certain categories of line-item expenditures which are believed to be "luxuries" —such as state travel, consultants' fees, and training program costs), training has found itself hard pressed to maintain any continuity—much less identity. Under these circumstances, trainers have had to abandon programs and jobs, to be replaced by new trainers who have subsequently become equally frustrated; so the cycle continues.

But even in the face of sporadic program development and intermittent resource availability, training as an organizational function has survived and even begun to prosper. Why this is happening now is less certain, but the most significant pressure probably comes from individual employees, who are interested in and demanding, training for both maintaining current work skills and developing new ones. Indirect pressure comes from supervisors and managers, many of whom have been troubled by their perception of an increase in the gap between what jobs require and what individuals are capable of doing.

This indirect source of pressure is a complex factor. In a sense, it is a lament along the lines of the "Johnny can't read" syndrome associated with our education system. Many work supervisors feel that Johnny and Joanna don't know how to type, weld, write, analyze, *etc.* Part of this is certainly a problem stemming from our educational system and its difficulties. But another part surely involves our obsession with credentials and certification which are often totally unrelated to entry level jobs and the specific skills required to perform adequately.

A further source of indirect pressure is that work responsibilities are changing more rapidly in the current dynamic social-technological environment. Work skills are subject to considerable obsolescence, a factor only barely discussed by most of the literature.

The consequences of the above pressures are more readily identifiable. Supervisors are more supportive of training programs (within reason, of course) and expect to receive a fair share of training opportunities to develop and reward their employees.

Employees want their "share" as well and they expect to have both formal training during work time and informal training on the job. Perhaps James O'Toole, in his book on quality of worklife, has said it best, "most workers have an innate desire to grow . . . Apparently being able to satisfy the desire to grow and to learn on the job enhances worker self-esteem, satisfaction, loyalty, motivation, and occasionally, productivity."[1]

Training has arrived and now constitutes one of the most significant personnel management functions. It's so significant, in fact, that many training offices are being established outside of the usual personnel organization, frequently under a separate title of *Human Resources Development*. A question of some concern to personnel managers is emerging—Where does the training and development function belong? and What should I do?

TRAINING AND PERSONNEL—TRADITION AND SECESSION

If there is such a thing as a traditional approach to personnel management, it clearly includes training. Train-

[1]James O'Toole, *Work, Learning, and the American Future*, San Francisco Jossey-Bass, 1977, p. 159.

ing is part of the process of development that advances and maintains individuals within an organization. It is essentially an activity sequence within employee development based on several key criteria—that training be job or career related, relevant to enhancing advancement potential, useful in improving organizational effectiveness, and of sufficient relevance and interest to employees. In the public sector, decisions about training programs are most often focused on the first criteria mentioned—job or career-relatedness. In fact, this criteria is generally used specifically by most personnel shops to approve or deny requests by employees for training.

But how do the objective of training and development fit into the objective of personnel management?

This can only be answered in organizational terms. First, What are the functions of personnel? What is personnel designed to do? Obviously the answer is to ensure organization continuity or organizational survival. What personnel is most concerned with is making sure that organizations, through the people in the organization who make it up, have "human continuity." It's long-range continuity that is the primary concern, and for most organizations, the way to long life survival is to be concerned with adaptability, flexibility, and organizational effectiveness, which essentially means a good productivity ratio with the use of people and a variety of other things. Why some organizations function more effectively (and survive longer) can be due to many things— motivation, creativity, management styles, acceptance of change, *etc.* This constitutes an ever-present management dilemma.

Unfortunately, personnel uses its responsibility in this area much too narrowly. Personnel generally understands its function to make sure that the organization can bring to bear on any type of problem at any point in time the right kind of people to provide the right kind of solutions. Personnel for its part purports to develop those people, place them in the organization in the right position, and insure that for those people who are leaving the organization, there are adequate replacements.

Training them has its place in this organizational human resources cycle—staffing, placement, advancement, training and development, replacement, and informational support. However, what seems conceptually logical falls far short in practice. Personnel management has so specialized its functions that its focus has become concerned largely with the impacts of its own functions. Personnel doesn't compare in any systematic fashion, how or even if it should face an organizational resource problem; for example, by new hiring, reassignment or transfer, training, or job redesign or some combination of these options. Rather, it prefers to solve recruitment, assignment,

training and work organization problems, as they are handed down to personnel management specialists. Personnel all too often and by its own choice prefers to facilitate the implementation of organizational solutions rather than actively help shape the decision in the problem-solving phase.

Trainers, on the other hand, have become increasingly concerned about what they view as self-proscribed isolationism. In many cases, this is moving them towards secession. Trainers seek autonomy in part to establish the credibility of their own function and in part to avoid the regulatory image that personnel often conjures up. In a sense, trainers want to disassociate themselves from "those people who have to say no because of the regulations," and establish their own image.

To accomplish the above, training is making a major effort to professionalize itself. This process begins with training staff who are being urged to move through a professional development process. The American Society for Training and Development (ASTD) has issued a recent statement on what this will entail. ASTD's activity categories include:

1. Analyzing needs and evaluating results
2. Designing and developing training programs and materials
3. Delivering training and development programs/ services
4. Advising and counseling
5. Managing training activities
6. Maintaining organization relationships
7. Doing research to advance the training field
8. Developing professional skills and expertise
9. Developing basic skills and knowledge.

Whether "professionalization" will secure a separate identity for training remains to be seen. Certainly such an effort takes training far beyond presenting orientation programs, explaining affirmative action policies, and providing forty hours of supervisory management training for new supervisors. Our own opinion is that trainers must first be concerned about human development objectives and then focus on upgrading the activities and techniques to be used. We believe that these objectives can be condensed down to three critical functions:

• To plan what people need to know—both now and in the future to facilitate dynamic change
• To stress the ability to communicate and apply— to ensure that what needs to be known is actually learned and used
• To be *seriously* involved with the whole process of Human Development in helping people learn more about themselves.

A RETURN TO BASICS:
AN AGENDA FOR THE 1980s

The 1980s already promises to be a tenuous decade for governments. It will surely be a time of diminishing finances with increasing problems, both in scope and complexity; and at the same time of vanishing credibility and greater cynicism among public employees. Governments will have to be more efficient, more effective, more relevant, and more accountable. On top of these requirements, they may well have to spend more time on public relations, building a better image and proving that they are worth the resources alloted them.

Learning to do more with less about bigger problems for an increasingly disbelieving and unforgiving public will constitute a severe test.

Ironically, Training and Development will face an even greater challenge. It must play a crucial role in preparing public employees for the 1980s *and* at the

An Agenda for Trainers in the 1980s

Items	Requirements	Items	Requirements
1. Better Planning	a. develop training needs assessment techniques b. interface with workforce planning to forecast future training needs	6. Increase Concern with Equity	a. reexamine affirmative action programs and how training assists in achieving EEO goals b. increase communication and information dissemination about all training programs
2. Increase Supervisory/ Employee Participation	a. involve all kinds of employees in training programs as instructors, planners, and evaluators b. develop training methods in training/instructional skills for supervisor and project personnel	7. Increase Learning Research Efforts	a. examine functional work areas and research most effective learning methods for each area b. examine age, sex, socio-economic considerations for possible adverse efforts of current learning techniques
3. Develop Basic Budgeting Techniques	a. develop actual training budgets that provide both functional and program cost breakdowns b. develop and use cost-effectiveness analysis techniques to assess specific training programs and alternatives	8. Better Evaluation	a. develop basic evaluation techniques that focus on content learning and job and career performance change as opposed to simple trainee reaction b. reexamine evaluation objectives to develop evaluation techniques that can provide validity and reliability measurements

4. Augment Career Development and Counseling Skills	a. research and develop basic understandings of career dynamics of current organizations and career planning needs of individuals
	b. research work socialization process and reexamine orientation and career counseling programs
		9. Increase Focus on Human Development and Individuation	a. develop more flexible, modular training approaches for individuals to enhance diversity and choice
			b. reexamine training and development programs and methods—Do they meet individual concerns about:
			  1. participation/ involvement
			  2. personal security
			  3. individuation
			  4. equity
			  5. human growth needs

5. Increase Organizational Coordination Efforts	a. increase communication with organizational units to demonstrate facilitator/ consultant role of training b. increase participation in training experiments geared to specific organizational units' needs.		

same time develop planning, research, communication, information, technology, budgeting, evaluation skills to manage and justify its own existence. This will be an immense undertaking but one that trainers should welcome. What will be required is a return to sound management, good analysis, and intellectual integrity. Training can no longer rely on good intentions and its inherent self-righteous character. This is no overnight accomplishment. Training and Development should set an agenda for the 1980s if it is to develop the basic management skills it will need for the coming decade. The chart [on page 6] lists some possible items on such an agenda. Since we believe that agendas should be kept short (the idea being to provide a basis for opening discussion as opposed to shutting it off), we've incorporated the agenda into the chart.

The agenda is hardly all-inclusive. We hope it will stimulate discussion and we would greatly appreciate comments and additional suggestions by trainers and or anyone with an interest in this area.

There remains a final problem to be considered. An agenda, by its nature, implies a systematic approach to problem solving. The proposed agenda is a large one, one that could easily exhaust the capacities of even the best staffed training organizations. The key is to be selective, and to focus efforts progressively. These are easy words to say but much more difficult ones to live by. Trainers, like their personnel management counterparts, are constantly besieged with an array of operational tasks, distractions, favors, oddities, and absurdities to be performed. As any organizational realist will tell you, it's easier to do them than to say no. The trick is to focus qualitative effort. As Dugan Laird, noted in a recent address, "Anything not worth doing is not worth doing well."[2] Given the tasks at hand, as training develops its basic management skills, this is imperative.

---

[2]Dugan Laird, currently a training consultant, has written extensively in the field of training. His most recent work is *Approaches to Training and Development*, Reading, Mass. Addison-Wesley, 1978.

Human Performance Problems and their Solutions

by Geary A. Rummler

Few people would argue with the statement that managers are more successful in solving machine and system problems than in solving problems involving human performance. Part of this lack of success can be attributed to the complexity, unpredictability, and general "uniqueness" of human beings. A major part of our failure at solving people-centered or people-related performance problems, however, is our failure to analyze these problems completely before we try to solve them. If we were more effective at analyzing people problems completely before we try to solve them. If we were more effective at analyzing people problems, we could significantly reduce the number of such problems.

There are several factors that contribute to our lack of success in analyzing human-performance problems. First, when people are involved, we react to our biases or assumptions about human nature. Second, we are led by all the training courses and programs available, and by the staff people who support them, to separate human-performance problems from the job—from the complex environment in which they occur.

We apparently assume the cause and solution of the problem are completely wrapped up within the individual—that the problem or the individual is in no way influenced by the unclear standards, the inconsistent interpretation of those standards by supervision, or the built-in conflicts surrounding most jobs in most organizations. Why else would we conclude that a manager "can't handle people" and send him off to a general course in "human relations" or "communications"?

Finally, there is really no useful, operational way for the manager to analyze performance problems, though there are some interesting theories about what makes people "tick." Perhaps, for example, it makes a manager more comfortable to hypothesize a problem-performer's "hierarchy of needs"—but it doesn't help him solve the problem. Such theories may be useful to corporate staffs, who can design policies and procedures sensitive to what are supposedly "satisfiers" and "dissatisfiers," but understanding people at some abstract level is a long way from solving performance problems, as most managers know.

The lack of any effective way of analyzing performance problems is reflected in the labels used by managers in describing "problems"—poor performance is the result of "poor motivation" and "poor attitude." These terms are not useful; they don't say anything, they don't lead us to any real solutions. Frequently, the result is that the performer who has the vaguely stated performance problem is exposed to a training program with an equally vague title, again, such as "communications" or "human relations."

This article is concerned with a viewpoint for analyzing human performance problems. It provides managers with a framework for examining performance problems—a framework that cuts through the level of generalities we are used to and in so doing identifies specific, workable, nonmagic solutions to problems. An integral part of this approach is to examine the performer in his environment. The approach in fact concentrates on the dynamics of the relationship between the performer and his environment.

Moreover, the approach has the potential of overcoming our personal bias about people by ignoring it. Concentrating on the performance desired, and those factors in the environment that influence it, makes bias and assumptions about human nature less relevant. If not totally irrelevant (thereby deemphasizing the need for the currently popular training in awareness, prejudice, and sensitivity).

COULD HE DO IT IF HIS LIFE DEPENDED ON IT?

For the most part, human performance deficiencies can be classified as deficiencies of knowledge, which result from an employee's not knowing what to do, how to do it, or when to do it; or as deficiencies of execution, which result from an employee's failing to perform because of factors in the work environment: or as some combination of the two.

Distinguishing between deficiencies of knowledge and execution is a critical step in analyzing people-centered performance problems. A frequent result of failure to make this distinction accurately is that extended and expensive training is conducted in a foredoomed attempt to solve a supposed knowledge problem that is in fact an execution problem—a nontraining problem. In addition to being a waste of money, such training tends to reduce the credibility of the organization with the employee being trained, and frequently leaves management with the dangerous illusion that the performance problem in question is being solved.

This critical distinction between a deficiency of execution (D/e) and a deficiency of knowledge (D/k) can usually be made by getting the answers to these questions:

1. What is the desired performance (job outcome)?
   What are the job standards?

Says who?
Does everybody agree on those standards?
Does everybody (anybody) know whether these standards are now being met?

2. What are the specific performance differences between actual and expected performance?
   Has anyone ever performed as required?
   Who?
   When?

3. Could employees perform properly if their lives depended on it?
   Did employees perform properly when they first came on the job?

4. Do employees whose performance is deficient know:
   What is expected of them?
   That they are not performing correctly and how far they are from expected performance?
   How to perform correctly?
   When to perform?

5. What positive/negative consequences of performing correctly/incorrectly can employees expect:
   From their bosses?
   From their subordinates?
   From their peers?

As an example of what can happen if these questions are not asked, consider the case of the personnel function of a large bank that was about to launch an extensive three day program for all managers on "employee appraisal," in order to revitalize the current three-year-old appraisal program. A day was to be spent exhorting the executives on the importance of accurate employee appraisal and two days were to be spent in skill-training for conducting appraisal interviews, complete with videotape feedback on interview performance. Fortunately, before this program got off the ground and valuable management time and training-development money were expected, someone asked these questions:

1. *What exactly was the problem? How did "poor attitude" toward the existing appraisal system manifest itself?* The problem indicators included the fact that the annual review forms were returned to the personnel office weeks and sometimes months later. More important, a recent review of the evaluations showed that of the possible ratings of "outstanding," "excellent," "good," "fair," and "poor" for each item, the rating "good" was checked for nearly all items. (The items being evaluated were personality oriented—e.g., initiative, ability to get along with others, thoroughness, integrity.) What had alarmed the personnel department was that the appraisal system did not discriminate among

good and poor employees and was useless as a guide for manpower-planning and promotion. The conclusion was that managers didn't know how to evaluate performance properly.

2. *Has anyone ever performed as required? When?* Yes. When the program first began three years ago, the managers did a good job, as reflected in the evaluations, which showed a distribution of employees along the scale "outstanding" to "poor." Even now, a new manager will occasionally conduct an "accurate" appraisal when he first comes on the job.

3. *What are the consequences to a manager of performing correctly and incorrectly—i.e., of accurately recording a subordinate's performance versus "going down the middle" with "goods"?* The answers to this question were not easily articulated by the organization. Through observation and informal discussions with individual managers, it was learned that these consequences were frequently forthcoming.

- Predictably, subordinates did not like being told they were below "good." Their reactions to such a rating were unpleasant, to put it mildly. The nature of the personality items on the form left considerable room for judgment and frequently made the review session with a subordinate more of a negotiating session.

- Over time, it became apparent that employees whose overall performance was considered excellent or outstanding were promoted out of the department and that any employee whose overall performance was fair or poor attracted attention from Personnel and resulted in time-consuming explanations and commitments to develop the substandard performer.

- Finally, Personnel came to use the appraisal as a cross-check on the raises recommended by managers. The theory was that an outstanding performer should get a larger raise than a fair performer. The reality facing the manager was that he had to respond to better job offers from other organizations and the need to attract and keep new people. By rating everyone approximately the same (no large deviations), he had more flexibility in awarding raises.

In short, managers received basically positive consequences for their "poor" performance in appraising employees and fairly negative consequences for performing as desired by Personnel. Performance had deteriorated over the three years, not because managers forgot—but because they learned. All the refresher training in appraisal interviewing in the world would not help. Instead, the appraisal system underwent a major overhaul, the first step being to provide for appraisal along dimensions other than the vagaries of personality.

The managers in this example would have been able to perform properly "if their lives depended on it"—as could most problem-performers. In fact, performance problems caused by deficiencies of knowledge are by far the smaller category. It is a safe bet to say that of those problems initially identified as "training" problems, only 15 to 20% can in any way be solved through some form of training, formal or informal. The big problem area, and the area in which we are the least effective, is the deficiency of execution.

ANALYZING DEFICIENCIES OF EXECUTION

Part of our ineffectiveness in solving deficiencies of execution is that we have few useful models for looking at performance. As a result, we conclude that people don't care, aren't motivated, have lousy attitudes, and so on. Although such conclusions may be true to a certain extent, a majority of problems initially diagnosed as attributable to such causes can be solved by using a more refined model.

Deficiencies of execution, or the failure to exhibit learned behavior on the job, can further be classified as resulting from (see Figure 1):

- Lack of feedback. This problem arises when the person either does not know that the behavior is important or does not know that he is failing to perform to standard. The solution to this problem is to design and implement an adequate feedback system.
- Task interference. Here, the person cannot perform as desired because he lacks the tools or because the layout or organization of the job is such as to interfere with proper performance. The solution to this problem is job engineering.
- Punishment or unfavorable consequences. In this case, the person has no incentive for performing as desired; frequently, even it is against his own best short-term interests to do so. The solution to this problem is to *change the consequences* attendant on the job so as to encourage proper performance.

Another example will help illustrate this further classification of D/e's: A major manufacturer and distributor of typewriters was lamenting the poor motivation of its repair service men because of their lack of enthusiasm for a program by which they were to report sales leads to salesmen in their district offices. The program had begun with great fanfare a year ago and had netted a sizeable number of sales leads the first several months, but had slacked off to nothing.

FIGURE 1
Performance Symptoms: Classification and General Solutions

Symptoms	General Class of Solutions
Tasks are not being done up to the desired standard.	
Desired performance gradually deteriorates over time.	IMPROVE (or INITIATE) FEEDBACK
Employees don't believe it is necessary to perform as desired.	
Work is seldom done on time.	
There is a backlog of work to be done.	JOB ENGINEERING
Work is done, but seldom well.	
Tasks are not being done at all.	
Employees do the task correctly when first on the job, but their performance deteriorates after a short time.	
Employees do the job correctly only when a supervisor or other authority figure is present.	CHANGE THE CONSEQUENCES
Employees appear to be "lazy" or "not motivated."	

The procedure seemed simple enough. When a repairman identified a potential sale, he was to complete a card requesting several lines of basic information and drop the card in a box at the office next time he was in. Management was frustrated at the lack of performance and was considering quietly dropping the program altogether or "upping the ante" by providing a bonus for leads or a commission on ultimate sales.

A quick analysis showed the following:

- No feedback to the repairmen. The cards were picked up from the box by a clerk and were supposedly distributed to the salesmen—without any word to the repairmen. Sometimes cards were discarded because the information was incomplete. In such cases, the repairmen were never notified of the incompleteness in the data supplied.
- No positive consequences to the repairmen for completing and turning in the cards. The consequences necessary were not extravagant. One repairman said: "At least he could acknowledge that he got them." Another observed, "The cheap guy didn't even buy me a bottle at Christmas." There were, however, some negative consequences in the form of salesman rebuffs, such as, "Thanks for nothing. I chased clear across the country to follow up on that 'lead' and found they were going out of business. Don't do me any more favors." It took

only a couple of remarks like this to bring a repairman up short.

This "motivation" problem becomes something else when you look at it more closely. There is no feedback on the results of the desired behavior, there are no particular positive consequences for doing as desired, and in fact there is a risk of mild "punishment" for doing as desired. Perhaps the ante does have to be upped now to get and maintain the desired behavior. But this could have been maintained initially at little cost by providing feedback to the repairmen—in the form of as simple a thing as returning the card with a salesman's notation: "Made sale on 11/2/71. Customer appreciated your suggestion. Thanks."

This feedback / task-interference / consequence framework is extremely powerful. It can be used to analyze existing problems, predict problems before a job or system change is made, or solve problems. It provides an alternative to using labels such as "motivation," "communication," and "attitude" to describe problems. Now let's look more closely at each of the three causes of D/e's.

Feedback Problems

The individual performer is guided by the feedback he receives about his performance. In most cases where an individual agrees with the work goals, he will improve if he knows: 1) He is off target. 2) How to correct or get on target. If an individual fails to get feedback on his performance, he will begin to develop his own explanations of good and bad performance, of cause and effect—and he will inevitably develop superstitious behavior (i.e., he will erroneously attribute effects to certain causes).

The critical characteristics of effective feedback include:

- Frequency. Generally, the more frequent the feedback, the better.
- Immediacy. There should be little delay between the performance error and the feedback concerning it.
- Specificity. The feedback must in essence be "constructive criticism," in that it should differentiate the effects of various dimensions of performance.
- Understandability. The units used in stating the amount by which performance falls short should be clear to the person receiving the feedback.
- Positive orientation. The feedback should stress attainable performance subgoals, rather than punitive consequences—that is, reinforcement, rather than enforcement.

Most organizations abound with examples of poor feedback—computer printouts on last month's performance received three weeks into the next month (too infrequent, too late); production figures that lump all shifts together and memos to field noting " . . . a drop in overall performance which must be corrected" (not specific), and top management comment only when there is a negative exception, which means, "no news is good news."

Frequently, performance can be dramatically improved by improving feedback. Usually this requires collecting no new data, but simply redistributing existing data in a more useful format. Witness the following case. A vice president of an international freight company was concerned with the infrequency of container use by dockmen. Containerizing shipments represented a possible $20 saving in shipping costs for each container used. At one location, however, only 10 out of a possible 30 containers were being used on an average day. The 20 containers not used each day represented a $400 per-day lost saving. Multiplying by 260 working days yields a possible $104,000 annual saving through containerization that the company was failing to capitalize on. After observing freight handlers' performance at one location, the vice president concluded that workers were sufficiently familiar with the criteria for using containers. He found, however, that the freight handlers were unaware of the cost-benefits of containerization and had no specific standards against which to measure their performance.

The vice president's remedy was amazingly simple. He established 95% as the standard for containerizating shipments. (He maintained that no task can be done perfectly 100% of the time.) He made workers aware of the standard through their supervisors. The feedback system centered on a chart posted conspicuously in the freight terminal. On a typical day it read: OUT OF A POSSIBLE 30 CONTAINERS WE USED 25 TODAY. In this way, freight handlers knew exactly how well they had performed in relation to standard.

The results? One week after the feedback system was implemented, performance soared from 30% to 86% of standard and it's been improving ever since. When examining a performance problem that might be caused in part by lack of feedback, the following checklist of possible actions should point to effective corrective action.

Can Performance Be Improved by
1. Setting standards?
2. Stating existing standards in a shorter time frame (e.g., units per hour rather than per day)?
3. Providing feedback on:
   a. Fewer dimensions of performance?
   b. Different dimensions?
   c. Additional dimensions?

4. Designing the job so the performer can tell whether he is not performing properly (and if not, why not)?
5. Making the feedback message:
   a. More specific (e.g., by foreman rather than shift)?
   b. Less full of "noise" (e.g., on a single sheet, not as two inches of computer printout)?
6. Having the message delivered by a more objective and positive source?
7. Changing the format to show:
   a. Cumulative performance record (a history)?
   b. Composite of various performance indicators (for comparison)?
8. Increasing frequency?
9. Providing permanent storage for comparison by performer (a memory system)?

Consequence Problems

A person's performance is strongly influenced by the consequences he suffers or enjoys as a result of that performance. The consequences of performance may be positive, negative, or, for all practical purposes, nonexistent. They may also be immediate or long-term, and real or potential. Finally, they come simultaneously from a number of sources, including the work itself, subordinates, peers, bosses, and the organizational establishment. The result is that a person's "performance system" is a dynamic multi-dimensional set of factors that significantly influence his behavior.

It follows that proper management of consequences is critical in maintaining desired performance. This is particularly true in organizational settings where a complex environment of people, equipment, and events continuously metes out consequences. The frequent, random, and arbitrary consequences that naturally occur in the organization must be brought under management's control, balanced, and managed in a way to support the desired performance.

Poor performance can frequently be traced to the fact that the organization (system, situations, procedures) inadvertently provides negative consequences for—that is, "punishes"—the desired behavior. Earlier, we reviewed the appraisal-interviewing case, where managers received negative consequences for accurately recording the performance of subordinates. We realize that "good" managers and employees should rise above this adversity and do what is correct. And most try to for a while, but are worn down over time or by the unrelenting nature of the negative consequences.

The long-term results of these inadvertent punishers are usually extremely costly. For example, the negative consequences of having more than 4% when he was 7%—and to do extreme things to "bury" that remaining 3% scrap. The result to the company will be excessive metal costs, an inventory shortage, scheduling headaches, and overtime to meet the inventory shortage.

A more subtle but frequent problem is exemplified by the airline manager who sought training in "decision-making" for his airport-terminal ticket-counter supervisors. When pressed for an example of poor decision-making, he was able to cite only the failure to add additional staff to the counter when the passenger lines extended beyond a certain point. The training analyst asked the counter supervisors why they didn't add staff under these circumstances. One replied that he had done so once, but got "burned" because it caused an overrun in the overtime budget. Now when he sees a need for additional staff, he calls his supervisor and asks him to decide. Not surprisingly, the supervisor's supervisor said much the same thing. Now he asks the manager, rather than run the risk of all that "heat." There are several costs that result from this set of negative consequences. One is the loss of service to customers and the possible loss of revenues. The other—the more insidious one—is that the manager is now bogged down making all manner of decisions that should be made two levels below him.

Sensitivity to the power of consequences will not only help analyze problems, but also will help predict problems. For example, the marketing function of a bank decided that it would launch a major training program for tellers in all its branches. The objective was to have tellers "sell" additional bank services, with particular emphasis on personal loans. Although the marketing staff was convincing in its argument that personal loans were extremely profitable, the program was doomed to failure because of the existing structure of consequences in the branches. First, there were immediate negative consequences to the tellers for errors in handling money. Failure to balance out at the end of the day and taking bad checks. This, coupled with long lines, kept the tellers' mind on the essentials: no fancy stuff. Second, there was no support from branch management for the personal-loan emphasis. The positive consequences for the branch manager (attracting attention downtown) were for building up a sizeable loan portfolio—which could be done quicker and at less cost by making a $1,000,000 loan to a small corporation. It takes a lot of $3,000 personal loans (and considerable expense per loan) to equal $1,000,000.

Given these two sets of consequences, thirty weeks of training in "selling services" would have negligible effect on personal loans as long as the balance of consequences itself was unchanged.

The following principles are basic to analyzing the balance of positive and negative consequences to performers.

- A consequence may be positive, neutral, or negative, depending on the individual, the time, and the circumstances.
- If a behavior continues, the balance of consequences is positive.
- If there are positive consequences for two mutually exclusive behaviors, the one with the greater positive consequence will occur.
- The further removed in time a consequence is from a behavior, the less effect that consequence will have on the behavior.
- The consequences that control the behavior are those that have value to the individual.

These principles can be restated as the following guidelines for analyzing the consequences of an act to a person:

1. Frequently, people don't just not do something; they do something else instead. There is value, therefore, in looking at the consequences of both what is desired and what is currently happening (i.e., undesired).
2. Do not mistake company policy and platitudes (e.g., "You will get promoted") for real consequences to the individual (e.g., missing lunch with the fellas, having to do extra paperwork).
3. Separate immediate consequences (e.g., a sale today, holding up the car pool) from long-term consequences (e.g., week-end scrap report, monthly budget statement).
4. Consider the certainty of the consequence. We will often elect to engage in behavior with a high probability of immediate results (e.g., taking an extra 10 minutes for lunch, padding the call report) and low probability of negative consequences—i.e., getting caught.
5. Finally, remember that what one man considers a positive consequence, another man may consider very negative. Some people will bust their backs to get a chance to give a group presentation; others in the same office will go to extreme lengths to avoid such an "opportunity."

When trying to identify consequences and assess their power, you must be careful not to impose your value system on the analysis. You must look at what in fact is happening in the way of consequences and infer from your observations whether the consequences are positive or negative to the individual.

Task Interference

A number of very common causes of poor performance can be classified as "task interference"—that is, something interfering with the person's making the proper response in the desired situation. For a salesman, forms of task interference range from having to use a large, poorly laid-out parts or price manual to having more customers to call on than can possibly be done well in the time available.

In a manufacturing plant, task interference may range from a shortage of hand tools to an inadequate inventory-control system. Task interference describes those factors that make it either difficult or impossible to perform as desired. In addition to poor physical layout of a job, the major source of task interference is the lack of adequate resources—of time, tools or support equipment, or personnel.

Such problems can be identified by asking:

1. Is there enough time to perform the task?
2. Is there enough equipment to perform the task?
3. Are there enough support people and services to perform the task?
4. Are there competing tasks?
5. Are there things that distract the employee from the task?

Task-interference problems constantly creep into jobs as procedures are modified, assignments subtly change in scope, and systems slowly evolve. The problems can usually be solved by some form of job engineering. Although these kinds of problems are relatively straightforward and the solutions are far from profound, it is important that a manager identify and correct these problems. An employee may be slow to admit that such a problem exists or quick to work around it, assuming that it is "just one of those things." (In fact, human beings are generally so adaptive that they will be up to their ears in "just one of those things" unless someone keeps clearing them out of the way.) It is important that a manager identify task-interference problems and get the interference removed, or at least help a subordinate figure out the optimal way to get around the interference.

"TROUBLESHOOTING" PERFORMANCE PROBLEMS

We have presented a framework for looking at performance problems and some guidelines for analyzing them. A number of questions can be added that will make this framework into a troubleshooting guide for managers. First, we must determine whether there is in fact a real problem (e.g., is the symptom of "can't make decisions" in fact backed up by a performance discrepancy such as not enough ticket agents at the counter?) and whether the problem is in fact worth

solving (e.g., what is the impact, economic or other, on customer wait time extending beyond X minutes?). Obviously, these are preliminary steps to forestall spending too much energy on solving a performance problem that either is no problem at all or is not worth solving. The second addition to the framework is the following very specific list of questions for probing a performance problem. The result is a troubleshooting guide for human-performance problems.

SUMMARY

As we have indicated, this D/k-D/e framework can be used to analyze existing problems and to predict problems that might occur if changes in procedures or changes in emphasis on some performance variable are being considered. The value of this framework or template for viewing people-related performance problems is that:

1. It makes possible (in fact requires) a closer look at the problem. It forces us to get off the "communication" and "doesn't care" level of abstraction and to get down to specifying what exactly is desired and how what is desired is different from what we are currently getting. In so doing, we then examine systematically the variables that influence performance—the consequences, the feedback, and the barriers to performance.

2. If provides real and specific solutions. The solutions are not grand abstractions such as "Change his attitude" or "Motivate him," nor are they vague preambles to training-course titles such as "He needs some training in 'communication'" or "Train him in 'human relations.' He can't handle men." The solutions that result from looking at performance problems from this viewpoint are specific ("He needs to have information on X and Y and in Z form" or "He will not do X as long as his supervisor persists in making him do Y every time he does"), and their implementation is frequently well within the domain and authority of management. There is little need to lateral the problem to staff—unless, of course, management doesn't want to face the problem, or really doesn't want it solved.

The value of this approach is considerable. Organizations and managers who have systematically applied it have accumulated an impressive list of results. It is a useful tool for the individual manager, but it is all the more powerful when used as the common approach by all the management of an organization.

A Guide for Troubleshooting Performance Problems

A. IS THERE A PROBLEM?
What do you observe that indicates there is a problem?
1. How long has this been a problem?
2. How general a problem is it?
    - Where does it occur?
    - When does it occur?
    - How frequently does it occur?

- Does it ever not occur in some locations or at some times?

3. How will you know when the problem is solved?
    - How will things look different?
    - What numbers will increase or decrease?

B. WHAT IS THE PROBLEM?
1. Who is the performer in question?
2. What is the desired action?
3. What specifically does he perform incorrectly?
4. Does he ever perform correctly?

If yes: When?
If no: Has anyone ever performed correctly?
           When?
           Where?

C. IS THE PROBLEM IMPORTANT?
What impact does the incorrect performance have on:
1. The product or service?
        Quality   Cost   Quantity
2. The company?
        Procedures   Image

3. The performer or his department?
        Safety   Ease of work
4. Other workers or departments?
        Safety   Ease of work

D. WHERE HAS THE PERFORMANCE SYSTEM BROKEN DOWN?
Questions   *Action*

Does the performer:

Questions		Action
1. Know he is supposed to take the desired action? • How do you know?	If no:	Instruct him.
2. Know what the desired action is? • How do you know?	If no:	Instruct him.
3. Know when to take the desired action? • How do you know?	If no:	Instruct him.
4. Know how to take the desired action? • How do you know?	If no:	Instruct him.
5. Know the standard or level of performance expected? • Are there standards? • Does everybody agree on them? • Is anyone meeting them now?	If no standards: If standards:	Set them. Instruct in them.
6. Know whether he is taking the desired action or not? • How can he tell whether he is doing correctly?	If no:	Redesign job. Instruct in observing. Provide feedback.
7. Have adequate resources (e.g., time, equipment) to take the desired action?	If no:	Provide resources.
8. Receive negative consequences for taking the desired action? • Consider such sources of consequences as superiors, peers, subordinates; and the system.	If yes:	Remove negative consequences.
9. Receive no consequences for taking the desired action?	If yes:	Provide positive consequences.
10. Receive immediate, positive consequences for doing something other than the desired action? • Do "good" things happen to him if he doesn't do it?	If yes:	Remove positive consequences.
11. Receive no information on the consequences of taking the desired action? • Does he know it makes a difference to do it right?	If no:	Provide feedback.
12. Receive wrong information on the consequences of his actions? • Does information lead him to conclude he's doing okay when he is not?	If yes:	Correct feedback.
13. Receive information on consequences that is not sufficient for him to correct his performance (i.e., not clear, not specific, too late, too infrequent)? • Does he receive enough information to know how to correct?	If yes:	Provide better feedback.
14. Know how to interpret information in order to correct his performance? • Given good information, can he figure out how to change?		Instruct on how to interpret data.

Analyzing Performance Problems: Quick-Reference Checklist

by Robert F. Mager and Peter Pipe

Key Issues	Questions To Ask
I. He isn't doing what he should be doing. *I think I've got a training problem.*	
1. What is the performance discrepancy?	Why do I think there is a training problem? What is the difference between what is being done and what is supposed to be done? What is the event that causes me to say that things aren't right? Why am I dissatisfied?
2. Is it important?	*Why* is the discrepancy important? What would happen if I left the discrepancy alone? Could doing something to resolve the discrepancy have any worthwhile result?
3. Is it a skill deficiency?	Could he do it if he really had to? Could he do it if his life depended on it? Are his present skills adequate for the desired performance?
II. Yes. It is a skill deficiency. *He couldn't do it if his life depended on it.*	
4. Could he do it in the past?	Did he once know how to perform as desired? Has he forgotten how to do what I want him to do?
5. Is the skill used often?	How often is the skill or performance used? Does he get regular feedback about how well he performs? Exactly how does he find out how well he is doing?
6. Is there is simpler solution?	Can I change the job by providing some kind of job aid? Can I store the needed information some way (written instructions, checklists) other than in someone's head? Can I show rather than train? Would informal (i.e., on-the-job) training be sufficient?
7. Does he have what it takes?	Could he learn the job? Does he have the physical and mental potential to perform as desired? Is he over-qualified for the job?

From *Analyzing Performance Problems* by Robert F. Mager, (Belmont, CA, 1970), pp. 100–105, by permission of Pitman Learning, Inc.

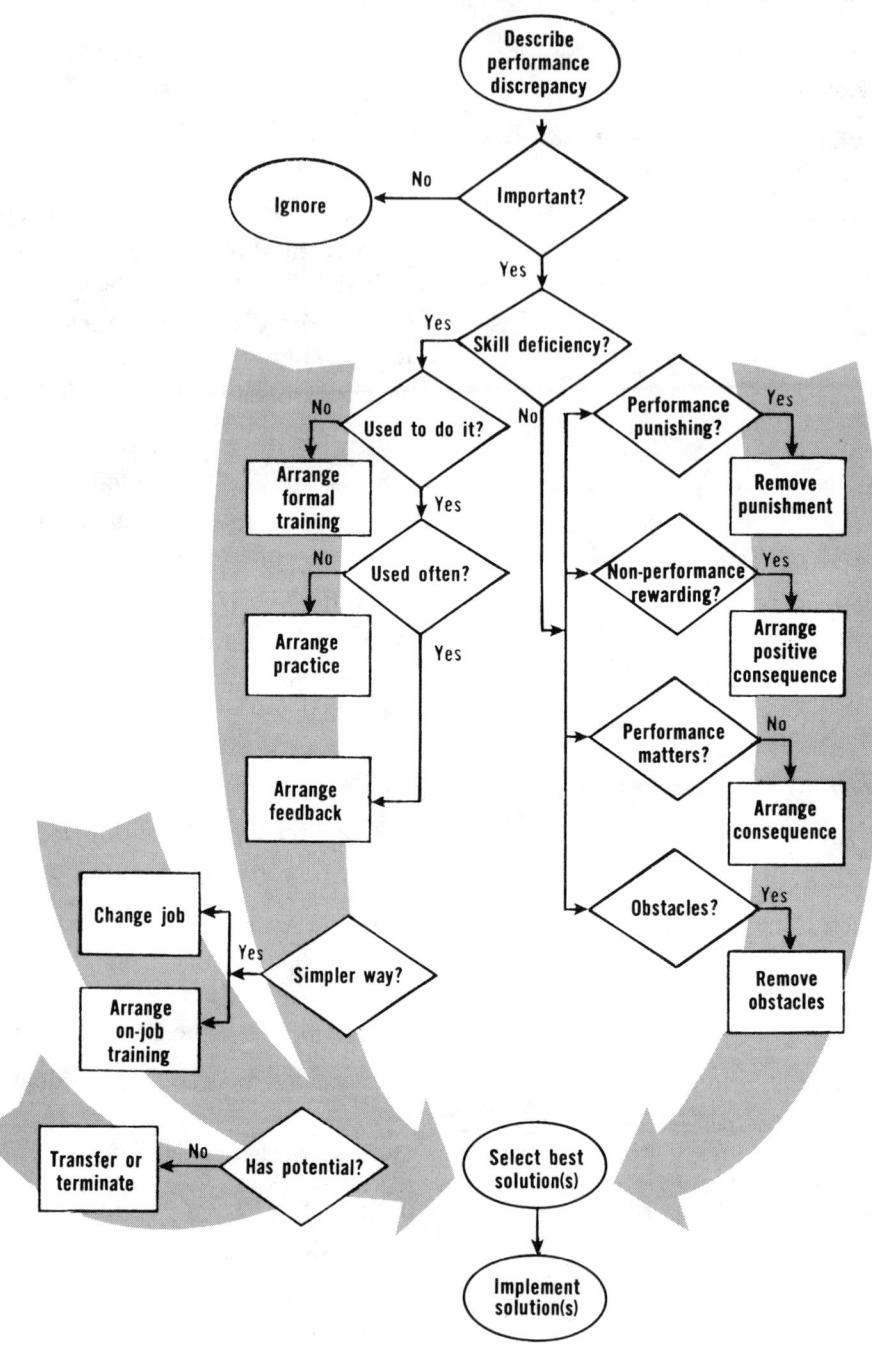

Key Issues	Questions To Ask

III. It is not a skill deficiency.
He could do it if he wanted to.

8. Is desired performance punishing?

What *is* the consequence of performing as desired?

Is it punishing to perform as expected?

Does *he* perceive desired performance as being geared to penalties?

Would his world become a little dimmer (to him) if he performed as desired?

9. Is *non*-performance rewarding?

What is the result of doing it his way instead of my way?

What does he get out of his present performance in the way of reward, prestige, status, jollies?

Does he get more attention for *mis*behaving than for behaving?

What event in the world *supports* (rewards) his present way of doing things? (Are you inadvertently rewarding irrelevant behavior while overlooking the crucial behaviors?)

Is he "mentally inadequate," so that the less he does the less he has to worry about?

Is he physically inadequate, so that he gets less tired if he does less?

10. Does performing really matter?

Does performing as desired matter to the performer?

Is there a favorable outcome for performing?

Is there an undesirable outcome for *not* performing?

Is there a source of satisfaction for performing?

Is he able to take pride in his performance, as an individual or as a member of a group?

Does he get satisfaction of *his* needs from the job?

11. Are there obstacles to performing?

What prevents him from performing?

Does he know *what* is expected of him?

Does he know *when* to do what is expected of him?

Are there conflicting demands on his time?

Does he lack the authority?
   . . . the time?
   . . . the tools?

Is he restricted by policies or by a "right way of doing it" or "way we've always done it" that ought to be changed?

Can I reduce interference by improving lighting?
   . . . changing colors?
   . . . increasing comfort?
   . . . modifying the work position?
   . . . reducing visual or auditory distractions?

Can I reduce "competition from the job"—phone calls, "brush fires," demands of less important but more immediate problems?

Key Issues	Questions To Ask

IV. What should I do now?

    12. Which solution is best?

Are any solutions inappropriate or impossible to implement?

Are any solutions plainly beyond our resources?

What would it "cost" to go ahead with the solution?

What would be the added "value" if I did?

Is it worth doing?

Which remedy is likely to give us the most result for the least effort?

Which are we best equipped to try?

Which remedy interests us most? (Or, on the other side of the coin, which remedy is most visible to those who must be pleased?)

Guide for Designing Training Programs

When a training staff works together to design a program, it must achieve a high level of efficiency and creativity. A much-needed tool is a guide for staff members that not only describes what should be done but also suggests the sequence to be followed. Such a guide is provided here.

DESIGNING A TRAINING PROGRAM

If the staff members for a training program are new to one another, initial time (perhaps as much as an afternoon or an evening) should be scheduled for them to do their own team building.

    The staff typically must take up the following considerations, in approximately the order given, as it prepares a training event.

1. Assess needs.
2. Set training goal.
3. Assess staff resources and skills.
4. Select training strategies and place them in the order they will occur in the program (prioritize).
5. State the objectives for each module of the program.

6. Predict the time schedule for each element of the modules.
7. Allocate a staff member who will be responsible for each element.
8. Assess the logistical elements.
9. Define primary client concerns.
10. Provide for evaluation.

    Schedule time for future planning and checking sessions of the staff. Few programs run their course without alteration. When will the staff get together? Can it be done during working hours so that meetings will not consume all available free time or go on late at night?

1. Assess Needs

- What data do you have on the participants' jobs, back-home environment, age, sex, race, religion?
- What are the participants' expectations for the training program?
- Has a precourse questionnaire been administered? Have you seen the program announcement?
- What further information do you need to obtain at the beginning of the program?
- What can you anticipate from the participants in the way of mood, volunteerism, readiness?

Reprinted from *The Reflector*, a publication of the Los Angeles Unified School District, Staff Development Branch, Office of Instruction, December, 1980.

2. Set Training Goals

- Discuss and write a set of goals for the program, usually not more than five, and have them ready for use in the first session.
- Agree among yourselves on the difference between goals and objectives.
- Be explicit about values, the methods to be used, and any ground rules.
- Establish trainer responsibilities as seen by the trainer.

3. Assess Staff Resources and Skills

- What training aids and devices have staff members brought with them?
- What special skills and interests exist among staff members?
- If certain unusual modules are needed, who can handle them?
- Make a list of what resources are needed and the resources that are available to see if there are any gaps.

4. Select Training and Prioritize Them

- This is the heart of the design: what should come first, second, etc.
- Block out the time schedule on newsprint and start filling it in.
- Begin with known elements: meals, free time, and perhaps time for back-home planning and evaluation.
- As other elements are filled in, look at the schedule's balance, flow, and required energy level.
- Mornings are better for theory; afternoons for activity; evenings for nonverbal events and T-groups.
- If T-groups are included, theory sessions should be selected to enhance the T-group activity in its predictable phases.
- One thing should lead to another. Will the experience of the participants be one of growth and development, or will it seem to them that they are getting a series of unconnected inputs?

5. State the Objectives for Each Module

- This may be done by the staff, through discussion, or by the staff members responsible for a specific module.
- Ideally, the objectives should be specific and measurable: "By the end of this period you should be able to. . . ."

- Present the objectives to participants at the start of each session. Knowing where they are going will help them to learn better.

6. Predict the Time Schedule for Each Element

- This should be specific: introduction, ten minutes; forming groups and giving instructions, five minutes; working on the task, forty minutes, etc.
- On a larger scale, review the schedule to see that sufficient time is available for what is planned, for each element.
- Provide for "fillers." Is more time available than the work will consume? Avoid planning so much that the participants feel hurried.

7. Allocate Staff Responsibility

- Generally, all staff members participate in the first session, and all should be visible. Planning the opening session often takes a large portion of the total planning time.
- For subsequent modules, individual staff members or pairs can volunteer to take responsibility.
- All staff need not participate in planning every session.
- Often a staff member will want to try to conduct a type of session for the first time as a means of learning or stretching.
- No one should be overburdened or under utilized. This is a good time to establish a norm regarding when and how staff members can help one another. When a staff member is up front, presenting, is it OK for others to interrupt?

8. Assess the Logistics

- Space: large rooms, small rooms, comfort, convenience.
- Materials: handouts, pencils, newsprint, nametags, workbooks, masking tape, flipcharts on easels, magic markers, tape recorders and tapes, reference materials.
- Housekeeping details: breaks, meals, physician, sleeping comfort, etc.
- Administration: registration, money, travel, personal supplies.
- Recreation: bar provision, indoor-outdoor resources, alone time, and socialization.

9. Define Primary Client Concerns

- Who is the primary client? Who is paying for this?
- What are the client's expectations? How will you communicate?

- Does your design to this point meet these expectations?
- What contact will you have with the client before, during, and after the program?
- Will the client be expected to take action as a result of the program?
- Are you and the client clear on your contract?

10. Provide for Evaluation

- Will you evaluate as part of the design:
  By obtaining postmeeting reaction sheets for each module?
  By obtaining a daily rating of satisfaction or learnings?
  By obtaining an end-of-program evaluation?
- Each of these needs preparation. Who is going to *do it?*
- Any provision for follow-up?
- Is there a requirement for a report to the primary client?
- Do you anticipate that the design as planned will meet the goals stated?

SOURCES SECTION II
IDENTIFYING TRAINING AND DEVELOPMENT NEEDS

A. **Identifying Training Needs**
   by Kenneth Wexley and Gary Latham
   - Develops systematic method for determining training needs
   - Discusses three types of analyses: organization, task, and person

B. **Determining Managerial Training Needs**
   by Stephan Wall and Deepa Awal
   - Describes five phase process for determining managerial training needs
   - Explains objectives of assessment process

C. **An Alternative Approach to Assessing Management Development Needs**
   by Robert Oppenheimer
   - Presents a "decentralized" approach for assessing training needs

D. **How to Determine the Training Needs of Your Supervisors—When They're Spread Across the Map**
   by Patrick Germany and C. Von Bergen
   - Explains a method for assessing training needs for a large population spread out over several locations

E. **The Nominal Group Technique: Applications for Training Needs Assessment**
   by Dow Scott and Diana Deadrick
   - Discusses nominal group technique as a method for assessing training needs

Identifying Training Needs

by Kenneth Wexley and Gary Latham

Too often training and development programs get their start in organizations simply because the program was well advertised and marketed, or because "other organizations are using it." It makes little sense for any organization to adopt an expensive and time-consuming training effort simply to "keep up with the Joneses." However, because organizations tend to imitate one another, training techniques tend to be faddish. This faddish nature of training can be reduced by systematically determining training needs. In this way, organizations will use training and development interventions only for the people and the situations where needed. In this chapter we will cover what we consider to be the most comprehensive and sophisticated system of determining an organization's training needs. This approach consists of three kinds of analyses: organization, task, and person (McGehee and Thayer, 1961). These analyses provide answers to the following three questions: *Where* is training needed in the organization? *What* must a trainee learn in order to perform the job effectively? *Who* needs training and of what kind?

Before proceeding with this chapter, it is important to keep several things in mind about this approach. The three analyses require a lot of time and human resources to conduct properly. It is clearly not something that a few individuals in an organization can complete overnight. Instead, it takes the combined efforts of many specialists (e.g., job analysts and manpower analysts). It is also a process that may never really end because organizations may be continually changing their products and services, technology, and so forth. Another important point to realize is that the three analyses must be performed simultaneously since they interrelate so highly with one another. Even if an organization cannot financially afford to carry out each step mentioned in this chapter, it should attempt to do whatever it can to approach this ideal. Now, we begin by discussing organization analysis.

ORGANIZATION ANALYSIS

Organization analysis is concerned with examining the organization as a whole. This involves examining its interface with the external environment in which it operates, the attainment of its stated objectives, its

human resources, and its climate. The primary purpose of an organization analysis is to determine *where* in the organization training activities should be conducted (i.e., "Are they needed?") and could be conducted (i.e., "Will they be successful?"). It is unusual for all units within an organization to have the same training and development needs. To implement an organization-wide training program without assessing where the training is needed makes little sense from a cost/benefit standpoint. Nevertheless, the authors have seen organizations adopt expensive "organization-wide" programs with little or no regard as to where the training was actually required.

The environment in which an organization operates can be a critical factor in determining whether training and development should be conducted. For one thing, if a training function is to survive it must be financially supported by the organization. The amount of support the organization gives can be affected by its overall profitability or vitality in the competitive market, as well as by the resources available (i.e., manpower, raw materials, capital, technology, markets) for its continued success (Hinrichs, 1976). Further, the larger environment in which an organization operates can affect the organization itself which, in turn, can affect training needs. For one thing, the environment can affect the way the organization's managers design jobs, supervise their employees, and make decisions (Schneider, 1976). The environment may also influence the structural nature of the organization itself. Those organizations operating in dynamic, uncertain environments where there are frequent scientific discoveries, technical inventions, and changes in market conditions (e.g., electronics firms) need structural features (e.g., flexible roles, open communications that cut across hierarchical levels, coordination by committees) that will allow them to adapt rapidly to changing environmental conditions. On the other hand, those organizations functioning within relatively stable commercial and technological environments (e.g., banks, insurance companies) can function well using a more bureaucratic or mechanistic structure (Burns and Stalker, 1961). Designing a bureaucratic structure may involve clearly defining roles and responsibilities, instituting a one-way chain of command from the top to the bottom of the authority hierarchy, and delegating sufficient authority to each manager to carry out his or her responsibilities.

Unless it is known what the organization and its subunits are trying to accomplish, there is little basis for determining where training is needed. Knowing, for example, that an organization's 90 retail stores had a net profit of 1 million dollars last year tells us little unless we can evaluate this outcome in relation to store objectives. Once we know the objectives, we can examine how closely these goals are being achieved.

An organization's overall objectives should first be stated in broad terms and then stated more specifically for the organization's various divisions, departments, and sections. In this way, training programs can be directed toward the improvement of those organizational units that are currently the weakest.

Furthermore, both short- and long-term goals must be established. Programs should not focus solely on solving immediate problems to the extent that long-term, preventive training is completely forgotten. For example, Table 1 presents a few of the short- and long-term objectives established by the medical records department and housekeeping department of a small midwestern hospital. Suppose that the medical charts of some patients had been misplaced in the past and that some members of the medical staff had voiced their complaints regarding the operation of the Medical Records department. Suppose, also, that the housekeeping department had been meeting or exceeding its stated objectives. All of this may suggest that members of the medical records department, but not the housekeeping department, need training of some kind.

It is important to remember, however, that not all inefficient operations can be dealt with by means of training. It could be that such nontraining factors as boredom with the work itself, low wages, inefficient work procedures, and poor physical working conditions are causing the problems. Further, if employees know how to engage in certain behaviors but do not want to engage in those behaviors, the problem may be one of motivation rather than training. The important point here is that the individuals performing the organization analysis must ultimately decide why a particular organizational unit is not meeting its stated objectives (i.e., training versus nontraining causes).

Another aspect of organization analysis is the estimation of *how many* people need to be trained immediately and in the future. This can be determined by conducting a process called employment planning or manpower analysis.

TABLE 1
Short- and Long-Term Objectives of the Medical Records and Housekeeping Departments of a Small Hospital

Medical Records Department	*Housekeeping Department*
• Develop 5-year capital and manpower plan in accordance with long-range plan for hospital	• Compliance with WisPRO and JCAH requirements for audit activities
• No more than 1 complaint per month as to the organization, operation, or attitude of personnel in department from members of medical staff	(a) No deficiencies on audit cited by survey (b) Be in compliance within current standards
• No more than 3 formal grievances per year from members of the department	• Maintain all necessary records for: (a) Infection control
• Written and current policies and procedures for the operations of the medical records department will be maintained, "current" being defined as semi-annual	(b) State license (c) Legal documents
• No medical record shall ever be lost	• Annual operating budget will be prepared according to timetable presented by the director of finance. Year-end variance will not exceed ± 5%
• Medical records shall be completed within time frames set up in Medical Staff Bylaws	• Monthly status report will be turned in to administrative head by the 10th of each month
(a) All charts will be assembled and deficiency slips made out and put in physician's box within 48 hours of discharge	• Develop 5-year capital and manpower plan in accordance with long-range plan for hospital
(b) If chart is still incomplete 1 week later, physician will be notified that he or she has 8 days to complete the chart	• No more than 4 complaints per month as to the organization, operation, or attitude of personnel in department from members of medical staff
• All registered and professional employees will maintain continuing education requirements	• No more than 5 formal grievances per year from members of the department
• All other employees to receive some form of continuing education at a minimum of 1 hour per month	• All employees to receive some form of continuing education at a minimum of 1 hour per month
	• Educational activities to include at least 12 hours of management education per year for the housekeeping supervisor
	• Written and current policies and procedures for the operations of the housekeeping department will be updated during the next 5 years in accordance with the hospital's projected expansion

FIGURE 1
A Manpower Analysis of One Hypothetical Department

1.	Number of employees in the job classification: 37								
2.	Number of employees needed: 38								
3.	Age levels:	29	33	45	47	50	51 53	55	69
	No. per age group:	2	8	7	10	3	2 2	1	2

Factors	Satisfactory	Questionable	Unsatisfactory
4. Skill	32	2	3
5. Knowledge	33	3	1

6. Skill and knowledge levels for other jobs within the company:

Classification	Number	Jobs
No other jobs	35	x
One other job	1	Job Z, Dept. Y
Two or more other jobs	1	Job Z, Dept. Y; Job A, Dept. B

7. Potential replacements and training time:

Outside Company	Within Company	Training Time
0	1	Less than 1 week
0	1	3 weeks to 6 weeks
10	0	12 weeks to 16 weeks

8. Training time on job for novice: 12 to 16 weeks
9. Turnover (two-year period): 5 employees; 13.5%

Every organization performs employment planning, either on an intuitive or a formal basis. Formal planning is especially necessary for large organizations with high growth rates, high employee turnover, and rapid changes in technology and product lines. The techniques used in forecasting vary from guesses by experts to sophisticated mathematical approaches.

Figure 1 presents hypothetical information to illustrate how manpower analyses can be used to shed light on a department's training needs. Items 1 and 2 indicate that there is an immediate need to train one new employee. Item 3 shows that two employees will be retiring within the next year. Their replacements will require training and development. Items 4 and 5 indicate that as many as nine present employees are either "questionable" or "unsatisfactory" in skill and knowledge about their jobs. This suggests that they may need retraining to improve their current performance levels.

It is evident from item 6 that the problem with these employees cannot be simply solved by transferring them to other jobs, since so few of the employees in this department have the skill and knowledge levels for other company jobs. Items 7 and 8 show that most replacements will have to come from outside the company and that their training time will take 12 to 16 weeks. Finally, item 9 indicates that, assuming the current rate of turnover, five new employees will have to be trained within a two-year period.

A final aspect of organization analysis sometimes involves an organizational diagnosis. A diagnosis is used to determine the way employees perceive specific aspects of their work (e.g., compensations, op-portunities for advancement, supervision received) and their membership in the organization (e.g., policies, goals, procedures, benefits, concern for human resources). If a group of employees perceive the company and their jobs as congruent with their own personal needs, goals, and aspirations, then the environment within their organizational unit will be one of trust and willingness to cooperate. On the other hand, if employees see the company and their jobs as being antagonistic to their personal needs, goals, and aspirations, then the environment in their unit will be characterized by mistrust and resistance to change.

Why would one want to diagnose an organization's environment? First, the environment may affect whether training can produce changes in behavior which will contribute to organizational effectiveness. Often, if the environment is very poor, employees will resist any kind of training given by the company. We have witnessed excellent training and development programs doomed to failure because the social-psychological environment basically made employees say to themselves, "I refuse to change." Second, a careful examination of an organization's environment using a technically sound attitude survey can help pinpoint "problem" areas within the organization.

An organizational diagnosis is typically conducted by using a questionnaire that is completed by all employees. One such organizational diagnosis questionnaire is known as Perspectives,* a computer-

---

*Perspectives, © Organizational Consulting Group, Akron, Ohio. Reprinted by permission.

scored 82-item instrument that yields the following dimension and subdimension scores:

- Overall Job Satisfaction
- Satisfaction with the Work Itself
- Satisfaction with Co-workers
- Satisfaction with Compensation and Advancement
  Satisfaction with Pay
  Satisfaction with Benefits
  Satisfaction with Promotions
- Overall Attitude toward Leadership and Supervision
  Considerateness
  Promotes Teamwork
  Supervision of the Work Itself
- Evaluation of Communication
- Attitudes toward the Organization
  Policies
  Concern for Human Resources
  Concern for Productivity
  Physical Working Conditions

- Individual's Relation to the Job
  Job/Person Match
  Identification with Work
  Organizational Stress
  Job Contribution to Quality of Life
- Relative Importance of Various Job Aspects

Table 2 shows some of the items found in this questionnaire. As you can see, all of the questions employ a multiple-choice answer format. Table 3 presents some of the data obtained after computer scoring of the questionnaire. The table gives summary data for all 879 respondents from one organization as to their satisfaction with pay, benefits, and opportunities for promotions. The table also compares the attitudes of the office clerical employees with those of all 879 respondents.

To summarize, organization analysis focuses on the organization as a whole. It attempts to answer the question, "*Where* is training and development needed

---

TABLE 2
Sample Content of an Organizational Diagnosis Questionnaire

The following questions are to be answered using the number associated with the choice that comes closest to your own feelings:

> 1 = not at all, or none
> 2 = very little
> 3 = somewhat
> 4 = quite a bit
> 5 = a great deal, or to a great extent

1. Does your job make the best use of your own particular skills and abilities?
   1 2 3 4 5
2. Are the people in your work group encouraged to work together as a team?
   1 2 3 4 5

In this section several aspects of your job are listed. Please indicate the importance of each of these for your overall job satisfaction by selecting one of the five choices below:

> 1 = very unimportant
> 2 = unimportant
> 3 = neither important nor unimportant
> 4 = important
> 5 = very important

1. Promotions   1 2 3 4 5
2. *Benefits*   1 2 3 4 5

The following questions are to be answered using the number associated with the choice that comes closest to your own feelings.

> 1 = almost never
> 2 = seldom
> 3 = sometimes
> 4 = often
> 5 = almost always

1. How often do you leave work with a good feeling of accomplishment about the work you did that day?   1 2 3 4 5
2. Do you get conflicting orders or instructions and, as a result, don't know what you are supposed to do?   1 2 3 4 5

From *Perspectives,* © Organizational Consulting Group, Akron, Ohio. Reprinted by permission.

TABLE 3
Sample Data from an Organizational Diagnosis Questionnaire

Summary Data for all 879 Respondents from
Consolidated Corporation

| | Percentage Responding | | | | |
| | LO | | | | HI |
Attitude Dimension	1	2	3	4	5
SATISFACTION WITH:					
Pay	9	11	34	32	14
Benefits	3	3	11	34	49
Promotions	13	28	28	24	8

Comparative Summary of
136 Office Clerical (C)
879 Overall Company (O)

| | | Percentage Responding | | | | |
| | | LO | | | | HI |
Attitude Dimension		1	2	3	4	5
SATISFACTION WITH:						
Pay	C	14	33	25	25	3
	O	9	11	34	32	14
Benefits	C	3	0	3	39	56
	O	3	3	11	34	49
Promotions	C	16	38	25	18	3
	O	13	28	28	24	8

and *where* is it likely to be successful within an organization?'' It consists of an analysis of the following:

1. How the organization relates to its external environment, in order to assess how these external variables influence the need for training and development
2. How well the organization and its various subunits are achieving their stated objectives
3. The organization's human resources, to determine current and long-range training and development needs
4. The organization's environment, to determine those problem locations that can be dealt with through training and development, and to determine where within the organization one can expect to experience unusually strong resistance to change

Once the question of *where* training is needed has been answered, the design or content of the program itself can be considered. This is done through a systematic task analysis.

TASK ANALYSIS

As shown in Figure 2, the first step in task analysis involves describing in rather general terms what the worker does when performing his or her job. Step 2 is

the most crucial since it entails identifying the specific tasks of which the job is composed. Finally, course objectives for the training program are derived from the job information gathered in these two steps.

Job Description

The first step in determining the content of a training and development program is to develop a description of the target job. A job description is essentially a narrative statement about what a person does on the job, including the conditions (e.g., cold weather, excessive time pressures, dealing with irate customers) under which the job is performed.

Some organizations already have written job descriptions that can be found in the personnel department. Often, however, these descriptions are not comprehensive enough for course preparation purposes. Thus, the training staff must frequently rewrite them. This entails observing current employees performing their jobs and questioning them about what they are doing. In some instances, the training analyst may perform some of the job duties himself or herself in order

FIGURE 2
Steps in Course Development Using Task Analysis

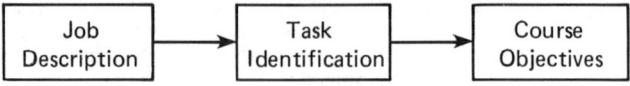

to obtain firsthand knowledge of exactly what is involved in doing the work. More often than not, this cannot be done because the work is either too complex or dangerous for a novice to perform.

Two examples of job descriptions are presented in Figures 3 and 4. The first one, a description of an investment specialist, comes from the securities department of a large life insurance company. The second one describes the job of a medical librarian in a small hospital. In writing these two descriptions, the training specialists tried to include those things that are critical to performing these jobs satisfactorily, no matter how infrequently or briefly they occur. Moreover, the training specialists took care to describe these jobs as they exist now, not as the training specialists or the supervisors would like them to be in the future.

Task Identification

As you saw in the last section, a job description portrays the job in some detail, but it does not give us enough specific information to put together a training and development course. This is where task identification comes in.

Task identification focuses on the overt, observable behaviors that are involved in performing a job. A task listing of a home telephone installer might include the following behavioral statements:

1. Reads and interprets service orders
2. Climbs pole to hook up the drop wire
3. Runs drop wire from pole to house
4. Checks protector to make sure it is functioning correctly
5. Uses ladder on side of house to hook up drop wire

Several different approaches can be used for identifying tasks. Although the procedures differ somewhat from one another, they all break down human work into task units that can then be used for determining the content of a training and development

FIGURE 3
An Example of a Job Description for the Job of Investment Specialist

The incumbent reports to a Manager of Investments and an Investment Officer. The Manager, along with three other Managers, an Assistant Manager, the Investment Research Officer, the Investment Officer (Markets), and the Assistant Treasurer-Assistant Secretary, reports to the Vice President-Securities and Treasurer.

The incumbent frequently accompanies the Manager or Investment Officer on trips made to the site of borrowing corporations, and may occasionally make such trips alone. She or he actively participates in negotiation conferences both in the Home Office and in the field between JMW and potential borrowers and/or their investment banking representatives. After mutually satisfactory terms have been reached and the investment has been finally approved, the incumbent works closely with the Law Department to review the loan agreement and assure that it conforms to the conditions and stipulations approved by the Finance Committee.

The incumbent spends much of his or her time performing various necessary service and analytical functions for JMW's offshore oil and gas project. She or he is required to maintain liaison with joint venture partners for the purpose of acquiring and updating information. He or she is further responsible for authorizing the disbursement of funds, updating the project budget periodically, and projecting future expenditures. Finally, the incumbent performs various research activities for the project such as computing the probable rate of return on JMW's investment.

The incumbent also has major responsibility for evaluating consent requests for changes in existing investment loan agreements. She or he pursues the financial and legal aspects of the requested changes to assess their investment consequences. The incumbent then presents oral and/or written recommendations concerning the requested changes to a Manager of Investments and/or an Investment Officer for approval.

The incumbent occasionally prepares special projects related to portfolio analysis, Securities Department procedures and activities, etc. He or she is generally expected to be knowledgeable about the portfolio, and to monitor its status periodically in order to identify and anticipate problem areas.

The incumbent assists a Manager of Investments and an Investment Officer in the analysis of new investment opportunities. This involves an appraisal of the credit worthiness of potential borrowers, including the general state of the borrower's industry, a thorough understanding of the terms of the loan agreement, and analysis of the yield required to make the deal attractive to JMW. The incumbent is expected to research and analyze these investment offerings with minimum supervision, developing and incorporating meaningful data on her or his own initiative. Based on this research, the incumbent's recommendation on a proposed investment is presented orally and in a detailed written memorandum to the Manager and Investment Officer for approval. They direct any necessary revisions, and accompanied by the incumbent, present the proposal to the Vice President-Securities. Investment proposals approved by the Vice President are subsequently presented to the Finance Committee by the Manager and/or Investment Officer.

FIGURE 4
An Example of a Job Description for the Job of Medical Librarian

---

General Responsibilities

Under general, but limited, supervision the librarian assumes responsibility for the administration, operation, organization and expansion of a professional hospital library providing document delivery, bibliographic and reference services and containing current books, serials, other appropriate print material, audiovisual material and bibliographic tools necessary for the use of the medical staff, medical and nursing students, and employees serving the hospital.

Specific Responsibilities

---

1. Works with and makes recommendations to the Library Committee in the selection of appropriate books, serials, and audiovisual material for acquisition through purchase, gift and/or exchange and in the establishment of library policies and procedures.
2. Classifies, catalogs and indexes books, serials, and audiovisual material.
3. Issues materials to qualified library users and keeps pertinent records of lending in order to locate material when necessary or prevent material from remaining outside of the library for undue periods of time.
4. Performs reference services for library users including requests for factual information and for subject or bibliographic searches to be done manually and or with MEDLINE terminal.
5. Provides document reproduction/delivery services as requested consistent with the Copyright Law of the United States (Title 17, U.S. Code).
6. Contacts other medical libraries and/or intertype library networks with shared services arrangements for material requested but not available in the hospital library.
7. Performs routine library clerical procedures including taking care of the library mail and correspondence, recording acquisitions and checking in journals.
8. Coordinates through all medical center departments, the purchase and/or subscription of reference materials or journals.
9. Develops annual departmental budget recommendations.
10. Develops annual plan of short-term and long-range departmental objectives.
11. Develops and establishes coordinated program of library service with the Director of Staff Development and the Hospital Education Council for in-house and community education.
12. Keeps all staff aware of library services and materials and orients the new medical staff, students and employees to use of the library, its services and materials to assure that effective use is made of the library.
13. When possible, participates in the professional organization, medical library consortia and intertype library networks for the purpose of continuing education in librarianship and to be aware of and/or influence legislation, activities and programs that may affect the hospital library.

---

program. In this section, we will present the following five procedures:

1. Stimulus→Response→Feedback
2. Time Sampling
3. Linear Sequencing
4. Critical Incident Technique
5. Job Inventories

The *stimulus-response-feedback* method was developed by Miller (1962). He argues that each task activity consists of the following components:

- An indicator on which the activity-relevant indication appears
- The indication or cue that calls for a response
- The control object to be activated
- The activation or manipulation to be made
- The indication of response adequacy, or feedback

An *indicator* may be any object that provides the cue for making a response. It may be an aircraft instru-

ment, a pressure gauge, a millivoltmeter, a circuit tester, or even a written message. The *indication* or cue that triggers the response may appear all at once, or it may have to be pieced together by the worker from recall through periods of time. In its broadest sense, it is an out-of-tolerance signal that there is a difference between present conditions and how conditions ought to be. Examples here might include the excessive vibrations of a piece of machinery, loud exhaust sounds from an automobile, or a clock that runs too slowly. The *control object* refers to any means the employee uses to correct the out-of-tolerance situation. It may require the use of a tool, a piece of machinery, or even another worker. The *activation or manipulation* deals with the employee's actual use of the control object. Here, Miller recommends describing the actual use of the tool or machinery or even the message conveyed by one employee to another regarding the situation. The indication of *response adequacy* is the feedback that the employee receives regarding the adequacy of his or her behaviors. The indication of response adequacy may be proximal (as by the feel of a

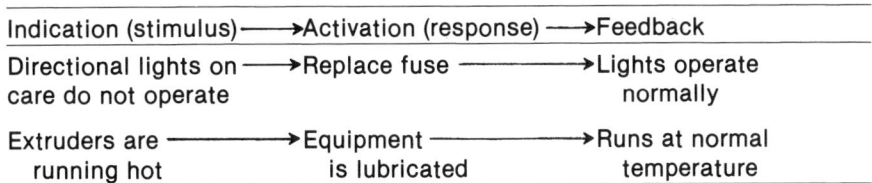

Indication (stimulus)	→ Activation (response)	→ Feedback
Directional lights on care do not operate	→ Replace fuse	→ Lights operate normally
Extruders are running hot	→ Equipment is lubricated	→ Runs at normal temperature

switch when a machine is being adjusted), or distal (as when one hears the machine starting up again). In short, Miller's approach basically calls for the analysis of each task in terms of a stimulus-response-feedback framework. This paradox is illustrated above for two different tasks.

This approach to task identification is of value when describing simple structural tasks that are amenable to a stimulus-response-feedback dissection. However, the method is limited with complex tasks (e.g., executive management) because of the difficulties in specifying the cues, responses, and/or feedback involved (Cunningham and Duncan, 1967). Nevertheless, the approach can be particularly useful in training where equipment simulators need to be developed. Imagine how much easier it would be to design a truck simulator or a punch press simulator after identifying the exact stimuli and responses involved in each aspect of the truck driver's or press operator's job.

A second task identification approach is called *time sampling.* Here, direct observations of work activities are made by trained observers. Time sampling enables trainers to determine through direct observation exactly what employees do on the job and how frequently they do it. By making randomized observations of employee behavior, trainers can learn in a relatively short time how employees perform their jobs. For example, in an analysis of entry-level clerical jobs, 37 clerical workers representing 10 clerical positions were selected for observation (Blood, 1975). At 25-minute intervals, an observer made "rounds" of observations that took him or her past the work stations of each of the 37 persons being observed. As the observer passed each work station, he or she simply noted the job duty (e.g., filing, checking, typing, receiving information, giving information) the worker was performing. Each observer's "rounds" were begun at random times throughout the work day. Over 1900 individual observations were made in all. This information enabled the organization to identify the tasks performed in each of these clerical positions.

In another organization, four observers were trained to monitor customer contacts of telephone company service representatives for a three-day period (Wexley, 1975). Well over 100 service representatives in two district offices were monitored while handling almost 1000 telephone calls. The monitoring procedure required the observer to follow a "new" call through to completion (a "new" call was signaled by a light on a switchboard in an observation room). When the contact was completed, the observer switched off that representative, recorded the behavior(s) engaged in by the service representative, and waited for the next call. Randomization of service representative positions was ensured because the positions were connected to the central switchboard on a rotary number basis; i.e., the next call was automatically connected to the next service representative available. Several inter-observer agreement checks were conducted to assess the consistency of their task identification procedure. Correspondence between pairs of observers listening to the same 30 telephone calls was found to be quite high, ranging from 90% to 100% agreement.

The third task identification procedure, called *linear sequencing,* has been designed expressly for specifying training content (Dean and Jud, 1965). The method is applicable for the trainer who wants to analyze the basic steps of any job so that he or she can successfully teach these steps to someone else. To do this, the task description must be sufficiently detailed so that trainees who know nothing about the procedure to be performed can read the analysis and perform the job correctly without guidance.

The approach can best be illustrated by using another telephone example and asking you to imagine for a moment a person who has never seen or used one. The trainer would use the following procedure:

1. Write each step on a card, with each card containing a stimulus and a response.
   Stimulus: When the phone rings,
   Response: pick up the receiver (that part of the telephone that is attached to the base by a wire).
   Stimulus: If you hear no voice
   Response: say "hello."
2. Make certain that the response portion of the card begins with an imperative verb telling the reader to do something. For example, when making an outgoing call some of the response cards could read:
   Next, *turn* the DIAL clockwise until your finger is stopped by a small silver bar.
   Next, *pull* your finger out of the dial.
3. Technical terms commonly used by subject-matter experts should be included in the write-up and defined.

Example: If you do not hear a DIAL TONE (Steady buzzing signal), HANG UP (replace the receiver on the phone as you found it).

4. If it seems desirable to record the rationale for a step (i.e., the reason why the step is performed) for future reference, the rationale should be recorded on the back of the card.

5. The trainer places the cards in the proper sequence. A series of steps that follow one another without any alternatives is called a *linear* sequence. If the steps are not always followed in exactly the same manner, and the trainees are required to make procedural decisions, the procedure is known as *branching*. Shown below are examples of these two types of sequences:

Linear: (5) Next, insert the letter in the envelope. (6) Next, close the envelope. (7) Next, moisten the stamp. (8) Next, affix the stamp to the envelope.

Branching: (5) Next, insert the letter in the envelope. (6) Next, close the envelope. (7) Next, determine if there is a postage meter in the office. (8) If there is a postage meter, . . . (instructions telling how to use it). (8a) If there is no postage meter, moisten a stamp.

As you can imagine, branching sequences occur more frequently as jobs become more complicated. The amount of time and labor needed for this method can, therefore, become exhaustive as jobs increase in complexity. Nevertheless, this is an excellent method for determining training content with any job involving certain prescribed procedures (e.g., orthopedic surgery, dentistry, pipefitting) since it specifies the exact things to be taught.

The fourth approach to task identification is known as the *critical incident technique* or CIT (Fivars, 1975; Flanagan, 1954). The CIT requires observers who are aware of the aims and objectives of a given job and who frequently (e.g., daily) *see* people perform the job, to describe to a task analyst incidents of effective and ineffective job behavior that they have observed over the past 6 to 12 months. This means that supervisors, peers, subordinates, and clients may be interviewed about the critical requirements of a specific job. The specific steps in conducting a task identification based on the critical incident technique are listed below:

1. (*Introduction*): "I am conducting a job analysis to determine what makes the difference between an effective and an ineffective _____ (e.g., foreman, pipefitter, secretary). By effective performance, I mean behavior you have seen in the past that you wished all employees would do

under similar circumstances. By ineffective performance I mean behavior which, if it occurred repeatedly or even once under certain circumstances, would make you doubt the competency of the individual.

"I am asking you to do this because you are aware of the aims and objectives of the job, you frequently observe people in this job, and you are able to discern competent from incompetent performance. Please do not tell me the names of any individual to whom you are referring."

Job incumbents are not interviewed concerning their *own* behavior. This is because incumbents are usually objective in describing their effective behavior, but there is sometimes a tendency for them to attribute their ineffective behavior to factors that were beyond their control.

2. (*Interview*): "I would like you to think of specific incidents that you yourself have seen occur over the past 6 to 12 months." The emphasis on the past 12 months is to ensure that the information is currently applicable. For example, behaviors that were critical for a salesperson in the 1950s may no longer be critical in the 1980s. Moreover, memory loss may distort the facts if the analysis is not restricted to recent incidents. The requirement that the interviewer report only firsthand information maximizes the objectivity or factual nature of the information to be reported (Latham and Wexley, 1981).

For each incident that is recalled, the same three questions are asked, namely:

a. "What were the circumstances surrounding this incident?" In other words, what was the background? what was the situation? This question is important because it establishes *when* a given behavior is appropriate.

b. "What exactly did the individual *do* that was either effective or ineffective?" The purpose of this second question is to elicit information concerning *observable* behavior.

c. "How is the incident an example of effective or ineffective behavior?" In other words, how did this affect the task(s) the individual was performing?

Generally, an interviewee is asked to report five effective and five ineffective incidents. Attention is given to both effective and ineffective incidents because an effective incident is not necessarily the opposite of an ineffective incident. For example, setting a specific goal has been found to be effective for increasing productivity in many jobs, but not setting goals does not necessarily decrease productivity (Latham, 1969).

A total of 10 incidents are collected because they can usually be collected within one hour. This is the maximum time period that many employees can be away from the job without disrupting their work day. No more than 10 incidents are collected from any one individual so that the data are not biased by talkative people. In order to obtain a comprehensive sample of incidents, it is recommended that at least 30 people be interviewed for a total of roughly 300 incidents (Latham and Wexley, 1981).

The interviewer must be skilled in collcting information describing observable behaviors. If the interviewee responds to question b with the answer, ". . . the employee really showed initiative in solving the problem," the interviewer must ask "what exactly did the individual *do* that indicated initiative?"

This procedure has particular utility where training specialists want to develop programs that concentrate on critical tasks. For example, a restaurant's waiters and waitresses may know how to set up tables and clean them after customers have left. The same waiters and waitresses may have difficulty, however, taking customer orders and relaying these orders accurately to the kitchen. Therefore, the training program should be concerned with these critical tasks.

The final approach to task identification involves the development of a *job inventory* (sometimes referred to as a task inventory). A job inventory is a structured questionnaire that consists of a listing of tasks comprising a particular job. Once the questionnaire is constructed, it is administered to employees who currently perform the job since they are considered to be among the most knowledgeable about it. In many cases, supervisors are asked to describe the job as well.

In brief, one or more small groups of persons (8 to 12 in a group) are initially selected to generate an exhaustive list of job tasks necessary to perform a particular job adequately. The individuals in these groups are not randomly selected, but are chosen on the basis of their exhaustive knowledge of the job. A technique known as group brainstorming is used by the training specialist during the meetings to encourage the group members to list as many tasks as possible. Employees and supervisors usually participate in separate meetings, as the presence of a supervisor may inhibit the employees from speaking openly. Listed below are several tasks that were generated during group sessions held by the authors with tire store managers:

- Takes a physical inventory monthly
- Reviews salespersons' expense reports
- Arranges for outside collection of bills through independent agencies

- Holds safety meetings with store personnel
- Informs employees of all company benefits
- Assigns sales quotas to sales and service personnel
- Makes certain that customers are informed of all warranties and guarantees

Following the group meetings, a job inventory is constructed by the training specialist and mailed to a random sample of employees. These employees are asked to rate each task in terms of both importance and amount of time spent. An example of a typical job inventory is presented in Figure 5. Both low and high performers can be used to complete job inventories, since both groups of employees provide similar ratings of importance and time spent (Wexley and Silverman, 1978).

After the questionnaire is completed by a number of employees, the training specialist calculates the mean (i.e., average) rating for each task for both importance and time spent. The end product of this analysis is a comprehensive picture of the job's tasks as seen by not just one person or a few people, but by many knowledgeable employees currently working on the job.

Summary

Five different task analysis procedures have been described. Any of these methods can be recommended for determining job tasks. The *stimulus-response-feedback* and *linear sequencing* methods are extremely time consuming and microanalytic. With these methods, the training specialist essentially observes employees at work and records stimulus-response links. Of the two methods, stimulus-response-feedback is more microanalytic, since tasks are broken down even further than in linear sequencing. *Time sampling* is a sound method of ascertaining what employees do and how frequently they do it simply by making direct observations of their behavior. The soundness of this approach, however, depends upon the randomness of the "rounds" and the comprehensiveness of the checklist on which job duties are noted. The *CIT* involves interviewing individuals who have themselves made direct observations. This method is particularly useful when one is interested in identifying critical aspects of the job. Finally, the use of *job inventories* is quite appealing, because employees participate in the construction of the inventory. The inventory is mailed to a large sample of employees who report their opinions about the importance and the relative amount of time they spend on each task. The end result is their averaged view of the job.

FIGURE 5
An Example of a Job Inventory Used with Tire Store Managers

	Importance	Amount of Time Spent
Instructions: For each task activity, *circle* the number corresponding to its importance for *your* job and the amount of time you spend on it.	1–*Not at all* important 2–*Slightly* important 3–*Moderately* important 4–*Very* important 5–*Extremely* important	0–*Never* do this task 1–*Very little time* compared to other tasks 2–*Somewhat less time* compared to other tasks 3–*Same amount of time* as other tasks 4–*More time* compared to other tasks 5–*A great deal more time* compared to other tasks

		Importance	Amount of Time Spent
1.	Assign and define duties to *all* new store employees.	1 2 3 4 5	0 1 2 3 4 5
2.	Take a physical inventory monthly.	1 2 3 4 5	0 1 2 3 4 5
3.	Assign accounts to salespeople for collection.	1 2 3 4 5	0 1 2 3 4 5
4.	Monitor overtime payments to employees.	1 2 3 4 5	0 1 2 3 4 5
5.	Make sure the inside and outside of building is maintained in a presentable condition.	1 2 3 4 5	0 1 2 3 4 5
6.	Schedule and place advertisements in newspapers and radio.	1 2 3 4 5	0 1 2 3 4 5
7.	Make certain customers are greeted when coming into store and properly handled upon leaving.	1 2 3 4 5	0 1 2 3 4 5
8.	Establish a probationary period for new hires and review their performance periodically.	1 2 3 4 5	0 1 2 3 4 5
9.	Advise staff accountant of store claims.	1 2 3 4 5	0 1 2 3 4 5
10.	Arrange promissory notes payable at customers' bank if deemed necessary.	1 2 3 4 5	0 1 2 3 4 5
11.	Ensure that trucks are routed profitably.	1 2 3 4 5	0 1 2 3 4 5
12.	Hold safety meetings with store personnel.	1 2 3 4 5	0 1 2 3 4 5
13.	Make telephone solicitations to customers.	1 2 3 4 5	0 1 2 3 4 5
14.	Ensure that advertised products are available to customers.	1 2 3 4 5	0 1 2 3 4 5
15.	Discuss career goals with employees.	1 2 3 4 5	0 1 2 3 4 5

Course Objectives

The information obtained from the job description and the task identification is used to construct the course objectives. The course objectives consist of statements that specify the desired behavior of the trainee at the end of training. That is, these statements explicate what the training specialist expects the trainee to know and do after participating in the training program. Listed below are a few of the many course objectives that participants are expected to achieve upon completion of a four-week tire store manager training and development program:

1. Set down conditions of employment for new hires (i.e., spell out exactly what their jobs are)
2. Maximize one's employees through efficient scheduling and use of part-time people
3. Critique the appearance of different stores, and offer cost effective solutions to any problems discovered
4. Fill out a customer invoice
5. Be familiar with the proper use of safety cages for safely dismounting and mounting split run truck tires
6. Effectively handle customer complaints
7. Make a complete diagnosis of any car malfunc-

tions so as to handle customer service questions

8. Handle radio advertisements, newspaper ads, and direct mailings

9. Be familiar with some of the more critical OSHA (Occupational Safety and Health Administration) guidelines affecting store operations (e.g., proper stocking of aisles, storage of flammable materials, use of safety equipment in service area)

10. Be familiar with all types of store inventory (i.e., truck tires, passenger tires, brake and mechanical parts, and paperwork)

Although course objectives are based on the task identification, they differ in two important ways. First, task identification describes all of the components involved in performing a job. Course objectives do not include those things that trainees know before entering a course. For example, if prospective store managers already know how to complete a monthly inventory, there would be no need to include this task as a course objective.

Course objectives also do not include those tasks called for in performing a job that are impractical to teach during training and are better left to job experience. For example, handling of certain store operations may not be taught during a four-week store manager program since the training specialist may feel that it can be learned better on the job. Second, the task analysis describes the job as it is performed by an experienced employee. Objectives describe the kind of performance one can expect at the end of a training program. For example, an experienced store manager may be totally knowledgeable about all safety regulations affecting his or her store operations. It would be unrealistic to expect a trainee to know all of this upon course completion. It is far more realistic to expect the graduate to know some of the more critical regulations and learn the remainder of them through managerial experience (Mager and Beach, 1967).

It is important to remember that course objectives are tailored to people who will take the training course. Their level of motivation and their abilities will influence the quality of terminal performance that can reasonably be expected at the conclusion of the course.

PERSON ANALYSIS

Person analysis focuses on the individual employee. It deals with the question, "Who needs training and of what kind?" For example, one company found that its salespeople spent, on the average, only three hours a day with genuine sales prospects. The rest of the time was spent on various nonsales activities. The vice president of marketing decided that the entire salesforce needed a course teaching them how to make more productive use of work time. Although the one-day workshop on time management was effective for most people, it was obvious to the trainer that not everyone needed this training.

What is involved in doing person analysis? Step 1 of person analysis is concerned with how well a specific employee is performing his or her job. The term "performance appraisal" will be used to refer to the techniques employed by training specialists to measure an employee's job proficiency. The results of the performance appraisal determine whether or not Step 2 (referred to here as "diagnosis") is needed. If the appraisal indicates that an employee's work performance is acceptable, there is no need for Step 2. If, on the other hand, the employee's performance is found to be below standard, this is a signal that diagnosis is needed. The diagnosis involves carefully determining what specific skills and knowledge must be developed if the employee is to improve his or her job performance.

Step 1

Since Step 1 involves employee performance appraisal, let us turn to an overview of some of the methods that are available for evaluating whether or not an employee is performing a job adequately. These methods can be conveniently categorized into three general areas: (1) behavioral measures, (2) economic measures, and (3) proficiency tests.

Behavioral Measures. These measures involve ratings based on observations of an employee's on-the-job behaviors by superiors, peers, subordinates and/or outside evaluators. A major characteristic of behavioral measures is that they are dependent upon human observation, and accuracy in reporting observations is often affected by factors irrelevant to job performance. For example, an individual's physical attractiveness, race, seniority in the organization, personality, and level of education may contaminate the performance appraisal. Simply warning or lecturing raters about judgmental errors does not reduce them to any appreciable degree (Wexley, Sanders, and Yukl, 1973).

Fortunately, managers and supervisors can be taught to eliminate certain errors when observing and evaluating their employees (Latham and Wexley, 1981). For example, in one program, corporate managers were trained to eliminate the following judgmental errors: halo error (the tendency to rate an employee either high, average, or low on many factors simply because the rater believes the employee is high, average, or low on one single factor); similarity effect (the tendency on the part of a rater to judge more favorably individuals perceived as similar to him/herself); first impressions (the tendency to evaluate another person on the basis of a judgment made primarily after an initial meeting); and contrast effect (the tendency to evaluate subordinates in comparison to one another rather than against preestablished job requirements).

During the one-day workshop, trainees saw videotapes of hypothetical employees being appraised by a manager. The trainees estimated how the manager in the videotape evaluated the employee, and how they themselves would rate the individual. The program provides an opportunity for trainees to actively participate in discovering the degree to which they themselves are prone to making judgmental errors, to receive immediate feedback as to the accuracy of their own ratings, and to practice job-related tasks so as to minimize any errors being committed (Latham, Wexley and Pursell, 1975).

The training specialist has a number of behavioral procedures available for appraising employee proficiency. Two of the better behavioral procedures for appraising employee performance are known as behavioral expectation scales (Smith and Kendall, 1963) and behavioral observation scales (Latham and Wexley, 1977). Figures 6 and 7 provide examples of BES and BOS rating scales. The two procedures are similar in that both are variations of the critical incident technique, both are based on observable job behaviors that are viewed by others as critical to job success, and both take into account the multifaceted nature of job performance.

The BES and BOS methods differ, however, in at least one important way. Behavioral expectation scales require that each dimension be arranged on a continuous vertical rating scale with a behavioral anchor listed near each of the seven points ranging from ineffective to effective behavior. Raters simply examine the respective dimension and place a checkmark beside the one behavioral anchor that they believe best describes the behavior that the employee could be expected to demonstrate. This expectation is based on what the rater has seen the employee do over a period of time. Thus, the manager is required to extrapolate from actual behaviors observed to those that could be "expected" as defined by the scale anchors. The BOS requires no such extrapolation. Each critical behavior is listed in a questionnaire format and the rater indicates the frequency with which he or she has observed each behavior. An employee's total score on each dimension or criterion of job performance is then determined by totaling his or her scores on the five-point BOS scales. Although the example in Figure 7 contains only effective behaviors, in practice ineffective ones are listed as well.

The frequently heard complaints of managers and supervisors that the items on performance appraisal instruments are either sufficiently vague to defy understanding or completely inappropriate can be minimized with BES and BOS. The behavioral statements used are expressed in the rater's own terminology. In addition, by actively participating in the construction of the scales, the raters are more inclined to complete the ratings carefully and frankly.*

Economic Measures.   Here, the individual simply records the number of units produced in a given amount of time, sales volume, number of injuries, scrappage weight, and so on. In general, economic measures can be broken down into two subcategories: those dealing with production (e.g., units produced, number of rejects, dollars earned) and those dealing with personal information (e.g., absenteeism, tardiness, grievances, training time needed to reach some acceptable standard of performance).

These variables may serve as excellent indicators of an organization's effectiveness, but they often present problems as measures of an individual's job performance. First, they cannot be meaningfully applied to many organizational positions. They are usually appropriate for such jobs as assembly-line worker or press operator, where an employee's performance can be evaluated by recording the number of units produced in a given time period, the number of rejectable items produced, or the scrappage weight. However, on such nonproduction jobs as manager or chemist, neither quantitative measures of output nor job-related personal information are typically available (Latham and Wexley, 1981; Wexley, 1979). For such jobs behavioral measures should be used.

Proficiency Tests.   An entirely different approach to measuring employee proficiency is to use proficiency tests. One variant of this approach is to take a *work sample* whereby, in either the actual work setting or a simulation of it, the employee is asked to perform the duties required in a job. Examples of this approach would include simulated telephone calls to operators, typing tests for secretarial personnel, and flight simulators for pilots. The *assessment center* illustrates the use of simulation devices for evaluating the proficiency of managerial personnel. Another variant of this approach involves the use of written tests to assess employees' current job knowledge. For example, pipefitters might be given a battery of tests measuring such things as knowledge of fittings, accessories, and tools.

---

*See Latham, G.P., and Wexley, K.N. (1981) for a detailed discussion of the strengths and weaknesses of BES and BOS.

FIGURE 6
Example of a Behavioral Expectation Scale (BES)

Directions: First read the name of the behavioral dimension and its definition. Then notice the examples that illustrate various points on the rating scale. These examples are included to give you clear anchor points to help you make more accurate evaluations. Don't worry about whether or not your employee has actually exhibited the behavior described in the example. By knowing your employee, you should be able to judge whether he or she "could be expected" to display the type of behavior described in the example. After reading all the examples on a dimension, decide where on the rating scale the individual belongs by making a checkmark in the appropriate box. The box you check can range anywhere from the bottom of the scale, which represents low or poor performance, to the top of the scale, which represents high or good performance. Finally, on the next page, describe actual behaviors you have observed that support your rating. This same procedure should be followed for each dimension.

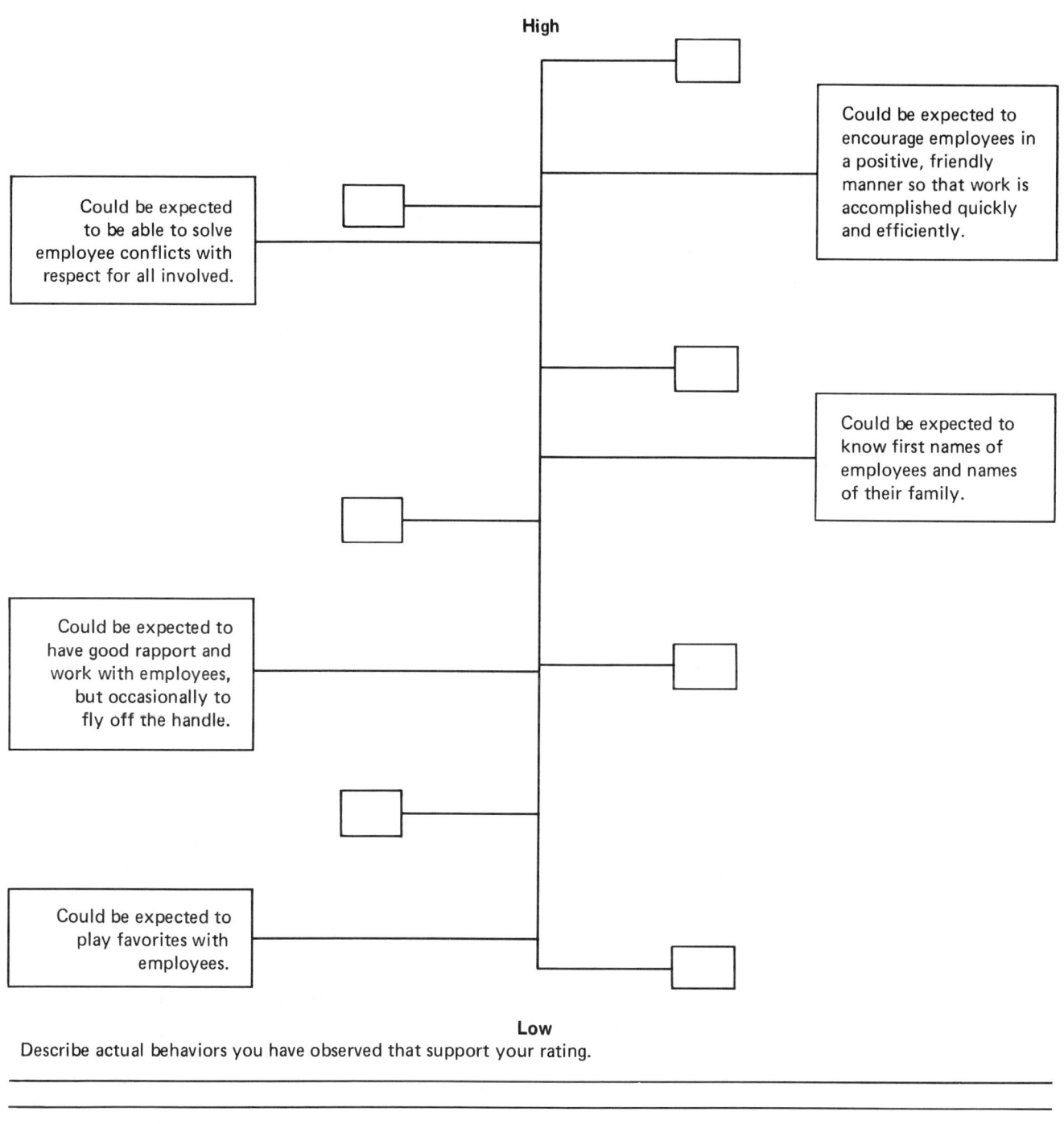

Describe actual behaviors you have observed that support your rating.

FIGURE 7
Example of a Behavioral Observation Scale (BOS)

Directions: This checklist contains performance-related job behaviors that foremen, their supervisors, and their subordinates have reported as critical to the foreman's job success. Please consider the above-named individual's behavior on the job for the past three months. Do not consider other foremen or this individual's behavior at other times in the past in making your ratings.

Read each statement carefully. On the basis of your actual observations or on dependable knowledge (e.g., hard evidence or reliable reports from others), circle the number that indicates the extent to which this particular foreman actually demonstrated each of the following behaviors. For each behavior, a 4 represents "Almost Always" or 95 through 100% of the time. A 3 represents "Frequently" or 85 through 94% of the time. A 2 represents "Sometimes" or 75 through 84% of the time. A 1 represents "Seldom" or 65 through 74% of the time. And a 0 represents "Almost Never" or 0 through 64% of the time.

Dimension I. Interactions with Subordinates

1. Asks an employee to do a job rather than tells him or her.
    Almost Never 0 1 2 3 4 Almost Always
2. Tells workers that if they ever have questions or problems with their jobs to feel free to ask him or her.
    Almost Never 0 1 2 3 4 Almost Always
3. Gives employees suggestions on how to do the job more easily.
    Almost Never 0 1 2 3 4 Almost Always
4. After assigning a difficult job, checks back to see if the worker is having any problem.
    Almost Never 0 1 2 3 4 Almost Always
5. When there is conflict (e.g., between two employees, between foreman and worker), takes the time to sit down and discuss the causes and potential solutions.
    Almost Never 0 1 2 3 4 Almost Always

Total = _____

Below Adequate	Adequate	Full	Excellent	Superior
0-4	5-8	9-12	13-16	17-20

In the space below, record observations to support your rating:

_____

_____

_____

_____

The major advantage of using proficiency tests is that they permit the employee's skills and knowledge to be compared to known standards under controlled and uniform conditions. Their main drawback is that the employee's performance during testing may not accurately reflect daily performance on the job.

We have now reviewed some of the performance appraisal methods that can be used in carrying out Step 1 of person analysis. This step involves determining whether each employee in the organization is adequately performing his or her job. By using a combination of behavioral, economic and proficiency measures, the training specialist can make an astute assessment of who is not fulfilling job requirements. If an individual is performing satisfactorily, there is no need for training. However, if an individual is not performing satisfactorily, then the next step in person analysis is warranted.

Step 2

Step 2 in person analysis involves determining the specific skills and knowledge that an employee needs to acquire in order to perform the job acceptably. This step requires a systematic diagnosis of each employee's strengths and weaknesses using the performance appraisal information collected during Step 1.

Consider an example of how diagnosis can help pinpoint the kind of training and development that an employee may need. Betty is employed as a copy editor for a medium-sized southwestern newspaper. Her job involves writing headlines, editing copy, selecting stories and other news material, laying out pages, and managing production flow. Betty's performance has been below standard ever since she was hired six months ago from another newspaper. Her performance has been evaluated using BOS by both her city editor and the paper's managing editor. Their evaluations indicate that Betty's weaknesses are primarily in the area of writing headlines. Specifically, she often writes inaccurate headlines, misses the point of a story with her headlines, occasionally misses deadlines, and uses poor grammar in headlines. As a result of this diagnosis, Betty is currently being coached by one of her department's most capable copy editors on headline writing. She is also taking a grammar course several nights per week at a junior college.

FINAL COMMENTS

We have presented several approaches that organizations can use for systematically determining training and development needs. Obviously, not all organizations will be able to afford the time and money to do every phase of organization, task, and person analyses as presented here. Yet, we offer these approaches as an ideal to strive for. Even a reduced application of these approaches is *better than* what many organizations are doing today to determine training and development needs.

Let us look for a moment at a few current organizational practices. Some organizations break down each of their jobs into a list of detailed parts or steps arranged in a logical sequence. A copy of this list is given to those employees whose opinions are valued. The employees check off those items on the list in which they would like to have more skill. Lists of all kinds are assembled. The one for salespeople might include prospecting for new business, conducting a fact-finding interview, sales closing, and sales follow-through. The list for retail store managers might include credit management, inventory control, building maintenance and security, sales management, customer relations, expense control, and community relations. One for industrial truck mechanics might include assembling distributors, changing generator brushes, replacing contacts and coils, reading blueprints, and so on.

Other organizations have a committee established for each special area of training such as orientation, sales, clerical, technical, supervisory, and executive. Each committee advises the training staff as to what particular training and development programs they think are needed. Sometimes the advisory committees also get involved in constructing the content of the courses and even evaluating course results.

Still other organizations purchase canned training and development programs from vendors who call on them periodically. The salesperson may be promoting programs on effective reading, improved human relations skills, increased assertiveness, or whatever. A vice president of manufacturing, marketing, or personnel may decide that this type of program is "needed" and purchase it on the spot or after giving it a short trial run.

Although these methods of determining training needs have their merit, it should be obvious that they are not as rigorous as the approaches presented in this chapter. Their biggest drawback, in our opinion, is that they are based solely on the assumption that someone can simply look at a list of training needs and accurately indicate what they themselves need or someone else needs in the way of personal development. Further, these methods tell us nothing about *where* within the organization a particular type of training is needed nor *who* needs it. The end result is the indiscriminate use of a training and development program across company locations and people. It is no wonder that employees are often heard making statements such as: "I have no idea why I've been told to go to that training course," "I know just about everything they taught in this program," and "Why doesn't the company just leave me alone and let me get on with my work!"

REFERENCES

- Blood, M. R., *Job Analysis of Entry-Level Clerical Jobs in the South Central Bell Company.* American Telephone and Telegraph Company, 1975.
- Burns, T. and Stalker, G. M., *The Management of Innovation.* London: Tavistock Publications, 1961.
- Cunningham, D. J., and Duncan K. D., "Describing Non-Repetitive Tasks for Training Purposes," *Occupational Psychology, 41*(1967), 203–210.
- Dean, E. C., and Jud, R. A. "How to Write a Task Analysis," *Training Directors' Journal, 19*(1965), 9–22.
- Fivars, G., "The Critical Incident Technique: A Bibliography," *JSAS Catalog of Selected Documents in Psychology, 5*(1975), 210.
- Flanagan, J. C., "The Critical Incident Technique," *Psychological Bulletin, 51*(1954), 327–358.
- Hinrichs, J. R., "Personnel Training," in Dunnette, M. D. (Ed.), *Handbook of Industrial and Organizational Psychology.* Chicago: Rand McNally, 1976, 829–860.
- Latham, G. P., "The Development of Job Performance Criteria for Pulpwood Producers in the Southeastern United States," unpublished Master's thesis, Georgia Institute of Technology, 1969.
- Latham, G. P., and Wexley, K. N., "Behavioral Observation Scales for Performance Appraisal Purposes," *Personnel Psychology, 30*(1977), 255–268.
- Latham, G. P., and Wexley, K. N., *Increasing Productivity through Performance Appraisal.* Reading, Massachusetts: Addison-Wesley, 1981.
- Latham, G. P., Wexley, K. N., and Pursell, E. D., "Training Managers To Minimize Rating Errors in the Observa-

tion of Behavior," *Journal of Applied Psychology,* *60*(1975), 550–555.

- Mager, R. F., and Beach, K. M., Jr., *Developing Vocational Instruction.* Belmont, California: Fearon Publishers, 1967.
- McGehee, W., and Thayer, P. W., *Training in Business and Industry.* New York: Wiley, 1961.
- Miller, R. B., "Task Description and Analysis," in Gagné, R. M. (Ed.), *Psychological Principles in System Development.* New York: Holt, Rinehart and Winston, 1962.
- Schneider, B., *Staffing Organizations.* Santa Monica, California: Goodyear Publishing Company, 1976.
- Smith, P. C., and Kendall, L. M., "Retranslation of Expectations: An Approach to the Construction of Unambiguous Anchors for Rating Scales," *Journal of Applied Psychology,* *47*(1963), 149–155.

- Wexley, K. N., *A Job Analysis Study of the Position of Residential Service Representative.* American Telephone and Telegraph Company, 1975.
- Wexley, K. N., "Performance Appraisal and Feedback," in Kerr, S. (Ed.), *Organizational Behavior.* Columbus, Ohio: Grid Publishing, 1979, 241–259.
- Wexley, K. N., Sanders, R. E., and Yukl, G. A., "Training Interviewers To Eliminate Contrast Effects in Employment Interviews," *Journal of Applied Psychology,* *57*(1973), 233–236.
- Wexley, K. N., and Silverman, S. B., "An Examination of Differences between Managerial Effectiveness and Response Patterns on a Structured Job Analysis Questionnaire," *Journal of Applied Psychology,* *63*:5(1978), 646–649.

Determining Managerial Training Needs

by Stephen J. Wall and Deepa Awal

ABSTRACT

The paper describes a process for determining managerial training needs that involves five phases: input, data collection, analysis and synthesis, recommendations for training and output. The process described accomplishes four important objectives:

1. *Provides a basis for placing the needs analysis process within an organizational context.*
2. *Identifies training needs by collecting and integrating information from different perspectives using multiple methods.*
3. *Uses existing knowledge of managerial work and skills from a behavioral perspective.*
4. *Clarifies assumptions associated with determining training responses.*

The ideas presented are based on current empirical findings and the authors' experience as practitioners.

This paper presents a framework for determining managerial training needs and examines the major assumptions underlying the process of needs assessment. Current theory focuses on organizational analysis, task analysis, and person analysis as the three

critical components for determining managerial training needs (McGehee & Thayer, 1961; Goldstein, 1980). The process employed assumes an open system perspective within the context of a "presenting problem." It also assumes that managerial training needs are addressed to increase the effectiveness of the organization and the individual.

The importance of doing needs assessment, or needs analysis, has been well documented in the training literature. In recent years much of the research on the subject has adopted a systems framework (Hinrichs, 1976; Goldstein, 1980). Few conceptual articles on needs assessment, however, have focused on the process from the viewpoint of implicit assumptions, characteristics, and problems in practice.

A framework for determining managerial training needs may be conceptualized as having five phases. What follows is a description of the key assumptions, characteristics, and problems associated with each phase in the process.

PHASE I: INPUT

The input phase defines the problem, identifies the level at which the problem exists, and establishes tentative standards against which subsequent efforts will be measured.

FIGURE I
Determining Managerial Training Needs

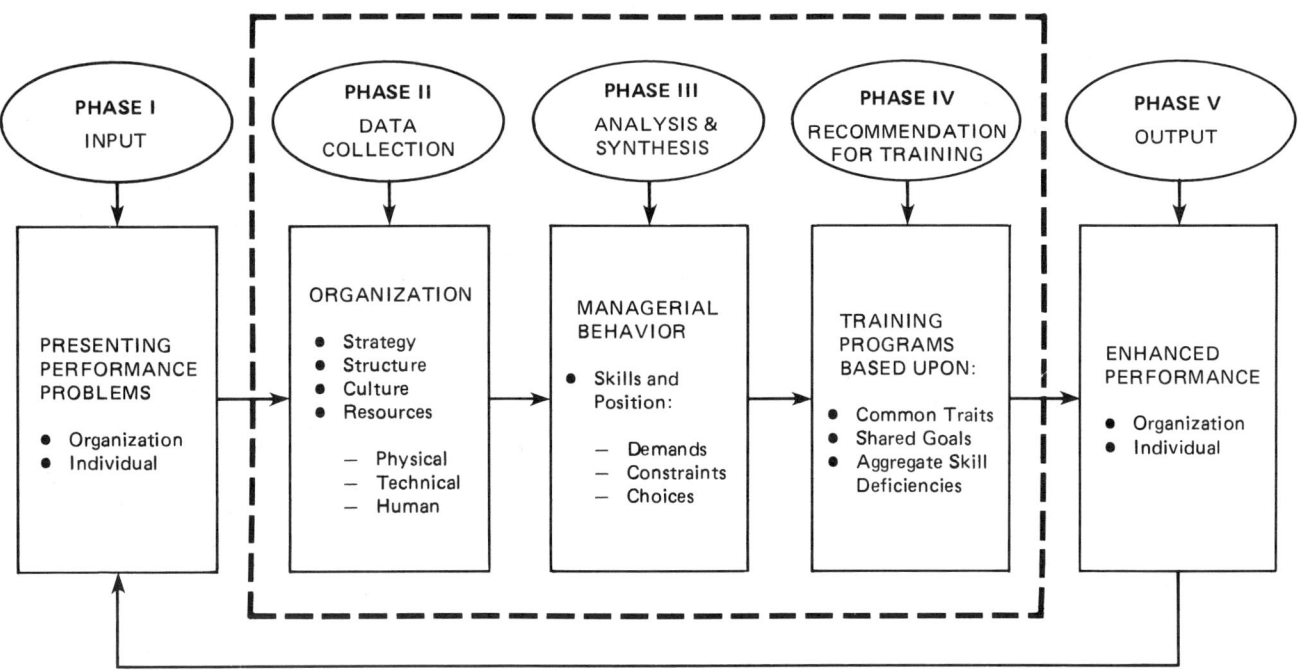

Assumptions

There are three major assumptions underlying the input phase.

1. Every needs assessment is undertaken in the face of a 'presenting performance problem.' In other words, "If it ain't broke, don't fix it."
2. In every needs assessment situation there is a client who engages the practitioner to undertake the project.
3. Managerial skill deficiency is at least considered a possible cause of some organizationally defined need (i.e., "the presenting problem").

Characteristics of Phase I

The input phase is primarily a description of the presenting performance problems which are the raison d'être for the needs analysis. There are two major characteristics of Phase I.

1. The presenting problem contains within it standards against which the output can be evaluated. This is a simple notion which merely states that the output can and should be evaluated against the needs defined at the Input stage.

Reduced probationary period, for example, or increased quality are instances of standards reflected in the presenting problem. The Input phase and Output phase then are similar to each other in terms of their desired outcomes, and some of the standards for evaluating output are expressed in the requirements of the input phase.

2. The nature of the presenting problem can vary widely ranging from an ill-defined conglomeration of trends, events and symptoms at the organizational level (e.g., increasing turnover, conflict and poor communications) to a well-defined, specific need of a group of individuals with similar work (e.g., training in marketing planning). This, to a large extent, determines the design of the next phase, i.e., Data Collection. When the problem is nebulous and large, different methodology would be used and different data would be collected than if the problem were specific and small.

Problems in Practice

1. Presenting problems may not be well defined. Very often the causes, symptoms and solutions of problems are not separated by the client. Assumptions about causes may not be valid and/or problems may be dressed like solutions.

2. Even if the problem is well-defined, pressures to act quickly may be driving the client to find quick apparent solutions, training being one of them.
3. Gaining the client's commitment to allocate the necessary resources especially in terms of time, energy, and money may not be easy.

PHASE II: DATA COLLECTION

The purpose of the data collection phase is to collect data with a view toward determining the managerial work to be done and the skills required to do it. In addition, it tests the hypothesis that managerial training will contribute toward resolving the presenting problem. Data is therefore, collected to appraise the situation and identify specific training needs. The former is at least as important as the latter since the "prescription" will only be as good as the "diagnosis."

Assumptions

There are three major assumptions underlying Phase II:

1. While training may at first seem appropriate, further analysis may show that this is not the case (Hinrichs, 1976; Mager & Pipe 1970; DiLauro, 1979). Requests for managerial training typically arise when the organization is not doing what it is supposed to be doing, e.g., actual performance deviates from desired performance. Training of managers may or may not be a solution to the problem.
2. Data should be collected using multiple methods and multiple sources. While the effort in this phase can be small or large, depending on the needs of the situation, the use of several methods (i.e., interviews, observation, unobtrusive, records, questionnaires) and sources (self, superior key informant) is essential (Goldstein, 1980).
3. There are two levels to be examined: the organization and the individual (Hinrichs, 1976). Each contains both formal and informal systems. These include organizational structure, strategy, work to be done, norms and values which guide the informal organization, skills required of and possessed by individuals and their needs, personal goals and expectations.

Characteristics of Phase II

1. The major characteristic of phase II is the emphasis on a wholistic view of the situation. While

boundaries need to exist for data gathering and interpretation, the practitioner nevertheless needs to avoid being dogmatic since the theories which underly our techniques cannot explain all of the variance in any organization situation. In most needs assessment approaches, the emphasis is on identifying the techniques and instruments for data collection. The typical response from the training departments is to collect information on training needs via questionnaires or interviews. As soon as techniques and instruments are identified, the boundaries for data collection are established.

2. The data collection phase can range from a smaller scale, more specific appraisal to a full-blown situation appraisal of the entire system. Some of the criteria for making this decision are:
    *   nature of presenting problem (e.g., an ill-defined problem vs. a well-defined one; or individual versus organizational)
    *   nature of the organization: its size, clarity of purpose, environmental constraints and opportunities, leadership, etc.
    *   inclinations and biases of client
    *   resources available
    *   willingness of client to use data in different ways, i.e., change other support systems in addition to managerial training
    *   culture with respect to extent and types of data collection

    Once these issues have been dealt with the techniques for doing needs assessment can be identified. While there are few meaningful guidelines for choosing techniques for conducting needs analysis, there are a number of tools and techniques available which permit analysis of the factors and variables described above (Gepson, Martinko & Belina, 1981).

3. Assuming that training is a whole or part of the solution to the presenting problem, the data collection phase enables three specific objectives to be achieved:
    *   to pin-point job-related training needs
    *   to ensure that appropriate training programs are developed
    *   to ensure that the recommendations are in keeping with the environment so that use of learned behaviors are supported by the organizational systems

Problems in Practice

The major problems encountered in Phase II are:

1. Defining and measuring relevant elements of organizational variables like strategy and structure.

Both the conceptualization and operationalization of these variables is inadequate at this point in time and much of this information must be collected from "members of the system." The practitioner, therefore, often needs to rely as much on judgment and intuition as on empirical findings to integrate the information regarding these variables.

2. The client's willingness, and ability to allocate resources to data collection in large part determines how this phase takes shape. The ability to persuade and inspire others' interest in the project is at least as important as formal authority.

3. Data collection methodology needs to be consistent with the organization's culture. The culture imposes boundaries upon what kind of information is collected, from what sources, and how.

PHASE III: ANALYSIS AND SYNTHESIS

With the data collected in Phase II now in hand, the next question is how to use the information to identify managerial work and skill requirements. While we continue to test the viability of managerial training as a possible solution for the "presenting problems" we remain openminded about "probable causes" and "possible solutions." At this point we narrow the focus by using the data collected in Phase II to describe the managerial behaviors required in the performance of that work.

Assumptions

A number of working assumptions guide the analysis at this point:

- Maintaining a distinction between work and skills is essential. Work refers to an activity which results in performance, while skills refer to the capacity of an individual to perform. Work describes positions while skills describe people and their capabilities.

- Using an understanding of the work to be done and the skills required rests on describing managerial behavior. Behavior ties both concepts together at the level of observable action. Without this behavioral foundation the ability to respond to a need for learning is severely limited (Gagné 1974).

- The work of managerial positions varies in a predictable fashion and useful information is available regarding the nature of managerial work and the behaviors required of those who hold managerial positions (Mintzberg, 1973; McCall et al, 1980; Yukl, 1980).

Characteristics of Phase III

This phase usually involves sharing the information gathered during Phase II with members of the organization. This includes the initial requester(s) of the training assessment, potential recipients, and those who will select participants for training. The information collected is reviewed and each offer their opinions regarding the managerial work implied and the behavior required of those who must do that work. This is the point when a shared model of managerial behavior is helpful. A common understanding and a common vocabulary regarding managerial behavior insures that the training system designers and training system users are communicating regarding the desired "end-product"; i.e, the behavior changes expected from managers who are trained. Thus, the building block for understanding both the work to be done and the skills required to perform that work is the ability to describe managerial behavior and how it systematically varies. Here existing taxonomies of managerial behavior are useful to describe positions and the capacities required of the individuals in those positions to do the work.

Behavioral terminology is used to speak of positions and individuals at different levels of abstraction. For instance, terms such as task, job, work and roles are used to describe positions, while terms such as activities, skills, dimensions and traits are used to describe individuals. The particular choice of terms is less important than agreement about meaning. From the viewpoint of the organization, work behaviors are used to develop and describe managerial positions, while skill dimensions stated in behavioral terms are used to describe the qualities possessed by individuals who staff positions. From the perspective of any training program ultimately developed, understanding the skills to be learned in behavioral terms allows us to prescribe the methods to be employed for the development of the individual. As Stewart (1982) points outs, only synthesizing managerial work and skills in terms of broad categories leads one to ambiguous conclusions which may be supported at a high level of abstraction but are misleading when applied to positions and individuals.

A considerable body of quite recent work does provide a useful point of departure. A review of diary and observational studies by McCall (et al., 1978) and longitudinal research by Yukl and his colleagues (1980) have provided a useful starting point for identifying the behavior requirements of managerial work. McCall et al. (1980) have extended our understanding of the work to be done in managerial positions by further elaborating Mintzberg's approach to describing managerial positions in terms of roles and the behaviors required to perform these roles. Yukl and his colleagues (1980) have developed an excellent behavioral base line for the description of managerial skills. Thus, we use existing taxonomies of managerial behavior to describe positions and the capacities required of the individuals in those positions. It is often not recognized that observable behavior is the "criterion" for both.

Problems in Practice

The number of problems and practice at this particular stage actually go beyond the scope of this article, however, we will list a number of the more salient.

- The nature of managerial work is simultaneous, frenetic and inherently political.
- It is difficult to measure managerial behavior per se.
- It is difficult to relate managerial behavior to individual performance.
- The actual standards of performance that are relevant to managerial work are organizational in nature and are therefore distal even when available.
- This is an area of evolving practice and theory and there is a considerable lack of consistency in the use of even simple terms like work, skills, and behavior.

PHASE IV: RECOMMENDATIONS FOR TRAINING

Phase III has produced an understanding of the behavioral requirements from both the perspective of the managerial work to be done and the skills required. This information provides the base upon which an effective and efficient training curriculum can be developed. With the work to be done defined in behavioral terms, the analysis now proceeds to an identification of the skills and knowledge which are amenable to development through training. The purpose of Phase IV is twofold:

- To determine what methods are appropriate for developing the behaviors required for task performance.
- To determine which individual managers should be developed given the data about the existing managerial skill base of the organization.

Assumptions

There are two major assumptions underlying Phase IV.

1. A number of training experiences are open to managers, other than formal training programs.

For example, project assignments, job rotation, coaching on the job are all available to develop skills/knowledge.

2. There is a common behavioral base underling the three important taxonomies at this stage; viz, the learning, the instructional and the managerial behavior taxonomy.

Since this stage of the analysis demands the specification of learning taxonomies and the matching of instructional systems, it requires a taxonomy of managerial behavior.

Characteristics of Phase IV

It is possible to examine the individual behavioral data collected in Phase III from at least three perspectives to determine what skills to teach to whom through formal training experiences:

- common tasks to be performed by individuals in similar positions
- shared goals held by managers in different functions
- skill deficiencies shared by a number of managers

These perspectives are seen as a logical foundation for drawing groups of people together for training programs. When based on shared work, the primary objective of the program is to teach managers specific functional skills. These programs could range from such topics as managerial finance and accounting, to managing sales people, to data processing management. These are programs for which the behavioral base is a common repertoire of activities demanded by work performance.

Programs based on shared goals would result from a decision to develop a common understanding for courses of action especially regarding policy and strategy. Such programs often have the secondary goal of establishing contact between managers who would not normally interact on a routine basis. There are often managers who establish a "mutual relationship" and are thus better equipped to handle some future problems or unusual occurrences by drawing upon this network for help.

The third basis of managerial training—shared skill deficiences—consists of people who have a common need with regard to the development of a particular skill such as "decision making" or "leadership." Since attendance at training would be based upon an identified skill deficiency basing training content on this dimension does require an effective supervisory management system where goals are being set in relation to agreed upon parameters (usually between a boss and a subordinate). This process should include a regular review of progress toward work goal attainment.

In addition to identifying the appropriate bases for training programs, recommendations need to be made in the context of existing human resource management systems in the organization. It is important to identify organizational variables which are required to support an effective training effort and integrate the training process with existing managerial selection, development, reward and planning systems. At this stage, it is likely that the needs assessment data analysis will serve other purposes as well. For example, appraisal is facilitated as a result of having identified the work to be done within managerial positions and the behaviors which are considered desirable by the organization for effective performance; development overall is enhanced as a result of having examined a wide range of options, including training; the effectiveness of the reward system is enhanced as a result of forging closer links between the rewards provided and the performance observed during the appraisal process, etc.

Problems in Practice

1. The major problem in this phase is to ensure that the recommendations are implemented effectively. In other words, the purpose of training is to bring about change. Very often the kind of things that should be in place to make training effective are not in place. Recommendations will be effective only to the extent that the other variables in the system support it.
2. Formal training competes with daily work demands for the manager's time.

PHASE V: OUTPUT

The output from a needs assessment should enhance managerial performance both at the individual and the group level.

Assumptions

1. The output reflects the presenting problem(s) expressed in Phase I. For example, if the presenting problem at the start was low quality of the product produced by the organization then the criterion to determine the effectiveness of output would be improvement in product quality.
2. The output phase assumes evaluation of the process in terms of (i) how well the requirements made explicit in Phase I are met, and (ii) how well resources have been used to obtain the output.
3. It also assumes a continuous feedback from output to input in order to monitor and/or change the process if necessary.

Characteristics of Phase V

The output phase is characterized by evaluation of two things:

(a) The extent to which resources have been used efficiently in the previous four phases; this is, the efficiency criteria.
(b) The extent to which the presenting problem in Phase I is eliminated or some opportunity goal attained. This is, the effectiveness criteria.

The efficiency criteria is reflected in such things as efficient use of resources perceived value of training on the part of participants, meeting competitive standards for similar types of training, etc. The effectiveness criteria is reflected in how well the problems described in Phase I are resolved both in the immediate and long term.

At this point, due to the inherent difficulties in measuring dynamic processes, and understanding causal relationships in complex organizations it may be sufficient to accept little more than some indication that the initial presenting problem and its effects have been dissipated. The evaluation, therefore, is limited in that success can only be judged by the system "designers" and the ultimate recipients of the training intervention.

Problems in Practice

An accurate assessment of output presents a number of problems for the practitioner. Major among these are:

1. There is an inherent resistance to allocating resources to evaluation.
2. In most business organizations needs assessment is seen as a one shot effort at a point in time for a specific purpose. The feedback from the output phase is therefore hardly ever washed against the input phase in a systematic manner to suggest changes in the process. This reduces the usefulness of assessing output.
3. It is difficult to measure dynamic processes and control for factors other than the ones under consideration.
4. Enhanced managerial performance represents the ultimate criterion for the needs assessment process. However, the construct of managerial performance is elusive and not well-defined. This necessitates assessing the output against more specific and often less adequate criteria.

CONCLUSIONS

We have attempted to describe a process of needs assessment which is both comprehensive and yet problem-focused. The framework described in this paper addresses the complex problem of determining managerial training needs within the constraints imposed by the nature of managerial work and the need to allocate organizational resources efficiently.

Throughout the process of needs assessment the practitioner is very much dependent upon the members of the system to understand how their system works, both in terms of defining the relevant variables and understanding the causal relationships between these situational variables. This is often done intuitively primarily because theory and methodology do not provide us with adequate tools. It is still possible, however to initiate action. As Weick (1979) has pointed out, " . . . people don't need to know the territory inch by inch to do something about it or in it".

The major contributions of this paper are:

1. In a review of the personnel training literature Hinrichs (1976) states that " . . . the major emphasis . . . tends to be on the training program . . . in the rush to 'do something' the (training) practitioners all too often lose sight of the problem." The ideas in this paper respond to this concern.
2. A second major contribution of this paper lies in attempting to clarify the basic concepts of managerial work, skills, and behaviors and how these concepts relate to each other. There are at least two reasons why this is considered important—(i) managerial work, skills and behaviors form the underpinnings of any kind of managerial training needs assessment (Campbell, 1971; Goldstein, 1980; Hinrichs, 1976) and (ii) the words, behaviors, skills, and work are often used in different ways by different authors; a common understanding of the terms is therefore necessary.

The scope of the paper is defined by the process of needs assessment and the variables within that process. It does not speak to instructional design and technology, program objectives and content, type of training program, etc. To the extent that the dimensions of managerial work are incompletely identified, the final output of a managerial training needs assessment will also be incomplete. The primary purpose of the paper has been to present a process for determining managerial training needs, to identify some fundamental assumptions that a practitioner needs to make in doing a needs assessment, and to present key characteristics and problems associated with the operationalization of each phase.

REFERENCES

- DiLauro, T.J. Training needs assessment: current practices and new directions. *Public Personnel Management*, 1979, 8, 350–359.
- Gagné, R. M. *Essentials of learning for instruction.* Hinsdale, IU.: Dryden Press, 1974.
- Hinrichs, J. Personnel Training. In M. D. Dunnette (Ed.) *Handbook of Industrial and Organizational Psychology.* Chicago: Rand McNally, 1976.
- Mager, R. F. and Pipe, P. *Analyzing Performance Problems, or You Really Oughta Wanna.* Calif: Fearnon, 1970.
- McCall, M. W. and Segrist, C. A. In pursuit of the manager's job: building on Mintzberg, *Center for Creative Leadership,* Technical Report No. 14, March 1980.
- McGehee, W. and Thayer, P. W. *Training in business and industry.* New York: Wiley, 1961.
- Mintzberg, H. *The nature of managerial work.* Englewood Cliffs, N.J.: Prentice Hall, 1973.
- Nadler, D. A. and Tushman, M. L. *A congruence model for organizational problem solving.* NY: OR & C Inc., 1980.
- Stewart, R. A model for understanding managerial jobs and behavior. *Academy of Management Review,* 1982, 7, 7–13.
- Yukl, G. *Leadership in organizations.* Englewood Cliffs, N.J.: Prentice Hall, 1981.
- Weick, K. E. Cognitive processes in organizations. In B. M. Staw (Ed.), *Research in organizational behavior* (Vol. 1). Greenwich, Conn.: JAI Press, 1979, 41–74.

An Alternative Approach to Assessing Management Development Needs

by Robert J. Oppenheimer

Under normal conditions, training and development is matched with deficiencies in employee skills. This usually entails an organizational analysis which identifies the organization's goals, resources and environment, followed by a task analysis which determines the skills, knowledge and attitudes needed to perform the job successfully. Finally, a performance analysis (perhaps by reviewing performance ratings) identifies skill areas in which deficiencies are relatively widespread and consist of those skills found important to task performance. (Goldstein, 1974; Bass & Vaughan, 1966.)

Cascio (1978) points out that training needs and training content usually are determined by the professional training and development staff. They gain the required information by such methods as surveys, job analyses, critical incidents, performance appraisals, manpower analyses and organizational analyses. Another method is to accumulate requests for training in specific areas made by line managers, and then respond by offering programs. (Miner & Miner, 1977.)

A difficulty with the usual approaches to assessing training and development needs seems to be the requirement for centralizing program initiation, conceptualization, definition and interpretation. Training and development professionals may become reactive to filling training and developmental needs, rather than anticipatory. Further, from what is known about participatory management methods, a more active solicitation from employees could prove effective. When assessing the development needs of middle and senior managers, assumptions about similarities in duties and performance-related activities may not be valid.

THE COMPANY AND NEEDS ASSESSMENT

The organization in question is a large, multi-plant, urban-based company. The company is a well-established firm experiencing only moderate growth, along with the rest of its industry. Their managerial ranks consist of basically loyal, long-tenured employees who have in-depth knowledge of their company and their industry. The managers occupy a large number of different positions, almost all of which have fairly high levels of responsibility. In essence, this is a highly mature, responsible, stable, knowledgeable and loyal population.

It was not considered feasible to conduct formal task analyses of the jobs of the middle- and senior-level managers. This was because most of the 150 jobs were unique. Those that had similar titles were in different locations and had different job requirements and would therefore need to be analyzed individually. The staff to conduct such an analysis was simply unavailable and unobtainable. Further, having one or a few individuals conducting analyses of individuals' training needs was even further removed from the realm of possibility. A different method of gathering this important information seemed necessary. After discussions with appropriate representatives, the job incumbents and/or their bosses were to conduct their own task and person analyses, resulting in a decentralization of data gathering.

After considerable discussion and pooling of opinions within the organization, it was decided that job incumbents (and not their bosses) would be consulted. This was done in part to decentralize the process to those affected by the analysis. The decision was based on the assumption that managers at these levels would have as good, or better, an understanding as their boss as to what additional skills, abilities or knowledge would be helpful in their present or future job.

Involving the incumbents rather than their bosses was also done to increase the incumbents' commitment to the training programs to be developed. This was based on our assumption that the more the managers felt the training programs centered around their needs as they perceived them, the more likely they would be to participate in the training programs. An important consideration in this decision was our opinion that the managers involved were knowledgeable, loyal and mature.

The alternative of building the analysis into the annual performance review was considered, but rejected on the basis that these had been recently completed, and therefore, close to a year would pass before this could be done. Further, there was some reservation as to the quality of the information which would be obtained if it was "simply" another part of the performance appraisal process.

Concurrent with the decision to involve the incumbents directly was to consider the method of data collection, what questions to ask and how to analyze the results. The data collection method was the easiest of these questions to answer. Given a limited number of people and the desire to compare responses readily, questionnaires were determined to be the method for collecting information.

THE ASSESSMENT PROCESS

Designing the Questionnaire

The questionnaire listed a number of skills and knowledge areas believed to be relevant for a senior- or middle-level manager. Subtopics that further defined each of the skills and knowledge areas were also pro-

vided. As an example, "time management" had subtopics of "scheduling one's time," "setting priorities" and "delegating." In total, 21 skills and knowledge areas were specified. Space was also provided for other areas.

The skills and knowledge areas included were obtained by reviewing the management literature, analyzing the attributes commonly examined in assessment centers and "arm-chairing" additional general requirements for the positions to be assessed. This list was then distributed for review by seven other people in different departments or locations within the company. Based upon their comments, three additional areas were included; none were deleted. These steps were taken to assure the content validity of the questionnaire. The final 21 areas are shown in Table 1.

An initial draft of the questionnaire was distributed to a test group of 10 managers, to ensure that the questionnaire was unambiguous and understandable. This procedure resulted in simplified instructions. The revised instructions are shown in the appendix.

TABLE 1
Summary Analysis of Management Development Needs

Skill and Knowledge Areas	(Question 1) See Appendix Ratings (Number Responding That Training in Area Would be Considerably or Extremely Helpful.)	(Question 2) See Appendix Total Ranking (Number Ranking Training in Area as One of their Top Five Priority Areas.)	Possible Priorities
Motivation	69	46	6
Industrial relations	40	21	
Accident	20	10	
Communication	101	79	1
Teamwork	100	65	2
Planning	92	51	3
Organizing	62	29	
Controlling	66	25	
Problem solving	65	40	6
Decision-making	70	41	6
Time management	84	43	4
Goal setting	85	48	4
Performance appraisal	74	43	6
Selection skills	57	24	
Improving the working environment	57	33	10
Job evaluation	44	20	
Employee benefits	18	5	
Marketing strategies	38	16	
Production processes	52	25	
Financial planning	63	32	10
Basic computer concepts	41	18	
All "additional topics"	47	21	Follow-up indiv.

The purpose of the first question (asking how helpful training in each area would be) was to differentiate between considerably/extremely helpful areas and other areas. The second question (asking the test group to prioritize the five major areas which would be most helpful) was included to help further differentiate which areas were considered most important. The third question (asking for any additional areas) was included to facilitate the response to specific individual needs. The final question (requesting the more important subtopics to be circled) was included to help sharpen the focus of any course or seminar directed at improving a particular skill or knowledge area.

Analyzing the Responses

The issue of how to analyze the data was examined before the questionnaire design was completed. It was relevant for this organization to obtain information based on geographical location, job function (production, marketing, etc.) and the language preference (English, French, other) of the respondents. Questions to elicit this information were included in the questionnaire.

The number of people who responded that training would be "considerably" or "extremely" helpful was compiled for each of the 21 skill and knowledge areas. This information was summarized and is shown in column 2 of Table 1. The number of people who ranked a particular skill or knowledge area was also compiled. This is summarized in column 3 of Table 1. As an example, 46 of the participants ranked "motivation" as one of their top five areas (of the 21) for which they believed additional training and development would be most helpful. In addition to performing these analyses for the entire organization (shown in Table 1), the compiled data by geographical division, job function and language preference were provided.

The analyses were conducted using the subprogram "crosstabs" from the *Statistical Package for the Social Sciences* by Nie, Hull, Jenkins, Steinbrenner and Bent (1975). A further analysis, using the subprogram "frequencies" provided the same type of information on an individual basis. That is, each questionnaire, after it was returned, was number-coded. A listing was then provided for each of the 21 areas as to who rated that area as considerably or highly important (question 1) and who ranked it as a priority for training (question 2). This could then be used as a quick reference to determine who should be informed (or specifically invited) to a seminar in any given area. It was possible to do this because almost everyone signed their questionnaires even though it was not required.

Results

A clear and consistent pattern of results emerged (see Table 1). The four highest rated areas were communication, teamwork, planning and goal setting. These were also the four areas ranked with the highest priority. That is, they were seen as the areas where additional training would be most helpful.

The Spearman Rank Order Correlation between Ratings and Rankings is .96 (p < .001) for the 22 skills and knowledge areas (which include "all additional topics"). This means that the order in which the rankings appeared was extremely similar to the order of the ratings (i.e., those in the top five priority groups). The practical implication of this result is that either the ratings (question 1) or the rankings (question 2) could have been used, and that both were unnecessary. Usually, participants find it easier to rate rather than rank their choices.

The "possible priorities" column of Table 1 was determined by the author by subjectively evaluating the ratings and rankings in the second and third columns. Those areas rated and ranked highest were shown as having the top priorities. The "possible priorities" column was created to interpret and further summarize the data in columns 2 and 3. This information served as a basis for discussion during a series of meetings within the company. The back-up information, including the geographical divisions, job functions and language preferences was examined with respect to these possible priorities.

This process included conducting a number of follow-up telephone calls and informal discussions with the respondents to ascertain if the responses were being interpreted accurately. This increased our confidence that the measures were reporting what they were intended to report—that is, to test the construct validity of the measures.

FOLLOW-UP

One year after this analysis, the vice president of personnel described it as having effectively identified the general training needs of the middle- and senior-level managers. His evaluation was based on the written and personal comments of those who participated in the training programs which were designed and implemented based on this analysis. No systematic research was undertaken to determine whether the training had any effect on actual on-the-job performance.

A disappointing outcome was that participation was predominantly from one of the four major locations. The process of designing the needs analysis included the active participation of the personnel managers from the different regions. This was done to gain their ideas and commitment. Apparently this was accomplished; however, their bosses (regional general managers) were not involved in the process and two of them decided not to participate in what they perceived as a "head-office" training program.

In trying to evaluate why this occurred, the following explanations are provided. The general managers, although participants in the analysis of training needs, were never committed to the need for training. That is, no effort was made to convince them that there were deficiencies that training would rectify, nor was there an attempt to justify the training costs in terms of performance payoffs. The general managers were not involved in the process of designing the questionnaire, nor in decisions regarding its implementation. Therefore, they were not committed to the results it generated. Finally, the history of the "protectionist" attitude of the regions with regard to "interference" from the head office was not addressed.

IMPLICATIONS FOR USE

The approach described was successful in identifying the management development needs considered most pertinent in this particular company, and it may be relevant in other organizations. The specific characteristics of the company and of the population should be considered before contemplating the use of this approach elsewhere.

We believed these middle- and senior-level managers were capable and willing to identify those areas in which training and development would be helpful to themselves and to the organization. Thus, these considerations were instrumental in suggesting this "decentralized" approach to assessing management development needs. The approach was effective in this particular company, and although different organizations face other conditions, it may also be helpful elsewhere.

An alternative to test validity of the questionnaire would be to use an alternative data-gathering method and to compare the results. This could be done by conducting an organizational, task and person analysis in a part of the organization or by asking the immediate supervisors to evaluate their subordinate's development needs. In this organization these strategies were considered unnecessary and were not pursued. Greater confidence, however, may be placed on the results when two or more methods converge. Therefore, this approach is recommended if the time and resources are available.

The result of this needs analysis process was a mixed success. It provided an understanding of management development needs and a basis for the design and implementation of a training program that, based on testimonial-type reports, met the participants' needs. However, the process failed to enlist the support of two key general managers. These results, both positive and negative, may provide insights for others facing similar circumstances.

BIBLIOGRAPHY

- Bass, B. M. and J. A. Vaughan. *Training in Industry: The Management of Learning.* Brooks/Cole Publishing Belmont, Calif., 1966.
- Cascio, W. F. *Applied Psychology in Personnel Management.* Reston, Reston, Va., 1978.
- Goldstein, I. I. *Training: Program Development and Evaluation.* Brooks/Cole Publishing, Belmont, Calif., 1974.
- Miner, J. B. and M. G. Miner. *Personnel and Industrial Relations,* 3rd ed. Macmillan, New York, 1977.
- Nie, N. N., C. H. Hull, J. G. Jenkins, K. Steinbrenner and D. H. Brent. *Statistical Package for the Social Sciences,* 2nd ed. McGraw-Hill, New York, 1975.
- Oppenheim, A. N. *Questionnaire Design and Attitude Measurement.* Basic Books, New York, 1966.

APPENDIX

Instructions for questionnaire on management development needs.

The purpose of this form is to help identify what type of *general* management training and/or development activities would be beneficial for our management personnel to help them perform their jobs better. Since an overall evaluation of our training needs is sought and since we are anxious to ensure that the information provided is as complete and accurate as possible, you are *not* required to sign this form.

You are welcome to discuss your development needs with your immediate supervisor, as well as to retain a photocopy, should you wish to use this as part of your personal development plan in the future.

Specifically, what is requested is that for each of the skill and/or knowledge areas identified on the following pages, you answer the following four questions.

1. To what extent would training, designed to increase your skill or knowledge (for each particular area), help you to do your present job better and/or prepare you for other job responsibilities? Please use the following scale when answering in Column A of the attached form.

1—Not at all helpful
2—Somewhat helpful
3—Reasonably helpful
4—Considerably helpful
5—Extremely helpful

2. In which of these major skill and knowledge areas would additional training or development be most helpful to you? Select only the five major areas (not subtopics) that would be most desirable areas and rank them from 1 (most desired) to 5 (fifth most desired). Please answer in Column B on the attached form.

3. What additional aspects would you like to see included in a training program and/or what other topics would you find helpful, if any? Please add your suggestions directly to the attached form.

4. Within each of the major skill and knowledge areas, please circle those subtopics which are of particular interest or importance to you.

How to Determine the Training Needs of Your Supervisors—When They're Spread Across the Map

by Patrick J. Germany and C. W. Von Bergen, Jr.

Training competent managers and supervisors is a vital and important task, especially in a growing organization. And we all know the most effective training programs begin with a careful, systematic assessment of needs. Yet how do you assess management/supervisory training needs—efficiently and effectively—in a geographically dispersed organization? Here's how we did it at Western Petroleum Services division of The Western Company of North America, a land-based oil well servicing company employing over 2,000 people in five geographical regions.

Many approaches are available for determining the training needs of supervisors. D. L. Kirkpatrick, in "Determining Supervisory Training Needs and Setting Objectives" (*Training and Development Journal*, 1978) summarizes various methods:

1. Analyzing the supervisor's job.
2. Analyzing problems.
3. Asking the supervisors themselves.
4. Asking the superiors of the prospective trainees.
5. Asking their subordinates.
6. Testing knowledge and/or skills.
7. Observing supervisory behavior.
8. Analyzing performance-appraisal information.
9. Conducting exit interviews.
10. Using an advisory committee.

A combination of several of these methods—an approach Kirkpatrick endorses—is often the most effective way to determine needs, and it is the approach taken by the training department of Western Petroleum Services.

In 1978, the training staff decided to undertake a supervisory/management needs analysis to determine if existing training programs reflected actual training needs and to identify areas in which additional training might be required. The needs analysis was structured to include numbers 2, 3, 4 and 10 of Kirkpatrick's methods. The staff felt that these items would yield a thorough list of needs without being overly cumbersome and time-consuming.

The target audience in this case was 40 middle-level managers, 55 foremen and 176 first-line supervisors. The needs analysis included developing a questionnaire and appointing an advisory committee (Figure 1). After a review of literature in various training-related publications, a 72-item needs analysis questionnaire was developed by the training staff to measure the importance and frequency of tasks engaged in by supervisors. Respondents were asked to rank the importance of a task on a three-point scale from high to low and the frequency of a task on a four-point scale from often to never.

HELP FROM THE TASK FORCE

While the questionnaire was being developed, the training staff and the regional vice-presidents appointed managers from each of five geographical regions to serve on the analysis task force. The objectives of this group included interviewing key managers and supervisors in each region to identify expressed

FIGURE 1
Needs Analysis Flowchart

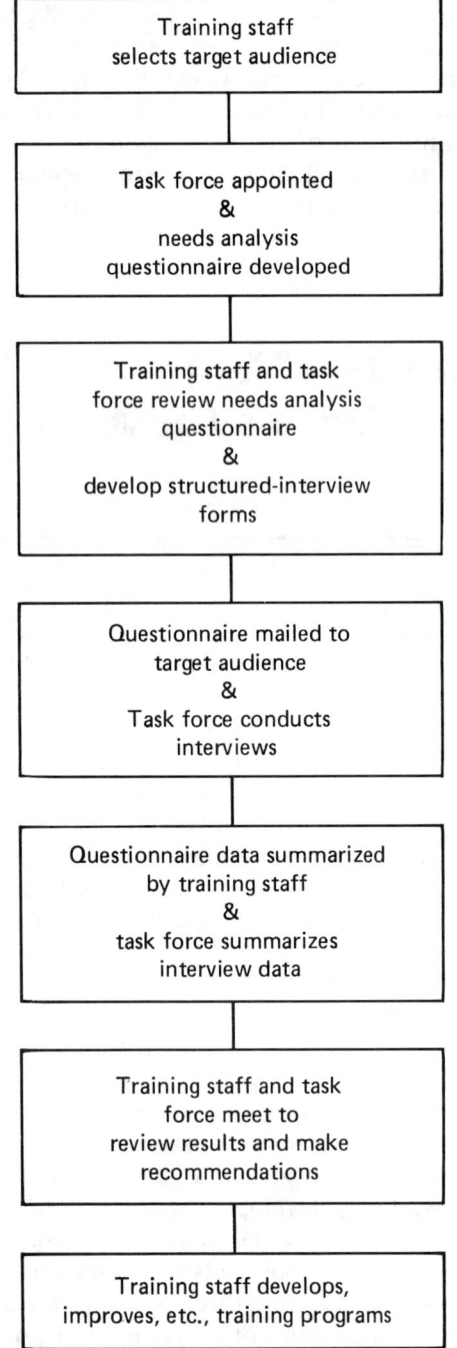

training needs, reviewing all data accumulated by the training staff and making recommendations concerning any training which might be needed in the future. This group of managers met with the training staff to review the needs analysis questionnaires and to develop a structured interview form. The form (Figure 2) was considered necessary to ensure reliability and standardization among interviewers.

The task force then spent a month interviewing supervisors and their managers. A total of 93 first- and second-level managers were interviewed. The interviews yielded a rank order list of specific areas of needs: Human relations, financial profit & and loss/ preparing budgets, planning, safety, sales, interviewing, policies/procedures, performance appraisals, communications, sales management.

At the same time the interviews were conducted, the needs analysis questionnaires were sent to all supervisors and their managers. The response rate was 82%, with 222 questionnaires returned. The questionnaires were then keypunched and a computerized, statistical analysis was conducted to determine the mean and standard deviation for each item on the scales of frequency and importance. Several of the more important tasks, according to the target group, were: Employee safety rules, planning the work, training employees in policy/procedure compliance, checking on the work of employees, giving instructions to employees, giving safety instructions, problem solving, handling dissatisfied employees, involving employees in decisions, controlling expenses.

THE RESULTS

The results of the questionnaire and the interview data were summarized by the training staff and the task force, and a second meeting was held to analyze the findings and make recommendations concerning future training programs. One problem encountered at this time was that the results of the questionnaires differed somewhat from those of the structured interviews. For instance, although problem solving was a task engaged in frequently and deemed important by supervisors, the topic was not mentioned in even a single interview. Sales training was mentioned frequently in inter-

FIGURE 2
Structured Interview Form Sample Questions

1. Think back to when you first started your present job. What type of training would have helped you at that time?
2. What training would benefit you now in your present job?
3. What training do you need to become a promotable candidate for the next position up? What job is that?
4. What would the prerequisites for your job be? What is the minimum experience level of a candidate for your job?
5. How should you receive training, i.e., seminars, on-the-job, etc.?
6. Where should we have training, i.e., resort, hotel, work location?

views but the questionnaire, by virtue of its design, did not yield this need. However, the task force was able to deal with these differences by allowing discussion and arriving at a decision based upon the staff's knowledge (derived from the questionnaire and actual training conducted) and the experience of the task force members. For the most part, the questionnaire results were compatible with those of the interviews.

The group developed a list of areas of need, and these were compared to topics included in existing training programs. Areas identified as needing additional attention included training in human relations, finance, planning and safety.

A new program, advanced management, was developed to include the following human relations topics: Orientation for new employees, employee motivation, employee counseling, effective discipline and handling employee and customer complaints. Two existing programs were revised to increase from seven hours to sixteen hours the time spent on planning and finance for supervisors.

No action was taken to add more safety training, since the group felt that existing training in that area was sufficient. The analysis pointed out that more managers and supervisors needed to attend safety training sessions and that more management people needed to attend at least one of the three in-house sales training programs in order to better supervise their sales personnel.

This needs analysis design proved to be an efficient, cost-effective way to evaluate existing training and identify needed programs. One improvement suggested was that the members of the task force serve as content-area specialists, to monitor new and existing training modules to ensure that each reflects a specific training need.

This approach could be used by most moderate to large organizations. It is recommended for those that are geographically dispersed, but it could be applied, with minor modifications, to a large manufacturing organization on one site.

The Nominal Group Technique: Applications for Training Needs Assessment

by Dow Scott and Diana Deadrick

Performing a needs assessment is recognized as a fundamental first step in the development of a training program (Stein, 1981; Leach, 1979; Moore and Dutton, 1978). In the face of rapidly changing markets and technologies, organizations must make periodic adjustments in their mode of operation to survive. Training programs based on previously developed materials, such as the training director's old notes or reruns of previously successful programs, will at best be discontinued for irrelevance, or at worst will be offered and will burn up scarce training resources.

Although numerous methods of conducting a training needs assessment have been proposed, the authors believe that the Nominal Group Technique (NGT) can be used for such assessments and may represent the most effective method in many situations.

NOMINAL GROUP TECHNIQUE

The nominal group was originally developed by Andre Delbecq and Andrew Van de Ven in 1968 as a technique to involve disadvantaged citizens in community action agencies under funding by the Office of Economic Opportunity. Since then, it has been widely applied in health, social service, education, industrial and government organizations as a method for generating ideas in situations where the participants do not fully understand or agree upon the nature of the problem or how to solve the problem. More specifically, NGT is a special-purpose group process appropriate for identifying elements of a problem situation, identifying elements of a solution program and establishing priorities. It is extremely useful when the judgments of several individuals must be clarified and aggregated into a group decision.

Actually, NGT has become more than a "nominal" group. The term "nominal" is derived from earlier researchers' work with groups in which no verbal communication existed between individuals. Since verbal exchange was excluded, these were groups in name only, or nominally. Now, the NGT structure contains both nonverbal and verbal stages which has increased the effectiveness of the group problem-solving process. Van de Ven and Delbecq (1974) provide empirical evidence that nominal groups can generate twice as many ideas as conventional groups.

The NGT is a structured group meeting conducted by a group leader or facilitator. Five to nine individuals sit around a table in full view of one another, but initially no talking takes place. Each individual has a sheet of paper with the ''nominal question''* at the top, and then, independently and silently, writes down as many answers to the question as possible.

After five to 10 minutes of controlled and intense work effort, each member, in round-robin fashion, presents one idea from their listing. The responses receive a sequential number and the leader writes them on a large flip chart for all members to see. No discussion takes place during this recording session, other than to clarify ideas presented. The leader encourages the ''hitchhiking'' of ideas, yet group members should not evaluate each other's suggestions. This recording continues until members have no more ideas to offer, thus concluding one ''nominal'' phase of the meeting.

The next stage consists of a structured discussion of each recorded idea, in sequence. The leader asks for clarification or expressions of support or nonsupport for each idea and encourages all group members to participate. The suggestor, however, is not required to explain his or her suggestions; anyone in the group is free to do so. The leader must be sure each item is thoroughly examined.

At the conclusion of this non-nominal phase, the group returns to a nominal stage with independent, private and silent balloting, in which each group member selects priorities by rank ordering, or rating, the listed ideas. The pooled outcome of the individual votes represents the group's priorities or decision. Thus, in approximately 90 minutes, five to nine individuals focusing on a single topic generally produce 25 or more ''solutions/problems'' with ranked priority judgments.

NGT & TRAINING NEEDS ANALYSIS

Undoubtedly, training needs assessment is essential to the development of training programs. Information collected in this stage is necessary for identifying specific problem areas on which the program will focus, obtaining commitment from participants and top management and determining which criteria to use for evaluation purposes. Emphasis on the cost of training versus no training will aid in determining the necessity of a training program. Furthermore, training assessment can provide meaningful examples and illustrations for the training program and signal employees that organizational changes are in the making.

McGehee and Thayer (1961) suggest that the needs analysis be performed on three analytical levels:

- *Organization analysis*: determining where within the organization training emphasis can and should be placed;
- *Operations analysis*: determining what should be the contents of training in terms of what an employee must do to perform a task, job or assignment in an effective way;
- *Person analysis*: determining what skills, knowledge or attitudes an individual employee must develop if he or she is to perform the tasks which constitute the job in the organization.

The applicability of NGT is examined in terms of its ability to extract information effectively at each one of these analytical levels.

At the *organizational* level, the analysis focuses most broadly on which training areas can and should be implemented. NGT participants examine such organizational factors as goals and objectives, resource allocations, efficiency standards and organization climate to ensure that the training programs are congruent with overall organizational needs. The use of NGT in this phase forces a clarification of long- and short-term objectives, determines the degree to which middle managers understand the organization mission, determines what human resources are available versus what are needed and emphasizes the impact of external forces on the future business operations. Moore and Dutton (1978) discuss the importance of this type of analysis, but indicate it is often not accomplished. The NGT process provides an efficient method of extracting this information from top level managers. In addition to linking the organization's needs for human resources to training, it provides an excellent mechanism for involving top managers in program design and facilitates an exchange of ideas. The diverse, sometimes conflicting, perceptions and equal participation of members ensures a shared analysis and decision as to what training programs are necessary in order to improve the overall operations of the organization.

The *operations* analysis focuses on specific jobs or groups of jobs, performance standards and job spec-

---

*The nominal question provides the primary focus of the meeting. This question is carefully constructed prior to the meeting in order to generate the required information.

ifications. Through the nominal group process, a thorough examination can be made of how managers, supervisors and employees perceived the actual duties of the job, the importance of the job and the environmental factors involved. NGT can be a method of identifying important job elements and development required to attain performance standards. Information generated by the group will provide management with more accurate employee inventories and more descriptive bases for employee placements and advances. In addition, career paths and retraining programs may be identified through the collective insights of the "family" work groups. Again, joint involvement permits a shared data analysis and builds emotional commitment for the training programs.

The *employee traits* analysis is an extension of the operational analysis, and the objective is to determine what personal traits and skills are necessary to perform the job at a desired performance level. During this phase of analysis, NGT groups specify the abilities and behaviors required for the job. Although discrepancies will surface, an on-the-spot synthesis of these opinions will take place to mesh the diverse views and lead to a group consensus. Personal attributes such as responsibility, analytical ability and stress threshold will emerge to indicate where training is needed and whether individual and organizational objectives are being achieved. Furthermore, the NGT process strengthens both awareness and commitment for the programs designed to alleviate problem areas. Thus, NGT will result in a training plan that is directly related to specific employee training needs. Care must be taken, however, to prevent NGT participants from identifying specific "problem" individuals, since this could result in personal attacks on individuals rather than on the problem itself.

EVALUATING NGT

As discussed previously, NGT is directly applicable as a method of assessing training needs analysis. With the multitude of other methods available, however, NGT should be examined in terms of its effectiveness and efficiency relative to other assessment methods. Newstrom and Lilyquist (1979) provided criteria for this evaluation. The following is a discussion of how each criterion relates to the NGT:

- *Employee involvement.* The nominal group process involves potential trainees in problem analysis as well as goal-setting. Typically, employees participate in training programs without a clear understanding of the organizations's reasons and expectations. The shared approach of nominal groups motivates employees by actively involving

them in the needs analysis. Furthermore, the NGT process ensures that certain participants to not dominate the discussions or force their ideas on less powerful or aggressive participants.

- *Management involvement.* The participants in the nominal group process can be selected to include all hierarchical levels of management. This involvement is a major factor in stimulating true commitment to the resulting training program implementation. The NGT process is designed to obtain consensus and to deemphasize the origin of individual ideas.

- Time required. The time it takes to complete an NGT training needs assessment compares favorably with other assessment techniques. For instance, it is unnecessary to construct and test a questionnaire. The total time span of interviewing individuals will be considerably longer than this group meeting, which typically requires less than two hours for seven to 10 participants. Although this method does not decrease participant time as compared to an interview, it substantially reduces the time required to collect the information. Furthermore, the data are quantified during the nominal group process so this step is alleviated. Job observation would be more time consuming depending on the job cycle.

- *Relevance and quantifiability.* The relevance of NGT is determined by the nominal question and the people selected to participate. Care must be taken in selecting appropriate people to participate, which will depend on the level of analysis. Unique insights may be provided from members who do not typically deal at the target level of analysis. For instance, if a nominal groups is considering organizational issues such as mission, an employee from the productions department can articulate his or her interpretation of the mission after it has filtered down through the organization. Because the NGT process protects minority views and people who are reluctant to express their ideas, it is more likely that diverse ideas will at least be considered.

The reliability of the information gathered is increased in the NGT process because a number of people are involved in each session. Furthermore, once the ideas are generated, a priority setting process encourages consensus. The data are qualified into a priority ranking, based on evaluation of importance, feasibility, cost, etc.

- *Cost.* In an absolute sense, the costs of NGT are moderately low. It does not require a questionnaire, group facilitators can be easily trained, professional staff members do not have to review interview data. Cost is relative, however, since quantity and quality of the data obtained from the process must be considered.

The strengths of nominal groups include:

- The process allows all participants to have an opportunity for influencing the group decision, which imposes a burden on all to work and contribute their ideas. Furthermore, it stimulates the generation of ideas by not allowing the evaluation of those ideas until later in the process. Thus, the structured format prevents closure and evaluation while problem dimensions are generated.
- The NGT avoids the dominance of group output by strong personalities. In addition, it encourages and uses minority opinions and views. In this sense it reduces political group maneuverings. The recording process provides ample time and opportunity for individuals to engage in reflection and consider diverse views.
- NGT encourages a shared commitment to objectives and implementation. The group process induces a sense of responsibility to achieve group success by taking individual ideas and making the group responsible for those ideas.

As with any managerial technique, NGT has several potential weaknesses. First, if the nominal questions are improperly framed, the groups may waste time attempting to clarify the questions. The ideas generated may not be appropriate. Second, facilitators must be interpersonally skilled. The facilitator must not allow the group to evaluate each other's ideas or allow certain people to dominate group discussion. At the same time, however, the facilitator must not alienate the group and cut off the flow of ideas. Finally, like other techniques for obtaining input, participants must receive timely feedback. If participants in nominal groups do not perceive that their ideas were used, future use of NGT is jeopardized.

A principal value of the NGT is the emotional commitment developed by involving not only supervisors but also potential trainees. When considering this process, a trainer should devote attention to the group formation, the range and relevance of nominal questions and the solicitation of feedback. With these factors in mind, the NGT will improve the training needs analysis by increasing synergy among participants and actively involving employees in both analysis and goal setting. The increased cohesion of the group results in a greater motivation to achieve the goals of a training program.

BIBLIOGRAPHY

- Leach, J. J. Organization needs analysis: a new methodology. *Training and Development Journal.* September 1979, *33*, 66–69.
- Moore, M. L. and Dutton, P. Training needs analysis: review and critique. *Academy of Management Review.* July 1978, 532–545.
- Newstrom, J. W. and Lilyquist, J. M. Selecting needs analysis methods. *Training and Development Journal.* October 1979, 52–56.
- Stein, D. S. Designing performance oriented training programs. *Training and Development Journal.* January 1981, 12–14.
- Van de Ven, A. H. and Delbecq, A. L. Nominal versus interacting group processes for committee decision-making effectiveness. *Academy of Management Journal.* June 1971, 203–212.

SOURCES SECTION III
GAINING COMMITMENT

How to Get Top Management Support

by William N. Yeomans

"To make this work, we really need top management support."

How many times have you heard that? How many times have you said it yourself?

Managers throughout every organization crave high-level support for their functions, projects and programs. Yet, somehow, most find that kind of support elusive and hard to grasp.

Certainly, those of us in training and development feel a strong need in this area. Unlike other functions in the company that want backing from the top but can function without it, we can't very well—especially in the area of developing managers for the company.

Top management support is not a speech or a memo. That sounds obvious, but it's important to remember. Mention of training and development in a presidential speech represents nothing more than something nice to say. It will not change anything that happens in the company, nor will it give you license to do anything different.

WHAT IS TOP MANAGEMENT SUPPORT?

Top management support is a continuing commitment, backed by words and deeds over a long period of time. Management truly committed to training and development will demonstrate that commitment by strong personal involvement. Managers will hammer away at its importance in speech after speech, report after report and meeting after meeting. They will continually ask how training and development is working in trips to the field and in their visits to headquarters. They will ask for periodic reports on progress in the departments. Managers will address training and development in articles in the company newspaper, and will comment on it publicly, outside the company, and will probably devote space in the annual report to it. They will begin appraising and rewarding supervisors on their skills at developing people. They will recognize the need for training and development to support and facilitate company change and will involve the T&D function early in the planning stages. They will assure adequate resources, both people and dollars, are allocated to training and development in the departments and in the training and development department itself, even in bad business years.

Management will do these things long enough, over a continuing period of time, until managers all through the organization begin to believe that the top people seriously believe that developing people is important and they must pay attention to it. That's when things begin to happen. Top management support is essential to set the tone and provide the resources, but it is the managers below that level, all throughout the organization, that make things work . . . managers at headquarters, at plants and branches, first-line supervisors, middle managers and department heads. When they believe top management is serious, they are likely to:

- Become more interested in doing performance appraisals, on time, with some thought behind them.
- Start thinking more seriously about identifying and developing back-ups.
- Be more eager for their people to participate in seminars, university courses, in-house workshops and other developmental activities, and even help them identify the right ones to improve performance.
- Be more willing to let their people participate in developmental assignments, such as transfers, task force membership, special projects and on-loan assignments. They even may become more receptive to interdepartmental transfers and promotions.
- Become more interested in helping their people with career planning.
- Begin to see training and development as part of their job responsibilities, and not just something somebody else takes care of in a classroom. That is top management support, or more correctly, complete management support. Sound idealistic? Perhaps, but it's not unattainable. Some organizations have that type of support, and they are stronger because of it.

HOW DO YOU GET SUPPORT?

Top management people are not much different from the rest of us. They support things that make sense and that will make them look good by helping them accomplish their objectives.

You will not convince management that training and development makes sense by waiting and hoping, writing a memo, asking for support now and then, complaining when you don't get it or sending an occasional report. You must actively pursue support.

First, *start thinking of T&D as part of the business.* Discard any notions you may have that training and development is separate and apart from the organization. It has to mesh with and be an integral part of the ongoing operation. If you want attention, begin first by doing those programs and activities that help the organization meet its objectives. Get copies of strategic plans and "mine" them for ideas. Meet with key managers to talk about their plans. Determine where the company will need training support and begin with high priority, high impact work first. Look for new technology, organization changes, new product lines and new company directions.

Second, *learn the business!* If you want to talk coherently with managers about what is happening, you had better learn the business, especially the financial end. Many staff people don't bother to do that. Do you know what your company's earnings per share were last year? Net profit as a percent of sales? Contribution of the major divisions? Take a course, get to know the financial people so you can ask questions, study annual reports, quarterly reports and everything else you can get your hands on until you are comfortable with financial objectives, ROI, sales figures, operating profit, debt-equity and cash flow. Then go back to those strategic plans to make sure you're conversant with new business ventures and company direction. Know your company's products and services. Learn what's selling and what's not and why. Talk with line people.

When you start identifying with the line personnel, rather than with your own specific staff discipline, you'll be able to relate your programs to business objectives. You will also be able to build more credibility into the work you do, and people will start believing in you. And senior management will hear about that.

Third, *develop programs and activities that line managers want*, that satisfy their needs and will help them make money for the company or otherwise further the goals of the organization. Start with line departments first; worry about staff departments later.

Use your study of strategic plans and operating reports and your discussions with managers as starting points. You can and should give guidance as to what training you think is necessary in your discussion of needs with managers. But be sure whatever you do reflects what they really want and need, what they want to accomplish, what behaviors they feel are needed and what skills should be developed. Implement only those programs and activities that have been ordered by managers.

Fourth, *involve top management.* Ask them which needs they consider important. After you've done your homework, at all levels, develop a master plan covering level or general type of position. The plan should encompass all activities either in place or to be developed, including programs, developmental assignments, appraisal and succession planning. Get top management's agreement on this and you will have gotten them involved, made yourself and T&D more visible and built a road map for future development activities—instead of trying to identify them by bits and pieces.

Involve other managers as much as you can. Use them as subject matter experts to assist you in developing needs, objectives and content and in reviewing programs as they develop. When possible, bring line people into your organization. Nothing builds your credibility faster in the plant than a well-regarded supervisor on your staff.

Fifth, *develop programs that are practical, how-to types of courses*, that give people tools they can use to help them on the job right away. Move away from any academic image you may have. Stay clear of theory and fads. Get your job training in place first, and when you've got that all done, you can move into more esoteric kinds of activities. When you help people do their jobs better, you will start getting the publicity you want—and top management will begin hearing that programs you produce are hard-hitting, useful and realistic. Top management will like that.

Sixth, *get a handle on ROI.* Identify existing programs or activities that have a direct measurable impact on performance. Design evaluations of those programs and carry them out. Use before and after results and results compared to control groups. Use long periods of time (six months after the program), and publish the results—hopefully most will be positive. This will show your programs have an impact and that you are concerned with ROI.

Seventh, *make some "hard-nosed" decisions.* Say "no" to training requests that represent problems that training can't solve. Drop a program that didn't evaluate well or doesn't further company objectives. Find ways to train less expensively. Look at how you produce materials, where you train, where people travel from and where they stay. When you save money, write it up for the company newspaper.

Finally, *get away from a program orientation.* Think of learning on the job, where most of it happens anyhow, and train managers as trainers so that they can do a better job helping people learn. Help identify developmental assignments or work experiences that will develop people.

Build a training orientation into ongoing communications in the company, field meetings, annual meetings and the company newspaper. Gather clues wherever you can, such as officer speeches, press releases and your research. Decide what is the most needed skill to foster company objectives and propose it be made into a day or half-day workshop at the next company meeting. Supply an outline with your proposal, showing objectives and content, and propose that you'll train line people to run the sessions. People will probably tell you, "We don't have staff like that in our meetings." Keep trying. If your other strategies

are beginning to take hold, this one will too and T&D will be woven into the company operating process.

This is not easy! It takes a lot of work and persistence, a large tolerance for rejection, at least at first, and the good fortune to be blessed with a top management that will listen and observe. It will not happen overnight and it will not happen without setbacks and frustrations. But it can be done. Starting is the toughest part!

Gaining and Keeping Management Support

by Kenneth E. Hultman

As a staff person responsible for providing support services to the line operation, the training manager has little, if any, direct authority to implement programs. Usually decisions affecting the fate of training are made by key people elsewhere in the organization and political factors limit the training manager's power.

Statements such as "I know exactly what this organization needs, but no one will let me do it," or "I have to go through so many people to get a program approved, sometimes I wonder if it's worth it," are all too common. This doesn't mean that their impact must be confined to wishful thinking. Quite the contrary. To accomplish their objectives they need to get as much mileage as possible out of the methods available to them. Persuasion, although frequently misused, is still the most potent tool at the training manager's disposal.

This article will focus on how persuasion can improve one's effectiveness in gaining and keeping management support for training.

We all know people whom we consider to be persuasive. They seem to know exactly what to say at the right time. We say to ourselves that they have "finesse" or possess some unique intuitive quality. With this kind of thinking it is all too easy to conclude that persuasiveness is an art beyond our grasp. Nothing could be farther from the truth. Actually, persuasiveness is not an innate talent, but a learned skill. The problem is that people who have this skill can't remember the specific life experiences enabling them to acquire it. All they know is that they have it, perpetuating the belief that it is the prerogative of a

lucky few. A training manager can learn the skill of using persuasion by following a deliberate course of action. We will first talk about gaining management support and then focus on keeping that support.

GAINING MANAGEMENT SUPPORT

Gaining management support is a process of (1) defining what it is you want to accomplish, (2) identifying whose support you need, (3) gathering data about those people, (4) using this data to decide how to persuade them, and (5) evaluating the results of your efforts. Let's examine each of these steps in some detail.

What Do You Want To Accomplish?

It is essential for you to be as thorough as possible in delineating what it is you want to achieve. Whether you want to conduct a needs analysis, gain approval for technical or management training, increase the training budget, add staff to your department, or implement a new procedure for evaluating training results, you must be clear about what you want to do and why. Without this, it will be difficult for you to convincingly articulate your views to others. The effort you invest up-front in defining your objectives will be well worth it when the day of reckoning arrives and you are called upon to justify your recommendations.

Whose Support Do You Need?

After defining what you want to do, the next step is to identify whose support you'll need in order to get your recommendations accepted. To do this, you must understand the political realities existing in your organization, have a knowledge of influence centers, and be aware of how decisions are made. Every organization has a formal structure outlining reporting relationships and an informal network of power and influence. Frequently, the latter is more important in determining how things get done than the former. Obviously, you need to be aware of these dynamics in order to cultivate the support of the right people. Many recommendations have been doomed because the training manager underestimated someone's power and neglected to seek his or her support—a costly way to find out who runs the organization. Keep your eyes and ears open to discover who the key people are before doing anything else.

What Do You Need to Know About Key People?

It's difficult to influence people if they don't know who you are. In order to get key people on your side, you must have access to them. If it isn't possible to have direct access, then you need to settle for indirect access through someone else. For example, if you report to the vice president for human resource development and he or she has access to key line managers but you don't, then your persuasive efforts should be focused on your boss. In this case, your boss is the key person.

Once you gain access to key people, relevant information must be gathered before you can do an effective job of influencing them. Elsewhere,[1,2] I have described a systematic approach to collecting and organizing information about other people. Essentially, I said that the behavior of people is a function of their facts, beliefs, and values. A *fact* is something that can be proven with absolute certainty ("I've never attended a management training program before"), while a *belief* is a subjective description or opinion ("Management training programs are interesting but they don't change behavior"). A *value* is a belief about what's worth pursuing in life ("Training isn't important to me unless it increases profits").

The problem is that the facts, beliefs, and values held by a person are invisible and must be inferred from what they say or do. Therefore, when listening to or observing someone, ask yourself the question, "What fact, belief, or value is being represented here?" By doing this consistently you can identify the facts, beliefs, and values most important to a person and use this information as you attempt to influence them.

As a training manager, everything you say and do has an effect upon your ability to gain management

support. There's no such thing as behavior with a neutral impact. If we can assume that people will respond to different methods of persuasion because they hold different facts, beliefs, and values, then we should be able to increase the probability of success by taking this information into consideration before selecting our approach. Failure to do this not only results in rejected recommendations, but it also lowers the training manager's credibility and self-esteem.

A problem shared by many training managers is that they simply aren't familiar with enough approaches for getting their ideas across. In order to do a better job of responding to key people, they need a larger repertoire of potentially effective behaviors at their command. Generally speaking, we can place all approaches of influencing people into four categories:

1. *Active Facilitative*—By engaging in behavior, persuasive results are fostered.
2. *Passive Facilitative*—By refraining from behavior, persuasive results are fostered.
3. *Active Inhibiting*—By engaging in behavior, persuasive results are hindered.
4. *Passive Inhibiting*—By refraining from behavior, persuasive results are hindered.

Some examples of each category are:

Active Facilitative. Being prepared and organized; stating views with conviction; providing information; asking for information; making recommendations; being willing to negotiate; taking the initiative; paraphrasing.

Passive Facilitative. Being able to remain silent; being able to wait patiently; allowing others to speak.

Active Inhibiting. Trying to "wing it"; stating views tentatively; being unwilling to negotiate; being aggressive; discouraging feedback; discouraging discussion; criticizing; changing the subject; rejecting ideas; giving advice prematurely.

Passive Inhibiting. Withholding information; not paying attention; being submissive; ignoring others or their ideas; failing to respond with empathy; leaving issues ambiguous; failing to give praise or appreciation; failing to give recognition; failing to offer help or support; failing to ask for help or support; allowing others to define your role.

It's important to recognize that no approach is guaranteed to have successful results. Any facilitative approach used to gain management support could backfire. The objective is to lower the probability of this occurring by matching your approach to relevant information collected about key people. In contrast, inhibiting approaches are almost always doomed to failure. This is precisely why it's so crucial to gain access to key people, pay close attention to what they say, and use this information in formulating your approach.

As you go about the task of gaining acceptance for your programs, remember that you need the support of management and not vice versa. Since many line managers place a low priority on training ("Do you want my supervisors to sit in a classroom or get the product out the door?"), it is necessary to convince them that your programs relate to their values. Unless you can successfully respond to their implicit question, "What's in it for me?", you can't expect their support.

Let's say you want to implement a training program for first-level supervisors but you first need the support of two key line managers. One says, "I want a program that will improve communication between my supervisors and their employees," while the other one says, "Unless your program can correct performance deficiencies, I'm not interested."

Two different values, better communication and improved performance are represented here. In this situation, your best bet is probably to use an active facilitative approach and recommend a program that relates to both values. Recent studies have shown that supervisory training based on behavior modeling learning theory[3,4] is an effective approach in dealing with both of these concerns. By negotiating values in this way, you can achieve your objective at the same time that you meet the needs of two important managers. Equally important, you can increase the chances of gaining their future support, which might prove to be vital if economic conditions lead to scrutiny of the training budget.

Managers typically hold at least some facts, beliefs, or values that hinder their support of training programs. In most of these situations, active facilitative approaches can be very effective in clarifying facts, correcting mistaken, inaccurate, or incomplete beliefs, changing values, and in modifying the priority assigned to values. There are times, however, when a passive facilitative approach is the preferred course of action. For example, let's say your company had 10 preventable accidents last year at a cost of $40,000. Currently, the company safety program consists of cash awards for a good safety record, safety posters, a suggestion box and immediate corrective action by supervisors when they see employees using unsafe work procedures. You believe that the number of preventable accidents could be cut in half, saving approximately $20,000 by initiating a training program designed to increase employee awareness of potential safety hazards.

After submitting a report to the plant manager suggesting that employees meet with their supervisors for two-hour, monthly awareness training sessions, he formed an ad hoc committee of four department heads to study the matter and make a recommendation. You were asked to serve as an ex officio member of the committee.

Prior to the first committee meeting, you had individual discussions with the four department heads. Three of them believed the current safety program was adequate, that it wasn't realistic to expect a decrease in the number of accidents, and expressed concerns about the loss of production resulting from the two-hour, monthly training sessions. The fourth department head, however, believed that the proposed training was exactly what the company needed and offered to support it 100 percent.

Frequently, training managers attend meetings where decisions are made about their programs without gathering important information about the beliefs and values of key people who will attend. They make the mistake of assuming that a well organized presentation of data supplemented by impressive visual aids will result in management support. When they hear, "Yes, but . . . ." repeated over and over again, they respond with more and more data. Gradually, they create feelings of resentment toward themselves and their programs and end up leaving bruised and defeated. The approach of using more and more words can lead to an outcome opposite of the one intended.

There are times when the best approach is to say nothing and let someone else with more clout fight your battles for you. In the safety training illustration given previously, the probability of getting your program approved by the ad hoc committee will be increased if you remain quiet and allow the one manager strongly in favor of the training to deal with the negative beliefs of the other three. The use of such "creative silence" can be a very effective passive facilitative approach when it appears that by talking you might jeopardize your own recommendations. If you do your homework and have the necessary information about people available, you can make better decisions regarding whether to use an active or passive facilitative approach.

Training managers seldom use active inhibiting approaches deliberately. These are usually the unintended consequence of poor planning, lack of information, inadequate listening skills, or the inability to accurately assess one's impact upon others.

Frustration, impatience, and other feelings can also result in active inhibiting behavior. Regardless of how you might feel about daily work events, it's a wise practice to carefully evaluate the potential effects of each alternative before acting.

In contrast, passive inhibiting approaches result from failure to act when appropriate. It's very important to let key people know precisely what you can do for them. For best results go out and search for support rather than waiting for others to come to you. If you don't do this, it is possible that others will narrowly define your capability and the scope of your job out of ignorance. Indeed, they may even conclude they can do without you. Also, potential support may go untapped. Preventing these outcomes must be a high priority. Effective training managers should constantly be looking for opportunities to enhance relationships, build teams, and create a receptive climate for their programs.

As mentioned previously, any approach can potentially lead to negative results. The goal is to minimize the chances of this happening by selecting a facilitative approach that matches the needs of a specific situation. In addition, timing is a key factor that can make or break efforts to gain management support.

In training we use the expression "teachable moment" to describe a time when participants are most receptive to learning. Similarly, in gaining management support, a "persuadable moment" occurs when others are most open to your ideas. By listening very carefully, you can tell when such a moment arrives and implement a facilitative approach.

For example, if the organization were going through a major upheaval, such as a union attempt or drastic budget cuts, this would be a poor time to unveil your plan for an executive training program. You would be better off waiting until things settled down. One of the realities of our field is that a good idea introduced at the wrong time can be a disaster.

Gaining management support is a step-by-step process beginning with initial efforts to identify a need for your programs or services and ending up with an accepted recommendation. Normally, this requires a series of actions on your part. Therefore, it is essential to evaluate the impact of your approach each step along the way. This is done by "reading the signals" or paying close attention to both verbal and non-verbal feedback indicating whether or not the approach is succeeding. If results are not what you want, reassess the situation and try something else. Perhaps some key people were not consulted or you don't have enough information about the relevant facts, beliefs, or values of people.

Another possibility is that an approach other than the one originally selected would be more effective. In these instances, there is no substitute for flexibility and a willingness to vary your approach based upon relevant feedback. That is why the ability to use a variety of facilitative approaches is so essential.

Management support is elusive. It cannot be won permanently, but must be earned continually. The reason is organizations are dynamic rather than static. Everything about them is constantly in the process of change, including political factors, influence centers, economic conditions, priorities, people, and so on. To avoid losing support, training managers must be able to sense change and modify their approach by taking new information and conditions into consideration.

If you've done a good job of gaining support, it will be easier to keep it, but you can never afford to sit back and rest on your laurels. The expression, "If you don't use it you lose it" certainly applies to management support.

The active facilitative approach of soliciting input from key people on a regular basis is a useful method. One effective way of doing this has been described by Coffman[5,6] and is called Training Impact Auditing. Key people are asked to collect information regarding training program results and participate in small group discussions where strengths and weaknesses are listed and prioritized. This process, requiring minimal time, provides key people with a deeper understanding of program benefits and involves them in helping you overcome deficiencies.

Systematic approaches such as this demonstrate your responsiveness to organizational needs and provide the access needed to keep the support you worked so hard to obtain.

REFERENCES

1. Hultman, K. E., The Path of Least Resistance: Preparing Employees For Change, Austin, Texas: Learning Concepts, 1979.
2. Hultman, K. E., "Identifying and Dealing With Resistance To Change," Training and Development Journal, February, 1980.
3. Goldstein, A., and Sorcher, M., Changing Supervisory Behavior, New York: Pergamon Press, 1974.
4. Byham, W. C., and Robinson, J. C., Interaction Modeling: A New Concept in Supervisory Training," Training and Development Journal, February 1976.
5. Coffman, L., "An Easy Way to Effectively Evaluate Program Results," Training and Development Journal, August, 1979.
6. Coffman, L., "Successful Training Program Evaluation," Training and Development Journal, October, 1980.

How to Sell New Training Programs to Management
by David Chesnut

Many human resources development (HRD) directors know only too well the frustration of seeing good training programs stymied for lack of management commitment. Although it may seem too obvious to be true, the problem can often be traced to the poor manner in which the program was presented to management. If you make it difficult for non-HRD executives to evaluate the merits of a proposed program, you make it equally difficult for them to approve and fund it.

The problem is inadequate communication. Most HRD directors are experts in designing and organizing material for classroom instruction. But many fail to see that the same kind of planning and organization is necessary for a successful funding presentation to upper management. This situation can be corrected by following a logical presentation procedure. If you develop and use a logically structured proposal as a vehicle for presenting your next training program to management, you'll find you can give the executives involved all the information needed to assure an intelligent—and favorable—decision.

There is no better way to make a presentation to management than to put the request for approval and funding in the form of a written proposal. A proposal, however, must be developed carefully and properly, with enough of the appropriate information given to allow for a favorable evaluation. Your objective is not to sell the general merits of HRD. You simply need to convince one or several executives that what you propose to do is in the organization's best interest. Think of your proposal as a selling document: the training program is the commodity to be sold.

A good training program proposal will cover five areas.

1. *Need* for the particular program.
2. *Objective* in terms of benefit to the organization.
3. *Design* elements and facility requirements.
4. *Evaluation method.*
5. *Cost breakdown.*

NEED ANALYSIS AND OBJECTIVE

To demonstrate need for a training program, you want to provide information to show an analysis has been made that indicates there is a need to address a particular problem through a course of training. The problem could be in management, operation, skill acquisition, knowledge acquisition—the initiating department will have most of the necessary data. Ordinarily, of course, you would be using this information anyway in the construction of the training program. And you would also usually give the department head a number of training alternatives to consider so a mutually agreeable objective may be selected. Where your proposal is concerned, however, the need statement establishes the legitimacy of your involvement, while the objective will indicate not only what is to be accomplished by the trainee, but also how the organization will benefit.

Any training program must be designed to fit the trainee. You know this. Your management may need to have it demonstrated. A *trainee profile* should be prepared to indicate particular learning requirements; of specific interest will be the physical, mental and skill abilities of the typical trainee. For example, training techniques for those for whom English is a second language, not the first, may differ markedly from techniques used in programs designed for college-trained managers. Where special training procedures in addition to the usual procedures will be required, it is important to justify the added cost.

PROGRAM DESIGN

The design of the training program will be determined by the level of instruction, which in turn will dictate whether or not there will be a requirement for subject matter experts, text material, visual material or hands-on instructional devices. Use an outline format for the description of the program and briefly describe the teaching methods—lecture, discussion, seminar, self-instruction. Keep the program design in broad terms so the outline remains flexible enough to allow for revision after review. You don't want to lock yourself into a rigid design if situations change for the department or trainees involved.

State the number of persons to be trained and the facility requirements necessary. This is especially important from a management standpoint. The length of time each trainee will be away from regular employment and whether or not training will be done in-house or off-site should be included. If you plan to go off-site, be sure to explain where and why. You might also provide short biographies of those who will deliver the instruction, but emphasize only those qualifications necessary to the training program under discussion.

EVALUATION METHOD

Undoubtedly the most important question to be asked about any course of instruction concerns its validity—the degree to which it measures up to what it purports to accomplish. The determination of validity is an arcane science that does not, and need not, concern non-HRD management. What will be expected of you is an indication of how you intend to measure results and judge the relative success of the program.

You may have decided, for example, to design pre-test and post-test material to indicate knowledge gained, or to establish a norm by testing a representative group of employees in the department who now have the skills the new program is supposed to help others gain. Perhaps you plan to judge success by evaluations submitted by trainees themselves. The method used will be less important for management considerations than the prospect of a useful report on the results to be prepared on completion of the program. Don't promise more than you can deliver, and don't promise to deliver something management will have little interest in or need for.

COST ESTIMATE

The last section of the proposal describes in some detail the cost of the program. One way to present this cost breakdown is in tabular form, similar to Table 1. Indicate, as precisely as possible, what the actual costs will be to implement the program. You can find valuable help in the organization's comptroller's office, particularly where information in regard to salaries, indirect labor costs and overhead expenses is concerned. You must offer enough information to allow management to make a meaningful analysis. At minimum, include the cost of direct labor, materials, overhead and program preparation costs. Cost of program preparation is especially appropriate when a program is being developed for a particular department.

Direct labor and material costs are charged directly to the program. They include such items as instructor salaries, consultant fees and travel expense. Indirect labor charges and overhead expenses come under general and administrative costs, usually referred to as G&A. These include facility space charges, executive salaries, legal and accounting services, depreciation, and so forth. The HRD director's salary is part of G&A.

A chart should be drawn up to show how the program will be scheduled, from development stage

TABLE 1
Cost Breakdown

Cost Elements	Total Cost
1. Materials charges	
• Special equipment	
• Textbooks	
• Workbooks	
2. Direct labor charges	
• Instructor	
• Consultant	
• Travel expense	
3. Overhead expense	
• Facility charges	
• G&A	
4. Total	

through completion. The simplest form is probably a bar chart showing the time span for each of the scheduled items in the development of the training program. Take special care in preparing the cost section: it's your last opportunity to review program costs and correct any that seem to be out of line before submitting the proposal to management.

APPEARANCE

Don't overlook or underestimate the physical appearance of the proposal. You do not want a flamboyant piece of sales literature, even though it is a sales document. You want a presentation that is both attractive and easy to read. The body of the proposal should be typewritten, perhaps typed space-and-a-half or double-spaced, on a good grade of bond paper. If copies are made, be sure they are clean and extremely readable. Proposals get fairly rough usage when passed from person-to-person.

The format of the proposal should show organization. The divisions discussed above serve as chapters in the main body. Preceding them is material classed as front matter—which should, incidentally, be written last—title page, abstract and table of contents. The title page includes the name of the proposal, the name of the HRD director who prepared it, department affiliations and a date. Use an abstract only if the proposal is a long one. An abstract should be short and to the point, concentrating on the key topics to follow.

Remember the old saw about first impressions. The physical presentation is not as important as the contents, but your "consumer" in management will start reading with some initial reaction already forming. If you can learn to see your programs as services to be sold within the organization, and present them accordingly, you will go a long way toward gaining the approval and funding support you need.

Learning Theories and Training

by Leslie E. This and Gordon L. Lippitt

PART I

Attempts are often made to distinguish between training and education. Some educators feel that training directors are not engaged in education. Most training directors believe they are. Educators tend to make this distinction: training is narrow in scope and involves only learning that is directly related to job performance, while education is concerned with the total human being and his insights into, and understanding of, his entire world. These attempts to distinguish between training and education seem petty inasmuch as both are concerned with the process of human learning.

Berelson and Steiner define learning as "Changes in behavior that result from previous behavior in similar situations. Mostly, but by no means always, behavior also becomes demonstrably more effective and more adaptive after the exercise than it was before. In the broadest terms, then, learning refers to the effects of experience, either director or symbolic, on subsequent behavior."[1]

For the training director, learning would seem to imply these kinds of things:

a. Knowing something intellectually or conceptually one never knew before.
b. Being able to do something one couldn't do before—behavior or skill.
c. Combining two knowns into a new understanding of a skill, piece of knowledge, concept, or behavior.
d. Being able to use or apply a new combination of skills, knowledge, concept, or behavior.
e. Being able to understand and/or apply that which one knows—either skill, knowledge, or behavior.

Since the training director is concerned with learning, it follows that he should be concerned with learning theory. Training directors often talk about the learning theory that underlies their training. However, most of us do not have a good understanding of learning theories and their application to our training efforts. It is through the eyes of the training director

that the authors have ventured into an overview of learning theory.

As they design training programs, training directors are confronted by many factors about which they must make decisions:

a. Desired Outcomes for the Learning Experience.
This can range from complex comprehension of organizational dynamics to simple manual skills.

The *managers* who underwrite training programs normally stipulate an entirely different set of training outcomes. These usually are identified as reduction of costs; increased productivity; improved morale; and a pool of promotional replacements. Sometimes these are confused by training directors as outcomes of training that are affected by learning theory. It seems to us that these may be results of training but that learning theory does not directly relate to these as outcomes.

b. Site for Learning.
Training directors are concerned whether learning best occurs on the job; in a classroom; on organizational premises or off organizational premises; university or other formal site; cultural island; or at home.

c. Learning Methods.
These are on a continuum from casual reading to intense personal involvement in personal-relationship laboratories.

d. Grouping for Learning.
Our grouping of learners can involve all combinations from dyads to audiences of 1,500.

Theory vs. Corollaries

As we work with, and manipulate, the kinds of variables listed above, we tend to confuse them with learning theory. For example, a training director will say "My theory of learning is that employees learn best when placed in small discussion groups at a training site removed from the plant." What is not clear to most training directors is that the variables identified above result in a myriad of devices and techniques that stem from, and are most effectively utilized by, a given learning theory. In and of themselves they are not learning theory.

Just as we confuse learning theory with the variables discussed, the use of the terms "learning theory" and "learning theory corollaries or principles" can be confusing. Usually the learning theory can be stated very broadly—for example, "Learning occurs when a stimulus is associated with a response."

From this generalization about how learning occurs, a number of specific learning laws, rules, or statements are derived—for example, "Repetition of a response strengthens its connection with a stimulus." Thus, the statement, "problems are difficult to solve when they require the use of the familiar in an unfamiliar way" is a corollary of the Behaviorist Learning Theory School. It is the learning theory corollaries that most often serve as the application guides to the trainer.

Some research findings about learning seem to be unrelated to any particular learning theory and will be found in the literature as isolated pieces of research. Two examples follow:

a. Sleep immediately following learning results in more retention than when the subject stays awake after learning (even if he gets the same amount of sleep before the retention test).
b. Simple facts do not seem to be learned during sleep, even when they are presented throughout the night by tape recording.

We have discussed corollaries in detail because a training director sometimes chances upon one or more of these and incorporates them into his training design. He then says "Here is the learning theory that I am employing in my training activity." Sometimes the corollaries he employs have been borrowed from, or are derived from, several learning theories and so would appear to be inconsistent. However, this may be quite valid. This is so because the content and training objectives for a given training program may include both skill and conceptual training. Each of these kinds of training would tend to borrow techniques from different learning theories.

Our major point here, however, is that training directors frequently confuse a learning theory corollary with a basic learning theory. A learning theory is always greater than the corollary. In using the corollary, the training director is often unaware of the major learning theory which lies behind it.

What is Motivation?

As one plows into the learning theory literature, one is confronted by the problem of motivation. Can you motivate a learner to learn? Is understanding learning motivation a prime requisite of the training director and instructor? Immediately one runs into difficulty. It becomes obvious that learning theorists do not agree what motivation is or how it is accomplished. Generally speaking, you find these premises:

a. The learner must be self-motivated.
b. The trainer must motivate the learner through an effective learning climate.
c. We do not know enough about causes of motivation to discuss its role in the learning process.

Most training directors believe there is a factor called motivation. They seem to be evenly split as to whether the learner must be self-motivated or whether the training situation or trainer motivates the learner. Those who believe that learning must be self-motivated usually believe the trainer must provide the conditions under which self-motivation can occur. In practice, there is little to distinguish the training designs of trainers who subscribe to differing philosophies. Designed conditions under which self-motivation can occur look very much like the designs of those who attempt to motivate learners.

As the training director explores learning theory, he is confronted with another discouraging task. If anything is in print discussing, in layman terms, individual or comparative learning theories we have not found it.

Learning theories are to be found in courses in educational psychology and require a strong background in psychology, research, and statistics to understand them. Some of the differences seem to a training director to be very subtle. It is extremely discouraging to attempt to understand either the individual theories or the difference between the schools embracing several theories.

Animal Experiments Valid?

The first thing that strikes the training director is that most of the research on learning theory has been accomplished using animals and fowls for subjects. Several authors comment that at least 95 per cent of learning research has been accomplished on data received from experiments on rats, chickens, pigeons, monkeys, dogs, and cats.

It is also interesting to note that research on animals and fowls inevitably occurs under one or both of two conditions: the animal or fowl is very hungry or sex is deprived. It may very well be that training directors have been overlooking some excellent motivational factors in this area.

Two other immediate problems present themselves. First, it is often difficult to distinguish learning theories differentiated as to general schools. Second, it is even more difficult to distinguish between individual learning theories within the general schools.

This difficulty is compounded because of the technical language and equations used to express the theories or portions of the theories. Usually aspects of the theories are stated mathematically and then expressed in prose. Neither of these are done in such a way that a training director can easily comprehend them. He is then faced with the problem of trying to determine what the technical language expresses and restating them in words he can understand.

Learning Theory Schools

Generally, learning theories seem to fall into six general schools.

The first school is known as the *Behaviorist School*. Primarily, these theories hold that learning results from the rewards or punishment that follows a response to a stimulus. These are the so-called S-R Theories.

E.L. Thorndike was one of the early researchers into learning. Generally he held that learning was a trial-and-error process. When faced with the need to respond appropriately to a stimulus, the learner tries any and all of his response patterns. If by chance one works, then that one tends to be repeated and the others neglected. From his research he developed certain laws to further explain the learning process—for example, the Law of Effect: if a connection between a stimulus and response is satisfying to the organism, its strength is increased—if unsatisfying, its strength is reduced.

E.R. Guthrie basically accepted Thorndike's theory, but did not accept the Law of Effect. He came up with an "S-R Contiguity Theory" of learning. His position was that the moment a stimulus was connected to a response—the stimulus would thereafter tend to elicit that response. Repeating the connection would not strengthen the association. Thus, if I am learning a poem and learn it sitting down, I can probably recall that poem best when sitting rather than standing. Generally he did not attach much significance to reward and punishment—responses will tend to be repeated simply because they were the last ones made to a stimulus.

Clark Hull introduced a new concept—not only was a stimulus and response present in learning—but the *organism* itself could not be overlooked. The response to a stimulus must take into account the organism and what it is thinking, needing, and feeling at the moment. We now had the S-O-R concept.

B.F. Skinner is usually identified with the Behaviorist School. Rather than construct a theory of learning, he seems to believe that by observation and objective reporting we can discover how organisms learn without the need of a construct to explain the process.

He depends heavily upon what is called operant conditioning. He makes a distinction between "Respondent" and "Operant" behavior. Respondent behavior is that behavior caused by a known stimulus—operant behavior is that behavior for which we cannot see or identify a stimulus, though one may, and probably does, exist.

If we can anticipate an operant behavior, and introduce a stimulus when it is evidenced, we can provide the occasion for the behavior by introducing the stimulus—but the stimulus does not necessarily evoke the behavior. Thus the emphasis in learning is on correlating a response with reinforcement. This is at the heart of programmed instruction—a correct response is reinforced.

Other researchers have developed variations of the theories described above. Some assume that the organism is relatively passive but that the response is in the repertoire of the learner. Other theorists pay particular attention to instrumental conditioning. They assume that the organism acts on his environment and that the response may not be in his repertoire.

Still others talk about mediating responses in which a period of time may elapse between the stimulus and the response—or the response may be a series of responses that stretch over a period of time. For example, a man may be desirous of marrying a girl but will work for 10 years to save enough money to support her adequately before proposing.

Gestalt School

The second grouping is the *Gestalt School*. These theorists believe that learning is not a simple matter of stimulus and response. They hold that learning is cognitive and involves the whole personality. To them, learning is infinitely more complex than the S-R Theories would indicate.

For example, they note that learning may occur simply by thinking about a problem. Kurt Lewin, Wolfgang Kohler, E.C. Tolman and Max Wertheimer are typical theorists in this school. They reject the theory that learning occurs by the building up, bit by bit, of established S-R connections. They look at the phenomenon of insight, long-coming or instantaneous. To them, "the whole is more than the sum of its parts."

"Central in Gestalt theory is the Law of 'Pragnanz' which indicates the direction of events. According to this law, the psychological organization of the individual tends to move always in one direction, always toward the good Gestalt, an organization of the whole which is regular, simple, and stable.[2]

"The Law of 'Pragnanz' is further a law of equilibrium. According to it, the learning process might be presented as follows: The individual is in a state of equilibrium, of 'good' Gestalt. He is confronted by a learning situation. Tensions develop and disequilibrium results. The individual thus moves away from equilibrium but at the same time he strives to move back to equilibrium. In order to assist this movement back to the regular, simple, stable state, the learning situation should be structured so as to possess good organization (e.g., simple parts should be presented first; these should lead in an orderly fashion to more difficult parts). The diagram in Figure 1 represents the movement toward equilibrium in the learning process."

The third school is the *Freudian School*. This is a difficult school to capsulize. "It is no simple task to extract a theory of learning from Freud's writings, for while he was interested in individual development and the kind of re-education that goes on in psychotherapy, the problems whose answers he tried to formulate were not those with which theorists in the field of learning have been chiefly concerned. Psychoanalytic theory is too complex and, at least at the present time, too little formalized for it to be presented as a set of propositions subject to experimental testing."[4]

A fourth school are the *Functionalists*. These seem to take parts of all the theories and view learning as a very complex phenomenon that is not explained by either the Gestalt or the Behavioral Theories. Some of the leaders in this school are John Dewey, J.R.

FIGURE 1[3]

Equilibrium

1. The learning situation is presented to the individual.

2. He moves away from equilibrium.

3. But attempts to move back to equilibrium.

4. He organizes the new material in an effort to integrate and systematize it.

5. He moves to equilibrium.

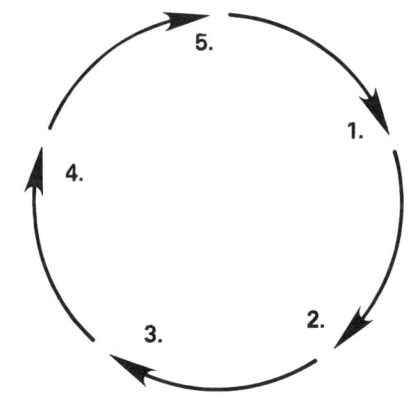

Angell, and R.S. Woodworth. These men borrow from all the other schools and are sometimes referred to as "middle of the roaders."

A fifth so-called school are those who subscribe to *Mathematical Models*. To these researchers, learning theories must be stated in mathematical form. Some of these proponents come from different learning theory schools but tend to focus on mathematical models such as the Feedback Model, Information—Theory Model, Gaming Model, Differential Calculus Model, Stochastic Model, and the Statistical Association Model. As one tries to understand this school, it occurs to one that they seem to have no theory of their own but are expressing research findings of other theorists in mathematical terms.

A sixth school is more general in nature and can best be characterized by calling it *Current Learning Theory Schools*. These are quite difficult to classify and seem to run the range of modifying Gestalt Theories, modifying Behavioral Theories, accommodating two pieces of both theories, assuming that training involves the whole man—psychological, physiological, biological, and neurophysiological. Some of these are the Postulate System of Mac-Corquodale and Meehl and the Social Learning Theory of Rotter.

Some of the more exciting kinds of current research seem to be in the neurophysiological interpretations of learning. One example of this was shown on a national television program, "Way Out Men," February 13, 1965. In this research, flatworms are trained to stay within a white path. If they deviate from the white path, they receive an electrical shock. After the flatworms learn to stay within the prescribed path, they are then chopped up and fed to a control group of worms. This control group learns to stay within the white path in about half the learning time. This has led some theorists to talk about the possibility of eventually feeding students "professorburgers."

Additional research is going on in this area and we have recently seen two or three other related pieces of research. It seems to indicate a key as to where memory and instincts are stored so that they can be transmitted to offspring.

One is intrigued by this research when one remembers popular beliefs such as "Eating of the Tree of Knowledge," eating fish is a good brain food, and the practice of cannibals eating the brain of an educated man to become smart or to eat the heart of a brave man to become courageous.

Transfer of Learning

One of the problems that often confront a training director is the transfer of learning. Some of the major ways in which learning theories attempt to provide for the transfer of that which is learned to the work situation are the following:

1. *Actually doing the "that" which is being learned.* In this instance, we believe transfer is best when learning occurs on or in live situations. This is so because little or no transfer is needed—what is learned is directly applied. Instances employing this technique are on-the-job training, coaching, apprenticeship, and job experience.

2. *Doing something that is similar to that which is to be learned.* This transfer principle is applied when we use simulated experiences—the training experience and techniques are as similar to the job as possible. Sometimes we let the trainee discover the principles and apply them to his job. In other instances, particularly in skill training, he works on mock-ups which closely resemble the actual equipment on which he will work. Other techniques employed would include role playing, sensitivity training, and case studies.

3. *Reading or hearing about that which is to be learned.* In this instance, the trainer or a book gives the trainee the principles and then discusses and illustrates them. The trainee must now figure out the ways in which he has heard or read applies to his job and how he can use it. Illustrative training techniques would be lectures, reading, and most management and supervisory training programs featuring the "telling" method.

4. *Doing or reading about anything on the assumption it will help anything to be learned.* In this instance there is an assumption that a liberalized education makes the trainee more effective in whatever job he occupies or task he is to learn. This might be termed the liberal arts approach. It assumes that a well-rounded, educated person is more effective, and more easily trained in specifics, if he understands himself, his society, his world, and other disciplines. Obviously, this would be a somewhat costly way of training. It would involve perceptual living and generalized education.

Much research has gone into the transfer of learning. Most of this occurs in the S-R Theories. It seems to be less of a problem in the other major theories. This is quite understandable as one compares the theories of learning. For example, the S-R Theories become quite concerned with questions like "Will the study of mathematics help a person learn a foreign language easier and more quickly?" This has led to much research regarding the conditions under which the transfer of learning best occurs. It is also applicable to conceptual learning. For example, will learning how to delegate responsibilities to children be useful in the delegation process in the work organization?

Adult Learning

Recent research at the University of Nebraska indicated:

1. The average older adult in an adult education program is at least as intellectually able, and performs as well, as the average younger participant.
2. Adults who continue to participate in educative activity learn more effectively than similar adults who do not. This would simply seem to indicate that learning skills require practice to be maintained.
3. Adults learn far more effectively when they are permitted to learn at their own pace.[5]

The concerns about motivating individuals to learn, and the recognition that there is such a thing as a learning process, have led training directors and training psychologists to explore the condition under which learning seems best to occur. Numerous lists of conditions for learning exist. They vary depending on the learning theory school to which the author subscribes. However, there is a remarkable acceptance of some general conditions that should exist for effective learning regardless of the learning theory employed. One of these composite lists follows:[6]

1. *Acceptance that all human beings can learn.* The assumption, for example, that you "can't teach an old dog new tricks" is wrong. Few normal people at any age are probably incapable of learning. The tremendous surge in adult education and second careers after retirement attest to people's ability to learn at all ages.

2. *The individual must be motivated to learn.* This motivation should be related to the individual's drives.

a. The individual must be aware of the inadequacy of unsatisfactoriness of his present behavior, skill, or knowledge.
b. The individual must have a clear picture of the behavior which he is required to adopt.

3. *Learning is an active process, not passive.* It takes action and involvement by and of the individual with resource persons and the training group.

4. *Normally, the learner must have guidance.* Trial and error are too time-consuming. This is the process of feedback. The learner must have data on "how am I doing" if he is to correct improper performance before it becomes patternized.

5. *Appropriate materials for sequential learning must be provided:* Cases; problems; discussion;

reading. The trainer must possess a vast repertoire of training tools and materials and recognize the limitations and capacities of each. It is in this area that so many training directors get trapped by utilizing the latest training fads or gimmicks for inappropriate learning.

6. *Time must be provided to practice the learning;* to internalize; to give confidence. Too often trainers are under pressure to "pack the program"—to utilize every moment available to "tell them something." This is inefficient use of learning time. Part of the learning process requires sizable pieces of time for assimilation, testing, and acceptance.

7. *Learning methods, if possible, should be varied to avoid boredom.* It is assumed that the trainer will be sufficiently sophisticated to vary the methods according to their usefulness to the material being learned. Where several methods are about equally useful, variety should be introduced to offset factors of fatigue and boredom.

8. *The learner must secure satisfaction from the learning.* This is the old story of "you can lead a horse to water . . . " Learners are capable of excellent learning under the most trying of conditions if the learning is satisfying to one or more of their needs. Conversely, the best appointed of learning facilities and trainee comfort can fail if the program is not seen as useful by the learner.

9. *The learner must get reinforcement of the correct behavior.* B.F. Skinner and the Behaviorists have much to say on this score. Usually learners need fairly immediate reinforcement. Few learners can wait for months for correct behavior to be rewarded. However, there may well be long-range rewards and lesser-intermediate rewards. We would also emphasize that rewarded job performance when the learner returns from the training program must be consistent with the learning program rewards.

10. *Standards of performance should be set for the learner.* Set goals for achievement. While learning is quite individual, and it is recognized that learners will advance at differing paces, most learners like to have benchmarks by which to judge their progress.

11. *A recognition that there are different levels of learning and that these take different times and methods.* Learning to memorize a simple poem is entirely different from learning long-range planning. There are, at least, four identifiable levels of learning, each requiring different timing, methods, involvement, techniques, and learning theory.

At the simplest level we have the skills of motor responses, memorization, and simple conditioning. Next, we have the adaptation level where we are gaining knowledge or adapting to a simple environment. Learning to operate an electric typewriter after using a manual typewriter is an example. Third is the complex level, utilized when we train in interpersonal understandings and skill, look for principles in complex practices and actions, or try to find integrated meaning in the operation of seemingly isolated parts.

At the most complex level we deal with the values of individuals and groups. This is a most subtle, time-consuming, and sophisticated training endeavor. Few work organizations have training programs with value change of long-standing, cultural or ethnic values as their specific goal. Many work organizations, however, do have training programs aimed at changing less entrenched values.

The reader will recognize that this listing of conditions under which people learn contains concepts and principles from most of the learning theory schools. Most training directors are generalists, and seldom do their training programs focus on a constant single-objective outcome. It is perhaps inevitable that his own guiding training concepts and principles will be a meld from many theories. It is important, however, that he understand the theories of learning so that he is using those concepts and principles which can best assure he will accomplish his organization's training objectives in specific training programs.

PART II

As the training director explores learning theory, he finds the following points of view:

a. There are individual exponents of a given theory who insist that their theory alone accounts for the way people learn.

b. There are those who insist that we do not know what learning theory is and that learning theorists do not contribute to the real problems of training.

c. There are those who will be frank in saying to a training director, "You are heavily on your own. Learning theory in its present state will not materially help you. Experiment. If it works and gets you the results you want—don't worry about what learning theory lies behind your success."

It is encouraging to note that some social scientists are aware of this breach between research and practice:

". . . Knowledge is not practice and practice is not knowledge. The improvement of one does not lead automatically to the improvement of the other. Each can work fruitfully for the advancement of the other but also, unfortunately, each can develop separately from the other and hence stuntedly in relation to the other."[7]

"It should be clear that the linking of social theory to social practice, as well as the development of a practice-linked theory of the application of social science knowledge to practice, is an intellectual challenge of the first magnitude. But it is one that many social scientists—particularly those who rarely leave the university system—have neglected."[8]

"Lewin is credited with remarking that one can bridge the gap between theory and reality only if one can tolerate 'constant intense tension.' Roethlisberger and his colleagues described these tensions all too well for the person trying to improve the practice of administration when they wrote on 'Training for a Multi-dimensional World'[9] which I have already recommended to anyone seriously planning to enter this field."[10]

In relating learning theory to learning goals, learning theory corollaries, and the designed learning experience or training program, Figure 2 provides a model that is useful in visualizing their interrelationship and their time sequence. Two points are critical regarding the model in Figure 2:

a. The model describes either a single training program or a series of training programs separated by a span of months or even years.

b. The dashed lines indicate that the process is not a single revolution—but a continuous process. In the life of a single training program, the learning goals may be modified—or the design, learning corollaries, or even the learning theory employed may undergo on-the-scene modification if they are not producing the desired learning goals.

The model does not exist in a vacuum, nor is the choice of its component parts a matter of whim, preference, or intellectual selection. It is always related to the forces within the organization, the

FIGURE 2

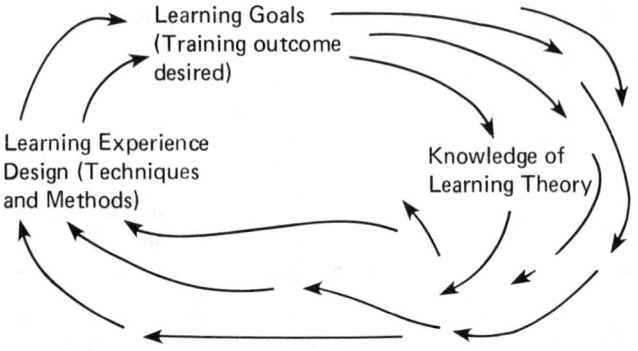

Learning Goals (Training outcome desired)

Learning Experience Design (Techniques and Methods)

Knowledge of Learning Theory

trainees, the trainers, and the situation, as is indicated in Figure 3.

A simplified mathematical statement of this model is:

LEARNING GOAL(s) =

$$\frac{\left(\begin{array}{l}\text{Present state of the organization } + \text{ present}\\ \text{state of trainees } + \text{ recognized need for change}\end{array}\right)}{\left(\begin{array}{l}\text{Appropriate learning theory } + \text{ appropriate training}\\ \text{design } + \text{ supportive climate for changed trainee behavior}\end{array}\right)}$$

If we accept (1) that effective training always takes into account the major forces impinging upon it and (2) that trainees have insights into factors that facilitate their learning, then it follows that we should listen attentively to trainee observations. Some of the more frequently mentioned are:

a. Participants almost always rate very high, as a training benefit, their interactions with each other. This seems particularly true in heterogeneous groups. They comment that they have become aware that their problems are not peculiar; it has been helpful to learn about other programs; they have learned from each other; and they have become more perceptive and broadened in the understanding of their role. We have, in the past, looked upon this as a minor side benefit of heterogeneous training. We are not inclined to believe this may be one of the major benefits of such training.

b. Participants always complain that they need time to internalize, digest, reflect, and to be left alone. We usually answer by scheduling more night meetings. Perhaps we need to experiment with two hours of training and six hours of internalization.

c. Participants like "bull sessions."

d. Participants say they need more recreation to release some of their emotional and physical energy.

e. The use of dyad conversations seem useful —even if these are forced. They seem to serve a helpful purpose of reaction, clarification, and feedback.

f. Time for reading pertinent articles and books seems to have excellent payoff. Training directors generally feel that managers would not accept training time being used for reading purposes.

g. Some limited experimentation seem to indicate that it is desirable to attempt to bring all participants up to a minimum level of knowledge before placing them in a training program. This can be accomplished by preliminary reading or programmed instruction.

FIGURE 3

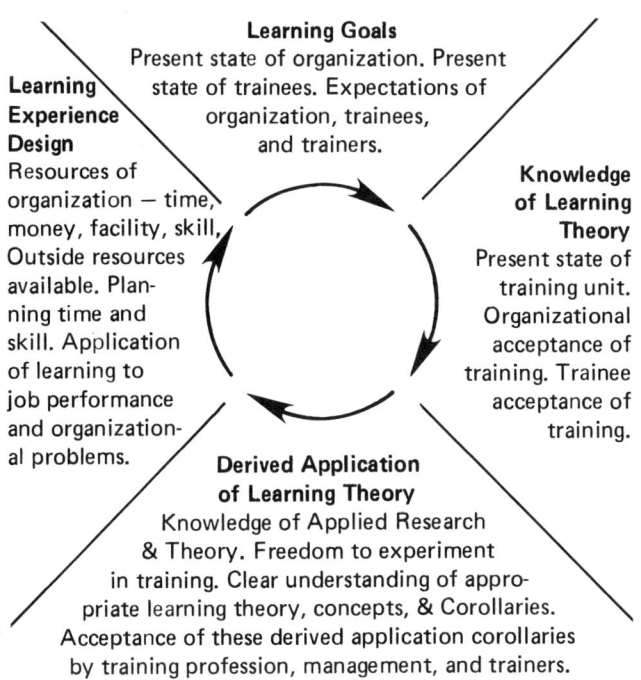

Learning Goals
Present state of organization. Present state of trainees. Expectations of organization, trainees, and trainers.

Learning Experience Design
Resources of organization — time, money, facility, skill, Outside resources available. Planning time and skill. Application of learning to job performance and organizational problems.

Knowledge of Learning Theory
Present state of training unit. Organizational acceptance of training. Trainee acceptance of training.

Derived Application of Learning Theory
Knowledge of Applied Research & Theory. Freedom to experiment in training. Clear understanding of appropriate learning theory, concepts, & Corollaries. Acceptance of these derived application corollaries by training profession, management, and trainers.

No Single Theory

We are inclined to think that by listening to the comments of participants as to what *they* believe enhances their learning, and designing training programs to meet these expressed needs, might have very excellent payoff in training programs even if the training director could not find support for the technique within existing learning theories. What we suspect is that there is no *single* learning theory that should be embraced by a training director or a training program.

This feeling seems to be supported as one surveys the current trends in training programs. These trends would seem to borrow from most of the Schools of Learning Theory. To illustrate, the authors believe that the following trends can be identified:

1. A trend toward a focus on *improved performances* rather than on increased individual knowledge.
2. A trend to *train situations* rather than individuals.
3. A trend to see training as the way *management gets its job done* rather than a function of the training department.
4. A trend toward building up *in-house* capabilities rather than dependence on outside experts.
5. A trend toward insistence on *evaluation* of training rather than accepting it on faith.
6. A trend toward designing learning that will focus on *learning-how-to-learn.*
7. A trend toward training that is *reality-based* as

against training that is highly unrelated to the learners' life experience.
8. A trend toward training that has an *action-learning* base rather than based on one-way communication.
9. A trend toward training that provides *reinforcement* and follow-up experience for trainees rather than "graduating" them from a training program.
10. A trend to depend more on the learning to be *self-motivated by the learner* rather than imposed on the learner by the trainers.
11. A trend for training to be *goal-oriented* rather than vague assurance that it will be "good for you."
12. A trend toward greater *homogeneity* in the persons being trained.[11]

Fitting Specific Needs

There would appear to be different learning techniques and conditions that are applicable to different kinds of training and learning. The training programs within a work organization are not all aimed at the same kind of learning. Perhaps different learning theories apply according to the nature of the subject to be taught and learned, the nature of the organization, the nature of the trainees, and the available teaching resources. This would indicate that no single learning theory can be applied across-the-board to all learning activities.

We suggest the following format as one that would be useful to a training director:

Step 1: What is the learning outcome desired? This will indicate what is to be taught—orientation, problem solving, decision making, knowledge, memorization, changed attitude, changed behavior, manual skill, creativity, self-insight, lessened resistance to change, person-to-person relationships, group-to-group relationships, technical knowledge, communication, self-development, executive development, or understanding principles and theory.

Step 2: Based on what is to be taught, select the learning theory most applicable to that content; i.e., Behavioral Theory, Cognitive Theory, Functionalism, Mathematical Model, Psychiatric, Neurophysiological, or total man and environment.

Step 3: The basic learning theory should be utilized by examining the derived Corollary Theories and principles useful in effectively training toward the desired end. For example: knowing others better, knowing related programs better, reflection time, informal interaction, exercise, recreation, advance preparation, immediate reward, delayed reward, learning plateau, practice-rest-practice, reading with recitation, meaningful material, "A-na" phenomena, immediate use, material known previously, important material, pleasant material, concept formation, concrete concept, part-whole versus whole-part, positive instances versus negative instances, general to specific, maturation task relatedness, fatigue factor, and motivation.

Step 4: These considerations would then suggest specific decisions on the following factors:

a. The learning site—on-the-job; classroom-organizational premises; classroom-off organizational premises; university or other formal site, cultural island, or home.

b. The grouping. (1) Related to size—one, dyad, trio, groups 5–8, groups 9–15, groups 16–30, and audience style—any number. (2) Related to relationships of participants—all male, all female, mixed sex; little experience, much experience, mixed experience; old, young, mixed age groups; known to each other, not known to each other; same organization—vertical, horizontal, diagonal; other organization—homogeneous, mixed; same educational level, mixed educational level; and same task or mixed tasks.

c. The learning methods to be employed—lecture, panel, symposium, debate, laboratory, programmed instruction, experience, coaching, job progression, job rotation, job enlargement, apprenticeship, situational training, personal reading, correspondence, liberal arts, formal school, formal outside program, workshop, conference, institute, seminar visitation, or discussion groups.

d. The training aids to be used—movies, instantaneous replay movies, telephone—loudspeaker, TV, role play, exercises, in-basket, gaming, film strips, slides—transparent, tape recorder, blackboard, newsprint easel, flannel board, magnetic board, self-administered instruments, tests and quizzes, case studies—no printed discussion, case studies—printed discussion, case studies—incident process, experiments, models—mock-ups, and group—generated data.

e. The type of resource persons or instructors—written material, experience, instrumentation, self, organizational technical expert, outside technical expert, organizational resource people, professors, industrial resource people, training department, supervisor, or peers.

f. How much attention needs to be paid to transfer of learning: direct transfer; live, simulated reality; principle to be applied; no direct application; known stimuli—opposite response; familiar to be used in unfamiliar way; or principle to be learned and applied.

Change on the Job

As training directors, we strive very hard to establish response patterns that hopefully will be carried over and continued in the work situation. This is at the heart of one of the criticisms managers level at training programs—the behavior of participants back in the work situation too often seems relatively unchanged.

As one examines this phenomena, one is struck that most training programs in the conceptual areas of supervision and management lean very heavily upon Theory "Y" assumptions. We do not know of any programs that pointedly train toward Theory "X" assumptions. Conversely, organizations still have a goodly amount of Theory "X" assumptions underlying both their operations and supervisory and management practices.[12]

This raises two questions:

1. In our zeal to get away from the mechanistic approach to organizational dynamics, we have underplayed the role of these factors in the total organization as they affect training outcomes. We have tended to train as if such realities did not exist and that the only dynamics that were operable were the human factors in the training. This has created a breach between the training office, the operating people, and management.

2. The S-R phenomenon not only operates within the training situation but is very much operable within the work situation. People react in the direction of the rewards they receive. The S-R patterns initiated in a training session have very little chance of survival when they come up against different S-R patterns of rewards in the work situation. For example, among the work situation S-R patterns rewarded are the following:

   "Research paper production gets you promoted—not supervisory ability or a skill."

   "Promotions depend on who you know—not what you know."

   "I don't give a damn how your people feel—we've got a job to do."

   "OK, you've been to a training program. Say something new."

   "Seniority is what really counts around this place."

Reward Patterns

If a S-R pattern, initiated in a training program, is to be maintained in the work situation, then it must be rewarded by the organization. If the pattern is in conflict with rewarded patterns, the newly-learned patterns do not have much chance to survive. We believe that this accounts for a great deal of supposedly poor results of training. The training is not in harmony with the reward patterns of the organization. As training directors, we would have much better success if we would train according to the pattern rewarded, and apparently desired by the organization.

The research into learning theory has indicated a need that has not been recognized fully by the training profession. We are amazed that a critically needed overview of the field of learning theory has not been written to assist the training director.

We need an identification of the existing learning theories that appear to be best researched and validated, the statement and comparison of these theories in language that the training director can comprehend and understand, and suggested guidelines for ways in which the training director can utilize these learning theories to the enhancement of his training activities.

We believe such a publication is long overdue and would be highly welcomed by almost all training directors. We believe it would add much to the professionalization of the training job. More importantly it would very well make our training programs more effective in meeting the needs of our organizations.

Helpful Guidelines

Beyond the implications for training directors that this exploration into learning theory has suggested, there seems to be some guidelines from such an exploration that are useful to a manager:

1. The sophistication needed to understand and utilize the implications of learning theory have much to say about the kinds of qualifications and skills a training director should bring to the job. The naive assumption that the bestowal of title and salary makes one a training director is tragic.

    Similarly, the managerial assumption that an employee who has the knack of making cute speeches or who once taught elementary school is training director material is inadequate. We would even go further and suggest there are some questionable implications of taking an employee who never managed even a small subunit and entrusting him with the training of other managers.

2. We have already commented on why we believe much of our training is not effective. Operational and organizational climate must support the training received. In addition, managers need to be much more realistic and expect that very few entrenched S-R responses can be changed in a week's training program.

3. We need to relook at the anxiety about evaluation of training. We are not even sure how people learn and this creates real problems in trying to evaluate the effectiveness of our learning process efforts. We know people do learn but we are not sure why.

When one looks at the tremendous number of complicated, tenuous, and conceptual ideas that are discussed within the span of one week in the average supervisory or management training program, it seems naive in the least to expect that very much by way of established new patterns of behavior could possibly emerge. The expectations of management are too high, and we as training directors have promised too much.

Enchantment of Theory

We see no other trap. As we become concerned with learning theory, we must expect to find conflicting theories and conflicting practices within the profession. We must keep our focus on our objectives and not become seduced by enchantment with the theories.

"Theories . . . attempt to organize existing knowledge, they attempt to provide guiding threads or hypotheses toward new knowledge, and they may also furnish principles by which what is known can be used. This practical outcome is seldom central in the thinking of the constructor of theory, and it is not surprising, therefore, that the person seeking advice from the learning theorist often comes away disappointed.

" . . . It turns out, however, that many of the quarrels of the theorists are internal ones, not very important in relation to immediate practical problems; there are, in fact, a great many practically important experimental relationships upon which the theorists are in substantial agreement . . . if the theoretical differences are irreconcilable, and one position eventually wins out over the other, there will ultimately be an effect upon practice. But advice for practical people today need not wait for the resolution of these theoretical controversies."[13]

This, then, is the challenge to those of us desiring to meet the critical problem of developing effective training programs to meet the changing manpower needs of today's organizations.

REFERENCES

1. Berelson, Bernard and Steiner, Gary A., "Human Behavior—An Inventory of Scientific Findings," Harcourt, Brace, and World, Inc., 1964.
2. Kurt Koffka, "Principles of Gestalt Psychology," Harcourt, Brace, 1935, p. 110.

3. Marsh, Pierre J., "Selected Learning Theories: Their Implications for Job Training," Masters Thesis, George Washington University, School of Business and Public Administration, Washington, D.C., August 6, 1965, pp. 56–57.
4. Hilgard, Ernest R., "Theories of Learning," Appleton-Century-Crofts, Inc., 1956, p. 290.
5. Knox, Alan B., and Sjogren, Douglas, "Research on Adult Learning," *Adult Education*, Spring 1965, pp. 133–137.
6. Composite drawn from: (a) Lippitt, Gordon L., "Conditions of Learning Affecting Training," unpublished notes; and (b) Miller, Harry L., "Teaching and Learning in Adult Education," The MacMillan Co., 1964.
7. Roethlisberger, Fritz J., in introduction to Clark, James V., "Education for the Use of Behavioral Science," Institute of Industrial Relations, University of California, Los Angeles, Calif., 1962, p. 4.
8. Clark, James V., Op. Cit., p. 89.
9. Roethlisberger, Fritz J., and others: "Training for Human Relations: An Interim Report," Division of Research, Harvard Business School, Boston, Mass., 1954, Chap. 9.
10. Clark, James V., Op. Cit., p. 91.
11. Lippitt, Gordon L., "Changing Trends in Organized Development," Talk before the Public Administration Society, University of Michigan.
12. McGregor, Douglas, "The Human Side of Enterprise," McGraw-Hill 1960. Chap. 3 and 4, pp. 33–57 for detailed explanation.
13. Hilgard, Ernest R., "Theories of Learning," Op. Cit., p. 485.

BIBLIOGRAPHY

- Bass, Bernard M. and Vaughan, James A., "Psychology of Learning for Managers," Graduate School of Business, University of Pittsburgh.
- Berelson, Bernard and Steiner, Gary A., "Human Behavior—An Inventory of Scientific Findings," Harcourt, Brace, and World, Inc., 1964.
- Blake, Robert R., Mouton, Jane S., Barnes, Louis B., and Greiner, Larry E., "Breakthrough in Organization Development," *Harvard Business Review*, Vol. 42, Nov.–Dec. 1964, pp. 133–155.
- Boudreaux, Edmond and Megginson, Leon C., "A New Concept in University Sponsored Executive Development Programs," *Training Directors Journal*, Vol. 18, Nov. 1964, pp. 31–41.
- Bradford, Leland P., Gibb, J.R. and Benne, K.D., "T-Group Theory and Laboratory Method," John Wiley and Sons, 1964.
- Goldiamond, Israel, "Justified and Unjustified Alarm Over Behavioral Control," In: Milton, Ohmer, "Behavior Disorders: Perspectives and Trends," J.B. Lippincott, 1965, pp. 237–262.
- Green, Edward J., "The Learning Process and Programmed Instruction," Holt, Rinehart, and Winston, Inc., 1962.
- Grose, Robert F. and Birney, Robert C., "Transfer of Learning," D. Van Nostrand Co., Inc., 1963.
- Guerin, Quintin W., "A Learning Theory Model," *Training Directors Journal*, Apr. 1965, pp. 40–45.
- Harris, Theodore L., and Schwahn, Wilson E., "Selected Readings on the Learning Process," Oxford University Press, 1961.
- Hilgard, Ernest R., "Theories of Learning," Appleton-Century-Crofts, Inc., 1948.
- Marsh, Pierre J., "Selected Learning Theories: Their Implications for Job Training," Master's thesis submitted August 6, 1965, School of Business and Public Administration, George Washington University, Washington, D.C.
- Miller, Harry L., "Teaching and Learning in Adult Education," The MacMillan Co., 1964.
- Morton, Robert B., and Bass, Bernard M., "The Organizational Training Laboratory," *Training Directors Journal*, Oct. 1964, Vol. 18, pp. 2–15.
- National Society for the Study of Education. Yearbook. 63d. ed. Pt. I., "Theories of Learning and Instruction," Hilgard, Ernest R. (edited by), University of Chicago Press, 1964.
- Rothschild, William E., "Practicing Managerial Skills," *Training Directors Journal*, Nov. 1964, Vol. 18, pp. 23–30.
- Skinner, B. F., "Pigeons in a Pelican," *The American Psychologist*, Vol. 15, No. 1, Jan. 1960, pp. 28–37.
- Weschler, I. R. and Schein, E. H., "Issues in Human Relations Training," (Sel. Reading Ser. 5), Memorial Issue. National Training Laboratories, 1962.
- Wight, A. R., "Translating Creativity Findings to Industrial training Programs," *Human Relations Training News.* Summer 1964, pp. 5–7.

Results-Oriented Training Designs

by Leslie This

Human resources development designers must look at their philosophy of training and education. Philosophy—even specifically a philosophy of training—is a very intangible and qualitative factor. However, it is that factor, above all others such as mechanical technique or detailed curriculum flow, which breathes spirit, life and true significance into a training effort. Program participants can only sense the existence of such a spirit in a program; they cannot, and do not, document it in an articulate way. They feel life in a program (and move off from it with enthusiasm and desire for organizational objectives and personal development of worth) or they sense lifelessness in mechanical movement of "paper perfect" curriculum design (and move off from it with cynicism, ridicule or, at the very best, apathy).

Training designers must ask themselves, "What is my philosophy of training?" Increasingly, training professionals are being faced with this question and too often have no answer because they are not aware, yet, of the question.

With a well-thought-out philosophy of training, the trainer knows what he is doing and why. At the present state of the "training art," it is difficult to conceive of professionals in training who have not asked, and answered, this question. Many training designers take into consideration possible reasons for the failure of their programs in order to anticipate and plan against failure. Some of the more common reasons for curriculum or program failure, which they identify, follow:

1. The trainees do not need the training.
2. The trainees need the training but do not know it or will not admit it.
3. The problem leading to the establishment of a specific training program is not one that can be solved by existing training knowledge and/or techniques.
4. The trainer is not knowledgeable or doesn't present his material properly.
5. The material being presented is too difficult to transfer and apply. It is too abstract to be readily applicable to the job situation of the trainee.
6. Neither the trainee's participation in the program nor his "changed job behavior" is adequately

reinforced by his superiors, associates or work situation.
7. The trainees need the training, know they need it, but resist it for various other reasons.

ASSUMPTIONS ABOUT TRAINING

More specifically, training planners might examine certain assumptions regarding training and explicitly identify their positions and the probable effect of their assumptions on training. The following are typical assumptions held by professional trainers:

1. Theory and principles have value insofar as they can be applied to the job. If one accepts this assumption, he will plan a curriculum in which theory for its own sake will be avoided and all theory will be introduced only insofar as it guides, explains the reasons for, and promotes successful performance.

2. Experience is as important a learning method as didactic exposition. This assumption has a 2500 year history in education theory, ranging between so-called "Platonic" and "Aristotelian" extremes. If one accepts this assumption, he will incorporate into his program design substantial amounts of participant (group) participation as distinct from an almost exclusive reliance on the seemingly more efficient coverage of material by lecture. This assumption also has critical implications for on-the-job training.

3. Communication is the most critical management skill. That is, every other managerial skill required for successful managerial performance depends on the ability to communicate. If one believes this assumption, he will build into the curriculum design a strong component of material dealing with interpersonal relations and underlying concepts from behavioral science; he will draw substantially from certain schools of management theory which stress the human skills of the manager. Obviously also, the curriculum design would reflect the above assumption in terms of generous allocation of time to the communication subject. (If the group being trained is not managers, some other skill would be substituted as the critical skill for that group. Or, for managers, the trainer might substitute what, to him, is the most critical skill—delegation, motivation, etc.)

4. Attitude changes follow changes in behavior. That is, one—and a most practical—method

of inducing desirable changes in attitude, as a product of a training program, is to first attempt to change the participant's behavior. One who accepts this assumption will incorporate into the training design a great deal of simulation, group and individual participation, role-play, case discussion and other methods designed to create, in the training room, participant behavior and provision for immediate feedback on the success or failure of that behavior. The trainer who believes strongly in this assumption will highly value laboratory, sensitivity and possibly encounter training.

DESIGN STEPS

To plan a design to improve performance on a job, it is necessary to have a thorough understanding of the nature of the job and the performance of the people in it. Several steps are required:

- Identification of the key persons in the system who define the tasks, roles and expectations of the participants.
- Continuous attempts to further define these tasks, roles and expectations and assign priorities, i.e., which are most important.
- Continuous efforts to identify and clarify factors which are associated with effective performance of the various aspects of the participant's job; e.g., knowledge of authority structure, educational background, etc.
- Determination of the desired and weighted characteristics of the participant's job related to performance.

Several people are concerned and should be involved in the process of defining the tasks, roles and expectations of the participant. Often there is a lack of clarity between what the job is and what it should be. This may be because of the multiple job definer situation.

The fact of multiple job definers should be discussed openly and evaluated in detail in relation to expected tasks and priorities as a part of training programs. Furthermore, the problem should be faced as to what extent and by what means others, not having formal authority over the participant's job, may influence task identification.

TRAINING OBJECTIVES

Once some understanding of the important characteristics that affect performance and alternatives to use in influencing them is developed, it is possible to proceed more effectively with the identification of broad objectives for the training itself. Subsequently, it is important to develop limited objectives for a specific period of time and for a specific set of training program activities.

1. To improve problem-solving capability
2. To handle new situations
3. To improve the ability to communicate
4. To improve attitudes appropriate to change
5. To learn why things occur in the organization's milieu
6. To recognize changes in the environment and that different responses are called for
7. To improve ability in involving others in the activities of the organization
8. To perform a specific task
9. To instill greater pride in being associated with the organization
10. To determine the present qualifications of the present group of participants
11. To find the critical incidents that indicate where present incumbents' performance is weak

For further specificity of objectives, several sources exist: the learner himself; the milieu or environment; the subject matter or content; and the instructor. It is suggested that these sources be used jointly to gather information systematically. Questions which should be asked include:

1. What are the critical incidents in his job?
    a. How are they best handled?
    b. What are the limits or restrictions?
    c. Whom does he relate to?
    d. Who determines his expectations?
    e. Whom does he have to persuade?
2. What are his career expectations? Locations? Type of Position? Length of service?
3. Who judges his performance? What criteria are really used? What should be used?
4. What types of people in what types of job situations are most effective?

It is important to keep in mind that a comparison of relevant points of view must be secured. Reality is what it is perceived to be by the perceiver. One must sample the perceptions of various populations to get at the "truth." Among these will be those of the superiors, the peer group and subordinates. In this way not only may the training program objectives be further clarified and specified, but additional ideas and inputs for curriculum content may be generated. This, of course, is a continuing process of determining objectives and content. One cannot wait until it is "finished." It never will be.

CURRICULUM MODELS

Any program design will be composed of various components, such as time blocs, training methods, training aids, content, training site, etc. Any particular combination of these components (among the almost infinite possibilities of such combinations and permutations) arranged and sequenced in a particular way will be referred to as a "curriculum model."

It seems axiomatic that one of the essential means to be used by program planners for effectively planning a curriculum is the systematic consideration of many possible curriculum models. The planners should consider the advantages and disadvantages of each in order to guide final selection. It is one thing to permit a particular model to constitute a curriculum which thus rejects all other models by implication; it is quite another explicitly to set many possible models before the mind, with the advantages and disadvantages of each, and explicitly select one while rejecting others for reasons, in each case, which have been examined thoroughly. The latter approach is strongly recommended.

The goal of a specific curriculum for specific results will be aided by the following considerations:

1. The Diversity of Program Participants.

Those for whom the training curriculum is being designed often represent an enormous diversity in terms of age, background, education, job experience and level. It is clear that the curriculum must ultimately be determined by the objectives decided upon for the curriculum; and that, in turn, these objectives must be established in terms of the behavior desired and required. That is, and must be, the classic approach to program development.

Much discussion often occurs around whether the training program should cut across vertical echelons, should include experienced and inexperienced participants, should include several functional groups, etc. No simple formula exists to answer these questions. The answer can only be found by tightly defining the program objectives and then asking, "Will the mix we are concerned about be useful or non-useful in attaining these objectives?" The answer then normally suggests itself. Of course, the planner sometimes will want, for example, the experienced to help teach the inexperienced. In this instance the methodology will suggest the answer.

One dichotomy of participants is often overlooked. Some participants learn best by lecture, note-taking and copious structure. This often is decried by professional trainers, but it seems to be true. Others learn best by analyzed experience and want methodology to allow for self-learning—role plays, discussion groups, etc. It is difficult to design a training experience that can appeal to both groups. If at all possible, participants should have some voice in determining the methodology best suited to their individual learning. Announced laboratory methods, for example, seem to "screen out" the more structured-learning participants. This is an area that has been down-played in recent years—most trainers have simply assumed that all participants can learn only by experiential training methods.

2. Concepts and Patterns of Career Development.

It should be noted that the design of a program should be established within a larger career development context. One, several, or all of the following patterns of career development might enter into a final and systematic career development plan, of which a specific program design would be but a part, although a most important part:

- Job rotation
- Management intern program
- On-the-job training
- Work-study
- Classroom training
- Situational training
- Simulation training
- Laboratory training
- Confrontation training
- Self-growth training

Each of these training concepts (and approaches) should be considered as planners develop a training curriculum.

3. Curriculum Content.

As curriculum planners develop a program design for participants, a principal concern will be the content. Although other classifications of subject matter might be used, the following are often typical:

- Technical material
- Managerial material
- Human relations material
  Other directed
  Self directed
- Community relations material

4. Curriculum Method.

Content is only one part of a total curriculum design, as any training professional knows. Another centrally-important part is choice of method. Here the philosophies and assumptions underlying training, referred to earlier, are critical.

At this point we move into an area that is not clearly defined in the training field. We may have a program of three days' duration that solely uses the lecture. What should this program be called? Is it a lecture program? Some programs of this nature use "canned" lectures on film and call the program a "film program." Is it film—or lecture? The film may include situational excerpts to illustrate some lecture points. Is it now lecture, filmed lecture or "live situations"— or even case study? The laboratory method may employ lectures, film, role plays, case studies or discussion. Is the key in the method most frequently used?

We feel comfortable with describing a one-day or more activity as a seminar, workshop, conference, symposium or institute. However, many of these look identical. No clearly-defined criteria seem to exist. We generally name the activity on such simple bases as "We've about worn out 'seminar,' let's call this one a 'workshop'." Or, "What will appeal to our audience— never mind what we'll be doing?"

Both usages appear in the following list. We have made no attempt to clarify an issue that has not yet been clarified in the training field. At some point it would be useful for the field to attempt clearly to differentiate and classify overall training designs, training methods and training aids.

Listed are the principal training methods with brief references to some advantages and disadvantages of each:

a. The Lecture Method.   The lecture method is, on the surface, one of the most efficient methods for imparting ideas. A lecturer, in an hour's time, can cover a great number of ideas and/or blocs of instruction. He can do this rapidly, efficiently, even dramatically. Thus, the advantage of the lecture method is speed of coverage and efficiency. Its disadvantage is that much, if not most, of the lecturer's input is lost on some ears that cannot understand or do not believe because nothing of their own experience is involved. Some of these disadvantages can be reduced when the lecture method is used in combination with other methods.

b. Case Discussion. Providing cases for participants to study and discuss has become a standard method over the past two decades. The cases may be "stock" items, or specially written, prepared by those designing the program and tailored to special purposes. The advantage is strong involvement of the participant and his own reactions. Often, too, concrete and controversial problem-solving is substituted for easy and platitudinous abstractions. A disadvantage is, of course, the relatively great time consumed in writing a good case and in encouraging free and full discussion.

c. Correspondence and Home Study. This method is inexpensive and convenient, and can accomplish much provided the material is excellent and the objective is primarily knowledge. Lack of immediate feedback and face-to-face contact is its obvious weakness.

d. Short Conferences, Institutes or Orientations. Often much can be accomplished by such one- or two-day meetings, especially in the form of rapid orientation of an audience which is alert, interested and anxious to learn.

e. Simulation. Simulation in training generally includes such techniques as role-playing, business and other games, computerized or manual, etc. It has, generally, the same advantages and disadvantages mentioned for case discussions.

f. Programmed Learning. This method has been a glamour technique in recent years. Its effectiveness, advantages and disadvantages have been argued roundly and are not summarized here.

g. Reading (directed and/or non-directed). Many training personnel insist reading changes nothing. Many participants are just as adamant that a good book or a good idea in a book has "changed my life." We need more hard data as to the relative effectiveness of reading and experience as change agents.

h. Laboratory Training. This learning method utilizes the behavior of the persons in the learning to analyze their "here and now" experiences as the prime focus of the content of their learning.

i. Sensitivity Training. One application of the laboratory method which uses an unstructured group learning experience to facilitate the participant learning the effect of his behavior on others, the effect of other persons' behavior on his and self-understanding.

j. Encounter Training. This is a recent adaptation of sensitivity training. It focuses on body movement, body touch and "internal feelings." Its major emphasis would seem to be on heightened awareness and enjoyment of feelings and emotions.

k. Confrontation Training. This method generally puts most of the burden of identifying training needs and meeting the training needs squarely on the participant. The participant is engaged in "diagnostic situations" that let him test his ability to cope with that situation. He may determine his preparedness—or he may be rated by "experts." He then, on his own, corrects his training deficiencies. The training staff provides whatever resources he needs. The participant determines when he is sufficiently "trained."

l. Situational Training.   This method usually begins with some formal program of training. The participants are in "family" groups that work and relate together on the job. Usually an outside trainer helps them to begin the process. More and more training responsibility is taken by the "work group leader" and on-going organizational problems are used as the learning vehicles. It is a learn-as-you-do process and one of the sought-after benefits is to learn how to handle similar future problems.

m. Multi-Media.   This seems exotic to many trainers but the basic concept is not new. Any program that has used role plays, film, cases, lectures, etc. has used the multi-media approach. The general idea seems to be to bombard every sense and "ram" the message home by sheer sensory overload. It would seem to hold promise, but currently is too often confused with sheer entertainment and psychedelic "noise."

Some idea of preferred methods may be ascertained from the experience of training directors of 45 large American companies, as indicated in the table by Wayne J. Foreman.[1] (See Tables 1 and 2.)

DESIGN VARIABLES

A number of variables must be considered in course design and course sequence. The arrangement of courses, course sequence, methods and other curriculum elements can vary along the following scales:

1. Number and Length.   The same material can be covered in six separate one-week courses, three two-week courses, or one six-week course. The advantages and disadvantages of each choice should be explored. As an illustration, it could be that more than a week away from the job would be virtually impossible for many participants and, thus, a curriculum design built on two- and three-week blocks of time would have a possibly fatal mechanical flaw.

TABLE 1

Training Techniques and Number of Times Appearing in Top Five Techniques According to Frequency of Use

Training Technique	Times Appearing in Top Five	Percentage
On-the-job	43	96
Conference	42	93
Job-rotation	34	76
Special projects	32	71
Case studies	22	49
Problem solving	22	49
Management games	8	18
Role playing	8	18
Programmed instruction	7	16
Sensitivity training	4	9
Brainstorming	3	7
Other	3	7

Foreman also points out that 96 percent of the companies used training courses outside the company and 41 percent used correspondence courses.

2. Subject Matter "Mix."   The same amount of technical, managerial and community relations subject matter might be covered over three separate courses by devoting the entirety of the first course to technical material, the entirety of the second course to managerial material, and the entirety of the third course to community relations material. An alternative would be to blend appropriate proportions of technical, managerial and community relations material into each of the three courses. Closely related to this decision, of course, is the even more basic decision as to the relative proportions of technical, managerial and community relations material to be covered over the entire curriculum.

3. Placement of Equivalency Tests and Other Evaluation.   One of the constantly recurring and plaguing questions raised by both training professionals and participants is "Why should I be required to take elementary work, or a program, in skills and knowledge I already possess?" This is a difficult question to answer. It is much easier to design a program that includes all needed components and require all participants to take the total program. However, in a management training program, a participant may feel he knows enough about motivation—or may have just completed a semester's course in that subject. Yet we require him to take our three hours of the subject. Our general rationalization is "You never get enough" or "You can always learn more."

We have no good way of determining what a participant knows and letting him select what he needs. Confrontation training attempts to get at this problem. The new leadership training program of the

TABLE 2
Rank Order of Frequency of Use of 18 Training Techniques by Type of Firm

| | Type of Firm | | | |
| | Manufacturing | | Non-manufacturing | |
Training Technique	Rank order	Mean value	Rank order	Mean value
1. Job instruction training	1	3.9	1	4.0
2. Conference or discussion	2	3.5	2	3.4
3. Apprentice training	3	3.1	6.5	2.5
4. Job rotation	4	2.8	3	2.8
5. Coaching	5	2.6	6.5	2.5
6. Lecture	6	2.4	5	2.6
7. Special study	7	2.3	4	2.7
8. Case study	8	2.1	10	2.2
9. Films	9	2.0	8.5	2.4
10. Programmed instruction	10	1.9	8.5	2.4
11. Internships and assistantships	11	1.8	11	2.0
12. Simulation	12	1.7	12	1.9
13. Programmed group exercises	13.5	1.6	16.5	1.3
14. Role playing	13.5	1.6	13	1.6
15. Laboratory training	15	1.5	16.5	1.3
16. Television	16	1.4	14.5	1.4
17. Vestibule training	17	1.2	14.5	1.4
18. Junior board	18	1.1	18	1.1

Consists of 63 firms.

Consists of 14 transportation, 13 finance, 10 retail, and 12 "other" firms.

Computed from the following values: 5 = Always; 4 = Usually; 3 = Average; 2 = Seldom; 1 = Never.

Stuart B. Utgaard and Rene V. Dawis[2] conducted another similar study with the above findings.

Girl Scouts of America also attempts to confront this problem for volunteer leaders. It is not an easy task to determine what a participant knows in such content areas as motivation, communication, delegation, managing, etc. For this reason we generally choose to ignore the problem. We believe this is an issue training professionals will have to face sooner or later—as will personnel people and our entire society. (For example, if the half-life of knowledge in the physical sciences is now eight years, how do we assess a man's knowledge and capability five years after he finishes school—10 years later—20 years later? How do we give credit and recognition to the concept that the most and best training occurs on the job?)

Testing, whether paper and pencil, point and factor ratings, and so on, might be used at many, all, or no stages of the curriculum sequence. They might be used as a criterion of satisfactory program completion and/or as a qualifying test. Satisfactory pre-determined scores might be required of all candidates applying for a particular later program at a particular stage of their career development.

4. Relationship Between the Curriculum and Other Possible Concepts and Patterns of Career Develop-

ment. A particular course or stage of the training curriculum might immediately precede or follow a man's relocation in a job rotation or career ladder pattern.

5. Curriculum Method.

The curriculum might blend some or all of the curriculum methods mentioned above such as orientation conferences, case study, home study, advanced reading, etc.

6. Individual Counseling.

The curriculum might provide for a certain amount of individual counseling of participants.

7. Composition of Participant Groups.

A particular group might be homogeneous or heterogeneous; that is, all might be participants from large cities of a certain region of the United States with similar educational and prior-job backgrounds—or group diversity might be sought.

The training designer, if he is to be effective, must consider that most employees will face three or four major retraining efforts in their lifetime. The development of his organization's human resources is a continuous, life-long process. The training designer must see each specific program as contributing to this continuous development—not as an end in itself. Within this broad context, he then deals with the variables, factors and components described in this article to exact the maximum contribution of a specific program to the total human resource development of the participants.

RESULTS-ORIENTED TRAINING DESIGNS: AN UPDATE

Were I re-writing this article today, I probably would pay attention to six very pragmatic things:

First, I would be much more sensitive to using generic rather than masculine terms when referring to participants and trainers.

Second, I would have referenced the book, "The Small Meeting Planner" as a helpful resource to the designer of training.

Third, when reviewing the design steps, I would reference the reality, when selecting a training design, of such mundane things as:

- The skill and knowledge of the trainer. Much design occurs within the limitations of the designer.
- The pressure on the in-house trainer to show he/she is "earning their salt." Training is sometimes designed simply because the trainer needs to show he/she is busy.
- Awareness that outside persons are also motivated to suggest training designs depending upon their own resources and the state of their organization's cash flow.

Fourth, if people see/recognize the need for training in their job or life much of the pressure on design is voided. If one really needs to know something, and knows they need to know, they will learn under even the most trying conditions. Much of our design efforts go into making people want to learn—or find learning palatable—when their major motivation is looking for entertainment, credit, or temporary escape from the job. This awareness has caused me to be much more careful in the selection of who attends a program. My attention can then go into designing a learning event—not a motivational event.

Fifth, there is a discussion of equivalency tests. This was being much discussed when the article was written. My observation is that almost all such attempts did not pay off. We spent more time testing people for what they knew than it took to give them the program. About as good a test as any is simply to describe the course content adequately and then let participants decide whether or not it would be helpful to them.

Sixth, as a training designer I am extremely interested today in knowing whether or not the client or sponsor really is interested in the training or any change in behavior, operations, or procedure.

Many sponsors simply see training as something that can do no harm and rewards employees or provides a temporary respite from the job. I have found it quite dysfunctional to train participants in one direction only to have them return to a work environment that operates quite differently.

People do behave where they perceive the rewards to be. I now spend much more time with the sponsor/client on this matter. If change is wanted, we agree on what and how much and in what direction. My design work now is heavily affected by this consideration. To do otherwise is simply to frustrate participants and often make them less effective when they return to the job.

Acknowledgement

Some of the concepts in this article were initially put together by the author and Dr. James Owens, Professor of Business Administration, American University, for the Office of Civil Defense. The author wishes to express his appreciation and acknowledgement of this initial work.

REFERENCES

1. Foreman, Wayne J., "Management Training in Large Corporations," *Training and Development Journal*, May 1967, p. 12.
2. Utgaard, Stuart B. and Rene V. Dawis, "The Most Frequently Used Training Techniques," *Training and Development Journal*, Feb. 1970, p. 41.

Training and Development Programs: What Learning Theory and Research Have to Offer

by Craig Eric Schneier

There is little debate among those interested in training and development in organizations that the principles of learning are basic to their programs' design and implementation. This view is evidenced by the fact that training has been equated with learning (e.g., Blumenfeld and Holland, 1971), and that many proponents of Organizational Development, notably those favoring laboratory training techniques, have stressed "learning to learn" as a primary objective (e.g., Golembiewski, 1972).

Recently, various authors have used learning theory and research effectively in their discussions of training and development programs. Such concepts as anxiety, punishment, and reinforcement are used to help evaluate training experiences. Schrank (1971) has used some learning theory research to help emphasize the degree of similarity between the teacher–pupil role and the supervisor–subordinate role. He has also shed some light on the importance of the teacher's role in determining the pupil's learning success. At least one learning theory, operant theory, has recently been explored as to its application to a wide variety of training and development problems (Murphy, 1972; Beatty and Schneier, 1972).

Despite this sampling of useful ideas generated from learning theory and a widespread recognition that training and development programs are primarily learning processes, there is still much validity in the following remarks by Goldstein and Sorcher (1972, p. 37):

Management training—in its several underlying philosophies, its specific conceptualizations and its concrete techniques—is a human learning process. Yet almost without exception, there has been remarkably little reliance in the development and implementation of management training on this vast and relevant body of research literature.

We agree with the statement that there are principles of various learning theories and findings from empirical research that are still relatively unknown and/or not utilized by specialists in training and development. While there is considerable disagreement among the experts as to which one of the several learning theories best explains the human learning process, many principles which logically follow from the various theories are supported by a considerable body of research. Obviously, not all of this research was performed with managers, or even with adults in work situations, but so much of it has been substantiated time and again that the findings are generally agreed upon in the literature.

This article will state some of these principles and findings which are thought to be useful in all phases of training and development programs. The statements will be grouped under the learning environment, the role of the teacher/trainer, characteristics of the learner, basic processes in the human learning activity, reinforcement and punishment, retention and transfer of learning, and practice.*

It will be stressed that these seven categories form the interdependent considerations in the design, implementation, and evaluation of effective training and development programs, that they represent the sources of possible contingencies to be dealt with in each unique learning situation, and that they form the conceptual base for many important organizational training and development programs, such as MBO, skill training, and performance appraisals.

PRINCIPLES AND FINDINGS FROM LEARNING THEORY AND RESEARCH

I. The Learning Environment

1. Objectives and success criteria for the learning program should be specified and communicated to all learners before the program begins (see V-7).
2. Tests of the learner's progress should be scheduled. If a learner is not ready for a test, he should continue practicing. The learner should have an idea of the types of questions or activities that will be on the test. The "ordeal" aspect of testing should be eliminated.
3. Tasks should be broken into component behaviors that can be learned directly. The

*For a more detailed explanation of these principles and findings, the reader is referred to any of the works on learning cited in the references.

behaviors should be sequenced in order of increasing difficulty toward a final target behavior (see V-5).

4. The value of teaching machines and programmed learning devices lies in their ability to help sequence learning, to allow the learner to progress at his own pace, and to help control attention by focusing the learner on the stimuli; their value does not lie in their gadgetry or hardware.

5. To measure learning, note observational changes in the frequencies of desired behavioral responses, not necessarily in the strength of responses, in intentions, or in attitudes. Baseline frequencies of behavior must, therefore, be established prior to the learning situation in order to note the differential effects of learning.

6. "Whole" presentation is usually better than "part" presentation. Therefore, give the learner a "feel" for the total task initially.

7. Learning can and does take place in every context, not only in specified locations and in formal programs. Undesirable and desirable behaviors learned in these "informal" settings should be noted.

II. The Role of the Teacher/Trainer

1. Teachers learn a great deal about their learners when they are actually teaching and given responsibility. Having students act as teachers in some situations increases their ability to learn, as well as their empathy for other teachers.

2. The teacher conditions emotional reactions in the learning program, as well as behavioral responses and should, therefore, attempt to condition favorable reactions to himself and to the subject matter.

3. The teacher establishes objectives, methods, sequences, and time limits in learning programs with varying degrees of participation by the learner. The teacher's knowledge of the learner, the situation, and the content of the learning program is vital for specifying both the proper methods and the appropriate degree of learner participation in each learning program.

III. The Characteristics of the Learner

1. People not only learn at different rates, but each person brings a different emotional state or temperament to the learning situation (see II-2). Assessment of temperament facilitates a more effective choice of teaching strategies.

2. The motivational level of the learner is relevant to the type and amount of stimuli to which he

will respond. Whether he finds the learning intrinsically or extrinsically rewarding (i.e., instrumental for internally mediated or externally mediated rewards), should be considered. The needs the learner has unsatisfied as he enters the learning program are also relevant.

3. Each learner's prior conditioning or learning background will influence the amount, frequency, and type of reinforcement and punishment which will be most effective, as well as the method of stimuli presentation (e.g., visual, auditory).

4. Individual learners should be encouraged to learn the skills or behaviors of which they are capable and in which they are interested. They should be able to specialize and demonstrate expertise in at least one area in order to take pride in their accomplishments.

IV. Basic Processes in the Human Learning Activity

1. Interest and attention come from successful experiences. These, in turn, facilitate learning as they are seen as rewarding experiences.

2. Attention and curiosity in learning are best facilitated by the use of moderate (not too high nor too low) levels of arousal, curiosity, or anxiety.

3. Learning can occur when the learner merely observes. Active participation is not always necessary, unless motor skills are being taught.

4. Learners should not leave the learning setting after giving incorrect responses. Final responses should always be correct.

5. There are several ways to learn: trial and error, perception-organization-insight, and modeling another's behavior, are all effective under certain conditions.

6. Learning usually progresses to a point and then levels off. This leveling (a "plateau" in a "learning curve") may be due to the fact that incorrect responses are being reduced or that small simple steps in learning were learned rapidly and now as the small steps are combined into complex tasks, learning slows. Incentives added in the "plateau" stage are helpful.

7. If motor responses are to be learned, verbal guidance, practice, and a favorable, supportive environment are helpful. If ideas or concepts are to be learned, active participation and the formation of meaningful associations between the new material and more familiar material are helpful.

8. Learning can be inhibited and therefore proper responses decreased if too much repetition or fatigue is evidenced (see VII-3).

9. Avoidance learning occurs when fear is felt and a response is made to eliminate the fear. This fear-avoiding response is often reinforced, and it therefore has little chance of being eliminated, as it is needed to avoid aversive stimuli (see V-2). To eliminate avoidance behaviors, the aversive stimuli must be removed.

10. Incidental learning is learning that remains dormant until the occasion for its demonstration arises (e.g., curiosity is stimulated or reinforcement is powerful enough to elicit the response) (see VI-1).

11. Imitation requires that the learner is directly reinforced for matching a model's behavior. "Matched dependence" occurs when the learner models a model. "Same behavior" occurs when two learners respond to the same stimulus, not to each other. Vicarious learning is matching the behavior of another without receiving direct or immediate reinforcement from the model.

12. Complex human learning includes a proper degree of discrimination and generalization. Discrimination requires distinguishing between quite similar stimuli which require *different* responses. Generalization requires noting that similar, but not exactly the same stimuli often require the *same* response.

13. Attitudes can be learned and reinforced in much the same way as behavior is reinforced.

V. Reinforcement and Punishment

1. The "Law of Effect" states that behavior that is reinforced will increase in probability of future occurrence. A reinforcer is, therefore, any object or event that *strengthens* the probability of future occurrence of behavior.

2. Punishment occurs when the probability of a response is *weakened* by an object or event. Punishment leads to escape and avoidance behaviors, as well as frustration.

3. Secondary reinforcers (e.g., money) are those objects or events which are linked to or instrumental for receiving other primary reinforcers (e.g., food) and so also take on reinforcing properties themselves. The many effective secondary reinforcers should be identified and used.

4. Undesired behaviors can be extinguished if they are simply not reinforced and not punished, but ignored.

5. "Shaping" behavior occurs when desired responses are observed which are approximates of a target behavior, and are reinforced. The responses are continually reinforced as they become closer and closer to the target, until the target is imitated.

6. For punishment and reinforcement to be effective, they must be dispensed immediately and be appropriate in intensity for the particular response they follow.

7. Knowledge of results of performance is basic to learning and is often a reinforcer. It provides necessary feedback for corrective action, and should be related to goal levels which are predetermined standards of performance communicated to and understood by the learner.

8. A harder, more intense response will not be elicited unless a more intense, more powerful reinforcer is given.

9. If reinforcement is dispensed on a variable ratio schedule (after a random and changing number of responses unknown to the learner), behavior will be most difficult to extinguish. The variable ratio is thus more effective in sustaining desired responses than either a continuous reinforcement schedule (each desired response rewarded) or fixed interval reinforcement schedule (reinforcement given after the passage of an interval of time e.g., weekly).

10. Social reinforcement (e.g., approval, status given by others) can be effective in controlling behavior, depending upon the environment and personal attractions.

11. The personality and position of the reinforcing/punishing agent influences the effectiveness of the reinforcement or punishment he dispenses. Therefore, it is not only that he dispenses rewards, but his manner, sincerity, and tone in these instances that is noticed by the learner.

VI. Retention and Transfer of Learning

1. In transferring learning, the teacher/trainer should be aware of latent learning and offer reinforcement to prompt the demonstration of such learning.

2. Time does not cause forgetting per se; it merely allows for interfering learning processes to occur between what was learned and the time recall is desired.

3. Retroactive inhibition refers to the interference of new material on the ability to recall older material. Proactive inhibition occurs when old material interferes with the learning of new material. At times, therefore, it is wise to almost over-learn or repeat some material many times.

4. Some learned material is not recalled, as it is repressed in the subconscious of the learner because its overt demonstration is deemed to be harmful to the learner.

5. Identical stimuli presented in the learning and application settings should result in positive

transfer. The learning of principles that apply across situations also aids in transfer of learning.

6. Transfer is aided if responses are given in situations which are similar to those which will be encountered in the post-learning environment.
7. Transfer is aided if the learner is able to demonstrate generalization (see IV-12).
8. Retention is strengthened if a variable-ratio reinforcement schedule is followed (see V-10).

VII. Practice

1. The learner must be encouraged (i.e., reinforced) to take practice seriously.
2. Practice should include responses to different stimuli than those encountered in learning, but which may be encountered in actual application (see IV-12).
3. Distributed, rather than massed practice, with frequent short rests, is usually optimal.

USES OF THE PRINCIPLES AND FINDINGS

It is obvious that while not all of these findings and principles from learning theory and research are applicable to each type of training and development program, some are of obvious use. Depending on the type of program, exigencies of time and cost, and the characteristics of the trainees and trainers, some will be more relevant than others. Furthermore, the seven categories are not meant to be entirely separate. Many items necessarily overlap. The most important aspect of the categories is their *interdependent* nature. Program developers can benefit from some consideration of each category.

As with so many aspects of organizations, the effective design and implementation of training and development programs depend largely on the recognition of the contingencies the data from the seven categories present to the specialist. In each particular instance, the categories come together in a unique way to form a complex learning situation or set of contingencies to be managed. The use of a particular type of training program can depend upon the characteristics of the trainees, which can depend upon the learning environment and learning content, which may depend upon the role of the trainer, and so on. It can thus be seen that each of the seven categories may influence, or be contingent upon, any or all of the others in any given learning situation. The training and development specialist's success in facilitating learning will, therefore, depend in large part on his ability to properly *diagnose* a situation and then develop the most effective learning strategies for that situation. In

the diagnostic phase of the facilitation of learning in organizations, the seven categories represent the possible sources of data which can be gathered regarding a training situation (e.g., data regarding the environment, the trainer, the trainees, etc.) (see Figure 1).

After the diagnosis is completed, the actual *design* of a particular program or learning strategy can begin. The statements in each category can be scanned for their relevance to a specific type of strategy, such as programmed instruction, lectures, modeling, etc. For example, if a "skill" training program is required, statements concerning practice, knowledge of results, and reinforcement schedules would be helpful. Following design, the *implementation* of the strategy can be aided by the statements, as they suggest points to be noted which can deter or facilitate implementation in a particular situation. For example, as category three notes, certain characteristics of the learner are vital

FIGURE 1
Training and Development viewed as a four-phase process to facilitate learning in organizations.

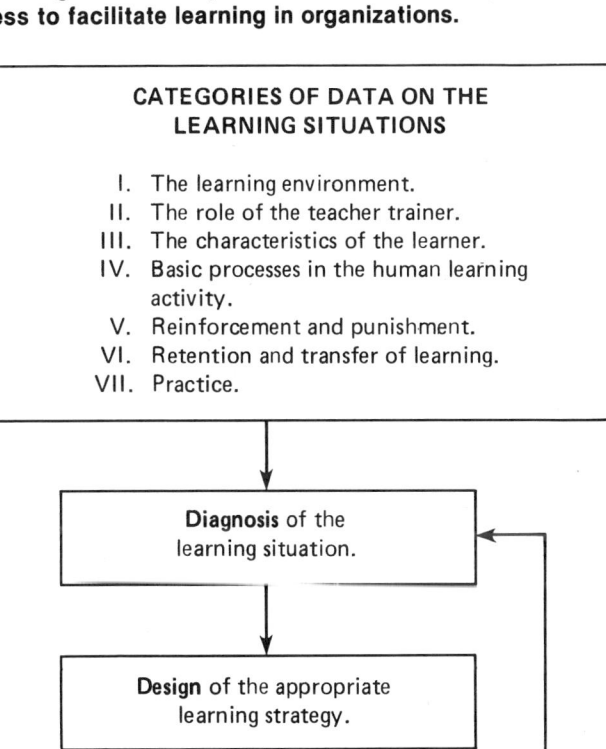

considerations which would make some strategies more effective than others. The last stage in training and development work is *evaluation* of the strategy and possible *redesign*. This stage can be aided as the seven categories again present the sources of probable success or failure.

The principles and findings from learning theory and research have been presented as an initial list compiled to help those engaged in training and development programs become aware of the scope of the learning literature which is applicable to their programs. The list is also designed for use in the following stages of training and development work: diagnosis of the learning situation, design of the learning strategy, implementation of the strategy, and evaluation and possible redesign. The seven categories are offered as possible sources of data which combine to form each particular training and development situation. Data gathered from the seven categories can facilitate a more rigorous diagnostic effort on the part of the training and development specialist. This diagnosis aids in tying the unique learning situation faced by the specialist to the learning strategy most amenable to that situation. Particular statements within the categories can also be scanned as to their obvious use as guides in implementing specific programs such as MBO, skill training, performance appraisals, and the many other training and development programs which are designed to facilitate learning in organization settings.

Our experience has been that employees are willing to answer quite lengthy mail questionnaires, if the survey is conducted properly. For example, the letters shown previously were sent to 1,200 employees at one of the divisions of a large corporation. Of this number 800 represented a systematic sample of their non-managerial employees, and they received a 12-page 8½ × 11 size questionnaire, while a 16-page questionnaire was sent to the managers. The percent of completed questionnaires was 80% from the managers and 72% from the other employees.

It takes thorough planning and hard work to get a high percent of response on any survey. The letters shown look simple enough, but they were written and rewritten several times and tested with two pilot studies. The same was true of the questionnaires. It is not only a high response that is important, the questions (and answers) have to be unbiased and unambiguous. Some questions were rewritten many times by several people before the right phrasing was found. It is often difficult to make sure that a question doesn't "lead" the respondent or appear to be an invasion of privacy.

For the purposes of meaningful analysis, it is very important to have detailed classification data, such as sex, age, marital status, family size, education, title, department, years with company, years at present job-level, etc. These questions can be asked, but then they will add a page or two to the already long questionnaire. If the company has these data, and the research house can get them with the mailing list, the questionnaires can be keyed and the classification data added to the responses.

Employee surveys offer many interesting possibilities for useful analyses. They must be approached with a sincere desire to find out, first-hand, the attitudes and opinions of employees on a "let the chips fall where they may" basis. Only in this way can management take a long, hard look at itself and the practices and procedures of the company as far as the employees are concerned.

REFERENCES

- Bass, B., and Vaughan, J. *Training in Industry: The Management of Learning.* Belmont, California: Wadsworth, 1968.
- Beatty, R. W., and Schneier, Craig Eric. "Training the Hard-Core Unemployed through Positive Reinforcement." *Human Resource Management*, Winter 1972, 11(4), pp. 11–17.
- Berrelson, B., and Steiner, G. *Human Behavior.* New York: Harcourt Brace, 1967.
- Blumenfeld, W. A., and Holland M. C. "A Model for the Empirical Evaluation of Training Effectiveness." *Personnel Journal*, Aug. 1971, 50(8), pp. 634–40.
- Bugelski, B. R. *The Psychology of Teaching*, second edition. Indianapolis: Bobbs-Merrill, 1971.
- Goldstein, A. P., and Sorcher, M. "Changing Managerial Behavior by Applied Learning Techniques." *Training and Development Journal*, Mar. 1973, 27(2), pp. 36–9.
- Golembiewski, R. T. *Renewing Organizations; The Laboratory Approach to Planned Change.* Itasca, Ill.: Peacock, 1972.
- Hilgard, E. R., and Bower, G. H. *Theories of Learning*, third edition. New York: Appleton Century Crofts, 1966.
- Logan, F. A. *Fundamentals of Learning and Motivation.* Dubuque, Iowa: Wm. Brown, 1970.
- Murphy, J. "Is It Skinner or Nothing?" *Training and Development Journal*, Feb. 1972, 26(2), pp. 2–9.
- Schrank, W. R., "Three Experiments in Education." *Personnel Journal*, Sept. 1971, 50(9), pp. 702–4.
- Skinner, B. F. *The Technology of Teaching.* New York: Appleton Century Crofts, 1968.
- Staats, A. W., and Staats, C. K. *Complex Human Behavior: A Systematic Extension of Learning Principles.* New York: Holt, 1963.

How Adults Learn

by Malcolm Knowles

An interview with Malcolm Knowles is a delightful experience. Less an interview than a conversation with a self-professed and bona fide lifelong learner.

For the record, Malcolm S. Knowles is a professor of Adult and Community College Education, North Carolina State University, Raleigh. Three of his books. The Modern Practice of Adult Education, The Adult Learner: A Neglected Species, *and* Self-Directed Learning *are cornerstones in the adult learning field. He is credited by many as The Father of Adult Learning. In truth, Malcolm Knowles seems a bit too unpretentious for so ponderous a title. People who wear the title "Father of . . ." seldom exhibit the good humor, rapacious wit and open eagerness of a Malcolm Knowles.*

But beware. Malcolm Knowles is, by his own report, a man with a mission: "I have been so impressed with the joy my students have found in self-directed learning that I want to spread the gospel. My motives are the motives of the missionary—so beware. I'll try to convert you."

Knowles, like the true believer he professes to be, has a rather broad witness. He can be found consulting with a medical college in Canada one day and a company in Colombia, South America the next. Somewhere between his various pulpits and parishes, Philip Jones and Ron Zemke, TRAINING's managing editor and research editor respectively, managed to buttonhole this trainer of 40 plus years long enough to ask . . .

TRAINING: What has changed in your thinking about adult learning since publication of your excellent 1973 book, *The Adult Learner: A Neglected Species?*

KNOWLES: The major changes or breakthroughs in my thinking deal with implementation processes. For example, I have found that the use of learning contracts is the magical answer to many of the problems that we were running into in helping adults organize and structure their self-directed learning. I use learning contracts in all of my course work here on campus, in all of my in-service training work with professional associations, and in the management development work I do in industry.

TRAINING: Aren't learning contracts increasingly popular in public education also?

KNOWLES: Yes, they are. For example, the reason public school educators ran into a lot of problems with alternative schools, open schools and ungraded classrooms is that they tossed out *content structure* without supplying a *process structure* in its place. Kids would come in and the teachers would say "what would you like to learn today" and not much would happen. Now the youngsters develop learning contracts which specify what the learning objectives are, what the resources and strategies are for accomplishing the objectives, and what evidence they will collect to demonstrate that they accomplished the objectives. This turns out to be a structure that the kids can use to have a systematic, articulated, sequential set of learning experiences. Well, the same thing's true with adults.

TRAINING: Isn't this "new concept" of learning contracts just another version of the behaviorist's "If . . . Then," "Behavior . . . Reinforcer," "First work . . . Then play" performance contract idea?

KNOWLES: There are similarities, but that's all. Allen Tough's research is pretty clear about what a learning contract needs to be to respond to the adult's needs. Those requirements distinguish the learning contract from the behavioral performance contract. One of the things he found is that when adults decide they want to learn something, they start organizing their thinking in terms of a project; not in terms of behaviors to be acquired. And so, the form of the learning contract is really the identification of a set of projects for accomplishing a particular set of learning objectives.

The objectives *may* be stated in terms of behavior, particularly for simple, motor kinds of learning, but I don't find terminal behavior statements to be very appropriate for the complex kinds of learning that involve the combining of a number of behaviors into a performance. What I do in my own practice is to give a lot of freedom to the learner to state the objectives in terms that are meaningful to him, and to use a variety of forms. As a result, some of the objectives might be behaviorally stated while others may simply be in terms of improving one's ability to do something.

TRAINING: When you don't state the performance change in behavioral terms isn't there an evaluation problem; simply stated, the problem of "knowing one when you see one"?

KNOWLES: The new thing in education in general, but particularly in professional education and management education, is competency based education. The competencies that are required for performing a particular role are described and evaluated in holistic terms. The problem the competency model approach avoids is the fragmenting and isolating of behaviors which must be seen in interaction with one another for the performance to make sense. In other words, a given performance might require a combination of knowledge, understanding, skill, attitude and value—and so the competency statement combines all the behaviors that are relevant to that particular performance.

Now to your specific question, "Isn't it hard to measure competencies?" Of course it is, but the device that is being found most appropriate is what is rather awkwardly being called a criterion-referenced performance test. For example, a critical incident is presented, the learner shows how he would solve that critical incident making use of the knowledge and skill a particular competency contains. Development of the criterion-referenced performance test is difficult, but for most competencies it makes evaluation very reliable and fairly easy.

TRAINING: "For most competencies" doesn't mean for all competencies then?

KNOWLES: No. For complex human behaviors we must often base attainment of competency on data from subjective judgments. For example, in assessing whether a person has in fact developed a certain competency, having a panel of judges observe him doing the performance and rating him according to a prescribed set of criteria on that performance is really better data than we get from paper and pencil tests that give a quantified score.

TRAINING: Where are people doing what you'd like to see done with adult learners?

KNOWLES: There are two institutions that have carried these ideas that we've just been talking about to the furthest degree. One is a little liberal arts college on Prince Edward Island, Canada—the name of it is Holland College, in Charlottesville. The president there is Don Glendenning. He's been the catalytic agent for converting their entire curriculum away from a course structured program to a competency based modular program.

TRAINING: The curriculum is completely by contract?

KNOWLES: By contract. They don't have any "classes" as we know them. They've identified the competencies that are required for a wide variety of roles, vocational and general. They have seriously addressed the question of what exactly it means to be a well-educated person. And they've constructed learning packages for each competency. The individuals write personalized contracts toward developing the established competencies they want to develop.

The other place, that has done a tremendous job of developing a self-directed learning environment is the School of Medicine at McMaster University in Hamilton, Ontario. The key person there is Dr. Victor Neufeld. I've been a consultant to both of those institutions on faculty development, which is why I know them so well. The McMaster School has developed what they call a problem-centered approach to medical education. They've identified a large number, a couple hundred, of the most common problem situations that doctors confront. For each problem situation they have developed modules that contain in them what a doctor needs to know about anatomy, pathology, pharmacology, prognosis, diagnosis, etc. necessary to handle that kind of problem situation.

TRAINING: Are they completely away from the bio-systems approach?

KNOWLES: Yes, except of course, where the problems have to do with intersystemic problems. But on the main, the learning is in terms of developing competencies for dealing with this wide variety of problems.

TRAINING: From our experience, it's pretty hard to bring people in professional education to agreement on process issues. They tend to agree on the goals and objectives, but disagree on the most appropriate steps for getting there.

KNOWLES: You're really getting to the problem of validation of the competency model. The process by which both Holland College and McMaster School of Medicine validated their models was a two-step process. First they involved experts from the field as well as experts on the faculty, former students and present students on a series of task forces, each assigned to develop a specific competency model. The second step was to field test that model through a jury system. These juries were comprised of a broad spectrum of people across the country. Ultimately, of course, the model can only be validated by the performance of the graduates. And that's what both colleges are now in the process of doing. Systematically collecting data about the performance levels of the graduates as compared to pregraduation predictors.

TRAINING: When a jury of experts begins discussing a competency model, isn't there a danger that the discussion will degenerate into arguments of specific processes rather than outcome—that how the students should look during the performance will become the topic rather than what result should be achieved?

KNOWLES: Absolutely. And the only way out of that is through negotiation. I had an experience as a consultant to the Hoffmann-LaRoche Drug Company helping to develop their multimedia system for training cardiological nurses. What they did was to assemble a panel of the country's outstanding cardiologists, sit them down and say, "We're not going to let you out of the room until this is settled." The panel simply had to argue through the taught criterion issues and come to a consensus. In a few cases consensus was achieved by majority vote. Going with the best judgment available at the moment is sometimes about all you can do. Incidentally, the meeting was held in Scottsdale, in the winter, so there was some additional motivation to resolve things within the allotted time period.

TRAINING: Are other medical schools showing an interest in McMaster's approach to training?

KNOWLES: Yes. In fact they're experiencing some problems due to the heavy number of outside consulting requests their faculty members receive. An interesting thing: They opened in 1969, so they've had a few graduating classes. Still, they had quite a hard time getting their first graduating class into internships. They had to go out and do a heavy sales job. They had much less difficulty getting their second class placed. Now, as I understand it, they have more applications from hospitals and clinics for interns than all the other medical schools in Canada put together. And there's great competition for McMaster's graduates. When the McMaster people ask, "Why do you want our people?" the answer they get is, "Well, your graduates come into an internship behaving like doctors. The graduates of other places come in behaving like graduate students."

TRAINING: If industrial trainers take this message to heart, the message that adults need lots of options and they need to be able to organize the learning environment in their own idiosyncratic fashion, shouldn't they then stop being trainers, accountable for learning, and become information presenters and communicators? Maybe they should revise their roles and just become brokers and librarians for various kinds of learning aids and materials.

KNOWLES: I see the required functions here being more than just brokering. In fact the new brokering agencies that are being established have found that more is needed than just giving the person information about where the resources are. Help is needed in structuring and planning the learning strategies. Help is needed in getting evidence as to accomplishment of the learning objective.

What I see happening is the redefinition of the role of teacher *away* from that of the transmitter and controller of knowledge and skills. I would describe that role as facilitator and resource person to self-directed learners. That's not a passive, permissive role. It's an active role that includes such functions as helping the learner diagnose his needs for learning. There are all sorts of strategies, tools and methods for helping the learner get some objective data about the competence he needs to learn to become what he wants to

become. The facilitator needs to have a big repertoire of tools and devices and procedures for aiding the learner in self-diagnosis.

Then, too, he needs to have a broad repertoire of strategies that he can give to the learner: how to make use of material resources, what strategies to use to go to various multimedia and print resources, how to make use of human resources. One of the greatly underused resources in a corporation are *peer* resources, other human beings in the environment. In my little book on self-directed learning, for example, you will see that I give quite a bit of attention to how one learns from another person. These are just examples of the kinds of tools and strategies and skills and knowledge that a learning facilitator and resource person needs to have. They're different from that of the simple transmitter.

TRAINING: Is another of the facilitator's roles to give me good evaluative feedback before I build my own?

KNOWLES: Oh, absolutely. I don't think of self-directed learning as isolated learning. In fact, a more descriptive phrase would be interdependent self-directed learning.

TRAINING: What impact is the adult life stages research, the sort of data reported in Gail Sheehy's *Passages* having on adult learning theory and practice?

KNOWLES: The adult developmental studies are having a tremendous impact. For example, there is a new section in the American Psychological Association called "The Life Span Developmental Psychology Section," which is indicative of the importance of this new field of study.* Until recently, we only had data on adult growth up through adolescence and after 65. There was a big void in the middle. In the last five years there's been a growing body of knowledge about the in-between period. *Passages* is a popular version of some of that research. A much more scholarly work is a book by Baltes and Goulet called *Life Span Developmental Psychology.* What we're finding out from that work, of course, is that there are various kinds of developmental tasks people face at different stages of their lives. Education or training has to be geared to those developmental tasks.

By the way, one of the early insights that we got from research on adult learning was that readiness to learn is a product of an adult confronting the need to know something or to be able to do something in order to perform a life task that he is about to undertake or to cope more effectively with a life problem. The point *Passages* makes clear is that crises are dramatic

---

*See Harry Levinson: "Adult Growth Stages Affect Management Development," TRAINING, May 1977.

manifestations of the confronting of life tasks. So, in a sense, *Passages* is saying, "If you want to engage an adult in a learning program in which he'll be highly motivated, highly ready, then find out what his life crises are, and build your learning around his life crises."

TRAINING: Is anyone doing that tailoring in an applied setting?

KNOWLES: Not in terms of the kind of crises Sheehy talked about, but there are a couple of parallels. One of them is what I think of as the most significant development in history in regard to the education of the under-educated, the illiterate, and the semi-illiterate. I'm referring to the work on coping done by Northcutt at the University of Texas. What Northcutt found in his initial study of the coping skills was that 39 percent of the adult American population is coping inadequately with typical life problems. The problems of getting work and holding a job, the problems of buying things and managing one's economic life. The problems of parenting. All kinds of problems. Given that finding, Northcutt and friends organized a curriculum for helping adults learn to cope better. The curriculum is exclusively based on those life situations people seemed to have the most trouble with.

For example, the Northcutt people no longer teach reading, writing and arithmetic to adults as subjects. They have a whole sequence of units on coping with the world of work. In one unit they ask "What's the first thing you need to be able to do to get a job?" Well, you need to be able to read a classified ad. The next task is to be able to fill out a job application form. Well, let's learn how to read the words in that. Then one has to learn to write on the application form. So, you see they're teaching survival skill content but only in relation to life tasks and problems.

TRAINING: That's a good example, though generally a public education example. It sounds as if you're saying that educators in business and industry don't yet see any relevance in the life stages/adult development work.

KNOWLES: I don't think it's had the impact on industrial trainers that it has had on some of the more public-serving institutions for the simple reason that most of the crises addressed in Roger Gould's research on life stages (reported in *Passages*) tend to be non-occupationally oriented. The most comprehensive attempt to gear a total, continuing self-development program to the concept of developmental stages that I know of is the program Walt Storey has worked out at General Electric. His career development program. That program starts with the new worker, the new exempt worker coming into GE. Right off, they engage him or her in a continuing process of career planning and career competency development. It moves through his whole career with GE. It's organized according to levels, and those parallel personal developmental stages.

TRAINING: Any final words of wisdom or wit?

KNOWLES: Let me make one point final that sort of gets at the feeling and tone of our conversation. In the 40 years that I've been in the business of training and educating adults I've seen a lot of innovation. But, I have seen more innovation, more new knowledge, more ferment in the last five years than in the previous 35. If that is any indication, the next 20 years are simply going to be revolutionary. We're on the verge of coming up with a whole new way of organizing our national educational enterprise. I believe the organizing concept for that enterprise will be lifelong education and the training and development of lifelong learners.

In terms of my own practice, the single most important innovation has been the bringing together of the new knowledge about adult development and adult learning into a comprehensive theory which we've labelled androgogy. A concept quite differentiated from the traditional comprehensive theories of learning that went under the label of pedagogy. Initially, I defined androgogy as the art and science of helping adults learn and I put that in opposition to pedagogy which I was defining as the art and science of teaching children. But in the last five years there's been enough experimentation with the application of the concepts of androgogy to the teaching of children and youth, that I am ready to assert pretty firmly that they also learn better when they're involved actively in the process. I'm now defining androgogy as the art and science of helping people learn, period!

We seem to be developing a general comprehensive theory, which yields guidelines for making decisions about organizing learning experiences and selecting methods and materials that are appropriate for learners in different stages of development, and under different environmental and personal conditions. Before that, before we had a comprehensive theory, we only could deviate from classical pedagogy by the intuition in the seat of our pants. Until we began formulating androgogy, adults in fact were taught as if they were children. And I think that is one of the reasons why adult education and training didn't make the impact that it was capable of until recently. Now that we've begun to treat adults like adults, it's making an enormous impact.

Beyond Modeling: Managing Social Learning Processes in Human Resource Training and Development

by Fred Luthans and Tim R. V. Davis

Each year, corporations and public agencies are spending an increasing amount on training and development, and consulting firms have sprung up to offer a wide range of training programs and organizational development interventions. Given this increasing commitment to training, one might expect to find substantial evidence supporting its effectiveness; unfortunately, this is not the case. Programs are frequently undertaken with no prior diagnosis, with unclear aims, with vague procedures, and with no thought given to assessing the effectiveness of the training.

We must begin to examine the need for training and the types of programs that are likely to produce effective results. Recent research in experimental, clinical, and personnel psychology offers important (but overlooked) insights for training and development in today's organization. For instance, the relevance of social learning theory for training has so far been limited to the social learning process known as modeling. We feel that there is much more to a social learning approach to training and development than just modeling; the purpose of this paper is to present a new social learning approach to training and development.

RECOGNITION OF THE EXPANDING ROLE OF TRAINING

Training has taken on a greatly expanded meaning and scope that goes far beyond the traditional notion of teaching a particular physical skill (e.g., drill press operator) or an area of technical knowledge (e.g., the organization's operating procedures). While job-based skill building remains an important area of training (especially in programs for the disadvantaged and the hard-to-employ), one of the largest growing functions of training and development in most organizations during the last two decades has been in the area of human relations (called more recently human resource) programs that attempt to improve employees' (both hourly and managerial) interpersonal behavior at work.

Practitioners have generally assumed both the need and inherent value of these programs. For the practitioner, it seems, training provides a ready-made solution to organizational problems (i.e., where a performance problem exists, there is a training program that can provide a solution). Consulting firms have cashed in on this assumption by making available an ever-expanding range of programs. Many of these programs trade substantive content and demonstrable advances in learning for intuitively appealing gimmicks and flashy presentations. Such programs run the gamut from over-the-counter "canned" audio-visual packages and/or one-shot presentations and workshops to prolonged interventions and extensive involvements with external consultants. The content varies from general discussions of methods for improving the quality of work-life, or overall OD interventions to reduce conflict and increase trust, to specific "dog and pony" programs dealing with improving communication, leadership, supervision, and time management. They also range from programs that are primarily designed to train more effective behavior in groups (e.g., sensitivity training or team building OD programs) to programs that are designed to improve individual performance behavior and satisfaction such as assertiveness training, biofeedback, and transcendental meditation. Although this traditional approach to training and development probably hasn't done any harm, there is little evidence to show that it has done any good either. The time seems ripe for questioning some of the assumptions and offering some new approaches.

ASSUMPTIONS ABOUT CHANGING BEHAVIOR

With each of the traditional training and development programs, the attempt is made to change organization members' behavior. In some cases, the content and direction of the training is relatively specific (e.g., a set of prescriptions for a time management program or the procedures to be followed in a stress management program using biofeedback); in other cases, the content and direction of the training is very vague (e.g., how to obtain trust and openness in many OD interventions, or the general sociotechnical or job redesign prescriptions offered for improving "the quality of worklife"). In the majority of cases, however, whether the training is relatively specific or general, very little attention is given to the *learning process itself*; i.e., the way in which people acquire new behavior.

It is generally assumed that people learn through verbal instructions or demonstrations. The assumption is that the trainees learn through hearing a persuasive presentation on leadership or transactional analysis, and that they will return to their place of work and put the prescriptions into effect. In addition, the assumption is made that behavior is learned through participation, that, for instance, through interacting with colleagues in an OD team-building session or by coaching from a supervisor, the organization members will be able to construct their own learning. The main weakness with these traditional approaches to learning is that a persuasive presentation or demonstration heard one day rapidly fades from the memory the next day. Similarly, participation in OD team-building sessions in a specially convened situation may be totally unlike interactions in the normal work setting. While these approaches to learning occasionally produce successful results, there is a transfer of learning problem. The main drawback is twofold: (1) This approach does not focus on integrating the new behavior to be learned with the organization member's existing pattern of behavior. (2) This approach does not take into consideration the need to modify behavior in the setting where it normally takes place. This is why new methods of leading, or of communicating with subordinates, new time management practices, and new ways of avoiding stress or being assertive, frequently never get put into effect. The newly-trained employees have to *remember* to use these new practices they were told about in the training session, and the practices have to fit within their existing work situation. What has scarcely been recognized is that new ways of *behaving* need to be carefully inserted into the existing training pattern. New behaviors must be linked in with existing behaviors in the setting where the existing behaviors normally occur. Most training programs do not make allowances for either the on-site cuing of the new behaviors (i.e., so people will remember to use them) or for the existing work environment to contingently reinforce the use of these new behaviors. These are fundamental principles of a social learning theory approach to behavior modification.

THE CONTRIBUTIONS OF SOCIAL LEARNING THEORY

Research in psychology being carried out by social learning theorists (see Bandura, 1977 for a summary of this literature); is providing improved understanding of how human behavior is learned and controlled. The work of the social learning theorists builds on the operant approach to learning which has shown that behavior is acquired and maintained by the stimulus

cues that precede it and the response consequences that follow it. Each individual learns from the effects that a particular response causes in the environment. However, the main difference between the social learning approach and the operant approach is that whereas the operant approach gives no significant recognition to the role of cognitive processes, the social learning theorists have shown that cognitive processes (e.g., thoughts, feelings, imagery) can play an important mediating role in learning and behavior control. Cognitive processes can affect both the stimulus conditions and the consequences that people attend to. According to the social learning theorist, Albert Bandura (1977), human learning may occur through direct learning, modeling, or self-control. Each of these processes plays an important role in human learning and potentially would seem to have significant implications for training and development.

DIRECT LEARNING

The direct method of learning is generally termed operant learning. Direct learning gives recognition to those occasions when learning occurs with no conscious awareness of the contingencies involved. Learning takes place in the presence of a cuing stimulus and in response to an environmental consequence. The person emits a behavior, learns from the immediate response consequences, and manifests new patterns of behavior. In direct learning, cognitive processes play no *instrumental* role in the acquisition and control of behavior. If the behavior is rewarding, the person learns to repeat it; if the behavior is punishing, the person learns to avoid it; and if nothing occurs after the behavior, the response tends to extinguish. The successful application of these acognitive principles of learning to training people in organizations has now been demonstrated in numerous studies of behavior modification (see Luthans and Kreitner, 1975; and Andrasik, 1979, for a summary of this literature).

IMITATIVE LEARNING

A second way in which learning may occur is through imitation or modeling. Imitative learning or vicarious learning gives recognition to the socializing influences of other people that affect learning and the acquisition of new or modified behavior. Here learning takes place through observing the effects of other people's behavior in the social environment. In other words, a person learns vicariously through observing the reinforcing or punishing outcomes of other people's behavior. Considerable research has demonstrated how people quickly reproduce the actions, attitudes, and responses exhibited by models, as noted by Bandura:

Although behavior can be shaped into new patterns to some extent by rewarding and punishing consequences, learning would be exceedingly laborious and hazardous if it proceeded solely on this basis. Environments are loaded with potentially lethal consequences that befall those who are unfortunate enough to perform dangerous errors. For this reason, it would be ill advised to rely on differential reinforcement of trial and error performances in teaching children to swim, adolescents to drive automobiles, and adults to develop complex occupational and social competencies (Bandura, 1976, p. 5).

Vicarious, imitative learning explanations account for the rapid acquisition of newly learned behavior more convincingly than the selective reinforcement of each discriminable response. The acquisition of most imitative learning is cognitively mediated. In other words, the person is usually conscious of copying the behavior of others. However, this behavior may be acognitively maintained by social cues and consequences in the environment. The application of the principles of imitative learning to training in organizations has been less frequently demonstrated than the principles of direct learning, but evidence of the usefulness of this approach (usually called modeling) is now beginning to appear in the literature (for example, see Kraut, 1976; Latham and Saari, 1979).

SELF-CONTROL

A third way in which learning may occur is through "self" control. A growing number of studies are providing evidence of the mediating role of cognitive processes in the regulation of behavior (see Thoresen and Mahoney, 1974, for a summary of this literature). These studies show how feelings, images, and symbolic processes can have an intervening effect on the stimulus conditions and response consequences that tend to regulate behavior. The contingencies affecting behavior may be observable in the environment (overt) or unobservable cognitive processes in the person (covert). Not only can people learn to change their behavior, they can also learn to defer immediate consequences in order to realize ultimately more rewarding outcomes. It is this ability to think through the consequences of a particular behavior in different social situations that allows people to "self" control their behavior. Rather than being dependent on immediate environmental consequences, each person is capable of deferring rewards or tolerating aversive conditions in order to achieve worthwhile long term outcomes.

The application of the principles of self-control or self-management to training in organizations is very recent. Preliminary studies which train managers to use these principles in diagnosing and changing their

own performance problems have provided initial support for the usefulness of this approach (see the article by Luthans and Davis, 1979).

THE TYPES OF LEARNING IN PERSPECTIVE

These three different ways of learning and acquiring behavior are not entirely separate and distinct. Behavior acquired through imitative learning may result from "self-controlled" imitation of others or it may be "directly learned" through socializing influences of which the person is largely unaware. Similarly, behavior acquired through self-control may involve the conscious imitation of others or it may involve goal-oriented behavior that has little to do with modeling other people's behavior.

The three different ways of *acquiring* new behavior (direct, vicarious, and self-controlled) may or may not be the way a behavior is then *maintained*. A behavior that was originally cognitively mediated may rapidly become *directly* controlled as certain physical or interpersonal cues in the environment consistently become associated with a particular response.

In summary, social learning studies provide evidence that learning can take place in three different ways: directly, through modeling, or by self-control. In each case, the stimulus conditions that set the occasion for the behavior and the consequences that follow the behavior have a powerful determining effect on the learning that takes place. With direct learning, cognitive processes play no significant role affecting the acquisition of newly learned behavior. The newly learned response is under the control of the stimulus conditions that immediately precede it and the response consequences that immediately follow it. Modeling or vicarious learning occurs through observing and imitating other people's behavior. It is usually cognitively acquired but may be acognitively maintained. Self control or self-management consists of cognitively learning to take charge of the immediate stimulus conditions that precede a behavior and the consequences that follow it in order to bring about more satisfying long-term outcomes. These stimulus conditions and consequences may be overt or covert.

THE IMPLICATIONS OF SOCIAL LEARNING

The different ways in which people learn is important not only for systematic attempts at improving the training process but also for understanding and effectively managing the ways in which people in general learn and behave at work. The number of behaviors impacted on in a training program is usually quite small when compared to an organization member's total behavior repertoire. The vast majority of organizational behaviors will be acquired on the job as a result of direct learning, modeling and self-control in the natural work environment. Many of these behaviors may be learned with *little awareness* through the *interactive influences* of the physical and social organizational environment. These interactive influences may be considered a type of "invisible hand" in today's organizations.

TRAINING IN ORGANIZATIONS: THE INVISIBLE HAND

Organization members are continuously creating stimulus conditions and consequences for one another as well as for themselves as they interact in the social setting. These moment-by-moment interactive influences can be expected to have a pervasive effect on their behavior. Over time, the same patterns of interaction are likely to result in a natural training process that can be expected to shape behavior far more extensively than formally-designed training programs. For instance, the interactions between superiors and subordinates frequently produce patterns of behavior that become very stable over time:

- Meetings take place in the corridor or when the superior and subordinate see each other rather than in a formally prescribed setting.
- Issues discussed are those of immediate importance when the superior and subordinate run into one another.
- Meetings or visits go on until someone else interrupts or walks into the office.

These types of naturally occurring behavioral events may never be thought about or discussed; they gradually come into being as the superior and subordinate interact with one another on the job. In fact, most formal training programs may be viewed as interventions that attempt to *change* this natural training process or "invisible hand training."

In addition to behaviors directly learned through such interactions, many behaviors will be vicariously learned through observing others. The shaping influence of models may be expected to have a pervasive influence on the natural training process. According to the social learning view, organization members literally learn how to behave from observing those around them. As Jabes (1978) has noted:

By identification with others in society, people not only come to imitate the behavior of others but also to internalize their values, ideals, and attitudes. The young employee who

begins to imitate the dress code and manners of the top brass of the organization soon may also begin to talk like them and to share their opinions, from political to managerial (p. 15).

From a vicarious learning perspective, training methods that tell people how to behave may frequently be less influential than the examples that others set in the work group. The dictum, "do as I say, not as I do," seems unlikely to be followed. Job descriptions, rules, and policies are more likely to be interpreted from watching what others do than from following written directives. In addition, the example that individual managers set for their subordinates may be more important than the instructions they provide.

GUIDELINES FOR APPLICATION TO TRAINING

The pervasive influence of training that takes place through direct or imitative learning in the natural setting makes it critical that these processes should not be ignored when designing formal programs that attempt to change behavior. From a social learning perspective, one of the major goals of training is to convert behavior inadvertently acquired through direct or imitative learning in the natural setting to self-controlled responses that are managed by the organization member.

A social learning approach would say that training programs in organizations should be regarded as "interventions in the natural environment." Fundamentally, this approach would be concerned with questions of how to change behavior in the natural setting. As has already been noted, the vast majority of formal training programs do not integrate new behavior with existing patterns of behavior in the organizational setting. It follows that this helps explain why these programs are frequently ineffective. To improve the potential for success, the social learning approach would suggest the following guidelines for formal training programs: (1) identify the performance behaviors that need to be changed in the natural setting; (2) systematically manage the cuing stimuli that set the occasion for the critical performance behavior; (3) manage the cognitive processes that influence the behavior; and (4) systematically manage the consequences that tend to reinforce the behavior.

Guideline 1: Identify the Performance Behavior to Be Changed in the Setting

Before commencing a formal training program, it is first necessary to specify what performance behavior needs to be changed. This involves a clear statement of: (a) what the performance behavior is now; and (b) what it should be. Most training programs do not investigate what specific performance problem presently exists. A need for the training is usually assumed (e.g., the need for training in leadership or communication) and specific behavior problems in the performance setting are seldom, if ever, clearly identified. Similarly, the desired change in performance (i.e., what performance should be) is rarely stated. Hence, the training program is not grounded in presently occurring behaviors and cannot be evaluated against the behaviors that should be occurring. For this reason, training can take place—and probably often does—that has absolutely no relationship to ongoing performance behavior.

The specification of performance behavior involves the translation of general terms, concepts, or metaphors (e.g., leadership, motivation, communication, etc.), that people wrongly tend to treat as the behavior itself, into specific events that can be observed in the organizational setting (for a discussion of this process in relation to leadership, see Davis and Luthans, 1979). Training goals should be stated in terms of changes in existing activity that can be observed in the setting. The behavioral content of the training program must be made very clear to the trainee and these behaviors must be integrated in very precise ways with the organization member's present performance activity.

Guideline 2: Manage the Cuing Stimuli That Set the Occasion for the Response

For training to be effective, organization members must remember to put the newly learned behavior into practice on the appropriate occasions (i.e., there must be a transfer to the job). This concerns the cuing of behavior at the time it is supposed to occur. A frequently-encountered problem with many training programs is that organization members do not remember to put the newly learned behaviors into effect. Arrangements for the cuing of appropriate behavior on those occasions when it is supposed to occur is an aspect of training that has been almost totally neglected.

According to social learning theorists, both stimulus cues in the setting and cognitive stimulus cues evoked by the person affect what a person attends to; they both can play an influential role in setting the occasion for behavior. Most training programs do not take into consideration the need to cue behavior or set the occasion for its occurrence. Most programs merely rely on cognitive learning in an instructional or experiential learning situation to change behavior in the ongoing work setting. "Once learned, always remembered" seems to be the operative rationale. The

organization member is expected "to carry around" cognitive instructions concerning the problem behavior and to remember to put these instructions into effect on appropriate occasions.

This assumption fails to take into consideration the large number of stimuli that compete for the organization member's attention in the setting. The awareness of a behavioral problem created during a training session does not generally stay with the organization member while he/she is working. Concentration on the task requirements of the job, ringing phones, paperwork, visits from colleagues, etc., provide constant distractions that compete for the person's attention. This is what makes dependence on memory and cognitive cuing an unreliable strategy for behavior control.

An analysis of the stimulus cues that affect behavior in the setting will generally be needed as part of the training intervention. In some cases, cognitive awareness of the stimulus cues that precede a problem behavior may be sufficient to eliminate the behavior. Through being made aware of the events that typically precede the behavior, organization members can become alert to the particular problem as it is about to occur and can change their usual response. However, in a large number of cases, awareness of the naturally-occurring stimulus cues that precede a behavior may not be enough to eliminate the problem response. Cuing stimuli may have to be introduced or taken away from the environment in order to support the occurrence of the appropriate behavior. Research by social learning theorists has shown that behavior can be modified by introducing or eliminating stimulus cues or through a process of controlling the exposure to stimuli (see Thoresen and Mahoney, 1974).

A study involving a manager who had to process a large volume of paperwork each day provides an example of how these stimulus control techniques may be applied in organizational settings (see Luthans and Davis, 1979). In this case, the paper that entered the manager's office at varying times throughout the day was the cuing stimulus that reliably set the occasion for a dysfunctional response. As paperwork (letters, memos, customers' orders, or requisitions) was delivered to the office, the manager had a tendency to pick up and read each item and put it to one side on various piles. The presence of incoming paper continually distracted the manager and prevented him from completing priority work. After analyzing the stimulus cues that preceded his behavior, the manager decreased the items of paper that entered the office (stimulus elimination), reduced the frequency with which paperwork was delivered into his office by his secretary (controlled stimulus exposure), and used a wall display (stimulus introduction) to remind himself not to stack the paper in piles. These changes improved the manager's daily performance effectiveness. Importantly, instead of the stimulus conditions managing his behavior, he was now beginning to manage the stimulus conditions.

Changes like these are important for training interventions. Stimulus cues may have to be introduced or eliminated from the setting in order to cue the new behavior. Most trainers have shown little concern for managing the stimulus conditions that precede the target behavior. For new behaviors to replace old behaviors, formal training programs must compete with "natural training processes" that are often stubbornly resistant to change. Training interventions must take into consideration the interactive stimulus environment that continually disrupts and distracts people's attention. The management of the stimulus environment to support newly learned behaviors will frequently be critical for effective implementation of training in organizations.

Guideline 3: Manage the Cognitive Processes that Influence Behavior

Many training and development programs depend solely on the influence of cognitive processes to control behavior. Not only is it assumed that behavior is cognitively acquired during the training or OD session, it is also assumed that behavior is cognitively controlled in the organizational setting. Programs like transactional analysis and sensitivity training place heavy reliance on *cognitive learning* during the training and *cognitive control* of the behavior on the job. While these programs sometimes produce the desired changes in behavior, several problems can arise when the training method merely relies on cognitive learning and cognitive behavior control.

First, organization members can be made aware of better ways of behaving during a training session but may have no awareness and recollection of this behavior when they are interacting on the job. The problem of memory and cuing cognitive awareness is frequently neglected in training programs. Here stimulus control techniques can be used to turn acognitive responses into cognitively-mediated responses by creating awareness of behavior while the person is interacting in the setting. In some cases, the removal of stimuli from the environment may be sufficient to prevent a dysfunctional response from occurring, thereby obviating the need to induce cognitive awareness.

A second problem goes considerably beyond the need to create awareness in the setting. The way people think and feel about how they want to behave during the training session may not be the way they actually think and feel about their behavior while on the job. Organization members may want to change their behavior during a training session, but they may not feel like doing so when interacting in the setting. This problem does not just involve creating awareness; it involves the influence of different social situations on the goals and purposes of organization members.

One of the principal contributions of social learning theory has been to stress the "situational" nature of learning. The term "social learning theory" is derived from the tendency for each person to acquire new behaviors in response to different "social situations." Most training and development programs neglect the role of the social situation in the acquisition and maintenance of behavior. Rarely is any distinction drawn between the training situation and the performance situation. Usually, the training program is designed to alter organization members' cognitive awareness in the training situation on the grounds that organization members will then exercise cognitive control over their behavior on the job. A "carry over" effect is assumed between the training situation and the performance situation, and the new learning that takes place in the training situation is assumed to transfer to the actual work setting.

The unquestioned acceptance of the view that behavior can be cognitively acquired in a training session *and* cognitively controlled in the performance situation is one of the major fallacies of most training and development programs. The stimulus cues and response consequences in the setting affect the occurrence of the target behavior, and the cognitions (thoughts or feelings) of the organization members will also influence this behavior; it cannot be taken for granted that organization members can exercise cognitive control over their behavior without attending to all the effects in the social setting: of stimulus cues, cognitions, and response consequences. The task environment, performance goals, rewards and punishments in a training session are usually very different from the natural setting. Organization members can be expected to focus their attention on a different set of purposes while interacting on the job than they would when participating in a training program.

The influence of different goals or purposes and the effects of the different organizational environments need to be carefully considered when designing training programs. Behaviors that are introduced in a training program must be integrated with the goals and purposes that organization members seek to accomplish in the setting.

Individual performance goals have been demonstrated to have a powerful motivational effect on behavior (see Locke, 1968; Latham and Yukl, 1975 for a summary of this literature). One of the main differences between social learning theory and the operant approach is the recognition of how individual goals and purposes can affect behavior (Bandura, 1977, pp. 160–165). Whereas the operant approach treats all behavior as a response to immediate environmental consequences, social learning theorists emphasize how an individual's cognitive goals can mediate the relationship with the environment. Cognitive processes allow the individual to exercise "self-control" by self-regulating interactions with the environment. Not only can the individual choose what aspects of the environment to respond to, the individual can also learn to delay gratification or withstand punishment (aversive consequences) in order to attain ultimately more rewarding outcomes.

Individual goal setting and self-control processes have a critical influence on behavior. These processes should support the use of the newly learned behavior. Goal setting can clarify the application of the training behavior in the performance situation and can have a guiding influence over individual cognitive processes. Self-control methods can be used to integrate the training behavior with the contingencies (stimulus cues and response consequences) in the setting and can greatly increase the likelihood that the new behavior will become established (for example, see Luthans and Davis, 1979).

Training programs must take the differences in performance situations and individual goals into account. Training must be tailored to the needs of the individual. Modification of behavior in the natural setting by the organization member employing individual goal setting and self-management techniques is likely to be a more effective means of eliminating a performance inadequacy than engaging in general, "cognitively-based" training that is vaguely related and poorly integrated with what the person actually does back on the job.

Guideline 4: Manage the Consequences That Tend to Reinforce the Behavior

The use of goal setting and self-control processes must be integrated with the environmental consequences that tend to follow the behavior. Unless individual goal accomplishment and self-control is ultimately met with some rewarding consequences in the environment, it is unlikely that organization members will exhibit the behaviors advocated in the training program.

A large number of training programs emphasize the importance of communication and feedback, giving recognition to the work of subordinates, or developing better interpersonal and group behavior skills. Organization members often realize the importance of these behaviors during a training session but then fail to put them into effect back on the job. The answer to this problem may be that many of these

behaviors are simply not reinforcing to the organization member back in the natural work environment. Verbal instructions, prescriptions, and experiences in training sessions compete with the natural contingencies operating back on the job. What is reinforcing to an organization member during a training session is frequently not reinforcing on the job.

An increasing number of management scholars have noted that human resource training and development programs frequently do not fit in with the existing behavior and environment of many organizations. "Human relations" assumptions about behavior in organizations are often far removed from reality. For example, managers on the job rarely set goals in terms of behaviors advocated in the training and development programs. Organization members do not focus their attention on these behaviors nor are rewards or punishments meted out for exhibiting or failing to exhibit these behaviors. Consultants and academicians frequently preach humanistic values in training programs that are not reinforced in the natural work setting. Until training programs are adjusted to meet this reality, it seems unlikely that training and development programs will become more effective.

AN S-O-B-C FRAMEWORK

These four suggested guidelines for improving the effectiveness of training programs can be briefly summarized in the form of these main caveats:

1. The behavior to be changed must be clearly *identified*;
2. Organization members must be reminded to use the behavior through *managing the cues* in the stimulus environment;
3. Individual organization members must *set goals* for the behavior and then *actively self-control* their own performance behaviors;
4. The behavior must be *reinforced* in the setting.

Based on the social learning approach, these concepts can be represented in a four-term S-O-B-C framework that can be used as a practical tool for analyzing behavior modification in organizations:

S	O	B	C
Antecedent	Organism	Behavior	Consequences
Stimulus	Cognition		

Each of the elements in the S-O-B-C contingency needs to be considered when attempts are made to change naturally-occurring behaviors irrespective of whether the training attempts to improve communication, leadership, time management, assertiveness, or problems with stress. Unless all of these contingency elements are taken into consideration and actively managed by the organization member, it is unlikely that new behavior will be successfully introduced and maintained in the work setting.

CONCLUSION

With the exception of organizational behavior modification programs (for example, see Luthans and Kreitner, 1975), training programs have given little attention to the stimulus conditions and response consequences that tend to control behavior. Locke (1977) and others would argue that even these behavior modifications programs can be limited in their application because they deny the instrumental role of cognitive processes—especially goal-setting—that tend to have a motivational influence on behavior. The social learning approach integrates the role of cognitive processes with the operant principles and therefore provides a more complete account of the contingencies controlling human behavior at work.

Individual cognitive processes and the social learning principles of self-control need to be integrated with operant models of training. The integration of operant training practices with goal setting and self-management methods recognizes that only the individual organization member is capable of exercising the most complete control over his/her own behavior. In the final analysis, no one can really manage other people's behavior; each individual must be relied upon to manage his/her own behavior. Thus, the fate of all organizational training and development eventually rides or falls on the various organization members' ability to take control of their own behavior. By recognizing the critical role that the individual must play in the adoption of new behavior, training programs can greatly contribute to the introduction of needed human change in organizations. A social learning approach to training and development may indeed help meet the major challenges facing public and private organizations now and in the future.

REFERENCES

- Andrasik, F. "Organizational Behavior Modification in Business Settings: A Methodological and Content Review," *Journal of Organizational Behavior Management*, 2 (1979), 85–102.
- Bandura, A. "Social Learning Theory." In J. T. Spence, R. C. Carson, and J. W. Thibant (Eds.) *Behavioral Approaches to Therapy.* Morristown, New Jersey: General Learning Press, 1976, 1–46.
- Bandura, A. *Social Learning Theory.* Englewood Cliffs, New Jersey: Prentice-Hall, 1977.
- Davis, T. R. V. and F. Luthans. "Leadership Reexamined: A Behavioral Approach," *Academy of Management Review*, 4 (1979), 237–248.
- Goldstein, A. P. and M. Sorcher. *Changing Supervisor Behavior.* New York: Pergamon Press, 1974.
- Jabes, J. *Individual Processes in Organizational Behavior*, Arlington Heights, Ill.: AMH, 1978.
- Kraut, A. I. "Developing Managerial Skills Via Modelling Techniques: Some Positive Research Findings—A Symposium." *Personnel Psychology*, 29 (1976), 325–369.
- Latham, G. P. and G. A. Yukl. "A Review of Research on the Application of Goal Setting in Organizations," *Academy of Management Journal*, 18 (1975), 824–845.
- Latham, G. P. and L. M. Saari. "Application of Social Learning Theory to Training Supervisors Through Behavior Modeling," *Journal of Applied Psychology*, 64 (1979), 239–246.
- Locke, E. A. "Towards a Theory of Task Motivation and Incentives," *Organizational Behavior and Human Performance*, 3 (1968), 157–189.
- Locke, E. A. "The Myths of Behavior Mod in Organizations," *Academy of Management Review*, 2 (1977), 543–553.
- Luthans, F. and R. Kreitner. *Organizational Behavior Modification.* Glenview, Ill.: Scott Foresman, 1975.
- Luthans, F. and T. R. V. Davis. "Behavioral Self Management: The Missing Link in Managerial Effectiveness," *Organizational Dynamics*, 8 (1979), 42–60.
- Thoresen, C. E. and M. J. Mahoney. *Behavioral Self-Control.* New York: Holt, Rinehart and Winston, 1974.

Competency-Based Management

by Alice G. Sargent

INTRODUCTION

To develop effective human resource management systems, organizations need to develop models of managerial effectiveness for use in recruitment and assessment, training and development, and performance appraisal. The development of these models requires both an assessment of the status quo as well as a look at problems to be faced by managers of the 80's and 90's, so competency models can be built that reflect both present and future needs. Reward systems in organizations then need to be brought in line to support these models.

Business and the nation face vast problems in the 80's. These include the transition from an industrial age to an age of communication, the transition from hierarchical organizations to more horizontal models. The transition in values also includes, according to Daniel Yankelovich (professor of psychology at New York University and head of a research firm bearing his name) moving from an ethic of self-centeredness to one of commitment. Those of us who grew up in the 50's were taught guilt and responsibility. The next generation became the "me generation." Now, the 80's call for commitment that is a blend of concern for ourselves, our community and others.

Surprisingly few organizations attempt to develop managers systematically for entry, mid-level, and executive management positions. Many rely on an apprenticeship model or a random learn-as-you-go process, neither of which are systematic or cost-effective. Among the better-known firms that do have programs are IBM at Armonk, General Electric at Croton, Xerox at Leesburg, INA in Philadelphia, the Federal Executive Institute (FET) in Charlottesville, and Texas Instruments in Houston. There are not many executive development programs except for FET, and now several major oil companies are looking at the problems of how to develop their managers to manage the companies' vast resources. The major training firms in the management education field are the American Management Association, particularly their new competency-based Masters in Management Program; the National Training Laboratories; and

some of the major universities who operate education centers and certificate programs. These include Harvard Business School, Sloan School at MIT, University of Michigan, Wharton, University of Southern California, and UCLA.

The education of managers is a critical issue. In an article in *The Washington Post*, Walter Mondale was quoted as saying that managers don't know how to manage because business schools have not figured out what skills managers need. The American Association of Collegiate Schools of Business arrived at the same conclusion—MBA programs lack an effective model for developing practitioner managers, partly because they have relied too heavily on the case study method. A number of firms are seeking to grant degrees—major businesses such as Arthur D. Little, Wang, and Massachusetts General Hospital have moved or are moving toward degree granting. While business currently spends $30 billion a year for training, it would seem that business believes schools and colleges have not done, nor are ready to do, the job of "growing" managers effectively.

William Ouchi, in *Theory Z*, concludes that the key issues facing American business today are not technology, investment, regulation or inflation, but that the Japanese know how to manage better than we do. The Japanese emphasis on intimacy, trust, subtlety in the workplace is more effective and enlightened than our own heavy focus on task and technology. Whether or not we put it as boldly as Ouchi, the task confronting us is to define a curriculum for practitioners in management.

This chapter focuses on competency-based management training as an assessment tool. Competency-based programs identify the key training and development targets for present and future managers.

THE NEED FOR A COMPETENCY MODEL

We have grown up without much education in psychology. What we learned in that area, we tended to learn at home or from our peer group, without the opportunity to select from options. Hence, our society is basically emotionally illiterate. Many people do not express feelings easily, are uncomfortable with conflict, and/or don't work effectively in teams. Instead they try to "problem-solve" feelings rather than be

Sargent/Ulschak, *Human Resource Development,* 1983, pp. 153–63. Reprinted with the permission of Reston Publishing Company, a Prentice-Hall Company, 11480 Sunset Hills Road, Reston, VA 22090.

empathetic. Many of these same people become managers without a lot of training in people management skills. They have been promoted on the basis of technical competence. Yet, we know that other competencies—interpersonal, entrepreneurial, self-awareness, analytical—are critical to effective management. What we need are competency models which encompass all those elements which make for effective management.

Engineers, particularly those who have moved into project manager positions, have understood the need for management education. Now politicians and doctors recognize that they never have had applied behavioral science courses, either. In fact, lawyers have been taught exactly the opposite of interpersonal competence; they have learned adversarial skills and mistrust. As lawyers and accountants are being organized in teams of organizations, they are found to lack the skills to work effectively in that mode.

The prevailing theory of management today is situational management or contingency management, which means selecting the appropriate behavior to get the desired results in any given situation. Therefore, the critical skills managers need are to be effective participant observers to diagnose the impact of their behavior.

Buried inside managers is a management curriculum which enables them to be valuable resources in building a model for managerial effectiveness and in developing a common language for organizational management. In developing the new competency-based model of management, it is critical to capture the language of each organizational culture, rather than impose language from outside.

DEVELOPING A COMPETENCY-BASED MODEL

There are a number of approaches to competency-based management. One approach is the "generic" approach. In this approach, general management competencies are overlaid on an organization. It is assumed that the general competencies will be applicable.

A second approach is based on a research model. Using a research approach, external or internal consultants identify the management competencies within the organization and then present them to the organization.

A third approach is based on organizational development. This chapter is built on this approach. The starting point with the organizational development approach is using the language of the organization.

If the language of the particular organizational culture is not used to build the competency model,

there may not be validation and ownership. The model may be treated as another instance of social science jargon. It is essential to develop different competency models for executives, for middle managers and for supervisors, and to involve those managers in the development of the model.

Many line managers feel apprehensive about embarking upon the task of building competencies. They may not recognize that they are capable of defining the needs of managers, particularly if they come from a technical specialty such as engineering or law. A half-day to a day should be set aside to work in small groups to build the first iteration of the model. It may be necessary to invite the response to the question, "What words would you use to describe effectiveness?" The intent of this discussion is to begin the process of defining what effectiveness means in the organization.

Subsequently, a refinement of terms can be attempted. The goal is to generate behavioral descriptors that are objectively verifiable but not necessarily quantifiable. Neither are we trying to return to the old-style traits, nor are we trying to come up with only characteristics that can be counted. We are trying to capture the language people use to describe effectiveness.

It is necessary to identify competencies for at least three levels of management: the first-line supervisors, mid-level managers, and executives. Robert Katz (in "Skills of an Effective Administrator") described the degree of competence required at each of these three levels for three competencies he labeled conceptual, human and technical. As we can see from the chart, technical competence diminishes in importance as one moves up the corporate ladder. The executive has really left behind his/her technical specialty, utilizing at best technical judgment, whereas the human or interpersonal competencies remain stable at each level of management.

	Executive	Mid-level	First-line supervisor
Conceptual	47%	31%	18%
Human	35%	42%	35%
Technical	18%	27%	47%

The Department of the Army has conducted one of the only studies available that differentiates competencies at different levels: those between the colonel (middle manager) and the brigadier general (executive) (see Figure 1). The colonel influences others with a personal style that is charismatic and highly visible. The brigadier general influences others with an interpersonal style that is confidently assertive, but not

FIGURE 1
U.S. Department of the Army Leadership Profiles*

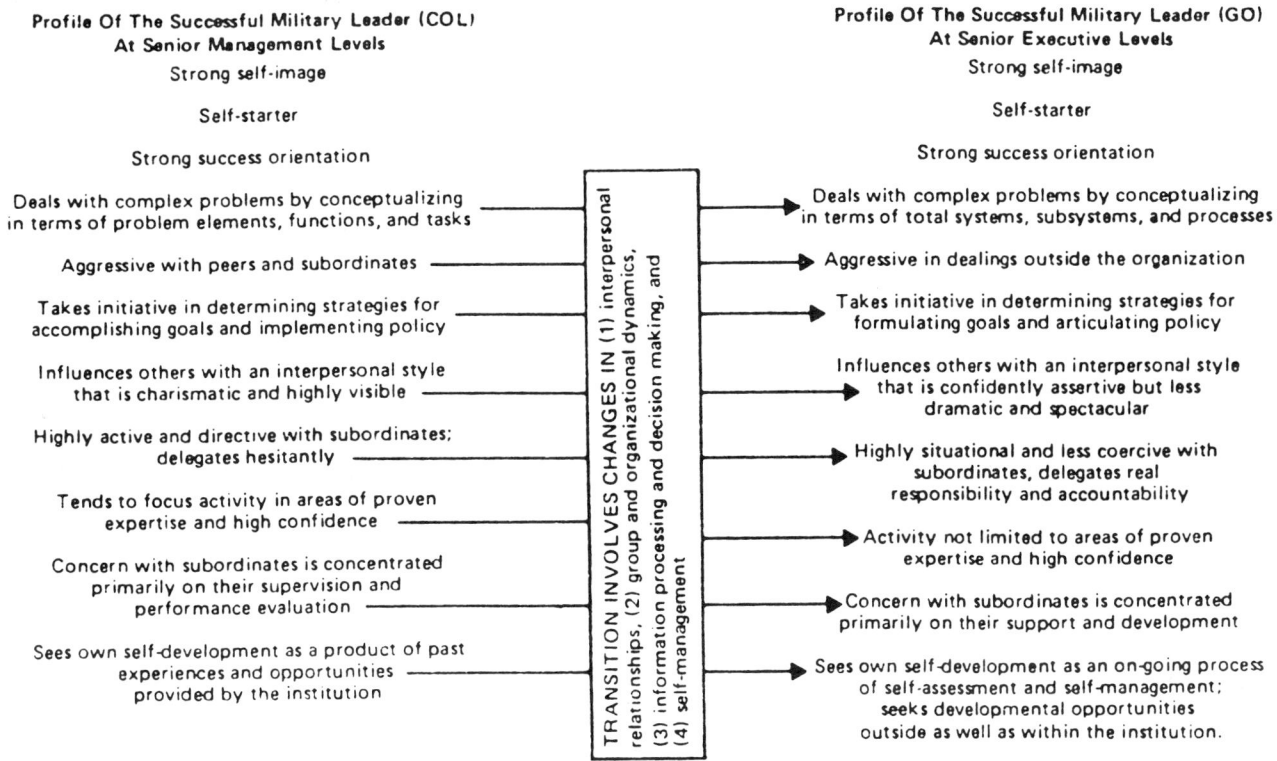

*From Bradford F. Spencer and Jerald R. Gregg, "Successful Behaviors Which Breed Failure," *University of Michigan Business Review* (1979). Developed by John Hallen, consultant, Washington, D.C., and Lt. Col. Frank L. Burns, U.S. Army.

so dramatic and spectacular. With that much power at the top, one need only say, "I want it this way."

For the colonel as middle manager, however, the concern with subordinates focuses on their supervision and performance evaluations. The executive is more concerned with support and development of employees. The mid-level manager looks after short-term issues, while the view from the top is longer range.

Richard Boyatzis, author of *The Competent Manager* and president of McBer & Company, has compiled an excellent competency list through research on critical incidents involving high performing managers (see Figure 2). The McBer model is useful to hold up to other models compiled in the language of the organization to see what might have been omitted.

The high-performing manager's number one characteristic is holding high standards for self and others. This manager produces compliance by being a role model, not via threats or punishment. Coaches often are held up as models of effective managers. People say, "He/she wouldn't ask the team to do anything that he/she wouldn't do." In the same way, the high performer gets compliance by doing a good job, which

others imitate. Old-style management used to be, "Don't do as I do, do as I say." Now we demand congruence in our role models, so they need to know that we will "do as they do, not as they say." Without alliances, cohesiveness and a focus on morale, employees are likely to burn out, to lose motivation.

The major part of the process of developing a competency-based model, then, is spending time building the competencies in the language of the organization. This happens in sessions where various levels of managers talk about what effective management means and what it may mean in the future.

THE ANDROGYNOUS MANAGER

From the beginning, management has been concerned with people and tasks, productivity and morale. The link between the two is becoming obvious. Morale and people are no longer simply frosting for task and productivity. We almost encourage alienation and isolation at work by thinking that business and personal lives should be kept separate. Yet, the critical interface at work is the manager/subordinate relationship and

FIGURE 2
Managerial Competencies

COMPETENCY: Some characteristic of a person which underlies or results in effective performance.

I. Knowledge competencies
   specific knowledge base

II. Emotional maturity
   self control
   spontaneity
   perceptual objectivity
   accurate self-perception
   stamina and physical energy
   adaptability

III. Entrepreneurial abilities
   efficiency orientation
   productivity—goal setting and planning
   proactivity—problem-solving and information-
      seeking skills
   concern for unique achievement
   task efficiency

IV. Intellectual abilities
   logical thought—perceive cause/effect
      relationships—inductive thinking
   diagnostic use of concepts—deductive thinking
   memory
   conceptual ability
   political judgment

V. Interpersonal abilities
   social sensitivity
   self-presentation
   counseling skills
   expressed concern with impact
   compliance producing skills
   alliance building skills
   language skills
   non-verbal sensitivity
   respect for others
   effective as team member

VI. Leadership skills
   presence
   persuasive speaking
   positive bias
   negotiating skills
   takes initiative
   management of groups—team building skills

Source: Richard Boyatzis, President, McBer & Co., Boston.

then the work team. These relationships must be characterized by trust if effective performance management, career development, team effectiveness, even strategic planning—which requires risk and creativity—are to result.

Amid rapid technological changes, people almost have been overlooked as the critical resource. We cannot be effective unless we pay attention to the management of people. If we rely on our current management model, we will end up with the status quo. What is wrong with that model? It does not respond to people's affiliation needs nor does it build the necessary teamwork to get the job done, particularly in a communication society. It may have worked at times to support a hierarchical, competitive model, but with shifts in forms of management, it is insufficient. We need to focus on self-awareness, competence, interpersonal competence, effectiveness as a team leader and member, and ability as a participant observer.

One model that offers some possibilities in the 80's is the androgynous manager, a blend of masculine and feminine skills and behaviors, of toughness and tenderness, of instrumental and expressive behaviors, of concern for both people and task, of caring for both productivity and morale, of analytical and intuitive thinking (see Figure 3).

The competencies labeled as masculine describe the way organizations have done business and managers have been rewarded. To date, the dominant style has been that of a rational, analytical problem-solver, an instrumental, direct, visible, results-oriented style. It emphasizes having a direct impact on people and producing compliance. Such a manager is effective through negotiation, competition, assertiveness, proactivity and thinking in a logical, linear fashion.

To date, however, the behaviors labeled feminine have not been as highly valued and rewarded in organizations. Nonetheless, a number of managerial functions require the full range of androgynous behavior—long-range planning, creative problem-solving, career development, performance management, and team-member effectiveness. These and other management functions require expressive behavior, self-disclosure, a vicarious achievement style in order to enjoy the development of others, mentoring, and skills in producing alliances.

Peter Block and Neil Clapp, consultants at Block Petrella Associates, presented good definitions for instrumental and expressive behavior (see Figure 4). Instrumental behavior is data based, rational and problem solving. It is planned, predictable, and certain. Instrumental behavior avoids surprises, where expressive behavior encourages spontaneity, strives to avoid boredom and welcomes self-disclosure.

Expressive behavior is critical to an intimate relationship at home. "Did you get the car fixed? Did you pay the insurance? Where should we go Saturday night?" all focus on instrumental behavior. It is the same when the parent/child relationship involves only, "Is your room cleaned up? Is your homework done? Did you brush your teeth?" But "How do you feel?" or "What is new?" is expressive behavior that is accepted as important at home. So, too, expressive

FIGURE 3
Androgynous Management Competencies

Masculine	Neutral	Feminine
Instrumental behavior	Command of basic facts	Expressive behavior
Direct achievement style	Balanced learning habits	Vicarious achievement style
Compliance producing skills	Continuing sensitivity to political events	Alliance-producing skills
Negotiating/competing	Quick thinking	Accommodating/mediating
Proactive style	Creativity	Reactive style
Analytical/problem-solving, and decision-making skills	Social skills	Self knowledge
Visible impact on others		Non-verbal sensitivity

The Androgynous Manager, A. Sargent, AMACOM © 1981; by permission.

behavior is needed at work to communicate between boss and subordinate, within work groups, and among work groups. Boss/subordinate communication needs to be characterized by conversations that involve "How are things?" "Where do you want to be two years from now?" "What new skills would you like to learn?"

The androgynous blend offers effective behaviors to both sexes to improve communications between male/male, female/female, and male/female, plus cross-cultural relationships: old/young, black/white, Hispanic/white, north/south, east coast/west coast.

NEXT STEPS

We are in the early stages of building competency-based management models. It may take several years to go through various iterations of building the competency model. The model needs to be tested by putting it on the performance appraisal form, to see if the organization will put its rewards behind it as well as to institutionalize the model as part of the management system. It also needs to be institutionalized in the assessment process and in training and development modules.

FIGURE 4
Managerial Behavior

Description	Instrumental Behavior	Expressive Behavior
Purpose	Problem solving to avoid failure, to achieve success	Self-expression: to get acknowledged, to get connected
Exchange	Services; information	Empathy
Basis	Data	Feelings
Needs served	Control; power	Spontaneity
Time orientation	Future-oriented; planned	Spontaneous
Structure	Predictable, certain, clear, agreed-upon negotiated, contracted	Flexible, ambiguous
Avoid at all costs	Surprise	Boredom

Neale Clapp & Peter Block, Block Petrella Associates. Source: see Fig. 3.

THE COMPETENCY MODEL:
ITS USE IN TRAINING

While the ultimate use of competency models relates to performance appraisals and effectiveness, it is very useful in training and development. The outcome of the competency process is a profile of an effective manager. This provides an excellent basis for assessment of managers for training and development needs.

The first step is to ask managers at different levels to do a self-assessment based on the competencies in order to select training modules that develop their flat sides. A number of already developed instruments can be used to assess a baseline competence level in interpersonal competence: Kilman Thomas, the Lead Self, the New FIRO, the Strength Deployment Inventory, Myers Briggs, the Androgyny Scale—all offer data in interpersonal competence.

Once competencies have been identified, the assessment process is readily completed by simply assessing the managers in light of those competencies. Then the individual manager's specific training needs can be targeted.

CONCLUSION

Competency-based management programs provide unique assessment possibilities. Since competencies have been identified, the process of assessment is readily done. By using a competency-based approach, training can be readily directed to the needs most vital to individual managers.

It is time for the human resource development professionals to involve line managers in building a competency model. In order for this model to be effective it must be institutionalized in the other HRD management systems (assessment, career development training and development, and performance appraisal); and it must be responsive to management issues of the future, not just the status quo.

One such model for the future is the androgynous manager. In effect, androgyny synthesizes the best of the feminine and masculine styles to develop a more complete manager and individual who can handle both technical and interpersonal issues. The androgynous manager is able to express emotions as well as to handle intellectual, analytical tasks. These are the values and behaviors necessary to carry us in the age of communication which requires interaction and understanding.

REFERENCES

- Boyatzis, Richard. *The Competent Manager*. New York: John Wiley and Sons, 1982.
- Katz, Robert. "Skills of an Effective Administrator." *Harvard Business Review*, Vol. 52 (September 1974).
- Ouchi, William. *Theory Z*. Reading, Mass.: Addison-Wesley, 1981.

ESTABLISHING TRAINING AND DEVELOPMENT OBJECTIVES

A. Course Objectives
by R. Mager and K. Beach, Jr.
*   Describes methods of establishing instructional goals

B. Develop Course Objectives
by R. Ribler
*   Suggests guidelines for stating objectives of the training course

C. Develop Enabling Objectives
by R. Ribler
*   Explains why enabling objectives are a priority

D. Individualizing Learning Objectives
by Gerald Miller
*   Presents individualized training process

E. Determining Supervision Training Needs and Setting Objectives
by Donald Kirkpatrick
*   Presents examples of knowledge, skill, and attitude objectives

Course Objectives

by R. Mager and K. Beach, Jr.

The statement of course objectives consists of as many statements, items, or examples as are necessary to describe the desired behavior of the student at the time he leaves the course. It is prepared in enough detail so another professional instructor could turn out a student who could do the kinds of things *you* want him to do at the proficiency levels you desire.

Course objectives differ from the task analysis in several ways. The task analysis describes the vocation or job as it is performed by a highly skilled person. Objectives describe the kind of performance that will be expected at the end of the course. For example: While a highly skilled person may be able to perform a particular machine adjustment in five or ten seconds without using any job aids to remind him of the steps, it might be unrealistic to expect a course graduate to perform that well on the day of graduation. It might be far more realistic to expect the new graduate to be able to perform the task without the use of job aids in ten or fifteen minutes. *If* he can perform all of the steps of the job, and *if* he can determine when the job is properly performed, *then* practice on the job will improve his proficiency.

The task analysis describes all of the steps carried out in the performance of the job, whether or not the student knows how to perform some of these steps before he enters the course. The objectives of the course differ from the task analysis in that they do not include those things that the student already knows.

Another difference between task analysis and course objectives is in the subject matter itself. It may be that some of the skills called for in performing an occupation are either unrealistic to teach in the classroom or are better taught on the job. An example of this might be the paper work expected of a skilled craftsman. This task is likely to be so different from one location to another, and so easy to teach (relatively speaking), that it might be a task better learned on the job.

The key question to ask is this: *What kind of things should the student be able to do at the end of the course that will most facilitate his becoming a skilled craftsman in the least amount of time?* In other words, what should the student be able to do at the end of the course so that all that stands between the student and skilled performance is practice?

Course objectives represent a clear statement of instructional intent, and are written in any form necessary to clarify that intent. In practice, you will have at *least* twice as many statements as you have tasks on your list. These statements will have the following characteristics:

1. An objective says something about the student. It does not describe the textbook, the instructor, or the kinds of classroom experience to which the student will be exposed.

2. An objective talks about the behavior or performance of students. It does not describe the performance of the teacher, nor does it describe what the student is expected to know or understand. Though you might begin an objective by a general statement such as "the student must understand the operation of the XYZ sewing machine," you would go on to explain what you mean by understanding by describing what the student will be expected to do to demonstrate your definition of understanding. In some cases the student may be expected to answer questions, or to solve some problems, or to describe a procedure, or to construct a gadget. Whatever it is *you* mean by understanding would be defined in the sentences to follow the general one. In any case, an objective describes what the *student* will be *doing* to demonstrate his achievement of your instructional intent.

3. An objective is about ends rather than means. It describes a product rather than a process. As such, it describes what the student is expected to be like at the end of instruction rather than the means that will be used to get him there. It talks about terminal performance rather than course content.

4. An objective describes the conditions under which the student will be performing his terminal behavior. In some cases the student will be expected to perform in the absence of any assistance provided by job aids; in some cases, such aids are acceptable. For example: Sometimes the student may be expected to solve problems with the use of a slide rule or calculator, and sometimes without these items.

5. An instructional objective also includes informa-

From *Developing Vocational Instruction* by R.F. Mager and K.M. Beach, Jr. (Belmont, CA: Pitman Learning, Inc., 1967). Reprinted with permission.

tion about the level of performance that will be considered acceptable. If a student will be expected to perform a task within five minutes at the end of the course, this will be stated as part of the objective. If his performance at the end of the course is expected to be error-free or if some error will be tolerated, this would be indicated. In most instances, the decision about what performance will be considered acceptable is an arbitrary one. This is one place where the experience and wisdom of the instructor is most important, because specification of satisfactory performance is one of the unique contributions that can be made only by the skilled instructor.

For convenience, it is possible to classify objectives into two broad categories, those that describe specific performances of the student and those that may be needed to describe his attitudes. For example: If it is important to send the student away more interested in the subject than he was when he arrived, this must be stated in an objective so that the course may be systematically organized to achieve it. If the student will be expected to perform with persistence, then the nature of this persistence should be spelled out so that the course may be designed to achieve this end. It may be that when the student is performing the job each failure on his part will be expected to result in another immediate attempt, as is often the case in jobs involving repair of equipment. If one attempt at fixing fails, another attempt is expected. In other words, each failure experience is expected to trigger another attempt to succeed. Unless this persistence objective is made explicit, it is possible that the procedures used during instruction will turn out a student who will give up after one or two attempts. (And this is just what will happen if, for instance, the instructor makes critical comments following every student attempt to come into contact with the very equipment he is expected to master.)

On some jobs it is important that a pleasant tone of voice be used, as well as a patient manner. When this is the case, it is important to specify this objective and design for its achievement. Most people do not know whether others perceive them as sounding pleasant or patient; this requires instruction. But such instruction may fail to be included in the curriculum unless the objective is made explicit.

In any case, it is important to describe as comprehensively as possible what the student is intended to be like when he leaves the course.

On the pages that follow are some examples of a variety of objectives. Notice that each is relatively specific and deals with either a single task or with steps within a task. Notice that each tells what the student will be doing when he is demonstrating that he

has achieved the objective, and that each says something about what will be considered as acceptable performance. Some are stated in a single sentence; others are wordier. The form isn't the important thing, *what is important is that instructional intent be made clear.*

Example 1

Given an unfinished metal casting, be able to surface, drill, and tap according to the specifications indicated on the attached blueprint.

Example 2

Provided with an outdoor television antenna kit and appropriate tools, be able to install the antenna and correctly connect the input lead to the television set. Performance will be judged correct if the antenna installation is completed according to trade standards and if the resulting TV picture is free of snow.

Example 3

Given a model XYZ sphygmomanometer, be able to take blood pressure to within 0.05 cm. The student must correctly complete five consecutive trials to this criterion.

Example 4

Goal: Be able to point out forest fire hazards in a forest area.
Behavior: Identify dangerous conditions by pointing.
Conditions: The student must have access to forest areas and be exposed to dangerous conditions determined by the instructor.
Criterion: The student must identify nine out of ten danger areas identified by the instructor.
Criterion: Given a descriptive list of dangerous situations, rank order them according to most to least dangerous.

Example 5

Goal: Be familiar with technical terms commonly used in nursing.

Behavior: Match term with correct definition.
      Conditions: Given list of terms and definitions.
      Criterion: 8 correct matches out of 10.
Criterion Test Item: Here is a list of . . .

Behavior: State meaning of sentence containing term "diastolic."
      Conditions: Given a sentence containing the word "diastolic."
      Criteria: Essential elements—rhythmic recurrence, expansion, dilation of heart cavities.
Criterion Test Item: Please read the following sentence . . .

Example 6

To be able to transcribe a business letter from a dictating machine of the following type (model indicated here) and be able to produce a typed letter with a minimum of three typing errors, with all typing errors corrected.

No doubt you noticed that these objectives do not all take the same form. Two consist of a single sentence, and two others are made up of two or more sentences. Two consist of a general statement followed by statements intended to clarify the nature of acceptable performance. Objectives should take whatever form will help make the instructional intent clear.

For a thorough discussion of objectives, and for further examples of the different kinds of objectives that might be written, the following references are recommended:

1. Bloom, B. S. (ed.); Engelhart, M. D.; Furst, E. H.; Hill, W. H.; and Krathwohl, D. R. *Taxonomy of Educational Objectives. Handbook I: Cognitive Domain.* New York: David McKay, 1956.
2. Krathwohl, D. R.; Bloom, B. S.; and Masia, B. B. *Taxonomy of Educational Objectives. Hand-book II: Affective Domain.* New York: David McKay, 1964.
3. Mager, R. F. *Preparing Instructional Objectives.* Palo Alto, Calif.: Fearon Publishers, 1962.

To prepare your own objectives, use your task analysis sheets as your guide. You might find it most convenient to write a task at the top of a sheet and then beneath it describe in more detail what the student will be expected to do at the end of the course in relation to that task. If that technique doesn't appeal to you, here is another used by some instructors. A sheet of paper is divided into three columns and a general objective statement is put in the left-hand column. The center column is used to describe the conditions (givens, constraints, etc.) under which the student will be expected to perform, and the third column is used to describe what the student will be doing to demonstrate his achievement of the objective.

As is true with the other steps in systematic course development, each step is not completed and then forgotten. Objectives are written before the course is prepared, but they are continually modified as experience reveals gaps, unrealistic expectations, or other ways in which they may be improved. But the statement of objectives is the key document to performance of all the remaining steps of course development. It is the blueprint describing the skills and performances we hope to achieve in our students. It is a description of the goal we intend to reach. Unless we know precisely where we are going, we might wind up someplace else . . . and never even know it.

With objectives in hand, you have established what you want the student to be like at the time your influence over him comes to an end. You have pinned down the endpoint and know what you want to achieve. But not everyone in the world is qualified to reach such a level of achievement . . . within the time likely to be available for instruction. And the nature of the persons accepted for the course will have an effect on the design of instruction. It is time, therefore, to specify the prerequisite behaviors that will be required for entry into the course.

Develop Course Objectives

by R. Ribler

Statements of objectives for the development of a training course should express the *performance* expected of the trainees upon completion of the program. The end-of-course objectives are stated in terms of *observable behavior* or *performance*, and do not simply describe what the trainees have learned.

A thorough analysis of the job is required to determine what behavior is necessary to perform the job completely and correctly. The training requirements analysis is the input to the process of developing objectives.

The second essential element in the definition of objectives is that they allow for *measurement*.

Thus, the essential features of objectives statements are that they are *observable* and *measurable*.

All objectives should include:

1. An input, or condition.
2. Disposition of the input, or how the condition is to be handled.
3. Performance criteria.
4. Disposition of the output, or result of the actions taken.

All the necessary information should be contained in the job description, in the task analysis, and in the training requirements analysis results.

DETERMINE INPUTS OR CONDITIONS FOR EACH TASK OF THE JOB

In virtually all jobs, there is an input or initial condition with which the trainee will have to do something. When you've identified the input or condition, it becomes the first part of the objective. For example:

> "Given the day's incoming mail . . ."
> "Given the day's outgoing mail . . ."
> "Given a postage meter . . ."

These kinds of opening phrases express the input or condition part of the objective.

Task statements in the job description should define the action required for different inputs or conditions. Most, if not all, of the course objectives will be related to the task statements in the job description. They should be expressed in enough detail so that there can be no doubt of the meaning.

DETERMINE WHAT THE TRAINEE MUST DO WITH THE INPUT

Here again, the job description is the source of the required information. This part of the objective statement identifies the specific action, decision, or process required of the trainee.

Examples of this segment of the statement are:

> ". . . will process according to the job description . . ."
> ". . . will process according to the job description . . ."
> ". . . will get it filled . . ."

Always state this part of the objective in terms of measurable performance. Use action verbs. In the long run, how well the objective is stated will determine whether or not the student has learned to perform.

Some job tasks will require that something be done with the output. However, most tasks and, therefore, most objective statements don't require information regarding what is done with the output. In this case, the completion of the process outlined previously will usually give the complete objective statement.

Putting together two of the examples already given, we have:

> "Given the day's outgoing mail, the trainee will process it according to the job description."

This is a statement of the objective in behavioral terms—the expected behavior is observable and measurable. The trainee must make a decision before processing the input, and we can measure that performance by presenting the learner with such a request and then determining if the mail is processed correctly.

DETERMINE THE OUTPUT OR RESULT OF EACH PROCESS

Some job tasks will call for disposition of the processed input. In such cases, the objective statement should

From *Training Development Guide* by R. I. Ribler (Reston, VA.: Reston Publishing Co., Inc., 1983). Reprinted with permission.

include that action. To continue the examples:

" . . . and deliver it to the post office."

" . . . and deliver it to the designated station on the appropriate floor."

Each objective should be examined to determine whether this part of the statement is actually required.

Again, it's important to remember that all parts of the objective should be expressed in *observable* and *measurable* terms.

The examples of course objectives below exemplify the differences between good and poor objectives.

WRITE COURSE OBJECTIVES IN MEASURABLE TERMS

Using the process just described, each objective should be written so it expresses the *behaviors* to be trained. Often there will be about the same number of objectives as tasks in the job, but this will depend on the job structure. When the list of course objectives is complete, it should represent all of the new behaviors expected of the trainee at the end of the course.

When you've finished writing your course objectives, you should check again to be certain your coverage is complete. This is a good time to go back and look at your training requirements analysis and your completed job description.

Examples of Course Objectives

Good	Poor
1. Given the day's outgoing mail, process it according to the job description and deliver it to the Post Office. *Criterion*: 100 pieces of mail per hour with an error rate not to exceed one percent.	1. Know how to process outgoing mail.
2. Given the day's incoming mail, process it and deliver it to the designated station on the appropriate floor. *Criterion*: 100 pieces of mail per hour with an error rate not to exceed one percent.	2. Understand how to process incoming mail.
3. Given a postage meter, get it filled when necessary. *Criterion*: Never run the meter so low that the day's mail will be delayed.	3. Learn how to get a postage meter filled.

Develop Enabling Objectives
by R. Ribler

Enabling objectives are related to, and often are derived from, the course objectives. They're usually expressed in a more detailed form and are addressed to the instructional unit, rather than to the entire course. They define for the trainee the information and knowledge needed to perform the tasks of the job. Enabling objectives are not usually tested at the end of the course,

since they simply enable the trainee to perform the tasks necessary to be able to perform the tasks defined by the course objectives. An example of the derivation of enabling objectives from course objectives is shown below.

COURSE OBJECTIVE

Given the day's outgoing mail, process it according to the job description.

From *Training Development Guide* by R. I. Ribler (Reston, VA.: Reston Publishing Co., Inc., 1983). Reprinted with permission.

ENABLING OBJECTIVES

1. Upon completion of this unit, you will be able to sort, without error, twenty-five pieces of the day's outgoing mail in fifteen minutes. You will sort the mail into groups of special delivery, certified, registered, air, and regular mail.
2. When you complete this unit, you'll be able to correct or add Zip Codes to the day's outgoing mail, using a Zip Code Directory.
3. Given mail of different weights, you'll be able to demonstrate how to weigh the pieces accurately on a postal scale.
4. Given the day's outgoing mail, you'll be able, in one hour and with ninety-nine percent accuracy, to sort one hundred pieces of mail into packets of local mail, out-of-town mail, and air mail.

As you can see, it would be impossible for the trainee to meet the criteria for the course objective without being able to satisfy the criteria defined in the enabling objectives. Therefore, if the trainee can perform the course criteria, you can assume the criteria for the enabling objectives have been satisfied.

Another way to define enabling objectives is to state that they ensure the requisite skills and knowledge needed to perform the more encompassing course objectives.

Individualizing Learning Objectives

by Gerald V. Miller

As trainers, we sooner or later come to the realization that one of the most critical factors in training practice is the fact that learning is an internal process.

Those methods, activities and techniques which involve the individual learner most deeply in self-directed inquiry will produce *internalization*, and the greatest learning. Related to this issue, Dr. Malcolm Knowles made the following comment:

> In fact, the main thrust of modern adult-educational technology is in the direction of inventing techniques for involving adults in ever-deeper processes of self-diagnosis of their own needs for continued learning, in formulating their own objectives for learning, in sharing responsibilities for designing and carrying out their learning activities, and in evaluating their progress toward their objectives.[1]

However, the question that immediately arises is: *"How do I, as a trainer, individualize when I have preset learning objectives to meet or a 'packaged program' to present?"*

To combine this need to present a specific concept with the need to individualize the training, I have developed and successfully implemented a learning design entitled, *The Individualizing Learning Objectives Instrument.*

The goal of this instrument is to aid the trainer and participants in the understanding of the learning objectives and the desired skills, which is necessary for a successful training event. In most cases, participants of a particular training event will have seen the preset objectives contained in the description of the training event. This instrument involves taking data, on site, from participants' own needs in order to find appropriate alternatives to what was planned prior to the training event.

This Individualizing Learning Objectives Instrument aids the trainer in the clarification of the goals for the training event, as well as in the identification of the specific learning needs of the participants. This instrument will also aid the trainer in keeping participants moving in the direction of the desired learning and skills.

The implementation of this instrument affords the trainer and participants with opportunity to formulate a contractual agreement. Since a contract is a specific document which spells out, as completely as possible, the expected performance of each and every party, a contractual agreement on the specific objectives should keep the trainer from forging energetically forward—alone. Chances of a successful training event are usually considerably better when everyone contracts or agrees on intended outcomes. This activity permits the contract to occur.

A contractual agreement on specific objectives provides participants with the opportunity to contribute, from the start, to the training event, thereby giving them ownership and personal commitment; enabling them to have influence on the desired outcomes. Therefore, this contracting also enhances the training event with "motivators" which should increase involvement of the participants.

Also, if for some reason the preset objectives do not match the expectations of the participants, the use of this instrument affords the opportunity for immediate change before plowing into the training event.

Furthermore, use of the instrument confirms the notion that objectives are adaptable. (The trainer and participants should keep in mind that objectives can change. Participants usually respond favorably to objectives that are flexible.) Objectives that are open to change are changed less often and therefore, more often achieved. The implementation of the Individualizing Learning Objectives instrument fosters the necessary openness to change.

Sidestepping for a moment, this instrument will demand of the trainer the ability to adapt preset material, resources presentation, and the general process of the training event. In most cases, the trainer can call upon the internal resources, the participants' experiences and personal resources, as an aid in this adaptation.

The following paragraphs detail the objectives and procedure, and provides the accompanying worksheet for instrument.

THE OBJECTIVES

1. To give the trainer an instrument for training that will enable the trainer to develop on site a learning design that is relevant to the needs of participants.
2. To give the trainer an instrument for training that will help to identify more specific learning goals for the training event.
3. To give the trainer an instrument for training that will help the trainer clarify his/her goals for a particular learning event or a particular part of a training event.
4. To give the trainer an instrument for training that will help to develop motivators for a particular learning event.
5. To give the trainer an instrument for training that will help the trainer and participants clarify their objectives within a particular learning event.
6. To give the trainer an instrument for training that will help the trainer and participants to call upon their own internal resources as sources for more effective learning.
7. To give the trainer an instrument for training that can function as an evaluation tool at the end of a particular training event by individualizing learning objectives at the beginning of the event.

THE PROCEDURE

1. The trainer begins the learning event with a general dialogue concerning the preset objectives.
2. Following the general dialogue, participants should form triads. (If there is a large number of participants, the small grouping should not exceed five per group or effectiveness will be lost.)
3. The trainer should proceed by distributing the *Individualizing Learning Objectives Worksheet* (Figure 1) to each participant.
4. The worksheet is completed by each participant and then shared with the other members of the triad.
5. The trainer should proceed by distributing newsprint and marker pens to each triad group for the purpose of recording their agreed-upon objectives for that triad.
6. The trainer should proceed by posting all the newsprints of each triad.
7. If applicable, the trainer may wish to briefly comment on the relevance of each objective to the broad goal of the particular learning event.
8. A general discussion for the purpose of modifying, combining, deleting, or adding to the preset objectives should follow. (Given the fact that the preset objectives, based on the original needs assessment, have been previously formulated by the trainer, the trainer now must see if the participants accept these objectives as accurate translations of their learning needs. The exploration of objectives for precision can be a fairly technical and time-consuming activity, especially if an extensive list of learning objectives results. Therefore, it may be prudent to limit the objectives developed to a particular day's activities or a specific number of objectives per triad.)
9. The above steps should bring the trainer and participants to a contractual agreement on the objectives and the goal of the learning event.
10. The agreed-upon learning objectives should be posted for observation for the duration of the learning event. This posting will enable the trainer and participants to keep a constant focus on the direction of their desired learning. The agreed-upon individualized learning objectives should be used at the end of the learning event as a tool for evaluation.

REFERENCE

1. Knowles, Malcolm S., *The Modern Practice of Adult Education: Andragogy vs. Pedagogy,* Association Press, New York, 1970, p. 51.

SOURCES

- Bergenin, Paul and McKinkey, John, *Participatory Training,* Bethany Press, St. Louis, 1970.
- Davis, Larry N. and McCallon, Earl, *Planning, Conducting and Evaluating Workshops,* Learning Concepts, Austin, 1974.
- Ingalls, John D., *A Trainer's Guide to Andragogy,* U.S. Department of Health, Education and Welfare, Washington, D.C., 1972.

FIGURE 1
Worksheet: Individualizing Learning Objectives

Preset Learning Objectives (PLO):
1.
2.
3.
etc.

Individualized Learning Objective (ILO) No. 1.

ILO No. 2.

ILO No. 3.

ILO No. 4.

ILO No. 5.

Determining Supervision Training Needs and Setting Objectives

by Donald Kirkpatrick

KNOWLEDGE OBJECTIVES

In supervisory training, we are frequently trying to accomplish knowledge objectives. A good way to state the objectives is to begin with the statement: "When the training is completed, the learner should be able to do the following:"

Subject	Knowledge Objective
1. Human Relations (Leadership & Motivation)	1. List in sequence "Maslow's Hierarchy of Needs".
	2. List in order for frequency, Herzberg's: a. Dissatisfiers b. Satisfiers
	3. Describe at least five assumptions of Theory "X" managers.
	4. Describe at least five assumptions of Theory "Y" managers.
	5. Give the name that Likert uses to describe each of his four systems of leadership.
2. Management By Objectives	1. Define MBO.
	2. List three objectives of an MBO program.
	3. List eight characteristics of good objectives.
	4. Describe the role of the subordinate in setting objectives.
3. Communication	1. Define the word "communicate."
	2. List six barriers that can be directly related to the sender.
	3. List six barriers that can be directly related to the receiver.
	4. List the five "c's" of an effective written communication.
	1. Differentiate between "personality-oriented" and "job-oriented" appraisals.
	2. List three possible objectives of a performance-appraisal program.
	3. List five characteristics of an effective performance-appraisal interview.

SKILL OBJECTIVES

Skill objectives are more difficult to accomplish than knowledge objectives. Knowledge objectives are understandings. Skill objectives require an ability to do something. Here are some possible objectives in a supervisory training program.

Subject	Skill Objective
1. Communication	1. Write a memo that is clear, complete, concise, correct and considerate.
	2. Give a five-minute oral presentation that receives an average rating of 4 (scale of 5) from the listeners.
	3. Listen to a five-minute presentation and list the three main ideas covered.

SKILL OBJECTIVES *(Continued)*

Subject	*Skill Objective*

2. Performance Appraisal	1. Complete a performance-appraisal form that accurately describes the performance of a subordinate.
	2. Conduct a performance-appraisal interview so that interviewee:
	  a. Understands parts of job he/she is doing.
	  b. Understands what one area of performance needs improvement.
	  c. Understands at least three things that can be done to improve performance.
	  d. Feels that the interview was worthwhile.
	  e. Has a positive attitude toward the interviewer.

ATTITUDE OBJECTIVES

Not all programs have attitude objectives that can be clearly identified. Here are some that might be appropriate:

Subject	*Attitude Objective*
1. Human Relations (Leadership & Motivation)	1. Believes that positive employee attitudes are necessary for maximum productivity. 2. Believes that minority employees can perform effectively. 3. Believes that employees have ideas that can contribute to the effectiveness of the department. 4. Believes that most employees will do what the supervisor expects.
2. Management By Objectives	1. Believes that MBO is worth the time and effort. 2. Believes that subordinates should be involved in setting their own objectives. 3. Is committed to doing MBO on a systematic basis.
3. Communication	1. Feels that employees should be told what they want to know and not just what they need to know. 2. Believes that upward communications depends on rapport between supervisor and employees. 3. Believes that listening to employees' problems is a wise use of time.

SOURCES SECTION VI
CHOOSING TRAINING AND DEVELOPMENT METHODS

A. Designing Meaningful Learning Situations in Management: A Contingency, Decision-Tree Approach
by W. Alan Randolph and Barry Posner
- Discusses variables for designing learning situations
- Provides a framework for matching these situations with various training techniques

B. Methods of Teaching
by John Randall
- Critiques common methods of teaching in training

C. Job Instruction Training
by Dugan Laird
- Discusses the importance of training in the boss-subordinate relationship
- Presents the structure of effective job instructional training

D. How Training through Behavior Modeling Works
by Stephen Wehrenberg and Robert Kuhnle
- Explains how behavior modeling works in a training program

E. The Miniature Job Training and Evaluation Approach: Additional Findings
by Arthur Siegel
- Discusses findings on the theory of training for the job following a demonstration of ability on the job sample

F. Assessment Centers: For Selection or Development
by Gary Hart and Paul Thompson
- Suggests the utilization of development-oriented assessment centers
- Provides detailed guidelines for an effective assessment center for career development

G. An Introduction to Computer-Based Learning
by Angus Reynolds
- Explains the basic terminology and technology involved in computer-based learning

H. The Five Most Frequent Questions (Plus One) About Computer-Based Learning
by Angus Reynolds and Richard Davis
- Answers common questions about computer-based learning

Designing Meaningful Learning Situations in Management: A Contingency, Decision-Tree Approach

by W. Alan Randolph and Barry Z. Posner

Management educators have long been concerned with selecting the most effective pedagogical technique for various management teaching and training situations, and interest in this issue seems to be growing. Presentations at national meetings of the Academy of Management, American Institute for Decision Sciences, and American Marketing Association, among others, continue to exhort the virtues of one pedagogy or another for teaching management.[3, 10, 13, 15] In the final analysis there is no one best pedagogical approach for all courses or classes in management. Indeed, each major approach—be it the case method, experiential exercise, or lecture format—has its own advantages and disadvantages. What has been lacking is a conceptual framework for determining when these various pedagogical techniques are most appropriate.

This paper represents a first step in developing such a framework. The framework is valuable regardless of teaching experience because it systematically brings into focus important pedagogical and situational considerations. It is useful not only in classrooms with management students but also in training practitioners. After some statements about the learning process, we discuss eight major input variables for designing learning situations in management. These variables are translated into a decision-tree format that provides a step by step approach to matching pedagogical technique and situation.

TEACHING AND THE LEARNING PROCESS

Rogers[30] suggested that teaching is probably a vastly overrated function. Conversely, thinking about and designing meaningful management learning experiences is definitely a vastly *underrated* function. Management faculty often feel that the material presented is what students actually learn. Unfortunately, the process is much more complex. What an effective teacher does involves not so much "stamping out ignorance" on the subject matter as it does creating a situation where learning can take place. Learning is something that cannot be taught or given by the teacher; it is something that takes place within the learner. Al-though there is *no* "one best way" to create conditions which maximize the opportunities for students to learn, there are better ways for given situations and learning objectives.[7, 16, 32]

The purpose of teaching is not simply to cover a given amount of subject matter but to produce some sort of change in human behavior. These changes can be assigned to five categories[14, 17, 18, 20]: (a) change in things known, or knowledge, (b) change in things done, or skills, (c) change in things felt, or attitudes, (d) change in things valued, or appreciation, and (e) change in things comprehended, or understanding. Teaching management is both a science and an art—a process of guided interaction between the teacher, the student, and the materials.[16, 17, 18] A teacher needs to focus considerable energy on the design of this guided interaction if it is to be effective.

SEVERAL IMPORTANT INPUT VARIABLES

In order to develop a useful model or framework for designing situations which are effective for teaching management, a way of classifying pedagogical techniques and a way of defining and categorizing the nature of the learning situation are needed. Additionally, a technique or algorithm is necessary in order to link the inputs (descriptors of the situation) of the model with the outputs (the pedagogical techniques). We begin by describing the major contingencies (input variables) affecting much of what goes on in the classroom. Next we present a typology for understanding the relationship between different learning styles and pedagogical techniques. We conclude by incorporating the input variables and pedagogical techniques into a decision-tree framework and discuss how this model might be used in the effective design of meaningful management learning situations.

The design of effective learning situations requires careful consideration of at least eight input variables or situational contingencies. They are: (a) course or class goals, (b) course or class content, (c) student motivation, (d) student skills, (e) facilities, resources, and norms, (f) institutional and professional pressures or concerns, (g) instructor skills and values, and (h) developmental nature of the learning process.

Course or Class Goals

The primary consideration in selecting pedagogical techniques and designing effective learning situations is determining and understanding what "changes" within the learner we hope will occur. This first input may be translated into: What is (are) the course goal(s)? What management skills and/or knowledge should the students take away from the classroom experience? Clarity about learning objectives for the students, often stated as behavioral objectives, is essential.[23]

The basic dimension underlying the goals input is the level of involvement in the learning process by the student. Learning (i.e., changes) in knowledge and appreciation do not require the same level of involvement that changes in skill and attitudes require. Statements about goals involve a continuum of reflective (respondent behavior) to implementation skills (operant behavior).[21]

Course or Class Content

A second input concerns the nature of the learning content: What is the state of the art of the subject matter? Is it well developed or not? In what form is it available? What skills, attributes, or characteristics do students need as a background or foundation for the desired change one hopes to effect? The basic dimension here is the level of abstraction (for the students) of the material extending from theoretical to applied. For example, if students are studying organization design, the concepts may seem rather theoretical and abstract, whereas the concepts related to perception may appear more applied and concrete because of direct student experiences with perception.

The next two major input variables relate to an assessment of the learners. The first concerns their motivation and the second concerns their level of skills. This assessment involves looking at both objective and subjective data.

Student Motivation

This input variable involves analyzing why students are taking the course. Is it required or elective? What do they want to get out of it? What do they want to put into it? To what degree is the group heterogeneous or homogeneous on these dimensions? While these questions are geared toward an assessment of the class as a whole, they are not meant to negate the importance of being sensitive to individual differences among students.

Most educational experts agree that the single most important prerequisite for learning is the motiva-tion or desire to learn.[6,18,22,31] Learning must be purposeful as perceived by the students. The effective instructor will be sensitive to the students' objectives and how they can be motivated to achieve them in concert with course objectives. This is facilitated when students clearly understand what the course objectives are: What will they know and be able to do as a result of this course? Where does it fit in with other courses (past or future)? Rogers[30] says:

When an individual has a goal he wishes to achieve and sees the material available to him as relevant to achieving that goal, learning takes place with great rapidity. We need only recall what a brief length of time it takes for an adolescent to learn to drive a car.

Hence, one way in which students' inherent motivational forces can be tapped and channeled is to structure learning tasks and experiences so that students will be intrinsically motivated by the work they actually do.[12]

The underlying dimension regarding motivation involves a sensitivity to the need which the student may have for learning the material. If the students are motivated to learn about leadership, for example, the pedagogical approach used is far less important than if the students have little motivation.

Student Skills

The other crucial assessment of students is their level of ability. Important considerations include: Where are they now in terms of ability and where are they likely to be capable of going? Are they fast or slow learners? What is their age and background? How much ambiguity can they tolerate? Again, while this assessment is geared toward the group as a whole it should not exclude being sensitive to individual differences.

The underlying dimension concerns the student's capability of becoming involved. Students with little skill and ability in a particular topical area (e.g., undergraduates learning about policy decisions) may by necessity have to be more reflective than students with a better background (e.g., experienced managers learning about policy decisions). Hence, teacher-centered negotiations of new material may have to precede learner-centered methods.

External Factors

The next two input variables are not often explicitly considered in designing learning situations. They involve the reality of the teaching environment in terms of: (a) the nature of the available teaching/learning facilities, resources, and norms, and (b) the nature of the institutional and/or professional pressures, rewards, and constraints.

The *first* issue focuses on class size, physical facilities, class time available, time the class meets, and availability of resources like graders, teaching assistants, films, computers, audiovisual equipment, etc. It also involves understanding the teaching norms at one's school and such practical matters as freedom in text selection and the nature and importance of student evaluations. In essence, this question regarding resources, facilities, and norms is a question of the degree of flexibility afforded the instructor in determining the particular pedagogical technique to be used. Reduced flexibility may tend to reduce the level of student participation which the instructor can allow, because other factors are likely to take precedence.

The *second* issue involves factors external to the classroom but which often have an important impact on the design of learning situations. These factors are categorized as institutional/professional pressures and include questions such as: What are the objectives of the department, faculty in general, school, AACSB, business community, trustees? What is the nature of competing pressures, like research, publishing, and service? What rewards or reinforcements are available in the system for being a good teacher? Do I have tenure?

In essence, these questions can be reduced to the issue of how much time can the instructor devote to teaching. If the instructor must offer a great deal of service to the institution and feels under considerable pressure to do research and to publish, then the time that can be devoted to teaching is obviously reduced. With limited time resources the instructor is often forced away from those pedagogies that actively involve students.

Instructor Skills and Values

The sixth input variable involves candidly appraising one's skills, abilities, and values. What is it that I, as the teacher, like to do and do best? What is my own background, training, and experience? How do I think people learn best and under what circumstances? How much control do I want in the classroom? How much ambiguity can I tolerate? Do I want respect, popularity, or both? What should be the nature of my interpersonal relationships with students? Taking a critical inventory of one's own skills and preferences may make the choices in pedagogical style easier to handle.[25] Teachers might realize that they cannot be effective in every situation with the same approach.

Contingency views of management already recognize this proposition.[8]

Recognizing and assessing one's own values and beliefs is important for another reason. McGregor[24] observed that people operate with a set of assumptions about the fundamental nature of other people, and these assumptions tend to produce self-fulfilling prophecies. "If teachers treat students as irresponsible, they will tend to do them the courtesy of behaving irresponsibly. If they are treated as able, mature and responsible people, they will tend to behave in such a way as to validate the prediction."[5] Consequently, the ramifications of one's teaching style are considerable.

Still, in designing a learning situation in management, consideration must be given to assessing what one is capable of doing well. It might be preferable to lecture in a situation where a case would be more appropriate, rather than to do an inadequate job presenting and discussing the case. The point is, a model may suggest which pedagogical technique is most desirable in a given situation, but it cannot *create* either the desire or the ability necessary to employ that technique.

Developmental Nature of Learning

The final input variable takes into account the developmental nature of learning. In many courses, the classroom situation changes over the term. Models of group development[2,11] can readily be applied to classroom situations. Not only is the subject matter generally becoming more complex, but the instructor–student relationship and interaction pattern are also changing. Both of these require shifts in teaching style, motivation, and responsibilities. The developmental aspects of learning situations are also affected by the time frame of the experience and the feedback process which exists. Applying a developmental perspective to the feedback processes and the learning environment requires that there be some flexibility and openness to change in order that pedagogical styles remain congruent and symbiotic with the learning mode of the students.[1] Explicit in this notion is the idea that instructors should also be developing and experiencing a concomitant sense of growth and learning as a result of the classroom experience.

Development of the Model

These eight input variables affect the effectiveness of possible teaching strategies and the creation of desirable learning conditions. They constitute an important set of questions which should be dealt with and considered in the selection of suitable pedagogical techniques. The input variables were developed and reviewed, along with the classification of pedagogical techniques explained in the next section, utilizing several processes of qualitative forecasting (e.g., panel consensus and cross-impact analysis).[4,33] The basic notions of the input variables and the two-dimensional framework for classifying pedagogies (presented in the next section) were originally presented at a national meeting of the American Institute for Decision Sciences.[28] Ten management educators met and discussed the input variables and the pedagogical classifications, leading to several modifications in the conceptual scheme.

The modified input list and classification set were verified at the Fourth Annual Organizational Behavior Teaching Conference by 25 Organizational Behavior/Theory professors.[27] In addition, the decision tree (presented later in this paper) for linking the input variables and the pedagogies was presented at this same meeting, as well as at the 1977 American Institute for Decision Sciences Meeting.[29] The inputs and model also went through several critical review interactions utilizing faculties at our respective universities. In all, the list of input considerations has been through a number of critical reviews and has met with acceptance as being representative of the issues which need to be considered in designing management learning situations. Likewise, the classification of pedagogical techniques and the decision-tree model have been through several critical reviews and appear to provide a generally valid and useful framework for classifying pedagogies and for analyzing learning situations in management.

A TYPOLOGY FOR CLASSIFYING PEDAGOGICAL APPROACHES

Before we can consider a methodology for exploring these situational contingencies and their associated tradeoffs, it is necessary to develop an appreciation of how pedagogical techniques might be related to different learning styles. Kolb[19] suggests that there are two major dimensions that need to be considered in understanding how people learn. Using this framework it is possible to effectively categorize the many different pedagogical strategies and techniques.

The *first* dimension is the degree of concreteness of the learning desired, as measured on a continuum from theoretical to applied, and the *second* dimension is the nature of participation and involvement required or desired of the learners, as measured on a continuum from reflective to active. Using these two dimensions of learning, pedagogical techniques available for teaching management can be classified as

one of four types: (I) reflective-theoretical, (II) reflective-applied, (III) active-applied, and (IV) active-theoretical (see Figure 1).

Quadrant I focuses on knowledge acquisition, where the student is expected to absorb certain theories and to be capable of rationally explaining those theories. Quadrant II focuses not only on knowledge acquisition but also on developing in the student an appreciation for the theories and an ability to use the theories in explaining real events.

Quadrants III and IV involve more active experimentation (i.e., actual doing). Quadrant III involves change in attitudes and development of skills, because the student is asked to act on the theories in experiencing and coping with actual or simulated events. Quadrant IV involves changes in understanding as the students become actively and personally involved in testing and developing theories and hypotheses (their own and others').

Two examples will illustrate the ideas in Figure 1. Suppose the learning situation involves a well-established conceptual body of knowledge such as motivation theory, and the goal is transmission of information about these theories. The degree of concreteness for the student is theoretical and the nature of participation required mostly reflective; hence, the pedagogical techniques presented in Quadrant I are the most appropriate.

Alternatively, suppose the learning situation involves the development of leadership skills of people about to become supervisors. The degree of concreteness for the learners in this instance is applied and they need to be actively involved; hence the approaches in Quadrant III are the most appropriate.

It is important to note that while the quadrants may appear discrete, this does not necessarily preclude more imaginative combinations where two or more approaches from different quadrants might be integrated. For example, Gadon[9] discusses ways to teach cases experientially. Nor does it preclude movement over time from the teacher-centered instructional methods in Quadrants I and II to the more student-centered methods of instruction in Quadrants III and IV.

We now have developed a set of input variables that can help in understanding the nature of the learning situation, and have presented a typology for classifying many of the pedagogical techniques used in management courses. However, these issues remain: How does one systematically consider each input variable and accurately diagnose contingencies affecting learning situations? How does one discover a feasible set of pedagogical alternatives? Answering these questions led to the development of a decision-tree model which translates the eight input variables into diagnostic questions and integrates them within

Figure 1
Conceptual Grid of Learning Styles and Pedagogical Techniques (Adapted from D. A. Kolb, "On Management and the Learning Process," in D. A. Kolb, I. M. Rubin, and J. M. McIntyre (Eds.), *Organizational Psychology: A Book of Readings*, 2d ed. [Englewood Cliffs, N.J.: Prentice-Hall, 1974], pp. 27–42.)

APPLIED

Degree of Concreteness to Students

THEORETICAL

Change in Appreciation
Movies
Applied lecture
Dialogue
Limited discussion
Cases
Problem exam
Programmed instruction
(skills)
                                        II III

Change in Skills and Attitudes
Role plays
Games
Structured exercises
Processing discussion
T-Groups
Diaries
Field Projects

                                        I IV

Change in Knowledge
Theory lecture
Required readings
Handouts
Programmed instruction
(concepts)
Theory papers
Content exam

Change in Understanding
Focused learning groups
Argumentative discussion
Experiments/Research
Suggested readings
Analysis papers

REFLECTIVE   *ACTIVE*

Nature of Participation
And Involvement of Students

the pedagogical typology. The result is a framework for designing meaningful learning situations in management.

A CONTINGENCY, DECISION-TREE FRAMEWORK FOR DESIGNING LEARNING SITUATIONS

The decision tree (shown in Figure 2) was developed to assist management teachers in matching an appropriate range of pedagogies with a particular learning situation, as described via the eight input variables. Several choices had to be made in developing this decision tree. It was necessary to restrict the number of alternative responses to each diagnostic question in order to prevent the analysis from becoming impossibly complex. Another important question was the order in which the eight input variables should be addressed. It seemed most logical to begin with the question of course objectives and content, as translated

into the two-dimensional framework in Figure 1. In so doing, one is in a better position to understand and calculate the tradeoffs associated with the other input variables.

Referring to Figure 2, the first two questions locate the course (or class) in one of the four quadrants in Figure 1 from an "ideal" perspective. The first question (moving from left to right) addresses the course objectives in terms of the Reflective-Active continuum of the learning model (Figure 1). The second question relates to course (or class) content, and it places one's response on the Theoretical-Applied continuum of the learning model. The responses to these two questions provide the ideal pedagogical category based solely on course content and goals. If all other input variables are ideal, the teaching modes shown in the particular quadrant should provide the most effective learning situation. However, if the other inputs are less than ideal it may be necessary to alter the ideal choice in order to cope with pragmatic issues such as student motivation, student skills, facilities, resources, norms, and institutional/professional pressures or concerns. These situational inputs are considered in the next four questions of the decision tree.

This part of the model is self-explanatory if one considers the basic dimensions of the various inputs, as described earlier. Still, after considering the ideal quadrant and then modifying this choice according to existing situational variables or contingencies, instructors need to refine that choice in view of their own skills and values. "What teaching styles (and techniques) am I willing and able to effectively utilize?" (shown at the far right side of Figure 2). One's response to this question leads to a consideration of whether there is a match between the teaching style one can comfortably and effectively use and the teaching style deemed most suitable for the present learning situation.

Assuming that there is a match, one can proceed with the desired teaching style but with *continual reassessment* of the maturing situation, because of the developmental nature of the learning process (the eighth input variable). This continual reassessment will help keep the instructor in step with a dynamic situation. If there is not a match between the most appropriate style and the style one can use effectively, the decision choice for the instructor becomes one of (a) trying to gradually alter the situation (i.e., input variables), (b) increasing one's pedagogical repertoire, or (c) reconsidering whether to teach the course at all (at this time).

FIGURE 2
Decision-Tree Framework for Designing Learning Situations
(ᵃNumbers refer to quadrants in Figure 1)

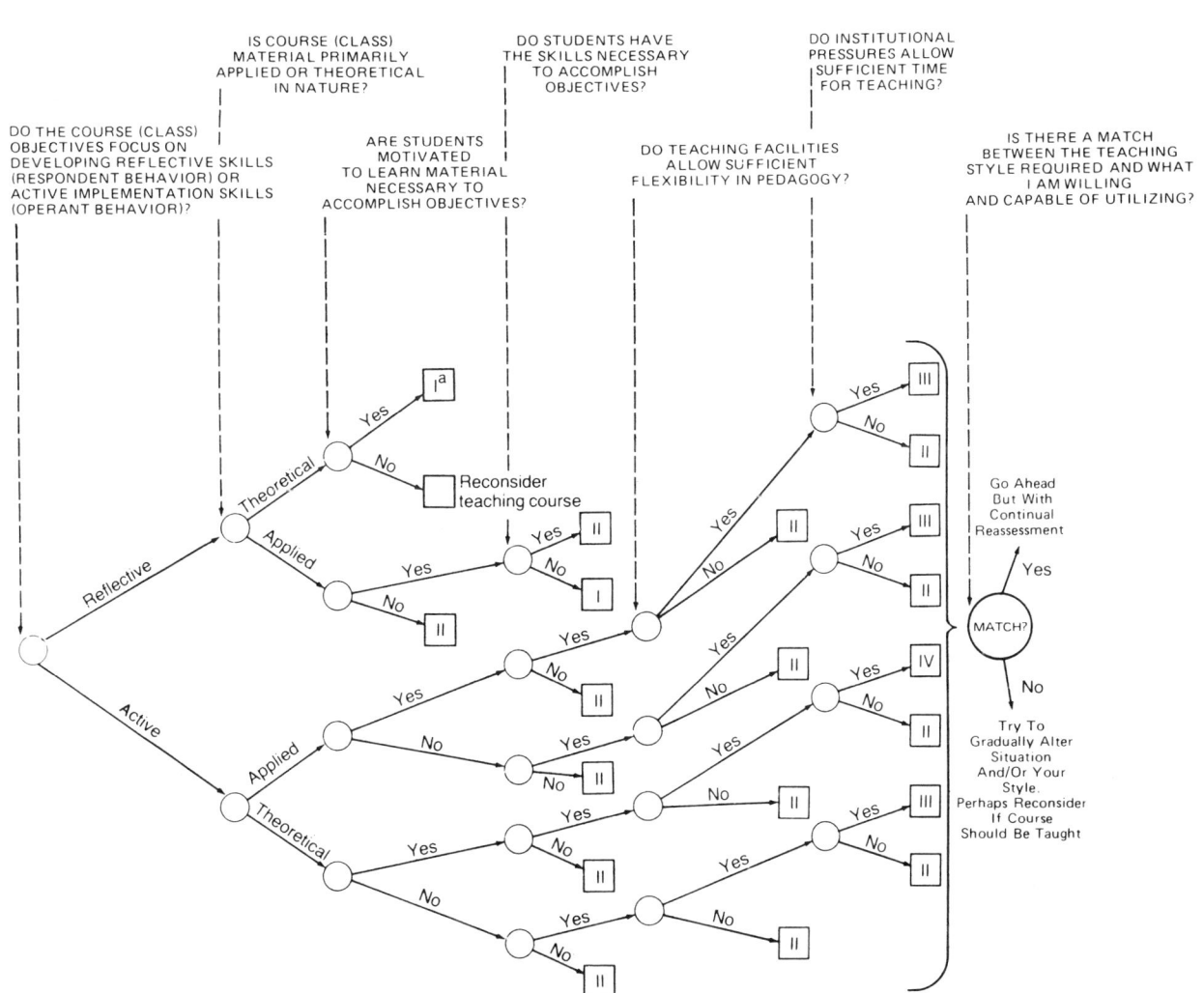

CONCLUSION

This contingency approach is not *the* answer nor is it the only approach that has been offered for becoming a better teacher, having happier or more productive students, or improving final course evaluations. Other frameworks are available.[14,16,22,26] The proposed conceptual framework and model are offered as one possible guide for systematically considering the contingencies critical to the pedagogical design of effective learning situations in management courses. It represents the kind of thinking about the design of learning situations which is needed to enhance meaningful student (and faculty) learning about management.

REFERENCES

1. Argyris, C. "Double Loop Learning in Organizations," *Harvard Business Review*, Vol. 55, No. 5 (1977), 115–125.

2. Bennis, W. G., and H. A. Shepard. "A Theory of Group Development," *Human Relations*, Vol. 9, No. 4 (1956), 415–437.

3. Certo, S. "Stages of the Kolb-Rubin-McIntyre Experiential Learning Model and Perceived Trainee Learning: A Preliminary Investigation," in R. L. Taylor, M. J. O'Connell, R. A. Zawacki, and D. D. Warwick (Eds.), *Academy of Management Proceedings*, 1977, pp. 21–24.

4. Chambers, J. C., S. K. Mullick, and D. D. Smith. *An Executive's Guide to Forecasting* (New York: Wiley-Interscience, 1974).

5. Davies, I. K. "Training in an Age of Change," in I. K. Davies, E. H. Hudson, B. Dodd, and J. Hartley (Eds.), *The Organization of Training* (London: McGraw-Hill Limited, 1973).

6. Dewey, J. *Experience and Education* (New York: Macmillan, 1947).

7. Douley, A. R., and Skinner, W. "Casing Casemethod Methods," *Academy of Management Review*, Vol. 2, No. 2 (1977), 277–289.

8. Fiedler, F. E. "Engineer the Job to Fit the Manager," *Harvard Business Review*, Vol. 43, No. 5 (1965), 115–122.

9. Gadon, H. "Teaching Cases Experientially," *Exchange: The Organizational Behavior Teaching Journal*, Vol. 2, No. 1 (1976), 20–24.

10. Guseman, D. S., and L. D. Dahringer. "Effective Teaching Techniques," in *Marketing: 1776–1976 and Beyond* (Chicago: American Marketing Association, 1976), pp. 540–543.

11. Hersey, P., and K. Blanchard. *Management of Organizational Behavior*, 3d ed. (Englewood Cliffs, N.J.: Prentice-Hall, 1977).

12. Herzberg, F. *Work and the Nature of Man* (Cleveland: World Publishing, 1966).

13. Hodgetts, R. M., D. E. Ezell, and P. M. V. Auken. "A Contingency Approach to Business Policy Pedagogy," in R. L. Taylor, M. J. O'Connell, R. A. Zawacki, and D. D. Warwick (Eds.), *Academy of Management Proceedings*, 1976, pp. 130–134.

14. House, J. *Management Development: Design, Evaluation, and Implementation* (Ann Arbor: University of Michigan Press, 1967).

15. Johnson, G. A., and J. N. Yanouzas. "Practicing What Is Practiced: Integrating OB and Production Management Experientially," in J. D. Stolen and J. C. Conway (Eds.), *American Institute for Decision Sciences Proceedings*, 1977, pp. 112–114.

16. Keys, B. "The Management of Learning Grid for Management Development," *Academy of Management Review*, Vol. 2, No. 2 (1977), 289–297.

17. Kidd, J. R. *How Adults Learn* (New York: Associated Press, 1973).

18. Knowles, M. *The Adult Learner: A Neglected Species* (Houston: Grid, 1973).

19. Kolb, D. A. "On Management and the Learning Process," in D. A. Kolb, I. M. Rubin, and J. M. McIntyre (Eds.), *Organization Psychology: A Book of Readings*, 2d ed. (Englewood Cliffs, N.J.: Prentice-Hall, 1974), pp. 27–42.

20. Lippitt, R. "The Neglected Learner," in I. Morrissett and W. W. Stevens, Jr. (Eds.), *Social Science in the Schools: A Search for Rationale* (New York: Holt, Rinehart, and Winston, 1970).

21. Livingston, J. S. "The Myth of the Well-Educated Manager," *Harvard Business Review*, Vol. 49, No. 1 (1971), pp. 79–89.

22. Lynton, R. P., and W. Pareck. *Training for Development* (Homewood, Ill.: Irwin, 1967).

23. Mager, R. F. *Developing Attitudes Toward Learning* (Palo Alto: Pearon Publishers, 1968).

24. McGregor, D. *The Human Side of Enterprise* (New York: McGraw-Hill, 1960).

25. Odiorne, G. "The Role of the Lecture in Teaching Organization Behavior," *Exchange: The Organizational Behavior Teaching Journal*, Vol. 2 (1976), pp 7–14.

26. Pfeiffer, W. J., and J. E. Jones. *Reference Guide to Handbooks and Annuals* (La Jolla, Calif.: University Associates, 1977).

27. Posner, B. Z., and W. A. Randolph. "A Decision-Tree Approach to Decide When to Use Different Pedagogical Techniques," *Exchange: The Organizational Behavior Teaching Journal*, Vol. 3, No. 2 (1976), pp 16–19.

28. Randolph, W. A., and B. Z. Posner. "Improving the Design of Learning Situations: A Practical Framework," in H. C. Schneider (Ed.), *American Institute for Decision Sciences Proceedings*, 1976, p. 299.

29. Randolph, W. A., and B. Z. Posner. "A Practical Decision-Tree Framework for Designing Learning Situations," in J. D. Stolen and J. C. Conway (Eds.), *American Institute for Decision Sciences Proceedings*, 1977, pp. 123–125.

30. Rogers, C. *Freedom to Learn* (Columbus, Ohio: Charles E. Merrill, 1969).

31.   This, L. E., and G. L. Lippitt. "Learning Theories and the Training Director," *Training and Development Journal*, Vol. 20, Nos. 4 and 5 (1966), pp. 2–11 and 10–18.

32.   Ulrich, R. A., and W. Manley. "The Contributions of Selected Instructional Modes to Management Education," *AACSB Bulletin* (1976), pp 1–6.

33.   Wheelwright, S. C., and S. Makridalis. *Forecasting Methods for Management* (New York: Wiley-Interscience, 1973).

Methods of Teaching

by John S. Randall

The lecture is a very common method of instruction. In it the leader or instructor does all of the talking. Lecturing is a relatively inefficient way of instruction because it does not actively involve members of the group. It can be effective only if in some way the group "thinks through" the information as it is being presented. This can be accomplished by having the individuals take notes, or the instructor can secure attention and hold interest by using communication aids.

Lectures may be used to introduce a new subject. You can motivate as you introduce the subject. You arouse interest and set the stage for what is to come. A lecture can be used also as your summary at the end of a session. It does permit you to cover a great deal of material in the least amount of time—you have no interruptions, no questions, no discussion. It also enables you to go directly to your desired objective. You will not be diverted. When you have a large group, a lecture may be mandatory.

With the lecture method, the individuals in the group play a passive role. There is no exchange of ideas, no participation, nor practice. You appeal to the fewest senses, and you have little opportunity to evaluate group reaction and adjust your material accordingly.

When you use the lecture method, start by motivating the individuals immediately. Make your introduction challenging and stimulating. Use language that is easy to understand . . . preferably short, correct sentences. Use "you" and contractions to make your presentation conversational. Keep in mind that your main purpose is to communicate ideas to others.

THE DISCUSSION METHOD

The discussion method may be referred to as the conference or seminar method. In it members of the group and the leader take part in a discussion and an exchange of ideas and information. You, as the instructor, air or steer the group toward a predetermined objective. Group participation is the main basis for the discussion method.

This method stimulates thinking and involves individual members of the group. It is usually done on an informal basis which is conducive to learning and retention. It can be quite interesting and informative if properly conducted.

The discussion method is, however, more time-consuming than the lecture. It is more adaptable to a small group of 25 or less. In a large group usually only a few participate; the shy or timid individuals remain quiet.

The discussion method necessitates that you control the group very subtly. You have to be alert and constantly on your toes. You should have a good background in the subject, and you should be able to question skillfully.

The discussion method can be used to solve problems after a lecture, after a film has been shown or after demonstrations.

THE DEMONSTRATION-PERFORMANCE METHOD

The demonstrative method includes an actual portrayal of procedures or operations, and practice by the individual. In this method, the individual is told what to do, shown how to do it, and then is given an opportunity to do it. It's a tell-show method. It could be called an acted-out lecture.

A well-planned demonstration, skillfully executed, is very effective. In this method you appeal to all the senses, provide actual practice, show the steps in a realistic manner, and you stimulate interest, and maintain attention.

This method is effective for small groups of 25 or less. It is not, however, practical for a large group, unless you can divide the group into small segments for the practice part, with an instructor or leader for each segment.

Planning for a demonstration requires that you break the skill or activity into various steps, arranged in logical order. You must become completely familiar with these steps and practice them so you can make a skillful, correct demonstration. You have to arrange also for the equipment and for the individuals to practice. Considerable time will be used for individual performances so you must consider this in arranging the session. A summary or review should be made after everyone has had the opportunity to practice.

By careful observation during the performance part, you can nip incorrect techniques in the beginning before they become established.

DRAMATIZATION METHOD

Participation and interest on the part of the group can be increased by using dramatization. This is actually a combination of demonstration and discussion with individuals from the group doing the demonstrating. To a certain extent, dramatization is unplanned demonstration. Certain guidelines, however, must be provided for the individuals taking part in the dramatization.

Dramatization involves the acting out by individuals, without a script or a rehearsal, job techniques needed in specific situations. Participants are told by the instructor what the situation is, what the desired outcome is, and in general terms, how each actor should move toward accomplishing the desired outcome.

You can use dramatization to stimulate the group to take a new look at familiar job techniques; or it can be used to help the group develop the confidence and skills needed for techniques that are new to it.

You can use dramatization if:

- The individuals in the group are completely at ease with one another and with you.
- A friendly atmosphere exists so no one will ridicule the actors or "ham-up" the acting.
- A number of individuals are willing to participate without rehearsal.
- You are completely familiar with the technique. You must be prepared to handle the possibility of an individual becoming embarrassed or upset.

The procedure for dramatization consists of the following steps:

- Describe the situation to be dramatized and the desired outcome. Make this as clear as possible.
- Ask for volunteers for the parts or select individuals to portray the roles. Do not force anyone to take part.
- Allow the actors a few minutes to discuss in a general way what they want to do. While they are doing this, tell the others what to watch for. Ask the audience to hold their comments until the end of the dramatization.
- When the important points have been sufficiently portrayed to provide a basis for discussion, stop the dramatization. Do this even if the desired outcome has not been reached.
- After the dramatization, conduct a discussion on it. Explore with the group the reason why the action took the direction that it did. You might ask: Was the desired result achieved or was it about to be achieved? How did each actor's behavior influence the result?

As the discussion is taking place, you can bring in points that you want covered. You can also help the group relate the dramatization to similar real job situations.

ROLE-PLAY

Role-play is similar to dramatization. In fact, the two are often confused. However, in role-play the leader does not determine the outcome in advance. He tells the actors how they *feel* and each actor tries to behave according to these feelings. The emotion of the actors determines the outcome of role-play. Role-play, therefore, is used to help understand human behavior and improve the skills involved in working with people.

The conditions for using role-play are the same as for dramatization. There must be a friendly atmosphere, individuals must be at ease with each other, and the leader must be familiar with the role-play technique. Since emotions are involved and are likely to be portrayed vividly, there is always the possibility that the actors and the audience will become disturbed. The leader must be able to work out these emotional problems in the discussion period.

The procedure for using role-play is:

a) Select a situation that will be meaningful to the group. If this is the first time role-playing has been used, select a situation that does not involve the job responsibilities of anyone in the group. This will permit participants to be more objective in their observations and analysis. In the discussion period, you can help the individuals relate the situation to their own jobs.

b) Ask individuals to volunteer for the role-play.

c) Give written instructions to each player. These should, in detail, indicate whom he is to portray, the mood he is to be in, and how he feels at the beginning. Remind the actors that they should act as the kind of people they are supposed to be. Allow the actors a few minutes to adjust to the mood of their roles, individually, not as a group.

d) While the actors are doing this, tell the others what the situation is. If you want to, you may tell them what emotions are to be portrayed. Let the group know what to watch for. Also, remind the group that the actors are not portraying their own emotions but the emotions of their roles.

e) Stop the role-playing when real feelings develop among the players. These usually develop within three to seven minutes.

f) Let the players tell why they behaved as they did, and how they felt about the behavior of the others involved in the role-play. The audience should be reminded that the actors are discussing the emotions of the people portrayed, not their own personal feelings.

g) In conducting a discussion, pattern your questions along the following lines:

1. Did any actor suddenly change behavior? Why do you think this occurred?
2. Did the actors seem to develop an understanding of each other? Why?
3. What do you think the outcome would have been?
4. Could the actors have improved their relationship? How?

h) After a discussion of the specific events that took place, encourage the group to relate the events to their jobs.

Your role as an instructor in role-play is very important, because you have to be alert to the emotional problems that can develop and to disturbing influences that may affect the actors and the audience. By skillfully handling the discussion, you can preserve each individual's dignity.

PROBLEM SITUATIONS OR CASE STUDIES

Presenting a problem situation or a case study gives participants an opportunity to apply new knowledge to specific situations. It stimulates discussion and participation.

To construct a case study, you should follow certain guidelines. First, the problem or case study should be so constructed that it is realistic as far as participants are concerned. They should be able to recognize it as pertaining to them and their jobs.

The statement of the problem or case study should be brief and simply worded. However, it should be complete enough to be understood. It can be made believable by including statements of individuals involved in the problem. These will be used to reveal attitudes and feelings. The problem or case study should be one that involves decision and action, and should suggest complex problems which are not evident. Finally, there should be definite instructions as to what is to be done. This is usually in the form of questions to be answered by the participants.

It's good to distribute a copy of the case study or problem to each individual so that he can refer to it as necessary.

The individuals should be given time to think on the problem and arrive at a solution. Then a discussion should be conducted. The purpose of the discussion is to help the individuals use problem-solving techniques.

You should guide the individuals to consider each of the following steps:

• Look for the real problem. By getting answers to questions such as who, what, when, where, why, you can pinpoint the problem and its causes.
• Gather all the facts. Guesswork and opinions must be eliminated.
• Evaluate the facts.
• Develop possible solutions.
• Select the best solution and apply it.

Although all steps may not apply to a particular problem or case study, the individuals should be aware of the steps.

THE SELECTION OF METHOD

You, as the instructor, should select the method to be used. No one method is best. The ideal is a combination of all three methods, lecture, discussion, performance. Many factors will influence your decision. You must consider the following determinants:

a. The subject.
b. Your objectives.
c. The size of the group.
d. The equipment available.
e. The time available.
f. The best way to present the subject.

g. The group's knowledge of the subject.
h. The kind of participation you want.

A combination of training methods will provide a change of pace and help maintain interest. It will help you emphasize the different facets of the subject, and make your sessions more stimulating and effective.

Job Instruction Training

by Dugan Laird

Every organization keeps saying, "When you get right down to it, the boss is responsible for training." Now there is more to this than meets the eye. It's not just a statement of responsibility, it's a statement of reality . . . a statement of inevitability. Why? Because in reality, as the boss you do train your subordinates all the time.

- You train them by the models you provide for them in the way you do your own work.
- You train when you coach and counsel.
- You train when you make comments about what you like and dislike in the work they do.
- You train in special sessions which you call "training," and in which you "tell and show" parts of their assigned duties.
- Above all, you train when you assign tasks, when you direct and when you follow-up. Yes, if you manage the work of others, you train those "others" by the sheer process of providing direction. Their productivity starts with your training.

ANYTHING YOU DO TO HELP THEM LEARN TO DO THEIR WORK THE WAY YOU WANT THEM TO DO THAT WORK— THAT'S TRAINING

Are you called "The President?" Then you train Vice-Presidents. Vice-Presidents in turn train Directors, who train Managers, who train Supervisors, Chiefs, or "Seniors." Call those positions whatever you like, a cascade of training, conscious or unconscious, is going on all the time at every level of every department in your organization. Training isn't like the weather, which everybody talks about, but nobody does anything about. Training isn't talked about very much, but everybody is doing it all the time.

So why not do it well? Why do it unconsciously, indirectly, clumsily?

One good reason for training well is that the best ways to train are also the simplest. They are the most efficient as well as the most effective and enduring. Another good reason for consciously training well is that since you are responsible for the output of those people who work for you, your best control of their output is through good training. Better that they learn what to do and how to do it from you than from someone else who doesn't know exactly what you want! If you train several people at one time, you get peer pressure (the "Japanese effect") reinforcing the new behaviors on the job.

Actually, this book is written for two very similar types of instructor: the boss who teaches just because "boss" is the title, and that great group of specialists known as "On-The-Job Trainers." Too often, the On-The-Job Trainer is a neglected specialist. Because he or she performed a task well, someone decided this was the logical person to train others. Great! Except nobody took the next step: teaching these master workers how to become trainers. The assumption that doing a task well qualifies someone to teach others to do that task is a risky and faulty assumption. We hope this book will help managers at all levels and On-The-Job Trainers to become professionals . . . to become professional trainers.

Now for many technical skills, or for skills required by huge numbers of workers in many departments, delegating training to a specialist called a "trainer" in the Training Department makes good sense. But for things which really matter the most, as a boss you'll want to maintain control. One trouble with sending people "off to training" is that distant instructors can't possibly know the peculiarities of your workplace, your individual people, or your own personal standards for getting the work done.

Besides, an effective trainer-subordinate relationship can be the foundation for a very rich boss-subordinate relationship. If you start an interactive, cooperative control, that makes being a "boss" a very satisfying experience!

Need we point out that if you are an On-The-Job Trainer, while you are training, you are "the boss"? At least you are the surrogate boss; the organization has charged you with responsibility for the work of others, and the "work" you are supposed to produce is the acquisition of the behavior or skill you are teaching.

Being a good trainer is not so difficult. Just remember that the structure of effective instruction is a simple six-step process:

1. ANALYZE THE TASK to be learned.
2. SET THE CLIMATE for the learning.
3. TELL the learners how to do the task.
4. SHOW the learners how to do the task.
5. LET THE LEARNERS DO THE TASK themselves.
6. REVIEW THEIR WORK in ways which reinforce their achievements and set goals for their improvement.

This basic process was developed (at least consciously identified) during World War II when many male workers went off to war and their replacements had to learn almost instantly how to carry on production in American factories. Overnight competence and excellence resulted from using the process.

The last four steps of the process are usually called Job Instruction Training, or JIT. We think of JIT most often when we think of manual tasks: welding, tying a shoelace, operating a machine, changing a tire. However, the JIT steps work just as well with mental operations such as determining the circumference of a circle, finding the square root, programming a computer, or interviewing. Executive decision making, financial planning, PERT (Program Evaluation and Review Technique)—any task which can be defined can be taught effectively if the trainer relates the content of the learning to the mental and psychological processes of the learner.

And that seems to be the power of JIT: it is consistent with the way human beings approach a new behavior. After the teacher has analyzed and defined the task, learners need the proper climate in which to learn. They need to hear how to do the task, then to see it in operation. (In many cases, these two needs can be met simultaneously.) After that, learners have a deep need to do the task themselves, and finally to review their own efforts with an authority figure.

Now of course not all people are alike, and research and experience since World War II indicate that the JIT process is enriched to precisely the degree

that the Boss-Trainer is sensitive to the needs and feelings of the individual learner. Setting the Climate thus becomes an important step in the learning process. Principles of feedback and reinforcement and humanistic psychology add meat to the bare bones of the Show-Tell-Do-Review formula: they make the act of training subordinates a thoroughly enriching experience for both boss and subordinate. There is mutual personal growth when bosses are the real trainers!

This humanistic enrichment makes the process of training more than a cut-and-dried application of the four-step formula. When the JIT system is operating at its best, it is merely a smooth interaction. Each of the steps is there—apparent to the Boss-Trainer, but evident to the learner only to the extent that each step is inevitable, comfortable, and logical. It's what they want to do and what they need to do to master a new behavior. Stated differently: as the Boss-Trainer you are aware that each step is being taken, but your learner-subordinate is merely sharing a logical and satisfying growth experience with the boss. And the satisfaction people get from growth is really something! Tiger and Fox, in a book called *The Imperial Animal* (1971),[1] point out that humans have a natural inclination to learn—and also one to teach. This should make the teacher-student relationship a very satisfying one. "That it often is not," they add, "May very well mean that . . . what is primarily a social relationship has become a technical transaction."

A view of traditional training would look something like this:

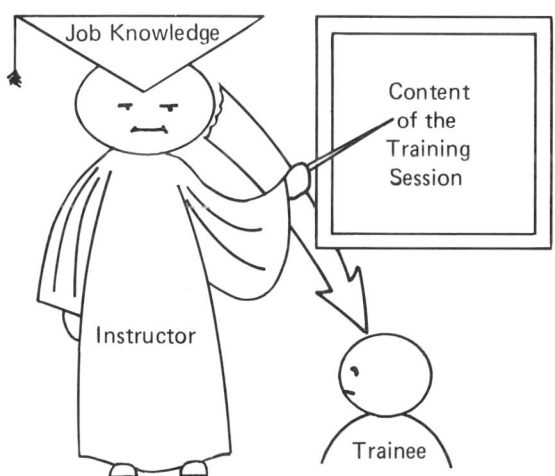

The object of the training was simply to transfer the knowledge from the head of the instructor into the head of the trainee. About all that is missing from the drawing was that the transaction pictured here may have been followed with a "practice session," at which the trainee tried out the new knowledge in a quest for skill in applying it. But even during such "exercises" the trainer acted like a drill sergeant, barking out orders, blowing the whistle, and leaving no doubt about who was in charge. Tiger and Fox (1971) describe such "dominance and attention" as "political rather than instructional" devices.

In interactive instruction, the process and the relationship between the teacher and learner are very different. They look more like this:

In this view of the learning process, the instructor and the learner cooperate and interact. Both dip into their existing fund of knowledge and experience to achieve new behaviors needed by the organization. The role of the instructor is not to control and command; rather it is to point the way and help the learner's growth.

Growth may be inevitable, but as recent research points out, it is not inevitably a comfortable thing. Psychologists like Dr. Carl Rogers have identified an "ambivalence"—a kind of mixed emotion we have about changing our behavior. Dr. Rogers (1969)[2]

says that humans have a natural potential for growth and learning, but that they also hate to give up old, familiar behaviors. Furthermore, they are a bit afraid of the new ways of doing things.

Malcolm Knowles has devoted much of his life to a study of the ways adults learn.[3] Freely translated, Knowles says that they feel they have "been around," and want to use their past experiences as the foundation for new learning. But unfortunately they sometimes use those past experiences as barriers to trying new ways to do things. Knowles has also found something that is good news to the Boss-Trainer and to On-The-Job Trainers; adults are anxious to learn those things which relate to their life roles—like being a parent, or a breadwinner, or a good employee. In other words, they want to learn the things you have to teach them because they know those new behaviors will help them fill their roles as employees in your organization.

Rogers (1969) has a similar discovery: "Significant learning occurs when the subject matter is perceived by the student as having relevance to his own purposes."

And B. F. Skinner, famous as a "behaviorist" psychologist, says that people will acquire and repeat behaviors for which they sense a personal reward. Well . . . you are the boss or you are the trainer, and as such you are the giver or withholder of on-the-job rewards! This will certainly influence and modify the way in which you administer the six-step JIT process: ANALYZE, SET THE CLIMATE, TELL, SHOW, DO and REVIEW. Furthermore, it offers still another compelling reason why you, the boss, are the best of all possible teacher-trainers.

REFERENCES

1. Lionel Tiger and Robin Fox, *The Imperial Animal* (New York: Holt, Rinehart and Winston, 1971), p. 152.
2. Carl R. Rogers, *Freedom to Learn* (Columbus, OH: Charles E. Merrill Publishing Company, 1969), pp. 157–158.
3. Malcolm S. Knowles, *The Adult Learner: A Neglected Species* (Houston: Gulf Publishing Company, 1973), p. 104.

How Training through Behavior Modeling Works

by Stephen Wehrenberg and Robert Kuhnle

Why does training through behavior modeling appear to work? Many theories have been proposed over the years to explain the determinants of human behavior and learning. Until recently, the major opposing theories were related to either internal drives (heredity) or external factors (environment). The heredity camp espouses the view that internal drives and inherited predisposition cause behavior. Achievement behavior is caused by an achievement motive, curiosity is driven by an inquisitive motive, etc. This argument becomes rather circular, however, when you consider that all we are doing is inferring a motive from the observed behavior.

This theory can be debated endlessly, but its empirical weaknesses cannot be ignored. Motive-behavior theories provide ready interpretation of past events, but are deficient in predicting future events.

The environmental camp believes that behavior is purely mechanical, caused by rewards for past behavior. The radical behaviorists say that we do what we do only because what we are doing has been somehow rewarded or shaped by rewards in the past.

This theory is rich in empirical research, but is still lacking in one important respect—learning becomes a very laborious and potentially dangerous process if we wait for the occurrence of random behaviors to be rewarded in order to elicit complex behavioral patterns. Behaviorist theories explain increased or decreased incident of behavior, but do less well in explaining the development of complex behaviors.

In the past few years, psychologists have reached some form of consensus, agreeing that both heredity and the environment play a part in causing behavior. This middle-of-the-road position is probably much more capable of explaining past events and predicting future behavior, even though the controversy still rages as to the exact relationship of heredity and environmental influences.

An even more general theory, probably a better representation of the "big picture" in behavior and learning, is that of social learning theorists, who agree that of course the environment affects behavior, and of course heredity affects behavior. Therefore, behavior does indeed seem to be a function of both.

There is another important relationship here, however: behavior impacts, and sometimes modifies, the environment as well. There seems to be a reciprocal interaction involved.

If we accept the concept that our interactions with the world around us are capable of modifying our basic "drives," this interaction becomes even more complex.

WHAT IS LEARNING?

But how do we learn complex social or cultural behaviors? Consider speech; we are born with the physical ability to make a wide range of sounds. These phonemes are somehow connected in combinations and related to events or objects around us. The chance of this occurring through reinforcement of random utterings is small at best. It is equally unlikely that we are born with the propensity to say, "Extraordinary!" after breast feeding. Most linguists agree that the development of language is imitative learning. Children imitate the sounds made by their parents or guardians and are usually reinforced for it. When baby finally says, "Da-da," mom excitedly gathers the entire family around the crib, cheering and awaiting the next profound statement.

The theory of imitative learning, more accurately called modeling, is not new. Studies date back to 1896. Modeling theory is very useful in explaining the learning process of complex behavioral patterns, and is so normal a procedure that we seldom even realize that we are involved in it. If we want our children to sharpen their own pencils, we get their attention (!), show them how to use the sharpener, let them try it, and then say "Good work! See, you can do it on your own. Aren't you grown-up!" We first acted as a model, and then reinforced the desired behavior that the tyke exhibited. This is a complex behavioral pattern: consider the difficulty involved in the process of waiting for Junior to randomly sharpen a pencil so that we could reward pencil-sharpening behavior!

Learning through modeling occurs constantly, all around us. Consider some of the imitative behaviors you have witnessed in children who are heavy television viewers. How does one learn to eat a lobster? By observing others. Drive a truck? Operate complex equipment? Shoot a bow and arrow? By observing others. Observational learning can add totally new behaviors to our repertoire and, when the model is punished or rewarded, can result in inhibitory or disinhibitory behavior as well. Research indicates that observing a modeled behavior coupled with punishment, such as the cheating gambler getting his just desserts, tends to reduce the likelihood of the observer exhibiting that behavior.[1]

Conversely, observing a modeled behavior coupled with a reward, such as a Girl Scout being patted on the head for helping an elderly person across the street, tends to increase this form of altruistic behavior. In sum, observing the response/consequences of others tends to give us expectations about rewards for our own future behavior. Modeled behaviors, plus anticipated rewards for those behaviors, will increase the incidence of those behaviors.

SHOW AND REWARD

This is a powerful concept with respect to supervisory training. If performance appraisal interviews are not seen as productive, we may either assume that supervisors do not have the necessary skill to conduct beneficial performance appraisal, or that the reward for doing so is either unknown or nonexistent. In order to develop this skill in supervisors, we must first show them how and then reward appropriate new behaviors. Seems simple, doesn't it? And yet, what a radical concept! We have assumed for years that managers and supervisors already possessed the requisite skills. Actually, the process isn't that simple. Any inattention to any of the components of the modeling process can reduce its effectiveness tremendously.

In general, the failure of the observer to match the modeled behavior may result from lack of attention to any of the processes involved: not observing the relevant activity, inadequately coding the modeled event, failure to retain the information relative to the event, physical inability to perform, or inefficient or nonexistent incentives.

At any rate, many organizations are putting their money on modeling to train their managers and supervisors. The list of users of this training process grows daily. Are the programs successful? It would seem so for those that follow the rules.

A MODEL TRAINING PROGRAM

A typical training program using behavior-modeling techniques as a foundation would be implemented in the following manner:

1) The Consultant/Trainer Conducts a Needs Analysis of the Organization. This consists of inter-views, surveys and statistical analysis in order to determine particularly weak areas in interpersonal relations. The results are clustered into specific areas for which this type of training is ideally suited. Some examples of the areas normally identified are: the conduct of performance appraisal interviews, dealing with rule infractions, reinforcement of appropriate behavior, reduction of tardiness and absenteeism, and orienting new employees. Ten or twelve critical skill areas are then selected by the consultant and top management to become the training topics.

2) Videotape "Models" Are Produced. This process consists of either shooting on-the-job videotapes in that organization or using prepared tapes. Each videotape addresses one specific skill area. It consists of an introduction by a high-level company officer, a listing of the "learning points" to be covered, and a portrayal of the situation by personnel from various areas in the organization. The learning points are followed exactly in sequence by these "actors," and the interpersonal encounter is always successful. The model does not address generalities or theories, but instead covers very specific job-related situations: for example, what to say and in what order to say it during a performance appraisal interview. The learning points are then reviewed.

3) Throughout the Entire Set of Videotape Models, Common Threads From Motivation Theory Tie the Process Together. Some common bonds are focusing on performance, building and maintaining people's self-image, using reinforcement, using reflective listening techniques, and setting concrete goals for changes in employee performance.

4) The Next Step Is the Selection of the Trainers. Trainers in most of the skills-training programs are line managers, not staff personnel. If the target population is shop heads and foremen, the trainers would be their supervisors (first-level managers). The managers are then given intensive training in the methods to be used when working with the foremen. This process may take up to four weeks (part-time), including video-taped practice sessions. When the managers are considered to be competent trainers, the training process begins.

5) The Managers Will Normally Train 6 to 12 Supervisors. Training sessions are usually scheduled one per week, taking either a full morning or afternoon. Ten modules therefore require ten weeks to complete. A typical training session follows this sequence:

The videotape model is shown. The trainer then reviews the learning points, writing them on a chart pad. The underlying principles (the common threads discussed above) are also listed on another chart pad.

A pair of trainees "rehearse" the encounter just as modeled on the videotape. One foreman plays the role of employee, and one acts as his or her immediate supervisor. During the rehearsal, the trainer stands behind the "employee" and steers the "supervisor" through the learning points, reinforcing appropriate responses and correcting ineffective ones. The trainer usually accomplishes this by using the two chart pads and hand gestures. The entire rehearsal is videotaped.

At the end of the encounter, the videotape is replayed. The trainer once again reviews the process, reinforcing the appropriate responses and correcting inappropriate ones. The other trainees are encouraged to comment as well, especially positive comments. These positive comments are also reinforced by the trainer. Another pair then rehearse the encounter, and so on, until each trainee has had the opportunity to imitate the model.

The instructor reviews both the learning points and the underlying principles again, this time facilitating discussion by the trainees. He or she then establishes a verbal contract with each trainee, having them discuss with whom and how they will apply their new-found technique during the week between training sessions.

At the next session, results of the on-the-job attempts at application are discussed. Once again, trainers reinforce successful encounters, and all participants talk over ways to correct unsuccessful ones. Then the next module is begun.

During this entire process, top-level management is indoctrinated in the basic principles of behavior modeling, which skill areas are being addressed, and how to recognize and reinforce those new behaviors that supervisors are expected to exhibit.

THE PLUS SIDE

Trainers involved in skills training through behavior modeling are inclined to agree that it is a superior method, mainly because it seems to address the pitfalls of past training. Transfer of new skills to the work place is enhanced because only specific, job-related problems are addressed. The "contract" phase of the training is also successful in this respect, while public commitment to a course of action acts as a strong motivator. This management support is enhanced by using line managers as trainers. Top-management commitment is shown through the introduction of each model by a top executive. Self-esteem and confidence

are built in the nonthreatening atmosphere of the classroom.

Rehearsal of the correct method of handling the interpersonal encounter is more effective than traditional role-play in which the trainees are typically allowed to "muddle through" the situation and are then criticized by the trainer and the class. The praise given by the trainer in the training process and the instantaneous feedback during rehearsal greatly enhance the trainee's self-esteem and serve as powerful reinforcers of new supervisory behaviors. Videotapes of the sessions enhance the quality and acceptance of the feedback.

One pioneer trainer thinks that his company's program is effective for several reasons.[2] For one, it affects supervisory behavior by teaching supervisors how to set goals through an iterative process (like MBO) by identifying tasks, establishing goals and standards, collecting performance data, and then reevaluating. Everyday, feedback skills are addressed (behavior-modification reinforcement techniques), and management support and reinforcement are provided for as well. The key issue in the system is performance appraisal, both ongoing and periodic.

Dr. Melvin Sorcher, now with Richardson-Merrell, Inc., was the staff psychologist for General Electric Company in 1970 when he developed a supervisory-training scheme using behavior-modeling techniques that was the model on which most trainers have based subsequent work.[3] The concepts are fundamentally the same as those discussed so far, addressing nine basic skills:

1. Orienting a new employee
2. Giving recognition (positive reinforcement)
3. Motivating a poor performer
4. Correcting poor work habits
5. Discussing potential disciplinary action
6. Reducing absenteeism
7. Handling a complaining employee
8. Reducing turnover
9. Overcoming resistance to change.

One difference in the process was the use of two trainers, one to facilitate the rehearsal sessions and one to ensure that the feedback given to the participants by the other trainees was positive and constructive. Sorcher thinks that managing the entire reinforcement scheme in the classroom is critical to retention of information and motivation to attempt new behaviors.

Sorcher claims long-lasting, measurable improvement in performance on the part of the supervisors, and a measurable difference in worker productivity as a result of the training. Sorcher also claims to have helped bridge the communication gap between white supervisors and predominantly black hourly workers.

Many other major companies have followed the lead of GE in instituting supervisory training based on behavior modeling. However, very few of these training programs have been assessed in a controlled, scientific manner.

ARE THE CLAIMS OF THE ENTREPRENEURS VALID

The claims made by the trainers involved with behavior modeling are not new. Every new supervisory-training scheme has had the same kind of fanfare, from Scientific Management to T-Groups. Unfortunately, few of the claims are empirically based. Only recently have any major studies been conducted in a scientific manner to assess the training of interpersonal skills.

One of the reasons for this is the lack of concrete, measurable factors of performance for managers and supervisors. Assessing the impact of an independent variable (training) is nothing more than noting the difference between the "before" and "after." This line of reasoning assumes that you can accurately measure supervisory skills in the first place. Of course, this is not as easy as it seems. How does one measure, accurately and objectively, performance as intangible as that of a supervisor? The concept of performance standards and evaluation of supervision is as hotly debated today as it was 50 years ago, and there are almost as many performance appraisal schema as there are companies to implement them.

For the purpose of assessing the impact and effectiveness of training using behavior modeling, we must either assume that the in-place performance appraisal system is accurate, or develop our own standards against which to measure performance and behavioral changes. Researchers have done either or both. Of course, it is recognized that behavioral changes could best be measured by direct observation, but this ethnographic approach is costly and time-consuming. One longitudinal study is currently underway in the U.S. Coast Guard, and another (of one-year duration) has been completed by Sorcher and Goldstein[4] as reported by Latham and Saari.[5]

Latham measured the impact of a program conducted at General Electric by Sorcher along four dimensions: participant reaction to the training, learning, behavioral change, and performance (using formal performance appraisal).

Reaction Measures.   Participation was mandatory for this experimental group of supervisors. Initial reactions were predictably unfavorable. But by the third session, comments such as "There's no way I can out-maneuver him when he sticks to those damn learning points!" were commonly expressed by the individuals taking the role of employee. A reaction questionnaire given at the end of the program yielded a mean response of 4.15 on a 5-point scale. This was supported behaviorally by the fact that some of the employees had scheduled vacations during the 9 weeks of the program, and all voluntarily attended the classes during their vacations. The questionnaire was administered once again eight months after the training and indicated that the initial positive reaction was sustained over time.

Learning.   However, reaction to training is not necessarily related to effectiveness, or even evidence of attempts at new behaviors. Prior to attempting new behaviors, one must at least retain a knowledge of those behaviors, in this case, the learning points and underlying principles. Latham's learning measure consisted of an 85-item situational test. Questions were phrased, "How would you handle the following situation. . . ."

The measured mean of the experimental group was 27.6 points higher than that of a control group. This indicates that there was a measurable knowledge increase in the interpersonal skills addressed. There was also considerable generalization to new situations, based on the underlying principles of the training.

Behavioral.   Reaction and learning measures, even when combined, do not necessarily reflect behavioral and performance changes, however. Behavioral measures are critical in determining if transfer of the skills from the classroom to the work place has occurred. Obviously, observation by trained psychologists would be preferable, but other measures are more easily implemented. Latham's report outlines the behavior measures used by General Electric, which were assessments of videotapes made of supervisors reacting to various scripted interviews. For example, the supervisor was instructed: "You have just called in the employee sitting in front of you to inform him that you are switching him from the day shift to the night shift. You suspect that he may not want to make the shift. Show how you would handle this situation." The employee, actually a trained supervisor from another part of the plant, was told: "Your supervisor has just called you into her office. You have heard that she wants you to work the night shift. You resent this very much. Show what you would do in this situation." None of the situations had been used in the training sessions, either on the videotaped models, or during the rehearsals.

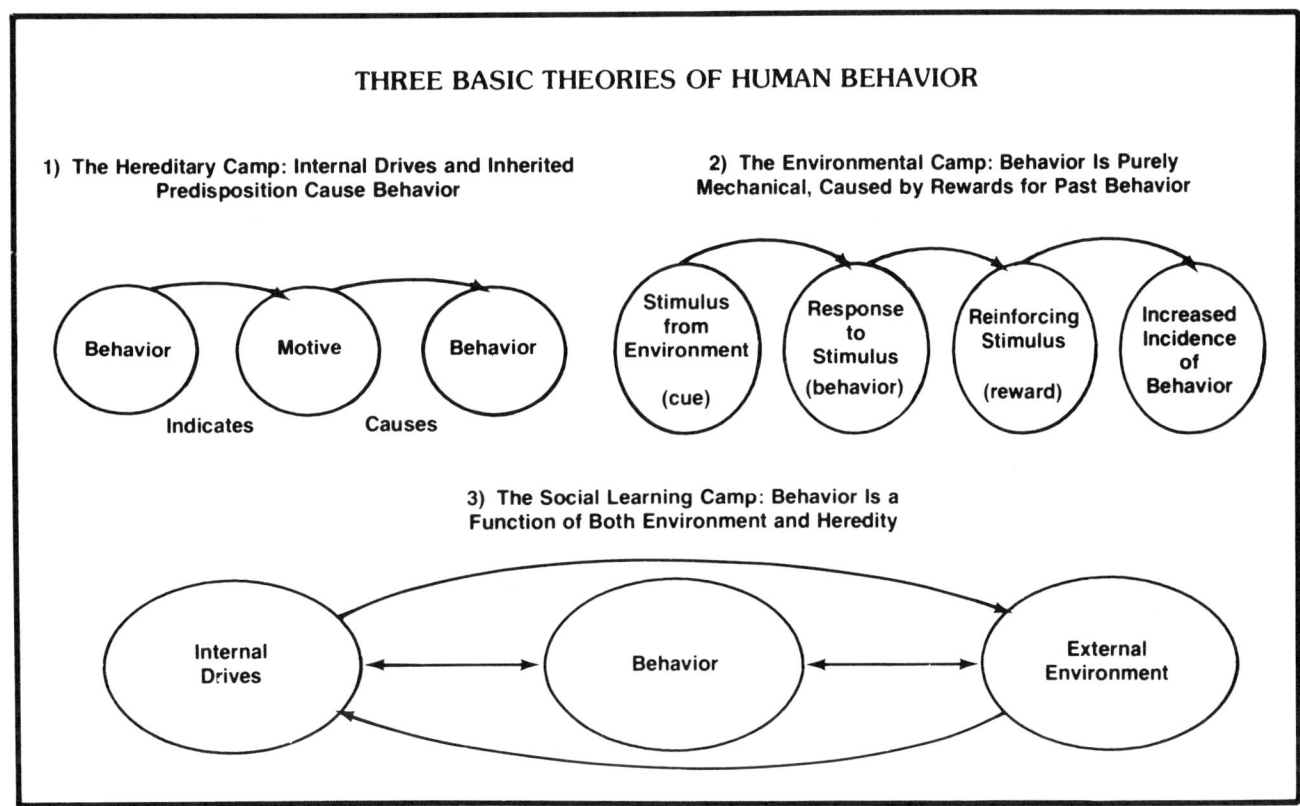

THREE BASIC THEORIES OF HUMAN BEHAVIOR

1) **The Hereditary Camp: Internal Drives and Inherited Predisposition Cause Behavior**

Behavior — Indicates → Motive — Causes → Behavior

2) **The Environmental Camp: Behavior Is Purely Mechanical, Caused by Rewards for Past Behavior**

Stimulus from Environment (cue) → Response to Stimulus (behavior) → Reinforcing Stimulus (reward) → Increased Incidence of Behavior

3) **The Social Learning Camp: Behavior Is a Function of Both Environment and Heredity**

Internal Drives ↔ Behavior ↔ External Environment

The videotaped sessions were evaluated by groups of superintendents from other parts of the plant. The employee's behavior was also rated in order to generate a "difficulty factor" in calculating the supervisors performance rating. Once again, the supervisors trained through behavior modeling were judged superior along the dimensions measured, scoring 1.27 points higher (on a 5-point scale) than a control group that was also assessed.

Thus, it would appear that not only was learning enhanced by the training, but also that the use of behavior-modeling techniques facilitated both transfer to the work place and generalization of the learning to different, untrained situations.

Performance.   All of the measures described thus far could be called internal criteria, since they only assess skill in performing the behaviors (or similar ones) that the program was designed to teach. A critical question is whether the training brought about any long-term changes in performance on the job.

The participants, and a control group, were evaluated one month before and one year after the training. The evaluative criteria were based on a job analysis, and the superintendents doing the rating were trained in minimizing rater error. The premeasure indicated no significant differences between the two groups, but the postmeasure indicated that the

trained group performed considerably more effectively as supervisors than the control group, by more than half a point on a 5-point scale. As a further check, the company's traditional performance appraisal system was used, and the results were basically the same.

Although the study by Latham and Saari is not conclusive evidence, it certainly indicates that supervisory skills training using behavior-modeling techniques may have a significant, positive, long-term impact on supervisor performance. To further support this contention, the control group used in the study was trained using the same program one year after the first group, and the results indicated that subsequent to this training, there were no significant differences between the groups in any of the four measures.

A rather interesting and reliable assessment of a supervisory relationships training program instituted at American Telephone and Telegraph was used by Moses and Ritchie.[6] Their technique was to validate the measurement of impact on the training through the use of an assessment center. The supervisors were trained in the skill areas discussed earlier. Four to seven weeks after the training, ninety trained and ninety-three untrained supervisors, matched in experience, age and sex, attended the center. The evaluators at the assessment center were professionals, trained in behavior observation and the use of specially constructed rating scales. The staff did not know which supervisors had been trained or even which skill areas had been addressed in the training.

Each supervisor was given three simulated problem-solving discussions to handle with an employee. Following each discussion, the staff independently completed a rating scale designed to evaluate the effectiveness of the discussion. Each supervisor handled two problem areas covered in the training, and one dealing with a new situation. The results of the individual assessments were then discussed by teams of evaluators, and consensus was reached as to overall ratings for each supervisor.

The overall ratings found that 84% of the trained supervisors achieved ratings of above average or exceptional, compared to 32% of the untrained group. Only 6% of the trained group were considered below average or poor, while 33% of the untrained group were in this category.

As an added benefit, management subjectively noted that the trained supervisors initiated more discussions with employees about performance. They also appeared better able to confront the face-to-face supervisor-employee communication that seems so difficult in most settings.

COMING FULL CIRCLE

At a casual glance, it would seem that we have come full circle in our concepts of manager training—from showing to showing. Proponents of the old "trait" school used to say, "If you want to build a good leader, show a good leader." That position has changed slightly, however. Now we say, "Show a good leader, *leading*."

The process of training using behavior modeling is very complex, and so a good foundation in social learning theory is prerequisite (but certainly not sufficient). Because of its measured impact on performance, modeling appears to be the new vogue in management training. Let's hope that it isn't just an ill-used fad.

REFERENCES

1. Albert Bandura, *Social Learning Theory* (Englewood Cliffs, New Jersey: Prentice-Hall, 1977).
2. J. Robinson, "Interaction Modeling: A New Concept in Supervisory Training," *Training and Development Journal*, February 1976.
3. A. P. Goldstein and M. Sorcher, *Changing Supervisory Behavior* (New York: Pergamon Press, 1974).
4. Ibid.
5. Gary P. Latham and Lise M. Saari, "Application of Social Learning Theory to Training Supervisors Through Behavior Modeling," *Journal of Applied Psychology*, Vol. 64, No. 3 (1979):239–246.
6. J. Moses and D. Ritchie, "Assessment Center Used to Evaluate an Interaction Modeling Program," *Assessment and Development Newsletter*, January 1975.

The Miniature Job Training and Evaluation Approach: Additional Findings

by Arthur I. Siegel

Miniature job training and evaluation situations were developed and administered to 1034 "low aptitude" Navy recruits. Checklist criterion data describing the on-the-job performance of the sample were collected after the recruits were on their fleet assignments: (1) nine months, and (2) 18 months. The results confirmed prior findings relative to the predictive validity of the miniature job training and evaluation approach and supported contentions favoring the power of the concept over a paper-and-pencil testing approach.

Siegel and Bergman (1975) described a job learning approach to performance prediction and concluded, among other things, that "The miniature training and evaluation concept appears to possess merit as a technique for predicting the performance of 'low aptitude' applicants." Cohen and Penner (1976) expressed con-

Reprinted with the permission of *Personnel Psychology*, Durham, North Carolina, © 1983. All rights reserved.

cern about some of the procedures employed by Siegel and Bergman and stressed the need for cross-validation. Accordingly, the miniature job training and evaluation concept was independently reevaluated employing a new and larger sample.

THE MINIATURE JOB TRAINING AND EVALUATION APPROACH

The miniature job training and evaluation approach was conceptualized at Applied Psychological Services as at least a partial answer to test relevance and test fairness issues. The approach is based on the conjecture that a person who can demonstrate the ability to learn and perform on a job sample will be able to learn and perform on the total job—given appropriate on the job training. This approach suggests both a training and a measurement aspect to the testing situation. Specifically, the job seeker is trained to perform a sample of tasks involved in the job for which he is an applicant and, immediately following the training, his ability to perform these tasks is measured. Within the training aspect, full attention is given to individual differences, "hands-on" training, minimization of literacy requirements, and the like. The test, similarly, is of the performance nature.

RELATED WORK

Since the work of Siegel and Bergman (1975), the results of studies into the miniature training and evaluation approach which have appeared in the open literature all support contentions favoring the potential of the approach.

Under the sponsorship of the Navy Personnel Research and Development Center (Siegel and Wiesen, 1977), the miniature job training and evaluation concept was extended to the assessment center context. The extension of the assessment center approach to technical jobs represents an elaboration of the approach to nonmanagerial jobs and was previously suggested as a possible area of investigation by Bray and Moses (1972).

Siegel and Wiesen developed a battery of nine miniature job training and evaluation exercises and administered the exercises to 140 recruits whose scores on Navy paper-and-pencil tests, employed for selection/classification at the time, caused them to be considered to be ineligible for assignment to a Navy school. Each recruit in the sample was evaluated by a team of assessors in terms of how well he would succeed in a selected job specialty. This allowed comparison of the actual miniature training and evaluation exercise scores with the combined overall opinion of

the assessors. To this end, a stepwise multiple linear regression analysis procedure was used. In other contexts, the approach has been termed "policy capturing."

Stepwise multiple correlation coefficients (six predictors) were calculated between the miniature training and evaluation situations and the composite estimate of the assessors for a "general rates" subgroup, a machinist's mate subgroup, and for the total sample. The resultant multiple correlation coefficients were, respectively: .68, .81, and .65. The corresponding multiple correlation coefficients for the Navy paper-and-pencil tests which were employed at the time were: .12, .41, and .23.

Cory (1981) studied the Siegel and Wiesen group after its members were assigned to duty in the Fleet. Cory's criteria were two sets of supervisory ratings of job performance. Cory employed multiple regression procedures to estimate the two criteria. The analyses were carried out using step-wise accretion and shrunken multiple correlations were computed by way of the technique recommended by Thiel (1971). Cory used a hierarchical selection procedure in which variables were made available to the regression program a set at a time for three sets of variables: (1) currently employed paper-and-pencil test scores, (2) biographical variables, and finally, (3) miniature job training and evaluation scores. Cory placed the following restrictions on the multiple regression computations in an attempt to limit the capitalization on chance and resulting over prediction: (1) the predictor sets were limited to those which had zero-order validity coefficients which were significantly different from zero, (2) the variables added as predictors during multiple regression steps were required to add to the validity of the battery at $p = .05$, and (3) no variable was selected as a predictor unless at least 30% of its variance was independent of the combined variance of the predictors previously selected. Cory found that batteries formed from the Navy paper-and-pencil selection/classification test scores and biographical scores had shrunken validity coefficients of .42 for the two criteria. Miniature training and evaluation variables "added from .12 to .31, which resulted in maximum shrunken validity coefficients for these criteria of .55 and .73."

There has also been prior work over the years on the trainability approach in the United Kingdom. Most of this work was reviewed by Robertson and Downs (1979) and was concerned with skilled and semiskilled trades in the civil sphere. The criterion in almost all cases was some type of training success. However, remarkably high validity coefficients were generally reported and, in the two cases in which an on-the-job rating measure was employed, validity coefficients of .69 and .45 were reported.

PURPOSES OF PRESENT WORK

The present work sought to reevaluate the miniature job training and evaluation approach by applying the approach to a larger sample and a greater number of Navy job specialties. As such, the results serve to address some of the concerns of Cohen and Penner about the prior work of Siegel and Bergman.

EXERCISES, METHODS, PROCEDURES, AND CRITERIA

Siegel and Wiesen (1977) previously developed a battery of miniature job training and evaluation situations for Navy recruits. These situations were, by and large, administered individually and, as a result, required considerable administrative time. A revision of this battery, to allow group testing, was determined to be a feasible and desirable goal. A one-half-day testing period was established as a goal for group administration of the battery. In the redesign of the components of the battery, four objectives were kept in mind: (1) establish a high degree of correspondence with actual tasks of Navy personnel, (2) minimize paper-and-pencil aspects, (3) establish hands-on training where possible, and (4) create an environment where individualized instruction and feedback are possible.

Nine group administered miniature job training and evaluation situations were created within these global objectives. Each of these is briefly described below.

Computation and Projection (CAP)

In the training aspect of the Computation and Projection (CAP) miniature training and evaluation situation, intercept course projection was taught. This included instruction about how to read a simplified plot diagram of the positions of two ships, their headings and speeds, and how to: (1) extrapolate the new position of each ship after one hour, and (2) evaluate the danger of collision. Simple addition, subtraction, and ruler measurement were required to perform the work. After a training and a practice session, problems were administered in a group session. Three subscores (projection, collision identification, and course change direction) were summed to derive a total subtest score.

Conceptual Integration and Application (CIA)

In the Conceptual Integration and Application (CIA) training session, the operation of an elementary, simulated electromechanical pumping system was ex-

plained and demonstrated. Potential malfunctions were diagnosed and the cause-effect relationships behind each diagnosis were explained. This ability to integrate facts and system relationships and to derive a conclusion about the cause of a malfunction is commonly termed "trouble-shooting." After the training session and a set of practice problems, 10 problems involving system malfunction symptoms were group administered. The task was to state the cause of each malfunction. Score on the subtest was right minus wrong.

Tool and Object Nomenclature, Use, and Recognition (TAO)

Ability to learn the name and use of objects was measured by the Tool and Object (TAO) exercise. Such a requirement is common to the entry level for most Navy job specialties. During the training, 10 different Navy oriented items were displayed and named. The use of each was also described. The items were passed among the group members who were encouraged to voice the name while they held and inspected each object. This holding and voicing of the name was considered to constitute practice. The test situation was based on the recruits' ability to remember the names and uses of the objects.

The evaluation was group administered and yielded three subscores (names, use, and recall) and a total subtest score. The total subtest score was the sum of the three subscores.

Dual Task (DT)

The ability to share time between the performance of two or more different tasks is required for many Navy jobs. Watch keeping and equipment operation are examples. The simultaneous performance of two tasks was consolidated into the Dual Task (DT) exercise: (1) simulated watch standing, and (2) fabricating a pipe assembly. In the watch standing aspect, the persons under evaluation attended to a series of "alarm" lights and recorded their time of occurrence. The pipe assembly task included assembly of a set of pipes in accordance with a schematic diagram.

During the training aspect of the exercise, schematic diagram interpretation and how to make the required measurements for completing the pipe assembly task were taught. In the evaluation aspect, the recruits were required to fabricate the pipe assembly while simultaneously monitoring the "alarm" lights and entering their time of activation on a simulated log form. The total score for the subtest was the sum of the pipe assembly and the alarm reaction scores.

Inspection/Sort (SOR)

In the training aspect of the Inspection/Sort (SOR) situation, recognition of "good" and of "defective" items was taught and practiced. The practice was monitored and feedback of results was provided. Then, the performance aspect was administered. In the performance aspect of the exercise, the ability to detect imperfections or deviations from standards in five categories of objects was tested. Nondeviant objects, from a pool of deviant and nondeviant objects, were sorted into the appropriate bin for that category while all deviant objects were sorted into a "reject" bin. The total score was the sum of three subscores (speed, good items—accuracy, and bad items—accuracy).

Record Keeping (RK)

In the training aspect of the Record Keeping (RK) situation, reading displays of ship's speeds and heading were taught along with how to log their values and "out of tolerance" conditions. In the evaluation aspect, 20 problems were presented. The score was the sum of five subscores (heading, heading out of tolerance, speed, speed out of tolerance, and time). Such an exercise measures general alertness, short-term memory for numbers, and ability to evaluate information against a structured criterion.

Social Interaction (SI)

Work group interactive and role assumption tendencies were measured by the Social Interaction (SI) exercise. There was no training aspect to this exercise. From three to six persons worked as a team to develop a plan of approach to folding a large tarpaulin into a form indicated on a schematic diagram. Four problems were included. Each involved both a planning and a plan execution phase. The behavior of each team member was rated on cooperation, leadership, motivation, rule breaking, shirking, and interference and these were summed to yield a total subtest score.

Precision and Planning (PP)

In the Precision and Planning (PP) exercise, training was administered on how to work with an orthographic drawing to produce an object. The evaluation involved fabrication of an object depicted on a second orthographic drawing. The medium of construction was clay. A T-square and knife were provided as tools. Successful completion of such an exercise involves planning an approach to work, careful measurement,

precise hand-eye coordination, and three dimensional visualization. The total subtest score was based on measurements of the quality (dimensions, surface quality, and angles) of the final object.

Relating Diagrams with Objects (ET)

In the training for Relating Diagrams with Objects (ET), symbols representing standard representations of electronic and electrical components were presented. The components were placed on a table together with their associated symbols. The trainees walked around the table and studied the associations. They were allowed further time to study a card showing pictures of the objects and the associated symbol for each component, side-by-side. Next, fabrication of a simple electrical assembly on the basis of a diagram showing interconnected symbols was taught and practiced. In the evaluation aspect, five somewhat more complex assembly tasks were presented. The final score was the sum of the individual scores for the five assemblies.

Administrators' Manual Development, Administrator Training, and Administration

With the tests on hand, a complete administrators' manual was developed. The administrators' manual was fully detailed and included for each miniature training and evaluation situation a full description of the procedures including a standardized text for the training aspect, standardized test administrative instructions, and full scoring and timing instructions. Other sections of the administrators' manual were concerned with such topics as: the nature, scope, and purpose of the present program, background information on the miniature training and evaluation approach, samples of various session management forms, the schedule to be followed, privacy rights of the individuals assessed, and special problems and how to manage them.

The battery was administered in two large rooms. One room was used largely for training purposes while the other was largely employed to administer the evaluation aspects. Individual test stations were provided for each person under evaluation. Chalk boards, projectors, and full training amenities were available for the purposes of the program.

The administrators' manual was developed as a partial basis for assuring full professionalism and standardization within the program. To assure further that these goals would be met, formal administrator training was implemented. This training involved three days and included: (a) a detailed formal review of and elaboration of the materials in the manual (the administrators studied the manual during the first four hours of the training), (b) practice exercise administration by each administrator with a critique by the exercise developers, (c) a "dry run" of one day's operation employing the precise methods to be employed in the conduct of the program, and (d) review and discussion of the "dry run" by the staff.

Sample

The miniature job training and evaluation battery was administered to 1034 male enlisted personnel at the Apprentice School, Naval Training Center, San Diego, during the period March 1978 through September 1978. These persons were in either the seaman, fireman, or airman ratings and were subsequently assigned to Fleet jobs. All persons in the sample had been previously judged by customary methods to be not A School qualified. The Navy A schools provide specialized job training in a number of specific skill areas.

VALIDATION

In order to assess the predictive validity of the miniature job training and evaluation battery, two followups were completed. The first followup was completed after the persons in the sample were in the Fleet for about nine months and the second was completed after the members of the sample were on their Fleet assignments for about 18 months.

Job Skill Technical Forms

To provide on-the-job performance criterion information, "job skill technical forms" were developed. The job skill technical forms attempted to gain information about the ability of the recruit to perform the technical aspects of his work. Three such forms were constructed—one for seamen, one for firemen, and one for airmen.

Each form contained a list of tasks (about 34 tasks per list) which an entry level seaman, fireman, or airman may perform. The tasks were taken from NAVPERS 18068D, *Section 1, Navy Enlisted Occupational Standards* and contained such tasks as: "steer by compass" (seaman), "use lubricating oils and greases" (fireman), and "make aircraft tiedown lines" (airman).

Each form required the immediate supervisor to rate, using the appropriate list, each person in the sample whom he supervised on the performance of each listed task. The rating on each task was performed on a seven category scale which ranged from "very poorly" through "very well." Scoring was completed by assigning a score of one to "very poorly," two to "poorly" . . . , seven to "very well." The final criterion score for any person was the average across all items (tasks) he performed.

Administration of Criterion Instruments

Approximately nine months after the members of the sample were on their first assignment, a set of criterion forms was distributed directly to each Commanding Officer at the appropriate location of each sample member along with a request that a job skill technical form be completed by each sample member's immediate supervisor. The materials were transmitted as individual packets (one for each sample member) and the information required for correct identification (e.g., name of sample member and his social security number) was on the cover sheet of the packet.

A parallel procedure was followed after the recruits were on their assignments for approximately 18 months.

For the first followup, 405 useable results packets were returned; for the second followup, 304 useable returns were received.

While this return rate (39% and 29%) is low by ordinary standards, it is not unusual for military work. While the first enlistment attrition rate in the military varies from year to year, a 50% attrition rate is not unusual. Additionally, a high mobility rate in the military makes followup studies difficult. There was no difference between the subjects from whom returns were received and for whom criterion data were not received on the usual Navy paper-and-pencil tests and the duty assignment process was equivalent for all subjects.

DISCUSSION

The present set of results substantially supports the prior findings (Siegel and Bergman, 1975) favoring the value of the miniature job training and evaluation concept.

However, the obtained validity coefficients should not be directly compared with the validity coefficients reported by Siegel and Bergman (1975) because the Siegel and Bergman coefficients are multiple correlation coefficients while the present validities are reported as zero order coefficients. Obviously, the multiple correlation of the miniature training and evaluation scores with the criteria would be higher than for any individual test score alone.

The decreased validity for the second followup, as compared with the first followup, is in accordance with prior findings (Siegel and Bergman, 1975; Robertson and Kandola, in press). While the predictive power of all selection instruments may attenuate over time, it is possible that performance oriented tests of the work sample and the miniature job training and evaluation nature, attenuate to a greater extent over time than the more usual type of predictor. As suggested by Robertson and Kandola, work methods and requirements may make such tests more susceptible to attenuation effects.

The obtained predictive validity correlation coefficients for the individual miniature job training and evaluation exercises must also be viewed against the perspective of a number of criterion problems. These include range restriction (only low aptitude personnel were included in the sample), possible rater error in the criterion data (it was not possible to train the supervisors in rating methods and some of the supervisors may have approached the rating task more seriously than others), and criterion unreliability (discussed earlier).

When one considers an approach such as that characterized by the miniature job training and evaluation concept, the person must, in the long run, come to grips with the feasibility of the approach. While the miniature job training and evaluation exercises were designed for group administration, their very nature limits the size of a group to whom the exercises may be administered. With their emphasis on individual instruction during the training aspect, miniature training and evaluation exercises place a heavier demand on the number of administrative personnel required and on the required level of the training of the administration personnel. Moreover, the facility and equipment requirements are more complex for miniature training and evaluation exercises than for the usual paper-and-pencil test. The question is whether or not such cost and convenience considerations should outweigh the benefits of the approach. Prior work (Siegel and Bergman, 1972, 1973; Siegel and Wiesen, 1977) indicated that Navy recruits accept the miniature training evaluation approach as "fair" and favor it over a paper-and-pencil testing approach.

As a personnel selection/classification test concept, the miniature training and evaluation approach possesses at least three important attributes: (1) job content relevancy, (2) construction based on accepted methods and all aspects of administration and scoring fully standardized, and (3) more acceptable to disadvantaged persons than the usual paper-and-pencil test.

Accordingly, a practical decision on the utility of the miniature job training and evaluation approach must counterbalance the cost considerations against the positive psychometric data, the social implications, the legal implications, and the importance of proper selection/classification. While the result will depend on the weight which one places on each of these diverse and complex issues, it seems that the scale will tilt in favor of the miniature job training and evaluation approach.

REFERENCES

- Bray, D. W. and Moses, J. L. Personnel selection. *Annual Review of Psychology*, 1972, 23, 545–576.
- Cory, C. H. *The assignment of general detail personnel in the Navy: Fleet followup of personnel appraised in a technical classification assessment center (NPRDCTN 81)*. San Diego: Navy Personnel Research and Development Center, 1981.
- Cohen, S. L. and Penner, L. A. The rigors of predictive validation: Some comments on "a job learning approach to performance prediction." *Personnel Psychology*, 1976, 29, 595–600.
- Guilford, J. P. and Fruchter, B. *Fundamental statistics in psychology and education*. New York: McGraw-Hill, 1978.
- Robertson, I. T. and Downs, S. Learning and prediction of performance: Development of trainability testing in the United Kingdom. *Journal of Applied Psychology*, 1979, 64, 42–50.
- Robertson, I. T. and Kandola, R. S. Work sample tests: Validity, adverse impact and applicant reaction. *Journal of Occupational Psychology*, 1982, 55, (in press).
- Siegel, A. I. and Bergman, B. A. *Nonverbal and culture fair performance prediction procedures. I. Background, test development, and initial results*. Wayne, PA: Applied Psychological Services, 1972.
- Siegel, A. I. and Bergman, B. A. *Nonverbal and culture fair performance prediction procedures. II. Initial validation*. Wayne, PA: Applied Psychological Services, 1973.
- Siegel, A. I. and Bergman, B. A. A job learning approach to performance prediction, Personnel Psychology, 1975, 28, 325–339.
- Siegel, A. I. and Wiesen, J. P. *Experimental procedures for the classification of Naval personnel (NPRDC TR 77-3)*. San Diego: Navy Personnel Research and Development Center, August, 1977.
- Thiel, H. *Principles of econometrics*. New York: Wiley, 1971.

Assessment Centers: For Selection or Development?

by Gary L. Hart and Paul H. Thompson

In recent years, many organizations have turned to assessment centers to improve their effectiveness in selecting managers. One study by Byham and Pentecost reported that between 1960 and 1970 more than 70,000 people were assessed by their employers. Since that time, assessment centers have proliferated, although there is little systematic information on just how many organizations are using them. One reason for their popularity is that most have increased their company's ability to select employees who perform successfully as managers.

For many organizations, however, the growth of the past 20 years has slowed and employee levels have become more stable. Career development is thus a more pressing issue in these organizations than is the selection of managers. In addition, there is increasing evidence that some assessment centers used for selection purposes are creating problems for the organizations involved. For example:

• In Germany a research laboratory for a large multinational corporation established an assessment center for selecting managers. After three years, the center had to be discontinued. A large group of unhappy engineers who had "flunked" the assessment center threatened to shut down the operation unless the assessment center was eliminated as a manager-selection device.
• A promising young accountant, who was highly respected by his superiors, was invited to participate in an assessment center. Unfortunately, he flunked. Whatever the reasons, he did not do well during the three-day assessment, and his supervisor was advised that the accountant would no longer be considered for promotional opportunities. All the evidence, except the assessment center results, indicated that he had outstanding technical, interpersonal, and management skills. But now this young accountant's future with his present company is no longer bright.
• A large engineering-based corporation in the United States invested a lot of money in developing an assessment center, but they dropped it after only two years. An executive of the company indicated that the assessment center demoralized the

Reprinted by permission of the publisher, from *Organizational Dynamics, Spring 1979.* © 1979 by AMACOM, a division of American Management Associations. All rights reserved.

managers and sometimes had a negative impact on their performance. Top management saw very few benefits and a lot of problems, so they decided to discontinue the center.

What went wrong in these organizations? Our investigation indicates that assessment centers are generating problems such as:

1. Too much faith in the results from assessment centers: A high-quality center can provide very useful information, but the results do not correlate 100 percent with future performance. A number of studies have been conducted that correlate assessment findings and subsequent performance. Byham's review of six studies showed that the correlations ranged from 0.27 to 0.64. These correlations are higher than the results from many other selection techniques, but no one has the right to dispose of other people's careers on the basis of a 0.64 correlation—let alone a 0.27 correlation. In the case of the young accountant, management placed too much emphasis on the assessment center results. With a lot of contrary evidence, why were they so willing to "write him off" as a potential manager?
2. Employees told that their future opportunities are limited by the assessment center results: The experience of the corporation in Germany illustrates the problems in such an approach. Managers not only used the center results as the sole and final word about the employees' management potential, but the employees who did poorly were told that they would never be offered managerial positions. Of course, the number of disappointed assessees grew as the program continued. Eventually the group became so large and disgruntled that they confronted management and forced it to drop the program.
3. Faulty methods of selecting people to attend the assessment center: The engineering company ran into this problem. The company's management assumed that managerial skills were self-evident and that people with high potential were easily recognizable. These employees were not invited to participate in the assessment program. Only those with questionable potential were assessed. Consequently, because the number of "graduates" who received promotions was practically

zero, participation in an assessment center was viewed as something to be avoided, and fewer people were willing to accept such an invitation. Top management began to sense the resistance to the assessment center, and agreed to discontinue the program.

One reason these problems have developed with assessment centers is that too much emphasis has been placed on selection and not enough on development. Most people who promote the assessment center approach have "sold" the company on its effectiveness as a selection tool, underestimating their value in developing managers. This is understandable, as selection has been a particularly pressing problem during the past 20 years. Many organizations have been growing rapidly and have been promoting people with relatively little experience. In that situation an assessment center can be of considerable help in selecting people with management potential. However, the problems have changed dramatically during the 1970s. Most organizations are no longer growing so rapidly, and promotions are less frequent. The focus is shifting from selection to development. For example, one manager observed:

Our division grew rapidly for fifteen years. We were adding new employees at a rate of 10 percent per year. But that stopped in the early 1970s, and now we're growing at 1 percent per year. That shift has created many problems. First, we have a group of supervisors between the ages of 40 and 50 who are stuck; they won't be promoted any further, and we don't know what to do with them. We also have a group of engineers between the age of 30 and 40 who are ready to be promoted to supervisory positions, but there are very few supervisory positions opening up.

This change is a little extreme, but similar shifts in growth patterns are common in large organizations. This manager is not worried about selection—he has a lot of information on all these people. The challenge now is to help them develop their careers.

In observing such trends, we have concluded that assessment centers should be used for development purposes rather than for selection of managers. This article describes one company's experience in using an assessment center for employee development. The organization involved is an IBM* research laboratory employing about 400 scientists, technicians, and administrative staff. The success of this program suggests that assessment center technology can be used for development and self-selection through career planning more effectively than for management selection directly. The center was developed in response to

a serious need for management development and career-planning activities in a research laboratory. While most of this article addresses itself to that experience, the same approach has been used in manufacturing and development environments with similar success.

THE CAREER DEVELOPMENT WORKSHOP

Prior to implementing the career development workshop, the participants in the laboratory were concerned almost exclusively with technical performance, paying little attention to management problems. Some were reluctant to accept managerial positions, while others accepted the positions but focused their efforts on technical problems and tended to slight many management responsibilities. Time allocated for training or development in managerial responsibilities was considered a distraction. Under these conditions, it was difficult to identify those employees most likely to develop into effective technical managers, and it was even more difficult to persuade them to devote time to managerial development activities. Managers were selected and promoted primarily on the basis of their technical prowess. Only minor consideration was given to their leadership and interpersonal skills. Some assessors assumed that anyone could easily learn in a short time what little was needed to know about directing the work of others. Consequently, technical performance was the principal selection factor used. With the concurrence of the senior managers of the laboratory, the career development workshop was started with the expectation that it would change the laboratory climate described earlier, while improving managerial performance.

Workshop Objectives

The career development workshop is based on an assessment center approach and was designed with the following objectives:

1. To help managers and potential managers discover the challenge involved in interpersonal relations, leadership skills, and administrative complexities and to provide them with an evaluation of their strengths and weaknesses in these areas. It was anticipated that this would stimulate a desire for training and development suited to their individual needs.
2. To provide a personal development opportunity, as opposed to the identification of managerial talent for selection and promotion. Therefore, no records were maintained (except those con-

---

*At the time this article was written, Gary Hart was employed as Manager of Manpower Planning and Development for IBM in San Jose, California.

trolled by the participants themselves) and management was not given a report on the individual's performance in the workshop.

3. To provide a development opportunity for assessors and assessees. Therefore, most of the staff were selected from the upper levels of management of the laboratory.

Workshop Activities

A one-on-one staff-to-participant ratio is used, and each session is limited to six participants and six staff members. To the extent possible, the group and individual problem-solving tasks were designed exclusively for scientifically and technically trained people, although administrative people have also been included as participants.

Each workshop requires four days of the participant's time (three days for assessment and one for career planning) and five and one-half days of the staff's time. Employees have been nominated by their managers to attend the workshop for a variety of reasons including the need to improve managerial skills, to accelerate development of high potential, and to obtain a better perspective for making career decisions. To date, approximately one-third of the nominees have been people in the high-potential category. Experienced line executives form the nucleus of the staff and are supplemented by management development specialists and frequently by one outside consultant.

Many of the participants arrive at the workshop tense and apprehensive, but these feelings generally subside rapidly. Most participants report that they soon feel more relaxed, although they still feel challenged. This tension-reduction phenomenon contrasts sharply with what happens at many (if not most) assessment centers. The participants in the workshop know that no performance results will be included in the personnel files or made available to management for selection purposes.

The workshop includes a variety of activities designed to reveal the participant's interpersonal, leadership, and managerial abilities. These activities include the following:

In-basket Exercise. The in-basket exercise deals with a variety of organizational problems typical of those a senior manager faces. Each participant is asked to assume the role of a new lab director who has two hours in his office before he must leave on a business trip. He is given background information on the organization and his in-basket is filled with typical items a lab director would have to handle, which he must take care of before leaving. Such an exercise provides the participants with an opportunity to demonstrate such leadership skills as planning and organizing, sensitivity to delegation and other issues, human relations skills, prioritizing, and analytical abilities.

Leaderless Group Problem-solving Discussions. Leaderless group exercises are designed to require that each group member convince the other members of the group that they should accept his ideas, proposals, or strategies. To succeed, the group must reach agreement. In one exercise their task is to select one candidate out of six for appointment to a second-level manager's position. In another they are to agree on the allocation of funds that fall short of the need. Each participant must be an advocate for one of six different needs.

Psychological Tests. The tests consist primarily of self-report inventories. That is, the scores reflect how the participants view themselves on such dimensions as need for control, acceptance, and affection as well as their responsibility, assertiveness, and sociability. These results are compared with the staff's observations.

Interviews. Interviews are conducted to determine how the participants handle themselves in one-on-one situations and to get more in-depth understanding of their behavior. One is a stress interview that tests their capacity to adjust to a fast-moving, demanding, and somewhat unexpected situation. Another interview provides an opportunity to identify the participant's deep-seated values, world view, management philosophy, and attitudes toward their job, the company, and their future.

Peer Evaluations. The participants prepare critiques of one another. They identify a minimum of three positive attributes and three suggested areas of improvement for each other. These critiques are summarized by the clerical staff and given back to each participant. The participants are given time to discuss the summaries among themselves. The staff do not have access to the data or to the discussions.

Participants consistently report a high acceptance of peer evaluations and a dislike for standardized self-report inventories. Generally speaking, the more immediate and comprehensive the feedback on an activity, the higher the satisfaction with that activity. But because the staff attempts to identify a broad range of the participants' behavioral characteristics in a short span of three days, feedback is held to a minimum *during* the session.

As was indicated earlier, the workshop staff is drawn primarily from senior management of the laboratory. This provides the managers with an excellent management development experience. However, it does present a difficult training problem because managers are reluctant to spend a great deal of time away from their jobs to prepare to serve as a staff member.

The training problem was resolved by conducting training during the workshop. Staff members arrive at the location two hours before the participants to receive an orientation. The schedule of activities allows an hour or more prior to each event for instructing the staff on their role, behaviors to look for, methods of evaluation, and the type of reporting required. After each exercise or interview, the staff participate in a critique of the event, thereby sharpening their observations, evaluation, and interview skills prior to the next activity.

Behavior Measurement

For the most part measurements consist of the staff members' narrative descriptions of each participant's performance on predetermined behavioral dimensions such as problem solving, communication, assertiveness, persuasiveness, sensitivity, and response to criticism. Interviews are conducted using a semistructured approach. That is, staff members are briefed on the objectives of the interview and provided with a suggested format. At the conclusion of the interview, staff members complete an interview report that covers some of the personal and interpersonal skills mentioned above.

Another area involves the assessment of performance in group problem-solving or leaderless group exercises. The six staff members observe all six participants in the group problem-solving exercises and are instructed to evaluate each participant on the same prescribed behavioral dimensions. As the workshop has been developed, many different rating and ranking schemes have been tried, most with marginal success. We found that the greater the number of behaviors rated in any one exercise, and the greater the attempt to quantify behavior through the use of rating scales, the less consistent and useful were the data. The most successful approach to generating useful evaluative data from observations of intragroup exercises has been to limit the number of behavioral categories to four or six, to rank participants and quantify their behavior on a 5-point scale, and to use narrative evaluative comments along with the rankings and ratings.

These two types of evaluations are examples of the problems involved in assessing behavior in the workshops. And even though the current approach is successful, it varies considerably as a function of the skill and motivation of the staff member. The more comprehensive the staff orientation, in which suggestions are made and pitfalls described, the higher the quality and greater the usefulness of the reports to the participants.

Report Preparation

The assessment portion of the workshop continues through the end of the third day, and then the participants begin their career-planning activity. At this point the staff members begin the difficult task of report writing. Each staff member analyzes and assimilates the data for one participant and writes the first draft of his or her report. The staff members then meet, and each report is read aloud and critiqued line by line. The reports are then rewritten, read aloud, and critiqued again—and again, if necessary. The objective is to be sure that each report receives the combined efforts and unanimous approval of the six staff members. Within a week or two after the workshop, each participant receives a comprehensive report consisting of a description of his or her strengths and limitations, as perceived by the staff, as well as a number of development recommendations. Unlike most assessment centers, the staff prepares *only one copy of the report and delivers that copy to the participants.* No other records are maintained. When the development recommendations contain one or more activities requiring management involvement, the participants are encouraged to share the contents of their reports with their management. However, the participant to whom the report is addressed has *total* control over the decision to share the information presented. Management has no other access to the report. To date, approximately one-half of the participants have shared their report with management.

A small number of the managers of participants who have not shared their reports have expressed their disappointment to the workshop director and a couple have assumed that the lack of sharing means the report was negative. The director's response to this concern (and the reason no further analysis of the issue is practical here) is that all the reports focus on the strengths *and* the limitations observed in the participants. There is no overall rating indicating that the participant did well or did poorly. Granted, some limitations described in the reports can be interpreted as more serious than others, and it seems logical that participants who in their own judgment did poorly would be less likely to share their reports with their managers than those who feel they did well. However, very few managers have expressed concerns about this issue.

The policy of providing the workshop report only to the participant was not arrived at without considerable debate among senior managers. On one side were those who believed that the considerable investment in time, money, and manpower could only be justified if management benefited by having the results available for management selection purposes. On the other hand, the intent of this program was for personal development. The policy prevailing was:

1. To maximize the validity of the results, the behavior evaluated should be truly representative of the participants. Participants will strive harder to be themselves during the workshop if they know the results are under their control.

2. Because most assessment center techniques have not yet been validated—and definitely not in this laboratory—and because people with little or no training in the behavioral sciences serve as staff members, the data will not be used for management selection purposes without the consent and participation of the participants themselves. Lab management generally accepts the policy of emphasizing the personal-development aspects of the program.

After the participants review their own reports, they meet individually with a trained workshop staff member to discuss any questions they may have regarding the contents of their reports and to begin their own development planning.

Career Planning

Recently an extra day was added to the participants' agenda for career-planning purposes. After three intense days of working together as a group, including completing peer evaluations and having discussions of those ratings among themselves, the groups become quite cohesive. As a result, the groups achieve a high level of openness and a willingness to share feelings, attitudes, and perceptions of one another's ideas and concerns. At this point, they are led through some career- and life-planning activities and discussions. They discuss the career stages described by Dalton, Thompson, and Price and attempt to determine in which stage they currently belong.

Then they are given time to reflect—to think about which stage they should now be in and which they want to be in by a given date. They are also encouraged to examine the relative costs and payoffs of moving from one stage to another and of remaining in a particular stage.

In summary, during the final day participants are introduced to a variety of life- and career-planning concepts, given time to reflect upon where they are now in their lives and careers, and encouraged to set goals and make plans and then to test these new goals and plans on their colleagues.

One other activity was developed to facilitate follow-through on the goal setting and planning done by the participants. Each participant is encouraged to identify a "mentor"—someone to share plans with, who could offer advice and assistance. To date, immediate managers, workshop staff members, and other senior members of the lab have been identified as mentors.

The authors estimate that about 30 percent of the participants have chosen a mentor but, as of this writing, we do not have enough data to evaluate the effectiveness of the mentor activity. The development of a relationship with a mentor is an informal process, and it is not clear that the organization can adopt formal procedures that will ensure the success of such a relationship.

RESULTS

After the first half-dozen workshops, all participants and staff members were interviewed by the lab director. After those interviews, the director said, "From what I could see of the workshop, it was worthwhile, but I wanted to continue it only so long as the participants found it beneficial. For this reason, I made it a practice to interview all of them, but only after they returned from the workshop and had enough time to digest their reports. Everyone I talked to felt it was well worth the time and effort. Every participant recognized that he wouldn't have a similar opportunity very often. Most felt that the reports were valid, offering the participants new insight into themselves. The participants *and* staff members grew personally. The working environment in the laboratory was improved and more productive. I think the program has been extremely worthwhile."

Reactions of the Participants

Reactions to the workshop have covered a wide spectrum, but most attendees have been very supportive. None has indicated that the program was not worth doing. Participants and assessors have made such statements as these:

I've never had such a meaningful development experience in my professional career.

I'm delighted (and amazed) that the company would sponsor such a significant development program.

I've had a great deal of management training and the career-development workshop was by far the most meaningful.

The following examples illustrate ways in which participants have reacted to the workshop:

Tom was a scientist who was technically outstanding and who also appeared to possess many leadership skills. He was under great pressure from his management to accept a managerial assignment but had successfully resisted for more than a year. When he was invited to attend a workshop, he accepted because he was curious, but he made it clear that if this was another ploy to get him to be a manager he would be unhappy. By the evening of the first day of the workshop he had decided to go home, but he was persuaded by the director to stick it out. At the conclusion of the workshop, the staff had considerable difficulty writing Tom's report. The strengths he had displayed were considerable, but so were his limitations. He had been rude, offensive, arrogant, and selfish at the workshop, but the staff was uncertain as to how candid they should be. What's more, since he had expressed such reluctance to be a manager, the typical rationale to change ("if you want to be an effective manager") was inappropriate. But the report was very candid. And because Tom had expressed a considerable desire to be active and effective in community affairs, the entire report was written to that end, making no mention of company management.

During the postworkshop interview, Tom said that the report described a person he would detest. However, he discussed the feedback with his wife, and she agreed with points contained in the report. He later indicated that the workshop experience had a profound impact upon him. His eyes were opened to the challenges in leadership positions and the limitations he would have to overcome before he could perform satisfactorily as a manager. After considerable introspection he decided to accept a management position. He worked hard to overcome his limitations as a manager and has since been promoted to a senior manager position. He has also returned to the workshop as a staff member.

Just before attending the workshop, Dick and his manager had discussed the possibility of Dick's accepting a managerial assignment. Dick was clearly regarded as *the* technical leader in his field in the laboratory. However, he was shaken considerably by his workshop report, which pointed to a number of interpersonal-skills limitations that would seriously impair his effectiveness as a manager. Dick expressed his disagreement with many of the observations pointed out in the report and shared both the report and his objections openly with management to get its reaction. As a result, Dick was appointed manager, but only after his potential skill and limitations were adequately discussed and plans were made to help and coach him. Since his appointment, he and his manager have doubled their efforts to overcome his limitations. Apparently, this has borne fruit: Several of his subordinates have indicated he is the best manager they have ever had. (Parenthetically, such intensive focus on managerial skills probably would not have happened had he

not attended the workshop, and had he not been willing to share the report with his management.)

Harry was the only participant who left a workshop early. The way he was invited to attend the workshop was probably the reason for his leaving early. Harry was on vacation at a mountain resort when he received a call from his manager directing him to report to the workshop the following day (24 hours later). Having had to drive about 300 miles to the site of the workshop, Harry arrived late. He missed the orientation but had time for the last part of the dinner. The director gave him a quick overview of what had been discussed at the orientation, and Harry seemed positive, confident, and willing to get started on his first assignment. But about an hour later Harry's roommate called the director and reported that Harry had dumped the workshop material on the floor and said something like, "This isn't for me," and then, as he went out of the door, "I'm going home."

The director found out later that Harry's boss was under pressure from his boss (a past, exceptionally enthusiastic staff member from another division) to provide a participant. After a last minute cancellation, the lot fell to Harry's boss and thus to Harry to fill the vacancy. The director was not made aware of this situation and, consequently, Harry was directed to attend a session for which he was unprepared.

An assessment center is hard work, and it is important that the participants be prepared emotionally as well as intellectually and physically. Normally the participants are invited to attend several weeks before the date of the workshop. The workshop director invited the prospective participants personally by phone or in an interview. Any questions the nominees have are answered, and if they seem overly anxious about the uncertainties of the experience, they are invited to talk with past participants. Great care is taken to make sure they can decline easily if they do not want to attend. Harry's experience, a rare exception, points out the importance of adequately preparing people for participation in an assessment center.

Reactions of the Staff

We indicated earlier that one of the objectives in creating the workshop was to provide a development opportunity for senior managers who would serve as assessors. It was anticipated that staff members would develop an increased awareness of the importance of leadership and interpersonal skills as well as improve their own skills in observing and assessing behavior in these two areas. The workshop has been very effective in achieving this objective. A large percentage of the staff members have indicated that they had been so impressed by their experience as assessors that they planned to change important aspects of their own management style upon returning to work. Several employees who attended the workshop first as participants and later as staff members indicated that even though their experience as participants was significant, the benefit as staff was even greater.

Senior managers have had very positive reactions as they have observed the program over time. They have nominated so many of their subordinates that there has always been a waiting list of people to attend the workshops. More importantly, after the first few workshops there has been no difficulty in finding senior managers who were willing to spend the six days necessary to serve as staff members. This is no doubt the most convincing evidence of management support for the workshop.

Employee Perceptions

It is not uncommon for people who participate in a management development activity to be full of praise for the program. After all, they've invested a lot of energy in the program and are reluctant to admit that it was not a good use of their time. However, it is usually more difficult to find evidence that behavior has changed or that management performance has improved. While no formal experiment was conducted to provide specific measures of the effectiveness of the program, there was a "natural" experiment that generated some evidence on this issue. Fortunately, a labwide opinion survey was conducted just prior to the first workshop (pretest) and another one was completed four years later (post-test). In the four-year period over 120 people had participated in the workshop either as participants or as members of the staff. More than 70 of those people were in management positions at the time of the second survey. When the results from the two surveys were compared, only one of six morale index factors had improved in the four-year period. Employees were much more positive about the performance of their managers on the post-test than they were on the first survey. Other indicators, such as job satisfaction, overall satisfaction, advancement opportunities, and so on, showed virtually no change. The item used as a measure for managerial effectiveness was: "How good a job is being done by your immediate manager?" This improved rating of management is particularly striking in the context of the rather stable measures on the other morale index items.
The recent survey data also indicate that employees managed by persons who had attended the workshop had more favorable attitudes toward their managers than did employees reporting to managers who had not attended. In departments managed by workshop graduates, 76 percent of the 140 respondents saw their managers as performing satisfactorily and only 6 per-

cent were dissatisfied; among the 68 employees reporting to managers without workshop experience, only 55 percent were satisfied and 17 percent dissatisfied. The data suggest that the workshop has had a positive influence on managerial performance.

It is obvious that employees working for managers with workshop experience rated them as more effective. But why? How did managerial behavior change so that subordinates (and others) perceived it as improved? What were workshop graduates doing that is different?

To help answer these questions, the questionnaire contained eight items related to specific dimensions of managerial effectiveness. With this additional information, it was apparent that employees perceived workshop graduates more positively in:

1. Dealing fairly with employees
2. Considering job concerns and complaints
3. Giving recognition for work done
4. Communicating with subordinates
5. Managing their people responsibilities

Employees made little or no distinction, however, between the two sets of managers on the basis of their availability, the criteria they used for evaluating their subordinates, and the effectiveness with which they managed their technical responsibilities.

Apparently, workshop graduates showed more interest in their subordinates' needs and concerns. Nor was this accomplished by sacrificing technical objectives: Both sets of managers were perceived as being equally competent in technical management.

An analysis of these survey data suggests two conclusions: (1) Something happened in that four-year period to improve employee attitudes toward their managers. (2) Employees gave higher ratings to managers who had been through the program than managers who had not. While not conclusive, this certainly provided evidence that the program has a positive effect on managerial performance.

IMPLICATIONS

What makes this program different from the ones described at the beginning of this article? Why have some assessment centers been discontinued and others been very successful? Clearly the assessment center described in this article is not the only one still in operation. A review of several successful and unsuccessful centers reveals some factors that executives should consider in a decision to make use of this particular technique.

FIGURE 1
Employee Attitudes Concerning Effectiveness of Their Immediate Managers
(Workshop Managers Compared with Other Managers)

	Percentage Responding			Total No.
	Satisfactory	Neutral	Unsatisfactory	Responding
Workshop Managers	76	18	6	140
Other Managers	55	29	17	68

Program Director

An assessment center cannot be "pulled off the shelf" and plugged into an organization on a moment's notice. A successful assessment center is the product of a complex set of technical and interpersonal skills. For example, it is vital that the right person be selected to direct the effort.

One of the authors, Gary Hart, served as the workshop director for seven years in the IBM division described in this article. However, other companies have had problems of turnover with their directors. One company dropped its assessment center after a relatively short period of time. When executives in the company were asked why, they said, "For one thing, we had problems with the directors. The first one couldn't relate to managers. In fact, he turned them off. Fairly soon they replaced him. But the new director had problems too. She had a Ph.D., and people felt she was trying to put them down. She had a need to act superior. So the program wasn't accepted by people in the field." A director must be able to win the support of line managers.

Other characteristics of a good director are as follows:

1. Has a sufficiently good grasp of the firm's needs, objectives, and sociotechnical systems to be able to select, modify, or develop a program to fit the environment.
2. Has above average adaptive and problem-solving skills. Each time the center operates, the personality mix of staff and participants differs. Must be able to solve problems and make changes on the spot.
3. Must be able to deal firmly and constructively with powerful people and intragroup conflicts. Senior managers serving as staff members may be difficult to direct and control, especially when conflicts arise over the ratings of participants.
4. Must be equipped to deal with criticisms. Must adopt a nondefensive, accepting response to suggestions for changes, but firmly resist invalid suggestions.

Top-level Support

As with any program touching all parts of an organization, this program needs the support of senior executives. Top management may be reluctant to make a long-term commitment. If so, then their full support and commitment for a trial period is needed. In our study, top management was aware of the problem of developing management talent and was willing to support the program on an experimental basis. For the first few workshops, the lab director interviewed each participant and staff member after the workshop. In addition, he (and subsequently his successor) attended nearly every workshop for one evening to hold an open discussion with the participants. This type of support increases the likelihood that people will attend the workshop and take it seriously.

Staff Selection

Choosing the right assessors is vital. Participants who feel that the assessors are not qualified will not be receptive to feedback. Some benefits of having senior line managers serve in this role are as follows:

1. They have credibility.
2. Serving this way affords them an excellent development experience (although they might not recognize this at first).
3. They acquire a greater sense of commitment to the program.
4. Participants learn that senior people value leadership and interpersonal skills.
5. The experience enhances the senior managers' desire and ability to move people across organizational boundaries.
6. Most important, the senior managers have an opportunity to:
   a. develop observational skills.
   b. discuss with other senior people the philosophical and theoretical concepts related to interpersonal and leadership behavior and examine their application to actual situations during the operation.
   c. get feedback concerning their own observational and evaluative skills.

In our experience, the problem of obtaining senior managers is minimal after the first successful workshop or two. Past staff members and participants become advocates, participants become advocates, and the program sells itself.

Participant Selection

Some assessment centers have failed because of inadequacies in their participant-selection process. Some invited only "super stars"; as a result, the invitation alone was a virtual passport to success. (Or so it was perceived by other contenders.) Some companies have invited only those with marginal to poor potential. Then the promotional record makes it clear to everyone that it is not wise to accept an invitation. In fact, the assessment center comes to be viewed as the cause of some people's failure—as indeed it may have been.

We suggest careful attention to the following ramifications of participant selection:

1. Invite people with a wide spectrum of potentialities, not just those with high or low potential.
2. Develop a nomination system that allows senior management to submit the names of people they would like to have attend, and make sure the senior managers understand the nomination criteria. (This will provide a data base from which the director can work.)
3. With the managers' approval, the director should invite each individual either by telephone or, where possible, in person. (This provides an opportunity to describe the general purpose and content of the program and to dispel anxieties and uncertainties.) For those willing to attend, a formal letter of invitation should follow.
4. Be certain that attendance is voluntary, that they can decline easily if they choose.

Participant Feedback

The results of the assessment should be fed back to the employee in as comprehensive, detailed, and helpful manner as possible. Although the assessment center itself provides considerable opportunities for learning through observation, interviews, peer-evaluation discussions, and the like, a comprehensive follow-up report is essential. The report provides the participant more opportunity for analysis, reflection, and introspection.

Development vs. Selection

Most assessment centers have been used for selection purposes and have paid little attention to the problems of management development. However, as we noted, this approach has led to a number of serious problems. Because there are important advantages to using the center for developmental purposes, more will employ that approach in the future. Some of these advantages are:

1. Participants are more likely to manifest genuine behavior because they know that the purpose of the experience is solely to help them develop.
2. The problems of who controls the report are greatly reduced. The assessment report only goes to the participant; it is up to that participant to decide who else sees it. It has been our experience that about 50 percent of the participants—and not just those whose reports are mostly positive—share the contents of their report with their superiors. When management controls the report, there are difficult questions as to who should have access to the information. An employee relations manager in a company that dropped its assessment center said: "We still have people asking to see those assessment reports. I don't know how to respond. How do you decide who should have access to that kind of information?"
3. Many people who attend a development workshop make the hard decisions about their career themselves rather than forcing management to make those decisions. Frequently when a report indicates that an individual's strengths are more technical than managerial and that a considerable amount of change and risk would be involved in pursuing a managerial path, that person elects to withdraw from managerial competition.
4. People are more willing to attend a development workshop than a program that can make or break their career.
5. When centers are used for development purposes, there is less tendency to place excessive faith in the results and in so doing to kill people's hope by telling them they have no future. These global judgments don't have to be made once and for all for people's careers. On the contrary, development workshops emphasize that people grow and change, and situations change as well.
6. More people are likely to benefit from attending a development oriented center than from a selection oriented center. Most selection centers are win/lose oriented. If the individual is rated above some threshold, and qualifies for advancement opportunities, he wins; otherwise he loses. Little if anything is done with the results for or by the "losers." The end was achieved, the attendees were separated into "winners" and "losers." By contrast, participants in a development-oriented

center are all winners: they all gain greater insight into themselves.

We have described an assessment center that has been operating for more than seven years. There are many indications that it is an effective program that has improved the performance of individuals as well as the overall operation of the organization. One key to its success is the focus on the development of all of the employees who have participated. A review of the problems that have been encountered with assessment centers indicates that almost all of those problems occurred when they were being used for selection purposes. We are convinced that the issue of selection or development will be critical in the future use of assessment centers. Our research indicates that the organizations that chose the development approach will be much more satisfied with the results.

SELECTED BIBLIOGRAPHY

Although several authors have treated career development as a by-product of the selection and identification process, very little has been written linking career development directly to assessment centers. The use of the assessment center as a management and career development tool is treated somewhat in William C. Byham's "The Assessment Center as an Aid in Management Development" (*Training and Development Journal*, December 1971, pp. 10–22) and Barry M. Cohen's "What the Supervisor Should Know About Assessment Centers" (*Supervisory Management*, June 1975, pp. 30–34).

Byham's "Assessment Centers for Spotting Future Managers" (*Harvard Business Review*, July–August 1970, pp. 150–160) and William C. Byham and R. Pentecost Egind "The Assessment Center: Identifying Tomorrow's Managers" *Personnel* (September–October 1970, pp. 17–29) offers a good view of the assessment center as a selection and identification device. An excellent critical review of assess-

ment centers is Allen I. Kraut's "A Hard Look at Management Assessment Centers and Their Future" (*Personnel Journal*, May 1972, pp. 317–326). An overview of the origin of the assessment center in the business setting is traced by Douglas W. Bray, Richard J. Campbell, and Donald L. Grant in *Formative Years in Business—A Long Term AT&T Study of Managerial Lives* (John Wiley and Sons, 1974). Allen I. Kraut's and Grant J. Scott's "Validity of an Operational Management Assessment Program" (*Journal of Applied Psychology*, 1972, 2, pp. 124–129) is one of several research studies performed at IBM on assessment centers. Research performed at Standard Oil of Ohio is presented in F. O. Carleton's "Relationships Between Follow-up Evaluations and Information Developed in a Management Assessment Center" (a paper presented at the 78th annual convention of the American Psychological Association, Miami Beach, 1970). The latter three studies are commonly used as evidence of the validity of the assessment center in selecting managers.

For a more thorough analysis of the career development side of this issue, see Edgar H. Schein's recent book *Career Dynamics: Matching Individual and Organizational Needs* (Addison-Wesley Publishing Company, 1978). This book looks at career development from the point of view of the individual as well as the perspective of the manager in the organization.

Douglas T. Hall's book *Careers in Organizations* (Goodyear Publishing Company, 1976) presents a thorough review of the literature on career development as well as current practices in organizations. A recent article by Donald B. Miller, "How to Improve the Performance and Productivity of the Knowledge Worker" (*Organizational Dynamics*, Winter 1977, pp. 62–80), describes a number of social and technical programs to help the knowledge worker becomes more productive. He includes a description of how these techniques are implemented in a division of IBM. A description of the career-stages model that is being used in the assessment center reported in this article can be found in an article by Gene Dalton, Paul Thompson, and Ray Price, "The Four Stages of Professional Careers—A New Look at Performance by Professionals" (*Organizational Dynamics*, Summer 1977, pp 19–42).

An Introduction to Computer-Based Learning

by Angus Reynolds

Computer-based learning (CBL) is a growing phenomenon, both in impact and in interest. The United States has provided the theoretical, technical

and practical leadership for this worldwide trend in learning.

Most human resource development practitioners recognize the need to become familiar with the basics of this new tool. Yet, to some CBL must be as alien as a spaceship. There is a definite need to demystify CBL, its terminology, technology and environment, in order to make it understandable to any HRD practitioner (see Figure 1).

SNAPSHOT OF CBL

A learner reports to the organization's computer-based learning area. There are other learners there. They all seem to be busy and hardly notice the new learner. There are CBL terminals and other resources such as audio-visual (AV) and test equipment. A facilitator welcomes the new learner, introduces the CBL terminal and explains how to proceed through the course. The first activity is a test. Then the learner reads some pages of a manual, views a videotape and returns to the CBL terminal to complete a lesson. One point is particularly difficult, so the learner makes a telephone call to get clarification. Then there is another test, something like the first one but not as long. The new learner seems to adapt readily to the CBL environment, and soon is as absorbed with the materials as the other learners.

This brief description of a typical computer-based learning encounter provides only a superficial glimpse of what is happening. An HRD professional must be able to see more deeply into the situation and understand it in much greater detail.

LEARNING ENVIRONMENT

The learner is a member of a work group that has been identified for participation in an HRD program. He or she is scheduled to use the CBL center for a block of time (one half-day every other day).

On the scheduled day, the learner reports to the organization's computer-based learning center. At first glance, it may look like the center is overscheduled because there are more learners than CBL terminals. This is intentional, since some of the time is spent using other resources such as the AV and lab equipment. The other learners have been in the program for varying periods of time. As one learner nears completion of the program, another is assigned and scheduled.

In traditional block instruction, all learners start and end together. In a CBL program, a learner studies only until the required learning is complete. An organization's computer-based learning center may range from a large facility to single terminals located in work areas. In cases where learners are remote or few in number, or the total HRD needs are limited, learning terminals are shipped to work locations for a period of time while the employees complete a planned program. Then they are shipped to another site.

THE LEARNING SPECIALIST

The learning specialist role continues to be important in HRD delivered through CBL, but not in the same way as in traditional instruction. A "facilitator" of learning performs the most enjoyable task in the learning specialist role, working with other people. Though it may seem incongruous, CBL provides the learning specialist with more opportunity to work with people.

FIGURE 1
Computer-based Learning Terminology

Computer-Based Learning (CBL)—The "umbrella" word. CBL includes all of the activities described by the terms: CAI, CMI and CSLR.

Computer-Assisted Instruction (CAI)—The use of a computer in the actual instructional process. For the technically inclined—CAI is a *medium of instruction* that may be applied in appropriate learning situations. Film, videotape and textbooks are also media. CBL, CMI and CBLR are not media.

Computer-Managed Instruction (CMI)—The management of instruction by computer. Management includes testing, prescription generation and record keeping.

Computer-Supported Learning Resources—The other supporting elements of CBL which neither directly teach as CAI, nor perform management functions. Usually limited to information storage and retrieval (data bases) and instructional communications.

Hardware—The physical items involved in the CBL process.

Software—The programs written in computer languages that make the computer components of a CBL system work as they should.

Courseware—The computer-delivered CAI lessons and CMI tests, as well as the video, audio, texts and other learning resources.

Source: Reynolds, A. Computer-based learning: Deciphering the alphabet soup. *Training*, January 1983, pp. 65–67.

In the CBL environment, facilitators coach, tutor and guide the learning activities of each individual learner, taking satisfaction from the increased opportunity to make a difference in the working lives of individuals in the HRD program.

CBL is, by its very nature, an individual form of learning. For that reason, there are areas where CBL is not the strategy of choice, for example, when human interaction is essential to learning. The obvious implication for the role of the learning specialist is expansion to accommodate this new tool.

COMPUTER-MANAGED INSTRUCTION

Computer-assisted instruction (CAI) always directly involves learning and teaching. Computer-managed instruction provides efficiencies through management. The modes of CMI are testing, prescription generation and record keeping. CMI is not yet as familiar to many as is CAI. This is not a reflection of its inherent worth or acceptance. CMI will eventually become better known to people in HRD because it offers considerable efficiency (see Figure 2).

Testing.   Testing is the CMI function used to measure the learner's knowledge of the learning objectives. It is the foundation of CMI, since it provides the information needed to prescribe "learning activities." Further, it offers learning efficiency by evaluating the degree to which the learner has mastered the objectives. After the learning activities are completed, the learner is again tested to measure mastery of knowledge. This test of the objectives already identified as important to knowledge of the subject may be somewhat more detailed. If the learner has mastered them, he or she goes on to the test for the second module. If he or she does not, another prescription will be given which uses different learning resources.

Prescription Generation.   The test for the first module of instruction results in a prescription of learning activities unique to individual needs. The prescription will be based on the instructional objectives which have not been mastered. The learner will then turn to learning resources. These can include lab equipment, manuals, audio-visual materials, instructor conference or CAI activity. Each is keyed to the objectives to be mastered to complete the module.

Prescription generation, as stated above, is the key to the power of CMI. The system generates an instructional prescription for unmastered learning objectives for each individual learner.

FIGURE 2
Components of Computer-Based Learning

Modes of Computer-Assisted Instruction (CAI)
   Tutorial
   Drill and Practice
   Instructional Game
   Modeling
   Simulation
   Problem Solving
Modes of Computer-Managed Instruction (CMI)
   Testing
   Prescription Generation
   Record Keeping
Computer-Supported Learning Resources (CSLR)
   Information Storage and Retrieval
   Instructional Communications

The prescriptions are designed along with the instruction (see Figure 3). Individuals can be expected to master different objectives. Each will only study the materials he or she needs. Each individual learner is directed only to those learning resources that support the unmastered objective(s). This selectivity shortens the time each learner must study.

Record Keeping.   This CMI system automatically generates and stores records of individual and group progress. The HRD department is freed from closets with shelves piled high with old records and reports. Records can be seen when, and if, desired.

The records of students or the entire HRD program can be printed out as needed. They can also be automatically posted to the organization's HRD or personnel system. In some cases, the data are available directly to the distant corporate headquarters using the same system.

COMPUTER-ASSISTED INSTRUCTION IN SIX MODES

When CAI is prescribed as a medium of instruction, it will actually be implemented in one of six modes (see Figure 4).

Tutorial.   Tutorial is the mode most familiar to those new to CBL. In a tutorial, the learner interacts one-on-one with the program. A good tutorial advances in the same manner as the best tutor would personally conduct the process. A typical tutorial lesson consists of a series of segments in which information is presented, and then the learner's understanding is checked. This

FIGURE 3
CMI Prescription Generation

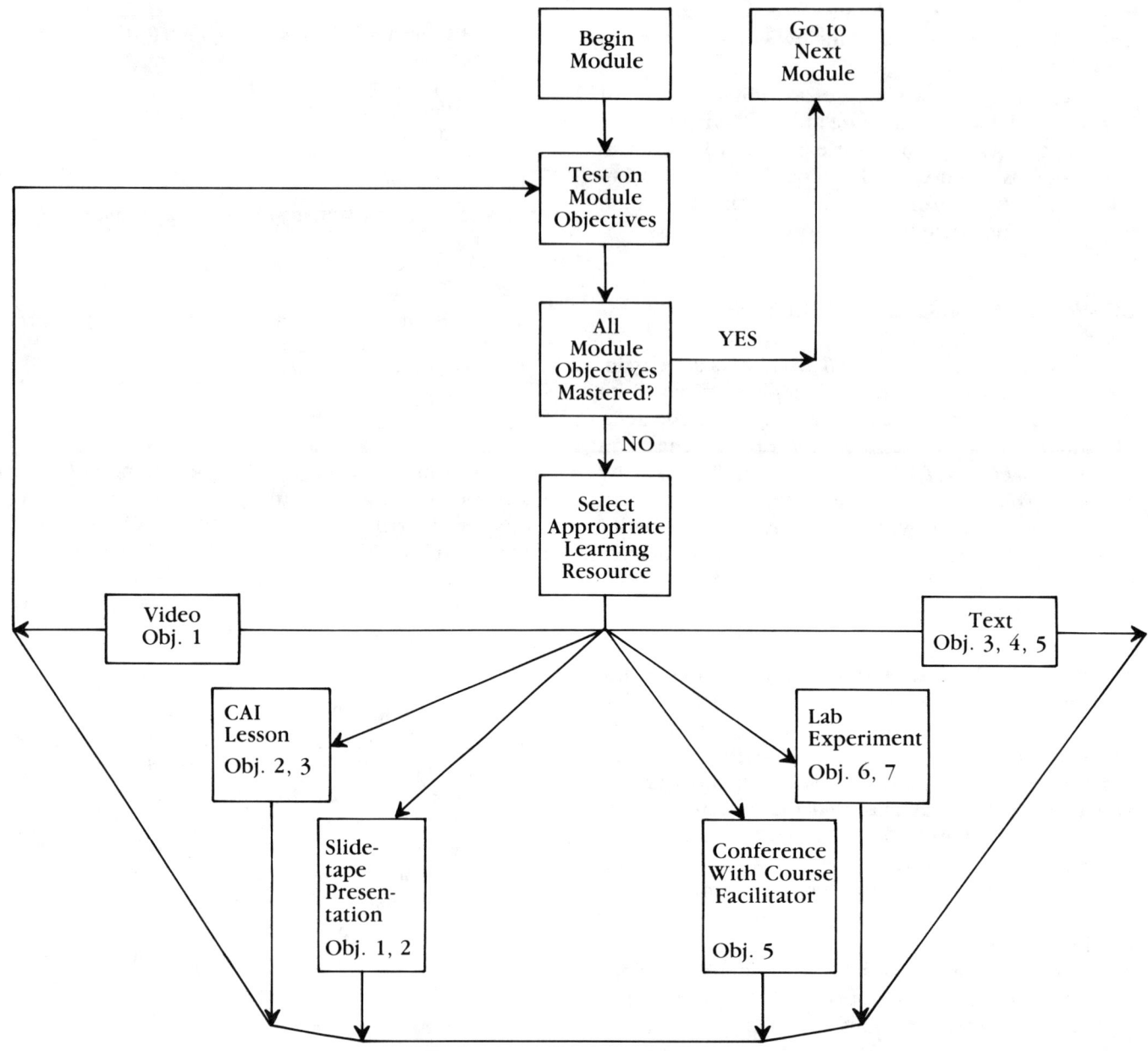

process is repeated throughout the lesson. Based on the demonstration of understanding, or lack of it, the learner's path continues to another segment, or the same information is presented again in a new way. The reinforcement process provides corrective feedback to the learner, who then proceeds.

A poor tutorial may take a form called a "page turner." An objective in designing a good tutorial is to keep the learner actively involved in the learning process.

Drill and Practice. Another familiar mode of CAI is drill and practice—the repetitive presentation of prob-

lems to the learner. In an elementary example, the learner is asked, "How much is eight times eight?" When the learner responds to the question, another is presented, such as, "How much is nine times nine?" After a given number of problems has been presented, the learner is informed of the numbers of questions answered correctly and incorrectly. This is not the only form of drill and practice. In HRD, drill and practice technique is used successfully with much more complex subject matter.

Instructional Games. Instructional games are a valid and professional method of stimulating learning.

FIGURE 4
CBL-Related Characteristics of Adult Learners

The rate of learning varies between individuals.

Adults enter the learning situation with considerable previous experience and learning.

Individuals have different learning styles and preferences.

Individuals may have a variety of goals for learning.

Adults need to feel confident that they are learning what is needed to meet their own goals.

Source: Knowles, M. *The adult learner: A neglected species.* Houston: Gulf Publishing Co., 1979.

They are well accepted by instructional technologists. Unfortunately, the term "game" is associated with frivolous activity. An instructional game is not necessarily recognized by the learner as a game at all, and it need not be frivolous. While instructional games often do contain an element of entertainment, the point is that learning while playing is, nevertheless, learning.

Modeling. When the CBL system is used to represent another system or process, it is called modeling or simulation. The learner can change values and observe the effects of the change on the operation of the system. For example, consider a population model. The learner can manipulate the demographic variables, such as infant mortality, birth or death rate in the model. The model calculates and displays the results that such changes would create, if they actually took place. The learner can observe the effects on the population over a period of time. A population model might be used in learning the techniques of planning. The essential difference between modeling and simulation is the degree of realism. Modeling usually implies that a realistic representation of the system modeled is either not attempted or impossible. The population model just described is one which is accurate but does not lend itself to a realistic form of representation.

Simulation. Representation of a system, sub-system, situation or device, with a degree of realism, is called simulation. The simulation mode enables learners to learn the operation of equipment without damaging it or harming themselves or others. Simulation can be done manually or in hybrid form, using both manual and computer methods.

Simulation is possible with a number of different levels of fidelity. It is possible to do some HRD simulation without a computer. However, the speed and complexity inherent in simulations prevented its use, as a practical reality, for most HRD organizations, until the availability of computing power.

Simulators are very expensive, special, single-purpose (computerized) instructional devices. They are typified by simulators of aircraft flight decks or nuclear reactor controls.

In an alternative form, the implementation of "part task" simulation on a CBL terminal is a proven technique for HRD. For example, since the entire instrument panel of a modern aircraft is so complex, a CBL terminal cannot represent all of it at once. Instead, the CBL terminal simulates the aircraft's systems one at a time. The learner can master each of the systems in turn. Then, when the learner enters the big simulator, time is not wasted learning. The simulator time is spent demonstrating mastery and gaining experience operating the entire aircraft system.

Problem Solving. Problem solving is not used extensively in HRD, outside data processing training, even though it has good applications in math and science instruction. Problem solving includes use of the computer itself, by the learner, as a tool to solve a problem. As computers become a more common tool on the job, we may see greater use of this mode.

The CAI lessons developed using any of the five modes become "learning resources." These are then used by the CMI component of CBL.

COMPUTER-SUPPORTED LEARNING RESOURCES

The typical computer-supported learning resource (CSLR) is a data base or source of information. Such a resource requires that the data exist, and currently there are no development tools for the implementation of a resource in HRD.

One aspect of CSLRs is communication. Communication is possible among users of a large or small network. The network can be used by learning specialists to exchange information between learners and a remote subject matter expert. Learner and instructor comments and notes can be recorded for later use. Files can be used for sharing information among users having similar interests. Individuals and groups can exchange notes.

THE ADULT LEARNER—HEART OF CBL

Learners, as a whole, seem to appreciate the way CBL handles their learning: as adults. It can make an effective contribution to nearly any HRD program because it is inherently compatible with adult learners. It handles instruction in a highly individualized way. It provides a very close match with what we know about adults in learning situations (see Figure 4).

The idea that computer-based learning is compatible with adult learning characteristics is not theoretical. It is supported by research, as well as by practical evidence that it works. Results of an analysis of more than 75 studies showed significant gains in achievement and positive attitude.[1] Most important for cost-effective programs, learning time was reduced by 25 to 50 percent!

The adult learner sees CBL as far less threatening than school and classroom experiences in general. Individualized CBL is able to deal with heterogeneous groups far better than does classroom instruction. In CBL, the person who can progress rapidly does so and is not forced to mark time while the instructor tries to present material on a level suited to most of the group. Others, who would not be able to keep up with that same presentation, proceed at a pace they can handle. The economic advantage of this approach has been demonstrated at United Air Lines.[2]

CONCLUSION

CBL is a growing phenomenon with strengths for use in HRD. It can be expected to debut in more organizations each year. Since CBL offers glamor as well as important strengths, it might be tempting to tack a CBL element onto one's next HRD program. Simply adding CBL to a conventional HRD project would not be a wise way to start. Consideration for, and application of, its strengths is absolutely essential. Otherwise, it will only add a cost.

Computer-based learning is a modern, technology-based tool, but it is not a sophisticated one. No magic or mystery is involved. Alien means "foreign or strange." CBL is certainly not foreign and remains strange only if you make it so.

The bad news is that CBL is not a panacea. Success with CBL comes from intelligent application. It must be used in situations where it will produce an overall outcome that is preferable to that which can be obtained with conventional methods. The good news is that there are many such opportunities.

REFERENCES

1. Kulik, J., Kulik, C. and Cohen, P. Effectiveness of computer-based college teaching: A meta-analysis of findings. *Review of Educational Research*, 1980, 50, 525–544.
2. Cain, J. Computer-based training at United Airlines. *Training and Development Journal*, March 1981, pp. 76–78.

The Five Most Frequent Questions (Plus One) About Computer-Based Learning

by Angus Reynolds and Richard Davis

To keep abreast of developments in the HRD field, to provide an organization with the best training services possible and to make best use of technological advances in the field, HRD professionals need to know about computer-based learning (CBL). In fact, HRD practitioners working in quite different industries and organizations ask remarkably similar questions about it.

It is an easy task to assemble the questions heard most frequently. It is less easy to answer them without the chance to ask qualifying questions, to clarify what is in the mind of the questioner and to apply them to organizational and situational variables. The following answers may be helpful in stimulating thinking about these five most asked questions.

HOW MUCH DOES IT COST?

Though more expensive than preparing lectures, CBL can be cost-effective and can become less expensive over time. Determining costs of any fledgling effort is difficult. One key reason is that computer-based instruction changes many aspects of the way business is done.

Davis: To help provide some perspective, here are some rules of thumb about CBL cost:

- Development—Compared to what now is being done, CBL development generally will be more expensive. In looking at several efforts, we have encountered costs ranging from 125 percent to 250 percent of the costs of the current effort. One way of thinking about this range is to consider the first 25 percent of cost as the expense of coding lessons and the rest as the cost of individualized instruction. Much of this remainder is simply the cost of good instructional development. If instructional development is good already, costs will be near the bottom end of the range.
- Delivery—If the development costs of CBL are higher than previous training methods, delivery costs generally are lower. In fact, many people see the tradeoff between development and delivery costs as the key economic factor in CBL. The biggest area of cost savings is that of reduced training time. It is essential to include the time saved by students in any cost analysis of CBL, yet many organizations fail to consider it.

Reynolds: CBL, is expensive, but the dollar amount of a proposed CBL effort is not the most important consideration. The big question is: How much does training really cost now? If that question can't be answered, it will be hard to demonstrate how anything that costs money can result in an overall saving to the organization.

A cost-effective program is the key to the success of CBL in an organization, and it is tied to the selection of the best possible application. A formal needs analysis is one way to ensure selecting the most promising application.

The principle of cost-benefit is simple. Spending money for a new way of doing things should bring a return to the organization. CBL can be used to reduce training time, reduce training costs, increase throughput of learners and improve effectiveness and productivity. Dollar amounts can be tied to these improvements. Within a reasonable period, such as five years, the value of the improvements should exceed the cost of the system. United Airlines provides an excellent example of how to select a cost-effective application.[1]

WHICH ONE SHOULD I BUY?

Davis: While picking a good "first system" for an initial CBL effort is critical, it should be recognized that needs change rapidly after the first project and that ultimately no single system can do everything that even a modest size organization wants to do. Here are some guidelines for selecting a first system:

- Data training should be put in the system that is being taught. If that isn't possible, the training should mimic the terminal response that the learner will see on the job.
- Choices are narrow for the unsophisticated user. Extensive vendor support will be needed to get started, as will good examples of lessons people have created for similar applications. In fact, there may not be a system which meets all an organization's needs and which has good vendor support.
- If the organization is committed to a long-term program rather than just a first effort, the key factors become the cost and the growth potential of the system. Even if a system can't do everything needed right now, it may be a good choice if it has shown steady improvement, or if it is relatively easy to adapt.
- If the user is sophisticated in computer use and has specialized needs, developing a custom system or working in a time sharing environment should be considered.

Reynolds: This is often the first question a person will ask. Yet, it should be the last. If the CBL effort is the result of a careful plan that considers the organization fully, the question practically will answer itself. It will be the system with the capabilities to meet needs for the current application as well as those which reasonably can be anticipated. A "state-of-the-art" CBL system has the following capabilities:

- Powerful authoring system with no requirement for programming and a high-level, user-oriented, education-specific author language with powerful authoring aids;
- Flexibility in instructional strategy;
- Powerful instructional management system;
- Micro ("stand-alone") delivery of courseware;
- Delivery of courseware on other systems;
- Line and vector graphics;
- Direct user access to computer through screen interaction;
- Auxiliary device control including electronic voice synthesis, random-access audio, random-access videotape and videodisc.

The urge to "start cheap" should be avoided. Hardware quickly will become the smallest part of the investment in most computer-based efforts. The system being selected should be able to handle future needs.

CAN I WRITE MY OWN LESSONS?

Good CBL lesson development follows the instructional system development pattern of activities: analysis, design, development (including lesson program coding for the computer), implementation and evaluation.

Reynolds: Theoretically, programmerless authoring allows anyone to create CBL lessons. In practical terms, the organization currently must carry out all of the steps listed above when training is developed. If the organization does this, then CBL lessons can be developed as well. If not, but there is sufficient need, an internal CBL organization can be developed.

It certainly is just as difficult to create good CBL lessons as conventional instruction. A good plan for an organization with a strong instructional development capability would be to have the first course developed out of house, but to participate in the process. Then the organization gradually can reduce its dependence on consultant help until it is entirely self-sufficient in those areas.

Davis: My experience suggests that once the area of need has been determined, the instructional analysis must be done internally, where needs are known best. Materials design and scripting require some special skills, but are certainly things that professional trainers can do well. Only the last activity, coding, involves skills so specialized that the current staff may not be able to do it. This may not be a huge problem. Many systems have sophisticated aids to help novices do coding, and coding specialists are available.

IS COURSEWARE AVAILABLE?

Computer-based training system vendors have devoted huge amounts of time and money to writing courses for general use. Whether or not a specific course is already available will depend on the area of interest. Extremely specialized skills and specific equipment and technologies mitigate against finding existing courseware.

Reynolds: There are thousands of hours of courseware available today. One company in the CBL

field has a staff of several hundred persons engaged full time in the courseware development process. Powerful authoring aids have come into general use relatively recently, and they can be expected to accelerate the development of courseware. Everyone's needs will never be met, but the body of off-the-shelf courseware will continue to increase.

If an organization cannot find the exact courseware it needs, it should:

- Determine if there is any courseware that exists. Some companies have developed CBL courseware in specialized areas that they will license.
- Use part of something that does exist, or use all of something as part of a needed course.
- If there is absolutely nothing, find another organization that needs the same course. A consortium of companies working together to develop courseware for their industry could be useful to the entire industry. An excellent example of this is a consortium of petroleum companies formed to develop a petroleum geophysics course.

Davis: There are two exceptions to our generalized answer. Most vendors offer basic skills programs in math, reading and such fundamentals as basic electricity. Some of these programs are excellent. The second exception comes in the areas of accounting and business computing where several companies are offering sophisticated programs.

CAN I USE MY EXISTING COMPUTER?

Davis: It is possible but not desirable, for two key reasons. Most companies exercise tight control over access to operations computers. There is rarely extra computer power floating around free. At three o'clock in the morning, the computer is easy to access; but during the day, the response time of most operational computer systems is slow by CBL standards. Most operational computer managers think four-second response time is fast, but CBL people think it is slow.

The other factor to consider is that data terminals generally make poor teaching terminals. So even if the mainframe could be used, the terminals would be inappropriate.

Reynolds: Trainers should remember that the systems and terminals that are in place meet a current need in the organization. The time hasn't arrived when most white-collar workers have a terminal at their desk. Current terminal settings make use by anyone but the regular user difficult.

The person who asks this question must have a group of terminals in mind, since running the CBL courseware on the organizational computer constitutes a cost. The power of a central system may be needed for instructional management, central record storage or computation. If these are not required, the central system may be desirable in order to use its powerful authoring utilities or flexible programmerless authoring.

The capabilities of the current computer must be examined and many different possibilities explored.

WHAT AM I GOING TO DO WITH THE INSTRUCTORS I HAVE NOW?

This question is voiced rarely, yet it is a concern of HRD practitioners. We are too much a part of the behavioral science discipline not to care about people.

This is one of the areas that is answered by examination of the many effects of CBL on an organization. The instructor is needed in a CBL organization. However, the title and function of the job will change. The instructor is set free from the imprisonment of the platform. As a facilitator of learning, the instructor doesn't just talk at a group of 30 learners. Since much of the routine instruction is delivered by a CBL terminal, the learning facilitator is free to interact on a one-on-one basis with learners. Records are generated automatically, removing a distasteful part of the job. Instructors still are needed, and they are going to enjoy their new job as learning facilitator much more.

REFERENCES

1. Cain, J. Computer-based training at United Airlines. *Training and Development Journal*, March 1981, pp. 76–78.

TECHNIQUES FOR IMPLEMENTING TRAINING AND DEVELOPMENT PROGRAMS

How To Prepare Your People

by Gregory H. Cripple and Harry E. Litchfield

Let's look at a typical discussion between a manager and subordinate prior to the subordinate attending a seminar:

Scene: The Manager's office, 4:25 p.m. Friday afternoon.

The manager *says:* "Hi! C'mon in and sit down. I just wanted to let you know that you're going to a management training program at headquarters next week. I think this is something that will do you a lot of good.

Now, first of all, I want you to come back with a better understanding and appreciation for your job. Try to develop a deeper awareness, too, so that you're better able to grasp the significance of your present assignment. Of course, I wouldn't mind a little more enthusiasm for your work either.

Well, this has been a good discussion; I feel good about it. You should too, now that you know what's expected of you.

By the way, don't forget to have a good time and get your batteries charged!"

The subordinate *says:* "OK, boss. Sounds good. See you in a week!"

The manager *thinks:* Boy, am I glad that's over. I'm not sure myself exactly what all that meant, but it sounded good. Now we'll let those "training types" whip him into shape.

The subordinate *thinks:* Good Grief! What kind of program am I going to? Why am I *really* going and why now? What's "deeper awareness" mean anyway? The boss must think I've been slacking off lately.

I thought I already was motivated and enthusiastic!

What is the program about? Should I concentrate on specific parts of it? If so, which ones? How is my work going to get done while I'm going? Who's paying the motel bill? Where will. . . . ?

Maybe this discussion is a little overdone, but probably not too much in reality. And similar conversations, often shorter and even more cryptic (if they happen at all), take place many times each day as managers "prepare" their subordinates for upcoming training programs or, "debrief" them upon return from recently completed ones.

WHY?

One answer may be that many managers feel the trainer is mainly responsible for their subordinate's development, not them. Thus, they tend to abdicate this responsibility. But, it seems difficult to accept this explanation given the emphasis in training and management literature on manager involvement in subordinate training experiences. The majority of managers are more than likely aware their support of subordinate training is at least in concept a desirable thing. Another possibility is the managers *think* they are doing what they should be doing. And the trainer may unknowingly be reinforcing this misconception.

HOW?

By committing a cardinal sin of training. Just as students have trouble performing when presented with a "fuzzy" training objective, managers also cannot be expected to "perform" when not told what is expected of them. Trainers set fuzzy expectations for managers when they in fact say, "Hey! You've got to support your subordinates' training," but don't tell them *how* they are expected to do it.

Managers engage subordinates in conversations similar to the one beginning this article. They're convinced they're fulfilling their support duties when in fact, they may be creating more questions in their subordinates' minds than answers.

To quote the warden from the movie *Cool Hand Luke,* "What we have here is a failure to communicate!" And it may be the fault lies with the trainers, not the managers.

At John Deere, one effort we've made to overcome this alleged communication gap is mentioned in "Professionalism vs. Salesmanship: Focusing on Evaluation at John Deere" (*Training and Development Journal,* April 1978). In that article, we described an evaluation procedure that encourages manager-subordinate discussion about seminar objectives prior to the subordinate attending a program. It also tends to spark a similar discussion about how well the objectives were achieved afterward.

A second technique we'd like to share is shown in Figure 1. What is displayed there is the "nuts & bolts" of a brochure entitled "How to Prepare Your People." It is sent to managers of participants in pro-

FIGURE 1
"How To Prepare Your People"
A guide to what managers can do to ensure their people get the most out of management development programs.

To the Manager:	Before Attending	After Attending	Some Tips to Help Participants Get the Most Out of a Program.
Think back to the training programs you've been to. How often did you have unanswered questions about the program? How often were you sent to a program not knowing exactly **why** you were going, **what** you were supposed to concentrate on, and what **changes** were expected of you when you returned? If you answer these questions as many managers do, one answer fits them all: "**Far too** often!" This guide is intended to provide you with some guidelines on how to prevent your people from having to give the same answer to these questions. Research has shown that training is more effective if it is preceded and followed by discussions with one's supervisor. For people to benefit most from a program, they should sit down with their supervisor to discuss the program they will attend and what they hope to gain from it in terms of changed job performance. Upon returning, they should further discuss what they learned and how they intend to use it. With these considerations in mind, this brochure has been designed to help you in your discussions with your people who are going to attend a program.	Participants will benefit more from attending a management development program if you show an interest in their participation and talk to them about it. Here are some suggestions for this discussion: ☐ 1. Let them know of their selection to attend the program well in advance and discuss **why** they were selected. ☐ 2. Look over the objectives and content of the program. Be able to give a brief picture of what they can expect. ☐ 3. Also, let them know what **you** expect them to gain and relate this to the objectives as well as to their specific job responsibilities. ☐ 4. Ask individuals to think of problems they might be able to find solutions to by interacting with other participants. This will help build a sense of purpose for attending. ☐ 5. Ask them to be prepared to discuss the program when they return. ☐ 6. Assure them that departmental arrangements have been made so that they can concentrate on the program without worrying unnecessarily about their job. ☐ 7. When appropriate, cover any necessary expense account arrangement with them.	If you want your people to get the most benefit from a program, talk to them about it after they get back on the job. Schedule plenty of time for it—free from distractions and interruptions. Here are some suggested points to cover: ☐ 1. Welcome them back. Ask if the program measured up to their expectations. ☐ 2. Ask, what was learned. ☐ 3. Ask how they intend to use this new knowledge or skill—especially look for concrete suggestions. Try to get commitments to apply within a set period of time. ☐ 4. Suggest that they present to other members of your group certain worthwhile materials or concepts. ☐ 5. Don't make this the last discussion you have about the program. Check back several times over the next three to six months to see how they have followed through with their plans. **Make them accountable for what they have learned.** ☐ 6. For out-of-company programs, ask them to complete an evaluation form which is available from your Personnel Department. (Forward a copy to Deere & Company.) These are analyzed and retained by the Management Development Department and form the basis for recommendations concerning these programs for other employees.	Much of the success of a program in terms of usefulness to the participants depends on their attitude. Encourage them to: ☐ 1. Enter into discussions and talk with other participants about common problems and their possible solutions. ☐ 2. Be willing to learn from the experience. Avoid being critical and insensitive to the aims of the group. ☐ 3. Meet new people and avoid "chumming" with people from the same unit. ☐ 4. Search for new ideas. Suggest they return from the program with an "action plan" with at least one new idea that will help improve their performance. ☐ 5. Listen carefully to learn new ideas from subject content and don't judge a session on the instructor's charm or funny stories. ☐ 6. Get involved as much as possible when there are participative activities. Don't be a passive participant. ☐ 7. Use time well. This is up to each participant—they can make friends, stimulate thinking, get new ideas, and strengthen their own thoughts—or **waste** time. ☐ 8. Continually refer to the objectives of the program and ask themselves: "What am I learning?" "How can I use this back on the job?"

grams offered by the Deere and Company Management Development Department about three weeks in advance of the program to be attended. It's also used as the basis for a module on the manager's role in the training process in our seminar for middle managers. Its purpose is to help managers effectively support the learning experiences of their subordinates with a checklist of suggestions for things to do and/or discuss both prior to and after attending a training program. Also offered are some tips on how to get the most out of a training experience for managers to pass along to their subordinates if they choose.

Use of a technique such as this does not ensure management support of training. However, in recent evaluation studies we've found an increasing percentage of participants having meaningful pre- and post-seminar discussions with their managers. Interestingly, we are finding this increase is even greater if the manager has attended our earlier mentioned seminar for middle managers.

Saul Gellerman has likened unsupported training to "expensive seed that is scattered on untilled ground and then left uncultivated and uncared for." If it is to successfully change performance and improve results, training must be *actively* reinforced and nurtured. Obviously, trainers cannot necessarily follow participants back to their jobs and that leaves the responsibility to the managers. But trainers cannot expect managers to succeed in this regard unless the managers know what they are expected to do. And we feel it's the trainers' responsibility to make sure they do through aids like "How To Prepare Your People."

REFERENCES

- Cook, James R., "Management Training? Don't Waste Your Money!" *Supervisory Management*, February 1978.
- Gellerman, A. W., "Training & Behavior Change." *Training and Development Journal*, February 1977.
- Sherer, W. R., "How to Get Management's Commitment For Training." *Training and Development Journal*, January 1978.
- Hickerson, K. A. and Litchfield, H. E., "Professionalism vs. Salesmanship: Focusing on Evaluation at John Deere." *Training and Development Journal*, April 1978.
- Phillips, J. J., "How to Improve Management Support for Supervisory Training Programs." *Training and Development Journal*, August 1978.
- Rackham, N., "The Coaching Controversy." *Training and Development Journal*, November 1979.

What Should Training Rooms Be Like?

by Dugan Laird

THE INFLUENCE OF THE T & D OFFICER

Perhaps we should think of the places where we meet to train as "learning rooms" rather than as training rooms, conference rooms or—above all—as classrooms. On the other hand, maybe the semantics are insignificant; maybe the important thing is just that the place where people gather should be conducive to the learnings.

It might seem at first that architects make all the decisions about those rooms. Things like the modularity of the building structure and building codes influence critical factors like dimensions and ceiling heights. T & D specialists can easily feel "out of it" when it comes to these key decisions. However, T & D officers can influence architectural decisions when buildings are in the planning stage; instructors can do a great deal to adjust the physical environment during training; everybody in the T & D function can observe key criteria when selecting hotels, motels, or conference sites.

CRITERIA FOR LEARNING ROOMS

Different kinds of learnings require different environments. For example, if contemplation and introspection are involved, then calm and quiet seem necessary. If the learning requires movement, lots of open space

is a must. Even so, there are general criteria. Experienced instructors will tell you they want flexibility, ventilation, isolation, and lighting control. Each of them is important enough to rate discussion by itself.

Flexibility

If instructors or course designers had to settle for just one quality in learning rooms, chances are they'd opt for flexibility.

Flexibility is an understandable criterion if you just stop to think about the wide variety of methods professional T & D specialists employ nowadays. Within a single room—probably within a single afternoon—class activities may vary from watching a filmstrip to fishbowling, from engaging in discussions to roleplaying to working on individualized programmed texts. The instructor therefore wants a room which can quickly and easily be rearranged.

Plenty of space is a "must" if buzzgroups are to work simultaneously in a learning center—and there's much to be said for their visible proximity to one another. The synergism produced by such nearness vanishes quickly (as do lots of precious minutes!) if the groups must commute to nearby break-out rooms. Besides, how often are these rooms truly "nearby"?

A major element of flexibility is size. Cramped quarters don't give the needed flexibility, or that sense of growth-potential needed for the learning experience. One way to estimate the adequacy of a room is to calculate the square-feet-per-participant. Such calculations need to allow for chairs, tables, access,

Dugan Laird, *Approaches to Training and Development,* © 1978, Addison-Wesley, Reading, Massachusetts, pp. 177–94. Reprinted with permission.

and capacity for course equipment. For "theatre type" sessions, nine or ten square feet per person is about right. Of course, this arrangement limits one to "tell-and-show" presentational types of methods. Classroom set-ups (rows of chairs, probably with arm-tablets) require 15 to 17 square feet per participant. Conference arrangements place learners at tables, and require 23 to 25 square feet per person. The table should allow at least 30 linear inches per person. It should also provide 18 to 24 inches of depth. This permits learners to spread their papers and learning materials during workshop activities.

For that reason, tables that are 60 inches long are excellent: they offer the minimum working dimensions for participants, but they can be easily shifted to new arrangements. Such flexibility doesn't apply to the six-foot tables often ordered for training rooms. The six-foot table offers an additional hazard: the temptation to crowd three people onto each side! It follows that tables 60 inches by 36 inches permit two people to sit at each side, providing both adequate table-top space and face to face seating for two-way communication during discussion and team task activities.

What does this imply for the total dimensions of the learning room? The Rocky Mountain Association of Meeting Planners recommends these specifications in *Training*, July 1976:

For this type of activity	Provide these dimensions
Conference	23–25 square feet per participant
Classroom	15–17 square feet per participant
Theatre	9–10 square feet per participant
Meals	11½–12½ square feet per diner
Receptions	8½–9½ square feet per guest

Another way to check adequacy of the dimensions is to base distances on the width of the screen used for visual presentations. Several critical judgments may be based on that single distance:

* The distance from screen to the last row of seats should not exceed 6W, or six screen-widths.
* The distance to the front row of seats should be 2W, twice the width of the screen. Participants who are nearer than that may be expected to experience discomfort and fatigue.
* The proper width of the viewing area is 3W, or one and one-half widths from a centerline extended perpendicular to the screen through the viewing area. If this criterion is met, no one will be farther to the right or left of the screen than 1W.

These figures (quoted or extrapolated from an article by Raymond Wadsworth in *American School and*

University Magazine, October 1971) indicate that another element in flexibility is the proportion of the room.

Optimum width-to-depth ratio is three to four according to Dr. Gerald McVey, quoted in *A User's Look at The Audio-Visual World* from the National Audio-Visual Association. The closer a room comes to this ratio, the more appropriate it will be for visual presentations.

Davis and Hagman of the National Conference Center advocate a room " . . . as nearly square as possible." They argue that square rooms bring people together "psychologically as well as physically." They continue by saying, "Both sight and sound, vital factors in verbal and nonverbal communications, are facilitated." In no case, they contend, should the length exceed the width by more than 50 percent. (*Training*, July 1976, p. 29)

An added virtue of either of these ratios is that the room can be changed on a functional or daily basis. The wall which is "front" today can be the side or rear wall tomorrow. Such reorientation gives a fresh viewpoint to the activities. It also causes participants to regroup. That's often healthy: more trainees get acquainted with each other, and the paralyzing impact of cliques is minimized.

If the screen is permanently mounted on the wall, that wall tends always to be the front. It needn't be. At sessions with no visual presentation, tables and chairs can face a different direction. This shift gives a "different feeling" and subtly underlines the theme that during training, change is the name of the game.

A special note: When the screen isn't being used, keep it rolled up. Participants inadvertently bump into, scratch, puncture, or otherwise deface screens; dust has a bad effect on any type of screen surface. Stored screens avoid these abuses.

Ceiling height is important. Anything under 10 feet poses problems for instructors and conference leaders. The screen should be high enough so learners in the rear can see it "above" and not "around" the heads of people in front of them. Experts urge that the top of the screen be as high as possible. Don't measure ceiling height from the center of the room. Enclosed airducts and indirect lighting lower the ceiling alongside some walls. Screens must then be placed too low, or away from the walls. This reduces total useful square-footage in the room.

Acoustical engineering is a special technology, beyond the range of most T & D officers. However, anyone can check a few things. Carpets should be a low pile, nonabsorptive. Ornamental ceilings and crystal chandeliers are good. According to Cyril M. Harris of Columbia University, they provide excellent "diffusion" and produce a desirable "sound decay curve." (*The New Yorker*, Nov. 8, 1976, p. 63) T & D officers can influence such details when designing new training centers; T & D specialists can check these features when selecting rooms in rented or leased facilities.

Dr. Gerald McVey, Associate Professor of Educational Media and Technology at Boston University, urges careful consideration of student chairs. They should have relatively flat seats, slightly dished in the buttocks area, about 17 inches from the floor. He recommends an inch of padding, plus a slight padding for the back. The back should be slightly curved, with major support in the lumbar area. Parts which contact the learner (seat and frame) should be constructed of material which does not conduct heat or cold. If desks, or tablet arms, are included, the writing surfaces should be slightly inclined and about 27 inches above the floor.

Davis points out, in *Planning, Conducting and Evaluating Workshops*, that "Adults are people who have relatively large bodies subject to the stress of gravitational stimuli . . . Most experience discomfort when they sit too long in hard chairs. Chairs that are too short or too narrow are worse. Some adults fall asleep in chairs that are just right."(p. 20)

Isolation

Isolation is another criterion. It doesn't mean that learning rooms are soundproofed and windowless—though those conditions sure do help! Soundproofing has an obvious value. Windowless rooms are excellent for visual presentations. They offer minimum distraction and external noise; there's less hazard from temperature shifts.

Isolation also implies that the room is sufficiently removed from the workplace so the learners know they are in training. If the proper policies prevail, such isolation can take place within a few feet of the workplace. Bosses of trainees should understand that when their employees are in training, the instructor is "the boss" and that all messages to trainees are routed through the instructor. Many organizations state policy clearly: nothing except personal crisis in the trainee's immediate family will be mentioned to trainees during learning sessions. They sometimes call this their "thousand-mile rule." Work-related messages or requests will not be delivered to trainees during the session unless the content is so critical that it would cause the manager to call the trainee back to the duty post were the trainee a thousand miles away!

Effective isolation is further achieved by a policy communicated before reporting to training: Instead of performing regular duties, for the period of the training trainees are expected to achieve the objectives of the program. "Learning" is their work.

Thus isolation is both physical and psychological. Considerations in achieving isolation range from getting far away from highways, airports, and loud plumbing to getting away from the boss!

Lighting Control

Lighting Control is a prime criterion for visual presentations. Although total darkness is required by only a few visual media nowadays, excess sunlight can dampen the sensory impact of even the most colorful films. As we noted when discussing flexibility, windows are thus something of a liability. (Some folks protest, saying it's unnatural to be away from the sun that long. But instructors who work in windowless rooms report that sunlight is usually available at coffee breaks, at lunchtime, or when the session breaks for the day!)

One dimension of lighting control is the ability to eliminate light; another is the ability to diminish it by degrees. The advantages of rheostat controls are obvious—especially if there are several. In some designs, different learners will be doing different things simultaneously. Thus, if the instructor can have bright light in one portion of the room and dim light in another, multi-method designs are easily executed. When the screen must be placed near permanent light fixtures, there's trouble. If there aren't rheostats to dim them, or switches to eliminate the light, then a ladder and a quick twist become the instructor's problem-solving materials!

For normal student note-taking, 30 to 50 footcandles are minimum. Some people, as the National Conference Center staff, recommend 70 footcandles at desk level. Dr. Gerald McVey notes that when taxing visual tasks are part of the student's activity, 100 or more footcandles should be available. This means that there should be lots of lumens available at worktables when participants work with minute diagrams or precise visual discriminations.

Within any learning room there is a potential problem of glare. It can best be prevented by removing naked lamps or glossy surfaces. Trainers who inherit rooms with glaring lamps and windows should install shades and drapes. Trainers who rent public rooms with glossy tables should insist on tablecloths. (By the way, here's a tip. When arranging for rented rooms: be sure to insist that there be a tablecloth for each table! Otherwise, when you go to move the tables to fit the changing activities of the design, you'll find that the cloths don't come out even . . . and waste lots of time adjusting the ashtrays and water glasses and pitchers.)

Ventilation

Ventilation is another criterion for learning rooms. An additional argument for high ceilings is that when the temperature goes up, so does the heat. But high ceilings will not guarantee good ventilation. Experienced instructors will tell you that ventilation is a "lose-lose" situation. "You can't please all the people any of the time—or any of the people for more than about 15 minutes at a time!" These old-timers say they prefer to keep things a little on the cool side: they'd rather have people alert than asleep!

A more scientific statement, again from Dr. McVey, says that when room temperature is between 68 and 76 degrees Fahrenheit (20° to 25°C) and relative humidity between 30 and 60 percent and air velocity is 12 to 25 feet-per-minute, "heat exchange between people and their environment generally takes place without discomfort." Most adults seem to be most comfortable when the temperature is between 73° and 75°F (22.5° to 24°C) and the relative humidity is about 50 percent. Current interest in pollution and anti-smoking movements has prompted many instructors and conference leaders to establish "Smoking" and "No Smoking" areas. This reminds us that Dr. McVey feels that ventilation is achieved best by keeping the air moving—and that if you must err, you should err on the side of coolness.

Let's emphasize that point about keeping the air moving. T & D officers who are getting new learning rooms would be wise to see that there is proper equipment to provide the minimum air velocity of 12 to 15 feet-per-minute.

There are some special problems associated with projection equipment. Many projectors generate lots of heat. It isn't that the machines make learners all that uncomfortable; it's that the efficient operation and their longevity is affected if the heat continues while the machines are in storage. Dr. McVey gives these guidelines for storing such equipment and material:

If housing	Keep the temperatures		And the relative humidity
	F	C	
Film projectors	65 to 70°	17.8 to 21°	25 to 40%
Film	Below 80°	Below 26.7°	25 to 60%
Audio tape	60 to 90°	15.6 to 32°	20 to 90%

In summary, by checking rooms for compliance with these four criteria—flexibility, isolation, lighting control, and ventilation—the T & D specialist is more likely to be in quarters where learning can easily happen. Beyond the room itself, there are some things instructors and conference leaders can do to make room arrangements conducive to the participation planned for each module of the training.

ROOM ARRANGEMENT

Flexibility is such a vital criterion for the training room because instructors will need to rearrange the furniture so it fits the variety of methods they will be using. The more andragogic the learning design, the more varied the furniture arrangements. This implies that the furniture will be moved—and quite often.

Even if the functional activities of the learning design don't demand a rearrangement, there are several reasons for changing the furniture from time to time:

- Individuals are given a new perspective on the activity by sitting in different parts of the room.
- Individuals get better acquainted with more of their peer-participants when they move around from time to time.
- Handicapped individuals are not consistently and permanently punished by being great distances from the screen or from the speakers.
- Small cliques do not arise. (There's nothing wrong with cliques per se, but in some cases they can become problems by forcing their norms or their agenda upon the entire group.)

The various functional arrangements often found in T & D learning rooms may be analyzed according to their facilitation of two-way communication. In this analysis we will look at them on that basis, starting with the least encumbering arrangements and proceeding to the more formal plans . . . plans which control rather than encourage free-and-easy communication between participants and communications between participants and the instructor. Finally, we'll consider arrangements which "deformalize" those rigid arrangements.

The un-furnitured circle in Figure 1 is probably the most democratic and unencumbered of all arrangements. There is no status symbol denoting a leader, and every participant has direct sightlines to every other participant. Since there is no table between participants, each person is in a sense "totally revealed." Subtle nonverbal communications are possible. This arrangement is typical for T-groups and sensitivity training, for data-gathering sessions in organization-development programs.

This circle (Figure 2) is uncluttered, but there is a clearcut leader. Consider this as a grouping for a brainstorming session. One person is in control, partly because of the standing position and partly because of a "scepter of authority": the pencil and the flipchart or chalkboard.

FIGURE 1

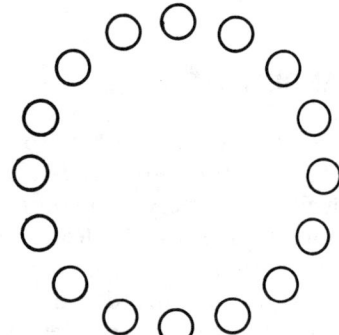

FIGURE 2

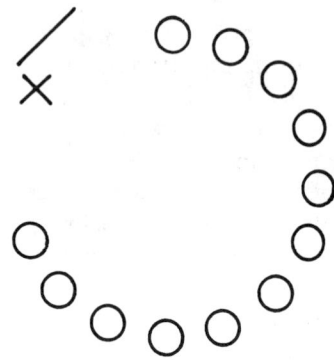

When the circular table is used (Figure 3), participants still have direct access to each other, including facial nonverbal communications. Remember the Paris peace talks? . . . when the nations argued relentlessly about the shape of the table? It apparently *does* make a difference! Informal studies show that there will be more conversation and shorter inputs, and that more members will participate, when the same people sit at round rather than at square tables!

Instructors can always arrange rectangular tables into various rectangular patterns. The square arrangement (Figure 4) produces several more worthy effects. Participants are now seated in rows, the first step toward formality. In rows (as opposed to arcs) nobody can see the faces of all the other participants. Depending upon where visual aids are placed. One side or another may become the "head" of the table. An interesting side light: informal studies show that a gap in the center, as shown here retards participation. A solid table (Figure 5) seems to encourage conversation. With a "hole in the middle," some people don't speak at all and some who do speak tend to talk for longer periods of time. It would thus seem that when instructors want more control, they should arrange the tables around a central "void." For more democratic conversation the tables should be joined to form a solid unit. This holds true with any rectangular arrangement.

If the rectangle becomes long and narrow (Figure 6), there are longer lines. Thus even fewer people can communicate face-to-face with their peers. The positions on the short dimension of the table are often identified as "leadership seats." Could this be because the father sat at the head of the table? Indeed,

FIGURE 3

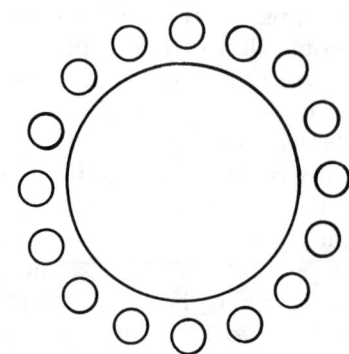

FIGURE 4

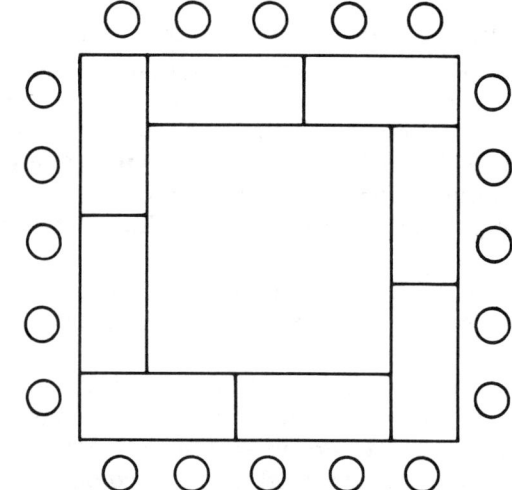

FIGURE 5

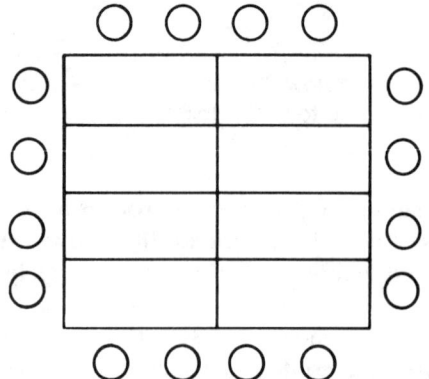

FIGURE 6

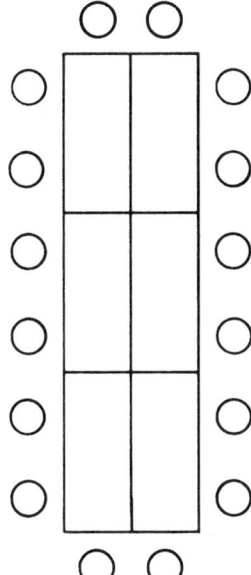

the conventional "U" there are only three rows of students. By placing the tables at an angle, as in Figure 9, the long rows are broken into numerous shorter rows and participants' mutual sightlines are improved.

FIGURE 7

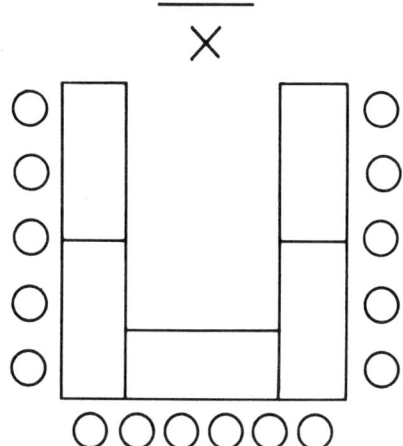

even when no leader is appointed, members along the sides tend to look to the end positions, expecting people seated there to dominate.

You'd probably win the bet if you wagered that more Management Development conferences use the "U" (Figure 7) than any other arrangement. It has a sense of the "senate" with equality of membership—but no doubt about who is presiding. It is frequently effective, even though it does have a formality and a constraint on participants. Since there are just three rows of people, a great many participants are blocked from viewing the faces of their peers.

Although some clutter results from placing people on the inside of the "U," as in Figure 8, such placement does open up more visual contact and bring the entire group into close physical proximity. That proximity cannot be ignored; the farther apart members are from one another, the more reserved their behavior—and the greater the control.

Whenever rectangles are used, the participants should be encouraged (or forced by the nature of the activity) to take distinctly different positions every now and then. If name cards exist, they can be shifted regularly. When such a practice is to be used, it's a good idea to start it at the first break or the first lunch break. This lets participants know that mobility is the norm for the entire program. Most instructors encourage participants to move on a voluntary basis in addition to the moves made with the name cards or the varying activity.

Simply "softening" the shape of the "U" can make considerable difference in the participants' ability to see and communicate with one another. With

FIGURE 8

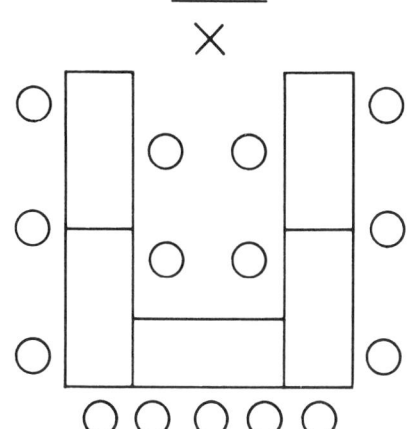

FIGURE 9

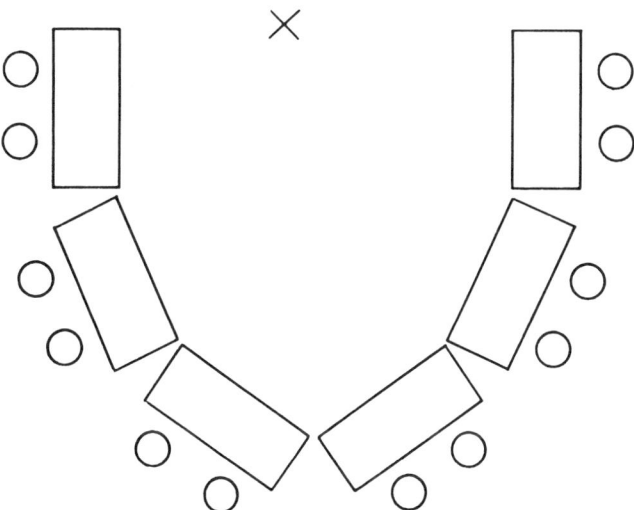

Tables can also be arranged in circular or semicircular patterns (Figure 10). An advantage is the return to the "arc." More people are able to see the faces of more peers than they can in some rectangular arrangements.

Cabaret arrangements, like the one in Figure 11, facilitate the establishment of buzzgroups for team tasks, games, or individual study. A cabaret setting is especially useful during workshop or programmed instruction modules within longer programs. Each table can be designated for a particular activity. At the same time, sight lines and the proximity of learners encourage free exchange of ideas. Discussions involving the entire group can occur as easily in this arrange-ment as in another. The instructors can easily assume a position of authority, yet can just as easily move among individuals or teams when they are working at tables. The cabaret plan reflects an informal, flexible type of learning environment.

The scattershot method (Figure 12) may seem extremely haphazard. It actually permits quick change of learner focus and produces tremendous investments of learner energy. It works very well in multiple role-plays, two-person team tasks, or highly synergistic action training. When necessary, participants can quickly form larger groups. The scattershot arrange-ment produces high interpersonal and intergroup com-munication. It's bad for notetaking, but the scattershot grouping is designed for experiential training when notes are rarely necessary.

The "classroom" set-up is almost the opposite. As shown in Figure 13 it reminds us of academic class-rooms—and is a bit undesirable. When students oc-cupy chairs with arm tablets, the arrangement does have great flexibility. It's easy to shift to scattershot groupings and to break up the "military" rows of seats found in most "schools."

FIGURE 10

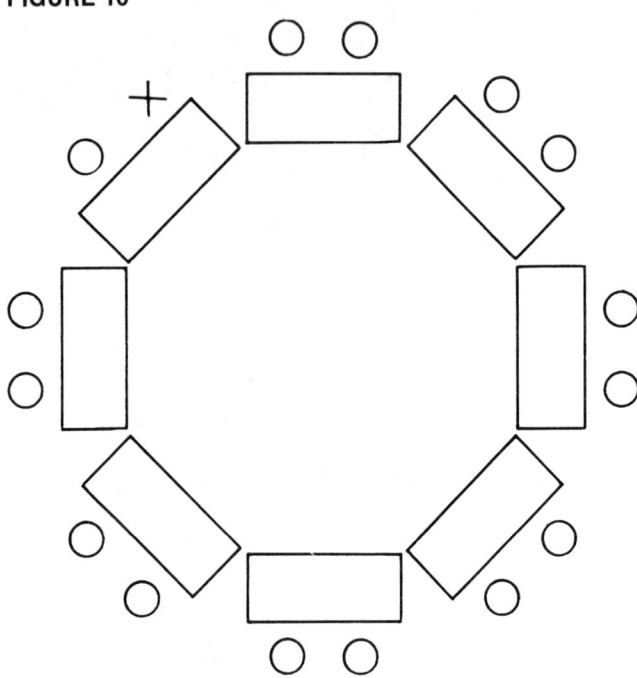

FIGURE 11

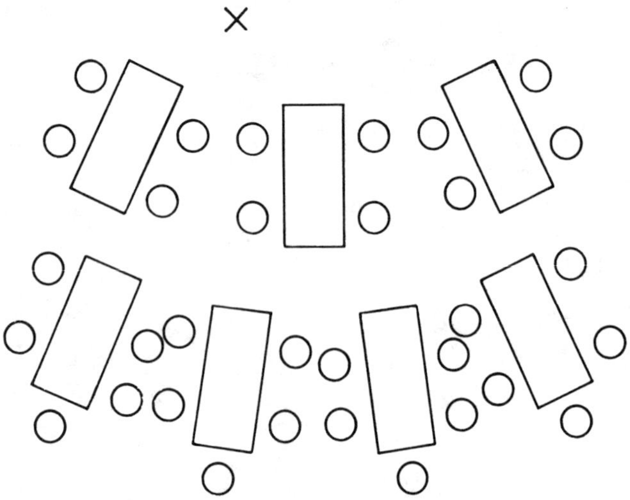

FIGURE 12

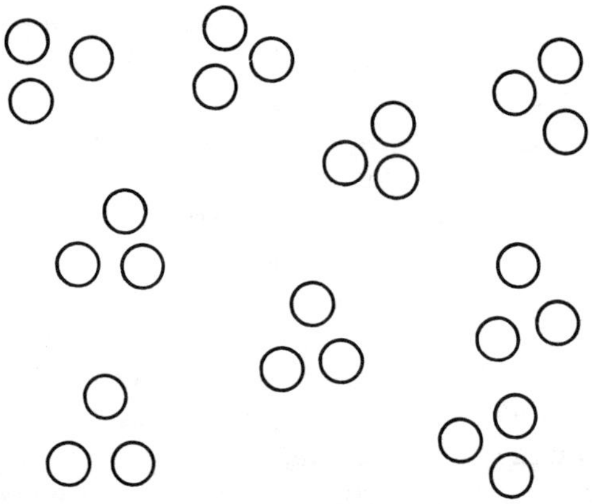

FIGURE 13

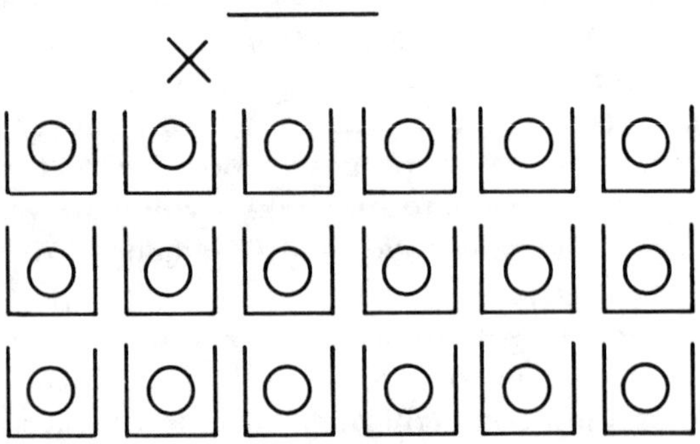

Organizational "classroom arrangements" (Figure 14) usually feature rows of tables. These indicate that there will be considerable control by the instructor. The rows limit face-to-face communication by participants, unless they twist a lot; it's hard to talk to anyone save the instructor or to the people right beside them. Unless there is ample room between the rows of tables, instructors cannot easily access individual learners to review progress with problems or projects. There is a barrier against forming natural groups for team tasks. There is no easy way for instructors to provide private or semi-private counseling.

An antidote for these limitations is a wide aisle between each row (Figure 15). If seating is restricted to the recommended two-at-a-table, instructors can have access to every learner without undue "nearness" of other participants.

Converting the rows to arcs, as in Figure 16, will enhance the learners' ability to communicate with one another. They can more easily see each others' faces, and the lines are bent—so the total environment seems less structured and less rigid. This "chevron" or arched arrangement isn't seen very often, but it's a useful plan in square rooms or in rooms with the recommended 3:4 ratio.

The modified chevron in Figure 17 permits a great deal of cross communication among participants without too much twisting and turning. Instructors are still able to access all parts of the room.

It goes without saying (but probably should be said anyway) that whenever possible the more formal arrangements should be set up so the main entrance is *behind* the learners. In such formal, presentation-type situations, control and focus are hard to maintain when participants are periodically stimulated by the arrival of the mid-morning coffee—or those outsiders who ignore the "Do Not Disturb" sign hanging over the doorknob!

SUMMARY

A "place to make learning happen" need not be a grand room, elaborately furnished. It needn't be

FIGURE 14

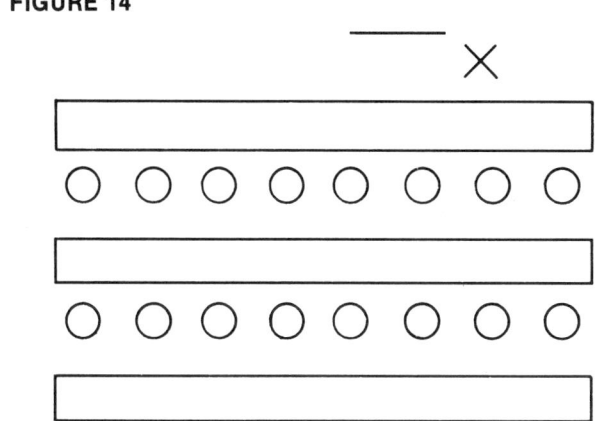

FIGURE 16

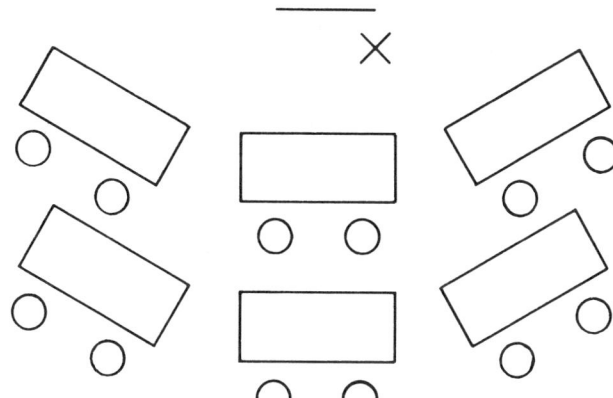

FIGURE 15

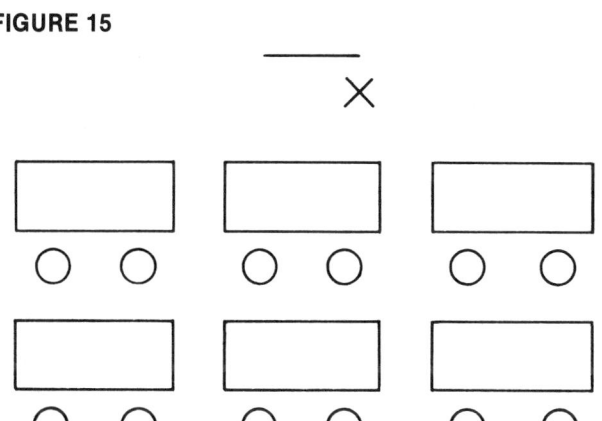

FIGURE 17

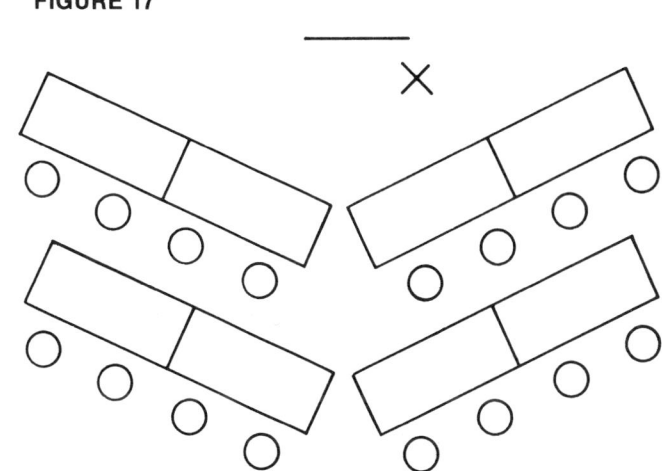

equipped with the latest electronic equipment, media machinery, and fancy control panels. Those things facilitate the mechanics of the support systems of learning. They shouldn't be ridiculed—but in themselves they don't guarantee learning.

A room where learning can happen is flexible—quickly responsive to the group's need for a new ar-rangement. It is isolated, so learners never doubt that their mission is to learn. Lighting and ventilation are not obstacles to maintaining that focus on learning.

But above all the room permits the creativity of the instructor to put things where trainee-participants can quickly use them as tools for their learning processes.

Uses of Silence

by Dugan Laird

When I read Carl Rogers, B. F. Skinner, or Malcolm Knowles, I expect to learn more about how to be a good instructor. But Thomas Carlyle? Just listen: "Speech is human, silence is divine. . . . We therefore must learn both arts." Carlyle might well be talking to us trainers! We are so often intent on the stimuli we send that we try to be stimulating every single second. We thus eliminate any learning that might have happened during silence.

Len Nadler understands this. If you've worked on his committees, you've seen him anguish over con-flict or digression, then heard him say, "I feel we need a few minutes of monastic silence." Len may not know that a John Donne elegy described a space where "harmless fish monastic silence keep," but he sure makes silence work. Participants stare into space, doodle, study their nails; they lay their heads on the table or their bodies on the floor. When discussion resumes, there is often new energy, new direction.

Here's my point: if groups can use silence for renewal, doesn't it follow that learners actually *need* silence to absorb, analyze, accept, or apply new learnings?

Suppose you've just asked a question of a stu-dent. Whether you want recall, analysis, or synthesis, the learner needs time—and deserves it! During that time empathic trainers stay silent. Yet too many of us think of better ways to phrase the question; we discover synonyms to clarify the things learners are trying to think about. So we ask what amounts to a dif-ferent question—right in the middle of the very think-ing we had intended to stimulate.

One Acting text calls the pause the "mind's measurement of thought." Astute trainers insure such uncontaminated silence for their learners. Silence is

thus appropriate after student questions too. Oh, you can establish yourself as a fountain of knowledge by instant answers; but that's very different from establishing credibility as an instructor. Besides, you need time to decide your most productive response. Do you (A) refer the question to the class, (B) refer it back to the asker, (C) combine A and B, or (D) answer it yourself? By thus "measuring your thought," you avoid the Answer-Man Trap. You also put the chance to learn where it belongs: somewhere above the shoulders but below the top of the learner's head.

Next, consider silence during team tasks. Often as the groups gather you hear an apparently painful silence. It seems to say, "We don't understand (or don't like) this task." It ain't necessarily so. They need time to clarify their roles and to ask what ideas and data each member can contribute. A good team project meets Keats's criterion: it's a "foster-child of silence and slow time."

The "Slow Time Syndrome" explains why you should wait for the second silence during team tasks. That initial silence gives gradual way to loud talk, then diminished noise, then almost total silence. It's temp-ting to hurry into the "reports." Beware! This is golden silence: learners are appraising their work, checking their assumptions, enriching their product. They need silence to complete these essential learning steps. After a few minutes, the talking reasserts itself. Not until it fades away a second time should you ask each group if they want more time or if they are ready to share their conclusions with other teams.

Silence is also a balm for conflict. Ben Jonson's Volpone says, "Calumnies are answered best with silence." It's true in front of a class. You can become a cheap debater by retorting to the skeptics and scoffers; you can facilitate with eloquent-but-honest silence. This gives cynics time to re-evaluate; it gives other students time to come to your support. That modern cynic, Dorothy Parker, described a "silence with things going on in it." What a delightful, productive thing to have happen in a classroom.

Finally (and "finally" is the appropriate word) near the end of every learning session trainees need silent, introspective time . . . time to put new information and new behaviors into perspective . . . time to contract with themselves about how often they will apply their new skills . . . how they will measure their effectiveness in doing so . . . how they will overcome the inevitable obstacles to change. Such commitment requires an unpressured environment, of which silence is one key ingredient. When I was in grade school, Miss Tribble made us put our heads down on our desks to "think about what we had learned today." I sometimes slept, but I often thought. Those were good and productive moments, representing what Old Tom Carlyle called "The Golden Gospel of Silence."

Well, those are my prejudices based on a perspective of too many years of trying to become adequate in applying that artscience called "Instruction." I vibrate to the Simon-Garfunkel hymn to the sounds of silence; and I cite one last maxim from Carlyle: "Silence is deep as eternity; Speech is shallow as Time. Under all speech that is good for anything, there lies a silence that is better." If only I could be like the man Thomas Hardy described when he wrote, "That man's silence is wonderful to listen to."

The Art of Questioning

by John S. Randall

Questions represent one of the most important and widely used tools of an instructor. They may be used for the following purposes:

- To arouse interest and curiosity. At the beginning of a session, questions can be used to secure interest and focus the attention of the group on the subject.
- To stimulate discussion. Questions that are thought-provoking can get the group to state reactions.
- To channel the thinking. By skillful questioning, you can steer the group to the objective you have established. You can keep them on the right track and guide their thinking. Also, you can help the group move from the known to the unknown by a series of well-prepared questions.
- To determine how well the group understands the material. By the response given to a question you can determine if the group has absorbed what you have been presenting. It gives you an opportunity to correct any misconceptions or to elaborate on points.
- To get the attention of an individual.
- To help a timid person to express his or her thoughts.

There are three general types of questions that can be used. First, there's the *overhead* question that is directed to the entire group. Anyone may answer. Its primary function is to stimulate group thinking and discussion. You may get an answer from one person at a time or several may attempt to answer. There is also the *direct* question addressed to a definite individual. The third type is the *rhetorical.* This type of question is addressed to the entire group, but an answer is not expected. It is used especially to stimulate thinking, quite often at the beginning of a session.

USE EFFECTIVE QUESTIONS

No matter which type of question you use, the question should require thinking in order to be answered. This rules out questions which may be answered by "yes" or "no." You want to develop constructive thinking and eliminate guessing. Each question should have a specific purpose and be pertinent to the subject.

Questions should be brief and easily understood. A long question is confusing. Your listeners will forget the first part or become so involved in thinking about the first part they won't hear the entire question. To be understood you should express the question in the language of the group. If you discover they do not understand the question, rephrase it or approach it from a different angle.

Each question should be restricted to one main thought. Don't link several questions together and be certain the question is neither too general nor too broad.

Although the art of questioning is being considered as a separate item here, your questions should be a natural part of your presentation. You should plan the questions you want to ask, but you should be flexible and adjust to the responses given by participants. You may have to change some questions; you may not ask all you have prepared.

Whether you use a direct or an overhead question, address the question to the entire group. If you want a certain person to respond, name him or her after you've stated the question. This requires the entire group to think about the question and the answer. If you give the name first, only that person will think about the answer.

Distribute the questions among the group; don't direct them to one or two individuals. Don't establish a definite pattern for asking questions. Participants will soon figure this out, and won't do much thinking about the subject until their turn comes.

Questions which arouse antagonism should not be used. These will cause the group to draw away from you.

Avoid questions which you know the group cannot answer. Don't put individuals on the spot by directing a question to them that they can't answer.

Ask questions in a friendly, sincere manner. The tone and manner should be such that participants are encouraged to express themselves. Your manner should encourage confidence and understanding. Tone of voice is very important. If your tone suggests indifference, lack of confidence, distrust, sarcasm, or a know-it-all attitude, your question will not be effective. A friendly tone, a pleasant expression, even a sparkle in your eyes can help insure the best reception to your question.

Why, where, when, who, what and how can be used in phrasing questions. Statements can be effective as questioning devices. For example: *Tell me why . . . Explain your reason . . . Describe how . . .*

Examples of effective questions would be:

- *How does this problem look to you?* This is an open question in that it invites individuals to express what they think. It doesn't make them feel that they must conform to a certain pattern or answer in a certain way.
- *How did you work out your solution?* This gives direction, and encourages students to think that their solution has merit.
- *What would you say the first step should be?* This appeals to reason. What are your reasons? Can you give us a specific example? Suppose we did this—

what would happen? Are there any other factors to be considered?

HANDLING RESPONSES

How you handle the responses to your questions is very important. You can alienate an individual or an entire group if you aren't careful. The incorrect handling of a response may cause an individual to withdraw mentally from the session.

You must give individuals time to answer. Remember they have to think about it and formulate their answers. If you think that the question is not understood, rephrase it, or break the question down into smaller parts. If you've used an overhead question, don't worry about the lack of immediate response. Someone will eventually break the silence. It may seem like a long time to you but actually it isn't. Don't answer the question yourself. If you start answering the questions without giving the group time to think, you will encourage the class to rely on you for all of the answers.

You should acknowledge all responses. If the answer is good, praise the individual or comment favorably on it—*"That's a good point." "That's important." "Yes." "You're on the right track."* If the answer is not clear to you or if it's incorrect, do some additional questioning. By skillful questioning, you can get a student to elaborate on an answer. You can also "lead" him or her to the discovery that the answer is not correct or that there's a flaw in his or her reasoning. You can rephrase your question or ask a leading question. Your main purpose is to help the individual with thinking, not to embarrass or make him or her feel foolish.

You can get comments from others by directing questions to individuals or to the group as a whole.

A relay question can be used to get comments from everyone. This is a question you ask of everyone, one at a time. It's an effective technique to get everyone involved and to get everyone to say something. It helps the timid person break the ice.

Questions will be directed to you. Many of these you will answer immediately; some you won't answer at all. You can expect to get two types of questions: those that are legitimate requests for information, and those intended to embarrass you. It is sometimes difficult to distinguish between them. However, as you become familiar with the individuals in the group, you learn how to handle them and their questions.

In answering questions, be certain that you reply to the question that was asked. *Don't* evade the question and don't ramble. Be as specific as possible. If the question is not clear to you, ask to have it repeated or ask for some additional information, perhaps an example or illustration. In a small group, everyone will probably hear the question. If the question is not heard by everyone, repeat it.

Don't answer the question so quickly that you give the impression that the individual should have known the answer. But don't take too long. Take just long enough to indicate that you are giving thought to your answer.

The reverse question technique can be used if you want to get the individual or group to do some thinking. This means that you should direct the question back to the individual with an appropriate comment. For example: *"That's a good question. I'd like to hear your comments on it, Mr. Smith."* Or *"What would some of you suggest?"* You can summarize the answers or opinions and add to them after the members of the group have expressed their views.

You may be asked a question you can't or don't want to answer. If you can't answer because you don't know, simply state that you don't know. You can offer to find out and let them know (be certain that you do), or you can ask if anyone in the group knows. If you know there's someone in the group who knows, you can refer the question to him or her . . . *"I don't know but Mr. _____, or Bill, has had considerable experience in that line. Let's ask him."* Most individuals will respond. There's nothing wrong with admitting you don't know or calling on someone else, but don't do it too frequently. If you do, the group's opinion of you and their respect for your knowledge diminishes.

If it's a question that will be answered later in the session or in another session, tell the group this. Just be certain that you do cover it. If it's an irrelevant question or one you shouldn't answer, simply state that it is something that does not pertain to the current subject, or it's something you are not qualified to answer. Do this as tactfully as you can.

Keeping your temper and not becoming upset or impatient are important to you as an instructor. Don't forget that what may seem to be an inappropriate or ill-timed question to you may be an indication of a need you have overlooked. The manner in which you handle questions can have an important influence on your effectiveness as an instructor.

Reinforcing Your Training Programs

by Herman Birnbrauer

A good training program will impart knowledge about the topic, develop reasons why trainees should want to master that topic and provide opportunity for practice. Trainees should return to the workplace able to use new "tools," correctly, with a high degree of self-confidence.

There are many obstacles trainers have to overcome to achieve maximum success. Trainers must be prepared to establish a *climate* for training to take place. This climate could be created much quicker if the trainees arrived at the program with a desire to participate. For this to happen, someone has to properly prepare the trainees for the program. The person best suited for this task is the immediate supervisor of the trainee. Unfortunately, in the "real world," most supervisors are not performing this important task adequately.

Our experience proves that Form A (page 179) is a good means of getting the proper climate started.

Using this process stimulates trainees into thinking about their reasons for attending, along with at least three topics they want to discuss.

We all too frequently hear responses to the question, "Why did you come to this session?", like these:

* Not sure.
* I must have done something wrong.
* It's a day off.
* It's better than night work.
* My boss was supposed to come—I'm just filling in.
* My boss didn't tell me yet.

Sometimes trainees are very unhappy at being forced to attend, and they proceed to do everything they can to interfere with the learning climate you are trying to establish.

Besides starting the process of getting the trainee thinking of the session, Form A also can be used to conduct a needs analysis of the group of trainees. The trainer should list the *"Three Things I Would Like To Discuss"* from each trainee as they are reported. The group, now, has an idea of their collective needs. Going through this list with the trainees, at the end of the session, makes the loop closer for the training program.

Additionally, there seems to be several problems that should be faced. For skills to be locked in, they must be applied back on the job. For this to happen, there will have to be active support and involvement by the supervisor. Our problem as trainers, is three-fold:

1. How do we get the supervisor's involvement in sending trainees properly?
2. How do we get the supervisor to know what these newly acquired skills are—when they haven't been to the training session themselves?
3. How do we get supervisors to support and reinforce these newly acquired skills?

The first and second phase of our problem can be corrected by using Form B. This form gets the trainee's supervisor involved ahead of time. After the supervisor has answered these questions (on Form B), the parting interview becomes easier and more successful for the supervisor.

When the supervisor discusses an upcoming training program with a trainee in terms of the questions on Form B, the trainee arrives at the program ready to participate. The climate of the program is vastly different.

We have found that most often the supervisor doesn't conduct the pre-session interview because they don't know how, or they do it incorrectly. If you find this, then you must provide a brief overview and some training in conducting the interview for the supervisors.

PROGRAM START

When the program starts, you, the trainer, explain the importance of learning new skills and their use back on the job. You might point out that each person will acquire different "tools/skills" because each person has different needs on the job.

You should say something like the following:

All too often people participate in a training session and like it. They also like the tools, and then return to the job, and never apply the new tools. This is, more often than not, the fault of the organization and not the participant.

Therefore, in this session we will take steps to make sure you have the opportunity to use the new tools, back on the job, that you learn here during the training.

Form C asks you to list the "tools" from the course. Some you already know, some you feel okay about, and some you want to try back on the job. The form also asks you how your supervisor can support and reinforce these tools. This form is provided to help you think through the tools, and how you can use them as the session progresses.

TRAINER AND SUPERVISOR MEETING

The trainer should approach the trainee's supervisor with several goals to accomplish. Start by mentioning that the trainee will be returning from the session, and success may very well depend on:

1. that new tools are acquired
2. that there is support for applying these on the job

Your task, now, is to get the supervisor to schedule a meeting with the trainee. During that meeting the supervisor should:

1. Find out what new tools were acquired
2. Find out how they could be used on the job
3. Discuss ways the tools may be best applied
4. Find out what support and reinforcement can be provided as they use the new tools. (New tools don't always work perfectly, right away, and for that reason, it will probably take added support and reinforcement on their part.)
5. During this meeting, the supervisor should also schedule a follow-up meeting. The supervisor may want to alter the support and reinforcement they have been providing, based on how it's going.

The next step is to get the supervisor's agreement for you, the trainer, to also follow-up.

It will be necessary for you, the trainer, to reinforce the supervisor for their efforts. People respect what is inspected! This model should establish some quality control, based on performance improvement. When we inspect for the use of new tools, they will be given attention and used.

Our experience has shown that many supervisors do not hold preattendance, or post-meetings properly. We have also found that it is because they are not familiar with the procedures of conducting an interview of this kind.

The trainer can be a great aid and resource to the supervisor by providing an overview of the program. You should read over and review the objectives, agenda and expectations with the supervisor to give them ammunition for their meetings.

FORM A

NAME:_____

Location of my plant is: _____

My department is:_____

I've worked as _____ for _____ years before promotion.

My reason for coming to this session is: _____

_____

_____

I would like to discuss:

A. _____

B. _____

My interests are:

1. _____

2. _____

3. _____

FORM B

TOPIC: _____

1. I see this topic as applicable to our company/department situation for this reason:

2. Our people can use this topic in the following areas:

3. To me, this topic consists of:

a) _____

b) _____

c) _____

4. The reason I am sending my people is:

a) _____

b) _____

c) _____

5. I expect from them:

a) _____

b) _____

c) _____

6. I can support/reinforce our people on this topic by:

a) _____

b) _____

FORM C
ACTION FORM

A course like "_____" provides many "tools." Every person attending acquires different tools, because we are all different with many different job needs. Many times you return to the "Alligator Swamp" after a course, and never get a chance to use your newly acquired "tools." As you go through this session, use this form to record several things:

1. those things you feel okay about—your development needs have been met
2. those things you would like to try, but will need your supervisor's support and reinforcement

I. TOOLS—I FEEL OKAY ABOUT

1. _____

2. _____

3. _____

4. _____

5. _____

II. TOOLS—I WOULD LIKE TO USE

1. _____

2. _____

3. _____

4. _____

5. _____

III. TOOLS—HOW I PLAN TO USE THEM

1. _____

2. _____

3. _____

4. _____

5. _____

IV. WAYS MY SUPERVISOR CAN SUPPORT AND HELP REINFORCE

1. _____

2. _____

3. _____

4. _____

5. _____

You may also find it advisable to share with the supervisor the guidelines that follow:

1. Don't argue.
2. Be prepared to listen. Get understanding of the trainee's point of view.
3. Seek clarification. Ask questions.
4. Mirror back the trainee's view—avoid giving advice.
5. Try to find out what the tool being discussed means to the trainee.
6. Find out how the trainee can, or plans, to use the tool.
7. Find out what support the trainee needs.

We have conducted sufficient research to prove that when these steps are taken there will be a substantially improved atmosphere in the training session. When the post-meeting is held, the performance of the trainee *does* change on the job, and the new tools get added to the trainee's repertoire.

SOURCES SECTION VIII
TRANSFERRING LEARNING

A. **Increase Training Benefits: Decrease Role Conflict**
   by Ruth House
   - Shows how training's success depends on shared accountability for results by three parties—trainee, supervisor, and trainer
B. **Why Aren't They Doing What We Trained Them To Do?**
   by Regis McNamara
   - Discusses how to build transfer into training programs
C. **Maintenance Systems: The Neglected Half of Behavior Change**
   by Karen Brethower
   - Discusses conditions which determine how long specific behaviors will continue after training has ended
   - Suggests ways of maximizing the effect of training

Increase Training Benefits: Decrease Role Conflict

by Ruth Sizemore House

. . . the stronger our feelings the more likely it is that there will be no mutual element in the communication. There will be just two ideas, two feelings, two judgments, missing each other in psychological space (Rogers, 1961, p. 331).

Sometimes both employee and supervisor have strong feelings about work requirements and about the employee's performance of those requirements. And their performance discussions may miss each other in psychological space . . . by light years. A training effort under these conditions is more likely to fall through the gap than to bridge it—unless you, as a training and development professional, build some abutments first.

How? You can shore up your training efforts by negotiating with supervisors of trainees *before* training begins. Your objective: To get supervisors to agree they will actively reinforce the newly-acquired skills of trainees during a specified trial period *after* the trainees return to work.

Ideally, your workshop will be based on an acknowledged need of your organization. But even under ideal conditions, some supervisors may (1) ignore their employee's new behavior back on the job or (2) actually punish the employee's new behavior because of a vague or mistaken notion of what the workshop objectives mean. You can promote another alternative—active reinforcement of the newly-learned behavior— if you include these two steps in your training delivery plan.

STEP ONE: NEGOTIATE WITH SUPERVISORS

Plan about 20 minutes to review workshop objectives and on-the-job expectations with each supervisor. Show the supervisor specific examples of what the trainee's output should look like after the training (a performance model). Try to "sell" him on benefits the model output could produce in his part of the organization.

It is unlikely that *every* supervisor will support *every* part of the model output. So you need to

- Reassure the supervisor that you will mention his objection when you deal with that part of the model in class.
- Make a note to be sure you let trainees know about parts of the model a particular supervisor says "will not fly" in his organization.
- Plan to discuss in class the trainee's role as a change agent (the potential "culture shock" of returning to the regular job and the need to continue negotiating performance expectations with supervisors).

Contract with the supervisor for his active reinforcement of parts of the model he does accept. Be specific about the meaning of "active reinforcement." In writing workshops, for example, I ask supervisors to

1. Approve of certain writing forms and verbally commend the writer for using them, and
2. Withhold the temptation to edit certain writing forms if the trainee can justify them based on a principle dealt with in training.

STEP TWO: SET UP PRE-COURSE MEETING BETWEEN SUPERVISOR AND TRAINEE

Require that the supervisor and the trainee review the behavior model, the course objectives, the on-the-job expectations, and the resulting benefits *before* the trainee goes to class. Follow-up to be sure the discussion actually takes place or require some product of the discussion as an "admission ticket" to class. (For example, course prerequisites could include a list of objectives initialed by both supervisor and trainee; a discussion checklist signed by both supervisor and trainee; or a letter from supervisor to trainee confirming the highlights of the discussion.)

THE RESULT: REDUCE ROLE CONFLICT

These two steps can help put employee-supervisor communications about work on the same track by reducing ROLE CONFLICT (the conflict a person feels because of his role—in this case at work).

This article was reprinted from the NSPI Improving Human Performance Quarterly, June, 1972 by special permission from the publisher, The National Society for Performance and Instruction, 1126 Sixteenth St., N.W., Suite 25, Washington, D.C. 20036.

Now there are three major kinds of role conflict:

1. Intersender role conflict: the conflict a person feels when he believes one authority figure expects one thing but another authority figure expects something else.
2. Person-role conflict: the conflict a person feels between his own expectations and the expectations built into his job.
3. Role overload: the conflict a person feels when he does not have the resources (such as time and energy) to do what is expected.

If you *decrease* the role conflict trainees feel about their work then you *increase* the odds they will demonstrate

- Increased Job Satisfaction, Tosi and Tosi, 1970
- Improved Effectiveness in Their Job Roles, Getzels and Guba, 1954
- Increased Levels of Participations in Activities at Work, Hamner and Tosi, 1974
- Higher Estimates of Their Supervisors' Effectiveness, Bible and McNabb, 1966
- Increased Conformity to Their Supervisors' Expectations, Rothman, 1974
- Decreased Job Tension, Lyons, 1971
- Lowered Rates of Turnover, Lyons, 1971
- Higher Continued Commitment to the Objectives of Training, House, 1980

Unless you intervene, intersender conflict and person-role conflict are likely to go up when trainees leave the classroom to return to work (House, 1980, pp. 48–50). And that could mean trouble! Why? An increase in role conflict is likely to be accompanied by

- Propensity to Leave the Organization, Johnson and Graen, 1973
- Goal Conflict and Inconsistency, Rizzo et al., 1970
- Delay in Decision
- Distortion and Suppression of Information
- Violation of Chain of Command
- Frustration, Sigel and Pindur, 1973
- Tension, Miles, 1975
- Sense of Threat and Anxiety, Tosi, 1971
- Psychological Withdrawal, Kahn et al., 1964
- Sense of Futility, Kahn et al., 1964
- Acting Out, Projection, Contrived Interpersonal Conflict, Hostility, Kahn et al., 1974

Why do I think the two-step negotiation with supervisors is a promising intervention? The two-step model has resulted from my study of role conflict experienced by trainees attending a writing workshop.

As an outside consultant, I negotiated with supervisors of 42 writing trainees (the experimental group). I had no contact with supervisors of 63 others (the control group). Then I measured intersender conflict and person-role conflict twice: first, at the beginning of class; second, at the end of class. Here is what happened:

1. Intersender conflict went up in both groups.
2. Person-role conflict went down in the experimental group, but it went up in the control group. The difference between groups was statistically significant.
3. Experimental group trainees participated significantly more in course follow-up activities.

Negotiations with supervisors of trainees had the desired effect on person-role conflict and on participation in course follow-up activities. But what about intersender conflict? My plan omitted that second important step that could have decreased levels of intersender conflict as well: Although I encouraged supervisors to discuss the results of our negotiations with trainees, I did not follow up to be sure the discussion actually took place. Kahn et al. (1964, 57) found that pressure from higher authority in the organization was an element in 88 percent of the instances of intersender conflict. In 36 percent of these cases, respondents identified their immediate supervisors as sources of the pressure. So it seems likely that trainees needed to hear about the negotiation from supervisors themselves—not from me.

Training is a common strategy for behavior change in organization. But the trainee is not the only person accountable for training's success. His role is linked inextricably with the role of his supervisor and the role of his training professional. In order for the training to pay off, all three must share accountability for results—just as Dugan Laird has been telling us for some time (1976, 1).

All three parties can be partners in the benefits of training when they share expectations about

- the objectives of training
- the on-the-job application of training
- the benefits to the trainee (including reinforcement by the supervisor), and the benefits to the supervisor (including increased effectiveness of his unit).

REFERENCES

- Bible, Bond L., & McNabb, Coy G. Role consensus and administrative effectiveness. *Rural Sociology,* 1966, 31(1), pp. 5–14.
- Getzels, J. W., & Guba, E. G. Role, role conflict, and effectiveness: An empirical study, *American Sociological Review,* 1954, 19, pp. 164–175.
- Hamner, W. Clay, & Tosi, Henry L. Relationship of role conflict and role ambiguity to job involvement measures.

Journal of Applied Psychology, 1974, 59(4), pp. 497–499.

- House, Ruth S. *Training and re-entry to work: The problem of role conflict* (Doctoral Dissertation, University of Georgia, 1979). Dissertation Abstracts International, 1980, 40, 3697A. University Microfilms Order No. 8001009.
- Johnson, Thomas W., & Graen, George. Organizational assimilation and role rejection. *Organizational Behavior and Human Performance,* 1973 10(1), pp. 72–87.
- Kahn, Robert L.; Wolfe, Donald M.; Quinn, Robert P.; Snoek, J. Diedrick; & Rosenthal, Robert A. *Organizational stress; Studies in role conflict and ambiguity.* New York: Wiley, 1964.
- Laird, D. *Training contracts: Tool of the future?* Paper presented at the first Annual Training and Development Leadership Symposium. Madison, July, 1976.
- Lyons, Thomas F. Role clarity, need for clarity, satisfaction, and withdrawal. *Organizational Behavior and Human Performance,* 1971, 6, pp. 99–110.

- Miles, Robert H. An empirical test of the causal inference between role perceptions of conflict and ambiguity and various personal outcomes. *Journal of Applied Psychology,* 1975, 60(3), pp. 334–339.
- Rizzo, J.; House, R.; & Lirtzman, S. Role conflict and ambiguity in complex organizations. *Administrative Science Quarterly,* 1970, 15, pp. 150–163.
- Rogers, Carl R. *On becoming a person.* Boston, Massachusetts: Mifflin Company, 1961.
- Rothman, Jack. *Planning and organizing for social change: Action principles from social science research.* New York: Columbia University Press, 1974.
- Siegel, Roberta S., & Pindur, Wolfgang. Role congruence and role strain among urban legislators. *Social Science Quarterly,* 1973, 54(1), pp. 54–65.
- Tosi, H. L. Organizational stress as a moderator of the relationship between influence and the role response. *Academy of Management Journal,* 1971, 14, pp. 7–20.
- Tosi, H. L. & Tosi, D. Some correlates of role conflict and ambiguity among public school teachers. *Journal of Human Relations,* 1970 18, pp. 1068–1075.

Why Aren't They Doing What We Trained Them to Do?

by J. Regis McNamara

As the issue of accountability becomes more important in human resources development, the question of what training accomplishes becomes increasingly relevant. Of particular concern is the impact training programs have on individuals back on the job. In other words, how much transfer of training or generalization (terms used synonymously here) took place? Transfer of training effects can be considered to occur when the relevant aspects of behavior altered under one condition or in one setting carry over in some form to nontraining conditions or settings. Transfer occurs, then, when trainees do what you trained them to do, where and when you hoped they would do it.

A system I believe can assist trainers in developing programs with more transfer elements in them is based on the Training, Resource, Assessment, Intervention and Network System, or TRAINS. A TRAINS analysis begins with a thorough examination of all elements connected with the training experience.

TRAINING COMPONENT ANALYSIS

The impetus for most training endeavors develops from the assumptions and models used in constructing a training experience. To analyze this component for transfer, the conceptual underpinnings of the training experience should be identified and assessed for their soundness in relation to achieving transfer objectives. A number of concerns related to this issue need be explored. The first question to pose is whether the training is derived from a *unimodal* or *multimodal* orientation. A management training program derived from behavior modification principles would be considered a unimodal system, whereas one that was jointly predicated on humanistic and behavioristic concepts is developed from a multimodal orientation. Unimodal systems are easier to deal with than those derived from a diversity of perspectives and viewpoints because of their greater theoretical integrity; also they usually have generated more extensive empirical evidence addressing the issue of external validity or generalization.

In unimodal systems, questions about what kind of discrepancies exist between the transfer procedures used to conduct a program and those implied by the theory are of particular concern.[1] An important associated issue is how discrepancies, when they occur, might influence the magnitude of desired transfer effects. For example, using a behaviorally based personalized system of instruction, more generalization in the use of concepts is achieved if the concepts are first defined, then elaborated on and finally worked through by learners using a concept formation program.[2] Failing to incorporate these elements into this type of instructional system may compromise generalization. For example, a program designed to enhance the counseling skills of trainees may be consistently derived theoretically. But its ability to change actual behavior in the counseling situation could be limited if the theory was developed to influence cognitive structures and attitudes of the counselee toward others.

Training is an eclectic field, where diverse orientations, philosophies and activities are accepted, and it is not unusual to encounter training programs that combine elements in ways that might seem, from a single perspective, unusual or perhaps even discordant. These multimodal systems pose vexing evaluation problems. When ideas from a social learning model, communication's theory and humanistic philosophy are tied together with the inspirational intuition of a program originator, an experiential tangle can be the end result. This is not to suggest that such a combination does not work from a participant's point of view, because it frequently does. It simply implies that the diverse orientations will contribute unevenly to the production of generalization effects. Whatever benefits might be evidenced from using procedures derived from one source probably will be compromised by adding less effective or counterproductive elements from another source. The synergism resulting from combining diverse theoretical orientations rarely enhances transfer effects, though the *chicken-soup, or the-more-ingredients-the-better, theory of training* asserts the opposite.

RESOURCE COMPONENT ASSESSMENT

Social factors and the physical training environment both influence transfer. The characteristics of both participants and trainers are one of these elements. One critical question pertaining to trainers is how much visibility, contact and influence they currently have and potentially will have in the post-training environment. To the extent that trainers are isolated from the rest of the organization, their ability to extend the gains made during training to other relevant organizational settings is unlikely to occur. If this situation exists, then it may be necessary to recruit, on a short-term basis, surrogate trainers from those settings to which the participants will return. By virtue of their continued presence around participants before, during

and after training, surrogates are likely to provide relevant social support for the newly acquired behavior in the appropriate organizational setting. Even if trainers are well integrated into other aspects of organizational functioning, a variety of trainers should be employed to increase transfer possibilities.

Personal investment and a feeling of some ownership of training content by significant participating figures in the transfer environment also contribute to successful generalization. When individuals with social and administrative influence participate in the development of the goals and objectives of the training experience, they feel more committed to carry through on transfer objectives and influence others to achieve similar results.

Another critical factor to assess is whether there is considerable hostile, negative or unconstructive sentiment among the participants for any particular training experience. If there is, transfer will be minimal. If the critical mass of negative opinion is not neutralized or balanced by careful participant selection during training, then participants will either be uninfluenced by the transfer program or will attempt to undermine it by poor role modeling and verbal innuendo. This aspect is particularly important to understand when the program in question deals with potentially emotional or controversial subjects, such as race relations, social skills training or performance counseling.

Trainers and participants are bound together by the social climate created during training. A persistent problem that compromises transfer effects is the special emphasis placed on developing social and emotional response patterns that are most adaptive within the training program itself.[3] Too often, participants conform to the demands of training, because it is functional to do so. Once these demands are removed, other factors influence a person's response, such as work load, new organizational priorities and so on. Examination of the discrepancy that exists between the social climate created *during* training and that which exists in the primary work setting of the participant is important. Large discrepancies between the two social climates decrease the likelihood of transfer, while small discrepancies increase the possibility of transfer effects.

Similar training and transfer physical environments are also important. Two aspects of the training environment should be considered—the physical space provided for training and the resources contained in the training space. The more common and salient stimuli that exist in the training and transfer environment, the greater the likelihood that generalization will occur. One way to accomplish this is by "vestibule training": on-the-job problems or situations along with their physical characteristics are recreated in the classroom.[4]

ASSESSMENT COMPONENT ANALYSIS

All program assessment can be divided into two types—process and outcome. Process-oriented assessments are structured to collect information on what happens to people undergoing a training experience. And outcome approaches focus on the changes (both positive and negative) that happen to the individual and/or organization as a result of training. Both types of assessment are frequently used to evaluate the success of a training effort. Neither of these assessment techniques to promote and better understand transfer effects is used often enough.

There are several issues associated with the selection and use of assessment methodology. A fundamental concern associated with drawing conclusions from assessment is whether the instruments or procedures chosen will reliably detect change back on the job. Since assessment for transfer will, by definition be conducted some time after training and in an environment different from that of training, the procedures used must demonstrate situational relevance and temporal stability. Relevance is established by identifying whether the measures used to assess the beliefs, behaviors or attitude during training are likely to detect these same characteristics in the transfer setting. The selection of particular dependent measures has differential utility for establishing outcomes related to transfer effects.[5] For instance, both video recordings and direct observations of selling behavior may be made during training. But when these same procedures are used in the field, in the presence of customers, the nature of the selling situation is likely to change so dramatically that an accurate representation of transfer to the field situation could not be made.

In order to strengthen transfer, special assessment procedures must be used. For example, an assessment strategy that can be used for both process and outcome purposes, as well as to promote transfer effects, is a self-monitoring data collection and feedback system. By recording their own behavior each day, individuals are motivated to change and progress, thus, positive change can be maintained in the transfer environment. Keeping track, in a diary, of the number of times employees are praised for their accomplishments reminds the supervisor to use principles of positive reinforcement taught during training. It also illustrates how dispensing such reinforcement affects improvement.

When self-monitoring systems are occasionally supplemented by means of external surveillance systems (which can corroborate or extend the information gathered by self-monitoring), even more sustained maintenance can be expected. One way to accomplish this is by having the employees also keep track of the amount of praise they receive from the supervisor. Periodic comparisons can be made to determine the correspondence between the two sources. The use of more automatic devices, such as television monitors, personal telemeters and electrical or mechanical counters, would also serve the same function.

Finally, we should consider the following factors when using assessment to promote transfer. First, how reactive are the procedures with the characteristic being measured? That is, will the mere process of having the behavior measured produce a predictable change in it? Second, are the cues associated with the assessment in the transfer environment obvious enough to remind individuals about their behavior? And is the feedback from the assessment delivered at appropriate intervals and in a practical way? And, third, are consequences provided to groups or individuals for meeting or failing to sustain adequate performance standards in the transfer environment? This last issue relates to the establishment of performance standards in the transfer setting and the creation of a motivational system that allows individuals to meet these standards. To the extent that much variation in transfer behavior is permissible, individually determined goals and reinforcement systems are acceptable.

INTERVENTION COMPONENT ANALYSIS

The procedures and operations used during training to create generalization are critical to the transfer process. For instance, the diversity, variety and novelty of tasks, responses and problems presented during training assist transfer.[6] Providing an adequate number of informational stimuli, as well as teaching sufficiently varied responses to them, is important. An underused method for programming generalization is to do the training in a number of organizational settings. For example, subgroups can be simultaneously trained in different environments with appropriate sequencing between them until training is completed; or the whole group can serially pass through training presentations in different settings. Both these approaches increase the logistical problems of scheduling and staffing, but they increase the transfer effects by weakening the association between the behavior learned and the environment it was learned in.

Although immediate reinforcement for correct responding is usually the operation of choice to facilitate a learner acquiring a new response, intermittent and delayed reinforcement ultimately assure better generalization. Thus during the latter part of training, both feedback and reinforcement should be delayed over time and varied in their amount so that the learner will maintain a reasonable level of persistence. This thinning of reinforcement and feedback to small amounts and at lengthy or unpredictable intervals approximates the usual state of affairs in most organizational environments.

The use of cues and consequences to bring forth generalized responses and then maintain them in the transfer environment is important, too. Written and verbal instructions form the principal basis for most cueing (or signaling of what comes next) that exists in organizations. The development of a commitment to perform in the post-training environment can be fostered through the use of contingency contracts,[7] while the use of policy control procedures[8] can assure that the posttraining behavior may be maintained through administrative means.

Consequences are those events that happen to a person after a behavior is performed. Positive consequences or reinforcement increases the likelihood that the behavior would be exhibited in the future; negative consequences or punishment decreases this likelihood. Those consequences that are useful during training—a passing grade in an examination or a certificate of attendance—may be entirely worthless in maintaining the behavior in the transfer setting. Therefore, it's important to identify payoffs in the transfer setting that are known to motivate employees effectively and to make these consequences contingent on the transfer behavior.

The transfer effectiveness of the procedures used to promote facts, skills and concepts presented during training also must be established. Generalization of factual material involves the ability to recall pertinent information at a later time in different surroundings. An effective way to enhance recall during training is to provide the participant with a set of retrieval cues and plans for the material to be recalled. A mnemonic scheme based on a memorized list of words associated with information to be recalled would be appropriate here. The use of live or videotape models to simulate the behavior as it will occur in the transfer setting is essential for skill carry-over. For concept generalization, an approach combining guided and discovery learning seems applicable. Using these combined procedures, participants are initially taught about the task; later on, they are allowed, through trial and error, to find out the answers for themselves.

NETWORK COMPONENT ANALYSIS

An examination of the arrangement and sequencing among the components in TRAINS is the focus in this part of the system. The adequacy of the linkages established between each component should be explored with special attention being given to how each component complements and strengthens the influence of the other. The identification and removal of in-compatible and counterproductive arrangements is of particular concern. The network analysis puts into perspective the entire transfer effort of the program and determines the effort's consistency and integrity. The network analysis finally attempts to balance transfer needs against other program and organizationally related factors, such as initial program learning, feasibility and cost/benefit to the organization.

CONCLUSION

Our knowledge of how to create transfer and generalization effects from training have reached a stage where formal recommendations for the use of such a technology is warranted.[9] The TRAINS system examines factors that have been identified as important in training programs. How widespread and effective the use of TRAINS becomes, however, will depend on two factors. First is the extent to which the ideas contained in TRAINS are incorporated into training programs. The second relates to the support this system receives from research that demonstrates its incremental benefit over other transfer systems and models.

REFERENCES

1. Leidecker, J. K., and J. J. Hall, "Motivation: Good theory—Poor application." *Training and Development Journal,* 1974, 28, 3–7.

2. Miller, L. K., and F. H. Weaver, "A behavioral technology for producing concept information in university students." *Journal of Applied Behavioral Analysis,* 1976, 9, 289–300.

3. Miller, F. D., "The problem of transfer of training in learning groups. Group cohesion as an end in itself." *Small Group Behavior,* 1976, 7, 221–236.

4. Luthans, F., and R. Kreitner, *Organizational Behavior Modification,* Glenview, IL: Scott Foresman, 1975.

5. McNamara, J. R., "Ways by which outcome measures influence outcomes in classroom behavior modification research." *Journal of School Psychology,* 1975, 13, 104–113.

6. Gagne, R. M., and L. J. Briggs, *Principles of instructional design.* New York: Holt, 1974.

7. Homme, L., A. P. Csanyi, M. A. Gonzales, and J. R. Richs, *How to use contingency contracting in the classroom.* Champaign, IL: Research Press, 1970.

8. Andrasik, F., J. R. McNamara, and D. M. Abbott, "Policy control: A low resource intervention for improving staff behavior." *Journal of Organizational Behavior Management.* 1978, 1, 125–133.

9. Stokes, T. F., and D. M. Baer, "An implicit technology of generalization. *Journal of Applied Behavior Analysis,* 1977, 10, 349–367.

Maintenance Systems: The Neglected Half of Behavior Change

by Karen S. Brethower

INTRODUCTION

Failure looms for programmed instruction projects in which there is inadequate consideration of maintenance systems. What happens to the trainee *after* training via programmed instruction is at least as important to job performance as the training itself.

The intent of this chapter is to enumerate the conditions in the job environment which determine how long any specific behavior will continue to be successfully performed after the training has ended. Ways of maximizing the effect of training through control of conditions in the job environment will be suggested. The conditions which will be in effect after training will affect the decision of whether to train and if so, what to train. Guidelines will be provided on how to make these decisions.

THE TWO HALVES OF CHANGING BEHAVIOR: ACQUISITION AND MAINTENANCE

Acquisition of Behavior

In acquiring a behavior one becomes proficient in a skill which he previously could not perform. The skill is often acquired through training of one sort or another, such as classroom lecture, text, programmed instruction or on-the-job coaching. At some point the trainee is tested and the decision is made as to whether he can perform up to standard. If he can, he is probably put out on the job.

Maintenance of Behavior

At this point the emphasis shifts from acquisition, or *getting* the performance up to standard, to maintenance, which involves *keeping* the performance up to standard. Some ways of maintaining the behavior are by providing the person with feedback on the quality of his work, providing positive consequences to the per-

son for performing at or above standard. Feedback and positive consequences are provided by structuring the job environment so that it provides them through supervision, other sources of recognition, discipline, social contact, money or other meaningful consequences.

MAINTAINING BEHAVIOR

Conditions for Maintaining Behavior

If a system is to maintain a behavior it must do four things: (1) allow the behavior to occur with sufficient frequency; (2) not punish it; (3) reinforce it; and (4) not reinforce behaviors which conflict with it. Two examples will illustrate specific ways in which the above four requirements may be met, and the slight cost involved.

Example 1: In an industrial production company, quality is of great concern. The Quality Control Department checks the quality of a worker's production at unpredictable times. When they find exceptionally high quality work they send a green card to the employee, which states, "The last four units you produced were of especially high quality."

For a very little cost a high level of quality and quantity is maintained.

Example 2: On a production line with a high accident rate the foreman agreed to a policy of (1) thanking production workers for reporting or altering unsafe working conditions and (2) refraining from comments about safety activities slowing down production.

By not punishing accident prevention behavior and, even further, by reinforcing it, the supervisors cut the accident rate.

Examining the world in which we live, we find the same people who state that a given behavior is important often suppress that behavior by advocating a system that does not support the behavior. The following example is a case in point.

Example of Not Maintaining a Behavior

Example 3: Freshman nurses calculate dosages better than experienced senior nurses. Examination of the

Reprinted from ["Maintenance Systems"/*Managing the Instructional Programming Effort*] by Karen B. Brethower, (Ann Arbor, Michigan: The University of Michigan), DIVISION OF RESEARCH, GRADUATE SCHOOL OF BUSINESS ADMINISTRATION, pages 60–72, by permission of the publisher, Copyright © 1967 by the University of Michigan. All rights reserved.

conditions in which freshmen worked and those in which seniors worked showed:

1. Seniors were in a hospital, under pressure to administer the correct dosage to a patient; freshmen were in a classroom and required to compute correct dosages on paper and pencil exams.
2. Seniors had a pharmacist available who was glad to calculate dosages for them; freshmen had to rely on themselves.

During the freshman year it was worthwhile for a nursing student to be able to compute dosages; her academic advancement depended on it. By the senior year, paper and pencil computation had been replaced by the more attractive alternative of calling a pharmacist.

Increased training for freshmen in calculating dosages would not solve this problem. Similar situations face managers and anyone else who works with people under a variety of conditions.

Principles of Behavior

Two basic principles will equip us to analyze and modify job behaviors. First, if a behavior leads to positive consequences for a person, he will continue to emit that behavior. Secondly, if a behavior leads to negative consequences for the person he will stop emitting that behavior. The key to using these two principles in analysis of a problem or deficient behavior is the phrase "consequences *for a person.*" No one can decide with certainty what will be a positive or negative consequence for another person. By observing what someone talks about and does in his free time, we can make fairly accurate predictions. But, in the final analysis, an event or consequence such as the opportunity to present a plan at a staff meeting may be something that John would work diligently to get and Bill would work hard to avoid.

Corollary Statements

From these two principles, some corollary statements follow, which allow us to see how the two principles specifically affect whether a job behavior will increase in strength, decrease in strength, or disappear. Each corollary statement below is accompanied by an illustrative example.

1. If one behavior is asked for and a second behavior is reinforced, the reinforced behavior will be the one emitted.

Example: A new supervisor attempts to handle all grievances at his level, as he has been told he should. Within a month he learns that if he passes the grievances up to the next level, he doesn't have to worry about them. If he tries to settle the grievances, he gets arguments from his subordinates and has to work overtime to make up for the time spent trying to come to an agreement.

He passes more and more of the grievances on to the next level.

2. If a behavior leads to positive consequences for a person under one set of conditions and negative consequences under another, he will emit the behavior when it leads to positive consequences and not when it leads to negative consequences.

Example: It's 20 minutes until the end of the shift. An accumulation of paper and broken cartons surrounds the work station.

Desired Behavior: Shutting down production and cleaning up debris.

Situation 1: versus	*Situation 2:*
Production is running at about standard. There's a cleanliness campaign on.	Production is running 6% below standard.
Unless the operator stops to clean up the mess, he'll get yelled at.	If the operator stops to clean it up, he'll get yelled at.
He shuts down the production line.	He does not shut down production.

3. If behavior is not called for on the job or has no consequences when emitted, it will eventually stop being emitted.

Example: The utility repairman dutifully submits equipment reports when first on the job. He hears nothing more of them; and when he forgets to submit one, nothing happens. He soon stops submitting the reports.

4. The more similar conditions of job performance are to conditions of training, the more likely a person is to perform as trained.

Example: The ROTC graduate trained in precision drill and tactics has a much more difficult time in his defense job of hand-to-hand combat than does the soldier trained in guerilla warfare and survival techniques in tropical jungles.

5. The further removed in time a consequence is from a behavior, the less effect that consequence will have on that behavior.

Example: A man whose boss compliments him on the tough contract he landed this week works harder on getting more contracts than he would if the boss waited until the annual appraisal (7 months hence) to mention it.

These two principles and the five corollary statements (1) explain day-to-day performance problems and (2) can serve as a guide in deciding what elements of the job environment must be changed to achieve the desired job performance.

IDENTIFYING THE FACTORS INFLUENCING MAINTENANCE

Programmed learning, designed to teach a job skill, is appropriately judged by whether or not that skill is later performed on the job. It is therefore important to consider the maintenance factors that will affect whether the skill is performed. The employee must not only *know how* to do the job, but also *perform correctly* on the job, in order for the programmed learning to be judged successful.

A Supportive Job Environment

A good maintenance system can make the difference between long-term success or failure for your self-instructional program. Stated job requirements must be consistent with the job conditions if they are to be met. When examining the job conditions which will be expected to maintain some specific bit of job performance, one should ask: "Will these conditions support or reward the behavior required?" For example, if we hire or train second line supervisors who can set up and administer a results-oriented appraisal system will the job conditions support the supervisors administering such a system?

Case Study of Maintenance System

The following case will illustrate how a good maintenance system made the difference between a job behavior being performed well and a job behavior being performed poorly. The good maintenance system reduced a company's illegible price markings by 15 per cent.

Case Study

A program designed to teach personnel to discriminate between legible and illegible price markings (*Price Marking; Why Care?*)* was evaluated in the following way: each of the three evaluation teams conducted an item investigation in the Grocery and Frozen Food Department of three different stores. They inspected 6000 items per store, examining the items most likely to be taken by the next customer. Each mismarked item was tallied, using the standards developed in the program. The number of mismarked items totaled approximately 20% of the entire sample.

Each store then used the program, *Price Marking; Why Care?* The performance of personnel was again evaluated after training. Figure 1 illustrates the differences between the program's effect on performance in the three stores.

By taking the programmed instruction materials the trainees improved their performance from an average of 20% unacceptable to price markings to an average of 5.5% unacceptable price markings. The acquisition phase was considered successful.

The maintenance phase varied in success from questionable to successful. Where the program was treated as one-shot remedy its effect "wore off" quickly. Where a thorough maintenance procedure (management follow-up) was used, the program was effective even four months after training.

If the program had been tried in *only* Store A, where there were 13.8% mismarked items three months after training, the program would have appeared to be of transitory value. As it is, the comparative results in the three stores indicate that if one uses the program, it is worth doing follow-up to support the skills trained. People quickly adapt to different conditions. If we train them in one job skill, such as quality of price markings, and then, on-the-job, pay attention to a different skill, such as rapidity of price marking, they will act as if quality is important in the training environment and rapidity is important on the job.

Training Behavior Compatible with Job

In order to make training effective, the training should be compatible with job goals. If, for example, we get all automatic stamping machine operators to agree that safety is more important than a several unit increase in hourly production, will their bosses accept and support that back on the job? The job environment should be analyzed to see in what ways it will support, and in

---

*Basic Systems, Inc., Educational subsidiary of Xerox Corporation.

FIGURE 1
Performance in Price Marking

	Before Training	1 Month After Training	Store Activity During Next 3 Months		4 Months After Training
	• Unacceptable Price Markings	• Unacceptable Price Markings	Turnover	New Employees Trained / Management Follow-up	• Unacceptable Price Markings
Store X	22.5	7.1	High	No / No	13.8
Store Y	17.7	4.8	High	Yes / Yes	6.1
Store Z	20.1	4.6	Low	No / No	8.8
Average	20.1	5.5			9.6

what ways it will punish the skill or behavior that we propose to introduce.

Identifying Rewards and Punishments

Identifying the reinforcement-punishment ratio may not be a one-step job. It can require the exploration of consequences of all levels, with some adding up of the final margin of reinforcements or punishment in the system. Although the exploration of consequences is a complex task, it is an essential one since without it we frequently *assume* that the system reinforces required job behaviors. Many training dollars and much time could be wasted in trying to change a job behavior via training if this assumption is wrong. The assumption could lead us to conduct a costly training program which would have only a temporary effect in a system which punished the behavior we trained.

The list of questions in Figure 2 illustrates the nature of the task of identifying the reinforcement punishment ratio. It is not an exhaustive or exclusive list of questions that should be answered but rather an illustration of the kind of questions that will help you decide whether any given skill would be maintained in a specific environment.

Decision to Train or Alter Environment

If you determine on the basis of questions such as those in Figure 2 that the job environment will support the skill or behavior you plan to introduce, you can go on to determining the most efficient means of acquiring personnel with the desired skills. If the job environment will not support the behavior, you have the choice of:

1. abandoning your plans for introducing the particular skill into that job environment; or
2. determining (a) what changes are necessary to maintain behavior in the job environment (e.g., changes in supervisory practices, redesign of a

job aid, or automation of some function); (b) what those changes would cost; and (c) whether it's economically more sound to make the changes or ignore the problem.

CHANGING BEHAVIOR THROUGH CHANGING ONLY MAINTENANCE

Problems can be solved by ignoring acquisition and working only with maintenance procedures. *It is worthwhile to work only with maintenance for any problem in which the personnel once knew or could not learn by themselves the skill or behavior* being considered. The following example *illustrates such a problem.*

Example: Warehouse employees didn't lift cargo properly when loading trucks. When they were told that the next item they lifted was going to be a test of whether they could lift properly, all men performed up to standard. A change in the job environment, i.e., the maintenance system, solved the problem—men lifted properly on the job with no changes in the means by which they acquired the skill.

You can determine whether your problem arises from a deficiency in acquisition or in maintenance by following the questioning in Figure 3 (the "Analysis of Type of Deficiency Form"). The question of whether the warehouse employees lifted improperly due to deficiencies in the acquisition or the maintenance system had to be answered to solve the problem. Solution of the problem in this case meant:

1. Reduced amount of money in medical benefits paid due to back injuries.
2. Reduced number of grievances on working conditions filed by warehouse employees who lift.
3. Reduced number of hours worked by substitutes hired to replace employees who are off the job due to back injuries.

FIGURE 2
Examining a Maintenance System

I. Goals and Standards
   A. Does the employee know what's expected of him and under what circumstances?
   B. Does the boss assess conditions and standards so that his appraisal matches the appraisal of the employee (and of the trainer).

II. Consequences of Behavior
   If an employee were to perform according to specifications what would be the:
   A. *Immediate* consequences for him?
      (1) from peers
      (2) from subordinates
      (3) from supervisors
      (4) in terms of distasteful things he'd get out of doing, or enjoyable things he would not be able to do
      (5) others
   B. Long-term consequences for him?
      (1) promotion, raise, recognition
      (2) reduced time on this part of his job
      (3) fewer crises
      (4) cut his budget
      (5) less/more contact with employees
      (6) more/fewer chances to be noticed by upper management
      (7) more/fewer grievances to handle
   C. Overall consequences for him
      (1) Immediate
         a. more positive than negative?
         b. more negative than positive?
      (2) Long-term
         a. more positive than negative?
         b. more negative than positive?
      (3) Overall

III. Feedback of Knowledge of Quality to Employee
   A. Would the employee learn that his performance was superior?

   If so,*
   (1) How?
   (2) From whom?
   (3) In what form? (print-out of quality control sheet, backhanded verbal compliment)
   (4) How long a delay between completion of job and feedback of quality to employee?
   (5) Is there a cumulative consequence of continued superior performance?
      If so,
      (a) What is that consequence?
      (b) What are the chances of getting it?
      (c) How long a continued superior performance is needed?
      (d) How long after the time requirement (c) is met does the consequence occur?
   B. Would the employee learn that his performance was inferior?
      If so,*
      (1) How?
      (2) From whom?
      (3) In what form?
      (4) How long a delay between completion of job and feedback of quality to employee?
      (5) Is there a cumulative consequence of continued inferior performance?
         If so,
         (a) What is the consequence?
         (b) What are the chances of incurring that consequence?
         (c) How long a continued inferior performance is required to incur the consequence?
         (d) How long after the time requirement (c) is met does the consequence occur?

*Repeat question sequence 1–5 as often as needed.

Use of the "Analysis of Type of Deficiency Form" revealed that (1) people knew what was expected of them; (2) the men performed adequately immediately after training; (3) there were no high and low performers who could be observed, and (4) men *could* perform the job if they had to do so.

Based on the fact that the men performed adequately just after training, job conditions were investigated further. On the job, supervisors reprimanded employees when they saw them lifting improperly. When they saw employees lifting properly, the supervisors didn't reprimand them and went on about their business.

Changes in the job environment followed this analysis. The plan was that a supervisor (1) would ig-

nore improper lifting, and (2) occasionally make a supportive comment when he noticed proper lifting. Under these conditions, men could no longer get their boss upset by lifting improperly; in other words, the positive consequences for improper lifting were removed. The supervisors were given some training and practice in the techniques of (1) and (2) and sent back to their respective warehouses.

After three months the division had only one back injury as opposed to an average of eight for the same time period in the past.

In this case restructuring only the maintenance system led to a dramatic improvement in performance. No changes were made in the acquisition system. If satisfactory performance of a given job behavior is

FIGURE 3
Type of Deficiency: Analysis Guide*

Objective: To determine if problem is an acquisition problem (can't do) or a maintenance problem (won't do).

Questions and Suggested Actions:

1. Do people know what is expected of them?

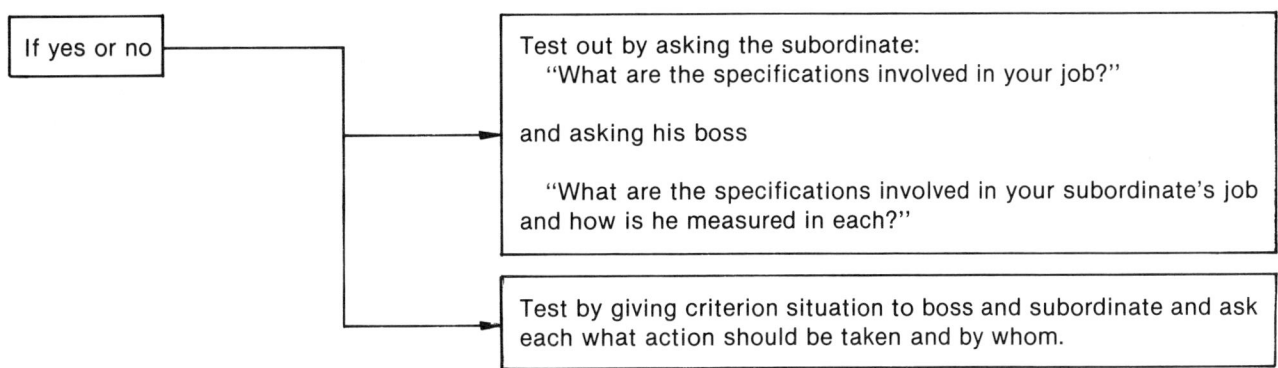

2. Do most men perform adequately when they are first on the job?

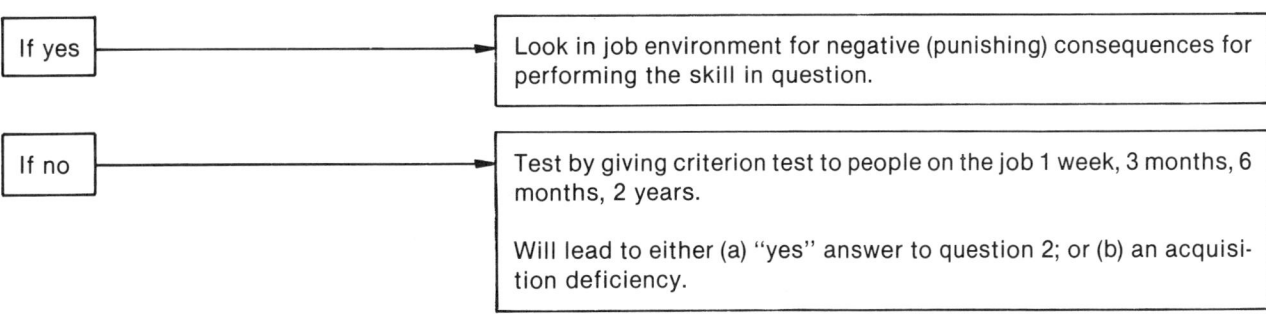

3. Are there high performers and low performers who could be observed to see the difference in behavior?

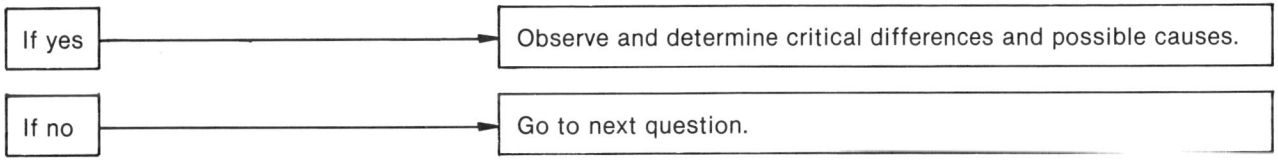

4. Could most men perform the job if they had to (i.e., their lives depended on it)?

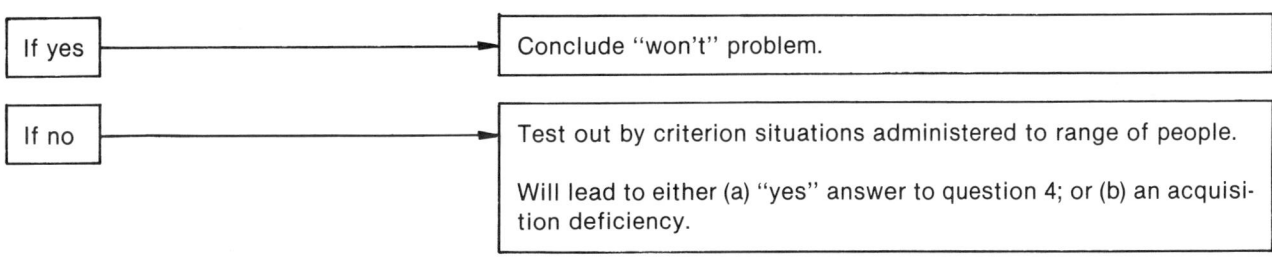

---

*"Type of Deficiency: Analysis Guide" designed by Geary A. Rummler, Center for Programmed Learning for Business.

ever exhibited, it's economically a sound decision to investigate maintaining that satisfactory level of performance by changing only the maintenance system.

SUMMARY

What does this mean to writers and users of programmed instruction?

Analyze any problem you face to see whether it stems from a deficiency in maintenance or from a deficiency in acquisition. If this analysis had not been done in the "proper lifting" example it would have been assumed that the problem was one of acquisition of proper lifting skills, and a programmed instruction course in "How to Lift Properly" would probably have been written for warehouse employees. Instead, the problem was analyzed, and turned out to be one of maintaining a previously acquired behavior. A programmed instruction course was written, but it was for *supervisors* to help them provide the job conditions necessary to support proper lifting by their subordinates. The analysis led to effective behavior change through programmed instruction, rather than "just another training course."

Analyze and restructure, as necessary, the job environment in which employees are to use the skills trained. If this is not done, programs can fail for lack of job support. In designing your program, keep in mind that programmed instruction is a means of acquisition and, as such, only the first part of a behavior change system. Without maintenance acquisition is temporary.

SOURCES SECTION IX
EVALUATING PROGRAM RESULTS

Evaluating Training

by Karen S. Brethower and Geary A. Rummler

A framework is presented for identifying evaluation alternatives and for deciding what evaluation is appropriate for a training system described in terms of inputs, processing system, outputs and the system receiving them. Guidelines cover four levels of evaluation, include an evaluation matrix, and extend to documentation of conditions surrounding training and other apsects of "real world" evaluation problems.

Most discussions of training evaluation we hear are not very satisfying. Nothing is ever resolved because each discussant seems to be talking about evaluating a different dimension of the training. When people can't agree on *what* they are trying to evaluate and why, they actually won't agree on *how* to evaluate.

In this paper we would like to present a framework for viewing evaluation alternatives and deciding what evaluation is appropriate. Included also are some guidelines for conducting evaluation studies.

EVALUATION AND THE GENERAL SYSTEM MODEL

A number of aspects of training might be evaluated. The range of reasonable alternatives is suggested by a general systems view of training, which shows the relationship between the training function and the organization it supposedly services. Figure 1 illustrates the key components of an ideal training system, consisting of the receiving system (in this case, the jobs or organization) and the processing system (the training function). The specific systems components are:

1. The inputs into the system (students or trainees).
2. The processing system, which converts inputs into outputs. Depending on the system in question, the processing system might be an instructional lesson, a classroom, a course, or a training department.
3. The outputs of the processing system (trained, or educated, students or trainees).
4. The receiving system, which is the area or unit into which the outputs immediately go. For a company apprentice program, the receiving system is the job. The processing system and the receiving system are always subsystems of some larger system (e.g., the school, the agency manpower planning system).
5. The mission goal, or stated goal, of the receiving system. This might be "All claims honored within X days with Y errors" where the receiving system is the claims office of an insurance company and the processing system is the training course for claims representatives.
6. The evaluation of the accomplishment of the stated mission goal (e.g., percentage of claims paid correctly within the stated time). This evaluation consists of measuring the output of the receiving system and matching that output against the stated criteria for the mission.
7. The evaluation of the quality and quantity of the outputs of the processing system (e.g., degree of mastery at the conclusion of the Claims Representative course). This evaluation requires measurement of the processing system outputs and their comparison with the product criteria.
8. The feedback to the processing system on the outputs of the processing system and attainment of the mission goal. Based on this feedback, adjustments can be made in the processing system itself, in the criteria for the product of the system, or in both. For example, feedback might indicate that even though Claims Representatives did exceptionally well in their class, Claims Representatives were deficient in knowledge that they were thought to have acquired in that class. Based on more specific data, it might be necessary to alter the content of the course, to raise the performance standard, or to do both.

The training function has these systems characteristics:

1. Its output is the input to another part of the system. It does not function in isolation. It must contribute to the larger, total system. If it does not contribute, then it will cease to function. Also, any attempts to maximize its output or effectiveness will be neutralized by the need for the total system to optimize all the subsystems. (Specifically, this is done through budget allocations.)

This article was reprinted from the NSPI Improving Human Performance Quarterly, 1976, by special permission from the publisher, The National Society for Performance and Instruction, 1126 Sixteenth Street, N.W., Suite 315, Washington, DC 20036.

FIGURE 1
A Model of a General System Applied to Education

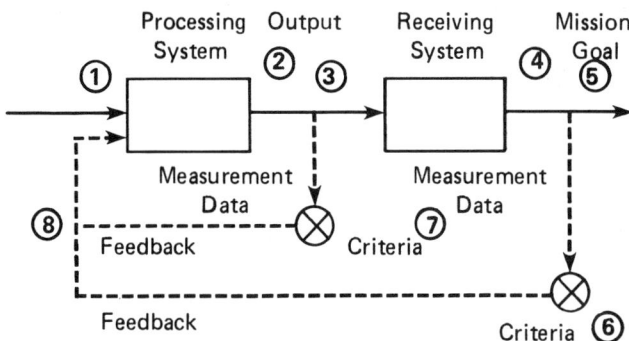

2. It responds to data. It must be correct. It must adapt or die.
3. It is controlled by the evaluation *criteria*, as it adapts. If it is evaluated on the basis of head-count and popularity, all adjustments will be made accordingly. If it is evaluated on its performance and contribution to the organization, it will correct toward that goal.

System Sophistication

Figure 2 illustrates three degrees of system sophistication, which point up the relative effectiveness of training organizations. The simple input-output training systems are characterized by those training departments that do no evaluation and pride themselves on having unlimited budgets. These are the training organizations that disappear in strenuous economic times because they are unable to show any apparent value to the organization when asked. They always cry "foul," explaining that they were never required to justify their existence before.

A more sophisticated system, the guided system, is still deficient, though somewhat better off. It evaluates its output. If it evaluates according to performance criteria ("Can the trainees *do* what we set out to have them do?"), then it may very well be an effective training organization. But if it chooses to evaluate (or gets lulled into evaluating) according to the criteria of the amount of training activity (e.g., bodies trained per budget dollar) and its popularity (e.g., "Did you enjoy the training? Do you think you will find it useful?"), then it is a little better off than the less sophisticated ballistic system. That is, its own internal evaluations do not measure what the organization needs.

Thus, the only truly effective training system is one based on the adaptive system model. Without the receiving system in the loop, there is no way of assessing whether the products of this training function

(however good they might be by behavior-change standards) are of any *value* to the organization.

Thus, a general system view of the training function or of a particular training course or experience exposes a number of dimensions which might be evaluated. Figure 3 combines four of the possible evaluation alternatives with the general systems model of training.

An evaluator might evaluate at any one of these four levels to determine whether the training is having the desired effect. The training action in response to the evaluation can be of two major types. He/she can:

1. Decide to continue or discontinue the training (summative evaluation); or
2. Decide to continue the training as is, or to revise any aspect of the training system until it meets the criteria (formative evaluation).

If the evaluation information is to be used to revise the training it must be much more detailed as to specific aspects that worked or failed.

FIGURE 2
General Systems Models

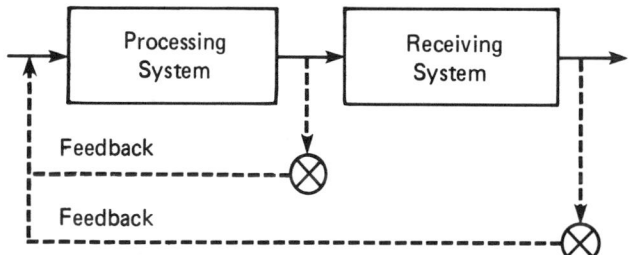

1. A BALLISTIC SYSTEM
(has input-output only)

2. A GUIDED SYSTEM
(has input-output
can correct its output)

3. AN ADAPTIVE SYSTEM
(has input-output,
can correct its output,
can change its goal)

FIGURE 3

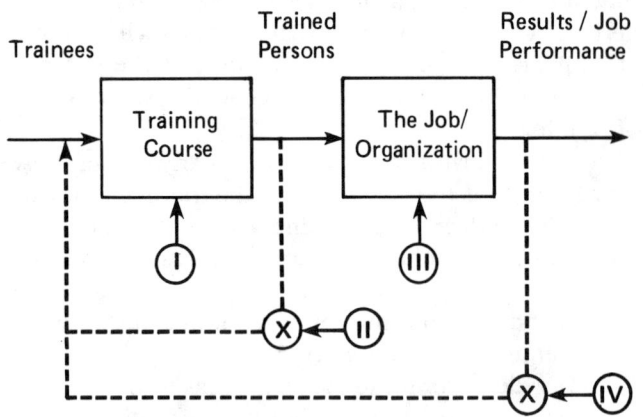

Four Levels of Evaluation:
I.   Are the trainees happy with the course?
II. Does the training course teach the concepts?
III. Are the concepts used on the job?
IV. Does application of the concepts positively affect the organization?

Evaluation Matrix

From the four levels of evaluation we have identified, we can form the evaluation matrix shown in Figure 4. For each level we can ask:

1. What question(s) do we want answered?
2. What might we measure to answer those questions?
3. What are the dimensions of learning or performance we are trying to measure?
4. What are the sources of the data to help measure?
5. What are alternative ways of gathering data for measurement?
6. What are the evaluation criteria we want to apply to each question?

Figure 5 is a partially complete matrix for one type of teaching activity, a management workshop. In the first column, alternative explanations of the "why not" have been made explicit for the workshop, e.g., I—"unhappiness" might emanate from the concepts not being relevant, inappropriate workshop (WS) design, or pre-workshop setting of expectations. The entries in each cell would vary depending on the course and the situation.

FIGURE 4

Degree	I	II	III	IV
What We Want To Know	Are the trainees happy? If not, why not?	Does the training do what it is supposed to? If not, why not?	Are the concepts used? if not, why not?	Does application of the concepts impact the organization? If not, why not?
What Might Be Measured				
Measurement Dimensions				
Sources of Data				
Data Gathering Methodology				
Evaluation Criteria				

Column headers above table: Trainees → Training Course → Trained Persons → The Job/Organization → Results/Job Performance

FIGURE 5

What We Want to Know	What Might be Measured	Measurement Dimensions	What To Look At (Sources of Data)	Alternative Data Gathering Method	Evaluation Criteria
I. Are the Trainees Happy? If Not, Why? a. Concepts Not Relevant b. WS Design c. Trainees Not Properly Positioned	Trainee reaction during workshop	Relevance Threat Ease of learning	Comments between trainees Comments to instructor Questions about exercises "Approach Behavior" to exercises	Observation Interview Questionnaire	
	Trainee reaction after workshop	Perceived "Worth" $\dfrac{V}{C}$ or $\dfrac{\text{Relevance}}{\text{Learning Energy}}$	"Approach Behavior" to project Questions about project, concepts	Observation Interview Questionnaire	
II. Do the Materials Teach the Concepts? If Not, Why Not? a. WS Structure b. Lessons •Presentation •Examples •Exercises	Trainee performance during workshop	Understanding Application	Learning time Performance on exercises Presentations	Observation Document review	
	Trainee performance at end of workshop	Understanding Application Facility Articulation	Action plan for project Use of tools on exercises Presentations	Observation Document review Interview Questionnaire	
III. Are the Concepts Used? If Not, Why Not? a. Concepts: •Not relevant •Too complex •Too sophisticated b. Inadequate Tools Environment Not Supportive	Performance improvement projects*	Analysis Action plan Results	Discussions Documentation Results	Observation Interview Document review Questionnaire (critical incid.)	
	Problem solving technique*	Questions asked Action proposed Action taken	Discussions Documentation Results	Observation Interview Document review Questionnaire (critical incid.)	
	On-going management approach*	Dissemination effort Language People management process	Discussions Meetings Documentation	Observation Interview Document review Questionnaire (critical incid.)	
IV. Does Application of the Concepts Positively Affect the Organization? If Not, Why Not?	Problem solving*	Problem identification Analysis Action Results	Discussions Documentation Results	Interview Document review Questionnaire (critical incid.)	
	Problem prediction and prevention*	Potential problem identification Analysis Action	Discussions Documentation Results	Interview Document review Questionnaire (critical incid.)	
	Performance measures*	Output measures Interim or diagnostic measures	Performance data	Document review	

*Specific to a particular workshop

There are several practical applications of the evaluation matrix. The first and most obvious one is as a guide to systematically determine *what* and *how* to evaluate training at the four levels.

However, a second application (which should be obvious to those readers who engage in performance analysis or front-end analysis) is as a test for the existence of a real problem which can be corrected by training (or anything else). For example, if someone in your organization has approached you to develop a report writing course and you are reviewing how such a course might be evaluated prior to designing it, you might quickly see how you would evaluate at levels I and II. However, if you sat down with the party re-questing the training to discuss how you might measure levels III and IV, chances are you would find them unable to help with IV because in fact there is no relationship between the perceived deficiencies of report writing and job performance. Or perhaps there is. The point is, thinking through the evaluation matrix prior to beginning the training effort is one method to approximate a front-end analysis.

The third practical application of the matrix is as a vehicle to gain organization support of a training effort. For example, you are approached to develop a training course on a "quality control" matter. Again, levels I and II should offer you no trouble. A discussion of evaluating III and IV with the management requesting the training will point up the need for management support of the trainees using the new skills or concepts on the job. The matrix makes it clear that all the training in the world around quality will be to no avail unless management takes the necessary steps to assure that use of these concepts will be supported on the job. In fact evaluation results that show passing grades at level I and II and failing grades at III and IV are an indictment of management, not the trainees or the trainers.

And that leads to application four—the use of the matrix to negotiate the degree of evaluation required. Frequently there is a mis-match between the expected or desired degree of evaluation by the requesting party and the training group. The matrix can help clarify how much (to what degree) evaluation is necessary or worth investing in.

Thus far, we have presented a model for training evaluation and some propositions related to that model. The propositions are:

1. The training system be viewed as a subsystem of the total organization.
2. There are four potential levels of evaluation.
   I. Do trainees like the training?
   II. Do trainees learn from the training?
   III. Do trainees use what they learn?
   IV. Does the organization benefit from the newly learned performance?
3. For each of these degrees of evaluation, there are basic considerations that need to be made for evaluation. These are listed in the EVALUATION MATRIX presented in Figure 5.

While a model is very important, it provides no benefit unless it is used in some way. The rest of this article will deal with issues in actually conducting evaluations.

Evaluation is frequently thought to be too difficult to do in the real world. Sometimes it is done in a way that undermines its utility. We, therefore, offer some suggestions for making evaluation easier and more useful.

- *Suggestion 1:* Be sure to describe all crucial elements in your training activity, not just program content.
- *Suggestion 2:* Choose an evaluation design that fits your situation.
- *Suggestion 3:* Seek out naturally occurring opportunities for evaluation.

What follows is a discussion of each of these suggestions:

DOCUMENTATION OF CONDITIONS SURROUNDING TRAINING

Needless to say, when evaluating job performance application and organizational impact, it is critical to specify *what* is being evaluated. If not, it makes both evaluation and transfer very difficult.

Example: A training program is tried out on a pilot basis and proves to be very effective as measured by desired changes in job performance measures. The program is then adopted organization-wide, but does not yield nearly as positive results. Why? In many cases, some crucially important aspect of the pilot situation was overlooked, and therefore not replicated in the other parts of the organization. The content and format of the training program itself are almost always described in great detail. However, some equally important aspects are often underrated. Each of the following conditions might have been critical to the process of the pilot but not specified as a necessary condition.

Before and During Training

Support
1. The program was introduced and supported by top management of the organization.

Perceived Need
2. The organization came to its own conclusion that it needed the training.

Group Make-up
3. Group make-up within training sessions is a special family group. For instance, X level manager and his or her direct or indirect reports experience training at the same time (and thereby share the vocabulary and opportunity to apply and provide mutual support to one another).

Scheduling
4. The program ran for 10 days—but the 10 days were spread over 10 weeks with extensive on-the-job application in between.

Location
5. It may be important that the program takes place off-site (away from interruptions) or on-site (where work materials are easily accessible).

After Training

Measurement
6. On-the-job application of learned behavior was measured.

Tools

7. Tools for on-the-job application were provided.

Opportunity

8. Trainees were placed in situations allowing for on-the-job application of learned behavior immediately post-training.

Ongoing Training

9. Personnel who entered the organization after the initial training are trained.

Communication of Success

10. Successful application of trained behavior is communicated throughout organization.

A good guide to what needs to be in the description of the training and situation is a document called "Request for Development of Training."

From Concept To Practice

To this point, we have presented several concepts important to evaluation:

1. The General Systems Model of training.
2. The Evaluation Model with its 4 degrees of evaluation.
3. The Evaluation Matrix.

Assuming that the decision has been made as to what questions to ask, some decisions still face the evaluator. How formal does the evaluation have to be? Will the organization allow evaluation activity? As with any other question, common sense is a large part of the answer to this one—the evaluation need be as extensive as necessary to convince whoever is the decision-maker. That will differ in each case, and one tries to do only as much as is necessary to make an informed decision.

In addition to common sense, there are several practical tactics that may help you in evaluation. There is one historical pitfall of training evaluation. That is, if a perfect laboratory type evaluation can't be done, then the organization falls all the way back to happiness index. In fact, there are a number of possible research designs for Degree III and IV evaluation which fit the dynamic nature of organizations and can often be used. In addition to the designs, some guides to converting *barriers* to evaluation into *opportunities* for evaluation will be suggested.

Some general suggestions for doing evaluation in the "Real" world:

1. Accept the fact that the evaluation will probably not be as clear-cut as laboratory research.

2. For purposes of formative evaluation research (in order to improve the training), limit yourself to a relatively small pilot group over which it is easier to gain control and get detailed information.

3. Conduct the simplest evaluation possible to answer the questions that the organization needs to have answered.

4. Take advantage of naturally occurring research opportunities.

EVALUATION DESIGNS FOR THE "REAL" WORLD

Most of the training evaluation today is classified as *action* research. That is, the research occurs in a real situation with all the constraints imposed by the organization going about getting its work done. This is articularly relevant to levels III and IV of the evaluation in which job performance and organizational value of job performance are the foci of the evaluation. It is crucial that levels III and IV be evaluated in the reality of the organization rather than in the laboratory. However, it is difficult to engineer and enforce all of the conditions necessary to the proper use of laboratory research design in the field setting. Some of the problems encountered in level III and IV evaluation and some suggestions for dealing with these problems are offered here.

A summary of several research designs and their applicability to level III and IV evaluation are presented in Figure 6.

Control Group Research Design

While one group receives training a *comparable* group does not receive the training. Each group is measured to see what the effect of the training has been.

Difficulties Encountered in the "Real" World.   It is difficult to find two *naturally* occurring groups that just happen to be comparable on the relevant dimensions. A group may be able to be selected in such a way as to provide comparability. Even when two such groups can be identified and used as the experimental and control group, the probability is very low that there will be identical environments and experiences for each group, so that training is the *only* variable that changes. One of the groups is very likely to have some important change occur—a local economic change, a local weather influence or an unpredicted influx of business.

FIGURE 6
Utility of Research Designs in the "Real" World

Designs	Applicability to Training Evaluation	When to Use
Control Group	Low	Very high cost program with support from high enough in the organization to hold *organization-controlled* factors constant in both groups.
Reversal (ABA)	Medium	As circumstances lead to stopping a critical element of the program (strick, workload influx, new manager, etc.)
Multiple Baseline	High	Any time you can get agreement on implementing the program area-by-area throughout the organization, rather than all at one time.
"Before and After" Measurement	It Depends	When there are no other possible factors influencing performance and/or it is impossible to use one of the other designs.

Suggestions. Use a control group to evaluate the on-the-job application and organizational impact of training only when the evaluation is seen as important enough to take extraordinary measures to ensure the continuing comparability of the groups. (Even then, factors outside your control may undermine the comparability.) Otherwise, seek other alternatives for evaluation.

Reversal, Or ABA Research Design

In a reversal or ABA design one evaluates by:

1. Taking a baseline measurement (how do things look now).
2. Implementing the training and measuring its impact (how do things look after training).
3. Return to the original condition by removing the training and measure (how do things look without the training).

The ABA design is intended to guard against the erroneous assumption that because two events occur at the same time one of the events *caused* the other. In other words, the fact that sales increased at the same time that a sales training program was conducted does not necessarily mean that the training *caused* the increase in sales—it might have been due to any number of other factors, such as the major competitor going on strike. If training caused the improved performance, then ceasing to train people should lead to deterioration of performance.

Difficulties Encountered in the "Real" World. If any action is implemented and there is an improvement in measured performance that can *logically* be tied to the action, it is very difficult to find a management group that is willing to stop doing what they think has caused the improved performance.

Suggestions. Seek out opportunities to use an ABA design due to naturally occurring changes that lead to removing the training or other practice being evaluated.

Multiple Baseline

In a multiple baseline design, the same program is used with different groups at different times. The design is an attempt to determine whether the change in performance is *caused* by the training or just concomitant (occurs at the same time) with the training:

Example: A training program is begun January 1st in Region A, and yields a 17% performance improvement. The same program is started February 1st in Region B and yields a similar performance improvement. This pattern is repeated March 1st in Region C, and April 1st in Region D. By starting the programs at different times, rather than all at once, factors such as changes in the marketplace, workload, quarterly business cycle, and personnel intake are spread. If, in each of 4 regions, the introduction of the training program leads to improved job performance, then one can attribute the change in performance to the training program with more certainty than if only one region had shown such an improvement.

Difficulties Encountered in the "Real" World. Organization may not be willing to spread out the introduction of something that has been proven successful in the pilot setting.

Suggestions. The decision to introduce progressively by area, rather than introducing the program everywhere at once, may be necessitated by the lack of staff to do it all at once. Or, one may be able to make the argument that careful high quality introduction more than compensates for the loss incurred by not installing the program all at one time.

"Before and After" Measurement

Performance is measured *in the relevant job setting* before the training and again after the training. Note that this differs from a pretest-postest design in that the performance is being measured *on-the-job* rather than in the classroom.

Difficulties Encountered in the "Real" World. The major difficulty is a limitation in interpreting the results. A change in performance might be attributed to training. It could equally well be attributed to any other change occurring during that same time.

Suggestions. Use this design only as a last resort, but if you do use it, try to have a detailed log of any changes which might be tied to the measured performance.

In summary, different situations lend themselves to different designs. Choose the one that is best suited to the current circumstances; and then try to build in the necessary conditions for the design to yield valid data.

NATURALLY OCCURRING RESEARCH OPPORTUNITIES

In addition to an evaluation design—conceived in the purity of an office atmosphere—there are often changes during a project which lend themselves to evaluation. Since the chance to conduct evaluation is limited, it is important that we learn to recognize these opportunities. Naturally occurring research opportunities present themselves very frequently. Unfortunately, these opportunities are often doing an excellent job of masquerading as barriers. It is the wise evaluator who can demask the barrier to find the subtle opportunity that lies beneath. The barriers/opportunities are situational, so no cookbook of hard-and-fast decision rules for conversion can be provided; but some examples are included as thought-starters.

Situation: Loss of Support. The person who was in charge of a group when training first was implemented gets promoted out of the area.

Barrier Interpretation. The support generated has been lost, and thus there is no point in continuing evaluation activities.

Opportunity Interpretation. Whereas previously the opportunity was to evaluate the program with a manager who followed the program through, there is now an opportunity to:

1. Evaluate the transferability of the program across managers.
2. Determine what different types of support building mechanisms are necessary when the manager inherits an ongoing program (than when he/she is there during start-up).
3. Determine if the program is applicable to the promoted manager's new area, whether it will be implemented and if so, what different kind of support (if any) is necessary.

Situation: Modification. People running the program have deviated from the original design in some way (changed the format; an example: the time frame, etc.).

Barrier Interpretation. They're not using the program as designed, so there's no point in conducting an evaluation.

Opportunity Interpretation.

1. There is an opportunity to evaluate the program *with* the modification.
2. Whether or not the modification "works," it would be very important to the interpretation

and use of evaluation results to find out *why* the modification was made. If the original design was felt to be unsatisfactory by this group, it might be unsatisfactory to other users for the same reason.

Situation: Interruption.   The program is interrupted for some reason (vacations, illness, personnel change, temporary crisis, etc.).

Barrier Interpretation.   This try-out of the program has been rendered useless since it has been interrupted.

Opportunity Interpretation.   This is a naturally occurring opportunity for an ABA design.

1. Continue to measure during the interruption to see if performance is maintained or drops off.
2. One would also want to check to see what new activities or priorities would logically be interfering with use of measured performance at this time.
3. Likewise, one would need to check to see what new or unusual support was being given to the measured performance at this time.

You will undoubtedly run into barriers/opportunities that are different from those presented here. The important thing is to constantly be on the lookout for conditions that allow for a type of evaluation that you feel is needed. Secondly, be alert whenever you curse a barrier that impedes evaluation (according to the original plan). It just may be an opportunity to do a different and equally useful evaluation.

SUMMARY

We have proposed a model for evaluation and suggested some ways of increasing the ease and opportunity to do evaluation.

If these ideas are used, it should lead to:

1. More clarity about *why* a given evaluation is being conducted.
2. More flexibility in evaluation design.
3. More evaluations that examine whether anything was learned, whether anything was used and whether that produced an organizational impact.

The better impact is measured, the easier it is to discuss the contributions of training to the critical results of the organization.

REFERENCES

- Brethower, Dale M., *A Systems Approach to Educational Problems,* Occasional Paper, Center for Programmed Learning for Business, University of Michigan, 1966.
- Rath, G. J., *Behavioral Planning Networks* ESD-TDR-63-607, Decision Sciences Laboratory, ESD, Hanscom Air Force Base, August, 1963.
- Rummler, Geary A., *Training System,* (Field Study Progress Report, University of Michigan—unpublished) 1964.
- Silvern, L. C., "Systems Engineering in the Educational Environment" a position paper for the STEMS PROJECT: Document 9.3.7, Northrop Norair, Hawthorne, California, March, 1963.

BIBLIOGRAPHY—BOOKS

- Mager, Robert F. and Pipe, Peter, *Analyzing Performance Problems,* Fearon Publishers/Lear Sigler, Inc., Belmont, California, 1970.
- Mager, Robert F. and Beach, Kenneth M., *Developing Vocational Instruction,* Fearon Publishers/Lear Sigler, Inc., Belmont, California, 1967.
- Mager, Robert F., *Goal Analysis,* Fearon Publishers/Lear Sigler, Inc., Belmont, California, 1972.
- Mager, Robert F., *Measuring Instructional Intent,* Fearon Publishers/Lear Sigler, Inc., 1973.
- Mager, Robert F., *Preparing Instructional Objectives,* Fearon Publishers, Belmont, California, 1962.
- Tracey, William L., *Evaluating Training and Development Systems,* American Management Association, Inc., New York, New York, 1968.

BIBLIOGRAPHY—ARTICLES

- Abbatiello, Aurelius A., "An Objective Evaluation of Attitude Changes in Training," *Training and Development Journal,* Vol. 21, No. 11, pp. 23–24 (November, 1967).
- Broadwell, Martin M., "Broadwell on Instructor Evaluation," *Training In Business and Industry,* Vol. 10, No. 10, pp. 25–28 (October, 1973).
- Burke, Ronald J., "A Plea for a Systematic Evaluation of Training" *Training and Development Journal,* Vol. 23, No. 8, pp. 24–29 (August, 1969).
- Catalanello, Ralph and Kirkpatrick, Donald L., "Evaluating Training Programs, The State of the Art," *Training and Development Journal,* Vol. 22, No. 5, pp. 2–9 (May, 1968).
- Chaddock, Carl and Gehrig, Bob, "On-the-Job Evaluation Shakes Up Training Program," *Training in Business and Industry,* Vol. 5, No. 8, pp. 31–35 (August, 1968).
- Denova, Charles C., "Research Is Not A Four Letter Word!," *Training and Development Journal,* Vol. 23, No. 11, pp. 24 ff. (November, 1969).

- Dubin, Samuel S., Mezack, Michael III and Neidig, Richard D., "Improving the Evaluation of Management Development Programs," *Training and Development Journal,* Vol. 28, No. 6, pp. 42–46 (June, 1974).
- Frederickson, Norman, "Proficiency Tests for Training Evaluation," Chapter II of *Training Research and Education,* University of Pittsburgh Press, Pittsburgh, Pennsylvania, 1962 (pp. 323–346).
- Furst, Hans, "The Economics of Training and Development," *Training and Development Journal,* Vol. 24, No. 10, pp. 30–33 (October, 1970).
- Gilbert, Thomas F., "Praxeonomy: A Systematic Approach to Identifying Training Needs," *Management of Personnel Quarterly,* Vol. 6, No. 3, pp 20–33 (Fall, 1967).
- Goss, William, "Teaching the Test," *Training in Business and Industry,* Vol. 7, No. 4, pp. 46 ff. (April, 1970)
- Habib, Waqar, "Problems in Determining Training Needs in an Organization," *Training and Development Journal,* Vol. 24, No. 7, pp. 44–48 (July, 1970).
- Jaffe, Cabot, "Diagnosis Before Treating," *Training in Business and Industry,* Vol, 6, No. 1, pp. 34–35 (January, 1969).
- Jones, A., and Moxham, J., "Costing the Benefits of Training," *Personnel Management,* Vol. 1, No. 4, pp. 22–28 (August, 1969).
- Laird, Dugan, "Notes From A Training Director," *Training in Business and Industry,* Vol. 8, No. 8 (August, 1971).
- Lees, D., and Chiplin, B., "The Economics of Industrial Training," *Lloyds Bank Review,* pp. 29–41 (April, 1970).
- Mollenkopf, W. G., "Some Results of Three Basic Skills Training Programs In An Industrial Setting," *Journal of Applied Psychology,* Vol. 43, No. 5, pp. 343–347.
- Rose, Homer C., "A Plan for Training Evaluation," *Training and Development Journal,* Vol. 22, No. 5, pp. 38–51, (May, 1968).
- Stander, Norman E., Townshend, Ralph, Jr., and Swartz, Gerald E., "A Quantitative Evaluation of a Motivational Training Program for Blue Collar Workers," *Training Director's Journal,* Vol. 18, No. 11, pp. 16–22 (November, 1964).
- Stewart, William J., "Determining First-Line Supervisory Training Needs," *Training and Development Journal,* Vol. 24, No. 4, pp. 12–19 (April 1970).
- Thorley, S., "Evaluating an In-Company Management Training Program," *Training and Development Journal,* Vol. 23, No. 9, pp. 48–51 (September, 1969).
- Underwood, William J., "Evaluation of Laboratory—Method Training," *Training and Development Journal,* Vol. 19, No. 5, pp. 34–36 (May 1965).
- Willing, Jules Z., "Are Your Problems Judged—Or Misjudged?," *Training Director's Journal,* Vol. 19, No. 4, pp. 29–31 (April, 1965).
- Wilson, Clark L., "On-the-Job and Operational Criteria," Chapter 12 of *Training Research and Education,* University of Pittsburgh Press, Pittsburgh, Pennsylvania, 1962, pp. 347–378.
- Wnuk, Joseph J., Jr., "Evaluation of Conceptual Training," *Training and Development Journal,* Vol. 20, No. 11, pp. 38–40 (December, 1966).
- Youmans, Charles V., "Testing for Training and Development," Chapter 4 of *Training and Development Handbook,* McGraw-Hill, New York, 1967, pp. 55–86.

CHAPTERS FROM BOOKS

- Brethower, Karen S., "Maintenance Systems: The Neglected Half of Behavior Change," Chapter from *Managing the Instructional Programming Effort,* Rummler et al. (ed.), 1967. For availability, check through Center for Programmed Instruction, University of Michigan, Ann Arbor.
- Kirkpatrick, Donald L., "Evaluation of Training," Chapter 5 of *Training and Development Handbook,* McGraw-Hill, New York, 1967, pp. 87–112.

Evaluation Procedures

by Irwin L. Goldstein

Rational decisions related to the selection, adoption, support, and worth of the various training activities require some basis for determining that the instructional program was responsible for whatever changes oc-

From *Training: Program Development and Evaluation*, by I. L. Goldstein. Copyright © 1974 by Wadsworth Publishing Company, Inc. Reprinted by permission of the publisher, Brooks/Cole Publishing Company, Monterey, California.

curred. Instructional analysts should be able to respond to the following questions:

1. Does an examination of the various criteria indicate that a change has occurred?
2. Can the changes be attributed to the instructional program?
3. Is it likely that similar changes will occur for new participants in the same program?

These questions could be asked about measures at each criterion level (for example, reaction, learning, behavior, results). Thus, evaluations of training programs are not likely to produce dichotomous answers. However, training analysts who expect results to lead to a value or no-value judgment are unrealistically imposing a simplistic structure and are raising false expectations among the recipients and sponsors of training research.

The unique objectives and constraints of each instructional setting make attempts to generalize results to other programs extremely hazardous. Kirkpatrick (1959) expressed this view by suggesting ". . . that one training director cannot borrow evaluation results from another; he can, however, borrow evaluation techniques" (p. 3). Before discussing particular methodologies for training evaluation, it is important to recognize that there are many different viewpoints about the desirability of evaluation, the approach to evaluation, and the effects of evaluation. The following sections discuss the most prominent of these viewpoints.

VIEWS OF THE EVALUATION PROCESS

Negativists, Positivists, and Frustrates

One continuum of thought revolves around the necessity for evaluation. As expressed by Randall (1960), negativists are those individuals who feel that evaluation of training is either impossible or unnecessary— that the value of formal instructional programs cannot be demonstrated by quantitative analysis. They feel that learning in an instructional setting is irrelevant and that improved performance in the transfer setting will be obvious without evaluation techniques. On the other end of the continuum are the positivists, who believe that scientific evaluation of training is the only worthwhile approach. This group suggests that instructional analysts should not waste time and money on anything other than a controlled study. In the center of these two groups are the frustrates, who recognize that training programs must be evaluated but are concerned with the methodology necessary to perform the evaluation. This group recognizes that all programs will be evaluated, either formally or informally; thus, it is concerned with the quality of the evaluation rather than with the decision whether to evaluate or not.

Each group's generalizations have a degree of validity. This text supports the view that the evaluation process is difficult but that the potential worth of evaluation remains undetermined because few evaluation studies are conducted. The negativist's viewpoint treats evaluation of programs in extremes—the pro-

gram is either good or bad. Instead, training programs should be considered dynamic entities that slowly accomplish their purpose in meeting predesigned objectives. Without systematic evaluation, there is no feedback to provide the information necessary to improve programs or quality information to make decisions. It is also difficult to accept the negativist's view that trainee improvements in the transfer setting will be obvious. A consideration of the difficulties associated with criterion contamination alone makes it clear that casual observations are not likely to provide much more than the observer's biased opinion. The positivists, on the other hand, would not permit a study except under completely controlled conditions. This view, if carried to an extreme, could result in research only in academic laboratories where systematic control of the environment can be maintained. While the data collected in these settings are important, the approach could have the undesired effect of reducing our understanding of instructional programs in real settings. The most reasonable approach is offered by the frustrates (the appropriate category for those participating in training research today). It is important to use the most systematic procedures available that fit the particular setting being investigated, to control as many of the extraneous variables as possible, and to recognize the limitations of the design being utilized. Thus, the better experimental procedures control more variables, permitting a greater degree of confidence in specifying program effects. While the constraints of the environment may make a perfect evaluation impossible, an awareness of the important factors in experimental design makes it possible to avoid a useless evaluation. The job of the training analyst is to choose the most rigorous design possible and to be aware of its limitations. These limitations should be taken into account in data interpretation and in reports to program sponsors.

TYPES OF EVALUATION

There are also varying opinions about the most appropriate type of evaluation. One dimension, discussed in this section, includes formative and summative evaluation. Another dimension, discussed in the next section, includes formal instructional research, action research, and casual research.

Formative and Summative Evaluation

As originally conceived by Scriven (1967), formative evaluation is utilized to determine if the program is operating as orginally planned or if improvements are necessary before the program is implemented. The major concern of summative evaluation is the evaluation of the final product with the major emphasis being program appraisal. Thus, formative evaluation stresses tryout and revision processes, primarily using process criteria, while summative evaluation uses outcome criteria to appraise the instructional program. However, process criteria (such as daily logs of activities) are also important in summative evaluation, because they supply the information necessary to interpret the data. Of course, both formative and summative evaluations can lead to feedback and program improvements. Design changes based on summative evaluations are determined by the degree to which program objectives are achieved. Improvements based on formative evaluations are more related to how closely the program is operating to the original design. The formative evaluation should be completed and judged adequate before summative evaluations are begun. Many research problems result from one-shot evaluation studies that attempt to combine formative and summative evaluations. Thus, the program is often appraised as if it is a completed product when it has not been implemented as originally designed.

A false concern with formative evaluations is that methodological difficulties might be caused by the continual changes adopted from collected data. But that constant modification is exactly the purpose of the formative period, and experimental design considerations should not prevent the necessary changes. Once the formative evaluation is completed, experimental design provides the foundation for the summative evaluation. On the other hand, satisfactory formative data indicating that the program is operating as designed do not mean that summative evaluations are unnecessary, just as the satisfaction of the personnel responsible for the implementation of the program does not mean that the program is meeting the stated objectives.

Formal Instructional Research, Action Research, and Casual Research

Borg (1963) developed an interesting comparison of these three types of research in educational settings. Table 1 shows that most of the categories are appropriate for all types of instructional settings. Since the remainder of this chapter will consider the methodological factors of these types of research (for example, sampling and design), this discussion will concentrate on more general considerations.

Practical, Statistical, and Scientific Significance. Analysts sometimes overemphasize the importance of statistically significant changes. It is quite possible to achieve statistically significant changes so small that they have virtually no meaning to the organization's objectives. On the other hand, the achievement of practical significant changes assumes that the differences are indeed reliable and will recur when the next instructional group is exposed to the treatment. Interacting with both ideas is the concept of scientific significance—that is, the establishment of meaningful results that permit generalizations about training procedures beyond the immediate setting being investigated. As Campbell, Dunnette, Lawler, and Weick (1970) suggest for managerial training, "Once the effects of such a program are mapped out for different kinds of trainees and for different types of criterion problems under various organizational situations, the general body of knowledge concerning management training has been enriched" (p. 284). If the instructional program is well designed, it should contribute to the solution of organizational goals, as well as add to the body of instructional knowledge.

METHODOLOGICAL CONSIDERATIONS

Each research design has different assets and liabilities in controlling extraneous factors that might threaten the evaluator's ability to determine: (1) if a real change has occurred, (2) whether the change is attributable to the instructional program, and (3) whether the change is likely to occur again with a new sample of subjects. Specific research designs will be discussed in a later section, but several general design concepts, including control groups and pre/post-testing, are mentioned here as background for the presentation of the sources of error that can affect the validity of the experimental design.

Pre/Post-Testing

The first question is whether the participants, after exposure to the instructional program, change their performance in a significant way. A design to answer this question would use a pretest administered before the instructional program begins and a post-test given after exposure to the instructional program. The timing of the post-test for the evaluation of an instructional program is not easily specified. A post-test at the conclusion of the training program provides a measure of the changes that have occurred during instruction, but it does not give any indication of later transfer performance. Thus, other measures should be employed after the participant has been in the transfer situation for a reasonable time period. Comparisons can then be made between (1) the pretest and the first post-test, (2) the pretest and the second post-test, and (3) the first

TABLE 1
Differences among Formal Instructional Research, Action Research, and the Casual Approach to Problem Solving in Education

Area	Formal Educational Research	Action Research	Casual or "Common Sense" Approach
1. Goals	To obtain knowledge that will be generalizable to a broad population and to develop and test instructional theories.	To obtain knowledge that can be applied directly to the local classroom situation and to give the participating teachers in-service training.	To make changes in the current procedure that appear likely to improve the situation.
2. Sampling	Research worker attempts to obtain a random or otherwise unbiased sample of the population being studied but is usually not completely successful.	Pupils available in the class of the teacher or teachers doing the research are used as subjects.	Some casual observation of pupil behavior may be made by the teacher after the change decided upon has been in effect for a while.
3. Experimental design	Design is carefully planned in detail prior to start of the study and adhered to as closely as possible. Major attention is given to maintaining comparable conditions and reducing error bias. Control of extraneous variables is important.	Procedures are planned in general terms prior to start of study. Changes are made during the study if they seem likely to improve the teaching situation. Little attention is paid to control of the experimental conditions or reduction of error. Because participating teachers are ego-involved in the research situation, bias is usually present.	If classroom testing of the decision is attempted, procedures are planned only in the most general terms. No attempt is made to establish common definitions or procedures among participating teachers.
4. Measurement	An effort is made to obtain the most valid measures available. A thorough evaluation of available measures and a trial of these measures usually precede their use in the research.	Less rigorous evaluation of measures than in scientific research. Participants often lack training in the use and evaluation of educational measures but can do satisfactory job with help of a consultant.	Usually no evaluation is made except for the casual observations of the teachers participating. The teacher's opinion as to whether the new procedure is an improvement or not depends almost entirely on whether the teacher approves the change.
5. Analysis of data	Complex analysis often called for. Inasmuch as generalizability of results is a goal, statistical significance is usually emphasized.	Simple analysis procedures usually are sufficient. Practical significance rather than statistical significance is emphasized. Subjective opinion of participating teachers is often weighed heavily.	Subjective opinion of the participants is usually the only procedure used. No attempt made at objective analysis.
6. Application of results	Results are generalizable, but many useful findings are not applied in educational practice. Differences in training and experience between research workers and teachers generate a serious communication problem.	Findings are applied immediately to the classes of participating teachers and often lead to permanent improvement. Application of results beyond the participating teachers is usually slight.	Decisions reached are applied immediately in classes of participating teachers. Even if the decision leads to improvement, it is often changed later because no evidence is available to support its continuance. This approach leads to educational fads and "change for the sake of change."

Adapted from Borg, W. R. *Educational Research.* Copyright © 1963, 1971 by David McKay Co., Inc. Reprinted by permission of the publisher.

and second post-tests. For convenience, this section will refer only to pre- and post-tests, but it is important to remember that one post-test immediately after training will ordinarily not suffice. An additional factor in the analysis of pre- and post-test scores is how scores on the pretest affect the degree of success on the post-test. One possibility is that the participant who initially scored highest on the pretest will perform best on the post-test. In order to examine this effect, some researchers (Mayo & DuBois, 1963), have suggested that the pretest scores should be partialed out of the post-test.

The variables measured in the pre- and post-tests must be associated with the objectives of the training program. The expected changes associated with the instructional program should be specified so that statistically reliable differences between the pre- and post-tests can confirm the degree to which the objectives have been achieved. This text does not attempt to treat the statistical considerations in instructional evaluation analyses except to warn the reader that statistical expertise is necessary to properly evaluate programs.

Control Groups

The specification of changes indicated by pre- and postmeasurement is only one consideration. It must be determined that these changes occurred because of the instructional treatment. To eliminate the possibility of other explanations for the changes between the pre- and post-test, a control group is used (treated like the experimental group on all variables that might contribute to pre/post differences except for the actual instructional program). With control procedures, it is possible to specify whether the changes in the experimental group were due to the instructional treatment or to other factors, like the passage of time, maturation factors, or events in the outside world. The particular kinds of errors that can occur will be specified in the next section, but, as an example of the necessity for control groups, we can consider the placebo effect. In medical research, the placebo is an inert substance administered to the control group so that the subject cannot distinguish whether he is a member of the experimental or the control group. This allows the researcher to separate the effects of the actual drug from the reactions induced by the subject's expectations and suggestibility. In instructional research, similar cautions must be taken to separate the background effects sometimes employed in the experimental setting and the actual treatment. It is possible that treatment effects in an experimental group in which videotape feedback is being investigated are caused by the presence of recording equipment and numerous observers (Isaac & Michael, 1971). Thus, the control group should be presented with similar attention. In medical and psychological research, there is concern about experimenters who unknowingly interact with subjects and shape their behavior, through subtle cues, toward the predicted results. While control groups do not provide a solution for this latter problem, researchers should be aware of these potential dangers.

Before discussing specific research designs, it is necessary to consider those factors that contribute sources of error. D. T. Campbell and J. C. Stanley (1963) have organized and specified these threats to experimental design, and, for the most part, their labels and organization are utilized.

INTERNAL AND EXTERNAL VALIDITY

Internal validity asks the basic question "Did the treatment make a difference in this particular situation?" Unless internal validity has been established, it is not possible to interpret the effects of any experiment, training or otherwise. External validity refers to the generalizability or representativeness of the data. The evaluator is concerned with generalizability of his results to other populations, settings, and treatment variables. External validity is always a matter of inference and thus can never be specified with complete confidence. However, the designs that control the most threats to internal and external validity are, of course, the most useful.

These threats are variables other than the instructional program itself that can affect its results. The solution to this difficulty is to control these variables so that they may be cast aside as competing explanations for the experimental effect. Threats to internal validity include the following.

History. History refers to the specific events, other than the experimental treatment, occurring between the first and second measurements that could provide alternative explanations for results. When tests are given on different days, as is almost always the case in instructional programs, events occurring between the testing periods can contaminate the effects. For instance, an instructional program designed to produce positive attitudes toward safe practices in coal mines may produce significant differences that have no relationship to the material presented in the instructional program because a coal-mine disaster occurred between the pre- and post-test.

Maturation. Maturation includes all biological or psychological effects that systematically vary with the passage of time, independent of specific events like history. Participants become older, fatigued, or more or less interested in the program between the time of the pre-test and the time of the post-test. Thus, performance can change for reasons unrelated to the instructional material.

Testing.   This variable refers to the influence of the pre-test on the scores of the post-test. This is an especially serious problem for instructional programs in which the pre-test can sensitize the participant to search for material or to ask friends for information that provides correct answers on the post-test. Thus, improved performance would occur simply by taking the pre- and post-tests, without any intervening instructional program.

Instrumentation.   This threat to validity results from changes in the instruments that might result in differences between pre- and post-test scores. For example, fluctuations in mechanical instruments or changes in grading standards can lead to differences, regardless of the instructional program. Since rating scales are commonly employed as a criterion in training research, it is important to be sensitive to differences related to changes in the rater (for example, additional expertise in the second rating, bias, or carelessness) that can cause error effects.

Statistical Regression.   Participants for instructional research are often chosen on the basis of extreme scores. Thus, students with extremely low and extremely high intelligence-test scores may be chosen for participation in a course using programed instruction. In these cases, a phenomenon known as statistical regression often occurs. On the second testing, the scores for both groups regress toward the middle of the distribution. Thus, students with extremely high scores would tend toward lower scores, and those with extremely low scores would tend toward higher scores. This regression occurs because tests are not perfect measures; there will always be some change in scores from the first to the second testing simply because of measurement error. Since the first scores are at the extreme ends, the variability must move toward the center (the mean of the entire group). Students with extremely high scores might have had unusually good luck the day of the first testing, or students with extremely low scores may have been upset or careless that day. On the second administration, however, each group is likely to regress toward the mean.

Differential Selection of Participants.   This effect stems from biases in choosing comparison groups. If volunteers are used in the instruction group and randomly chosen participants are used in the control group, differences could occur between the two

groups simply because each was different before the program began. This variable is best controlled by random selection of all participants, with appropriate numbers of participants (as determined by statistical considerations) for each group. Random selection is a particular problem in educational settings where one class is chosen as the control group and another class as the experimental group. Establishing experimental and control groups by placing individuals with matched characteristics (for example, intelligence, age, sex) in each group is still not the best alternative. Often, the critical parameters that should be used to match the participants are not known, and thus selection biases can again affect the design. One alternative is a combination of matching and randomization in which participants are matched on important parameters; then, one member of each pair is assigned randomly to the treatment or control group.

Experimental Mortality.   This variable refers to the differential loss of participants from the treatment or control group. In a control group of volunteers, those persons who scored poorly on the pretest may drop out because they are discouraged. Thus, the group in the experimental program may appear to score higher than the control group, because the low-scoring performers have dropped out.

Interactions.   Many of the above factors—for example, the selection and maturation—can interact to produce threats to internal validity. When younger students are compared with older students over a period of a year, there are differences in initial selection and differences in maturation changes that could occur at varying rates for each of the different groups.

Threats to External Validity

External validity refers to the generalizability of the study to other groups and situations. Internal validity is a prerequisite for external validity, since the results of the study must be valid for the group being examined before there can be concern over the validity for other groups. The representativeness of the investigation determines the degree of generalizability. For example, when the data are initially collected in a low socioeconomic setting, it is difficult to claim that the instructional program will work equally well for a high socioeconomic area. Campbell and Stanley list the following threats to external validity.

Reactive Effect of Pretesting.   The effects of pretests often lead to increased sensitivity to the instructional procedure. Thus, the participant's responses to the training program might be different from the responses of individuals who are exposed to an established program without the pretest; the pretested participant might pay attention to certain material in the training program only because he knows it is covered in test items.

Interaction of Selection and Experimental Treatment.

The characteristics of the group selected for experimental treatment determine the generalizability of the findings to other participants. The characteristics of employees from one division of the firm may result in the treatment's being more or less effective for them, as compared to employees from another division with different characteristics. Similarly, characteristics of school students, like socioeconomic status or intelligence level, may make them more or less receptive to particular instructional programs.

Reactive Effects of Experimental Settings.

The procedures employed in the experimental setting may limit the generalizability of the study. Observers and experimental equipment often make the participants aware of their participation in an experiment, which can lead to changes in behavior that cannot be generalized to those individuals who will participate in the instructional treatment when it is nonexperimental. The Hawthorne studies have become the standard illustration for the "I'm a guinea pig" effect. This research shows that a group of employees continued to increase production regardless of the changes in working conditions designed to produce both increases and decreases in production. Interpreters believe that the experimental conditions resulted in the workers' behaving differently. Explanations for the Hawthorne effect include: novelty; awareness of being a participant in an experiment; changes in the environment due to observers, recording conditions, and social interaction; and daily feedback on production figures (Isaac & Michael, 1971). Since the factors that affect the treatment group will not be present in future training sessions, the performance obtained is not representative of that of future participants.

Multiple-Treatment Interference.

The effects of previous treatments are not erasable; therefore, threats to external validity occur whenever there is an attempt to establish the effects of a single treatment from studies that actually examined multiple treatments. Thus, trainees exposed to role playing, films, and lectures may perform best during the lectures, but that does not mean they would perform in a similar manner if they were exposed to lectures all day long without the other techniques.

EXPERIMENTAL DESIGN

This section presents some of the many designs that examine the effects of experimental treatments. The previous sections on internal and external validity discussed some of the factors that make it difficult to determine whether the treatment produced the hypothesized results. As we shall see, these threats are differentially controlled by the various designs. Given a particular setting, the researcher should employ the design that has the greatest degree of control over threats to validity. Certainly, it is possible to avoid choosing a useless design. In many cases, the main difficulty has been the failure to plan for evaluation before the program was implemented. In these instances, the utilization of a few procedures—for example, pre/post-testing and control groups—could dramatically improve the quality of information.

For convenience in presenting the experimental designs, T_1 will represent the pretest, T_2 the post-test, X the treatment or instructional program, and R the random selection of subjects. Campbell and Stanley (1963) have organized a detailed examination of the variables that should be considered when choosing a research design. The designs in this text, organized into several different categories, provide examples of the numerous approaches available. The first category includes pre-experimental designs that do not have control procedures and are valueless in analyzing cause-and-effect relationships. Experimental designs, the second category, have varying degrees of power that permit some control of threats to validity. The third category includes quasi-experimental designs that are useful in many social-science settings where investigators lack the opportunity to exert full control over the environment.

Pre-Experimental Designs

1.   The one-shot case study:

$$\boxed{\quad X \qquad T_2 \quad}$$

In this method, commonly called the case-study approach, the subjects are exposed to the instructional treatment (without a pretest) and then are tested once. This design has a total absence of control, and all threats to internal validity are present. Thus, there is no scientific value to this approach. The only bases for comparisons are intuitions and impressions. As Campbell and Stanley have observed, these studies often involve a tedious collection of specific detailed data that cannot substitute for a more rigorous design. The only purpose that this design can serve is to collect preliminary information for a more thorough investigation.

2.   The one-group pretest/post-test design:

$$\boxed{\quad T_1 \qquad X \qquad T_2 \quad}$$

When this design is employed, the participants are given a pretest, presented with the instructional program, and then given a post-test. This design is widely utilized in the examination of instructional settings, because it provides a measure of comparison between the same group of subjects before and after treatment. Unfortunately, without a control group, it is difficult to establish whether the experimental treatment is the prime factor determining any differences that occur between the testing periods. Thus, the many threats to internal validity, including changes in history, maturation, testing effects, changes in instrumentation, and statistical regression, are not controlled. This design does, however, control biases due to subject mortality.

Research Example of Pre-Experimental Designs

Golembiewski and Carrigan (1970) carried out a training program that utilized a pre/post design without a control group in one of a series of investigations designed to change the style of a sales unit in a business organization. They had a series of goals, including: the integration of a new management team, an increase in congruence between the behaviors required by the organization and those preferred by the men, and a greater congruence of individual needs and organizational demands. The training program consisted of a laboratory approach using sensitivity training to encourage the exploration of the participant's feelings and reactions to the organization. The program also included confrontations in which management of various levels were given an opportunity to discuss their ideas and feelings. The instrument used to measure pre-and postexperimental changes was Likert's profile of organizational characteristics, which includes items related to leadership, character of motivational forces, communication, interaction influence, decision making, goal setting, and control.

After statistical analyses, the authors concluded that the learning design had the intended effect in terms of the measured attitudes. Golembiewski and Carrigan indicated that they had included all the managers in the treatment and so did not have a control group. Thus, their design did not permit them to

be certain that the effects were a result of the training program rather than of random factors or the passage of time. This design uncertainty is expressed by Becker (1970) in an article entitled "The Parable of the Pill":

There once was a land in which wisdom was revered. Thus there was great excitement in the land when one of its inhabitants announced that he had invented a pill which made people wiser. His claim was based on an experiment he conducted. The report of the experiment explained (1) that the experimenter secured a volunteer; (2) the volunteer was first given an IQ test; (3) then he swallowed a pill which he was told would make him more intelligent; (4) finally he was given another IQ test. The score on the second IQ test was higher than on the first, so the report concluded that the pill increased wisdom.

Alas, there were two skeptics in the land. One secured a volunteer; gave him an IQ test; waited an appropriate length of time; then gave him another IQ test. The volunteer's score on the second test exceeded that of the first. Skeptic One reported his experiment and concluded that taking the first test was an experience for the subject and that the time between the tests allowed the subject to assimilate and adjust to that experience so that when he encountered the situation again he responded more efficiently. Time alone, the skeptic argued, was sufficient to produce the increase in test score. The skeptic also pointed out that time alone could have produced the change in test score reported in the experiment on the Wisdom Pill.

Skeptic Two conducted a different experiment. He held the opinion that most people were to some extent suggestible or gullible and that they readily would accept a suggestion that they possessed a desired attribute. He further believed that people who accept such a suggestion might even behave in a way such as to make it appear, for a time at least, that they indeed did possess the suggested ability. Therefore, the skeptic secured a volunteer; gave him an IQ test; had him ingest a pill composed of inert ingredients; told him the pill would increase his intelligence; then gave him another IQ test. Skeptic Two dutifully reported his subject achieved a higher score on the second test and, based on his hypothesis, explained how the disparity arose. He also pointed out that the increase in test score in the Wisdom Pill experiment could have been due to the taking of the pill and expectations associated with taking the pill rather than to the ingredients in the pill.

The inventor of the wisdom pill drafted a reply to the two skeptics. He wrote that, although he did not employ a control group or a placebo group, he is confident that the pill's ingredients caused the observed change because that change is consistent with the theory from which he deduced the formula for his pill [p. 94].[1]

The point in the parable is that Skeptic One, Skeptic Two, or the inventor of the pill may be right.

---

[1]From Becker, S. W. The parable of the pill. *Administrative Science Quarterly*, 1970, 15, 94–96. Reprinted by permission of *Administrative Science Quarterly* and the author.

There is no way of being certain, given the present design, what was responsible for the effect.

Essentially, pre-experimental designs do not provide good information about the impact of the treatment. They should be used only to collect preliminary data. The next group of designs shows how easily many of the pre-experimental designs can be improved. Design 1 can be strengthened by adding a pretest, and both Design 1 and Design 2 can be improved by adding a control group. Even where the environment makes a control group impractical, these designs can be improved by using the time-series approach (described in the section on quasi-experimental designs).

Experimental Designs

3. Pretest/post-test control-group design:

| Experimental Group (R) | T_1 | X | T_2 |
| Control Group (R) | T_1 | | T_2 |

In this design, the subjects are chosen at random from the population and assigned randomly to the experimental group or control group. Each group is given a pre- and post-test, but only the experimental group is exposed to the instructional treatment. If there is more than one instructional treatment, it is possible to add additional experimental groups.

This design represents a considerable improvement over Designs 1 and 2, because many of the threats to internal validity are controlled. The differential selection of subjects is controlled by the random selection. Variables like history, maturation, and pretesting should affect the experimental group and the control group equally. Statistical regression based on extreme scores (if subjects are chosen that way) is not eliminated but should be equal for the two groups because of the random selection procedures. However, any effects not part of the instructional procedure that are due to differential treatment of subjects in the control and experimental groups must still be controlled by the experimenter. This design is affected by external threats to validity, which are not as easily specified as the threats to internal validity. The design does not control the effects of pretesting; thus T_1 could have sensitized the participants to the experimental treatment in a way that makes generalizations to future participants difficult. Generalizations would also be hampered because subjects in the experiment might be different from those who will participate at later times and because the guinea-pig effect could lead to differences between the experimental and control groups. This latter concern is dependent on the ingenuity of the experimenter in reducing the differences between groups by treating the control group in the same manner as the experimental group (except for the specific instructional treatment).

The difficulties associated with external validity should not freeze the researcher into inactivity. While threats to internal validity are reasonably well handled by experimental designs, generalizations, which are the core of external validity, are always precarious. As Campbell and Stanley point out, experimenters try to generalize by scientifically guessing at laws and by trying out generalizations in other specific cases. Slowly, and somewhat painfully, they gain knowledge about factors that affect generalizations. (For example, there is now ample evidence that pretesting does sensitize and affect participants.) As shown in the following design, a control for pretest sensitization is relatively easy to achieve by adding a group to Design 3 that is exposed to the treatment without first being presented with the pretest.

4. Solomon four-group design:

Group			
1 (R)	T_1	X	T_2
2 (R)	T_1		T_2
3 (R)		X	T_2
4 (R)			T_2

The Solomon four-group design represents the first specific procedure designed to consider external-validity factors. This design adds two groups that are not pretested. If the participants are randomly assigned to the four groups, this design makes it possible to compare the effects of pretesting. (Group 4 provides a control for pretesting without the instructional treatment.) It also permits the evaluator to determine the effects of some internal-validity factors. For example, a comparison of the post-test performance for Group 4, which was not exposed to pretesting or instructional treatments, to the pretest scores for Groups 1 and 2 permits the analysis of the combined effects of maturation and history.

Research Example of Experimental Designs

Goodacre (1955) reported on an evaluative study of a supervisory training program at B. F. Goodrich Company that fits into the classification of experimental designs. The program consisted of conferences, lectures, and discussions for different supervisory and managerial personnel on topics related to the understanding of human behavior, decision making, employee selection, employee progress, and job evaluation. The experimental design was developed in conjunction with the program and built into the instructional procedure. The 800 participants were randomly placed into two groups—an experimental group and a control group. As Goodacre notes, random selection was necessary to assure that the groups would be comparable on variables like age, length of service, job level, and intelligence. The control group did not participate in the training program, but, in all other regards, it was treated similarly to the experimental group. Various criterion measures, including attitude scales, achievement tests, and ratings by immediate supervisors, were administered both before and after training.

As reported by J. P. Campbell et al. (1970), the control group did not show any significant changes, but the experimental group improved on the achievement tests, self-confidence ratings, and post-training performance measures. This is one of the few studies that not only used a rigorous design but also attempted to measure performance on the job and in the training program. Goodacre and Campbell et al. note that one problem with the performance ratings was that the raters knew who participated in the training program. Yet, even with that difficulty, the experimental design permitted the control of many threats to internal validity that plague pre-experimental design. However, it did not control for the external-validity threats of pretesting sensitization.

Quasi-Experimental Designs

5.   The time-series design:

| T_1 | T_2 | T_3 | T_4 | X | T_5 | T_6 | T_7 | T_8 |

This design is similar to Design 1, except that a series of measurements are taken before and after the instructional treatment. This particular approach illustrates the possibilities of utilizing quasi-experimental designs in situations in which it is not possible to gain the full control required by experimental designs. An examination of the internal-validity threats shows that this design provides more control than Design 1. If there are no appreciable changes from pretests 1 to 4, it is unlikely that any effects will occur due to maturation, testing, or regression. The major internal-validity difficulty with this design is the history variable; that is, events that may happen between T_4 and T_5 (such as environmental changes and historical occurrences) are not controlled by this procedure.

The use of the time-series design does not control most of the external-validity threats. Thus, it is necessary to be sensitive to any relationships between the treatment and particular subject groups (like volunteers) that might make results difficult to generalize to other groups, and it is also necessary to be aware that subjects might be sensitized to particular aspects of the instructional program through the use of pretests.

6.   The nonequivalent control-group design:

| Experimental Group | T_1 | X | T_2 |
| Control Group | T_1 | | T_2 |

The nonequivalent control-group design is the same as Design 3, except that the participants are not assigned to the groups at random. (The choice of the group to receive the instructional treatment is made randomly.) This design is often used in educational settings where there are naturally assembled groups, such as classes. If there is no alternative, this design is well worth using and is certainly preferable to designs that do not include control groups (such as Design 2). The more similar the two groups and their scores on the pretest, the more effective the control becomes in accounting for extraneous influences—for instance, internal-validity factors like history, pretesting, maturation, and instrumentation. However, the investigator must be especially careful, because this design is vulnerable to interactions between selection factors and maturation, history, and testing. Since the participants were not chosen randomly, there is always the possibility that critical differences exist that were not revealed by the pretests. For example, some studies use volunteers who might react differently to the treatment because of motivational factors. Thus, the investigator must be sensitive to potential sources of differences between the groups. The dangers of instrumentation changes and of differential treatment of each group (unrelated to the treatment) remain a concern for this design as well as for Design 3.

Although the external-validity issues are similar to those for Design 3, the nonequivalent control-group design does have some advantages in the control of the reactive effects of experimental settings. The utilization of intact groups makes it easier to design the experiment as part of the normal routine, thus reducing some of the problems associated with the guinea-pig effect. Since this design is not as disruptive, it is also possible, in some settings (for example, educational systems), to have a larger subject population, thus increasing generalizability.

Research Example of Quasi-Experimental Designs

A study by Canter (1951) illustrates a quasi-experimental design employing pre/post measures with nonequivalent control groups. The purpose of this investigation was to train supervisory personnel in human relations—that is, to establish facts and principles so that supervisors could become more competent in their knowledge and understanding of human behavior. The criteria consisted of a test battery including measures of supervisory behavior, social judgment, and logical reasoning.

The experimental group contained supervisors from one department, and the control group contained members from two other departments. Since the participants were not randomly chosen, Canter checked variables like age, sex, mental alertness, and years of service. While there were no statistical differences due to considerable variability in the scores, the author indicated that differences in number of years of service and mental alertness were discernible. The results of the study indicated that changes in performance favored the trained group.

While this design controls history and maturation factors reasonably well, there are problems related to selection interactions and factors like history and testing. The participants in this program worked under different supervisors and in different psychological and physical environments. The effects of these selection factors are unknown, but of special concern is the fact that the department heads for these participants did observe certain aspects of the training.

SUMMARY

Campbell and Stanley have summarized threats to validity for various designs (see Table 2). They warn us about using the summary table without a full understanding of the various designs and threats to validity. While it is often best to use regularly employed personnel in operating the training program, the design of the program and the statistical analyses require adept professionals. Experts working closely with the regular staff will create the most productive program, design, and analyses.

TABLE 2
Sources of Invalidity for Designs 1 through 6

	Sources of Invalidity											
	Internal								External			
	History	Maturation	Testing	Instrumentation	Regression	Selection	Mortality	Interaction of Selection and Maturation, etc.	Interaction of Testing and X	Interaction of Selection and X	Reactive Arrangements	Multiple-X Interference
Pre-Experimental Designs:												
1. One-shot case study X T$_2$	−	−				−	−				−	
2. One-group pretest/ post-test design T$_1$ X T$_2$	−	−	−	−	?	+	+	−	−	−	?	
True Experimental Designs:												
3. Pretest/post-test control-group design R T$_1$ X T$_2$ / R T$_1$ T$_2$	+	+	+	+	+	+	+	+	−	?	?	
4. Solomon four-group design R T$_1$ X T$_2$ / R T$_1$ T$_2$ / R X T$_2$ / R T$_2$	+	+	+	+	+	+	+	+	+	?	?	
Quasi-Experimental Designs:												
5. Time series T$_1$ T$_2$ T$_3$ T$_4$ X T$_5$ T$_6$ T$_7$ T$_8$	−	+	+	?	+	+	+	+	−	?	?	
6. Nonequivalent control-group design T$_1$ X T$_2$ / T$_1$ T$_2$	+	+	+	+	?	+	+	−	−	?	?	

Note: A minus indicates a definite weakness, a plus indicates that the factor is controlled, a question mark indicates a possible source of concern, and a blank indicates that the factor is not relevant.

Adapted from Campbell, D. T., & Stanley, J. C. *Experimental and Quasi-Experimental Designs for Research.* Chicago: Rand McNally, 1963. © 1963 by the American Educational Research Association, Washington, D.C. Used by permission.

A FINAL WORD

In summary, it is important to note that the literature abounds with studies of designs that do not justify the conclusions reached by their authors. Sadly, the majority of research utilizes pre-experimental designs (pre/post, no control; or post, no control). To add to the difficulties, most of this research employs criteria reflecting training performance (reactions and learning), with little attention to criteria that may be available at a later time in the transfer situation. The studies sometimes reflect a lack of sophistication, but, in most instances, the evaluators appear fully knowledgeable about the inadequacies of their design and even comment about the uncontrolled factors before going on to justify their conclusions. It is difficult to interpret data from training and educational settings because of the many possible contaminants. In many instances, the researchers simply could not impose strong experimental designs (such as Design 4). However, many of the quasi-experimental designs could have been utilized with little extra effort. The difficult process of properly evaluating our instructional programs must be undertaken. Dunnette and Campbell (1968) summarize the important minimum requirements for evaluation.

What needs to be done?
The *scientific* standards necessary for properly evaluating training experiences are few in number and disarmingly simple, but . . . they are almost never put into practice.

First, measures of trainees' status should be obtained *before* and *after* the training experience. Ideally, the measures should sample, as broadly as possible, trainee *behaviors* relevant to the organization's problems and/or to the aims of the training procedures, but attitudinal, perceptual, and other self-report measures may also prove useful. Second, measured changes shown by the trainees between pre- and post-training periods should be compared with changes, if any, occurring in a so-called control group of similar, but untrained, persons. Using control groups is the only way to assure that changes observed in the experimental (or trainee) groups are actually the result of training procedures instead of possible artifactual effects—such as the mere passage of time, poor reliability of measures, Hawthorne effects, or other spurious components. Finally, a third standard necessary for most training evaluation studies stems from the possibility of interaction between the evaluation measures and the behavior of the trainees during the program. For example, if trainees are asked beforehand to answer questions about their supervisory "styles," they may be alerted to look for the "correct answers" during training in order to answer the same questions "more appropriately" (i.e., more in line with the desires of the trainer) when they are asked again after training. One way of estimating the degree of interaction between such measures and the training content is to provide a quasi-control group which takes part in the training program *without* first completing the measures.

Then, comparisons between the two trained groups (experimental and quasi-control) on the after-measures may give estimates of the relative amounts of change actually due to training or due simply to having been alerted by prior exposure to the measures.

Unfortunately, these three rather simple standards for learning what training accomplishes are actually very difficult to meet, and they have been applied only rarely . . . [p.8].[2]

The importance of the improvements that can be realized by rejecting pre-experimental designs and by considering the three factors stressed by Dunnette and Campbell—that is, pre- and post-tests, control groups, and a control for pretest sensitization—should be emphasized. In most instances, the inclusion of these procedures requires some planning, but it is well worth the effort in terms of the quality of information. Even in those cases in which it is not possible to implement all the procedures, a degree of forethought can provide dividends. Thus, in the situations in which a control group is not possible, a time-series design is preferable to a one-group pretest/post-test design. Thoughtful considerations can often provide solutions when the environment appears to dictate otherwise. For example, Rubin (1967) managed to obtain a control group for a sensitivity-training procedure while still providing the treatment for all participants. This was accomplished by having a selected number of trainees complete a pretest by mail several weeks before the treatment commenced. This group then completed the questionnaires again shortly before the treatment began for all participants. These pre- and post-test scores without an intervening treatment provided a control group that was later compared to pre- and post-test scores separated by the treatment condition.

REFERENCES

- Becker, S. W. The parable of the pill. *Administrative Science Quarterly*, 1970, 15, 94–96.
- Borg, W. R. *Educational Research*. New York: David McKay, 1963, 1971.
- Campbell, D. T., and Stanley, J. C. *Experimental and quasi-experimental designs for research*. Chicago: Rand McNally, 1963.
- Campbell, J. P., Dunnette, M. D., Lawler, E. E. III, and Weick, K. E., Jr. *Managerial behavior, performance, and effectiveness*. New York: McGraw-Hill, 1970.
- Canter, R. R., Jr. A human relations training program. *Journal of Applied Psychology*, 1951, 35, 38–45.

---

[2]From Dunnette, M. D., & Campbell, J. P. Laboratory education: Impact on people and organizations. *Industrial Relations*, 1968, 8, 1–45. Copyright 1968 by the Regents of the University of California, Berkeley. Reprinted by permission.

- Dunnette, M. D., and Campbell, J. P. Laboratory education: Impact on people and organizations. *Industrial Relations*, 1968, 8, 1–27, 41–44.
- Golembiewski, R. T., and Carrigan, S. B. Planned change in organization style based on the laboratory approach. *Administrative Science Quarterly*, 1970, 15, 79–93.
- Goodacre, D. M. Experimental evaluation of training. *Journal of Personnel Administration and Industrial Relations*, 1955, 2, 143–149.
- Isaac, S., and Michael, W. B. *Handbook in research and evaluation.* San Diego: Knapp, 1971.
- Kirkpatrick, D. L. Techniques for evaluating training programs. *Journal of the American Society of Training Directors*, 1959, 13, 3–9, 21–26; 1960, 14, 13–18, 28–32.

- Mayo, G. D., and DuBois, P. H. Measurement of gain in leadership training. *Educational and Psychological Measurement*, 1963, 23, 23–31.
- Randall, L. K. Evaluation: A training dilemma. *Journal of the American Society of Training Directors*, 1960, 14, 29–35.
- Rubin, I. Increased self-acceptance: A means of reducing racial prejudice. *Journal of Personality and Social Psychology*, 1967, 5, 233–239.
- Scriven, M. The methodology of evaluation. In *Perspectives of curriculum evaluation*. American Educational Research Association Monograph, No. 1. Chicago: Rand McNally, 1967.

Cost Effectiveness: A Model for Assessing the Training Investment

by James G. Cullen, Stephen A. Sawzin, Gary R. Sisson and Richard A. Swanson

Evaluation of training costs may be divided into two major categories: cost effectiveness and cost benefit. Cost benefit (CB) is the analysis of training costs in monetary units to benefits derived from training in nonmonetary terms. Examples of nonmonetary benefits would be trainee attitudes, health and safety. Cost effectiveness (CE) is the analysis of training costs in monetary units as compared to benefits derived from training in monetary terms. Monetary benefits such as production increases, production waste, scrap savings and production down-time savings, are considered.

Throughout training literature, money spent on training is defined as a monetary "cost." This term seems to automatically denote a loss of revenues for the company. This dire connotation may be softened in the minds of production managers by using the term "investment." This term denotes money and time used as an investment to help the company. Therefore, the gains or losses derived from training are identified as the "returns." These returns as compared to the investment result in the subsequent cost benefits or cost effectiveness of the training.

Whether training costs are technically "expense" or "investment" is a moot question. Money spent now to train someone will keep coming back in future years

in the form of greater efficiency and in other ways and, therefore, could be viewed as an "investment." However, it also requires recurring expenses to maintain and continue training which provides immediate return, and, therefore, could be seen as an "expense."

Financial experts and industrial managers view money spent for training in a way that fits their particular technical definitions. Whether it is viewed as expense or investment is academic, except for tax considerations. The important thing to realize is that money spent for structured training will be returned many times over, and this was the whole point of the Industrial Training Research Project at Bowling Green State University.*

The usefulness of the comparison of the investment to the return is the simplicity of the comparison and the specificity of the terms and units used in the comparison. These terms must be definable and in measurable units. This is most important in the cost-effectiveness comparisons. The cost benefit can also be in measurable terms such as attitude surveys, health and safety accident reports, and an increase in the

---

*An experimental study under the direction of Dr. Swanson at Bowling Green State University. Mr. Sawzin served as principal investigator on the project. The origins of the project and its financial support came from Johns-Manville Corp. Both Mr. Cullen and Mr. Sisson had continued involvement in the conceptualization and conduct of the research.

complexity and responsibility of work tasks assigned to the better-trained employee.

The literature abounds with CE models clouded in statistical models and mathematical formulas. Usually these models can be used only by the companies developing them. This is not to underestimate the complexity and importance in recording and accounting for training dollars. But, this complexity of formulas keeps the reader from fully understanding and utilizing the usefulness of the CE model. The reader stumbles through trying to first understand the statistics and mathematical language. Basically, this cost-effectiveness model reduced down to a comparison and analysis of the training investment to the training return.

To accurately estimate the resources that should be allocated to industrial training, the expected gains (returns) of that training must be known. One source of controversy over training is the inadequate knowledge of its economic returns. At face value, training costs appear to be an economic burden which reduces company profits. With some form of training being mandatory to maintain production, an economic cost-effectiveness model is needed in order to determine the relative economic returns of varying training strategies.

The calculating of training costs and returns is complex. There is no single formula. There are arguments for and against any formula or model. It appears that the one that works best for a given situation is the one to use. The model used in the Industrial Training Research Project[6] combined the economic reasoning of three cost-effectiveness models that have been utilized in the training profession.[4,5,7]

DEFINITION OF TERMS

Analysis Time: Total people hours to produce analysis of the job.

Design Time: Total people hours to design the training program.

Material Cost: All material costs incurred from onset through completion of one training program. These costs include supplies to facilitate training-program development (secretarial, graphics work, travel, duplicating, display boards, training aids, etc.).

Reproduction Costs: All costs incurred in duplicating additional copies of the completed training program for training purposes.

Trainee Time: Total people hours and resulting salary costs incurred for trainee to reach job competency.

Instructional Hardware: Shelf items that are purchased to facilitate the training program (e.g., pro-

duction machine to be used just for training; filmstrip projector, tape recorder).

Instructional Software: Shelf items of instructional content that are purchased to facilitate the training program (e.g., manufacturer's operating manual; filmstrip/transparencies).

Investment: Money spent now, usually on a one-time, lump-sum basis, for a return that will keep being realized in future years without further expenditure, such as for equipment purchase.

Training costs can be split into three groups: fixed, variable and total.[7] The ratio comparisons of these costs then determine the economic benefits of a training program. This method provides a detailed analysis of training costs. A broader look at training economics involves a process of calculating an investment cost for training and comparing it to certain returns from that investment.[4] The cost-effectiveness model used for the Industrial Training Research Project included the use of both the above plans. Also, information unique to Johns-Manville Products Corp. cost-effectiveness terms and practices were considered.

For this model the costs for training are classified as either fixed or variable. Fixed costs are costs that do not vary even though numbers of trainees, training time or training program development vary. Variable costs are costs that change as the number of trainees, training time and training program development vary.[1] Example: If regular production equipment (which is a fixed cost for production) is used for training, the losses in production are considered a variable cost.

STRUCTURED TRAINING PROGRAM TRAINING COSTS

The following are the training-cost categories for the structured training program as characterized in this study:

1. Training Development
   A. Analysis time
   B. Design time
   C. Material costs
2. Training Materials (expendable)
   A. Cost of reproducing copies of developed training program
3. Training Materials (nonexpendable)
   A. Instructional hardware
   B. Instructional software
4. Training Time
   A. Trainee time
   B. Trainer time
5. Production Losses Resulting from Training

A. Production rate losses
B. Material losses

The following are the training-cost categories for the unstructured training program as characterized in this study:

1. Training Time
   A. Trainee time
2. Production Losses Resulting from Training
   A. Production rate losses
   B. Material losses

TRAINING RETURNS

The training return of the training program (either structured or unstructured) is a competent production worker. To evaluate a competent production worker, one must detail the competencies and evaluate them. The combined component evaluations determine the total evaluation. The following outline is utilized to summarize the procedures for assessing the returns of training. The third-order headings contain information unique to the specific job of a plastic-extruder machine operator.

1. Production Task Performance
   A. Trainee has reached job competency via training (structured or unstructured training program)
      1. Trainee can successfully perform job startup
      2. Trainee can maintain set standard of plastic tubing
      3. Trainee can successfully perform in production malfunction performance tests
      4. Trainee can successfully perform job shutdown
   B. Trainee is satisfied with his or her training and the job
2. Collect Data on Task Performance Returns
   A. Measurements of task performance
      1. Time (to reach competency, production curtailed, startup)
      2. Production rate
      3. Performance test
      4. Product quality
      5. Raw material usage
   B. Measurement of trainee attitudes toward his or her training and the job
3. Monetary Value of Returns
   A. Convert trainee performance data to a monetary value
   B. Returns of structured training program and unstructured training program are totaled

DATA COLLECTION PROCEDURES (EXTRUDER OPERATOR)

1. *Time-job time* (time clock)
2. *Production Rate:* Number of three-foot lengths of quality pipe per hour of production (count the number of lengths per hour, clock time for each bundle).
3. *Trouble-Shooting:* Reaction to injection of machine malfunctions via performance test (down-time, loss of tubing, time of malfunction injection *vs.* time to respond to malfunction, time to correct malfunction).
4. *Training-Program Costs:* List total costs to develop structured and unstructured training materials and program.
5. *Production Down:* Time production is completely halted or interrupted.
6. *Material Efficiency:* Weight of raw material supplied to the machine versus weight of scrap and amount of quality product produced (weight raw material supplied, scrap, and hour bundles of quality tubing).
7. *Training Time:* Time consumed to train a trainee to reach job competency.

DATA ANALYSIS AND EVALUATION

The following comparisons will be used to evaluate the effectiveness of the two training methods:

1. Training time required of the unstructured training program as compared to training time required of the structured training program to produce a competent production worker.
2. A comparison of levels of production worker competency by time intervals between the two industrial training methods.
3. The total development costs and returns of the structured training program as compared to the costs and returns of the unstructured training program.
4. The production losses of the structured training program versus the unstructured training program.
5. The reactions of the structured training program operators to production problems (malfunction performance test) versus the unstructured training program operators.
6. The attitudes of the trainees in the structured program toward their training, trainer and job versus those in the unstructured program.

The following is the overview program procedure and model for evaluating the cost effectiveness of industrial training programs. The specifics of the costs, returns and analyses have been discussed previously. The graphic representation of the model is presented in Figure 1. For both the structured and the unstructured training programs, each variable under training costs and training returns should be quantified. For those that are expressed in nonmonetary indexes (e.g., time), their monetary equivalency should be calculated whenever possible. These figures can then be used for the analysis and evaluation stage.[2]

The cost-effectiveness comparison between the structured and unstructured training programs is determined by analyzing the training variables, converting them to monetary equivalents, and then conducting a cost comparison. Obviously, individual variables such as "time taken to reach competency" can also be compared and reported as separate indexes of effectiveness. This cost-effectiveness model developed and reported here has been utilized in several practical situations and has been proven workable.

REFERENCES

1. Cullen, J. G. and Sisson, G., Personal communication, April 19, 1974.
2. Cullen, J. G., Sawzin, S. A., Sisson, C. R., and Swanson, R. A., Training, what's it worth? *Training and Development Journal*, August, 1976.
3. Cullen, J. G., Personal communication, June 7, 1977.
4. Furst, H., The economics of training and development, *Training and Development Journal*, 1970, 24, 10, pp. 30–33.
5. Ghazalag, I. A., *The role of vocational education in improving skills and earning capacity in the State of Ohio: A cost-benefit study.* Athens, Ohio: State of Ohio Department of Education, Division of Vocational Education, 1972.
6. Swanson, R. A. and Sawzin, S. A., *Industrial Training Research Project.* Bowling Green State University, 1975.
7. Wheeler, E. A., Economic considerations for industrial training, *Training and Development Journal*, 1969, 23, 1, 14–18.

FIGURE 1
Industrial Training Cost-Effectiveness Model

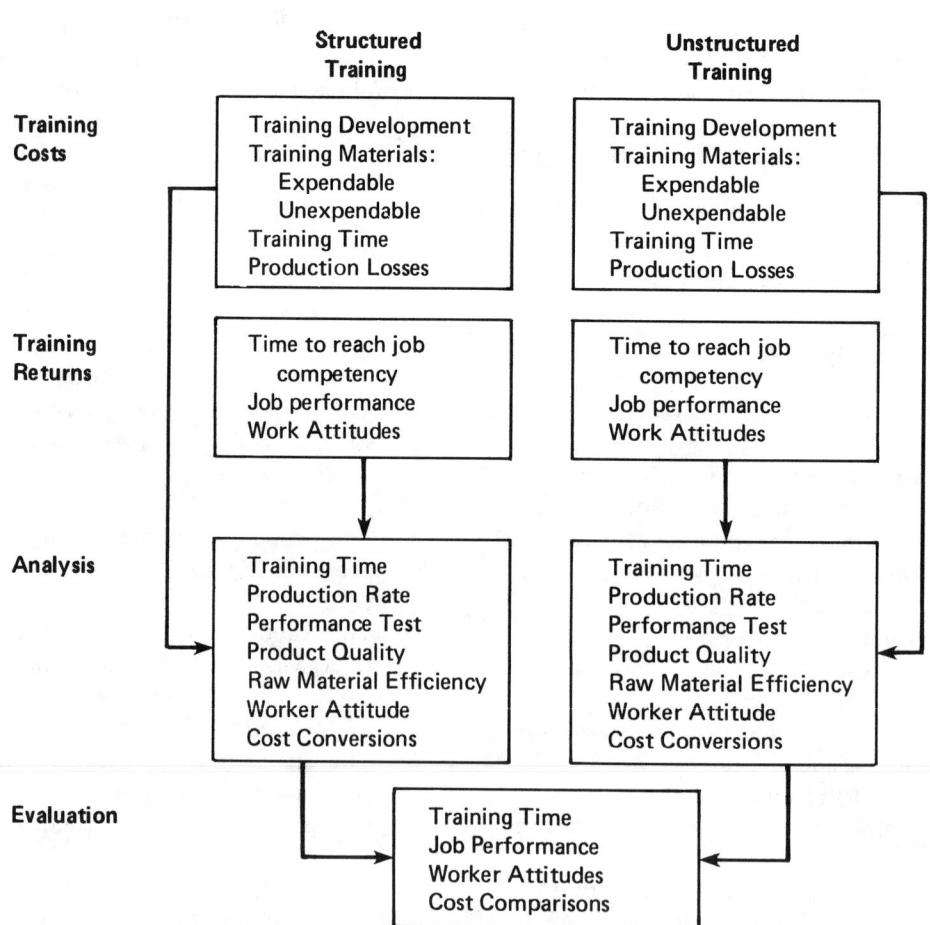

Evaluating Training Daily

by Gloria Stevenson

The end-of-course evaluations that many of us get from trainees can be immensely helpful in improving a training program—next time around. To improve an *ongoing* session, however, we need trainee feedback that will help us spot and resolve problems as they arise.

To gather this kind of feedback, the training office in the U.S. Department of Labor's Employment Standard Administration utilizes daily evaluation meetings, 20- to 30-minute end-of-day meetings attended by course trainers and representative trainees. Besides providing daily feedback on issues affecting course effectiveness, this mechanism encourages trainees to share responsibility for their own learning.

ESA first used the evaluation meeting approach midway through a 1974 course when a trainer invited trainees to the regular after-hours meetings that trainers were holding to go over each day's events. Trainee input proved so useful that the approach is now used in virtually all ESA skill-development courses. Such courses typically last between one and two weeks, emphasize specific skills for new or experienced employees, and rely heavily on small group exercises in which four to six trainees jointly complete tasks that simulate job behaviors. Courses are generally conducted by a team of two trainers and class size ranges from 16 to 24 persons.

Trainees learn about the evaluation meetings at the outset of the training session when trainers describe how the course will function. The trainers announce that they will meet immediately following close of business each day to assess the day's effectiveness and to try to solve any problems that are hindering learning. They explain that the meetings generally last about half an hour and they invite each small group to send one representative each day on a rotating basis. Trainees are then given a moment to decide whether they want to participate—and they nearly always do—and to select a representative for the first meeting.

The trainers then mention specific areas in which they welcome feedback. These include:

- *Pace.* Are we moving too fast or too slowly? Are any members of your group having trouble keeping up? Etc.

- *Problems with materials.* Is the information too easy or too difficult? Are you having any problems with the way materials are organized? Are instructions clear?
- *Problems with the small groups.* Are some trainees failing to participate in group work? Is one person dominating? Are any personality conflicts interfering with the group's functioning?
- *Problems with the trainers.* Are we doing anything distracting or irritating? Are we answering your questions satisfactorily? Are our explanations clear?
- *Housekeeping.* Is the room too hot or too cold? Should we break for lunch earlier or later? Are nonsmokers being irritated by smoke?

Some trainers suggest that trainees keep a list of these items handy and jot down problem issues as they arise during the day. The list reminds trainees to stay aware of specific areas that have an impact on learning.

IDENTIFY PROBLEMS AND SOLUTIONS

About 10 minutes before the close of the first day's session, trainers ask the members of each small group to tell their representative about any issues, problems, or questions they would like to have discussed at the meeting. This insures that the representatives have a chance to collect data from all members of the small group.

The meeting is held immediately after close of business, generally right in the training room. We have tried adjourning to nearby watering holes but find that while the meetings are often more enjoyable, they tend to take longer and be less productive.

One of the trainers opens the meeting by saying something like: "Our overall purpose here is to answer the following question: If we were going to do today over again—and in a sense, we are—what should we do differently?"

As problems are identified, trainers and trainees try to find solutions that will enhance learning. This often requires the trainers to probe for specificity and to see whether the problem is a concern to only one individual or small group or to trainees as a whole. As solutions are developed, both trainers and trainees take appropriate responsibility for making needed changes.

Suppose, for example, that a trainee says the course is moving too quickly. If this perception is shared by the entire class and if skills are consequently not being learned, the best solution might be for trainers to slow the pace. If, on the other hand, only one group is having trouble keeping up, trainers should probe for reasons. Perhaps one person in the group is slowing everyone down by arguing irrelevant points. In this case, an effective solution might be for the trainee from that group to take responsibility for informing other group members of the need to keep discussions on track and to refrain from irrelevant comments.

As the first item of business the next day, trainees who attended the meeting take five or so minutes to report back to their small groups the gist of discussions and/or decisions made at the first meeting. These reports are given simultaneously in each small group.

This form of reporting serves several purposes: It lets the whole group know what happened in the meeting. It enables each small-group representative to respond to specific concerns raised by his or her group. It lets other trainees know what they can expect if they attend an evaluation meeting. And it indicates to the trainees that this is a serious meeting, one that addresses real issues and is worth taking time for.

EVALUATION MEETINGS

After trainee representatives finish reporting to their small groups, the trainers reiterate to the whole class any commitments they made at the meeting. They might, for example, say they will take more time for each exercise, provide after-hours assistance in a learning area where many trainees are experiencing difficulty, or break for lunch earlier. This insures that both trainees and trainers have the same understanding of trainer commitments arising from the meeting. The small groups then select representatives for the second day's meeting, which is conducted the same way.

The evaluation meetings held on the first and second day of the session are generally the most difficult to conduct—and the most crucial. Trainees may hold back real concerns because they do not yet know what to expect or how genuine they can be in their comments. If this happens, trainers may need to probe for trainee input in specific areas. They might, for example, bring up problems they observed during the day or ask specific questions about items like pace, group interactions, and trainee's reactions to trainers' behavior.

Evaluation meetings tend to yield the most valuable information during the first three to four days

of a course, when any initial "bugs" are being worked out. On days that are problem free, the meetings may take only 10 minutes or so. Meetings are held even if the trainers think the course is going smoothly, since trainees may have different perceptions.

When evaluation meetings function effectively, both trainers and trainees:

- Know more about how the course is going than they would without the meeting dialog.
- Air issues, such as a trainee's refusal to participate in small group work or adverse trainee reactions to a trainer's behavior, that might otherwise go unvented and thus interfere with learning.
- Identify and solve learning problems as they arise.
- Assume specific responsibilities for ongoing course management.

Experience indicates, however, that effective evaluation meetings require several conditions. First and most important, trainers must take them seriously. They must want and value observations from trainees and encourage them by providing class time for trainees to share their concerns with their representatives and to hear the representatives' meeting reports.

Trainers must also be open to hearing negative comments about the course or about their own training styles and be willing to solve any problems in these areas. Follow-through on any commitments made at the meetings is also essential. If these elements are lacking, trainees will know that the meetings are merely symbolic and will not bring up relevant issues.

On the other hand, trainers must also be careful not to give up decision-making authority in their areas of expertise—methods and strategies that enhance learning and group process. However, evaluation meetings are *not* a forum for joint decision-making in all areas. Trainers can seriously harm course effectiveness by agreeing to trainee suggestions that violate established learning principles.

Trainers should also be clear on what aspects of the course are "givens" not subject to change during the session. Examples might be starting and stopping times, basic course design or location of the session. In some situations, of course, these items may be open to alteration.

In six years of conducting evaluation meetings, ESA trainers have found that most trainees welcome the opportunity to attend the meetings and to express their concerns about the course. Trainees attending sessions in their home cities are the major exception; transportation and babysitting arrangements or other logistics problems sometimes make it difficult for these trainees to attend meetings after close of business. Participants with such problems may work around them by planning to attend a meeting several days ahead.

In contrast, we have seen a fair amount of resistance on the part of *trainers* to whom the evaluation meeting idea is new. A frequent reaction is "Trainees can't tell me anything I won't have already observed. I'm the expert at spotting learning problems." If they can be persuaded to give evaluation meetings an honest try, then even skeptics may tend to admit that trainee reactions do supplement their own observations.

Several private companies holding training contracts with the Department of Labor have used the evaluation meeting approach in ESA programs, and some trainers from these companies now utilize this mechanism in other settings. One company, Applied Science Associates of Valencia, PA, has used the meetings in training conducted in Asian countries. An ASA trainer reports, "In some countries, the norm is that trainees don't express emotion or disagree with the trainer in class. If you set rules, people will always agree. It's only later in the meetings that people will say, often apologetically, that they need something different."

Through usage, some trainers have developed slight variations on the basic format described. For example, one person conducts evaluation meetings during the last half hour of regularly scheduled class time. His rationale is that the meeting is important enough to warrant the time expenditure.

The daily evaluation meeting thus appears to be a flexible course assessment tool that can be adapted to a wide variety of settings. Moreover, it requires little preparation time, is easily understood by both trainers and trainees, and can provide an ongoing means of evaluating course effectiveness while there's still time to make needed improvements.

Assessing Intervention Outcomes
by Robert R. Carkhuff

Typically, interveners simply assess one level of outcome without any notion of the relationship with other outcomes or any ultimate outcome. For example, most teachers and trainers are only interested in whether their learners or trainees acquire the skills involved. They have no idea of how skill acquisition relates to applications and transfers in real-life.

The key ingredient is intentionality. What level of outcome did they wish to affect? Whatever the level or levels they intended to assess should be the level or levels that they do assess.

Clearly, a systematic intervention approach should yield systematic outcome assessments. Each stage of the intervention relates to the other stages of the intervention. These stages are cycled from intervention development through delivery and then back again from delivery to intervention outcomes.

The systematic human intervention system begins with the development of productivity goals. It should, therefore, upon recycling conclude with the achievement of these productivity goals. In addition, each stage of development should be related to the next stage. All stages of intervention should be related to the achievement of our ultimate productivity goals.

The basic principle of human intervention evaluation is that you assess only those results your intervention was designed to affect. Perhaps the dumbest misinterpretation of research is the notion that the outcome measures must be independent of the intervention. To be sure, they must be independently measured. However, the outcomes must flow systematically from the intervention design or they are not outcomes at all—just simply random occurrences!

INTERVENTION OUTCOMES

In a systematic human intervention system, then, the stages of intervention development lead to the intervention delivery: 1) productivity goals lead to contextual tasks; 2) contextual tasks lead to skill objectives; 3) skill objectives lead to skills content; 4) skills content leads to the delivery plan; 5) the delivery plan leads to the delivery; 6) the delivery lead to the reception; and 7) the reception leads to the assessment of the various levels of process and outcome (Carkhuff and Friel, 1982).

The levels of outcome assessments involve a recycling through the stages of intervention and delivery (See Figure 1): 1) a process or interaction

FIGURE 1
The Levels of Effective Human Outcomes

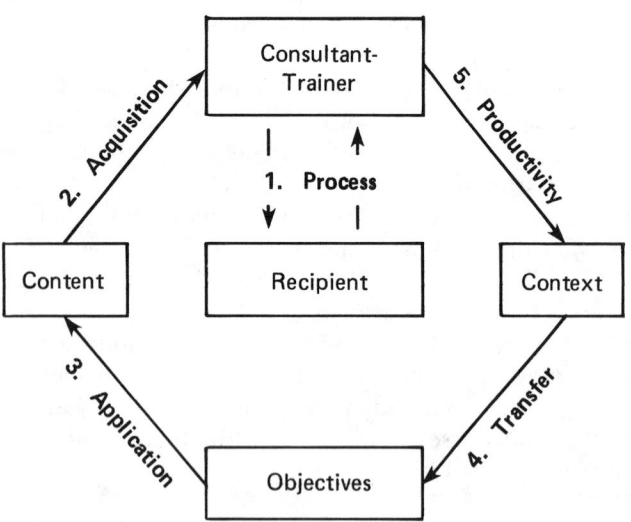

assessment determines how well the intervener facilitated the recipient's reception of the intervention; 2) an acquisition assessment determines whether or not the recipients acquired the skills content involved; 3) an application assessment determines whether or not the recipients applied the skill objectives; 4) a transfer assessment determines whether or not the recipients transferred their skills to contextual tasks; 5) a productivity assessment determines whether or not the task performance improved the recipients' productivity (Carkhuff, 1982; Carkhuff and Friel, 1982).

Clearly, in a systematic intervention system, each level of process or outcome relates to every subsequent level of outcome. However, while each level of process or outcome is necessary, it is not sufficient for the achievement of the next level. The results at every level must be programmatically developed.

Acquisition Outcomes

Where the process assessments answer the question of recipient movement, the acquisition outcomes answer the question, movement to what (See Figure 1)? The acquisition level of outcome revolves around the acquisition question: Did the recipients acquire the intervention skills content? In other words, do the recipients now have all of the tools which they need to perform the skill?

Thus, the acquisition outcome issues emphasize whether the recipients have all the skill steps and supportive knowledge which they need to perform the skills. Do the recipients know and can they do everything that they need to in order to perform the skill?

Again, a cumulative scale may be useful for assessing recipient acquisition (See Figure 2). As can be

seen, the levels of the scale reflect the steps and knowledge needed to perform the skill.

At the lowest level, level 1, we may ask and answer the factual question: did the recipients know what things are involved in the performance of the skills? Facts are names or labels—usually nouns—that identify what things are. For example, our assessment of acquisition outcomes involves the following facts:

- Facts
- Concepts
- Principles
- Skill Objectives
- Skill Steps

They help us to identify the critical things involved. We must know about these things in order to perform the skill.

At the next level, level 2, we may ask the conceptual question: did the recipients know what the things do in the performance of the skills? Concepts are the meanings—usually verbs, adverbs or adjectives—that we attach to things which tell us about those things and what they do. For example, our very process of defining levels of skill acquisition is a process of identifying concepts:

- Facts *label what things are*
- Concepts *identify what things do and what they mean*
- Principles *describe why and how things do what they do and why they are important*
- Skill objectives *define what we need to be able to do in order to perform the skills*
- Skill steps *detail how to perform the skill objective*

Concepts, then, help us to identify the critical things that can be done that we must know about in order to perform the skill.

At level 3, which we may consider a minimally effective level of knowledge, we may ask the principle question: did the recipients know why the things do what they do? Principles state relationships with and between facts and concepts. They tell us why things do what they do and why they are important. They also tell us when and where to use the skills. It is helpful to state principles in a hypothetical format which allows them to be tested: "If (*skill steps*), then (*skill*) so that (*benefit*)." For example, the following is a statement of principle for acquisition assessment skills:

> If we learn to define the levels of skill content, then we will be able to assess the recipients' levels of acquisition, so that we can assess the outcomes of systematic human intervention designs.

FIGURE 2
Levels of Acquisition of Skill Content

Levels of Acquisition		
5	*Skill Steps*	Recipient is able to *do* the steps of the skill
4	*Skill Objective*	Recipient *knows* the operations of the skill
3	*Principle*	Recipient *knows* how the things work
2	*Concepts*	Recipient *knows* what the things do
1	*Facts*	Recipient *knows* what the things are

Principles, then, help us to identify the critical ways that things are done. We must know about these processes in order to perform the skill.

At an operational level, level 4, we may ask the skill objective question: did the recipients define the operations needed to perform the skill? Skill objectives define what we need to be able to do to perform the skill. Skills define the behaviors in terms of *do* steps that are observable, measurable and repeatable. Basically, the definition of the skills objectives involves answering the question: who is doing what to whom and at what level? For example, the following is a statement of training skills objectives for acquisition assessment skills:

> The trainers will learn to discriminate with 100% accuracy the levels of intervention content acquired by the recipients following the implementation of all systematic human intervention designs.

Skill objectives, then, help us to define the operations that enable us to perform the skill.

Finally, at a technological level, level 5, we may ask the skill step question: did the recipients *do* the skill steps needed to perform the skill? Skill steps involve the steps we take to perform the skill objective. The steps emphasize the things we must *do* to perform the skill objective. They also emphasize the things we must *think* about before, during and after each *do* steps. For example, the training skill steps for acquisition assessment skills might be as follows:

1. Developing the acquisition assessment knowledge base:
   a. Facts
   b. Concepts
   c. Principles
2. Developing the acquisition assessment skills programs:
   a. Skill Objectives
   b. Skill Steps

3. Implementing the skills programs:
   a. Repeating the skill steps
   b. Applying the skill steps
   c. Transforming the skill steps

Skill steps, then, help us to achieve our skill objectives.

In training in interpersonal skills, for example, the skills content might involve responding. The content of responding skills might break down as follows:

Acquisition Outcomes (Illustration)	
Skill Steps:	1. Attending physically 2. Observing 3. Listening 4. Responding to content 5. Responding to feeling 6. Responding to meaning
Skill Objective:	Responding Skills
Principle:	*If* the trainees can attend and respond to another person, *then* the others *will* attempt to reciprocate interpersonally, *so that* there will be the basis of trust and understanding for constructive human relationships.
Concepts:	Attending, observing, listening, responding, content, feeling, meaning.
Facts:	Two or more humans in the presence of each other.

Similarly, the content of learning skills might break down in the same manner. For example, understanding skills might involve comparing and contrasting, classifying and categorizing, generalizing and operationalizing skills steps and their supportive knowledge. With working skills, the production skills might involve manipulating components, functions and process as well as their supportive knowledge.

In order to test the acquisition outcome, then, we need only to do the following: 1) determine whether the recipients can do the skills; 2) determine whether the recipients have all the skill steps they need to do the skills; and 3) determine whether the trainees have all the supportive knowledge they need to do the skill steps. The acquisition outcome issues are similar to the post-test of a teaching or training program. They reduce simply to whether or not the recipients can perform the skill.

Application Outcomes

The application outcomes give us an index of the recipients' abilities to apply the skills (See Figure 1).

The recipients have acquired the skills content. We must now determine whether they can apply the skills to simulated intervention experiences.

Recall that the purpose of the intervention is to enable the recipients to perform tasks required by the context in which they function. Assumedly, these tasks will relate directly to the productivity goals. The purpose in assessing application outcomes is to provide the recipients with an opportunity to perform the skills or achieve the skill objectives in experiences that most closely approximate the experiences in the real-life context.

Again, a cumulative scale may be useful for assessing recipient application in contextual simulations (See Figure 3). As can be seen, the levels of the scale reflect the systems of internal applications of the skill objectives. By internal applications, we mean those applications that are internal to the intervention experience, as for example, experiences in training that simulate real-life experiences.

At the lowest level, level 1, then, we may ask the systems' component question; did the recipients apply the skills in successive approximations of relevant systems' components? For example, with the employee communication tasks, we may involve the recipients with the components of the communications process, the unit personnel, in successive approximations of the full group of workers who are involved in the real-life context. Thus, we may move from interacting with individuals to small groups to a full group representing the personnel of the working unit. In other words, in our internal simulations, we are making the skill applications with successive approximations of the real-life contextual components.

At the next level, level 2, we may ask the systems' function question: did the recipients apply the skills in successive approximations of relevant systems' functions? For example, with employee communication tasks, we may involve the recipients in applying their skills to successive approximations of the functions in interaction with the components of the real-life context. Thus, with our individual, small group and full group components we may focus successively upon random tasks, assigned tasks and approximations of the real-life contextual tasks. In other words, in our internal simulations, we are making skill applications with successive approximations of the real-life contextual components and functions.

At level 3, our minimally effective level of application, we may ask the processes' question: did the recipients apply the skills in successive approximation of relevant systems' processes? For example, with employee communication tasks, we may involve the recipients in applying their skills to successive approximations of the processes in interaction with the components and functions of the real-life context. Thus,

FIGURE 3
Levels of Application of Skill Objectives

Levels of Application			
Internal Simulation of Systems' Factors	5	Initiation	Recipients apply skills initiatively to all relevant systems' factors
	4	Integration	Recipients apply skills integratively to all relevant systems' factors
	3	Processes	Recipients apply skills to successive approximations of relevant systems' processes, functions and components
	2	Functions	Recipients apply skills to successive approximations of relevant systems' functions and components
	1	Components	Recipients apply skills to successive approximations of relevant systems' components

with our individual, small and full group components and our random, assigned and real-life tasks, we may focus successively upon the communication skills involved in exploring, understanding and acting upon the real-life contextual tasks. Again, our internal simulations involve making skill applications with successive approximations of the real-life contextual components, functions and processes.

At the integrative level, level 4, we ask the integrative question: did the recipients apply the skills integratively to all relevant systems' factors? This level involves the repetition of exercises that involve the skills applications. Thus, for example, we can see the recipients applying their communication skills over and over to simulations of the tasks involving real-life contextual components, functions and processes.

Finally, at the initiative level, level 5, we may ask the initiative question: did the recipients apply the skills initiatively to all relevant systems' factors? This level involves utilizing a model for applying skills to initiate their use. Thus, we can see the recipients applying their communication or any other skills in contexts beyond the real-life contexts for which they are preparing. For example, the recipients may initiate using their communications skills with other units on the assembly line.

We can perhaps see the levels of application best in an example of a design for simulated applications of the communication skills (See Figure 4). As can be seen, levels of components, functions and processes of the simulated applications are presented. Thus, we see that the components involving personnel range from individual through small group to full group. The functions range from random through assigned to real tasks. The processes range from the communications affecting exploring, understanding and acting.

As can also be seen in Figure 4, the components, functions and processes are related programmatically in the design. Thus, the components interact with the functions in a programmatic way, i.e., the tasks are crossed with the personnel populations. Also, the processes interact with the components and functions. That is, the communication processes lead toward recipient action behavior with the different populations and tasks. In so doing designing these levels of applications, we have accounted for the components, functions and processes of the contextual simulation.

The level of integration, in turn, involves applying the skills integratively to all relevant systems' factors. We may find the level of integration in the culminating stage of the programmatic interactions (IIIC.3). This is the stage where the recipients engage in action behavior to apply their skills to real tasks in full groups approximating the real-life context. For the assembly line group, these integrative applications may be replicated in exercises to insure the preparation for transfer to the real-life context.

Finally, the level of initiation involves applying the skills initiatively to all relevant systems' factors. This involves applying the design model to initiate

new skill applications. Initiating new skill applications involves the components, functions and processes of different contexts. For example, for the assembly unit, it might involve a different means of communicating with other units on the assembly line about those tasks that are interdependent with the assembly unit's tasks.

Similarly, with the learning and working illustrations, the skills application might involve a series of approximations of integrating and initiating the components, functions and processes of the real-life contexts. Thus, the secretaries might practice movement toward learning to utilize the different technologies in approximations of their secretarial pool. In turn, the training and development section member might practice simulated training experiences that are more and more like those in the real-life context in which they will function.

Another way of looking at the application outcomes is as the exercises that are preparatory to real-life functioning. After the recipients have acquired the skills content, they must be provided with a series of application exercises that insure the probability of their successful transfer to the real-life context.

Transfer Outcomes

The essential difference between the applications and the transfers of the skills, involves the internal simulation versus the external real-life experiences. In training in communication skills, for example, the exact same components (personnel), functions (tasks) and processes (communication) may be replicated in the training context as appear in the real-life context. However, these factors interact in a continuous and naturalistic manner in the real-life context.

The assessment of transfer outcomes, then, involves transferring skills to the tasks required by the real-life context. You may recall that our needs assessments discriminated certain tasks required by the context within which the recipients function. Assessing transfer outcomes involves assessing the degree to which the recipients function effectively in those contexts.

Again, a cumulative scale may be useful for assessing recipient transfer to the real-life context (See Figure 5). As can be seen, the levels of the scale reflect the systems of external transfers of the contextual tasks. By external transfers, we mean those applications that are external to the intervention experience, i.e., they are the effect of the intervention experience.

At the lowest level, level 1, then, we may again ask the systems' component question, only now in a context external to the intervention experience: did the recipients transfer the skills to real-life contextual components? For example, with the employee com-

FIGURE 4
Example of Design for Levels of Application of Skill Objectives

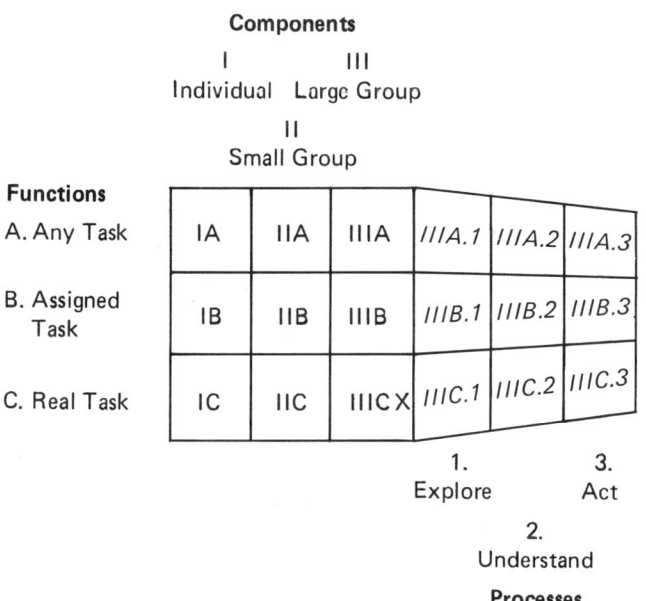

FIGURE 5
Levels of Transfer to Contextual Tasks

Levels of Transfer			
External Transfer to Contextual Tasks	5	*Initiation*	Recipients use skills initiatively with all factors of contextual tasks
	4	*Integration*	Recipients use skills integratively with all factors of contextual tasks
	3	*Processes*	Recipients use skills effectively with processes, functions and components of contextual tasks
	2	*Functions*	Recipients use skills effectively with functions and components of contextual tasks
	1	*Components*	Recipients use skills effectively with components of contextual tasks

munications tasks, the issue is whether the recipients use their interpersonal skills fully with all of the personnel in their units. In other words, the acid test of the intervention experience is whether the recipients transfer their skills to all contextual components.

At the next level, level 2, we may ask the external systems' component question: did the recipients transfer the skills to real-life contextual functions? For example, in improving employee communications, we want to know whether the recipients applied their interpersonal skills to the real-life unit tasks. In other words, did the recipients discharge the functions of the contextual components?

At level 3, our minimally effective level, we may ask the processes' question: did the recipients transfer the skills to real-life contextual processes? For example, in improving employee communications, we want to know whether the recipients applied their interpersonal skills to the real-life interpersonal communications process. In other words, did the recipients apply the processes that enabled the components to discharge their functions?

At level 4, we again ask the integrative question: did the recipients transfer the skills integratively to all relevant systems' factors? For example, in improving employee communications, we want to know whether the recipients applied their interpersonal skills integratively to all of the personnel, tasks and communication processes of the unit. In other words, did

the recipients integrate their skills with all the real-life contextual components, functions and processes.

Finally, at the initiative level, level 5, we may ask the initiative question: did the recipients transfer the skills initiatively to all relevant systems' factors? For example, in improving employee communications, we want to know whether the recipients applied their interpersonal skills initiatively with all of the unit personnel, tasks and communications. In other words, did the recipients initiate using their skills to different real-life contextual components, functions and processes?

Clearly, the integrative use of the skills with all components, functions and processes in real-life contextual tasks is the goal of the intervention. Thus, for example, assembly line workers communicate, secretaries learn and training and development personnel work integratively in their real-life contexts. The intervention has made a difference in their functioning and they have learned to make a difference in their real-life contexts.

When the recipients begin to use their skills initiatively, then they are adding bonuses to the desired effects of the intervention. Thus, for example, assembly line workers may engage in different communication processes with different personnel for the purpose of discharging different tasks. Similarly, secretaries may vary their learning with different machines for different tasks. Further, learning and development personnel may produce different kinds of training products for different tasks. When we vary one or more of our components, functions and processes, we may say that we are transferring our transfer skills.

Productivity Outcomes

The reason for the intervention is the productivity outcome. Recall, that we began by establishing productivity goals. Now, with the improvement in contextual functioning, we return to determine whether we achieved the goals.

It is important to recall that our productivity goals related to unit or agency productivity. Thus we introduced the intervention system in order to improve the performance of the recipients in the context in which they function. This contextual performance improvement should be reflected in improved unit or agency productivity.

The assessment of productivity outcomes, then, involves making determinations concerning the levels of productivity (Carkhuff, 1981). Again, it may be helpful to employ a scale in assessing these levels of productivity (See Figure 6). As can be seen, the levels of the scale reflect the levels of achievement in the relationship between resource input and results out-

FIGURE 6
Levels of Productivity

Levels of Productivity		
5	Incremental (+ +)	Agency results outputs are incremental (+) while resource inputs are decremental (+)
4	Effectiveness (0 +)	Agency maintains current levels of results outputs (0) while decreasing resource inputs (+) or Agency increases levels of results outputs (+) while holding resource inputs constant (0)
3	Efficiency (00)	Agency maintains a balanced relationship between current levels of results outputs (0) and resource inputs (0)
2	Maintenance (0 –)	Agency maintains current levels of results outputs (0) while increasing resource inputs (–) or Agency results outputs are decremental (–) while resource inputs are maintained at current levels (0)
1	Decremental (– –)	Agency results outputs are decremental (–) while resource inputs are incremental (–)

puts. The levels move from negative or decremental results outputs (–) and incremental resource inputs (–) to positive or incremental results outputs (+) and decremental resource inputs (+).

At level 1, we may diagnose a level of decremental productivity if the unit or agency performs in the following manner: its results outputs are decremental while its resource inputs are incremental. Both of these conditions indicate negative (–) productivity. Clearly, the continuation of this condition generates measurably different levels of decremental productivity culminating in a stage where the resource inputs are infinite and the results outputs are absent.

At level 2, we may diagnose a level of maintenance productivity if the unit or agency meets the following conditions: it maintains the current levels of results outputs while increasing the resource inputs. The current results outputs are a neutral (0) state of productivity while the incremental resource inputs are

a negative (–) state. This is a common condition in established agencies of business and industry and is reflected in declining profits. A variation of this theme is for results outputs to be decremental (–) while resource inputs are constant (0). Although conceived of as maintenance, it is not indeed maintenance but rather the first stage of decremental productivity.

At level 3, what we may consider as minimally effective levels, we may diagnose unit or agency efficiency if it meets the following conditions: the agency maintains a balanced relationship between current levels of results outputs and resource inputs. We may consider this level of efficiency a neutral state of productivity (0). It is perhaps the most common interpretation or misinterpretation of productivity in business and industry. It seeks only a one-to-one correspondence of resources to results. In other words, most businesses seek only to use their resources most efficiently in producing results outputs.

At level 4, the agency may be diagnosed as effective after meeting one of two conditions: either it maintains current levels of results outputs (0) while decreasing resource inputs (+); or it increases levels of results outputs (+) while holding resource inputs constant (0). For the elite few industry leaders, the effectiveness goals is the most desired goal: either to produce more or to invest less. Developmentally, this level of productivity leads directly to incremental productivity, i.e., producing more while investing less.

Level 5 or incremental productivity, then, may be diagnosed when the agency meets the following conditions: it increases results outputs (+) while decreasing resource inputs (+). Both of these conditions are positive states of productivity. Clearly, meeting these conditions generates measurably different levels of incremental productivity.

Incremental productivity is the only real productivity (Carkhuff, 1981). Other existing definitions of productivity are at best definitions of effectiveness. Incremental productivity concludes in intervention processes that generate infinite resource outputs while eliminating resource inputs. Incremental productivity makes something out of nothing. Indeed, it culminates like the universe in making everything out of nothing.

SUMMARY AND OVERVIEW

We made our interventions in order to achieve our productivity goals. Thus, we established our productivity goals; analyzed our contextual task needs; developed our intervention objectives; developed our intervention content; developed our delivery plan; made our delivery; and insured the reception of the delivery.

Now, in reverse order, we have assessed our various levels of process and outcome: the interactional process; the intervention acquisition outcome; the intervention application outcome; the intervention transfer outcome; and finally, the productivity outcome. At each level, the basic questions in relation to the intervention are the following; did the recipients receive, acquire, apply and transfer the intervention? At the productivity level, the question is: did it make a difference?

It may be helpful to use a scale to assess the levels of outcome (See Figure 7). Again, the scale is cumulative with each level incorporating the previous level. This means that the intervention experience cannot be rated at a level higher than it has achieved cumulatively. For example, it cannot be rated at acquisition (level 2) if it has not satisfactorily achieved process movement (level 1).

Thus, at level 1, the recipients demonstrate effective process movement toward receiving the intervention experience. At level 2, the recipients acquire the intervention content. At level 3, the recipients apply the intervention content to simulated tasks. At level 4, the recipients transfer the intervention content to real-life tasks. Finally, at level 5, the recipients demonstrate different levels of productivity based upon their improved task performance.

Another way of viewing the relationship of intervention to productivity outcomes may be seen in Figure 8. As can be seen, there are at least three levels of intervention. First, based upon the comprehensive intervention system design, the training intervention transforms naive trainees into skilled interveners. Second, the skilled interveners intervene to transform unskilled performers into skilled performers. Finally, the skilled performers functioning at their individual performance stations employ their newfound skills to process raw materials into finished products.

FIGURE 7
Levels of Outcome

Levels of Outcome		
5	*Productivity*	Recipients demonstrate productivity
4	*Transfer*	Recipients transfer intervention skills to real-life tasks
3	*Application*	Recipients apply intervention skills to simulated tasks
2	*Acquisition*	Recipients acquire intervention skills content
1	*Process*	Recipients demonstrate effective process movement toward receiving the intervention

FIGURE 8
The Relationship of Intervention to Productivity Outcomes

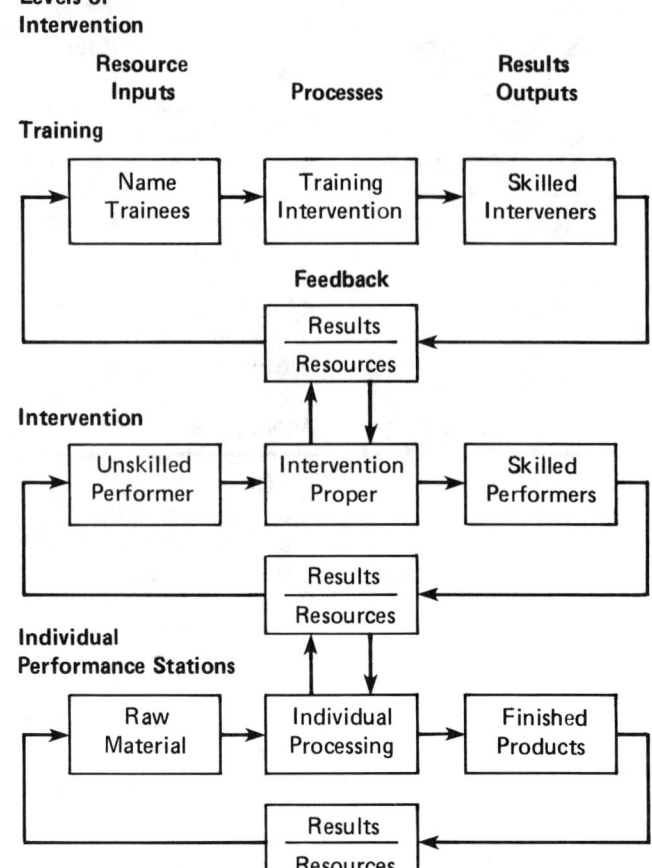

For example, based upon our analyses in a comprehensive intervention systems design, we may decide to train supervisors to implement an interpersonal skills-based performance appraisal system. At the training level, we will transform the naive supervisors into skilled appraisers. At the intervention level, the skilled supervisors will transform their unskilled supervisees into skilled performers. At the individual performance stations, the individual performers will employ their increased knowledge and skills regarding the performance that is expected of them to process the raw material into finished products.

Each one of these levels of intervention requires a systematic intervention design. Each one of these levels of intervention may be assessed in terms of its relationship to productivity outcomes. All of these interventions must be seen in a comprehensive intervention systems design. The phases of intervention will be the topic of the fifth in the series of papers on "Systematic Human Intervention."

REFERENCES

- Carkhuff, R. R. *Beyond Productivity*. Amherst, Mass.: Carkhuff Institute of Human Technology, 1981.
- Carkhuff, R. R. *Interpersonal Skills and Human Produc-*

tivity. Amherst, Mass.: Human Resource Development Press, 1982.
- Carkhuff, R. R. and Friel, T. W. *Toward Systematic Human Intervention*. Amherst, Mass.: Human Resource Development Press, 1982.

Evaluating the Effectiveness of Management Training: Progress During the 1970's and Prospects for the 1980's

by Ronald W. Clement

American business spends billions of dollars each year to train and develop employees, and business executives must often wonder whether or not this investment really pays off. Do these programs really work? Do trainees perform better on the job after returning? Does the organization reap such bottom-line benefits as improved profits, reduced costs, or higher productivity?

Similar concerns have been expressed by behavioral science researchers. Despite the many approaches to training evaluation that have been proposed in the training literature over the past two decades, this important training activity comes under frequent attack as being ineffective. For example, training professionals have been criticized for administering "happiness ratings" instead of trying to measure the effects of training back on the job; this particular failure, to evaluate the *effects* of management training, has been widely criticized.

This article reviews the progress of management training over the past decade and summarizes the state of training evaluation as we enter the decade of the 1980's. Most importantly, the article attempts to answer the following questions:

1. How effective is management training evaluation? Are we really doing a better job now of finding out what training approaches work?
2. What is the current outlook for management training evaluation in the 1980's? Is it likely to play a bigger role than in the past?
3. What are the implications of the findings for American business executives?

BACKGROUND

A 1970 review of the management training literature found that evaluation studies of management training courses tended to be inadequate (Campbell, Dunnette, Lawler, and Weick, 1970). The review focused on the studies published during the prior two decades and uncovered several shortcomings. First of all, less than a third of the studies had measured the effects of training on individual job performance or on results for the organization such as sales, profits, or productivity. Most had focused on training outcomes typically assessed *during* or *just after* a course, such as trainee reactions toward the course or improvement in knowledge. Second, very few studies had compared the relative effectiveness of two or more techniques of training in reaching a desired objective. For example, no one had attempted to determine which training technique worked best for improving interpersonal skills. Third, no studies had measured the influence of individual differences on the outcomes of training. For example, none had investigated how the success of training might vary with the level of a trainee's prior experience or education. Finally, few studies had investigated the effect that the organizational environment has on the transfer of training to the job setting. For example, none had examined the influence that a trainee's superior or subordinates might have on the success of the trainee in applying the new knowledge or skill on the job.

It is important to note that the 1970 reviewers had focused only on those evaluation studies that had employed a control group or—in the absence of a control group—both pre-training and post-training measures (e.g., of trainee knowledge or job performance). Only these studies could be expected to provide meaningful data about the effectiveness of a course. Studies employing no control group and only a post-training measure tell the training researcher essentially nothing about the effectiveness of his or her course. One positive finding of the 1970 review was that fully 87% of the pre-1970 studies had employed a control group or at least pre-training and post-training measures.

THE PRESENT STUDY

To allow for a direct comparison with the findings of the 1970 review, the current review also focused only on the studies employing a control group or at least pre-training and post-training measures. Use of this screening rule produced a most disappointing finding —an omen of further disappointments to come. A much smaller percentage of the post-1970 studies (only 68%) had met the desired conditions for producing meaningful data. In other words, 32% of the post-1970 studies employed no control group and only post-training measures of training outcomes. Discussion of the probable reasons for this finding, as well as of all the other findings of this review, is presented in the last section of this article.

Turning now to the progress of management training evaluation since 1970, it will be recalled that there are four issues of concern: 1) training outcomes measured in evaluation; 2) comparisons of relative effectiveness; 3) measurement of the influence of individual differences; and 4) measurement of the influence of the organizational environment. The findings regarding these four issues are summarized in Table 1, which is referenced in succeeding sections of this article.

Training Outcomes Measured in Evaluation Studies

After screening out the less meaningful studies, the 1970 researchers divided the remaining 73 studies into two categories. One category included studies that had measured trainee reactions toward a course or the trainee learning that had occurred; these outcomes are usually measured within the course before the trainee has returned to the job and will be called *internal outcomes* in this article. The second category included studies that had measured the improvements in the trainee's job performance or in the results for the organization; these outcomes, of course, tell us more about the effectiveness of a training course than do reactions and learning. Since they are measured outside the course, they are termed *external outcomes.*

Again, to allow for a direct comparison with the findings of the 1970 review, the same method of

categorizing studies has been used in the current review. In terms of the outcomes used to evaluate management training, some progress has apparently been made since 1970 (Table 1). Only 29% of the pre-1970 studies had focused on external outcomes, whereas 58% of the post-1970 studies had done so. However, one must remember that this finding is based only on the studies producing meaningful data— those employing a control group or at least pre-training and post-training measures. Apparently, those training researchers who take the effort to design a meaningful study also have tended, since 1970, to focus upon outcomes external to the course.

Comparisons of Relative Effectiveness

According to Campbell, et al. (1970):

A very valuable type of research effort, from both the scientific and the organizational point of view, is one which compares the relative effects of two or more training methods against the same criteria. For the organization, such a study directly attacks the question of cost versus utility for alternative approaches to the same goal (p. 315).

Unfortunately, of the 73 studies they reviewed, only four (5%) had attempted to compare the relative effectiveness of two or more training methods (Table 1). Despite this dismal finding, there was good reason for the current researcher to expect that comparisons of relative effectiveness had become a concern of training researchers since 1970. In particular, a survey of 200 training directors of *Fortune 500* companies (Carroll, Paine, and Ivancevich, 1972) found that they perceived each of nine training techniques to be differentially effective in achieving each of six common training goals. For example, case study was rated as most effective for development of problem-solving skills, and programmed instruction was considered best for retention of knowledge. Both role playing and sensitivity training were considered best for changing attitudes and developing interpersonal skills. More recently, Newstrom (1980) has replicated the 1972 survey and found similar results.

One might expect that these perceptions would generate controlled research to confirm those perceptions. Not so of the 26 post-1970 studies; only five (19%) had attempted to compare the relative effectiveness of two or more training methods in achieving a common goal. These are still too few to warrant making generalizations about which training method is best for a given objective.

As an aside, however, one of the five comparison studies (Smith, 1976) was also found to be one of the best-conceived post-1970 evaluations of

TABLE 1
Pre-1970 Versus Post-1970 Evaluation Studies

	Number of studies in review	Number (Percentage) of Studies That Had			
		Measured the external outcomes	Compared the relative effectiveness	Measured the influence of individual differences	Measured the influence of the organizational environment
Pre-1970	73	21 (29%)	4 (5%)	8 (11%)	5 (7%)
Post-1970	26	15 (58%)	5 (19%)	2 (8%)	1 (4%)

management training. Not only did this study compare the relative effectiveness of three training methods, it also employed equivalent training and control groups; it focused on both internal and external training outcomes; and it used pre-training and post-training measures of training outcomes—including measures several months after the course to determine the long-range outcomes. Training professionals would be well-advised to emulate this excellent evaluation study.

Measurement of the Influence of Individual Differences

Obviously, individual managers differ in their experience, education, abilities, attitudes, and values. It seems reasonable to expect, therefore, that a given training course would have different effects on different managers. For example, a 25-year-old college graduate, recently employed in a supervisory position, would probably respond differently to a training course on participative management than would an experienced 40-year-old peer with only a high school diploma. If this assumption is valid, then it also seems reasonable to assume that training researchers would want to discover the individual difference variables that might be determining factors in the success of management training. However, the 1970 researchers found that only eight (11%) of their 73 pre-1970 evaluation studies had attempted to measure the impact of individual differences (Table 1).

Despite this finding, the current researcher had good reason to expect that management training evaluations performed since 1970 had focused on individual differences. Clearly, the contingency approach to management which had gained wide acceptance over the past decade would support this expectation. This management concept merely postulates that there is no "one best way" to manage—that the appropriate management style (e.g., autocratic versus democratic) depends upon many variables, one of which is the nature of the individual to be managed (Gibson, 1980).

Acceptance of the contingency approach to management might lead one also to believe in a contingency approach to training. This approach would postulate that there is no "one best way" to train—that the appropriate training method also depends upon many variables, one of which is the nature of the individual to be trained.

Unfortunately, *no* progress has been made since 1970 regarding this issue. Of the 26 post-1970 evaluation studies, only two (8%) had attempted to measure the influence of individual differences. However, both of these studies lent support to the concept that individual differences can affect the outcomes of training. Each of these studies is described below.

Hayes and Williams (1971) measured the change in supervisory attitudes resulting from 12.5 hours of leadership training. They found the amount of attitude change to be inversely related to age, seniority, and span of control. They concluded that

. . . supervisory training programs are more effective when the participants are young, relatively new to supervisory ranks, responsible for a small number of subordinate personnel, and have a short period of total service. In order to achieve program effectiveness . . . among the older supervisory personnel having lengthy position and total service tenure and large span of control responsibilities a different type of program must be undertaken by training personnel (p. 38).

Unfortunately, they did not specify what this "different type of program" might be.

In another study of individual differences Schein (1971) measured the changes in attitudes, interests, and personality characteristics resulting from an eight-month management training course for college graduates. Among other things, she measured the extent to which the trainees learned a more favorable attitude toward business, a greater desire to exert a leadership role, and a more considerate leadership style. Furthermore, she attempted to determine if certain individual difference variables (i.e., intelligence, personality, and background) could be identified as predictors of these changes.

The course was found to have been successful in producing the expected attitude, interest, and personality changes. More importantly, the results showed that the individual difference variables—particularly the background variables—could be identified as predictors of the attitude, interest, and/or personality changes. For example, the higher the education level of the trainee, the greater was the favorable change in the trainee's attitude toward business.

The researcher concluded that individual difference variables—particularly measures of background and past experience—could be used to select those trainees who will most benefit from the training program. However, the researcher also cautioned that further research is needed to definitely establish the validity of the results. Both of these studies show that individual differences probably do affect the outcomes of management training. Clearly, further research in this training area would prove worthwhile.

Measurement of the Influence of the Organizational Environment

Earlier, it was suggested that there is probably no one best way to train, and that the appropriate approach to training depends upon many variables, one of which is the nature of the individual to be trained. A second variable that probably affects the outcomes of training is the organizational environment. In other words, the organizational environment to which a trainee returns probably influences the extent to which he or she is able to use the knowledge, skills, and attitudes learned in training. For example, in a rather extensive review of the research on leadership training and leadership behavior, House (1968) identified three organizational factors that influenced the transfer of training to the job. These factors were the formal authority system within the organization, the immediate superior of the trainee, and the primary work group of the trainee.

The first factor refers to the objectives, policies, and practices established by top management, within which the trainee must work. Obviously, training that runs counter to the formal authority system will not succeed.

The second factor refers to the immediate superior's right to administer rewards and punishments. If the superior encourages the trainee to apply principles taught in a training course, the training is more likely to transfer to the job setting.

The third influencing variable—the primary work group of the trainee—refers to the expectations of peers and the immediate subordinates of the trainee. No doubt, as House concluded, these " . . . will also help to determine [the trainee's] attitudes toward the

prescriptions taught in the training and his ability to transfer new knowledge and skills into job performance" (p. 562).

The House conclusions were based mostly on studies of leadership behavior and only incidentally on studies of management training. Still, his review definitely indicated the importance of additional research regarding the influence of the organizational environment on the outcomes of management training.

However, the 1970 researchers found that only five (7%) of their 73 pre-1970 studies had attempted to measure the influence of the organizational environment. They considered this to be the most negative conclusion to come from their review.

Although the current review uncovered several studies that had commented *post hoc* on the way in which the organizational environment *may* have influenced the outcomes of training, only Hand, Richards, and Slocum (1973) had focused *a priori* on this issue. Theirs was a longitudinal study of a human relations course that taught a consultative approach to managing. Two experimental groups were used: One consisted of trainees who perceived their organizational climate as favoring a consultative approach to managing, while the other group of trainees viewed their organization as less democratic and more structured. Eighteen months after the course, both experimental groups had experienced the expected changes in attitudes (i.e., toward consultative management). However, only the consultative experimental group was found to have transferred the consultative approach to their job performance. The organizational variable that apparently had influenced the post-training behavior of the trainees was the decision-making of top management with regard to salary increases and promotions. Whereas the consultative experimental group was encouraged by means of such rewards to apply the training on the job, the group of trainees from the less democratic organization was not encouraged in this manner.

Although more research is needed, it is clear that training courses should be designed and conducted with an eye toward the influence of the organizational environment. Influential factors within that environment should be identified during the assessment of training needs.

CONCLUDING COMMENTS

Evaluation studies of management training courses apparently are not much more thorough than they were in 1970. Few training researchers have attempted to measure the influence of either the organizational environment or individual differences upon the success of a training course. Further, we have added essentially nothing to our knowledge of what training method is most effective in reaching a given objective. The only positive finding to come from this review is that those post-1970 training researchers who bothered to gather meaningful data (e.g., by using a control group) also tended, more so than their pre-1970 counterparts, to measure external outcomes such as improvement in job performance and not just internal outcomes such as reactions toward the course. But even this favorable discovery is offset by the fact that a much smaller proportion of post-1970 training researchers made the effort to gather meaningful data; 32% had employed only post-training measures and no control group. In short, evaluation practices have not improved much since 1970.

Furthermore, the outlook for the 1980's shows that evaluation may continue to play a *lesser* role in management training. A recent survey of over 2000 training professionals (Clement, Walker, and Pinto, 1979) found them emphasizing non-evaluation activities as the important ones for the future. On the one hand, the respondents reported that the training functions in their organizations were growing in terms of breadth and depth of services provided; examples of this growth included the design of new facilities and the addition of capabilities for organization development, manpower planning, and the development of minorities. On the other hand, this growth meant they were spending more time on management activities such as planning and organizing, and less time on the more traditional training activities, including evaluation. Apparently, organizational management is demanding a wider array of programs but not necessarily a determination of their worth to the organization. The danger is the potential of growth without accountability—a proliferation of ineffective programs.

The overriding implication is that evaluation practices are unlikely to change until top management demands it. Such a demand is unlikely unless top management is willing to pay the cost of effective evaluation, which can be considerable. This cost, however, must be viewed as an investment in better training and, therefore, improved organizational performance. It simply makes no sense for American business to spend billions of dollars on training and development programs and almost nothing to determine their effectiveness.

REFERENCES

- Campbell, J. P., M. D. Dunnette, E. E. Lawler and K. E. Weick. *Managerial Behavior, Performance*, and Effectiveness, New York: McGraw-Hill, 1970.
- Carroll, S. J., Jr., F. T. Paine and J. J. Ivancevich. "The relative effectiveness of training methods—expert opinion and research." *Personnel Psychology*, 1972, 25, 495–510.
- Clement, R. W., J. W. Walker and P. R. Pinto. "Changing demands on the training professional." *Training and Development Journal*, 1979, 33 (3), 3–7.
- Gibson, C. F. *Managing Organizational Behavior*, Homestead, Ill.: Richard D. Irwin, 1980.
- Hand, H. H., M. D. Richards and J. W. Slocum, Jr. "Organizational climate and the effectiveness of a human relations training program." *Academy of Management Journal*, 1973, 16, 185–195.
- Hayes, W. G. and E. I. Williams. "Supervisory training—an index of change." *Training and Development Journal*, 1971, 25 (4), 34–38.
- House, R. J. "Leadership Training: Some Dysfunctional Consequences," *Administrative Science Quarterly*, 1968, 12, 556–571.
- Newstrom, J. W. "Evaluating the Effectiveness of Training Methods," *Personnel Administrator*, 1980, 25 (1), 55–60.
- Schein, V. E. "An evaluation of a long-term management training program." *Training and Development Journal*, 1971, 25 (12), 28–34.
- Smith, P. E. "Management modeling training to improve morale and customer satisfaction." *Personnel Psychology*, 1976, 29, 351–359.

Training and the Law: What You Don't Know Might Hurt

by Mark Giorgini

In the rush of putting together a new training program, it's easy to forget how many of your actions are governed by assorted federal and state laws and regulations. The fact is, of course, that almost everything connected with the training process is touched by the legal system at one time or another.

The materials used, the persons trained, the records kept . . . all are regulated in varying degrees by the legal system. To steer clear of litigious hassles, trainers need to know more than a little about copyright law, idea ownership, comparable worth, access to training and related equal opportunity issues and privacy law. There are also a growing number of regulations about reporting training practices, says Robert Craig, vice president for government and public affairs for the American Society for Training and Development, who notes that "employment selection guidelines and affirmative action guidelines both have training elements in them."

Large or small, legal issues impinge on the human resource development (HRD) professional's freedom of action. Following are outlines of specific issues bound to have increasing importance for trainers.

COPYRIGHT

Much has changed since the first federal copyright statute was enacted in 1790. That act was limited to protecting maps, charts and books. But today's trainers also work with computer software, videotape recorders, videodiscs, films, sound recordings and a variety of printed materials.

All those items are covered under the most recent copyright act, which took effect January 1, 1978. But coverage in the law doesn't necessarily mean safety for the person seeking copyright protection.

Hundreds of millions of dollars in movies alone are lost every year, says Ed Murphy of the Film Security Office of the Motion Picture Association. While a good portion of the losses concern commercial motion pictures, trade films also turn up when the FBI closes in on film bootleggers.

Writing Your Own Training Materials? Get 'em Registered

Even if you're not planning to market training materials that you have developed, it pays to have them registered with the Library of Congress Copyright Office in Washington, DC. Registration provides several benefits:

- It establishes a public record, necessary before an infringement suit can be filed.
- If registration is made within five years of publication, a prima facie copyright is established. As with any prima facie case, however, rebuttal evidence would be allowed.
- If registration is made within three months of publication or before infringement, statutory damages and attorney's fees could be asked besides actual damages. Otherwise only actual damages could be claimed.

With advances in technology come increasing headaches for the producers of training materials. Converting a film to videocassette is a pretty simple operation; duplicating cassettes is even easier, says James F. Denton, an FBI supervisory special agent in Washington, DC working on copyright violation investigations. Photocopying machines make improper use of printed materials a snap.

Even things which seem to be available for free public use could cause problems. For example, using the song "Happy Birthday" in a company film showing employees at an office get-together could make you a copyright violator unless you received prior permission from Summy-Birchard, a New Jersey-based publishing house.

If you don't know whether something you plan to use in a training session has been copyrighted, check with the Library of Congress Copyright Office. That office, which registers approximately 455,000 copyright claims per year, maintains several catalogs and indexes of protected items.

Training materials are protected, however, even if they're not registered with the Library of Congress, says Frank J. Evina of the copyright office. "But it's certainly to a trainer's advantage to go through the hassle and check," he says. In addition, it pays to get your own training materials registered, Evina says.

The heart of modern copyright law is the concept of fair use. "Unfortunately," Evina muses, "no one really knows what that means. You almost always need an attorney to sort out the facts on any particular copyright case."

The statute sets out four factors to consider in determining the fairness of any particular use: the purpose and character of the use, the amount and substantiality of the portion used in relation to the total work, the nature of the copyrighted work and the effect of the use on the potential market for or value of the copyrighted work.

Excerpts of copyrighted works can be used for the purposes of illustration or comment. But reproducing anything consumable to avoid buying it would be a clear infringement.

Trainers about to set up a consulting firm may often be tempted to borrow materials developed for a previous employer. But the copyright law specifically covers the situation. In essence, the law says that just because you develop something for an employer doesn't mean it's yours.

While a basic tenet of copyright law is that the author of the work should derive benefit from his or her labor, the principle is generally reversed in employment situations. The rationale for this flip-flop is that employers should benefit from work produced at their direction and expense.

Section 201(b) of the copyright law explicitly exempts situations where the employer and the employee have reached a different arrangement by written contract. But in the absence of an agreement to the contrary, section 201(b) vests copyright protection in the employer for any work done by an employee.

Idea Ownership

Closely related to the notion of copyright protection is the concept of idea ownership. The copyright law and supporting court cases clearly protect the particular manner in which ideas are expressed or described. But an idea itself clearly is not a tangible item.

Consequently, ideas are not covered by the copyright law. Section 102(b) specifically exempts ideas, procedures, processes, methods of operation, concepts and principles from copyright coverage.

If you're planning to set up a consulting firm, you'd probably be on safe ground if you took a pure idea from your employer. But if you plan to start using that idea in a way similar to your employer's use, you might encounter copyright problems.

Comparable Worth

Although implications for training are sketchy, comparable worth is going to be a hot issue for the personnel field in the 1980s, says Bob Farnquist, personnel

Remember These Tips When Figuring Out Comparable Worth

If you foresee squabbles over the tricky comparable worth issue, here are a few considerations from Bob Farnquist, personnel director for the city of San Jose, CA.

- Sit down and decide on a general company policy, keeping in mind that the comparable worth issue has political, psychological and sexual dimensions.
- Decide whether your company is prepared to make the shift from a compensation system based on external market factors to one based on internal comparisons.
- Think about whether you want to be a trendsetter.
- Evaluate the different compensation systems used in your company. Some union groups might want to be paid on a seniority basis while some might want to be paid on a comparable worth basis. And that means some inherent inconsistences.
- Decide what kind of system you'll use to determine comparable worth. Different point evaluating systems yield different results.

director for the city of San Jose, CA, which underwent the nation's first comparable worth strike in July. Comparable worth is generally defined as equal pay for comparable work, taking into account such things as supervisory responsibilities and educational requirements.

A study of the San Jose personnel system by Hay Associates, a consulting firm, compared predominantly male and female jobs within comparable job categories. Women made less money than men, according to the study.

The nine-day strike pointed up a number of problems managers and HRD practitioners need to think about, says Farnquist. Besides formulating a workable definition of comparable worth, a manager has to devise a system to make comparisons between jobs. In addition, he argues, the question of who will pay the bill also needs to be answered.

In San Jose's case, Hay Associates devised a point system against which all jobs were compared. The $1.4 million settlement cost will be paid for by the taxpayers—but fewer workers will also be hired, Farnquist adds.

Another significant—and unresolved—problem is how to handle comparable worth problems when they run up against other government-mandated rules and programs such as affirmative action. While affirmative action is oriented toward upward mobility, the comparable worth concept is horizontal in nature. "Who knows what will happen," says Farnquist, "when the two collide."

Caveat Tester—And Other Hints to Avoid Lawsuits

Case law gives a few general tips for avoiding the problems of access to training:

- Make sure all potential trainees know about training opportunities. Avoid using word-of-mouth or a "good-old-boy" network for communicating information to employees.
- If you don't genuinely need an item of information on an employee, don't collect it. Unwarranted information collection could result in improper data being collected. And that could serve as the basis for a lawsuit whether or not the information was used.
- By the same token, make sure that the training is genuinely job-related.
- Be wary of using tests. Tests may be culturally biased and that could lead to a legal complaint. Tests are subject to validity and job-relatedness standards.

Legal scholars aren't much help in answering that question either. The U.S. Supreme Court handed down a decision on June 8, 1981, which did little more than open the door a crack on the comparable worth issue. Almost everything else about the subject remains to be legislated or litigated.

Nevertheless, comparable worth will not pose itself as a legal issue for trainers for a number of years, according to some observers. Barbara Hanley, associate director of the Employer Education Service at the University of Minnesota's Industrial Relations Center comments that "comparable worth will not affect trainers until our career development systems and promotability systems are much more formalized and better defined than they are now." As these systems mature, she speculates, the linkage between the rewards and the preparation for jobs will become more obvious.

"If the reward is ultimately linked backwards to how the person was prepared for a particular position," Hanley says, "it would link comparable worth to training. But we're nowhere near that because statistically, people end up in their jobs by accident."

ACCESS TO TRAINING

Equal employment opportunity laws directly affect many human resources areas including the training field. Title VII of the 1964 Civil Rights Act and Equal Employment Opportunities Commission (EEOC) regulations and guidelines are the primary sources for determining acceptable behavior.

"The fundamental concept is fairness," says EEOC attorney Jacy Thurmond. "Any training test or selection procedure which has an adverse impact on a member of a protected class could get a company in trouble." Race, sex, color, religion and national origin are the protected class categories.

Two basic forms of discrimination exist in the human resources area: disparate treatment and disparate impact. Disparate treatment—where similarly situated individuals are treated differently—is the most obvious.

But disparate impact is much more subtle and dangerous for an employer, says Thurmond. This kind of discrimination is often proven in court by statistical comparisons showing protected-class members getting shorter shrift than their nonprotected-class colleagues.

If you think a particular action could have an adverse impact, consider using a less dangerous way to achieve the business goal, Thurmond advises. For an employer, it's always best to avoid a discrimination complaint. Once a complaint has been filed, the employer must show the action complained about was taken for legitimate business reasons.

PRIVACY

Privacy is one of the more rapidly expanding areas of law. Since the U.S. Privacy Protection Study Commission issued its report in 1977, there have been a number of developments. Meanwhile, several states have adopted statutes dealing with information collection and use by government bodies.

In the corporate world, however, privacy has not been the subject of as much action. Even though Michigan and California have statutes that regulate the employer-employee privacy relationship, they are the exception and not the rule, says Robert J. Tennessen, a Minneapolis attorney, state senator and member of the federal privacy commission.

But even in the absence of statutory privacy provisions, employees have a common law right of action against employers, Tennessen notes. As a practical matter, though, the common law right to privacy has not been fully developed either. The U.S. Supreme Court has considered a number of privacy-related cases, but they generally involve nonbusiness situations.

Respecting an employee's right to privacy might appear to conflict with the need to keep records of private information for government bodies such as the EEOC. But both objectives can be met if handled properly. The best solution in such a case is to specifically tell the employee that certain information is being collected for a limited purpose and that distribution will be limited to only a certain government agency.

If circumstances require that information be distributed or used for purposes beyond those originally told to the employee, an employer will be on safe ground only if the employee is told of the changed circumstances and gives consent.

Watch for the Private Side of Training Records

Trainers often come into contact with personal information concerning employees. How that information is used —or not used—can seriously affect someone's career.

Because of a national trend toward privacy legislation, trainers should be aware of some of the concepts underlying privacy claims. Business relationships are not governed by statute as much as government relationships, but businesses are still susceptible to suit on common-law grounds.

Following is a excerpt from the final report of the U.S. Privacy Protection Study Commission* laying out eight basic obligations for employers and trainers:

1. to limit the employer's collection of information about applicants and employees to matters that are relevant to the particular decisions to be made and to avoid items of information that tend to stigmatize an individual unfairly;
2. to inform all applicants, employees and former employees with whom it maintains a continuing relationship (such as retirees) of all uses that may be made of the records the employer keeps on them;
3. to notify employees of each type of record that may be maintained on them, including records that are not available to them for review and correction;

4. to institute and publicize procedures for assuring that individually identifiable employment records are (a) created, used and disclosed according to consistently followed procedures; (b) kept as accurate, timely and complete as is necessary to assure that they are not the cause of unfairness in decisions . . . ; and (c) disclosed within and outside the employing organization only according to stated policy;
5. to institute and publicize a broadly applicable policy of letting employees see, copy, correct or amend, and if necessary, dispute individually identifiable information about themselves in the employer's records;
6. to monitor the internal flow of individually identifiable employee record information;
7. to regulate external disclosures of individually identifiable employee-record information in accordance with an established policy of which employees are made aware;
8. to assess its employee record-keeping policies and practices, at regular intervals, with a view to possibilities for improving them.

*Personal Privacy in an Information Society, The Final Report of The Privacy Protection Study Commission, pp. 236–237, 1977.

SOURCES SECTION X
TRAINING AND DEVELOPMENT FOR TARGETED AUDIENCES

A. **Remember These Five Basic Topics When Training New Field Sales Reps**
   by Daniel K. Weadock
   - Previews areas of knowledge needed by sales representatives

B. **Visualizing Technical Training Programs**
   by Michael J. Bashista
   - Proposes methods for training low-tech workers for high-tech jobs
   - Suggests use of new technical media

C. **Vocational and Technical Education**
   by Arthur W. Saltzman, Raymond Maly, and Richard Hartshorn
   - Surveys vocational and technical educational resources available to training professionals

D. **In-House Supervisory Training Programs: High Caliber, High Impact**
   by Stanley Truskie
   - Discusses successful in-house management training programs

E. **Career Development Puts Training in Its Place**
   by Beverly Kaye
   - Suggests focusing training on individual career development

Remember These Five Basic Topics When Training New Field Sales Reps

by Daniel K. Weadock

Most training programs for newly hired salespeople either are cluttered with a great deal of unnecessary information or emphasize product knowledge while neglecting other selling information and skills. Actually, training in only five basic areas should prepare an inexperienced person to become effective quickly in field sales.

The five essential topics are:

1. The nature of the sales process.
2. The account distribution (geographics) of the territory.
3. Prospects in the territory.
4. Sales knowledge.
5. The competition.

A brief consideration of the nature of the sales position will show why. Sales is the most goal-oriented corporate function. Most professional sales job descriptions state a major objective in terms of increased total sales dollars, total profit and/or market penetration or share within a given sales territory. At the same time, in sales, unlike other line functions, the individual must achieve this main objective while working independently from the rest of the organization. In general, the salesperson is not closely controlled by management in the methods used to achieve the job objective.

At issue, then, is how to train a person who has a specific, visible objective and will be operating, to a degree, apart from the rest of the organization. What knowledge must this person have?

The information included in the five topics listed above should be sufficient. When training is organized this way, product knowledge becomes an equal in a group of five areas that must be mastered. Also, use of this compartmentalized approach will help the training group avoid stressing unnecessary information.

Upon closer examination, these five areas of knowledge look like this:

1/TRAINING IN THE NATURE OF THE SALES PROCESS

An attempt to make a sales neophyte into an effective salesperson by teaching him or her only one of the many sophisticated sales techniques probably would not work and might even be detrimental. Seldom will one approach to sales work with more than a handful of customers. The many situations a salesperson confronts on a daily basis are too varied to be accommodated by one approach to the sales process.

It makes much more sense to help the trainee understand the essence of the sales process so that the person can tailor his or her own approach to a given sales situation. It is far easier to teach this than to try to teach a person how to construct a conviction sales modulus or utilize a features-advantages-and-benefits approach. After the individual has had some exposure to selling and fully understands the nature of the sales process, it will be easier for him or her to learn sophisticated sales techniques.

The advantages of this approach for the company training the new salesperson are numerous. It saves time because it eliminates the need for early training in specific sales techniques that may not be useful. It allows the company to show the sales process in a mode suited to the image the company wishes to project. And it helps build the trainee's confidence because it's easy to understand and apply in numerous sales situations.

2/TRAINING IN THE GEOGRAPHICS OF THE TERRITORY

One of the first problems a new salesperson has upon taking over a territory, large or small, is that of traveling in an unfamiliar area. This can be frustrating and time-consuming and may cause an inexperienced person to waste considerable time and become discouraged.

While a person is in the initial stage of training to take over a sales territory, he or she should have an opportunity to study the best ways to travel that territory. There are numerous ways a sales trainee can develop an itinerary that will cover a territory efficiently. The trainer need not deal extensively with the techniques used to develop computer-generated itineraries. However, if the company does use a computer for this purpose, the trainee should be shown the principles underlying this procedure.

A valuable exercise for a sales trainee is to use zip code account distributions and zip code maps to develop a plan to cover a territory. First, the trainee should collect all the sales invoices that have been generated in this territory in the previous 6 to 12 months. Then he or she should collate them by the first three digits and five digits of the zip code. Using zip code maps, the person lays out the accounts by distribution and account size in the various zip code areas. Before long, the trainee will know where he or she should be spending time.

After the trainee has organized the accounts in the territory by zip code, he or she should be required to develop a travel program to cover these accounts efficiently. The district or regional manager to whom the trainee reports should then evaluate this travel itinerary and offer suggestions where necessary.

Completion of this travel itinerary, which will cover the first three to nine months, will offer the trainee a number of specific benefits. It will be a tremendous planning aid, enabling him or her to use time more efficiently and minimize frustration during the first months in the field. Furthermore, management will be able to judge the initial progress the trainee is making by watching his or her ability to stick to this initial itinerary.

3/TRAINING CONCERNED WITH PROSPECTS IN THE TERRITORY

While determining the account distribution by studying the sales invoices from his or her territory, the trainee can also be listing the specific products purchased by each account and the names of people shown on these invoices.

Again, many companies have computer capability to generate customer profiles of every product the customer purchases. However, during this initial learning process, the trainees should be required to do this themselves. They will learn and retain far more information about what specific customers purchase if they develop these profiles themselves than if these lists are handed to them.

Most salespeople keep personnel profiles on accounts in their territories. Among other things, these profiles list the key purchasing influences (people) at each account. They also include information such as phone numbers and days the client sees visitors. While trainees are developing product profiles on their accounts, they should be developing personnel profiles and general informational profiles as well. They can do this by taking the necessary names from their customers' purchase orders and/or their own company's invoices.

Once sales trainees have a good understanding of the major accounts in their territory, they will have far greater confidence contacting these clients and should be able to converse effectively with them during the initial sales calls. Also, management can be confident that the individual who has a solid background of knowledge on the important accounts in his or her territory will be able to make effective initial sales calls on these accounts.

4/PRODUCT KNOWLEDGE TRAINING

Most companies do a superb job in training their new sales representatives in the technical aspects of the products they sell. Companies have management, scientific and engineering personnel who "know" their products. For this reason, they can easily *overtrain* salespeople in the area of product knowledge.

Salespeople should understand the products they sell well enough to be able to converse intelligently about them with their customers. They should be able to answer routine questions and know how to get the answers to complex ones. In other words, sales trainees should acquire a thorough knowledge of their products, but *not* at the expense of sales skills. The salesperson's technical knowledge need not be at the expert level. A real sales problem arises when the salesperson is spending a great deal of time on esoteric technical problems and not enough time in face-to-face selling.

Companies know the types of questions their salespeople are asked. For example, in the specialty compressed gas business, a frequently asked question might be: What valve should be used with a specific gas? In the life insurance business, the question might be: What is the difference between whole life and term insurance? The company should provide the information necessary for trainees to answer the most common questions. It should also tell them how to obtain the answers to more technical questions.

This approach to product knowledge training allows a company to zero in on those product problems a new sales representative is likely to face in the field. It prevents overtraining in technical areas, yet gives the trainee enough product knowledge so that he or she will go out and meet the customer with confidence.

5/TRAINING THE CANDIDATE IN THE STRENGTHS AND WEAKNESSES OF THE COMPETITION

Both national and regional companies have competition that varies from one place to another. A given competitor may be strong in one area, region or part of the country and weak in another. How can a trainer familiarize the new salesperson with the strengths and weaknesses of the competition in his or her sales territory?

The sales representative who previously covered a territory is probably the trainee's most valuable resource for information on this subject. Discussions with the area, regional or national sales manager are another excellent way to become familiar with the specific strengths and weaknesses of the competition. Other experienced people in the company, such as plant, warehouse or depot managers, may also have valuable input about competitive strengths and weaknesses in a given territory.

While the trainee is studying the sales data on the territory being taken over, he or she can construct a picture of the competitive strengths or weaknesses of the accounts. Also, the trainee can study competitive catalogs and other advertising published by the competition. This literature will show the trainee where the competition has distributive and product strengths. Finally, business reference books sometimes provide detailed breakdowns on the types and dollar volume of products sold by the competition.

When a trainee has covered all five of the areas discussed, he or she should be familiar with the requisite sales skills and information. This practical and economical approach to training the newly hired sales representative stresses those skills that are most needed to achieve the main sales objectives: increased market share and profitable sales. It covers the matters a salesperson confronts on a day-to-day basis in selling in a territory. Therefore, sound training in these five areas will help a new salesperson become an effective field sales representative quickly.

Visualizing Technical Training Programs

by Michael J. Bashista

As the technology of the American work place continues to evolve, one of the looming problems facing employers is the question of how best to train low-tech workers for high-tech jobs.

The Center for Continuing Study of the California Economy in Palo Alto predicts that 45,000 to 50,000 new high-tech jobs will be created by 1990 in that state alone. The work will be there. But how does one design effective programs to upgrade and expand the skills of the people who will have to do it?

The need to provide technical training not only to new hires but to experienced employees is nothing new, of course. What is new is the challenge of merging technical training with the delivery media of the '80s such as video and interactive computer systems. With the military, in many cases, leading the way, training departments are turning increasingly to those media as a viable alternative to the classic, often-impenetrable volumes of high-density print.

The bottom line on the effectiveness of visual programs rests, of course, on the ability of the program designer to integrate complex subject matter with the new media. Technical training usually covers operational, maintenance-related and analytical skills. The challenges associated with developing and delivering technical training in a video format are formidable.

In the first place, the raw information the designer needs often exists only in those volumes of mumbo-jumbo he is trying to get away from. Basic questions such as "What is the critical content?" and "What are the important tasks?" may be hard to answer.

In the second place, the learners whom the designer is trying to serve will require a viewpoint—a "map" providing visual clues from which to uncover skills, knowledge and concepts. "Visualization" is the development of viewpoints, symbols, analogies, relationships and vehicles of presentation. Who is best qualified to do the developing? Do you hire a scriptwriter with visualization talent or ask a content expert to write the script?

The best answer probably is, refuse to treat this as an either/or decision: Use both as a team. Working together, the writer and a knowledgeable expert first should complete an analysis of the O.A.C.R.: Objectives, Audience, Content (including tasks) and available Resources. After the analysis stage, the content expert becomes a reviewer while the writer takes over conceptualization and visualization.

Although conceptualization and visualization are two distinct steps in the design process, experience indicates that they often merge: The designer tends to begin visualizing quickly, before completing the concepts. In any case, visuals are based on concepts, and concepts hang on the visuals.

Given the state of special effects, it is relatively easy to use animation, music and camera technology to add "bells and whistles" that spruce up a technical training program. Unfortunately, this usually is a mistake. The writer should take advantage of available technology, but only in the context of the O.A.C.R. analysis. The idea, remember, is to train the workers, not to distract them.

WORKING FROM THE BOOK

Ordinarily, the analysis will have uncovered the fact that visuals play a secondary or nonexistent role in the written material that you are trying to translate into video. The figures, charts, tables, exploded-view illustrations and complex diagrams are in there, all right, but they probably are comprehensible only to Ph.D. candidates. Beyond the dubious values of these, you may be faced with step-by-step procedures that continue for page after page, with the elucidating comment "See Fig.7" implying answers to all questions.

In other words, you often will have to design the visuals almost from scratch—and anything involving motion obviously will have to come from you. To reemphasize, the concepts and visuals you design must be based upon your analysis of the O.A.C.R. They must take advantage of the inherent advantages of video— particularly the ability to show motion—even at the additional expense of including special effects and animation *when appropriate.*

GUIDELINES

The key to visualization is controlled movement. There are three ways to create movement: Move what is in front of the camera; move the camera; or use editing and other post-production techniques, such as music and effects.

Keep the program tight and succinct. Use short sentences and, as a rule of thumb, restrict segments to less than seven minutes. Don't hesitate to incorporate support materials, allowing the video to present only core information.

Pay particular attention to the audio. Narration should not be used as a redundant backup for what the viewer sees ("As you can observe, the liquid rises"), but should amplify and expand upon visual elements. Special sound effects can be effective cues and are useful as punctuation. Silence can focus attention. And

music can be a bridge to a preview or review of the material.

Narration should employ the active voice. When possible, avoid the use of "we" or "I" in favor of the implied "you" (not "We remove the element," but "Remove the element"). Too much "we" can make a technical program sound like a kindergarten cooking class. The progressive removal of "we" and "you" as the program continues places more subliminal learning responsibility on the viewer.

Video-based technical training manipulates the same tools found in writing: character, plot, setting and theme.

Typically, individuals who appear in technical training programs are simply credible sources of information: They look the part but do not have complex personalities. Limited on-camera appearances or total voice-overs are the norms, with actual demonstrations usually provided by anonymous yet knowledgeable technicians. Time, money and the abilities of the talent determine the extent of character involvement.

Plot, which might more aptly be defined as "framework," is tied closely to the setting. Some frameworks include "a day in the life of . . . ," classroom instruction, an on-line tour or a network parody.

The program's theme is based on its objectives. And in just about every technical training program, one of those objectives is to teach people to do a job better.

A video-based course on troubleshooting and diagnostic procedures produced recently required a lot of flow charts and diagrams. A professional on-camera instructor was selected, and the initial proposal called for a newsroom set. The news set became a classroom due to cost and time restrictions.

As the material became more complex, so did the visuals. That created problems of format and detail resolution. To accommodate the complexity, the instructor explained some of the examples using a flip chart. The camera panned other diagrams from a copystand. Split screens, highlighting and wipes (to reveal information sequentially) also were used.

In the March 1982 issue of *Educational & Industrial Television* one producer described another way to show and explain complex diagrams. Using a key, the producer shrank the instructor, permitting him to walk like Gulliver through a land of giant flow charts.

A third video-based training package, this one on troubleshooting and repairing audio equipment, used the subjective angle extensively to eliminate mirror-image confusion. The package was based on printed troubleshooting guides, and many visuals had to be reformatted for the TV screen.

Exploded views and a few brief animated sequences illustrated data flow. To speed up repetitive disassembly procedures, jump cuts were used to create a cartoon effect, with screws and covers appearing to remove themselves.

Unlike the first example, on-camera talent appeared only during the opening two minutes, the segue between preventive maintenance and troubleshooting, and the close. Actual technicians demonstrated the close-up repairs. The lower third of the screen showed abbreviated, printed explanations of the steps being completed.

The audiences for the first and third programs are expanding, which points out a feature of video-based technical training that is attractive to the designer as well as the client: More and more companies are marketing in-house programs to outside clients—sometimes even to the competition.

Vocational and Technical Education

by Arthur W. Saltzman, Raymond J. Maly, and G. Richard Hartshorn

This chapter briefly surveys vocational and technical educational resources available to the training professional. It discusses special-purpose work-related programs offered by public and private educational institutions, with primary focus on public institutions. Such programs are designed both to qualify youth for entry-level positions in specific occupational categories and to meet the special skill training needs of designated groups of adults. Educational programs leading exclusively to college degrees are not discussed.

Four elements of the training professional's job will be considered:

1. Recommending policy for the organization relating to use of public funds and institutions
2. Establishing objectives that are mutually acceptable to the organization and the educational resource
3. Identifying and evaluating available community educational resources, including schools, programs, and services
4. Establishing mutually beneficial relationships with educational institutions

POLICY IMPLICATIONS

Policy considerations relating to the use of in-house and external training resources are, in part, "make-or-buy" decisions depending on available options and, in part, on philosophical inclination. The small business with limited space, overworked supervisors, and a part-time training staff obviously depends on external resources. Large firms, particularly those with sophisticated technical training support units associated with their sales or production activities, have other options. It is convenient and sometimes cost-effective for such firms to use these resources for in-house training.

There is no one best way, though, even for large companies. To illustrate, the Ford Motor Company has for many years followed a policy of using public educational facilities whenever possible to provide vocational and technical education. In contrast, the other two-thirds of the automotive "Big Three"—General Motors and Chrysler—operate large proprietary technical institutes.

As a result of changing manpower and vocational education legislation at all levels of government, the organization must decide (1) whether to use public educational services and, if so, on what terms and (2) how to respond to the pressures of immediate social priorities. These policy decisions must be made, if not deliberately, then by default. In either case, the recommendations of the training professional are usually critical.

In making recommendations about the use of public education, a rule of thumb is that older and better-established schools and programs are usually accepted by management, while newer institutions will be considered more carefully. Few managers remember that land-grant colleges were established to train specialists in the agricultural and mechanical arts under the Morrill Act of 1862. Enrollments in apprentice-related classes and similar offerings of technical institutes and vocational high schools are rarely challenged. These are available largely as a consequence of the Smith-Hughes Act of 1917 and subsequent categorical vocational legislation.

Management may be more skeptical about the merits of more recent programs. Those offered by the community colleges, which emerged in the 1950s, may need aggressive sponsorship. Still more care may be required in drawing on the institutions of the 1960s: Job Corps centers, skills centers, and regional vocational schools. These developed as a result of such laws as the Manpower Development and Training Act of 1962, the Vocational Education Act of 1963, and the Economic Opportunity Act.

Policy recommendations concerning the potential use of public resources associated with social-priority programs have additional dimensions. These, too, have a long tradition—for example, programs providing training and jobs for the physically handicapped and for war veterans (the GI bill following World War II was probably the largest of all government-sponsored vocational education programs). However, recent programs transcend traditional training. They are designed to provide "equal opportunity" for blacks, women, older workers, youth, and other groups considered excluded under usual employment practices.

Participation in these programs means dealing with several basic policy questions. Traditional employment standards may have to be modified, entry-level jobs may have to be restructured under the Economic Opportunity program, and the propriety of accepting government subsidies under the Job Opportunities in the Business Sector (JOBS) program may have to be examined.

Legal, social, philosophical, and economic issues are involved in such decisions. The astute training professional will assess management's attitude toward each of these before utilizing the vocational and technical resources associated with such programs.

ESTABLISHING MUTUALLY ACCEPTABLE OBJECTIVES

Needs analysis and the setting of training objectives are particularly critical in the case of vocational and technical courses and programs; these vary widely in content, quality, and degree of relevancy. Properly designed behavioral objectives and related skill and knowledge standards can provide the basis for planning jointly with, and evaluating the effectiveness of, the educational resource used.

Task Analysis

Task analysis, behavioral objectives, and related skill and knowledge requirement techniques are some of the better by-products of the programmed learning movement. There are a number of approaches to task analysis. Figure 1 is an illustration from the Upjohn Institute program, How to Use the National Task Bank.

Most educators participate enthusiastically in setting objectives. Their importance for the training professional can be readily illustrated by a discussion of the way in which objectives are used in three of the major types of vocational and technical education programs.

Preemployment Education

Preemployment education is usually offered on a full-time basis. It is designed to qualify youth for entry-level jobs such as that of typist, computer operator, automotive mechanic, or assistant cook. Graduates acquire certification or, in the case of high schools or junior colleges, diplomas. Since training is completed prior to employment, the behavioral objectives become standards for employment decisions.

Preemployment programs provide the basis for answering three critical questions: Can the graduate perform the entry-level tasks to the specified standards? Can he or she perform better than new hires with less specific education? To what extent will the training enhance the graduate's career progress? If behavioral standards enable the placement activity to obtain systematic answers to these questions, preemployment programs can be used in a cost-effective manner.

Special-Group Education

A second type of training includes courses and programs tailored to the needs of specific groups of employees or organizations. Such training may be designed by the organization itself, or it may be purchased from private vendors or, in some cases, the public schools. If objectives are accurately specified and can be met by the public schools, low-cost, effective training results.

For example, the Ford Motor Company and the Dearborn public schools have developed a program to qualify employees who have failed the selection test for a regular apprenticeship. In this program, the company diagnoses the employees' deficiencies. Each deficiency becomes an instructional objective and is corrected through an individually tailored learning plan. The employee uses self-instructional materials and studies segments needed to correct each specific deficiency. School counselors assist trainees with learning materials at the plant site to optimize employee involvement and commitment.

Trainees who satisfactorily complete the preapprenticeship program qualify for regular apprenticeship training without retaking the entire apprentice selection test battery. The program is of particular value for training disadvantaged employees who have inadequate educational preparation.

FIGURE 1
Task Analysis. (Functional Job Analysis. An Approach to a Technology for Manpower Planning. Reprinted by permission of the W. E. Upjohn Institute for Employment Research, Washington, D.C. Reprinted with the permission of Dr. S. A. Fine. All rights reserved.)

Data	People	Things	Data	People	Things	INSTR.	Reas.	Math.	Lang.	
WORKER FUNCTION – LEVEL			WORKER FUNCTION – ORIENTATION				GENERAL EDUCATION DEVELOPMENT			TASK NO.
3B	1A	2B	70%	5%	25%	2	3	1	4	

GOAL:
(To be completed by individual user)

OBJECTIVE:
(To be completed by individual user)

TASK: Types/transcribes standard form letter, including specified information from records provided, following S.O.P. for form letter, but adjusting standard form as required for clarity and smoothness, etc., in order to prepare letter for mailing.

TO DO THIS TASK

PERFORMANCE STANDARDS

DESCRIPTIVE:
· Types with reasonable speed and accuracy
· Format of letter is correct
· Any changes/adjustments are made correctly

NUMERICAL:
· Completes letter in X period of time
· No uncorrected typing, mechanical, or adjustment errors per letter
· Fewer than X omissions of information per X number of letters typed

TO THESE STANDARDS

TRAINING CONTENT

FUNCTIONAL:
· How to type: letters
· How to transcribe material, correcting mechanical errors
· How to combine two written sets of data into one

SPECIFIC:
· How to obtain records and find information in them
· Knowledge of S.O.P. for standard letter format: how/where to include information
· Knowledge of information required in letter
· How to use particular typewriter provided

THE WORKER NEEDS THIS TRAINING

Individual Courses and Programs

A third type of training draws on individual courses and programs offered as part of standard curricula. Schools, both public and private, offer basic courses in newer occupations, such as those generated by the computer industry, as well as in traditional areas, such as supervisory training.

Courses are many and varied, and the training professional's challenge is to learn what subjects are offered, where they are offered, what the quality of the courses is, and how relevant they are. With so many courses in so many subjects, the training professional is dependent primarily upon participant evaluation.

The most feasible quality check usually involves a brief written report from employees who have com-

pleted a course. Employees who know the behavioral objectives (i.e., what they should learn) will be able to report on whether such learning took place and whether the knowledge acquired was useful on the job.

EDUCATIONAL RESOURCES

Schools

Public High Schools. There are several distinct kinds of public schools which the training professional can turn to for vocational and technical courses. General, technical, and vocational high schools exist in most large metropolitan areas. Most high schools have a division of adult education or a person designated to coordinate vocational training. These schools typically offer a variety of occupationally related courses to prepare full-time high school students for jobs. Most schools also offer selected groups of programs at night for adults.

Curricula usually fall into three categories: (1) commercial or business, including typing, shorthand, and home economics; (2) vocational, typically including machine-shop work, metalworking, and carpentry; and (3) agricultural. In addition, the range of schools includes the special-purpose institutions that exist in the larger cities, such as the High School of Needle Trades in New York City.

Area Vocational Schools. These schools are relative newcomers to the educational community and are usually strategically placed to serve smaller communities and rural areas which cannot support a technical high school of their own. Most of them were built with funds available under the Vocational Education Art of 1963. Consequently, they are newer, have modern equipment, and frequently offer more flexible and relevant courses. An example of this type of school is the St. Paul Area Technical Institute, which is referred to in the discussion of continuing vocational and technical training.

Junior Colleges. Many junior colleges offer excellent vocational education and are well equipped, not only with machinery and equipment, but also with qualified staff using contemporary training technology. In addition to providing classroom instruction for apprenticeship programs, junior colleges also offer technician training in areas such as hydraulics, electronics, industrial technology, tool and die design, drafting, and specialized fields of engineering.

Colleges and Universities. Four-year colleges and universities also offer a variety of resources to the training professional. Publicly supported colleges frequently sponsor specialized programs directed toward adults who need updating in a particular area. Some private colleges sponsor such programs as well. These courses are usually offered through the senior college's division of adult or continuing education. They require that the school substantially alter its usual approach, which centers on tightly structured, conventional degree credit programs. Some schools custom-tailor programs and offer them at the workplace or on the school premises, frequently using qualified members of industry as instructors.

Independent Study

Independent study programs have been used in industry for a considerable period of time. International Correspondence Schools points out that more than 3,500 business and government organizations are using ICS independent training materials, programs, and assistance as part of their formal training programs.

Some large corporations use self-learning programs coupled with special-purpose educational media to reduce instructional costs and avoid premium payments after regular work schedules. Such courses range from those using commercially published programmed texts to those using lessons prepared on video tape and supported by program books which parallel and complement the video presentations. Some training packages also include hands-on training on simulators, which are training aids closely resembling equipment on the factory floor.

Company-operated Institutes

Some companies, such as General Motors, RCA, IBM, and AT&T, have established special institutes, programs, or classes to tailor-make educational programs to their own needs. These programs usually complement the more general and theoretical classes presented by local educational institutions and are aimed at updating technicians, skilled craftsmen, and engineers. The content usually focuses on the specific application of theories, something which is not usually covered as well in traditional adult education at the secondary, junior college, or college level.

Courses Sponsored by Unions and Trade Associations

Unions and trade associations also are utilized by many employers as educational resources. Building and construction trade unions, for example, offer apprenticeship training in many large metropolitan industrial areas. Several unions, such as the UAW, offer training to disadvantaged persons. The building and construction trades sponsor dozens of apprenticeships covering a multitude of classifications from bricklayer and carpenter to plasterer and tile setter.

Proprietary Schools

More than 7,000 private "for-profit" schools offer vocational training. Most of this is full-time pre-employment training in such trades as cosmetology, typing, or data processing. Many schools offer evening programs for upgrading employees as well. Since there is little published information available about the quality of such schools, each must be evaluated on its own merit. Specification of behavioral objectives and of systems through which participants can report is extremely important so that the training professional can separate the wheat from the chaff.

Skills Centers

These training institutions originated in the 1960s under MDTA to provide, in one school, both skill training and basic education for "disadvantaged" adults. The focus is on the adult; skills, job-hunting techniques, literacy, grooming, or whatever may be required is taught in modules with no fixed-time constraint. Centers now exist in many areas, and administrators usually willingly set up vestibule areas to meet the special needs of particular employers.

PROGRAMS AND SERVICES

Several factors affect the types of school programs and vendor training services and the terms under which they will be offered. Public school courses are usually structured to take advantage of funding available under law. Private technical institutes and colleges frequently separate vocational and technical programs to protect degree standards. Vendor offerings vary from straight classroom teaching to teaching-machine technology. Some of the most commonly used programs are apprenticeship, cooperative education, continuing vocational and technical education, and government programs for special groups.

Apprenticeship

A total of 264,122 persons enrolled in apprenticeship programs in 1972, with more than 60 percent in the building trades. Apprenticeship is the oldest continuing vocational and technical training system in American industry.

The importance of the apprenticeship training model transcends the program. It has evolved directly from the medieval guild system, as has training in the medical and legal professions. Further, the model has been extended and is used for a wide variety of vocational training: to develop foremen, technicians, and engineers, for example. The cooperative education program and that latest in federal manpower efforts, the "coupled work-study" program, are essentially variants of the same model.

In its present form, apprenticeship flourishes where unions flourish. The program is typically administered by a union-management joint apprenticeship committee (JAC). In essence, it is a system under which a trainee acquires vocational skills "on the job" by working with journeymen craftsmen for a designated period of time. In addition, the apprentice acquires related formal knowledge, usually in a classroom, but occasionally through self-study. Programs vary in length, typically from two to five years, and successful graduates are certified as journeymen in such trades as plumbing, electricity, die making, bricklaying, printing, and mechanics.

Both the federal and state governments supervise these programs and subsidize the related training aspects. The National Apprenticeship Act of 1937 (Fitzgerald Act) is the basic federal law, and the program is administered through the Bureau of Apprenticeship and Training (BAT) of the Department of Labor. In addition, 30 states have state apprenticeship councils (SACs).

Programs meeting BAT and/or SAC standards may be registered, and graduates are given certificates of completion by the appropriate agencies. Certificates are sought after since they assure the journeyman of greater job choice.

Standards include a minimum of 144 hours of related training per year, specified wage progress, and levels of supervision. Most related training is provided by public schools with designated subjects such as shop mathematics, blueprint reading, and electrical theory.

The effectiveness of the on-the-job learning phase can vary considerably. In small firms with few apprentices, success is obviously dependent upon the ability of journeymen and their willingness to share their skills. In larger firms, the training professional can help organize the work situation to increase program effectiveness. Apprenticeship assignments can be structured so that simple tasks are learned first and complex tasks later. Checks can be devised to assure that skills have been mastered.

In the Ford Motor Company an extensive task analysis of the nine most populated trades was undertaken. With this as a base, a vestibule school was established, and self-paced learning guides were designed. Apprentices perform each operation on production materials under the guidance of journeymen instructors until they demonstrate mastery. Tasks undertaken are increasingly complex, and skills are learned more quickly and completely. The task guide tells the apprentices what they must learn to do, and it lists the tools, materials, and equipment necessary to perform the task. It also defines when the task is being done correctly, directs apprentices to reference materials, and provides a check sheet on which ap-

FIGURE 2
Portions of Basic Training Guide for Apprentices. (Reprinted by permission of the Ford Motor Company.)

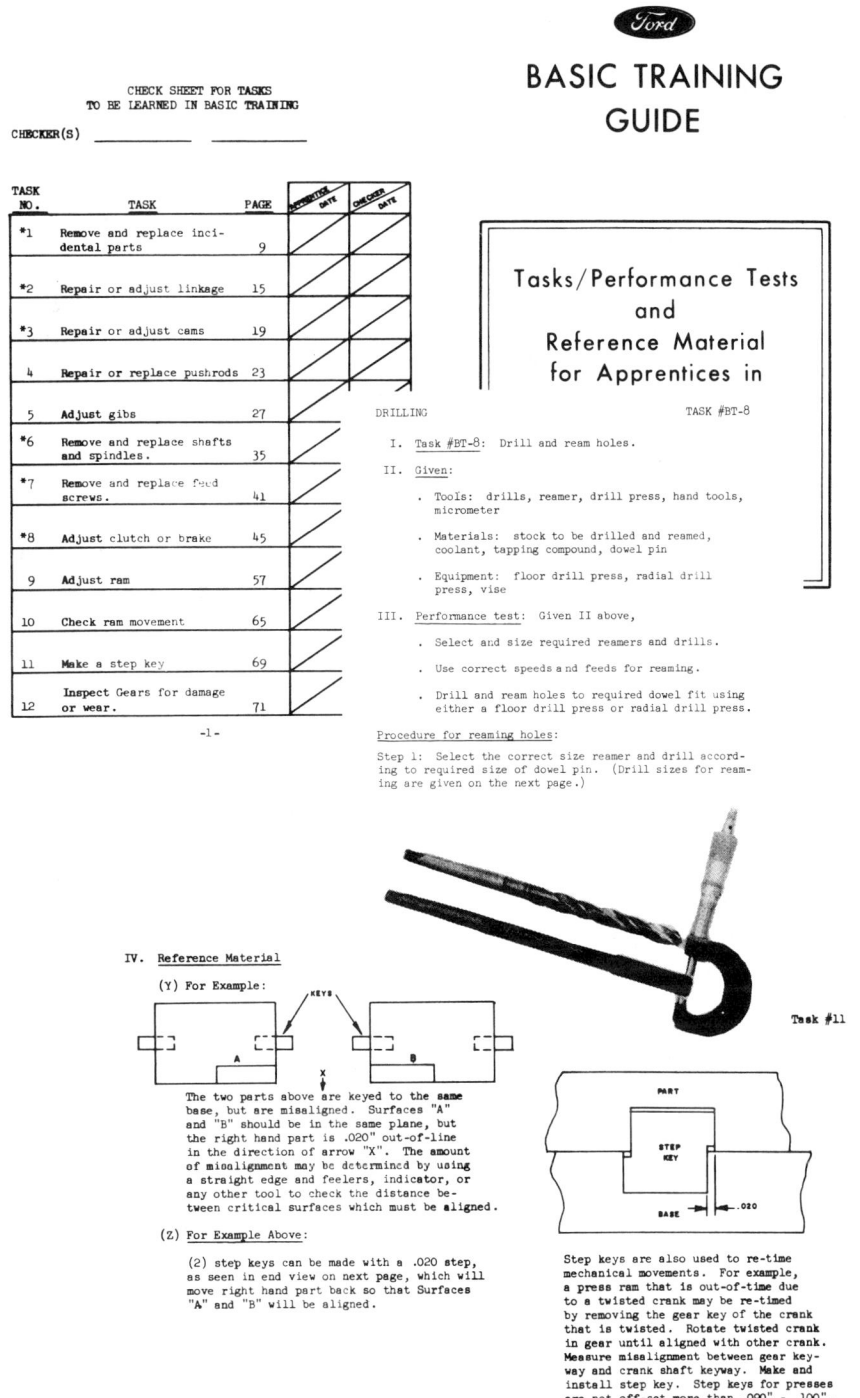

CHECK SHEET FOR TASKS
TO BE LEARNED IN BASIC TRAINING

CHECKER(S) _____ _____

TASK NO.	TASK	PAGE	APPRENTICE DATE	CHECKER DATE
*1	Remove and replace incidental parts	9		
*2	Repair or adjust linkage	15		
*3	Repair or adjust cams	19		
4	Repair or replace pushrods	23		
5	Adjust gibs	27		
*6	Remove and replace shafts and spindles.	35		
*7	Remove and replace feed screws.	41		
*8	Adjust clutch or brake	45		
9	Adjust ram	57		
10	Check ram movement	65		
11	Make a step key	69		
12	Inspect Gears for damage or wear.	71		

-1-

BASIC TRAINING GUIDE

Tasks/Performance Tests
and
Reference Material
for Apprentices in

DRILLING   TASK #BT-8

I. Task #BT-8: Drill and ream holes.

II. Given:

. Tools: drills, reamer, drill press, hand tools, micrometer

. Materials: stock to be drilled and reamed, coolant, tapping compound, dowel pin

. Equipment: floor drill press, radial drill press, vise

III. Performance test: Given II above,

. Select and size required reamers and drills.

. Use correct speeds and feeds for reaming.

. Drill and ream holes to required dowel fit using either a floor drill press or radial drill press.

Procedure for reaming holes:

Step 1: Select the correct size reamer and drill according to required size of dowel pin. (Drill sizes for reaming are given on the next page.)

IV. Reference Material

(Y) For Example:

KEYS

A   X   B

The two parts above are keyed to the same base, but are misaligned. Surfaces "A" and "B" should be in the same plane, but the right hand part is .020" out-of-line in the direction of arrow "X". The amount of misalignment may be determined by using a straight edge and feelers, indicator, or any other tool to check the distance between critical surfaces which must be aligned.

(Z) For Example Above:

(2) step keys can be made with a .020 step, as seen in end view on next page, which will move right hand part back so that Surfaces "A" and "B" will be aligned.

Task #11

PART
STEP KEY
BASE   .020

Step keys are also used to re-time mechanical movements. For example, a press ram that is out-of-time due to a twisted crank may be re-timed by removing the gear key of the crank that is twisted. Rotate twisted crank in gear until aligned with other crank. Measure misalignment between gear keyway and crank shaft keyway. Make and install step key. Step keys for presses are not off-set more than .090" - .100".

prentices record that they have learned to do each task. The task statement shown in Figure 2 is from *Basic Training Guide: Tool and Die Making*.

Cooperative Education

Schools use federal funds to offer cooperative work-study programs. Local and state funds supplement federal subsidies in some districts. These are programs under which students spend some time at school and some time at work. Schools are interested in these programs because they smooth the transition from school to work. Employers, in turn, have the opportunity to evaluate potential employees before full-time job commitments are made. Students also find the arrangement very helpful because it enables them to apply theory to work situations much sooner than they could otherwise.

Typically at the high school level, seniors split their days between class and job, with a minimum of 15 hours of work per week. At the junior college level, split days or whole days at work alternating with whole days at school may be the pattern. At the college level (outside the purview of this chapter) students spend an academic quarter or semester on campus and an equal period of time on the job.

Federal subsidies are given for cooperative programs in areas involving the distributive, trade and industrial, and office occupations. Information about these programs is usually available from the Cooperative Education Association, which publishes the *Directory of Cooperative Education.*

Continuing Vocational and Technical Education

Public schools in many areas offer a variety of vocationally related technical courses during the evening. Schools receive federal funds for these courses too, and offerings usually include the same courses as those for apprentices supplemented by other, more advanced programs. Subjects vary from computer programming to financial analysis and plant layout, and the courses are designed to help adults qualify for advancement.

Courses are offered by high schools, area vocational schools, junior colleges, and university extension programs, frequently simultaneously, in the same city. They may be organized into curricula leading to certificates, or, at the junior college level, to two-year degrees. For example, the announcement shown in Figure 3 is from the catalog of the New York University School of Continuing Education, Division of Business and Management.

Figure 4 shows one section of a poster announcing the courses offered in the evening by the St. Paul Area Technical Vocational Institute (St. Paul, Minnesota).

Government Programs for Special Groups

Federal manpower policy has emphasized increasingly that the work-providing community has a social obligation to employ special groups of individuals. Traditionally, these groups have included returning war veterans and the physically handicapped. Recently, the "disadvantaged," including minorities and women, have been added. A variety of approaches have been tried. These include retraining and prevocational training at new types of institutions, such as the skills centers. Included also are novel approaches such as the JOBS program, under which employers are

asked to hire submarginal trainees and are subsidized until the trainees can perform to commercially acceptable standards.

A number of state, federal, and local departments are involved, ranging from the Veterans Administration through the Department of Health, Education, and Welfare, the Department of Labor, and the local prison and school system. The number of federal programs alone can be mind-boggling. A recent publication summarizing federally assisted manpower programs in tabular form listed 18 programs.[1]

Programs change as new laws are passed. Regardless, programs which train individuals for vocations impact the work-providing community. Training professionals are well-advised to become familiar with current government manpower policy trends and areas of emphasis so that they can appropriately advise their management.

RELATIONSHIPS BETWEEN INDUSTRY AND SCHOOLS

Training professionals need to be aware of the special needs of the public vocational education system. Capital equipment is constantly replaced by industrial firms intent upon using new technology. Public schools do not have the money. Some reasonable system must be devised so that students do not find themselves trying to learn skills of questionable value on equipment which no longer is in use.

Some schools have difficulty getting business to provide work-related experience. This problem is not peculiar to vocational education. Schools of dentistry and medicine, for example, long ago faced the necessity of locating in or near hospitals so that interns could begin to apply the theories of the classroom to the ills of the hospital room.

Faculty members need to keep current. Their time is preempted, by the demands of students, administrators, and research. Occupations, however, develop at the workplace, not in laboratories or treatises. Somehow teachers must be given access to the workplace so that they can learn about new skill requirements and new technology. Several paths are open for building the necessary relationships. For one thing, teachers can be used as consultants. In this capacity, they may fill a real short-time need in organizations which have neither the expertise nor the manpower to provide training for themselves. A shop instructor, for example, who is an expert in electronics may be an invaluable asset to a plant struggling with the need for updating technicians to maintain and troubleshoot new equipment.

Joint committees of educators, industrial trainers, and engineers are another way of bringing

FIGURE 3
Continuing Education Announcement. (Reprinted with the permission of the New York State University Management Institute.)

education and occupation together. For example, in an industrialized Midwestern community, a technical school approached its local industrial and business committee for assistance in setting up an electronics program. As a result, an engineering manager was assigned to serve in an advisory capacity to the school. His contribution consisted of designing a curriculum and simulation equipment for classroom use.

Committees are also used to establish related classroom programs for apprenticeship training, to keep educators current on growing and contrasting career paths, and to develop awareness of equipment needs.

Training professionals play a pivotal role in these relationships, since they frequently interface with the schools. In addition, they have a vested interest in maintaining the competency of this lowest-cost educational resource.

REFERENCE

1. Levitan, Sar A., and Robert Taggart III: *Social Experimentation and Manpower Policy: The Rhetoric and the Reality.* The Johns Hopkins Press, Baltimore, 1971.

BIBLIOGRAPHY

• Cooperative Education Association: *Directory of Cooperative Education*, Drexel University, Philadelphia, 1973.

(A compendium of cooperative programs offered throughout the United States and Canada. Provides detailed information on the institutions in terms of program type, enrollments, graduates, etc.)

FIGURE 4
Course Listing From Technical Institute Announcement. (Reprinted by permission of the Saint Paul Area Vocational Technical Institute.)

No.	Class	Instructor	Room No.	Time	Days	Start Date	End Date	Hours	Fee
AIR CONDITIONING & REFRIGERATION									
1-01 710C4	Princ Refr & Elec I	Lawton	423/S-16	6:30-9:30	TH	1-24-74	5-16-74	48	15.00
1-01 715D3	Princ Refr & Elec II	Thomas	423 S-16	6:30-9:30	M	1-21-74	5-20-74	48	20.00
1-01 715D4	Princ Refr & Elec II	Vincent	423 S-16	6:30-9:30	W	1-23-74	5-15-74	48	20.00
1-01 721D2	Refrig & Elec III	Lawton	S-16/423	6:30-9:30	T	1-22-74	5-14-74	48	20.00
1-01 721D3	Refrig & Elec III	Dunbar W.	423/S-16	6:30-10:00	T,TH	1-22-74	3-14-74	56	20.00
1-01 726D2	Refrig & Elec IV	Vincent	S-16 423	6:30-9:30	M	1-21-74	5-20-74	48	20.00
1-01 726D3	Refrig & Elec IV	Caswell	S-16/423	6:30-9:30	W	1-23-74	5-15-74	48	20.00
1-01 730C2	Princ Air Cond V	Malaske	304	7-10	TH	1-24-74	5-9-74	45	20.00
CHEMICAL TECHNOLOGY									
1-03 720D1	Ind. Chemistry II	Bergstrom	327	6-10	T,TH	1-22-74	4-4-74	77	20.00
1-03 715D1	Organic Chemistry	Faye	325	6-10	T,TH	1-22-74	5-9-74	105	20.00
1-03 730C1	Polymer Chemistry	Various	325	7-10	M	1-21-74	5-13-74	45	15.00
1-03 725C1	Wastewater Lab Procedures	F. Osborn	327	7-10	W	1-30-74	5-15-74	45	15.00
CONSTRUCTION TECHNOLOGY									
1-04 710D3	Drawing	Tichich	331	6-9	M,W	1-21-74	5-8-74	87	20.00
1-04 710D4	Drawing	Schliek	201	6-10	T,TH	1-22-74	5-9-74	120	20.00
1-04 716C1	Adv. Construction Estimating	Roth	333	7-10	M,W	1-21-74	5-8-74	87	20.00
1-04 717D1	Advanced Surveying	Trence	203	6:30-9:30	M,TH	1-21-74	5-8-74	87	20.00
1-04 721C1	Basic Structural Design II	Tichich	331	6-9	M	1-21-74	5-6-74	42	15.00
1-04 726C1	Construction Model Building	Blesener	331	6-10	T	1-22-74	5-7-74	60	15.00
DESIGN TECHNOLOGY									
1-05 710D3	Fund Mech. Drafting	Spanovich	209	6-10	M,T	1-21-74	5-7-74	116	20.00
1-05 710D4	Fund Mech. Drafting	Raiche	205	6-10	W,TH	1-23-74	5-9-74	120	20.00
1-05 711C2	Assembly & Layout	Paulson	207	6-10	TH	1-24-74	5-9-74	60	15.00
1-05 717C1	Machine Design	Risch	203	6-10	T	1-22-74	5-7-74	60	15.00
1-05 745D1	Statics & Strength II	Skok	106	6-10	M,TH	1-21-74	5-9-74	116	20.00
1-05 746C1	Dynamics II	Reagan	226	7-10	T	1-22-74	5-7-74	45	15.00
1-05 742C2	Registration Refresher	Kallemeyn	208	6-10	W	1-23-74	3-3-74	44	15.00
1-05 723C2	Cost Estimating	Paulson	208	6-10	T	1-22-74	5-7-74	60	15.00
1-05 743C2	SME Certification Review	W. Schuldt	208	7-10	M	1-21-74	5-13-74	42	15.00
BASIC ELECTRONICS									
BASIC ELECTRONIC SERIES: THESE INTRODUCTORY CLASSES ALSO START NOV. 5, JAN. 14, MAR. 13, 1974. Every other meeting is spent in the lab. Intended for the beginner, these courses also provide an excellent review of modern electronic principles and basic applications. Qualified students may enter the series at higher levels.									
1-08 710C4	Elect. Fund I	Alnes	426/421	6-10	M,W	1-14-74	3-11-74	64	15.00
1-08 711C4	Elect. Behavior II	Martinson	427/424	6-10	M,W	1-14-74	3-11-74	64	15.00
1-08 712C3	Reactive Comp. III	Mickelson	424/427	6-10	M,W	1-14-74	3-11-74	64	15.00
1-08 712C4	Reactive Comp. III	Deeg	424/427	6-10	T,TH	1-17-74	3-12-74	64	15.00
1-08 713C3	Elect. Devices IV	McKinnon	422/431	6-10	M,W	1-14-74	3-11-74	64	15.00
1-08 720C3	Small Signal Amps V	Breault	431/422	6-10	M,W	1-14-74	3-11-74	64	15.00
1-08 721C3	Power Amps VI	Ritchie	416/431	6-10	T,TH	1-17-74	3-12-74	64	15.00
1-08 722C3	Pulse & Digital Circuits VII	Berdahl	431/426	6-10	T,TH	1-17-74	3-12-74	64	15.00
1-08 723C3	Special Device Appl. VIII	Schilling	416/419	6-10	M,W	1-14-74	3-11-74	64	15.00
APPLIED ELECTRONICS									
1-08 729C1	Medical Elect. Fund	Snegoski	420	6-10	T	1-22-74	5-8-74	64	15.00
1-08 745C1	MSI/LSI	Khambata	432	6-10	TH	1-24-74	4-18-74	48	15.00
1-08 743C2	Operational Amps	Zander	419	6-10	W	1-23-74	4-17-74	48	15.00
1-08 757C1	Logic Circuit Appl.	Khambata	221	6-10	W	1-23-74	5-4-74	56	15.00
1-08 780C1	Electronics for Maintenance Men	Schilling	421	6-10	M	1-21-74	5-13-74	60	15.00
1-08 782C1	Digital Instrument Fund.	Schilling	429	6-10	TH	1-24-74	5-9-74	60	15.00
1-08 784D1	Logic Laboratory	Schilling	419	6:30-9:30	T	1-22-74	5-2-74	33	20.00
RADIO & TV									
3-32 721C1	Radio Service II	Cervenka	429	7-10	M	1-21-74	5-20-74	48	15.00
3-32 713C2	FCC License	Snyder	426	6-10	T	1-22-74	5-28-74	72	15.00
3-32 735D1	TV Service II	Freeborg	425	6-10	M,W	1-14-74	4-29-74	112	20.00
3-32 745C1	Color TV II	Rubbert	425	6-10	T	1-22-74	5-14-74	64	15.00
3-32 745C2	Color TV II	Rubbert	425	6-10	TH	1-31-74	5-23-74	64	15.00
3-32 712C2	Tape Recorder Serv.	Rubbert	429	6-10	W	1-23-74	5-15-74	64	15.00
3-32 711C2	FM Multiplex	Rubbert	429	6-10	W	1-23-74	5-15-74	64	15.00
INDUSTRIAL HYDRAULICS/PNEUMATICS TECH.									
1-10 710C3	Basic Hydraulics I	Minogue	220	6:30-9:30	TH	1-24-74	5-16-74	48	15.00
1-10 715C1	Basic Hydraulics II	Mahle	220	6:30-9:30	M	1-21-74	5-13-74	45	15.00
1-10 715C2	Basic Hydraulics II	Walraven	220	6:30-9:30	W	1-23-74	5-8-74	45	15.00
1-10 725C1	Design & Function of Hyd. Circuits	Minogue	222	6:30-9:30	W	1-23-74	5-8-74	45	15.00
1-10 726C1	Systems Control	Walraven	222	6:30-9:30	TH	1-24-74	5-9-75	45	15.00
1-10 735C1	Maintenance & Testing	Wickoren	220	6:30-9:30	T	1-22-74	5-7-74	45	15.00
INSTRUMENTATION TECHNOLOGY (These classes are sponsored by the Instrument Society of America)									
1-12 720C1	System Applications II	Keseluk	309	6-9	M-TH	1-21-74	4-22-74	72	15.00
1-12 715C2	Test Technology	Snegoski	420	6-10	TH	1-24-74	5-16-74	45	15.00
QUALITY CONTROL (These courses are offered for the ASQC Certification Program) Obtain special registration form from ASQC or at TVI.									
1-15 711B1	Total Quality Control	R. Kane	206	6:30-9:30	M	1-21-74	5-6-74	42	
1-15 712B1	Inspection Engineering	McLellen	203	6:30-9:30	W	1-23-74	5-1-74	42	
1-15 713B1	Statistics in Q.C.	Hilliard	204	6:30-9:30	W	1-23-74	5-1-74	42	
1-15 720B1	Supervision for Q.C.	Schroeder	304	6:30-9:30	M	1-21-74	5-6-74	42	
1-15 731B1	Quality Costs & Audits	Sherwin	203	6:30-9:30	M	1-21-74	5-1-74	42	
DRAWING									
9-02 711B3	Related Drawing	Anderson	205	6-10	T	1-22-74	5-14-74	68	
9-02 711B4	Related Drawing	Anderson	205	6-10	M	1-25-74	5-20-74	68	
MATHEMATICS									
9-03 710B11	Basic Mathematics	Various	308	6-8	M	1-21-74	5-13-74	30	10.00
9-03 712B12	Adv. Mathematics	Various	308	8-10	M	1-21-74	5-13-74	30	10.00
9-03 710B13	Basic Mathematics	Various	102	6-8	T	1-22-74	5-7-74	30	10.00
9-03 716B14	Adv. Algebra	Various	102	8-10	T	1-22-74	5-7-74	30	10.00
9-03 710B15	Basic Mathematics	Various	103	6-8	W	1-23-74	5-8-74	30	10.00
9-03 714B16	Beginning Algebra	Various	103	8-10	W	1-23-74	5-8-74	30	10.00
9-03 710B17	Basic Mathematics	Various	204	6-8	TH	1-24-74	5-9-74	30	10.00
9-03 712B18	Adv. Mathematics	Various	204	8-10	TH	1-24-74	5-9-74	30	10.00
9-03 720B19	Metric Mathematics	Various		6-9	W	1-23-74	2-20-74	15	10.00
SUPERVISION & FOREMANSHIP									
1-18 710B1	Supervisory I	Various	326	6:30-9:30	TH	1-24-74	5-16-74	48	10.00
1-18 711B1	Supervisory II	Various	326	6:30-9:30	M	1-21-74	5-20-74	48	20.00
1-18 720B1	Supervisory III	Various	326	6:30-9:30	T	1-22-74	5-14-74	48	10.00
1-18 721B1	Supervisory IV	Various	326	6:30-9:30	W	1-23-74	5-15-74	48	10.00

- Evans, Rupert N.: *Foundations of Vocational Education,* Charles E. Merrill Books, Inc., Columbus, Ohio, 1971.

  (A well-organized, thought-provoking book extending from needs analysis and philosophical foundations for vocational education to teacher development and an examination of the future of vocational education.)

- Evans, Rupert N., Garth L. Mangum, and Otto Pragan: *Education for Employment*, Institute of Labor and Industrial Relations, Ann Arbor, Mich., 1969.

  (A reprint of a 1966 report of the Council on Vocational Education including a section on the 1968 vocational act amendments. The summary of vocational education in the United States was used for this chapter.)

- Fine, Sidney A.: *Functional Job Analysis: An Approach*

to Technology for Manpower Planning, W. E. Upjohn Institute for Employment Research, Kalamazoo, Mich., 1973.

- Hendershot, Carl H.: *Programmed Learning and Individually-Paced Instruction Bibliography*, Carl H. Hendershot, Publisher, Bay City, Mich., 1973.

  (A comprehensive listing of programmed learning materials, classified by subject and publisher. It includes price, length, level, and content of each program and is updated periodically.)

- Levitan, Sar A., Garth L. Mangum, and Ray Marshall: *Human Resources and Labor Markets*, Harper & Row, Publishers, Incorporated, New York, 1972.

  (An excellent textbook combining traditional labor economics with newer manpower materials. This chapter used information from chaps. 11, 16, and 17, on apprenticeship and manpower programs.)

- Levitan, Sar A., and Robert Taggert III: *Social Experimentation and Manpower Policy: The Rhetoric and the Reality*. The Johns Hopkins Press, Baltimore, 1971.

  (A reference—especially appendix, p. 108—for a list of federally assisted manpower programs.)

- Lovejoy, Clarence: *Lovejoy's Career and Vocational School Guide*, Simon and Schuster, New York, 1967.

  (Includes a description of more than 3,500 vocational schools.)

- Mager, Robert F.: *Preparing Instructional Objectives*, Lear Siegler, Inc., and Fearon Publishers, Inc., Belmont, Calif., 1970.

  (A programmed text to develop skills in defining and stating teaching objectives. Describes criteria for measuring learner accomplishment and determining what must be taught and discusses materials and procedures to improve instruction.)

- Mager, Robert F., and Kenneth H. Beach, Jr.: *Developing Vocational Instructions*, Lear Siegler, Inc., and Fearon Publishers, Inc., Belmont, Calif., 1967.

  (A programmed text which includes steps necessary to translate task analysis into instructional units. Provides examples and how-to methods for accomplishing job task analyses, designing measurement instruments, and preparing instructional units.)

- Mangum, Garth, and John Walsh: *A Decade of Manpower Development and Training*, Olympus, Salt Lake City, Utah, 1973.

  (Summarizes attempts to evaluate federal manpower programs and concludes that "MDTA has been worth the cost and effort." Chapter 3, on skills centers, was used as background to this chapter.)

- Olean, Sally J.: *Changing Patterns in Continuing Education for Business*, Boston University, Center for the Study of Liberal Education for Adults, Boston, 1967.

  (A survey of "higher-level" business programs which are or could be conducted at a college. Twelve firms and several educational consultants are included.)

- Patten, Thomas H., Jr.: *Manpower Planning and the Development of Human Resources*, Wiley-Interscience Publishers, a division of John Wiley & Sons, Inc., New York, 1971.

  (The most comprehensive book on manpower planning and development known to the authors. Particularly strong in industrial programs, including both historical background and present practice. Chapter 7, on apprenticeship and technical training, and chap. 13, on public policy, were drawn upon.)

- Smith, Harold T.: *Education and Training for the World of Work: A Vocational Education Program for the State of Michigan*. W. E. Upjohn Institute for Employment Research, Kalamazoo, Mich., July 1963.

  (An excellent study of vocational education in Michigan which also contains descriptions of vocational systems in 10 other states, including New York, California, Illinois, and Minnesota.)

- Somers, Gerald G.: *The Effectiveness of Vocational and Technical Programs: A National Follow-up Survey*. University of Wisconsin, Center for Studies in Vocation and Technical Education, Madison, 1971.

- Staley, Eugene: *Planning Occupational Education and Training for Development*, Frederick A. Praeger, Inc., New York, 1971.

In-House Supervisory Training Programs: High Caliber, High Impact

by Stanley D. Truskie

Most companies, large and small, are very much concerned with the development of their supervisors and managers. In an effort to support professional self-

Reprinted with the permission of *Personnel Journal*, Costa Mesa, California; all rights reserved.

development, companies enroll their management personnel in training programs conducted outside the company by colleges, universities and professional associates. These companies may be surprised to know they can do a much more effective job, for much less money, by developing and conducting some of these programs in-house. We do it for our supervisors and managers at the Metropolitan Edison Company, and we are extremely pleased with the results.

The Metropolitan Edison Company is an electric utility company located in Reading, Pennsylvania. As a member-company of the General Public Utilities System, it serves 350,000 customers in all or parts of fourteen eastern and central Pennsylvania counties. Its employee population numbers close to 2,700.

Prior to joining Met-Ed as corporate manager of employee education and development, I was deeply involved in planning and administering management seminars through Penn State University's Continuing Education Division. These programs ranged from week-long, supervisory development workshops to four-week senior-level executive seminars and included program titles such as Basic Supervisory Skills, Time Management, Arbitration in Labor Relations and Executive Management Series. Most programs offered through Continuing Education were open to the public, and brochures and announcements were sent to many companies who would enroll one or more of their supervisors or managers in these programs. Many participants often expressed thanks and gratitude for the opportunity to gain the information and skills presented during the programs. Many also expressed their eagerness to apply their newly acquired skills and information to the job once they returned to their companies.

HIGH CALIBER, LOW IMPACT

Although I usually had a good feeling about the quality of Penn State's programs, I was constantly concerned about program impact, wondering how much, if any, of the program material was actually put into practice once the program attendees returned to the job. My major concern stemmed from the fact that most program material was not tailored to one specific company. It couldn't be, of course, because of the many different companies being represented at most programs. This inherent condition required courses to present material in an over-view fashion which would enable participants to sample important management concepts, principles, theories and practices. It was the responsibility of each participant to process the material: i.e., sort out relevant information and skills, modify them if necessary and then apply them in a manner which would conform with the reality of the job back at the company.

Since I am now in a position to evaluate training results from the company viewpoint, I have recognized two major problems with enrolling employees in outside programs. One is the fact that companies vary greatly in terms of organizational structure, management practices, policies and procedures, and goals and

objectives. Modifying and applying the management concepts, principles, theories and practices presented in workshop settings in light of these dramatic variances means major obstacles for even the most enthusiastic supervisor or manager returning to the job.

The other major problem has to do with organizational change. Having one or two supervisors returning from a program with newly acquired skills and information isn't going to change the organization's management philosophy and practices at all. In fact, it usually results in the supervisor's tossing aside what he or she has acquired at a program because superiors and subordinates haven't changed *their* behavior through the same learning process. This is probably one of the most frustrating experiences for any supervisor who has recently attended a supervisory development program.

We took both of these factors into consideration when designing our own basic supervisory development program. We wanted a custom-designed program which taught supervisory skills within the context of our company's policies, procedures and practices. We wanted to present information which would be both company and job-related, hypothesizing that such a program would result in significant behavioral improvement of our supervisors.

AN IN-HOUSE MODEL

Planning

In the initial stages of our planning, we sought to gain the support and commitment of our senior management. This is an essential ingredient for the success of any program of this magnitude. Fortunately, our top management was sold on the concept before they were even approached. Once this commitment was confirmed, we interviewed officers, managers and supervisors in an attempt to establish factors which were important to the function of supervising employees.

The information we obtained was then analyzed and resulted in the formulation of the purpose, objectives and topics of our program. It was decided that our program format should be a workshop consisting of five and a half consecutive days, due to our supervisors' work schedules and their geographic dispersion.

Staffing

In staffing our program, we recruited primarily in-house instructors. These included officers and personnel staff specialists who were to present topics relating to company information, policies and procedures which would customize our program approach. One person from the training department and an outside consultant conferred in planning the presentation of other related management theories, concepts and principles in order to synthesize theory with practice. The final program staff consisted of one outside consultant, one training staff member and seven company personnel, including three vice-presidents. The president of our company has, by the way, addressed every group since we started this program in October, 1977. To date we have completed 10 groups of 20 to 24 participants each, or a total of 236 frontline supervisors and foremen.

Program Schedule

As mentioned previously, the program is presented in a workshop setting and runs for five and a half consecutive days. We start with dinner and an orientation Sunday evening, and we conclude Friday afternoon. There are evening sessions on Monday, Tuesday and Thursday. Topics presented during the week include: The Supervisor's Job at Metropolitan Edison; Planning, Organizing and Controlling; Controlling and Preventing Absenteeism; History and Organizational Structure of the Company; The Labor Agreement; The Grievance Procedure; Handling Discipline; Problem Solving and Decision Making; Employee Motivation; Company Position—Issues and Answers; EEO and Affirmative Action; Compensation and Benefits; Human Relations; Communication Skills; Developing a Leadership Style; and Training and Self-Development.

Program Evaluation

We made a study following the completion of the first four programs to determine the effectiveness of our efforts. In the study we looked at these 3 areas: 1) evaluation of the program by 88 supervisors who had completed it, 2) comparison of our program with similar programs conducted by colleges and universities and 3) any change in participants' on-the-job behavior after attending the program, as reported by their immediate supervisors.

The participants' evaluations of the program were overwhelmingly favorable. In 99% of the returns, the general comments ranged from very good to excellent. Many participants stated that it was the most meaningful course they had attended, and that included outside programs.

We also compared our program with similar courses offered by colleges, universities and other professional associations. This comparison revealed that our program contained more topics, presented by

more instructors, within an equal or greater time frame, for much less money. When comparing costs, we estimated that we were saving as much as 60 to 85% by conducting these programs in-house!

Although we were impressed with these findings, we still wanted to know if there was any improvement back on the job. To find out, we sent a questionnaire to each supervisor's superior, asking him or her to indicate any observed behavioral change they noticed in the supervisor following attendance at the program. The questionnaire contained fourteen specific areas which related to the program, such as problem solving and decision making, dealing with absenteeism, planning and organizing, and developing subordinates. Improvements, if observed, were to be reported in percentiles for each of the fourteen items.

The results of this survey indicated an average of 20% improvement in the overall performance of each supervisor who attended the program. Although this method of evaluation is not empirically pure, it did give us a strong indication that significant positive behavioral change did indeed occur as a result of the program.

Follow-up

I am happy to report that this is the beginning and not the end of our story. In addition to our plans to have every supervisor attend the program, we have developed and implemented a similar approach for managers. Our plans call for having every manager attend a similar program by the end of 1979. Additionally, there will probably be follow-up sessions, two- or three-day seminars covering timely management topics.

ULTIMATE BENEFITS

In summarizing, the benefits of designing and implementing in-house supervisory and management development programs are as follows:

- *They can be tailored to the company and the job:* They provide an opportunity to synthesize management theories and principles with company goals, policies and practices. This, in turn, provides immediate and direct application of required skills and information to the supervisor's or manager's job.
- *The organizational impact is pervasive:* Organizational and management improvement comes about through extensive and thorough participant involvement. If all supervisors and managers participate in the same or similar programs, the

likelihood of significant improvement throughout the organization increases dramatically.

- *In-house programming is cost-effective:* In analyzing costs, we have estimated that we can provide training for twice as many supervisors and managers by conducting in-house programs as compared with enrolling them in programs outside the company.
- *It can provide senior management participation:* In planning, designing and presenting the program, senior managers usually welcome the opportunity to participate. Whether they suggest, recommend, approve or actually present program material, their involvement adds an important dimension to the success of the program and assures participants of top-level support.
- *Organizational problems can be identified:* Conducting in-house programs can be instructive to management as well as to participants. Through our programs we have identified, and corrected, some inconsistencies and misinterpretations of our policies, procedures and practices.
- *Company unity is solidified:* Supervisors and managers from various parts of the company have an opportunity to meet each other, in most cases, for the first time. During the after class sessions,

they also have a chance to discuss mutual problems, thereby reinforcing the fact that everyone is on the same team, even though functions may differ significantly.

- *Employee morale is boosted:* Giving supervisors and managers the opportunity to interact with senior management has obvious morale benefits. For the first time, many supervisors have an opportunity to discuss issues, problems and goals with company officers on a personal basis.

We at Met-Ed continue to encourage our employees to attend outside programs sponsored by colleges, universities and professional organizations. We do believe, however, that the development of our supervisors and managers should include a common instructional base provided through basic programs designed and presented in-house. You don't need outside management experts to develop and conduct this kind of training. Most personnel departments have staff members who can competently plan, organize and conduct supervisory and management development programs in-house. I hope the example of what we have done at Metropolitan Edison provides some instructive assistance to those companies who want to begin such a program.

Career Development Puts Training in Its Place

by Beverly Kaye

TRAINING SHOULD BE MORE THAN A PLACEBO FOR UNDEFINED ILLS

For many, if not most employees, the opportunity to participate in training is somewhat analogous to the opportunity to take a sabbatical. It sounds like a good idea, but what would—or should—I do with it? Is it a time to relax, a time to learn, or perhaps a time to just get away from the routine of the job? Various individuals approach training—and sabbaticals—with vastly differing degrees of need and goal orientation. If the crucial question of "What am I aiming for?" is unresolved, training is little more than a placebo for undefined ills. Yet organizations tend to plunge ahead with training programs because, after all, they seem like "the thing to do."

The challenge for those who make decisions about employee training is to move it beyond the realm of "it might do some good and it can't do any harm." An important means for accomplishing this is to approach training as a strategy for individual career development that will benefit both the individual and the organization. If the link with career development is forged, training is put in a framework of employee goals and organizational human resource needs. With such linkage, both the trainee and the organization can make relevant decisions about the best use of training time and financial commitment.

WHAT ARE WE DOING HERE ANYWAY?

Why is it important to link training and career development? The need becomes clear if a majority of the following questions are answered with "no":

1. Has the organization substantially changed its training offerings in the past four years?
2. When changes have been made, has new training stemmed from employee needs, as opposed to general trends or pet ideas from the top?
3. Do we regularly schedule employees for surveys that can help us assess training needs?
4. Do employees and the organization have clear goals for the training that is undertaken?
5. Do employees have concrete plans for future professional growth that are reflected in their training opportunities?
6. Do employees know who to approach for counseling about training programs?
7. Are managers and supervisors knowledgeable about the organization's training programs and policies?
8. Do we conduct follow-up studies to assess the results of training?
9. Do we monitor who receives what training and determine how that training might be utilized by the organization?
10. Do our systems for compensation, transfer, promotion, etc., link into a system for monitoring training?

THREE TRADITIONAL APPROACHES

If the majority of your answers were in the negative, your organization may have adhered to one of three traditional (but not always effective) approaches to training: training as "nuts and bolts," training as "smorgasbord," or training as "reward." Although each of these concepts can offer appropriate training for certain circumstances, they fall short of achieving maximum human resource development and top return on expenditure of training dollars.

Training as Nuts and Bolts. Training that is directly aimed at skill building for the current job—generally through classroom instruction or an apprenticeship—is often essential for the organization and employee. Such training generally has the advantage of readily measurable results in terms of increased task abilities.

Eventually, however, employees who learn their jobs will wonder "What next?" Organizations that have not thought through this next step may find that they have put dollars into training and now are losing their investment. Newly trained employees may leave the organization due to lack of sufficient challenge in their jobs. If these employees are capable, the organization can benefit by expanding their job-

skill training to include meaningful career development training.

Training as Smorgasbord. This approach is common among many organizations. Here, training is viewed simply as a worthy fringe benefit, with some learning value on the side. Employees are offered a smorgasbord of possibilities ranging from in-house programs to courses at nearby colleges. They may select their own favorite training pastime within reasonable budgetary and time constraints. A well-balanced training diet, however, like an athlete's diet for building muscles, is bound to produce more effective growth than the "sample everything and anything" approach. By specifically targeting training to individual and organizational career development needs, there is less waste and more payoff for both the individual and the organization.

Training as Reward. Conferences, tuition reimbursement, advanced learning seminars, and other educational benefits may be granted as rewards for performance or promotion to top levels. Once again, however, decisions about training may be based on factors unrelated to organizational and individual needs, or future benefits. Rewarding through training can be a valuable strategy for organizational altruism, but it is generally less valuable in terms of the development of organizational resources.

A NO FRILLS APPROACH

The foregoing training approaches can become more effective when placed in the context of a planned, comprehensive career development program that integrates ends and means. Carefully planned career development programs give employees an opportunity to select training that contributes directly to future goals and immediate needs. It also allows the organization to assess, build, and utilize its work force by means of a productive match between individual capabilities and organizational tasks. When training is viewed as part of career development, it is no longer seen as an end in itself.

A traditional training program might be initiated in the following way: "We need an update on new civil rights regulations, so let's send some supervisors and personnel representatives to a seminar." A more expanded version of that statement, which reflects a career development orientation, might be: "We need an update on new civil rights regulations, so let's determine who would desire and need to use that information now, as well as in the future, and seek a program that's relevant to this situation. When they've completed the program, we'll give them projects—maybe even form an internal civil rights task force—to use their training and help us improve our civil rights status."

Thus, a career development link to training allows an organization to look backwards and forwards—to decide who is trained in what areas, how they are trained, and what use will be made of the training.

Because training in the career development context must take a long-term view and account for a vast array of individual needs, it is important to look beyond traditional methods of classrooms and seminars. Formal learning settings are only one resource. A full developmental effort should recognize that essential learning also can occur through informal processes. A career development program can garner resources from three categories:

Training and Education.   The resource here is programs that are designed to teach specific skills and capacities in topical areas—from technical abilities to interpersonal competencies. These programs may be conducted as on-site sessions or off-site courses and special programs.

Experience-based Training.   This category includes development that is truly "learning by doing," through on-the-job training, special project assignments, job rotation, and other opportunities for new experiences under the organizational umbrella.

Support-guided Development.   The third category includes formal and informal arrangements that encourage sharing of experiences and knowledge among individuals, such as mentor arrangements, professional organizations, instructional teams, and informal networks.

Career development program participants generally need some assistance in recognizing that resources outside the bounds of traditional training sessions are available to help them meet their goals. The organization may need to not only refine its existing offerings in terms of employee career development plans, but also to establish systems for informal learning through mentors, special project teams, and other arrangements.

A GREATER REALM OF CHOICES

Of course, this expanded view of training resources presents a greater realm of choices for employees who

may already be confused about what strategies will best implement their action plans. For example, should skills in writing job descriptions be learned by attending a community college course that touches on that area, by seeking out a personnel department mentor who has that responsibility, or by asking to take on a special project of revising job descriptions within one small division?

Some questions employees can ask themselves to help narrow the field of choices are:

1. Exactly what are my options for acquiring this skill or knowledge, both within and outside the organization? (Write down as many as possible—even those that seem a bit far-fetched—trying for one or more from each of the major categories listed above.)
2. Are any of these completely precluded by restrictions of time, cost, organizational policies, etc.?
3. Do I know enough about the options to make choices concerning them? If not, how can I find out and to whom can I go for advice?
4. How do the options rank with one another concerning the amount of time involved and the amount of potential progress toward my goals?
5. Do some options put me in a better position than others to eventually use the learning I will be gaining?
6. Thinking back to valuable knowledge and skills I've acquired in the past, do I seem to develop these more effectively through formal training, experience, or guidance from others?

DEVELOP INFORMAL RESOURCES

In assisting the employee to make choices, the training professional needs to be prepared to present information about both in-house and external resources, and to creatively develop informal resources that match employee needs with appropriate experiences and individuals. Some areas that are often overlooked or underused as fertile training grounds are reviewed below:

On-the-job Training.   When this route is selected, it is essential that supervisors and other on-the-job trainers be well versed in coaching and demonstration abilities. In addition, a specific training period should be determined, along with targets for competencies to be acquired and potential movement for trainees. (Example: An advertising copy writer may be able to learn media buying by assisting a person who has that responsibility, and by gradually taking on a greater portion of the work.)

Job Rotation. The movement of employees to various tasks at set intervals can be used to closely acquaint an employee with different areas of a particular operation, to cross-train in several skill areas, to assess employee capacities for various types of work, to prepare employees for advancement, or to provide opportunities for diversity and movement. Job rotation can be formally structured by the organization for specific groups of employees, or it can be less formally undertaken by individuals who have identified temporary movement as the best way to gain understanding and skills necessary for particular career goals. It is an especially valuable resource for employees whose goals indicate a need for exposure to a variety of management techniques, operational skills, and personal contacts. (Example: A supervisor in the purchasing department may rotate to the accounting department to assess and broaden financial skills.)

Special Projects. Valuable experience-based training can occur when individuals or teams take on temporary projects outside their normal work routine. Special projects can range from one person's research into a new budgeting system, to team problem solving to restructure paper flow. Generally, such projects are relatively easy to initiate without formal organizational policy setting or financial commitment. The results are as rewarding in providing immediate organizational benefits (information, decisions about change, strategies for increased productivity, etc.) as they are in contributing to individual development. (Example: An administrative assistant desiring to move to another department may gain access and knowledge by serving on an interdepartmental team exploring the realignment of several staff divisions.)

Mentor Relations. The mentor/protege relationship helps individuals gain direct access to advice, information, and counseling that can contribute to attainment of a career goal. The mentor arrangement can be informal, with mentors and proteges adopting one another because the relationship is comfortable. Or it can be formalized when the organization establishes a pool of volunteer mentors and matches them with proteges— usually employees who are relatively new to their jobs. These relationships are substantially strengthened by the career development process, since a protege who has set clear goals will better know what to seek in a mentor, and the mentor who knows a protege's goals will be in a better position to assist. (Example: A clerk whose goal is to become a paralegal secretary may gain useful advice and information from a mentor who is a lawyer in the general counsel's office.)

Groups and Associations. Professional associations and groups directed to member development and learning present such a substantial resource that many organizations finance employees' membership dues. Their value ranges from the personal contacts and seminars available to the direct experience and learning provided. In addition to direct and indirect skill development, such associations are good sources for interchanges of ideas and examples of how various tasks and problems are handled in different settings. (Example: A first-line supervisor who wants to advance to higher management can acquire skills for making presentations and handling meetings through membership in a public speaking group.)

It is also useful to further examine the resources themselves. Those discussed here offer varying degrees of structure and organizational involvement, which may indicate appropriateness to various employees and goals (see Figure 1). While it is useful for the organization to offer a healthy mix of options, it is also important that employees select a mix. Using only college courses or in-house seminars as developmental strategies is unlikely to provide the comprehensive learning required of a career development effort.

AN EFFECTIVE LINK

The link between training and career development will be more effective if each of the key players meets their individual responsibilities, as follows:

1. Top management is responsible for making policy decisions about the career development program committing organizational resources, and providing opportunities.
2. Training and human resource professionals are responsible for providing information, tools, and guidance that enable employees to plan and implement their career development, and for acting as program liaisons to top management.
3. Immediate supervisors are responsible for providing the first line of support, advice, and feedback.
4. Individual employees are responsible for initiating their own career development, undertaking training and development, and implementing results.

The training professional wears many hats and may be called upon to initiate and administer the entire process. The training professional defines and refines developmental resources to reflect employee goals and needs, provides information and guidance concerning resource choices, and establishes systems that monitor

FIGURE 1
Analyzing Training Options

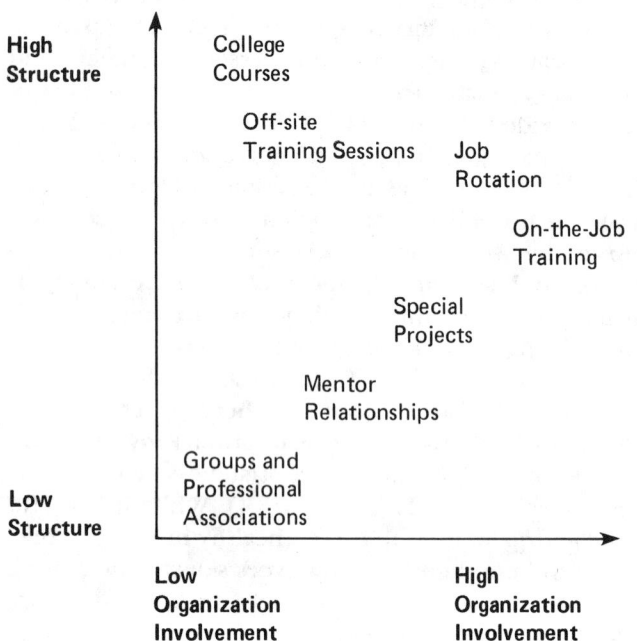

training results and provide for the utilization of new skills. At the same time, the training professional is informing and updating others in the organization, and working with those who may be called upon to counsel or coach career development program participants—from supervisors to mentors.

The training role emphasizes facilitating, coordinating, and monitoring, while taking care not to take too much responsibility out of the hands of employees themselves. Employees must take on the responsibilities of initiation and implementation, including seeking advice and information, determining the fit between developmental resources and career goals, demonstrating new capabilities, and self-nominating for tasks that are preparatory to career movement.

Without this clear separation of responsibilities, the training professional may find that employees participating in career development simply "go along for the ride," but leave the driving to others. When this happens, employees simply react to others' ideas and directions, without really taking charge of their own plans and actions, and, ultimately, without a commitment that assures career movement.

Figure 2 indicates the roles of the training professional that involve career development participants, others in the organization, or both. It demonstrates that the responsibilities of this position are not limited to working with participants, and do not include those things that participants could and should do on their own.

A FAIR RETURN ON INVESTMENT

Appropriately enough, most organizations are sticklers for insisting on a fair return on investment. Measurement of any investment in human resources—such as training—is fairly elusive, however. Yet there are ways of quantifying indicators. If the bottom line concerns results, rather than simply completion of a training activity, the career development link to training is likely to enhance the chances of a favorable return.

There are several ways of measuring the return on investment:

Earnings Orientation. One common method of measuring return on investment is to compare changes in company earnings to changes in personnel expenses (including training costs). If earnings increase by greater amounts than expenses during the timeframe of a career development program, it may seem successful. However, confounding variables operating during the same timeframe may make it impossible to link earnings changes strictly to training and career development.

Human Changes Orientation. Another means of measuring return is to assess changes in areas likely to be influenced by career development and training. Some areas to look for include reduced turnover, improved performance (measured differently, depending on tasks), and reduced grievances.

Time Orientation. Time spent—or wasted—is a readily measurable commodity that also can be useful in evaluating return on investment. Time might be influenced by developmental programs, and measured at before and after intervals, in areas such as time spent recruiting new employees from outside versus inside the organization, time taken off the job to attend training, time spent in training new employees versus moving existing employees to new jobs, and time wasted due to turnover.

Close program monitoring can increase the ability to measure return on investment, and will usually influence the return itself. By knowing what is taking place at all times, and by revising and correcting as progress occurs, the training professional can position resources to best fit the organization's goals. The monitoring system required is one that tracks individual goals, plans, and progress, while at the same time tracking organizational opportunities and the potential for employee movement that suits organization needs.

FIGURE 2
Roles of the Training Professional

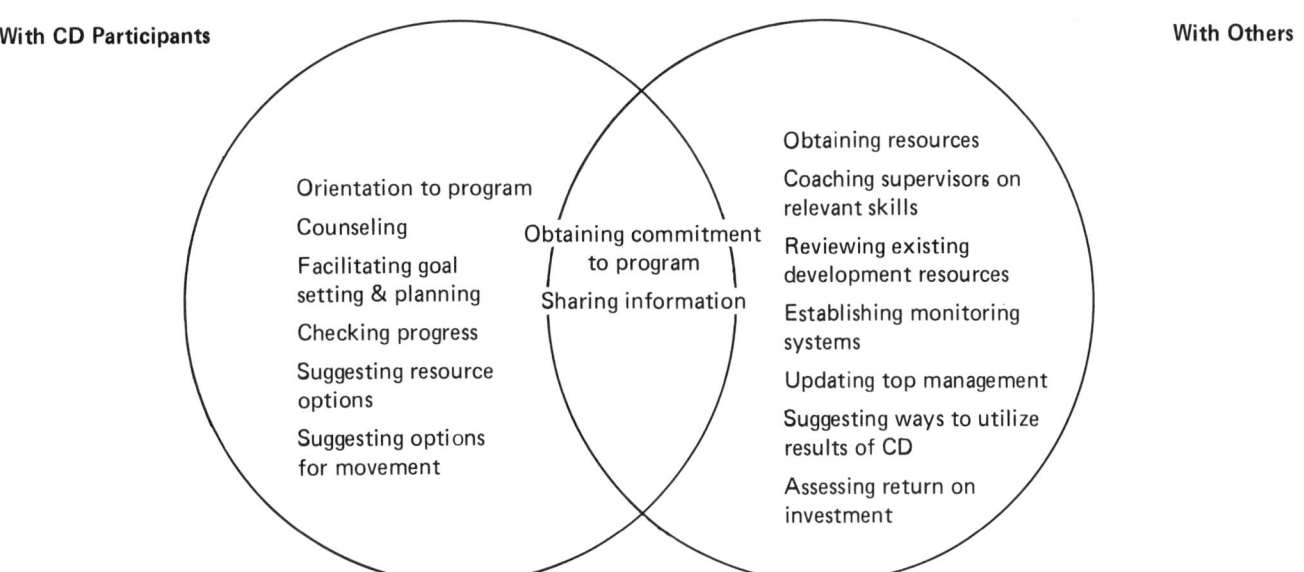

If training programs are to bring a fair return on investment for the organization and for the individual, then a link to career development is vital. Training programs that tie directly to the developmental needs of individuals will move those individuals towards their professional goals. As more time is spent in carefully planned and selected training events of all kinds, instead of training "for its own sake," training will become more cost effective, and individuals, managers, and training professionals will reap the rewards.

What Is Organization Development

by Michael Beer

Using the conceptual framework of congruence, organization development may be seen as a process for diagnosing organizational problems by looking for incongruencies between environment, structures, processes, and people. Following are some examples of how lack of fit arises between these components and how organization development deals with it.

An organization that has enjoyed a technological edge and a secure position in its market finds that, owing to decisions made by its competitors to introduce new products, it is operating in a more competitive environment. Previously the organization had been able to function effectively within a bureaucratic framework of centralized decision making and authority, fairly explicit rules and regulations, tight financial control, and a traditional hierarchical structure. Now the organization finds its structures, procedures, policies, and top-down management approach do not seem to work as well.

Poor fit exists between the organization's structures, processes, and its external business environment. For the first time, the organization needs to be more innovative, respond more quickly to changes in its market, and develop new products and technology. There is general frustration in the organization over an inability to get decisions made quickly. As they attempt to develop new products, top management is frustrated by continued and unexpected problems. There is conflict between groups who need to coordinate their activities. Top management finds too much of its time taken up by these conflicts.

Top management seeks the help of an OD specialist to perform a diagnosis of the organization. This specialist suggests that top management commission a task force to help with conducting interviews and administering a questionnaire. Information from these sources reveals that many of the frustrations are due to an inappropriate focus for decision making. All decisions being made at the top by a few individuals does not fit with the need for more rapid decisions. The task force's feedback of its findings and the resulting discussions lead to a plan by top management to change the formal structure of the organization to achieve more coordinated decision making at lower levels on new product development. Project teams are formed to coordinate new product development at lower levels.

These groups report directly to the top of the organization. People on the teams are evaluated by both the team leader and their functional bosses. The top group sets time aside for sharpening its strategic plan. All of these changes are announced widely and are followed by numerous meetings of the new project teams. Functional groups which must work together but are currently in conflict meet to resolve differences, and top management spends some time away from work with the OD consultant to discuss their roles in the new organization.

The organization has changed its more traditional functional structure to one which allows more coordination and decision making at the level where information exists. The new structure requires that individuals in the organization adopt less formalistic attitudes about management and that they be able to confront conflict more fully. New structures and processes are adopted despite the fact that many people in the organization cannot yet function in these new ways. Meetings, training, and other intervention methods are all aimed at helping them change or helping them find other positions if they do not want to change. These activities associated with managing the organizational change take place over a two-year period.

While we would expect OD efforts to move organizations to less bureaucratic structures because of the more dynamic environment in which organizations find themselves, OD can legitimately lead to centralization of decisions, more traditional organizational forms, and more directive management styles.

A small company headed by an inventor has developed a new product that it has just begun to manufacture. As the company enters the manufacturing phase, problems develop. The people in manufacturing become extremely frustrated as their manufacturing schedules and plans are changed by the engineering department. These changes are made without discussion with the purchasing department or the production manager. Customers become dissatisfied as promised delivery dates for the new product are missed. Manufacturing people are frustrated by their inability to get the work done efficiently and to deliver the products on time. They are particularly upset by the president's support of engineering and his unwillingness to provide structure and direction for the fledgling organization.

At a series of meetings in which interview findings are fed back to management by an OD consultant,

266

decisions are made. These include: formalized procedures for product changes and for coordinating changes with purchasing and customer service, clarification of how decisions on new products are to be made, and finally a series of personal counseling sessions between the OD consultant and the president regarding the need for clear direction. These and other changes move the organization from a loosely run R&D organization to a more highly structured manufacturing organization with more firm procedures, rules, and chains of command.

Organization development can also deal with problems at lower levels in the organizations where technology, guided by traditional industrial engineering principles, has created a work environment that is not congruent with the needs of more highly educated workers.

A plant manager asks for help from an OD consultant in solving turnover and absenteeism problems on the plant floor. Discussion indicates that morale is low and productivity is down. A task force of union and management people is formed with the help of a behavioral scientist to diagnose the problems and propose solutions. Interviews show that people find their work dissatisfying and unchallenging. With the involvement of additional task forces and help from professionals, jobs are redesigned to include more responsibility and information about quality and productivity. In some cases, groups of workers are given the responsibility for running a production line on their own. The span of control for each supervisor is increased and his role changes. To support these changes, supervisors receive training, coaching, and counseling in how to manage this new situation.

These examples of OD applications illustrate the diversity of directions an OD effort can take, the variety of techniques that fall under the umbrella of OD, and the many situations in which it can be applied. But the aim is always to surface concerns, attitudes, and views not normally discussed. Plans for action and change, based on the information surfaced and the problems identified, follow. This process is aimed at bridging the gap in communication and influence between those with less power and those with more, and between people who do not normally collaborate though they have common goals. The result is a more open organization in which effectiveness is under continuing scrutiny.

Organization development may begin because a manager senses problems that block organizational performance or employee satisfaction. Or it may begin because a manager wants to further improve his organization. Sometimes, organization development begins when a new organization is formed and there exists an opportunity to shape it in advance. Regardless of how it begins, the process described above ideally encompasses the organization as a total system. This means a variety of dimensions—individual performance, interpersonal relations, policies, supervision, organization and job structure, planning, communication, pay systems, and decision making—may all be examined and changed.

Organization development is ideally implemented by a manager knowledgeable and skillful in its use. Often, however, an organization may call in an OD consultant for help. He may be from inside or outside the firm, but he usually has had training in the behavioral sciences and in techniques of OD.

The consultant acts as a catalyst in helping organizational members define problems, develop alternative solutions, implement changes, and evaluate the effects. He supplies techniques for carrying out the process of change while at the same time providing the expertise needed to solve human problems. The consultant moves change along but does *not* control the change process. Indeed, he also trains members to do their own OD so that the organization can carry on without him.

To develop an organization, a number of roles are required. Someone must recognize the need for change and initiate the process. Someone must collect data and diagnose the organization. Someone must have expertise about organizational structures and processes which could increase effectiveness. Someone must be knowledgeable about various strategies and approaches to change. Someone must implement meetings, training programs, and other interventions needed to move change along. Someone must lead by setting expectations and modeling new behaviors.

While in some instances one person, the manager, carries out all these roles, in most organization development efforts the roles are mixed in different ways between two or more people. For example, recognizing the need for change and catalyzing the process itself is often the role of the manager, but internal staff people or outsiders could, and sometimes do, take on that role. Leading by setting expectations and modeling is usually the role of the manager, but occasionally these tasks are carried out by a staff specialist or outside consultant. While collecting data, diagnosing, and implementing the changes are often the responsibility of a staff specialist or consultant, they are sometimes carried out by the manager leading the organization.

Three different terms—*manager, change agent,* and *consultant*—will be used in this book to refer to individuals who might be involved in carrying out the various roles associated with change. Because of the many different ways in which the roles are mixed between individuals, the terms will be used somewhat interchangeably. The book's intention is to convey what is known about the total process of organization change and development. Who carries out various parts of the process, while of significance, is less important than a full appreciation of what has to happen for an organization to move successfully through major transitions. Nevertheless, to help clarify who typically carries out various change roles, the book will be consistent in the terms applied to different roles. The term *manager* will be used to refer to the person heading an organization. The term *change agent* is the most general term and will be used to refer to the individual, staff specialist, consultant, or manager, or a team of these individuals responsible for initiating and managing the organizational change effort. The term *consultant* will be used to refer to an internal or external organization development specialist, usually an applied behavioral scientist or a personnel specialist, who brings knowledge in organizational diagnosis, alternative organizational approaches, change strategy, and intervention methods.

OD DEFINED

This description of organizational development leads to a formal definition of OD that will guide us in the remainder of the book.

OD is a system-wide process of data collection, diagnosis, action planning, intervention, and evaluation aimed at: (1) enhancing congruence between organizational structure, process, strategy, people, and culture; (2) developing new and creative organizational solutions; and (3) developing the organization's self-renewing capacity. It occurs through collaboration of organizational members working with a change agent using behavioral science theory, research, and technology.

The material in this chapter has tried to convey something about the uniqueness of organization development compared with other approaches to organization improvement. Because what distinguishes OD from other approaches helps to define it more clearly, a list of its basic tenets follows:

1. *Organization development seeks to create self-directed change to which people are committed.*

Obtaining collaboration of people in the change is the means for obtaining commitment. Less participative approaches to change aimed at improving congruence are also used in organization development in situations which require rapid change or in which employees do not have the capacity to participate.

2. *Organization development is a system-wide change effort.* It starts with the assumption that organizations are complex systems and that its subunits, levels of management, and components (process, people, structures, etc.) are all interdependent. Changing one means that change in the others is inevitable.

3. *Organization development typically places equal emphasis on solving immediate problems and long-term development of an adaptive organization.* The latter objective is met by developing an organization in which individuals are encouraged and have competence to confront problems. However, change efforts which are aimed at only one of these objectives are also considered organization development so long as the goals are based on a valid diagnosis of the organization's needs.

4. *Organization development places more emphasis than other approaches on a collaborative process of data collection, diagnosis and action for arriving at problem solutions.* The assumption is that unless the process is "right," there will not only be low commitment to planned change but managers will not learn to use the OD process.

5. *Organization development often leads to new organizational arrangements and relationships that break with traditional bureaucratic patterns.*

6. *In organization development efforts, the change agent brings two types of competencies to the organization.* He brings *knowledge* about organization design, management practice, and interpersonal dynamics. He also brings *skills* in working with individuals and groups.

Starting and Managing System-Wide Change

by Michael Beer

WHERE SHOULD OD START?

A manager or OD consultant who would like to introduce OD to an organization and see it spread and encompass the whole organization, faces the choice of where to start change activities. Should the change begin at the top of the organization and work its way down? Should it start at the bottom and work its way up? Or, should the change start somewhere in the middle and work in both directions? Yet another consideration is with what kind of organizational unit is it best to start. Finally, what kind of problem is a good starting point for an OD effort?

Evidence indicates that change occurs and becomes relatively permanent when a number of important conditions are present in the target organization. The simultaneous presence of these conditions creates a "window" through which a change effort can move successfully (Franklin, 1976; Myerseth, 1977). The presence of only one or even two of these conditions may be sufficient to get a change started, but may not be enough to allow it to become institutionalized. If this is true, then the selection of the first change target is perhaps the most important decision for the long-term success of OD. If the first OD effort is not successful, the probability of success in other parts of the organization is significantly diminished.

Key Managers Must Be Dissatisfied

Management's dissatisfaction with the current state of affairs is an absolutely necessary condition for a successful long-term organizational improvement effort. The whole thrust of the entry and contracting process is to ascertain if sufficient dissatisfaction and commitment exist to warrant investment of change resources in an OD effort. Consequently, OD should start in that part of the organization where the best OD contract can be negotiated. Such a contract is one in which management is able to identify specific problems and to commit themselves to becoming involved in the OD process. OD contracts in which the interventionist is given license to work with any managers he can interest in OD or on a problem of his choosing, are likely to lead to failure.

Experience suggests that it is important to understand which of two major sources of dissatisfaction has triggered an interest in OD. Dissatisfaction may arise out of many internal and external pressures. These pressures and the crisis that they create comprise a *deficiency agenda* for OD. Under these conditions, OD is directed at eliminating deficiencies in organizational efficiency and effectiveness. However, dissatisfaction may also arise out of management's desire to introduce innovative and progressive approaches to management. This *growth agenda* for OD is motivated by management's design to develop a new alignment between social system components closer to their values or capable of producing even greater efficiency, effectiveness, and health.

Most organization development efforts are triggered by both sources of dissatisfaction and include both agendas (Franklin, 1976). However, of the two, a deficiency agenda is more likely to have the attention of top management, lead to a good OD contract, and produce an early success. These are the preconditions that will lead to perceptions that OD can improve organizational effectiveness. The result will be its acceptance throughout the whole organization. For these reasons, OD should probably start with an organizational unit that has an important deficiency agenda.

Finally, the level of dissatisfaction with deficiencies in the organization may also be an important factor in choosing the first OD target. Very high levels of dissatisfaction may create so much anxiety that managers are incapable of entering a process of inquiry prior to taking action. Under these circumstances, they are not open to diagnosing problems and learning about new approaches. They tend to want to take control and are not willing to involve others in organization development. Therefore, a moderate amount of dissatisfaction may be the optimum for starting an OD effort.

The Top Manager Must Be Committed and Lead

A system-wide organization development effort must have the intellectual and emotional commitment of the target unit's top manager. Without this commitment the manager cannot provide leadership for the change effort. He cannot model new behavior and attitudes, and he cannot adequately confront traditional wisdom

269

in the organization. In a period of transition, when traditional norms and structures are weakened, such leadership is crucial to the development of change momentum.

It will be possible to obtain commitment from the top manager if the direction of OD and its process are consistent with his basic values and assumptions about management. This does not mean that the manager must fully understand the new approach to management or be completely skillful in it. If he were, there would probably be no need for an organization development effort. It does mean that at a fairly fundamental level, OD goals and process are consistent with the manager's core values and beliefs about life and management.

For these reasons, the first OD efforts in a large multiunit organization should start with a unit whose key manager is friendly to the goals, process, and values of OD. Often managers support OD verbally but their behavior makes it clear that they will have difficulty with a collaborative process of inquiry and actions. The change agent must make an early assessment of the top manager on this issue before significant resources are committed to an OD effort.

Slack Resources Must Exist

Organization change and development requires "slack." That is, additional human and financial resources will have to be made available to execute a change plan while at the same time continuing with day-to-day operations. These slack resources are required to pay for training or consulting services, to staff the organization deeply enough so managers can have time and energy to learn new ways, and to provide a financial cushion if and when performance drops during the period of transition. Slack can be developed by improving the performance of the organization, by borrowing or budgetary allowances, or by lowering financial performance standards.

The need for slack resources, resources that the organization is not pressed to use elsewhere (other investments, contributions to corporate profits or dividends), suggests that whenever possible OD should start with an organizational unit that has these resources. Unfortunately, many organizations that need organization development do not have them. For example, a division of a large corporation found it difficult to budget for sufficient change resources. It could not obtain agreement from corporate headquarters for performance goals that would allow a significant investment in organization development. With pressures for profits, there was insufficient time and money for OD, people became disillusioned, and the thrust of organization development was blunted.

The years of delay in achieving an OD success slowed and endangered the spread of OD to other parts of the corporation.

Naturally, the question of resources presents a dilemma. Organizations that have such resources are generally not dissatisfied and do not need OD. Those who do not have the resources can't fund such efforts. A system-wide change effort should start with a unit that is dissatisfied with its performance but also is able to free-up sufficient resources to mount a reasonably effective OD effort.

Political Support Must Exist

The need for slack resources also highlights the issue of political support for the top manager of the target unit. If he is to obtain the budgetary allowances and support needed for organization development, the key manager must be in a strong position with the executives above his level. These executives need not have an intellectual and emotional commitment to organization development, but they must support the key manager and his OD efforts. Such support may exist because the key manager has credibility or it may exist because the next level managers understand and agree with the goals and values of OD, but the support must be there or be developed.

No top manager can deal with potential resistance to innovations unless he feels secure with those who control his fate. Nor can a change agent be effective for long without an opportunity to discuss his efforts with those above him. Such discussions provide the guidance and acknowledgment that he needs to sustain his thrust as a change agent, when unanticipated problems develop and support is needed. For example, many of the new plant innovations in work design have resulted in a slower learning curve than expected. If upper management pressures the key manager unduly during the critical start-up period, or if the key manager is removed for unfounded reasons, regression in organization development is likely. Moreover, political support is needed to obtain the cooperation of staff and line managers who do not report to the manager of the change target, but whose support may be needed to introduce change in the target organization.

Political support is more than a one-time directive to change or a one-time agreement to support innovation in management. The managers above the change agent must be willing to actively support him in the face of inevitable conflict and political infighting that surrounds most major change programs. It becomes important for the change agent to recognize early whether political support exists. The frequency and quality of communication about organization development between the change agent and upper levels is the best indicator of support. A distant and aloof stance is the best indicator that change is being tolerated but not supported. Case 1 contains an account of interchanges between a change agent and higher levels which indicates inadequate political support.

It is interesting to note that OD efforts in one large decentralized corporation were concentrated in several divisions and groups of the company and were almost nonexistent in others (Myerseth, 1977). Not surprisingly, the upper level managers in those parts of the company that did not have many OD efforts, were known to be unsympathetic to OD.

Change Resources Must Match the Size and Kind of Change

As a change effort unfolds it requires the time and energy of managers and the increasing support of consultants. Interventions must be made and followed-up. Some individuals may require counseling, others training. As unexpected problems arise, consulting help will be required. Finally, successful changes generally stimulate additional and more intense interest in organization development.

For a change momentum to develop, sufficient change agent resources must support OD initiatives. Furthermore, intervention skills and orientation of the change agents must be appropriate to the kinds of problems the organization is working on. Thus change agents should select the first target for organization development on the basis of the kind and amount of resources available. The problem should not be beyond the skill of the change agents nor should the size of the change target be larger than the available resources can handle.

It's unlikely that most corporations will be able to maintain an internal staff of OD specialists who have a full range of skills. Furthermore, organizations who are just getting started with OD may not have internal OD resources. Thus, when all the conditions for change are present, but *internal* resources are not, external consultants can be brought in. The external consultants can provide the skills and the effort needed to get things started, but they will have to train an internal staff to follow-up and support new initiatives. The timely availability of trained internal resources is critical to the successful evolution of an OD program.

The Organization Development Window

Where should OD start? It should start in that part of the organization that comes closest to meeting all of

CASE 1

The following account, provided by a top administrative officer in the State Department, indicates inadequate political support for an OD effort in the State Department that ultimately faltered when he, the change agent, retired.

One of the first things that happened to me was a summons from Robert Kennedy, the Attorney General, to come to his office. There was no greeting, no small talk, and no chance for response by me except, "yes, sir" to his cryptic monologue. He said:

First of all, get your loyalties straight. No matter whom you think you work for, the President appointed you and he is your boss. He will expect your absolute loyalty. Second, get your job straight. The State Department must be made to be loyal and responsive to the President. It must become more positive and proactive. It must be made to assume a leadership position in the Foreign Affairs Community. Your job is to make this happen. And thirdly, do you know how to make this happen . . . ?

While I was trying to think up an answer, he held up his hand to silence my response and added, "You will make it happen by giving orders and firing people who don't produce." The discussion was ended, and although I had numerous calls from him later in which he asked for this and demanded that, I never saw him in person again.

It is interesting that neither the President, who appointed me, nor Dean Rusk, who was my nominal boss, ever discussed with me whether this was my primary objective or how I might best pursue it. Neither outlined a goal or a program. Rusk's favorite admonishment to his subordinates' inquiries for direction and feedback was: "Work up to the horizons of your job. If you get too far out I'll pull you back." In the six years that I worked for him he never "pulled me back." He never gave me guidance, directions, or goals, nor did he give me much support for my efforts or acknowledgment for my accomplishments. There was one other bit of ominous warning in the beginning, when he once told his staff, "I won't support you if you become embroiled in bureaucratic dog fights with other agencies."

At the time Rusk's warning didn't bother me; neither did the absence of direction. Thinking back on those early days of my new job I now wonder at the fact that I accepted the Robert Kennedy direction so calmly. His authoritarian recipe for bringing about change didn't seem to bother me at all. Having risen from the ranks, I felt that I not only knew the problems of the Department but also the answers, and I soon set in motion the changes for achieving the results that I had in mind.

From W. J. Crockett, "Introducing Change to a Government Agency" in P. H. Mirvis and D. N. Berg, *Failures in Organization Development and Change* (New York: Wiley-Interscience, 1977), pp. 113–114. Reprinted by permission of John Wiley & Sons, Inc.

these major conditions for a successful change effort. When these conditions exist, the organization development window may be said to be open. The entry and contracting process determines the extent to which this window is open.

If all of the conditions described above are met, then obviously the place to start an OD effort is at the top. Unless the top man is in a weak political position with other key executives or the board of directors, starting at the top eliminates the problem of political support for the change and increases the chances that resources will be made available. However, starting at the top without all of the preconditions present can create a very visible failure from which there may not be a recovery for a long time.

In most organizations, however, the change window is not open at the top. In these organizations, OD consultants or personnel specialists will have to look for open change windows at the bottom or middle of the organization. Experience suggests that these are likely to be found in subunits which operate in rapidly changing market and technological environments, or in situations where people's needs and expectations are changing. These units are likely to be struggling with problems of motivation or coordination for which there are known and effective intervention methods.

However, starting at the bottom or middle is not without its risks. The first OD efforts must generally start without political support since managers who understand the process have not yet risen to the top. Under these circumstances, the possibility of developing a viable system-wide organization development effort rests on the hope that managers who have experienced OD and support it will rise to the top.

MANAGING SYSTEM-WIDE OD EFFORTS

Where OD should start in a large organization is only the first important strategic decision. The second concerns sustaining changes in that unit over time. The third concerns spreading innovative solutions coming out of the OD effort and the OD process itself to other parts of the organization. The experience of several large corporations suggests that these are crucial issues that have not been addressed creatively or effectively.

These problems occur because a large multiunit organization is itself a system. The organizational units in which early successes occur are interdependent with staff groups at headquarters, with units whose help they require to get the task accomplished, and with top management which allocates resources, determines policy, and decides who is to be rewarded. This section will explore the strategic considerations in managing an OD effort from initial success to ultimate adoption by the larger organization as a total system.

Looking for Regression: The Problem of Sustaining Change

It is almost inevitable that the enthusiasm and energy associated with the "take-off" phase of change will diminish as the organization stabilizes at a new level. As time passes, there is an erosion in the innovations that were instituted with the OD effort. Structural solutions developed are modified and new managerial practices are less consistently followed or dropped entirely. Sometimes such modifications are warranted, given change in people, task, or business. But just as frequently, the modifications represent real regression from original change goals and must be dealt with if gains from the OD effort are to be sustained.

Let us look at the longevity of one plant-level OD effort that resulted in enriched jobs and a more open participative culture (Beer, 1979). Within approximately thirteen years after the organization development program began, substantial regression in patterns of communication occurred. A number of meetings, such as problem-solving ones between supervisors and production workers, and general information and product information meetings held by the plant manager, had been discontinued or occurred only sporadically. Regular performance appraisals for production employees no longer took place. A policy that recognized performance and seniority in identifying people to be laid off evolved into a policy that considered only seniority. Production employees felt poorly informed and saw themselves as getting the least attention from management as compared with the most attention shortly after OD began. Job design changes that gave workers responsibility for the assembly of the total product were, however, still in place. No assembly lines existed in the plant. Nevertheless, some job design elements, such as self-scheduling by groups making the same product, had disappeared.

Why should such regression take place when management viewed the original innovations in the plant as a great success? First, none of the management people involved in the original OD effort were there any longer. They had all been promoted or moved to other jobs inside or outside the corporation. New plant managers were not selected on the basis of their support for the innovations. Indeed, they were not convinced that the innovations at the plant were appropriate. Transferring managers from one unit to another is a normal part of the manpower flow in most large organizations and is needed to develop managers and reward them. But in this plant, it eroded a philosophical base that guided the OD effort.

Similarly, all OD consulting support to the plant ceased some three years after the change started. The OD effort came from local initiative and never became part of the corporate OD strategy. As a result, new plant managers were neither chosen according to the compatibility of their management philosophy with the new plant culture, nor encouraged or rewarded for sustaining the original changes. Indeed, one of the new plant managers saw continued OD work as potentially damaging to his career. Furthermore, a number of corporate staff units created pressures to apply corporate policies (job evaluation, labor relations, and pay practices) that were not consistent with the goals and philosophy of organization development at the plant.

Regression of the type seen in this plant has occurred in many other organization development efforts (Hinrichs, 1978). It might have been avoided at the beginning if the change agents and managers worked to obviate the potential causes of regression. The following conditions seem important in sustaining change (Beer and Driscoll, 1977; Walton, 1974).

1. *Manager replacement.* When key managers leave, they must be replaced with people who are compatible with the evolving culture of the change target. Similarly, managers in the change target who cannot keep up with the evolving culture need to be transferred to other units. One of the best ways to deal with the compatibility problem is to bring new people in at the bottom of the change target, develop them within the culture, and place them into key management positions only when they have been socialized into the culture.

2. *Management orientation and education.* New managers should receive orientation training on the history of the OD effort, the stimulus for its origin, and the rationale that has guided it. Often a lack of knowledge about previous events in the organization's evolution, particularly strategic decisions that guided the organization's adaptation, can cause regression (see Case 2).

3. *OD consulting support.* Because conditions and managers are continually changing, it is doubtful that OD's consulting support can ever be completely eliminated. This is contrary to much of the literature which stresses that termination of consulting support signals the end of a successful OD effort. Continued consulting support must be made available to an organization as it moves through new transitions. For this reason, appropriate corporate staff groups should follow-up and check for regression.

4. *Corporate interfaces.* To achieve their change goals, organizational units undergoing OD efforts often deviate from corporate policies and practices. Functions such as personnel, control, planning, and engineering can help OD efforts by allowing exceptions to corporate policy and

CASE 2

Seven years after a consultant had played a major part in developing innovative work structures in a manufacturing plant, he was asked to educate the plant's managers in the history and philosophy of this effort. Since none of the managers had been involved in the original innovations, none of them understood the theory underlying them. They had all heard about the OD program in the plant. They knew that workers in the plant tended to be managed differently than in traditional plants. They saw that assembly lines did not exist and wondered why not. They accepted a work organization in which individuals or groups took responsibility for assembling a whole unit. But they did not understand why this approach was undertaken or the theory behind it.

This lack of knowledge evidenced itself in the many questions they asked the consultant when he arrived. "Aren't assembly lines the best way to get efficiency? We hear from employees who have been here since the plant opened that the good old days were better. What do they mean?" This lack of knowledge reflected not only the complete turnover of the management staff but also the lack of a continual orientation program which briefed managers about the plant's history and philosophy.

The consultant's visit had been arranged by the current plant manager in an effort to revitalize the OD effort. The consultant described the history of the effort in some detail. He conveyed the assumptions underlying innovations, the many discussions that had led to their acceptance, early efforts to innovate, and the learning that came from these experiences. The struggles, problems, and successes of the OD effort in the first three years were described candidly. These descriptions served to give the current managers a "feel" for how the plant had evolved to its present state and why some employees talked about the good old days. The briefing and the discussions which followed lasted a half-day and were a precursor to a diagnosis aimed at starting a new cycle of improvement efforts.

practice. Encouragement for such exceptions can come from top management or through education of corporate groups.

5. *Periodic assessment.* Regression sometimes occurs because new and interesting approaches become familiar and routine. Periodic assessments of OD efforts and the development of action plans to further innovations can help sustain change.

6. *Rewarding new behavior.* Changes can only be sustained if managers in the change target are rewarded (promotion, formal recognition, and pay) for maintaining new managerial approaches. If managers perceive that there are career risks in continuing OD efforts, regression is a certainty. Formal organizational rewards to managers for sustaining change are even more important than

those to early innovators. The latter group often obtains intrinsic rewards for getting change started. Furthermore, strong beliefs and values may carry them through the early phases of change despite potential risks. None of these conditions exist for managers who have to maintain change (see Case 3 for an example).

Developing and Maintaining Management Support

Top management can influence virtually all of the conditions just listed. They create reward systems, influence the policy of staff units, and make money available for OD consulting. Perhaps the most important condition under their control is the political climate for organization development. If managers perceive that OD is looked on favorably by top management, they will become involved in it and continue changes begun by others. If they perceive that top management doesn't support it, managers will find ways to discontinue these activities and avoid starting new ones.

If OD starts at the top and is successful, the problem of top management support doesn't arise. However, the vast majority of OD efforts have started at lower levels such as a plant, division, or branch. In these cases, the OD effort will be sustained only if at the very beginning, top management understands the goals and is kept informed about progress and results. Their involvement is likely to lead to their support. One reason to involve top management early is to find out if there are conflicts between its interests and values and ODs. It is better to discover a discontinuity during the planning stages, before too much effort has gone into the implementation of changes doomed to fail.

Organization development means changes in attitudes and behavior, which can be threatening to the values and beliefs of upper level management. Furthermore, changes in the status quo in a lower level unit can demand that upper management behave in ways of which they are not capable. This inability understandably threatens top managers' sense of competence.

Numerous times, the failure to communicate with top management and develop their understanding have resulted in a lack of support for organization development. In one instance, a laboratory training program undertaken by lower level management was abruptly terminated when the top manager learned about it (Bennis, 1977). Evidently, the top man had not been told about the change program and the values underlying sensitivity training conflicted with his own.

CASE 3

A manager who had taken over a division which was on the leading edge of OD applications, described his reasons for slowing down these efforts. "I basically believe that the managerial approaches being used in this division are the right way to go. But frankly, I don't think they are being supported by the corporation. Some of the staff groups think this approach is poor and I have to work with them. I also don't believe the president thinks we are on the right track. I was at a meeting at corporate headquarters the other day, and during a break the president and I began talking about the approaches taken in my division by my predecessor. He pointed to several problems these approaches might create. I could sense immediately that he had reservations. He didn't say stop, but I know he didn't say go. I have to watch out for my career. It won't be helped by pushing ahead. I am just letting the current approach to management continue because I know changing it would result in a lot of resistance from my people. But I am not putting a lot of effort into further innovation and change. Why should I?"

In another instance, a program was started by the head of a department, and was continued with the support of a vice-president, despite the failure of a two-day conference to gain the support of the president and a hostile corporate management group. Sometime later, shortly after the vice-president left the company, top management discontinued the program, even though it was going full swing (Buchanan, 1967).

The second case illustrates the importance of top management commitment even when middle management is already supportive. One never knows when a middle management's protective umbrella might disappear as a result of transfer or turnovers. Both cases illustrate the importance of early communication and the need to weigh the risks of continuing changes not supported by upper management.

Obtaining top management support for a change effort can sometimes blind change agents to the need for getting the support of middle managers immediately above the subunit in which an OD effort is being undertaken. For example, a middle level manager terminated a new and innovative pay incentive plan that had significantly reduced absenteeism soon after the external change agents had ended their personal involvement in the project. A retrospective analysis showed that this manager had not been helped sufficiently to gain an understanding of the project (Porter, Lawler, and Hackman, 1975; Scheflen, Lawler, and Hackman, 1971). His intolerance for the project led him to take the relatively risky step of reversing the change, even though it had been successful, and top management (who initiated the project) had supported it. Clearly, "management support" means the support of managers at all levels above the subunit undergoing OD.

Efforts to gain the support of as many key management people as possible is important for other reasons as well. As the first OD effort achieves the prominence often accorded successful innovations, factions unsympathetic to the changes taking place will attempt to block, consciously or unconsciously, the people supporting change from achieving their objectives. Detractors can take subtle, but potentially damaging, political steps to discredit and weaken the leading edge organization and its supporters; corporate constraints, that the leading OD unit needs lifted to move change along, don't budge; negative information about the OD effort is publicized and blown out of proportion. In any case, conflict between the innovative unit and some key people in the larger organization develops and escalates. This conflict has negative consequences, not only for the spread of innovations, but also for the innovators (Marris and Rein, 1973).

In one plant, which undertook major innovations in work restructuring, several key managers associated with initiating the OD effort found themselves no longer employed by the company. The plant manager was asked to leave, the manager of organization development, who was associated with this and other similar innovations, was "forced" to leave. Several other managers left voluntarily because they did not see advancement opportunities. The terminations occurred despite the fact that the plant's financial performance was significantly better than an older plant making the same products.

How could this happen, given the success of the plant? A pattern of conflict between change agents and the larger organization has been noted in other OD efforts and, indeed, in the introduction of most significant innovations (Pettigrew, 1976; Walton, 1974). The managers who are involved in OD often have different beliefs from top management about how to manage. These beliefs drive them to innovate, and success leads them to deepen their beliefs. Their commitment to OD sometimes approaches religious zeal. Thus a value gap develops between the subunit undergoing OD and the larger organization. This gap leads to the negative cycle of attitudes typically found in any severe intergroup conflict. Secure in their beliefs, the plant people communicate disdain and arrogance to corporate people who do not share these beliefs. Corporate management's negative reaction leads the plant's managers to feel unappreciated and underrecognized, especially given the results and high interest by outsiders in their innovations.

In these circumstances, each side sees itself as right and develops negative stereotypes about the other. At a time when it is most needed to create a positive political climate, frequency and quality of communication decreases.

If changes brought about by organization development are to be sustained and adopted by other parts of the larger organization, the relationships between the innovators and the supporters of the status quo must be managed effectively. Because of the dynamics described, the change agents associated with leading edge OD effort will probably not be capable of managing these relationships. While we do not yet know how to deal with these dynamics more constructively, some kind of integrator is probably needed (Lawrence and Lorsch, 1967b). This person can be a manager, or a corporate OD group could act in that role. The integrator needs to have a corporate perspective, credibility, and the trust of all constituencies. Such a person or group can facilitate the communication process and help the change target and management deescalate their conflict.

Spreading Organization Development

In a system-wide OD strategy, early change efforts are spread to other parts of the company until eventually all units and levels are in some way engaged in the process. The spread entails the whole organization, adopting (1) innovative solutions to management and organizational problems that have emerged from early OD programs and (2) the process and methods of OD.

When OD has spread, intervention methods such as team building and survey-feedback will be increasingly used as means for solving and preventing organizational problems. An increasing cadre of change agents will be found working and living in various parts of the organization. It is important to recognize, however, that these change agents may not and should not always be professional behavioral scientists identified by the title OD consultant. They may be line managers, personnel specialists, corporate planners, or external consultants.

Unfortunately, evidence indicates that organization development does not spread very easily from one part of an organization to others. Walton (1974) investigated twelve plants in eleven companies that undertook innovations in work design and management at the shop-floor level. In three of the cases, there was regression back to more traditional states, and in several others the innovation in the experimental plant was sustained but did not spread to other parts of the corporation. In the few large corporations that have had OD efforts for at least ten years, there are still many divisions and subunits not engaged in organization development.

If OD is to survive where it started, a system-wide organization development strategy must find ways to spread OD to the whole organization. A momentum of change must develop across the whole system so that some of the conditions for sustaining innovative changes, listed earlier in this chapter, can develop. If OD does not spread, the units where it started become more and more isolated. Those opposed to OD begin to successfully marshall their opposition. Managers of compatible managerial philosophy, needed to replace those in leading edge units and/or needed to start OD in new units, will be hard to find.

An effective system-wide OD strategy must include a plan for how to spread organization development. Such a plan would include the following elements (Beer and Driscoll, 1977; Walton, 1975).

1. *Communication about OD.* Research on the spread of innovations has shown that it depends on communication from innovators to potential innovators about the new approach (Havelock and Havelock, 1973, Rogers and Schoemaker, 1971). Similarly, the leading edge unit must mount an active program of communication about its organization development activities. Preferably, this communication comes from credible managers. Regular forums of communication, such as company meetings, may be used or special conferences for those interested might be organized.

   However, merely communicating knowledge has been found to be insufficient (Myerseth, 1977). In order for other managers to seriously consider involvement in OD, they will need to get a "firsthand feel" for what it is like. Arranging visits for these managers to organizations leading in OD applications is one way to do this. Talking to managers who have experienced team-building or other OD interventions is another.

2. *Top management involvement.* An earlier discussion highlighted the importance of developing top management understanding so that leading edge innovations can be sustained. To spread OD, top management involvement in the development of a strategy is a key factor. A statement of policy, support for expansion of OD resources, approval for lifting traditional constraints, and a periodic review of progress are all needed. Without these, OD is not likely to spread. If it does, it is likely to regress when top management belatedly becomes aware of its substantial impact. Yet, top management involvement cannot be so heavy-handed as to force managers into OD. Such OD efforts, not meeting the conditions of readiness and internal commit-

ment that are so important, would result in failure.

3. *Continued use of the contracting model.* The importance of readiness and internal motivation in the target unit is no less important for later OD targets than it was for early ones. This fact is often forgotten by change agents who have experienced early success. They fall prey to the lure of success, try to spread OD too rapidly, and rely on top-down pressure to open new doors. This can often result in failure, resentment, wasted time and resources, and a slowed momentum of change. Continued use of the entry and contracting model is important.

4. *Manpower flows.* The most effective way to spread OD and to create readiness in other units is to transfer experienced OD managers to other parts of the organization. The careful seeding of these people can be the single most important step in spreading OD, provided they are supported when they get to their new location.

5. *Preventing religious fervor.* The tendency of early innovators to acquire religious zeal and commitment to new approaches has already been discussed. This is a natural by-product of successfully creating change against resistance and constraints in the larger organization. However, this zeal polarizes believers and nonbelievers and prevents managers unfamiliar with OD to make an informed choice. Such religious fervor must be prevented at all costs if OD is to spread.

6. *Removing bureaucratic barriers.* Units undergoing OD will develop more and more congruity within themselves, but this will run headlong into standard practices and procedures that usually pervade large organizations. As OD spreads, staff groups—who often create these standard practices—will have to be persuaded and/or directed to make more and more exceptions. Top management's support is critical for making this happen.

7. *Rewarding the application of OD.* If OD is to spread, managers must perceive involvement in it as beneficial to their careers. If early users of OD are promoted and recognized, other managers will be more prone to explore the potential benefits of organization development. In one company, the promotion of an early OD user and advocate to the presidency of the corporation created a climate of acceptance in which OD flourished. While this climate is desirable, change agents must be careful that managers do not become involved in OD for political reasons. Such OD efforts are likely to fail because the motivation and readiness to create real change will be lacking.

8. *Organizing change agent resources.* The spread of OD, particularly in the early phases of a system-wide strategy, depends on the effective development and organization of change agent resources. Many of the conditions for spreading OD that have been discussed in this section can be created or managed by an effective network of OD consultants and managers. The change agents, often located in different parts of a large organization, must meet regularly to review the status of OD and develop a system-wide strategy. Such a strategy assumes that the needed specialists will be hired and developed so that the rising demand for OD services can be met with effective consulting resources. If such resources are not available when managers need them, the "window of conditions" which make these managers and their organizations potential clients, will disappear. Similarly, meeting these demands with ineffective change agents will result in failures that will close these windows.

In the long run, organization development cannot succeed in a large multiunit organization unless it spreads to many parts and levels. As the numbered triangles in Figure 1 show, OD may start (1) in the middle and move to other parts of the organization before it finally reaches the top (8). But it must ultimately reach the top and help managers at that level with their problems. Similarly, spread to a critical mass of divisions, departments, branches, or plants is important to ensure both sufficient influence on corporate policy and a pool of managers who can fill top positions in the increasing number of units undertaking OD.

Centralized vs. Market Strategies in Spreading OD[1]

The discussion in the previous sections has emphasized the importance of managing a system-wide OD effort. Finding an appropriate first target, sustaining change in this and other change targets, and spreading change through manpower planning and other methods requires some degree of planning and coordination aimed at developing a wider and wider circle of success. In the end, organization development becomes an integral part of the organization's adaptive coping process. There are different strategies for achieving this final goal.

At one end of a continuum is a *centralized approach*. This approach would probably include a staff OD department at headquarters reporting to the chief executive offices (CEO) or the corporate vice-president of personnel. The OD activities would be

FIGURE 1
Typical Diffusion Pattern for OD

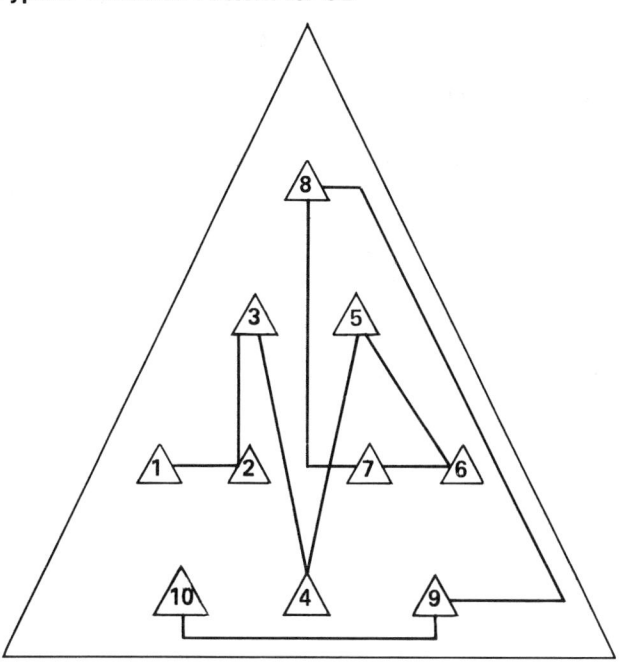

NOTE: Numbers indicate sequence of entry into various parts and levels of the organization.

initiated and budgeted by the larger system and they would be planned and reviewed with close involvement of corporate management (the CEO or the vice-president of personnel). Such an OD effort is essentially an arm of the corporation. The problems and parts of the organization which receive attention, do so as a result of top management's definition of priorities and problems. With this strategy, OD spreads primarily because top management is committed and only secondarily because of its perceived benefits at lower levels. The advantage of this approach is faster spread and better management of all the forces that shape culture change. The disadvantage is that commitment to OD at lower levels may be questionable and OD takes on a top management perspective rather than a systems perspective.

At the other end of the continuum is a *market strategy* for managing OD. With this approach, subunits are encouraged to undertake OD efforts, but they must find their own consultant (internal or external) and pay for their own programs. There is no corporate OD department nor is top management heavily involved in planning and reviewing OD activities. If a corporate OD staff group exists, its services are bought and paid for by line and staff units on a charge-back basis. Top management's assumptions are that people ought to be held accountable for results, but not for how they manage their organization. Centralized review and guidance of OD activities is thus seen as inappropriate meddling in the personal affairs of lower level managers. The advantage of the market approach is that it is quite consistent with the values of free and informed choice. Thus if OD spreads at all, it does so because of its perceived value. The disadvantage of this approach is that OD will spread extremely slowly, if at all, because there is minimal management of the many forces so important for sustaining and spreading it. A market strategy is essentially a decision not to actively manage the cultural development of the corporation.

Of course, these two approaches represent extremes that are not likely to be found in pure form in many corporations. Nevertheless, they clarify the strategic choices which top management must make about its posture toward OD. Like other management dilemmas there is no one answer. Some of the situational factors that must be considered in arriving at an appropriate balance between these two strategies are listed below (Coleman, 1973; Morris, 1964; Rogers, 1973).

1. *To what extent is the organization authoritarian, hierarchical, controlling, and centralized?* If it is authoritarian then a more centralized strategy for managing OD is appropriate.

2. *Do all parts of the organization have common goals and values?* If the organization is homogeneous in terms of values and goals, a centralized strategy is possible without incurring resistance and hostility.

3. *To what extent do people in the system desire freedom and participation?* If people desire participation, a market strategy is more appropriate.

4. *To what extent are the costs of delaying the adoption of OD greater than the costs of low commitment inherent in a centralized strategy?* If delay is more costly, a centralized strategy, which spreads more rapidly than a market strategy, is desirable.

5. *To what extent are various subunits of the organization (divisions, groups, etc.) similar in their tasks, people, and problems?* If subunits are dissimilar, a market strategy is more appropriate because each unit requires unique solutions.

6. *To what extent is OD likely to threaten the power elite's basic values and power?* If OD is potentially threatening to management, a more centralized strategy with early involvement is appropriate. When the top begins to feel threatened, it will squash a successful market strategy.

7. *Is the organization centralized in its operations?* A centralized organization requires a centralized strategy, while a decentralized organization requires a market strategy.

Relative emphasis on a centralized or market strategy is likely to shift and should shift according to changes in the situational factors listed above. For instance, in a highly centralized and authoritarian environment, a market strategy is not likely to get anywhere. In such an environment, managers are not mature or sophisticated enough to make informed choices. Only after extensive involvement in OD would a market strategy be more appropriate than a centralized one. The reverse can also occur. In one company, as the structure became more centralized, the market strategy was dropped even though it had been successful when the company was decentralized. Before the change, the OD department provided services to line divisions on a charge-back basis; afterward, the personnel division was in charge of its budget and its activities.

How Fast Should OD Spread?

From the perspective of the change agents interested in moving OD across an organization, the spread of OD should be as rapid as possible. Much of what has been said, however, implies that OD should spread at a rate consistent with its successes, the availability of competent OD resources, understanding of top management, and their willingness to become appropriately involved. That is, those who manage a fledgling OD effort must make sure that their plans for spreading OD activities are consistent with management's readiness and the availability of OD resources.

Controlling the growth and spread of OD is critical. If it spreads too rapidly, its emergence as a major force for change in the organization can become extremely threatening. Rapid spread means that some managers are not involved while others are pressured to change without sufficient involvement. Large budgets (for internal or external consultants) and large OD staff groups become targets for an anti-OD constituency. Pressures for cuts in OD resources build, particularly during periods of poor profitability. In one recent example, top management arbitrarily cut a large budget for external OD consultants when it became aware of its size. Case 4 illustrates one change agent's account of rapid change.

There are several ways to deal with this problem. Perhaps the most basic is to spread OD efforts more slowly than the needs of change agents and clients dictate. The problem with this approach is that professionals and managers engaged in OD work often thrive on change, and look for progress as a sign of hope. To these groups, the measure of success is the degree to which OD has penetrated the larger system. Slow or moderate progress becomes frustrating and does not meet their needs. McClelland (1978), in a

CASE 4

It is of little import that there was a grand design and that all of the changes fitted together neatly into the mosaic of the final objective. The important thing is that far too much was attempted. We did not have the time to oversee them all. We did not have the energy to nurture them all. We did not have the power to push them all. We did not have the insight to involve all the people who should have been made a part of them. It was far too ambitious an effort for the organization to digest and implement.

If I were to do it over, I would be more patient with the process. I would involve a great many more people and groups. I would include all the interested constituencies from the inception of the problem and try to make it their problem for their solution. Instead, I thought that I knew all the problems and had all the answers (which I probably had), but this attitude does not elicit broad support. I met my needs—not theirs.

I would have started earlier to ensure that my personal assistants and those responsible with me for bringing about change also worked through the participative mode instead of the authoritarian: "the boss wants so-and-so to be done." I suspect that there was much of that by fine, loyal subordinates who fell into this trap as a means of getting things done for me.

From W. J. Crockett, "Introducing Change to a Government Agency," in P. H. Mirvis and D. N. Berg, *Failures in Organization Development and Change* (New York: Wiley-Interscience, 1977), p. 143. Reprinted by permission of John Wiley & Sons, Inc.

discussion of an analogous problem, has suggested that many social scientists developed feelings of failure about the social change program of the 1960s, because they raised everyone's expectations, including their own, about immediate success.

To avoid these frustrations, change agents must spend much more time setting realistic goals (given the constraints outlined in this chapter) for change. They need to learn to derive satisfaction from small achievements rather than from impact on the whole organization. One way is to set goals for the research and development of more effective organization development methods. Unrealistic goals for penetrating the organization can only result in disillusionment. The many cycles of growth and decline in OD efforts are likely to be a function of the "mismanagement of hope."

The importance of change agents managing hope more effectively, raises issues about the selection and career development of change agents. For example, is it realistic for innovative plant managers or consultants, who pioneer the introduction of work restructuring, to stay in the same corporation for their whole career? If this is desirable, what career goals and paths make the most sense for them and the corporation? What help can they be given to mesh their own career needs with the reality that organizations change

slowly? Their needs for progress and success must somehow be met. The career issues that OD creates for professional change agents and managers may explain in part the repeated rise and decline of OD efforts in several large corporations over the last twenty years.

Thus far the discussion has centered on what change agents and organizations can do to limit the rate of OD growth. An alternative is to manage rapid growth wisely. Political realities suggest that visible entities, like large staffs and budgets, are more likely to come under scrutiny and be cut in difficult times. It would seem wise, therefore, to disperse OD resources throughout those parts of the organization that use their services.

This scattering of OD resources not only makes them less visible, but it places responsibility for those resources in the hands of managers who derive the most direct benefit from OD and have the most valid data about its effectiveness. Giving these managers such control enhances the quality of decisions made about OD resources and increases commitment to OD.

SUMMARY

This chapter has dealt with the question of where OD should begin in a large complex organization and how it might be spread. If OD is a fundamental managerial process by which an organization can maintain its vitality, then institutionalization of the process, not just the innovations which it delivers, becomes an important goal. The emphasis in this chapter has been on the kind of commitment, communication, involvement, political support, education, manpower planning, and rewards that are needed to start and spread OD. However, research aimed at evaluating OD programs can also help spread and sustain OD. Furthermore, specially designated departments, sensitive to the politics of managing change and innovation, can be a major force for institutionalizing OD.

NOTES

1. This section is based in part on Beer and Driscoll, "Strategies for Change" in J. R. Hackman and J. L. Suttle, *Improving Life at Work, Behavioral Science Approaches*, (Santa Monica, Calif.: Goodyear, 1977).

REFERENCES

• Beer, M., "The Longevity of Organization Development," in B. Lubin, L. D. Goodstein, and A. W. Lubin, *Organization Change Sourcebook I: Cases in Organization Development*. La Jolla, Calif.: University Associates, 1979.

- Beer, M., and J. W. Driscoll, "Strategies for Change," in J. R. Hackman and J. L. Suttle (eds.), *Improving Life at Work: Behavioral Science Approaches to Organizational Change.* Santa Monica, Calif.: Goodyear, 1977.
- Bennis, W. G., "Bureaucracy and Social Change: An Anatomy of a Training Failure," in P. H. Mirvis and D. N. Berg, *Failures in Organization Change and Development.* New York: Wiley-Interscience, 1977.
- Buchanan, P. C., "Crucial Issues in Organizational Development," in *Change in School Systems*, N.T.L. Institute for Applied Behavioral Science, 1967.
- Coleman, J. S., "Conflicting Theories of Social Change," in G. Zaltman (ed.), *Process and Phenomena of Social Changes.* New York: Wiley, 1973.
- Crockett, W. J., "Introducing Change to a Government Agency," in P. H. Mirvis and D. N. Berg, *Failures in Organization Development and Change.* New York: Wiley-Interscience, 1977.
- Franklin, J. L., "Characteristics of Successful and Unsuccessful Organization Development," *Journal of Applied Behavioral Science*, 1976, 12, 4, pp. 471–492.
- Havelock, R. G., and M. C. Havelock, *Training Change Agents.* Ann Arbor, Michigan: Institute for Social Research, 1973.
- Hinrichs, J. R., *Practical Management for Productivity.* Unpublished manuscript, 1978.
- Lawrence, P. R., and J. W. Lorsch, "New Management Job: The Integrator," *Harvard Business Review*, 1967(b), 45, 6, pp. 142–151.
- Marris, P., and M. Rein (eds.), *Dilemmas of Social Reform: Poverty and Community Action in the United States* (2nd ed.). Chicago, Ill.: Aldine, 1973.
- McClelland, D. C., "Managing Motivation to Expand Human Freedom," *American Psychologist*, 1978, vol. 33, no. 3, pp. 201–210.
- Morris, R. (ed.), *Centrally-Planned Change: Prospects and Concepts.* New York: National Association of Social Workers, 1964.
- Myerseth, O., "Intrafirm Diffusion of Organizational Innovations: An Exploratory Study." Doctoral thesis, Graduate School of Business Administration, Harvard University, 1977.
- Pettigrew, A. M., "Conference Review: Issues of Change," in P. Watt (ed.), *Personal Goals and Work Design.* London: Wiley, 1976.
- Porter, L. W., E. E. Lawler, and J. R. Hackman, *Behavior in Organizations.* New York: McGraw-Hill, 1975.
- Rogers, E. M., "Effects of Incentives on the Diffusion of Innovations: The Case of Family Planning in Asia." In G. Zaltman (ed.), *Processes and Phenomena of Social Change.* New York, Wiley, 1973.
- Rogers, E. M., and E. F. Shoemaker, *Communication of Innovations: A Cross Cultural Approach.* New York: Free Press, 1971.
- Scheflen, K., E. E. Lawler, and J. R. Hackman, "Long-Term Impact of Employer Participation in the Development of Pay Incentive Plans: A Field Experiment Revisited," *Journal of Applied Psychology*, 1971, 55, pp. 182–186.
- Walton, R. E., "Innovative Restructuring of Work," in J. M. Rosow (ed.), *The Worker and the Job: Coping with Change.* Englewood Cliffs, N. J.: Prentice-Hall, 1974.
- Walton, R. E., "The Diffusion of New York Structures: Explaining Why Success Didn't Take," *Organizational Dynamics*, Winter 1975, pp. 3–22.

Training To Be Ready for the '90s

by George S. Odiorne

One of the neatest rationalizations of the teacher's job is the old saw: "The full effect of the teacher's work is never known." This adage is often used to cover up the fact that nothing really happens in class, and thus accountability can be escaped by suggesting that the clients simply haven't waited long enough. If you will only be patient, you will see some big payoffs in a few more years.

Meanwhile everyone will either have forgotten or have expired, and this prevents a measurement which is uncomfortable to the teacher. Trainers likewise have been known to fall back upon the same argument. You can't measure what I produce, so therefore just keep paying and paying for training, and have faith that what I am fooling around with today will have a giant dividend at some undisclosed future time.

THE LABOR FORCE IS ALREADY IN VIEW

While this principle of deferred rewards for training might work in some companies which are somewhat removed from recessions, cost pressures, and the need for accountability by trainers, for most of us it isn't a sure-fire basis for justifying training expense. For an increasing number of firms expect some clear definitions of results to be obtained from any form of staff expenditure, including training. This forces the trainer in many instances to limiting the programs offered to those which are short term in effect. This, sadly, leaves the necessary investments in human capital which are involved in certain long-range development plans to be abandoned or postponed when times are tough.

The antidote to this kind of short-range forecasting and planning is for the training professionals to assume more of the mantle of the firm's captive labor economists, and do some predictions and shape programs to meet the strategic human-resources needs of the future. Fortunately for trainers, the raw materials which are our stock in trade are *people*, whose existence and changing dimensions as groups and individuals are more predictable than some other areas of the business: for example, economic trends or consumer tastes.

One of the major needs of strategic management in training then is to self-declare that you are a manpower (personpower) expert, and begin to emit useful reports, facts and opinions which are documented from already existing sources. U.S. Department of Labor figures, census data, and similar data counts are already well in place and with a moderate amount of study and considerable practice the trainer who wishes to usurp this labor economist or human-resource analyst role for the firm can easily acquire the skills and reputation to capture this function. If, of course, there is actually somebody in your firm who already holds such a position (a very rare occurrence) it would be a sensible and decent thing to await that person's departure before declaiming your new function. Otherwise you might try to get closer to that person and his or her outputs to find some strategic goals for training.

Strategic goals for training, in contrast with operational programs, are usually multi-year in time span, and are designed to change the character and direction of your training efforts to fit predictable future needs, or avert impending and potential problems. Here is how you get started.

1. Don't forget that your are engaging in job enlargement and perhaps job enrichment of your own job, but don't forget to continue to do your day-to-day operational job skillfully. Reform movements and revolutions can produce countereffects which must be watched for and dealt with as they arise.

2. Keep up to date on the three major elements of human resources planning and forecasting:
   * *Supply* of human resources, both in aggregate amounts and in the quality of that labor, including sources.
   * *Demand* for human resources: Not only the demands of your own firm, but of the labor market at large, for no organization operates on an island populated only by its own employees.
   * *Price*: The confluence of the first two is largely affected by the price which is offered and the price which is accepted by employees for work and employers for labor. Higher wages bring new people into the labor markets. Lower wages drives them off the labor market into alternative sources of income such as welfare, or further schooling.

3. Get your hands upon the basic manpower and human resources documents which are available, and master them. Then you can start collecting special reports, and minute details about special markets and prices.
   * *The Manpower Report of the President* published in March each year should be obtained, including several back issues. It's the master source of aggregate information about supply and demand for labor.
   * *U.S. Labor Department publications* starting with The Labor Market Bulletins of your state employment service. Then add the Monthly Labor Review published by D.O.L. in Washington, and a selected list of other labor department bulletins and reports which are obtainable from the U.S. Government Printing Office at nominal costs. Get on the distribution list for their periodic catalogs or reports. They are authoritative, informative and arm you with authority of information you never had before.
   * *The Statistical Abstract of the United States* and the *Survey of Current Business* (U.S. Department of Commerce) will comprise the third leg of your human resources planning stool. These are reference sources which you should familiarize yourself with and use on a regular basis.

     Once you get your feet on the ground with these, you can start picking up other sources. Every 10 years the *Decennial Census* should be added to your bookshelf. The most current one was completed in 1980 and makes fascinating reading. Later, when your reputation is established, you can opt for some of the more pertinent services such as those published by Bureau of National Affairs, Prentice-Hall, Commerce Clearing House and the like. There are others which are even more costly, but don't go overboard all at once. Take them on as you find them necessary and useful.

THE LABOR FORCE OF THE '90s

Getting ready for the changes in the labor force will be easier if we can get a grip on what will happen before it occurs. While there will be many important quantitative changes in the composition and size of the labor force, there will also be some qualitative changes, which will undoubtedly bring even tougher problems which can be alleviated by skillful training and human resources development.

Quantitative Changes During the '80s—A report by the U.S. Department of Labor in December of 1979 lays out a rather clear view of what changes in the shape of the labor force to expect during the coming decade. To name a few of the more important ones:

1. White-collar jobs will be up 24 percent which means that the already existing ratio of white collar to blue collar will increase. The rising cost of labor will accelerate automation, robotics and the substitution of machines and devices for laborers. As labor costs rise to the range of an average salary of $20,000 a year for an average employee, it will become increasingly economic to replace people with capital equipment during the '80s.

   It will also make it easier to substitute foreign labor—through imported products, and to operate in foreign locations such as Taiwan, Korea and jointly in Mexico. The future for plant supervision and skilled occupations isn't as gloomy, for it will require more skilled people such as machinists, technicians, carpenters, electricians, electronics experts and the like to keep the new automated plants running at full tilt. Labor relations as a profession won't grow in factories as fast as in white collar and office occupations, and many supervisors in such worksites won't be ready unless they are trained in labor management relations.

2. White-collar occupations are more likely going to be filled with people with different expectations, and participative management and motivational problems will take precedence over the old style leadership of hard-nosed supervision, even more rapidly than in the past.

3. The total size of the work force will rise from 98 million to 114 million workers, which is actually a lower growth rate than occurred during the '70s. Service industries will rise to 16.1 million workers, an increase of 30 percent over today. This will create some tough problems in productivity, for gains in service industry productivity call for different methods of attack than factory or distribution based industry. Productivity training will become a hot item for the '80s, and some innovative ideas would be welcomed in most service organizations.

4. Even with the higher age of retirement under Age Discrimination in Employment Act (ADEA), there will be 47 million replacement jobs for workers who die or retire during the decade. Getting new workers in place, ready to work, and upgrading them for higher levels of responsibility will produce some giant training problems.

5. More people will be working for large corporations, and there will be fewer self-employed people during the decade. Small companies are gobbled up by larger ones as concentration of industry continues despite periodic bursts of antitrust activity by government. The trend will be especially true in retail and distribution where chains are taking over small hot dog stands, department stores taking over specialty shops, and nationally franchised businesses replace individual shops.

6. There will be more professional managers required, and they will be called upon to do things supervisors 10 years ago were never called upon to do. A lot of this will be due to qualitative changes in the work force, plus new laws, and the changing nature of the work force. Blue-collar jobs will decline 25 percent during the decade, and the model manager will be directing more clerical, technical and managerial staffs of workers.

QUANTITATIVE CHANGES IN THE WORK FORCE

Even more importantly for training will be the changes in the character and expectations of the work force by 1990. The current census results are still incompletely analyzed, but some of the important changes which will affect the character and direction of training effort can be seen.

1. There is already a significant upgrading of the number of blacks and women in colleges of business and engineering, who will start entering the work force by 1982 and whose number will continue to grow rapidly. Black students enrolled in colleges of business rose from 41,000 to 221,000 between 1970 and 1978 with com-

parable figures for engineering and medicine as well. There are now some 1 million blacks in college, up from 282,000 in 1970. This population will not only diminish the number living at lower socio-economic levels, but will bring people with higher expectation for upward-mobility into the work force, which must be reckoned with in the coming decade.

2. Women entering business schools have leaped as well and will continue to do so through 1990. Not only are more women in college, up from 2.8 to 4.71 million, but they have abandoned the field of education as a career goal as schools shrink in enrollment. Enrollments of women in business schools has risen from 204,000 to 819,000 and will rise even more rapidly as up to 60 percent of the applications in some business schools are now from women.

Furthermore, deans and admission directors report that they are winning a disproportionate number of the top academic achievement spots in business colleges. This too will alter what is needed in induction, training and management development during the decade of the '80s. Setting aside any pressures from government commissions, the pressures from these good students upon the labor market for opportunities and challenges will be irrepressible. As they form caucuses, their internal lobbying will be very powerful. Among the opportunities which they will undoubtedly demand will be for equal training opportunities in the prestigious company programs and off-campus assignments to executive development programs.

THE RISING LEVELS OF WELFARE PAYMENTS

One of the important factors in changing the quality of the work force will be the presence of some 50 million people who now receive some form of welfare, supported and advised by some five million people in public and private employment whose major function is facilitating and administering welfare of various types. In-kind transfer payments, especially in food stamps, medical services and housing have created a kind of *de facto* end to much poverty, and people who are unable or not disposed to work don't really have to. These in-kind transfer payments according to a recent report by Professor Paglin of Portland State University have risen from $1 billion to over $14 billion since 1970 and haven't leveled off. This often translates into a shortage of available workers at the lower levels of the work force in such jobs as waiter-waitress, hospital workers, taxi drivers and the like.

If a person can live without working for almost as much as they could by taking a job, it is only rational behavior on their part—as Milton Friedman points out—that they should abstain from the work force and join the welfare population. Apart from any social significance we might overlay upon these hard facts, it also has a significant impact on the work force and labor supply.

It simply won't be easy to find American workers to take lower-level jobs. Women and blacks are now opting out of this level if they can attend college, and those who can't will not make the irrational choice of working for nothing.

There will be a significant rise in the number of bilingual employees and language training for supervisors and managers alike will become more important as the rising service occupations are increasingly required to use foreign workers. There will be so few unskilled American citizens in the work force that we will face a shortage of some five million unskilled workers by 1990, according to Professor Clark Reynolds of Stanford in a recent report. Thus, the "undocumented aliens" who seem to be a national worry will be recognized as a welcome addition to the work force.

Mexican workers as part of the American work force could rise to as high as 15 to 30 million from the present three million by the year 2000, Reynolds states. In many Southwestern sunbelt states, in Florida and in other states as well, the required absorption of Spanish-speaking workers will increase the problems of bilingualism in the work place, which will place a training burden on employers and the school systems surrounding the plants and offices. Cubans, Puerto Ricans and Mexicans are among the most rapidly growing segments of the population. The average age of Spanish-surname people is below 20, and their education and integration into the work force will comprise a major problem for trainers as well as industry generally.

Mexico itself doesn't hold much promise of restraining the immigration for its population is growing faster than its ability to create jobs for its people, oil-based prosperity notwithstanding. Not only will Spanish-speaking workers abound, but lowered immigration gates may be expected for such groups as the Vietnamese, and perhaps French-Canadians, and other refugee and disaffected groups around the world enter the United States to take up our slack in unskilled workers.

The barber in Mexico gets 50 cents for a haircut, compared with $5.00 in the U.S. It can be expected that, like the Cubans, many Mexicans with higher than minimal credentials will make the trek northward to seek the new affluence which comes with the demand for unskilled workers and semiskilled workers. Many of them will work in the new "In-Bond" plants in Mexico near the border (Maquilidoras) creating up to one million jobs by 1985.

THE NARCISSISTIC AMERICANS

Several writers, including Christopher Lasch (*The Culture of Narcissism*) and Tom Wolfe (*The Me Generation*) have noted the increasing trend toward self-obsessiveness which has overtaken middle class, college graduate Americans. The very face of mental health has been shaped away from conversion hysteria to narcissistic-founded hang-ups. We are obsessed with ourselves, our likes and dislikes, and our loves and hates. Our training is often centered in encounter groups, organization development (OD), est, rolfing, dietary fads, jogging and exercise, and other self-centered behaviors which they propose is a change in the American character with which employers must deal during the coming decade.

People are committed to finding a life style, and then a job to support it rather than the reverse which was characteristic of a depression-raised generation before them. This will call for new participative styles of leadership, more listening, and considerable democracy in the work place if these people are to be made productive and creative.

Tomorrow's supervisor will need skills which cover a wider range of supervisory situations than many supervisors of the past required. The idea of contingency management will come closest to being the supervisory style of the '80s. This means that the supervisors consider the entire situation—its objectives, the people involved, the environment in which they are working—rather than adhering slavishly to a single style.

You can't be just a roughneck, nor simply a facilitator, but must have a wider repertory of managerial behaviors to fit different situations. The supervisor managing the high talent young staff of professionals must handle that group differently from the unschooled and bilingual labor group. This means that supervisory courses will be tooled to present good human relations but also some methods of being firm, and of knowing the difference between them.

There will be a lot more sensing of the opinions of various employee populations in the future before the training needs are assessed. Already there is within the OD training technology considerable know-how in such method. Sometimes called "data based intervention," they call upon the group to help define its own needs.

TOWARD A BILINGUAL AMERICA

In 1980 in many parts of the country a substantial impact on the work force has occurred in the form of Spanish-speaking people as a significant part of the work force, especially at the lower levels, and in service jobs. This promises to become a near torrent by the end of the decade and will have considerable affect upon the supervisory skills and behavior required. Mexican migrants to the United States now account for some 10 percent of the annual growth in the work force, and this is but the first stage. Professor Reynolds suggests that America faces a shortage of five million workers by the turn of the century, and the demand for migrants to fill the gap may run as high as 15 million workers by the year 2000, he suggests, if our economy grows at an annual rate of three percent.

Fretting by some American citizens and the Immigration and Naturalization Service to the contrary, the pressures for more Spanish-speaking workers from Mexico, Cuba, and possibly other Latin American nations can be expected to grow to fill this need as more college education and rising expectations of Americans continue to make menial work unattractive. Furthermore, for many, this kind of work isn't economically justifiable when welfare and similar programs provide in either food stamps, housing, medical benefits and other transfer payments almost as much income for not working as would be available from working at one of the least desirable jobs in the labor market.

Reynolds concludes that Mexico must sustain a national rate of growth of seven percent to provide jobs for all of its people. The results will probably be a northward migration, pushed by unemployment below the border, and drawn by the need of such labor above it. The high wages in the U.S. compared with Mexican wages make it attractive to the best people in the underdeveloped neighbors to migrate.

All of which produces a substantial number of people whose only language is Spanish or something other than English. This creates problems for employers. It calls for one thing for a wider effort in school systems under present federal laws to provide bilingual education for children. This will add to taxes, and create demands for different kinds of school systems. It will also require that many firms in the southern tier and beyond will have to study the impact of bilingualism upon the work place.

Supervisors who can deal with Spanish-speaking employees, not only in language skills but in cultural expectations will be needed. Labor relations will be different than the traditional collective bargaining in places like Detroit and Philadelphia in the 1950s and '60s and will call for some new skills in union relations, at both line and staff levels.

There will be a greater demand for bilingual people in staff and upper management positions as well. Such ordinary matters as signs, publications, and instructions will tend to be more bilingual, which calls for people who can both read and write in two or more languages in many firms.

This will become even more important as we try to find new cheap labor by moving plants to overseas locations, or set up more "in-bond" assembly plants close to the U.S.-Mexican border on the Mexican side, which could employ as many as one million Mexicans by 1985. These language courses could be farmed out to colleges, universities and private language schools, but for the major corporations may find more language labs being established in-house by corporate trainers.

THE RAPID RISE OF SOCIO-TECHNICAL CHANGES

One particular kind of change which has already established a minor foothold in the late '70s and early '80s will probably increase by 1990. Often identified by the elegant title of "socio-technical change" it is best known by the addition of new classes of people on boards of directors.

Trustees and management committee containing worker representatives, or advocates of certain activist positions such as environmentalists, will increase. There are two distinct groups who press for such radical kinds of participation. In Germany, Yugoslavia and elsewhere, worker and union delegates to the board of directors of corporations already have been in place for many years. This socio-technical change of the European type has made little advance in this country, but predictably will gain considerably in the '80s and by 1990 will have attained significant gains. As the ultimate form of participative management, it is a form of industrial democracy which is relatively unfamiliar here.

Douglas Fraser was elected a member of the board of Chrysler in 1979 as a condition of some large loans by the union to the corporation. In other firms, women and blacks have been added to the board of directors. While they have by no means come close to a majority, and probably will never attain that status, their very presence on the board makes the issues of women's role and black status in the firm a matter which can be invited regularly into the board room in inescapable ways. It was the presence of Dr. Leon Sullivan on General Motors' board which shaped their South African employment policies without doubt.

Having women as directors substantially enhances the likelihood of accelerated programs of career development and planning for high-talent women within the personnel department of the firm on whose boards they sit. This in turn will call for better and more sophisticated training and development plans for talented women.

Still another form of participative management of the socio-technical character will be increased employee ownership of businesses. In some cases this will be through the long run operation of employee stock ownership plans (ESOP's). In other instances it is the actual purchase of the firm by employee groups.

When the Youngstown plant of a major steel company was closed, the employees through the union sought to buy and operate the mill, but without much success to date. In another more widely publicized case, Rath Packing Company of Waterloo, Iowa, a $300 million firm, was turned over to the employees of the board, and Local 46 of the United Food and Commercial Workers voted to buy the company, and now hold 60 percent of company stock. The 2,000 workers in the plant contribute $20 a week from their paychecks to purchase their shares.

This case, if extended to other plants threatened with closure, or sold to workers for other reasons would add considerable strength to the need for participative management in the way supervisors and managers relate on the shop floor. It would have considerable effect upon training programs for supervisors, for in such cases the term "management" also refers to the workers, and has more poignancy and impact than in an ordinary supervisory worker relationship where management consists of absentee owners and stockholders. While new forms are employee participation through safety committees, productivity committees, team problem-solving and quality control circles will become rampant where they are now often present in a desultory or spasmodic fashion depending mainly upon the preferences of the management. Every trainer has been exposed to situations where a change in management from a humanistic to a hard-nosed style has resulted in a cutting off of training, or an abandonment of humanistic programs in times of economic distress.

CHANGED LABOR MANAGEMENT RELATIONS BY 1990

The decline of the hourly rated, blue-collar work force by 1990 will have a serious impact upon the face of unionism. The population base upon which traditional unions were founded will have shrunk through automation and the export of jobs to a small minority of the work force, but nonetheless influential.

The greatest rise on unionism has been and will continue to be in white-collar occupations. The rise of the white-collar work force makes it more likely that this segment of the work force will be the target for organization, if unions are to survive. Already it is the school teacher, the airline pilot and the government employee who has assumed the strongest role in unionism, especially in union-political action programs. Over 300 of the delegates to the Democratic convention in 1980 were school teachers.

As time produces retirement of the old-fashioned industrial union leader, it is predictable that new union leaders will emerge from the white-collar technical and professional membership. Such people will not always act like teamsters and bricklayers, but will produce more sweeping policies and demands for participation in the decisions which affect them.

Unlike the traditional industrial unions, which have been quite cold to many of the newer behavioral science approaches to management, the new unionist in professional types of unions will insist upon participating in decisions which affect them. This will come under the rubric of working conditions, but in fact will be a demand for involvement in managerial strategies rather than simply narrower working condition demands. It will extend to supervisory-subordinate relations, leadership styles, and general planning practices of the organization.

As America moves toward improved productivity through research and development, budgets for scientists and engineers will increase, which will produce not only more of them, but a heightened significance of the employed professional. For trainers this will create a demand for special kinds of training programs for managers of engineering and scientific organizations. Traditional supervisory courses which rely upon assembling magnetic horses to illustrate group management principles won't fly as well with such people and will call for more sophisticated models of training programs and instructional

materials. The shortage of engineers which began as the decade of the '80s came in sight will continue as defense budgets rise, industrial research gets more attention, and courses in managing technical work will be in greater demand.

Changes in health care delivery will likewise produce a need for new forms of training in the supervision of health professionals. The growth of health maintenance organizations (HMO's) and the rising costs of professionals in health care will present a better educated and higher paid group of people for training in this giant industry. In 1980 the Congress has raised the pay of Veteran's Administration doctors into ranges of $50,000 to $75,000 a year, which confronts trainers in that organization with a new class of students from the past.

The realities of training and development are already emerging in 1980. A new and more professionally trained trainer, higher paid, and closer to the central strategies of the organization will be more completely achieved by 1990. This means that the apprenticeship for training management will be longer. People will stay in training and development longer, and training as a vestibule entry position for personnel management will become less common. More and more employees will see training as a right rather than an amusing and interesting sideline which is a diversion from doing their ordinary job. It means that trainers must raise their sights and scan the world around them through systematic obtaining of information. It will produce a maturity and professionalism in training never realized in the past.

Impact-Directed Training

by William M. King and Robert A. Roth

Corporate managers at all levels direct their efforts at achieving the goals of the organization. In organizations that are profit-oriented, the overall purpose is *return on investment*. In other situations, such as government and certain health-related organizations, the purpose is to improve services provided to the client group served. In all of these situations, however, the goals of the organization are derived from its purpose, and the efforts of the corporate manager are

directed at achieving these organizational goals and missions.

The role of the corporate manager can be summarized as managing resources to have maximum impact on the company's goals. In essence, this is what they are paid to do. Corporate managers are evaluated on this basis, and managers can be differentiated by their ability to do this. Good managers are able to do this better than others, and this is the critical factor making them better managers. They are rewarded because they have impact on corporate goals and because the organization knows about their contribution and its value.

The role of the manager or administrator is basically the same in all environments. Executives in business and industry are the same in this respect as hospital directors, managers in government and college/university administrators. Although the specific goals and techniques to achieve these (the tools of the managers) will differ, the fundamental role of the manager is essentially the same in all environments.

In addition to the role of manager/administrator, there is the role of trainer, teacher or educator, which supports the manager. A function of this role is to maximize human resources by developing this resource potential in terms of the needs or goals of the organization. This is what human resource development is all about.

Although the role of training is also essentially the same across environments, as is the role of management, this role is not fulfilled to the same extent in different environments. In K-12 schools, the teacher contributes directly to the goal of the organization, which is education of the students. Since this contribution has a direct impact on goals and is clearly recognized by the organization, teachers have this type of credibility in their environment. They are an integral resource in achieving the goals of the organization. Faculty at colleges and universities likewise are an essential contributor to the goals of the organization. Their contribution is extremely visible and valued in their environment.

ROLE OF TRAINERS

What about the role of trainers in their environment? *Trainers do not automatically enjoy a highly credible role in the business and industry environment.* They do not necessarily impact directly on the goals and mission of the organization. When they do make this kind of contribution, it is not always very visible or recognized by the organization. Corporate managers and teachers in other environments purposely focus their efforts on goals of the organization and thus have an impact on these goals. Trainers do not necessarily focus directly on these goals and thus do not impact directly on organizational goals as do corporate managers and other educators. For example, a trainer may focus on training employees on new equipment, while a corporate manager may focus on increasing sales. Increasing sales impacts directly on the corporate mission and probably is an explicitly stated goal of the organization. In contrast, while training on new equipment may be important, its relationship to goals may not be direct or its contribution to goals may not be fully recognized.

There are some very important implications of the situation in which many trainers find themselves.

These implications are so critical that they completely alter the ability of the trainer to function in the organization. An obvious implication is that trainers tend to lack credibility in their organizations. They are perceived as not being able to make a contribution to company goals, and even as a liability or expense rather than a revenue generating activity. When viewed in terms of return on investment, they are not perceived as making a contribution. They thus have little credibility in a profit-oriented environment.

How important is credibility to the trainer? An ASTD survey of 2,800 trainers asked them to identify the most important behavioral requirement for trainers. These experienced practitioners overwhelmingly identified credibility as the most important behavioral trait. Forty percent selected credibility, whereas the next highest trait, flexibility, was selected by only 18 percent (Clement, Walker, Pinto, 1979). Clearly, credibility is a critical factor in the performance of the role of trainer.

In view of the critical role of credibility, it is important to understand what it is. When trainers are credible, they are viewed with confidence that they can get the job done. They are believable, trusted and reliable in contributing to the organization. This means knowing what to do to get the job done and being able to do it. In other words, those for whom services are performed (corporate managers) believe that credible trainers know how to contribute to the organization's objectives and have had a direct impact on the organization at some time in the past.

Another very important implication of trainers not focusing and impacting on the goals and mission of the organization is the role of the trainer. The role that trainers usually play in business and industry has developed as a consequence of their perceived impact on corporate goals. Trainers and training directors are not usually part of the organizational decision making process. They are not part of the management team either organizationally or operationally, and thus are not an integral part of strategic planning. They are not viewed as playing a contributing role in goal achievement. They are not given sufficient resources in terms of staff or budget. This is not hard to understand when there is little documentation of return on investment (ROI). In effect, the trainer and training director generally play a minor or secondary role in the corporate organization.

For the most part, trainers are not content with this traditional role that they have inherited. They are looking for a broader role and a more important place in the organization. The training function can and frequently does play an important part in enabling the organization to achieve its objectives. Management is increasingly requiring that the training function be accountable and demonstrate its results. The emerging role of the trainer will require that he or she contribute to corporate goals in a direct, meaningful way. The training function which cannot do this, and does not demonstrate that this has been done, will not survive in most corporate environments in the future!

In order to gain credibility and change their role in the organization, those involved in the training function must look at what corporate managers do. Training directors are managers in their own right, and must recognize that their function is to manage resources and direct efforts at organizational objectives. As trainers and training directors, we must realize that we must perform much in the same way as managers do if we are to survive or perform any meaningful role.

The key factor in gaining credibility and achieving a new role is to have a direct impact on the organization's goals and mission, and to demonstrate that this has been done. Managers do it, educators in other environments do it, and trainers and training directors must also do it. The question, of course, is *how*.

IMPACT-DIRECTED TRAINING

As a response to this need, a model for the training function was designed and is called *impact-directed training* (IDT). Impact-directed training is patterned after the role that managers perform, and in fact the manager's function may be referred to as impact-directed management since what he or she does focuses on having an impact on the organization. IDT, therefore, uses this same basic concept and applies it to the training function. IDT is thus a key survival strategy. There is a growing need for this role of the trainer, and certainly this will be the role of the future.

What is IDT? It is an overall strategy for conducting the training function. It integrates several basic techniques which have been tested by successful trainers, with new techniques, and forms a new model. It also integrates the varied functions of the trainer into a more efficient method of performing the trainer's and director's role.

A general area of concern involves conducting the training function in an efficient and effective manner. Obviously, the more efficient and effective, the greater one's credibility. Efficiency means doing things right; effectiveness means doing the right things. The relationship between effectiveness and efficiency is illustrated in Figure 1.

Efficiency is addressed in the IDT model by coordinating functions of the trainer. By coordinating these functions into a common purpose and directing them in this way, a synergistic effect is produced. For example, by focusing on organizational goals rather than isolated problems, needs analysis, program design

FIGURE 1.
R-K Efficiency Effectiveness Impact Grid

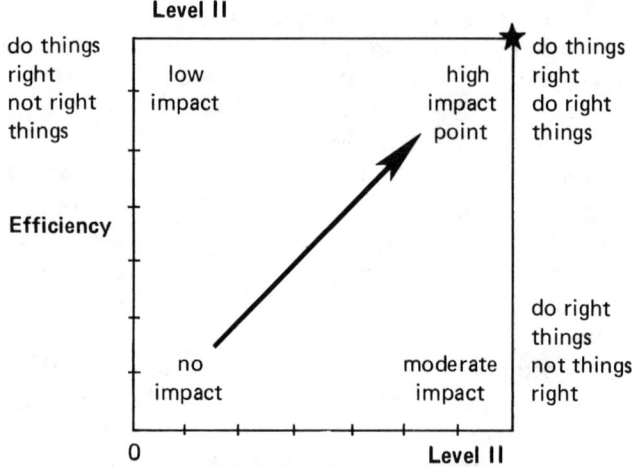

Effectiveness
0 = no effectiveness, no efficiency
level I = no effectiveness, high efficiency
level II = high effectiveness, no efficiency
impact point ★ = high effectiveness, high efficiency

and program evaluation are better coordinated within this framework. The total effort is greater than the sum of the individual efforts. The various functions of the trainer are frequently viewed and exercised in isolation from each other. A needs analysis might be conducted in a different way if it is focused on explicit current organizational strategic goals rather than on isolated problems of different departments. Instead of just conducting a general needs analysis, the analysis should be focused on organizational goals and objectives—otherwise it may even be counterproductive. By combining certain functions, focusing efforts in the same direction and performing only tasks and assignments which impact on this direction, a more efficient training function results.

The most important contribution of the IDT model is the potential for greatly increasing the effectiveness of the training function. Training is most effective when it has a more direct impact on the mission of the organization (ROI, service) and the goals established to achieve this mission. The IDT model does exactly that—it programs the training function to impact directly on the goals of the organization. The IDT model combines three factors—*results*, *visibility* and *credibility*—to achieve impact. These factors are depicted in Figure 2.

FIGURE 2
The Impact Triangle

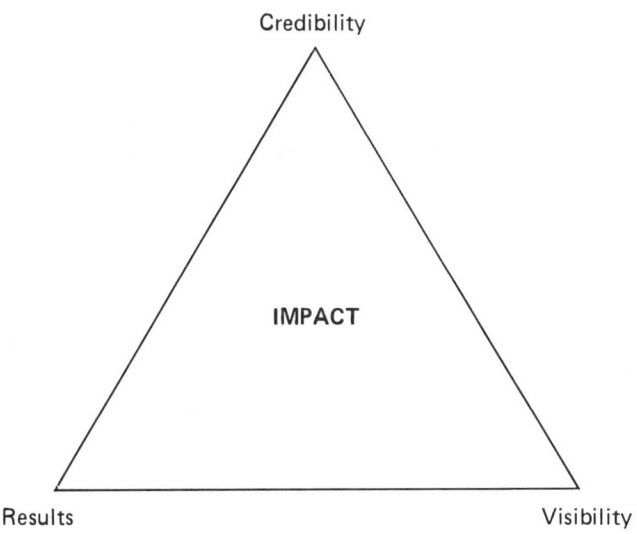

Credibility

IMPACT

Results   Visibility

Visibility + Results + Credibility = Impact

OBTAINING RESULTS—A CRITICAL FACTOR

Obtaining results of the training effort is obviously a critical factor. But all trainers would argue that they obtain results, so how is the IDT model different? The difference is in the kind of results that are achieved in IDT. Training may achieve results, but if we focus training efforts on isolated problems, misdirected needs analyses and low pay-off activities, the results have little real impact on the organization. A supervisor's request for an effective writing program may not have much organizational impact. By focusing on those activities which more directly enhance achievement of the organization's goals, the training function has greater impact. A program directed at increasing client retention rates is one example.

An important concept in targeting results to have greater impact is leverage. Use of leverage means to concentrate on activities which you get the most from in terms of organization impact. This is the effectiveness factor referred to previously. There is an efficiency aspect as well, in that activities are pursued which give a greater impact for a given amount of effort or the same impact for less effort. Although training activities produce results, those activities whose results have greater organizational impact provide leverage.

There are several strategies which will enhance leverage to produce results with impact. The essential first step, which is fundamental to the entire IDT model, is to identify and translate organizational goals into operational terms. The key to this phase is to take broad goals and step them down to more specific activities which are factored into human performance functions. For example, increasing the company's share of the market may be a strategic goal, and the role of training is to determine which human performance factors (new product design, more effective sales, penetration of new client groups) contribute to this goal and if training can improve these factors. A basic issue at this point is to determine how training can contribute to these human performance functions.

The next strategy in this procedure is to screen the translated goals. The purpose of the screening is to determine which training activities will provide the greatest leverage. Criteria need to be established which select these activities. The criteria include: relationship to goals, feasibility and measurability; degree of effort/resources required; and extent to which training is the best means of achieving the activity's objectives.

ACHIEVING VISIBILITY

In addition to achieving results which have impact, the training function must have visibility. If you expect to gain credibility you need to not only achieve meaningful results but the organization must know it. If management doesn't know it, then it's the same as not having done it, from management's perspective. Management must know not only what training has done, but also the significance of what was done in terms of its contribution to achieving organizational goals. Trainers and training directors must promote the fact that they have had an impact on the organization. If they do not advertise what they have done, no one else will do it for them!

A technique used to enhance visibility is to continuously evaluate activities in terms of their payoff. Every assignment or activity you propose should be evaluated in terms of its potential for visibility. Key questions are: How can these results be used? Who will see these results? Who *should* see the results? In what form should the results be reported—by whom, to whom and when?

Two factors which significantly enhance the potential for visibility of results are measurability and "next-level application." If results are measurable and reported in quantitative terms, they are generally more easily understood and accepted, and their relationship to organizational goals can be more readily devised. Quantified results also have greater credibility. Given these characteristics, such results would more likely be used, transmitted to others and publicized. This is visibility.

Another factor is "next-level application." This refers to results which are of value to the next higher level of management. If the training director reports to a vice president, then training results which can be applied by that vice president are more likely to be used and are much more noticeable. If that vice president is able to use training results and show how these results have aided in achieving organizational goals (particularly goals for which he or she is responsible), and he or she can use these in reporting to their next level, the trainer/director will have considerable visibility and at more than one level. Such an activity has great payoff for the trainer.

It is not only of value to select activities with visibility payoff, but the trainer should review activities currently assigned to determine payoff. You as a trainer may already be doing a number of things whose results should be publicized because of their impact. You should endeavor to get all the mileage you can out of these activities, particularly if you know they will be assigned to you on a continuous basis.

Another technique to generate visibility is to take the initiative and suggest training activities. This is particularly effective when you can demonstrate how the training results will have impact on the organization's goals. If this can be documented after having conducted the training, your visibility will be greatly multiplied. Look for ways to affect the organization's goals; these are great opportunities for visibility. Have you ever viewed an organizational problem given to you to resolve through training as an opportunity? Have you ever asked yourself the question: "How can I take a typical new employee orientation program and use it as an opportunity to impact on an organization goal?"

GAINING CREDIBILITY

Credibility has been identified as an extremely important factor in the role of trainer or training director. The IDT model also aids in achieving this characteristic. IDT has been devised as a reponse to this critical need. As indicated earlier, the key factor in gaining credibility and achieving a new role is to have a direct impact on the organization's goals and mission, and to demonstrate that this has been done. As we have seen, IDT aids the trainer in doing precisely that. IDT focuses the trainer's efforts on results with impact, and on visibility. Leverage and payoff are important strategies in achieving impact. They also maximize efficiency and effectiveness. Thus, by combining impact results and visibility, credibility is highly likely to be achieved. Use your high impact results and visibility to achieve credibility.

There are other strategies which will enhance achievement of credibility. Look for opportunities to achieve and demonstrate credibility. Remember that part of the definition of credibility is reliability. If you were asked to do a job, point out that you did it, and that you did it according to expectations and specifications. When you consistently perform in this way, you gain a reputation as being reliable. This contributes to your credibility.

When the organization is faced with new problems, look for ways you can contribute. Relate the new problems to successes you have had in solving similar problems in the past. Past successes go a long way in building credibility, but you may need to make them known. Eventually, management may turn to you when faced with problems or when working toward goals, instead of your needing to take the initiative.

Do not be hesitant to take the initiative in establishing credibility. Show what you have done, point out how and where you can help, and offer your assistance when you think you have a training solution and can handle the job. This will also contribute to changing your image and eventually your role.

Also, try to involve management in your overall training program. Get them involved in establishing training objectives, even if it is just a sign-off indicating concurrence on your direction. Getting management involvement in all phases of the training function can provide a great boost to credibility, particularly when you make a contribution. Management will become very much aware of the degree to which you contribute to the organization, and that training can be counted on to meet certain needs. Training directors may then be called on to help make decisions. These are indicators of credibility.

SURVIVING IN THE FUTURE

If you want to have impact on the organization, and you will be required to at some point in time, the IDT model offers several advantages. In general, you should screen all of your training efforts to determine the degree of impact each one provides. The screening matrix in Figure 3 may be helpful in this regard. You may wish to rate each factor on a scale from one to ten. You may also wish to weight each factor in terms of its importance on a scale of one to five. For instance, the leverage derived from an activity may be the most important factor to you, and thus you assign it a weight of five. This may be many times as important as the amount of effort required, and thus effort is assigned a weight of one. Visibility may be assigned a three and credibility a four.

Each activity is then rated on each of the factors. Orientation training, for example, may be rated

FIGURE 3.
R—K Impact Screen

	Factor				
Training Activity	Results: Leverage	Visibility: Payoff	Credibility Payoff	Effort	Total or Impact
Orientation					
Sales					
Management					
Stress					
Writing					

as three on leverage (little direct impact on goals), a four on visibility, a three on credibility and three on effort. (Note that the greater the effort required the lower the score on this factor. What you are searching for are activities with the highest impact for the least effort or use of time and resources). The total is thus the assigned weighted value for each factor multiplied times the rating given. In our example totals would be as follows: results/leverage—$5 \times 3 = 15$; visibility/payoff—$3 \times 4 = 12$; credibility potential—$4 \times 3 = 12$; and effort—$1 \times 3 = 3$. The total or impact rating of the activity is thus $15 + 12 + 12 + 3 = 42$ (Figure 4).

FIGURE 4.
Rating a Training Activity

Orientation Training			
	Assigned Weight	Assigned Value	Weighted Value
Leverage	5	3	15
Visibility	3	4	12
Credibility	4	3	12
Effort	1	3	3
Total			42

This score can then be compared to scores for other activities in order to determine priorities. Eventually a base score may even be established, below which you should reject an activity if possible. It may be of value to establish such minimum scores for one or more of the factors. For example, you would reject any activity which has a leverage score below a certain value.

An important message in this article is that impact on organizational goals is a critical dimension of the training function. Another important message, however, is that control of your role as trainer/training director is in your own hands. You can create your role within the organization; you can have an impact on the organization's goals. You can increase leverage and visibility payoff, and you can create your own credibility. By using the IDT model and adapting it to your particular situation, you can survive in the organization in the future.

REFERENCE

• Ronald W. Clement, Jones W. Walker and Patrick R. Pinto, "Changing Demands On the Training Professional," *Training and Development Journal*, 33, 3–7, (March 1979).

Training Programs: Pulling Them into Sync with Your Company's Strategic Planning

Richard P. Nielsen

This article shows the relationship between effective strategic planning and the management of training programs. To understand the relationship, one must understand how strategic planning is distinguished from comprehensive planning and short-run operations planning.

In comprehensive planning, resources are allocated to all sectors of an organization within the context of a long-term model that tries to optimize and integrate nearly all input-output relationships. At the other extreme is short-run operations planning in which an organization responds on a daily or even an hourly basis to changing internal processes and external market conditions. Strategic planning and management, on the other hand, is the process of continuously adapting in large and/or small ways in key decision areas to an organization's evolving environment as well as to changes caused by the organization's internal processes.

In a sense, strategic planning is something of a synthesis between the extremes of comprehensive planning and short-run operations planning. Strategic planning is similar to comprehensive planning in that it recognizes the need to order and coordinate long-term decision making. However, strategic planning also recognizes that markets and internal processes are continuously, and often quickly, changing and evolving. Strategic planning recognizes that key decision responses are much more practical than having to make comprehensive and coordinated changes in every aspect of the organization.

THE NEED FOR STRATEGIC HUMAN RESOURCES MANAGEMENT OF TRAINING PROGRAMS

Professor Wickham Skinner in his 1981 *Harvard Business Review* article, "Big Hat, No Cattle: Managing Human Resources," which reviews the human resources management field, concludes that:

Acquiring and developing the right talents for the business as it changes strategy, technology, and products requires more

shrewd, wise, long-range planning than any other corporate endeavor . . . the lack of long-range planning in human resources is frequently disastrous. So the ultimate irony is that the personnel function—which deals with the most fundamental and central corporate competitive resource and that has the longest time horizon of any function—is left with no long-range strategy and allowed to react merely to transient pressures and events.

Noel Tichy, Charles Fombrun, and Mary Anne Devanna in their article "Strategic Human Resource Management" (*Sloan Management Review,* Winter 1982) identify four key areas that are of necessity involved in effective strategic human resources management: selection, appraisal, rewards, and development. *Selection* refers to finding people who are best able to perform required jobs. *Rewards* are those characteristics associated with a job and job performance that help motivate employees—for example, salary, bonuses, benefits, praise, career opportunities, responsibility, and the opportunities to learn and to be creative. *Development* is the process of helping employees to realize and improve their work and career potential. *Appraisal* refers to the process of measuring and evaluating employee performance and potential for selection, reward, and development. Strategic human resources planning and management is concerned with planning and managing these areas so that they are consistent with and helpful to realizing both the organization's strategy and employee needs.

Can strategic human resources management of training programs in these four areas help an organization realize its overall institutional and relevant lower-level planning unit strategies? I contend that the answer is yes, but it might be useful to consider this question in relation to prototype strategies.

Although they come from different but related research traditions, the business and economic historian Alfred duPont Chandler and the industrial organization economist Oliver E. Williamson have independently identified five types of prototype strategies: specialized expansion, related diversification, unrelated diversification, vertical integration, and geographic expansion within and across countries.

For those unfamiliar with these strategies, a few illustrative examples may be of interest. An example of *specialized expansion* would be *The Boston Globe* newspaper company's expanding its share of the

Boston area newspaper market. *Related diversification* would be *The Globe*'s starting or buying a magazine. *Unrelated diversification* would be *The Globe*'s buying or starting a hotel business. *Vertical integration* would be *The Globe*'s buying or starting a paper-making factory. *Geographic expansion* would be *The Globe*'s buying or starting a newspaper in California or England. An institution can adopt a combination of these strategies simultaneously as well as chronologically.

To better understand how strategic human resources management of training programs can help an organization realize its strategy, several case studies are outlined below. These involve the following companies: Dayton-Hudson Corporation, IBM, AT&T, Delta Airlines, Inc., and Rockwell International. The human resources functions of selection, development, rewards, and appraisal are considered in each case.

Dayton-Hudson

The Dayton-Hudson Corporation (DH) is a retailing organization. Its strategy in the 1960s and 1970s was to expand geographically through acquisition while maintaining a high-quality image and product line. DH owns and manages retail stores under these names: Dayton, Hudson, Target, Mervyn, B. Dalton Bookseller, and several others. An important part of Dayton-Hudson's strategy is to maintain a consistent delivery and an image of providing high-quality products and service. Training programs play an important role in this strategy. Because DH acquired several of its retail stores and store chains through acquisition and plans to continue doing so, it is important for DH to develop employees who use the DH approach rather than the many different approaches of the acquired stores.

Through training programs DH is able to develop employees and employee behavior and attitudes consistent with the DH strategy and philosophy. DH gives its trainees written statements about and training in the company's strategic mission and direction, corporate purposes, merchandising philosophy, and so forth. The written documents are quite specific. For example, with respect to fashion and value DH states that:

Fashion is at the heart of our business. Fashion is change—change with direction. Newness and change can be predicted, however, through Trend Merchandising. Our aim is for each company to be the fashion leader within its markets . . . Our companies seek to provide maximum value to customers by acting aggressively as their buying agent . . . we are sensitive to the expanded meaning of the term *value*: customer time spent locating products or waiting for service, energy costs incurred in a shopping trip, ser-

viceability of durable goods, and the psychic and emotional value of the shopping experience itself. (William G. Ouchi, *Theory Z: How American Business Can Meet the Japanese Challenge,* Addison-Wesley Publishing Co., 1981)

When trainees are placed in DH's many and different types of stores, they help transmit this message and philosophy. They help provide unity and continuity across stores with respect to the central corporate strategy. Again, this is particularly important because many of the stores owned and managed by DH were acquired from previous owners and management systems with different philosophies and strategies and employees who were used to those strategies and philosophies.

Not only do training programs stress the development of employees with the DH approach, they are also used to select those employees who have best demonstrated performance that is consistent with the DH strategy for permanent employment and careers with the company. In the appraisal system that is used to evaluate trainees, specific attention is paid to trainees' performance and potential with respect to the DH strategy and philosophy. Trainees are rewarded with promotions, salary increases, and offers of permanent positions and careers with DH in large part on the basis of how well they learn and perform in a manner consistent with the DH strategy and philosophy.

IBM

An important part of the IBM strategy for the 1970s and 1980s is vertical integration. More specifically, IBM is building robots to help build computers. Training has an important role to play in this strategy. IBM has increased its recruitment of mechanical and industrial engineers as well as electrical engineers for its training programs. IBM training programs help trainees develop robotics skills that cut across electrical, mechanical, and industrial engineering skills that are needed to help IBM realize its strategy.

Trainees are appraised on how well they can combine such skills as well as on many other dimensions. Trainees are rewarded in significant part on the basis of how well they can apply their learning and skills in the vertical integration robotics strategic area. This is not to suggest that a good electrical engineer who fits other IBM criteria would be rejected because of a difficulty with integrating electrical and mechanical engineering skills. Instead, and more to the point, the training programs can help locate, develop, and select trainees who have the particular skills, potential, and interests in the robotics area that are important for IBM's vertical integration strategy.

AT&T

Important to AT&T's strategy (beginning in the late 1970s) is related diversification into information processing and telecommunications from its more specialized base in telephone services. This represents an important shift in strategy with important human resources and training implications. Before the adoption of this strategy AT&T had to worry less about competition and marketing than it will in the future when it tries to compete with such firms as IBM. Consequently, AT&T is placing greater emphasis on a marketing orientation in its training programs and trying to select more trainees who demonstrate that they have potential, talents, and interests in marketing issues and approaches.

Delta Airlines

With respect to its physical product, Delta Airlines is essentially the same as its competition. Yet over the last 20 years, Delta has been the most consistently profitable of U.S. airlines. The chairman of Delta, Thomas Beebe, attributes Delta's great success in large part to "the Delta family feeling," which translates in behavioral terms to a highly motivated and friendly workforce that provides superior service.

Delta emphasizes its "family feeling" and places a high priority on superior service, friendliness, and motivation in all its training programs. Trainees are also interviewed by psychologists to help determine whether they are appropriately cooperative, motivated, and interested in furthering Delta's strategy of superior service in a specialized industry as one of the primary approaches toward increasing and maintaining market share and profitability. A Delta psychologist, Dr. Sidney Janus, explains: "I try to determine their sense of cooperativeness or sense of teamwork because at Delta 'you don't just join a company, you join an objective'" (quoted by Janet Guyon in *The Wall Street Journal*, July 18, 1980).

Training is an important part of this strategy. Training programs give Delta the time to thoroughly introduce trainees to "the Delta family" concept. It enables Delta to appraise trainees and determine which ones are best suited to continue developing their skills and potentials as trainees and as permanent employees and members of the Delta "family."

Rockwell International

Rockwell International (RI) is one of the 50 largest U.S. industrial corporations. It owns and operates hundreds of related and unrelated businesses. In a corporation with hundreds of different businesses, it is normally very difficult for its thousands of employees to relate to an overall corporate strategy that includes unrelated diversification. In significant part because of this, RI has been trying to develop strategic human resources management that is consistent with corporate and division strategies. For example, in its largest division, Automotive Operations, RI concluded that:

In order to maximize our ability to handle rapidly changing market, government, and people complexities, we must continue to modify and develop our culture (beliefs, traditions, values, management systems) in a manner which will provide the overall framework to approach the eighties and nineties. The development, implementation, and communication of our culture will provide a key ingredient in promulgating an environment characterized by: innovation, prudent risk taking, value congruence, progressive management styles. (From William Ouchi's Theory Z book cited above.)

To this end RI has implemented what it calls a culture audit—through which for various specific issues, such as "individual orientation" and "information sharing," the division identified where it was in the mid 1970s, what it had done to make improvements since then, where the division was currently, and what future directions were needed. This audit has become an important part of RI's training programs. Trainees are presented with a history of where the division has been, what has been done to make improvements, where the division is now, and what future improvements are planned.

The purpose of sharing this audit with those at the training level is both to help potential long-term employees understand and gear their actions toward the improvements identified in the audit and to select those employees best suited for the culture that the division is trying to develop. In addition, the sharing of the audit with trainees is intended to enable them to better adjust their behaviors to the division's strategies. Over the longer term, if they become long-term employees, they may continue to use the audit mechanism as an effective mechanism for helping socialize newer employees.

The cases described above illustrate how strategic human resources management of training programs can help organizations realize their strategies.

IMPLEMENTING STRATEGIC HUMAN RESOURCES MANAGEMENT OF TRAINING PROGRAMS

Because strategic human resources management of training programs is desirable, a reasonable next step would be to consider how to implement such an approach. It is my contention that implementation involves at least six key steps.

Step 1. The director of training needs to be informed about the organization's overall and lower-level planning unit strategies. To adapt and design training programs that help realize organization strategies, the director of training needs to know what those strategies are. This may seem obvious—but unfortunately, human resources and other middle managers frequently do not know the organization's strategies. Sometimes this is because the human resources managers themselves do not appreciate how they can help realize such strategies; sometimes it is because higher-level corporate management does not understand that human resources managers can play a positive role in strategic planning and management.

Step 2. The specific ways in which training programs can teach trainees about organization strategies must be identified and articulated. It is not enough to know what an organization's strategies are. Implications in terms of specific needs and requirements for training programs and trainees should be articulated. This means that there has to be effective dialogue between training managers and those line and staff managers who will be supervising the trainees on the job.

Step 3. Strategies for the ways in which training programs can help institutions realize their overall strategies need to be developed. Training managers need to develop their own strategies for helping the larger institution realize its strategies. They must design specific selection, development, reward, and appraisal strategies that are consistent with and helpful in the achievement of the institution's overall strategies.

Step 4. Training operations need to be organized to facilitate the implementation of the training strategies designed to help realize larger institutional strategies. As the literature on relationships between general strategy and organization structure suggests, the way in which an institution is organized can facilitate or retard the achievement of strategy. The same is true for training programs. How a training department or division organizes itself can influence how well it is able to implement its strategies for delivering training programs.

Step 5. Training staff need to be trained to carry out the strategies that will further the institution's strategies. As an institution's strategies evolve, the needs that training is trying to serve tend also to evolve. While it may seem obvious that as training needs evolve and change, the people doing the training will have to retrain themselves, this is not always the case. Just as investment analysts may not manage their personal finances well, doctors are frequently overweight and smoke, and long-range planners are not able to plan their own lives very well, trainers sometimes forget or postpone their own retraining.

Step 6. Reward and evaluation mechanisms for training personnel need to be adjusted to reflect newer training strategies. Human resources and training managers are not unlike other managers in that they respond to evaluation and reward mechanisms. If a training strategy changes, but the rewards and evaluation criteria for managers and staff do not also change, there is a natural tendency to behave in a way that would meet the older criteria rather than the new ones.

CONCLUSION

Case studies from five well-known organizations have illustrated how the strategic management of training programs for human resources can enhance business strategic planning and management. For organizations that are interested in adopting such an approach, six implementation steps have been outlined.

PART TWO
TRAINING AIDS

SECTION I

Training Roles, Competencies, and Vocabulary

In the early 1980s, the American Society for Training and Development launched a study to identify the tasks performed by and the skills needed by training and development specialists. They eventually determined that there are 15 distinct roles which involve a total of 38 competencies. Of course, proper and complete performance of any role involves the use of more than just one competency. Three exhibits represent summary findings of that study:

1. The 15 roles.
2. The 38 competencies.
3. "The Human Resources Wheel," which depicts graphically how the roles and competencies work together to form what is increasingly called Human Resource Development.

Preliminary Roles and Outputs
ASTD Training and Development Competency Study

EVALUATOR: The role of identifying the extent of a program's impact.
- Instruments to assess individual change in knowledge, skill, attitude, behavior, results.
- Instruments to assess program and instructional quality.
- Reports (written and verbal) of program impact on individuals.
- Reports (written and verbal) of program impact on an organization.
- Evaluation designs and plans (written and verbal).

GROUP FACILITATOR: The role of managing group discussions and group process so that individuals learn and group members feel the experience is positive.
- Group discussions in which issues and needs are constructively addressed.
- Group decisions where individuals all feel committed to action.
- Cohesive teams.

INDIVIDUAL DEVELOPMENT COUNSELOR: The role of helping an individual assess personal competencies, values, goals and identifying and planning development and career actions.
- An individual with career development plans.
- An individual able to identify his/her own development needs/goals.
- Referrals to professional counseling.
- An individual with new knowledge about where to get development support.

INSTRUCTIONAL WRITER: The role of preparing written learning and instructional materials.
- Exercises, workbooks, worksheets.
- Teaching guides.
- Written proposals.
- Written case studies.
- Scripts (for video, film, audio).
- Textbooks.

INSTRUCTOR: The role of presenting information and directing structured learning experiences so that individuals learn.
- An individual with new knowledge, skill, attitudes or behavior in his/her repertoire.
- Case studies, role plays, games, tests and other non-technological but structured learning events directed.
- Lectures, presentations, stories delivered.
- Video tapes, films, audio tapes, computer aided instruction facilitated.

MANAGER OF TRAINING AND DEVELOPMENT: The role of planning, organizing, staffing, controlling Training and Development operations or training and development projects and of linking T&D operations with other organizational units.
- T&D department or project operating objectives.
- T&D budgets.
- Positive work climate in the T&D function or project group.
- Optimal staffing for department or projects.
- A fully productive T&D staff.
- T&D standards, policies, procedures.
- Selections of outside suppliers/consultants.
- Solutions to department/project problems.
- T&D actions congruent with other HR and organization actions.

MARKETER: The role of selling Training and Development viewpoints, learning packages, programs, services to target audiences outside ones own immediate work unit.
- Promotional materials for T&D programs and curricula.
- Sales presentations (developed and delivered).
- Program overviews (developed and delivered).

MEDIA SPECIALIST: The role of producing software for and using audio-visual, computer and other hardware-based technologies for training and development.
- T&D computer software.
- Lists (written/verbal) of recommended instructional hardware.
- Slide programs.
- Video tapes.

- Audio tapes.
- Films.
- Computer hardware in working order.
- AV equipment in working order.

NEEDS ANALYST: The role of defining gaps between ideal and actual performance and specifying causes for the gaps.
- Reports (written and verbal) of performance problems and discrepancies.
- Reports (written and verbal) of knowledge, skill, attitude problems/discrepancies.
- Tools to assess the knowledge, skill, attitude and performance levels of individuals and organizations.
- Needs analysis strategies.
- Data analyses.
- Documentation/justification of conclusions about causes of competency and performance gaps.

PROGRAM ADMINISTRATOR: The role of ensuring that the facilities, equipment, materials, participants and other components of a learning event are present and that program logistics run smoothly.
- Facilities selected, scheduled, equipped.
- Participant attendance secured, recorded.
- Material for the T&D library obtained and stored.
- Hotel/conference center staff managed.
- Faculty scheduled.
- Course materials distributed.

PROGRAM DESIGNER: The role of translating learning needs into objectives, content, learning activities and designs for a specific program.
- Lists of learning objectives.
- Written program plans/designs.
- Specifications for training content/activities/materials and methods.
- Sequencing plans for training content, activities, materials and methods.

STRATEGIST: The role of developing long-range plans for what the training and development structure, organization, policies, programs, services and practices will be in order to accomplish the Training and Development mission.
- T&D long-range plans included in the broad human resource strategy of the client organization.
- Identification (written and verbal) of long-range T&D strengths, weaknesses, opportunities, threats.
- Descriptions of the T&D function and its outputs in the future.

TASK ANALYST: The role of identifying activities, tasks, sub-tasks, human resource and support requirements necessary to accomplish specific results in a job or organization.
- Lists of key job/unit outputs.
- Lists of key job/unit tasks.
- Lists of knowledge, skill, attitude requirements of a job or unit.
- Descriptions of the performance levels required in a job/unit.

THEORETICIAN: The role of developing and testing theories of learning, training and development.
- Theories of learning and behavior change.
- Articles on T&D issues/theories for scientific journals.
- Articles on T&D issues/theories for trade publications.
- Research designs.
- Research reports.
- Learning/training models.

TRANSFER AGENT: The role of helping individuals apply learning after the learning experience.
- Individual action plans for on-the-job/real world application.
- Plans (written and verbal) for the support of transfer of training.
- Job aids to support performance and learning.

ASTD Competency Study
T&D Competencies

1. *Adult Learning Understanding* . . .
Knowing how adults acquire and apply knowledge, skills, and attitudes. Understanding individual differences in learning.

2. *Assessment Competence* . . .
Devising/selecting methods and materials for measuring individual difference factors (e.g., knowledge, skill, interest, attitudes, values) and learning needs.

3. *Audio/Visual Equipment Skill* . . .
Selecting and using audio visual aids.

4. *Career Development Knowledge* . . .
Understanding the personal and organizational issues and methods relevant to individual career planning.

5. *Climate Management Skills* . . .
Establishing and maintaining an environment where individuals are satisfied, growing and productive.

6. *Competency Identification Skills* . . .
Identifying the knowledge and skill requirements of jobs/tasks/roles.

7. *Computer Competence* . . .
Understanding how computers work and being able to use them in T&D applications.

8. *Cost/Benefit Analysis Skills* . . .
Assessing the financial, psychological and strategic advantages and disadvantages of various courses of action.

9. *Counseling Skills* . . .
Helping individuals identify, analyze, and explore personal needs, values, problems, and goals; supporting them in implementing actions.

10. *Data Reduction Skills* . . .
Scanning, analyzing, synthesizing, and drawing conclusions from data.

11. *Delegation Skill* . . .
Assigning task responsibility and authority to others.

12. *Evaluation Methodology Understanding* . . .
Knowing/being able to use techniques and approaches which can be used to measure and assess training and development impact.

13. *Facilities Skill* . . .
Planning and coordinating staff and logistics in an efficient and cost-effective manner.

14. *Feedback Skills* . . .
Communicating information/opinions such that it is understood.

15. *Futuring Skills* . . .
Projecting trends and being able to visualize possible and probable futures and their implications.

16. *Group Dynamics Understanding* . . .
Knowing how groups form, develop and terminate. Recognizing what is happening in a group at a given time.

17. *Group Influence/Leadership Skills* . . .
Affecting individual actions and decisions in a planned way such that group members are committed to a course of action.

18. *Industry Understanding* . . .
Knowing the products, services, processes and structure of the sector/industry (e.g., utilities, government, banking) being served, and the most critical forces affecting it.

19. *Intellectual Versatility* . . .
Recognizing and exploring new ideas and practices; being able to think both creatively and logically without undue influences from personal biases.

20. *Interaction Versatility* . . .
Recognizing values and needs differences across groups; adjusting behaviors in order to be effective across diverse situations (including cross-cultural).

21. *Library Skills* . . .
Gathering information from printed and other recorded sources. Identifying and using information specialists and reference services and aids.

22. *Model Building Skills* . . .
Developing theoretical and/or practical frameworks which described complex ideas in a usable way.

23. *Negotiation Skills* . . .
Securing win-win agreements while successfully representing a special interest in a decision situation.

24. *Objectives Preparation Skill* . . .
Preparing clear statements which define target outputs of an experience.

25. *Organization Change Understanding* . . .
Knowing what aids and inhibits individual, group, and system changes in organizations.

26. *Organization Understanding* . . .
Knowing the formal and informal structure, strategy, and systems of a SPECIFIC organization and their impact on individual and organization effectiveness.

27. *Performance Observation Skills* . . .
Tracking and describing behaviors and their effects.

28. *Personnel/HR Field Understanding* . . .
Knowing the technological, social, economic, professional and regulatory issues, resources and trends in the Human Resource field and their implications for training and development.

29. *Presentation Skills* . . .
Presenting information in a manner such that the intended purpose is achieved.

30. *Questioning Skills* . . .
Gathering information from and stimulating insight in individuals and groups through the use of interviews, questionnaires and other probing methods.

31. *Records Management Skill...*
Storing and retrieving data.
32. *Relationship Building...*
Establishing, strengthening, maintaining credibility, trust and confidence with individuals and groups.
33. *Research Design Skills...*
Selecting a methodology, statistical and data collection techniques for a formal inquiry.
34. *Role Versatility...*
Adjusting one's own behavior in order to be effective within and among groups and with individuals.
35. *Systems Analysis Skills...*
Taking a big perspective on events and actions; being able to identify causes, effects and values operating in a situation.

36. *T&D Field Understanding...*
Knowing the current and emerging technological, social, economic, professional and regulatory issues, resources and trends in the T&D field.
37. *Writing Skills...*
Preparing written material which follows generally accepted rules of style and form.
38. *Training and Development Techniques...*
Knowing the characteristics and critical attributes, advantages and disadvantages of the techniques and formats used in training—such as case studies, role playing, discussions, text material, and programmed instruction.

The Human Resource Wheel

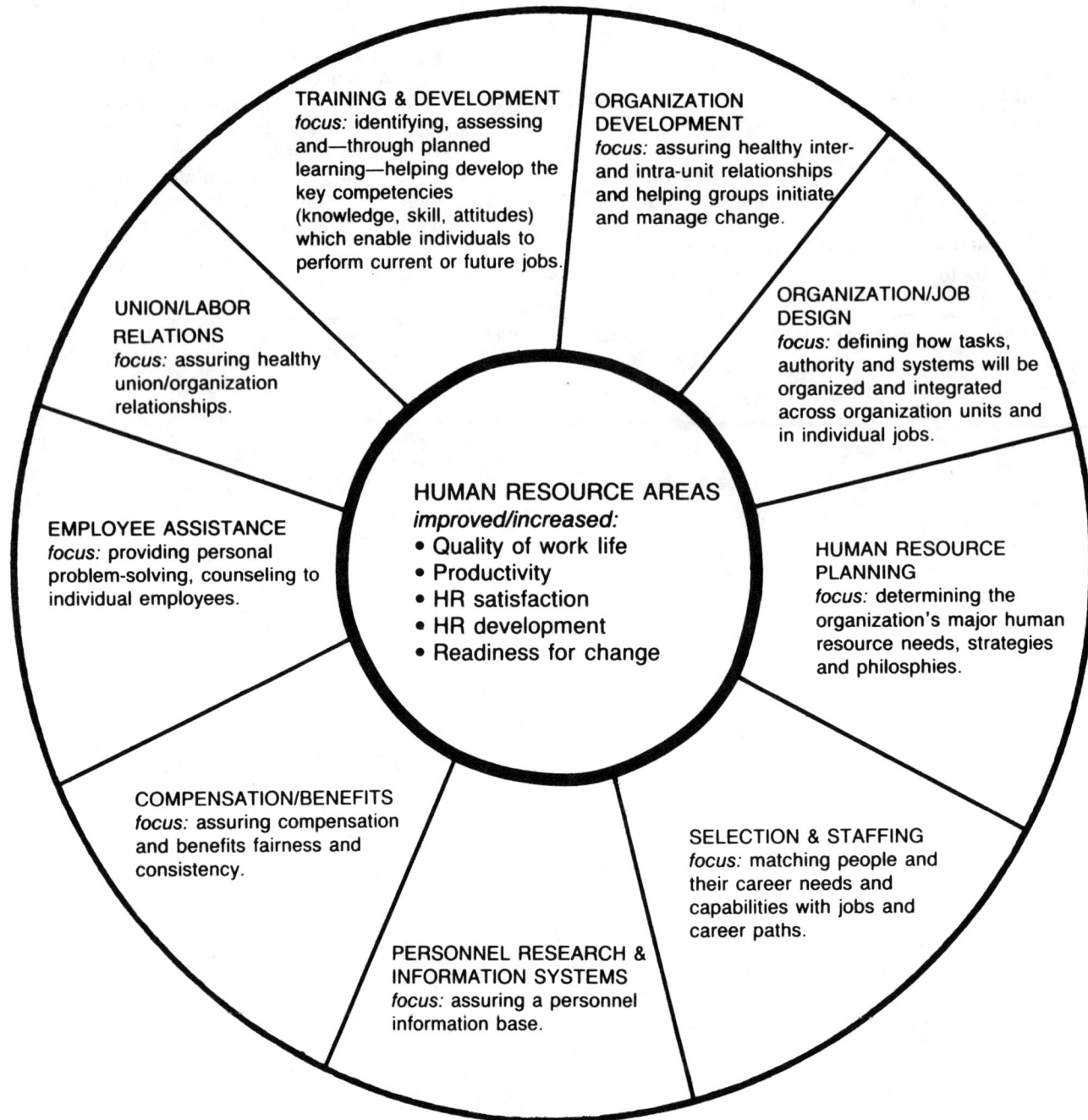

TRAINING & DEVELOPMENT
focus: identifying, assessing and—through planned learning—helping develop the key competencies (knowledge, skill, attitudes) which enable individuals to perform current or future jobs.

ORGANIZATION DEVELOPMENT
focus: assuring healthy inter- and intra-unit relationships and helping groups initiate and manage change.

UNION/LABOR RELATIONS
focus: assuring healthy union/organization relationships.

ORGANIZATION/JOB DESIGN
focus: defining how tasks, authority and systems will be organized and integrated across organization units and in individual jobs.

EMPLOYEE ASSISTANCE
focus: providing personal problem-solving, counseling to individual employees.

HUMAN RESOURCE AREAS
improved/increased:
- Quality of work life
- Productivity
- HR satisfaction
- HR development
- Readiness for change

HUMAN RESOURCE PLANNING
focus: determining the organization's major human resource needs, strategies and philosphies.

COMPENSATION/BENEFITS
focus: assuring compensation and benefits fairness and consistency.

SELECTION & STAFFING
focus: matching people and their career needs and capabilities with jobs and career paths.

PERSONNEL RESEARCH & INFORMATION SYSTEMS
focus: assuring a personnel information base.

SECTION II

Training Aids and Tips on Determining Training Needs

Training needs are determined through some form of communication between a training person and the client, or user in other parts of the organization.

Interviews and questionnaires are the common media for gathering the data, upon which to base decisions about what training to offer.

This raises questions such as "Which medium is better?" and "What questions should one ask?" Four exhibits will deal with these questions:

1. *DESIGN* of Needs Survey, prepared by Geoffrey M. Bellman.
2. "Questions To Ask in Determining Training Needs."
3. "While You Are Collecting Needs," a few tips from an experienced training director.
4. A "Needs Survey Checklist," developed by Sally Fitz of *Successful Meetings* magazine.

DESIGN Of Needs Survey

Design your approach to surveying needs by using the written material the client (or others) gives you, along with data collected in your brief interviews with the client and a few others named in the *CONTACT* session.

- Gather historical paper data. Make copies of your own that you can mark or cut up.
  Good sources:
  Organization plans and objectives
  Performance appraisals
  Training programs
  Audit reports
  Exit interviews
  Attitude surveys
  Industrial engineering
  Employment figures
  Job descriptions
- Common survey methods: Questionnaire, interview, test, observation
- Survey design considerations:

IF MORE . . .	Collection Time Available	IF LESS . . .
Open-ended, interviews	*Collection Time Available*	Closed ended, checklist
Less structured approach	*Experience of Data Collectors*	More structured approach
Mail instrument	*Geographic Spread*	Face-to-face
More structure	*Participants*	Less structure
Less notes	*Confidentiality*	More notes
More coding	*Amount of Data*	Less coding

- Simpler methods are easier for you to use and for the client to understand.
- Focus the questions in the survey on individual, group, or organization performance problems or opportunities—*not* on training needed.

Questions to Ask in Determining Training Needs

When you encounter symptoms of training needs, you need a repertoire of questions to use in validating the training need. Here are some samples for you to rate as USEFUL or NOT USEFUL, indicating the degree of usefulness by a check in the proper place.

Useful					Not Useful		
Very	Quite	Somewhat			Trivial	Ambiguous	Dangerous
___	___	___	1.	What are your training needs?	___	___	___
___	___	___	2.	What are the training needs of your employees?	___	___	___
___	___	___	3.	What are your big problems?	___	___	___
___	___	___	4.	What are the big "people problems" in your span of control?	___	___	___
___	___	___	5.	Do your employees have attitudes that need changing?	___	___	___
___	___	___	6.	What visible behaviors do these attitudes produce?	___	___	___
___	___	___	7.	Can you be more specific?	___	___	___
___	___	___	8.	What are they doing that they shouldn't do?	___	___	___
___	___	___	9.	What aren't they doing that they should do?	___	___	___
___	___	___	10.	What do you feel you need to know in order to do your job better?	___	___	___
___	___	___	11.	In what skills do you need practice so you can perform better?	___	___	___
___	___	___	12.	*(Add your own! On the rest of this page, and the reverse side, jot down helpful/fatal questions from your own experience. We'll have time to discuss these.)*	___	___	___

While You Are Collecting Needs . . .

- Ask questions about what organization and individual performance is needed—that's what people know about, have expertise in. Respect and listen to their thoughts on performance.
- Don't ask questions about what training is needed. Training questions can imply they have the training expertise to respond and that you are going to act on their training suggestions.
- While collecting data, just collect; don't analyze. Keep the separation clean.
- Collect and code data on cards (one data bit per card) for easy sorting.
- Collect only as much data as you can analyze.
- Help others understand the "how" (process) and "why" (objective) of what you are doing with them.
- Be as open with them as you expect them to be with you.

Needs Survey Checklist

Directions for use: Read this list over carefully. Circle the "Yes" for areas you want training in. Circle the question mark if you are uncertain, or "No" if you need no improvement on your own job or for promotion to a better job.

1. How to train people quickly and easily . . Yes ? No
2. How to lead or direct others . . . . Yes ? No
3. How to plan . . . . Yes ? No
4. How to control . . . . Yes ? No
5. How to organize . . . . Yes ? No
6. How to interpret and apply company policies and procedures . . . . Yes ? No
7. How to get out more work—motivate people . . . . Yes ? No
8. How to discipline workers . . . . Yes ? No
9. How to improve job methods . . . . Yes ? No
10. How to do research work . . . . Yes ? No
11. How to learn a new job . . . . Yes ? No
12. How to understand yourself and others—sensitivity . . . . Yes ? No
13. How to break down a job into elements . Yes ? No
14. How to work out new ideas . . . . Yes ? No
15. How to develop your own manual skill . . . . Yes ? No
16. How to keep machines in working condition . . . . Yes ? No
17. How to keep things in order . . . . Yes ? No
18. How to evaluate and rate employee's performance . . . . Yes ? No
19. How to reduce waste (time, materials, supplies) . . . . Yes ? No
20. How to improve your performance on the job . . . . Yes ? No
21. How to improve the morale of your unit . Yes ? No
22. How to sell ideas to a superior . . . . Yes ? No
23. How to manage the boss . . . . Yes ? No
24. How to delegate authority . . . . Yes ? No
25. How to hold people responsible for results . . . . Yes ? No
26. How to get people to work together—cooperate . . . . Yes ? No
27. How to be diplomatic—tactful . . . . Yes ? No
28. How to improve your written and oral expression . . . . Yes ? No
29. How to recognize details that count . . . . Yes ? No
30. How to read blueprints and drawings . . . Yes ? No
31. How to read charts and tables . . . . Yes ? No
32. How to improve reading and speaking ability . . . . Yes ? No
33. How to improve your memory . . . . Yes ? No
34. How to recognize causes of fatigue . . . . Yes ? No
35. How to reduce disagreeable factors on jobs . . . . Yes ? No
36. How to sell safety to your workers—prevent accidents . . . . Yes ? No
37. How to work more comfortably . . . . Yes ? No
38. How to avoid tensions—conflicts . . . . . . Yes ? No
39. How to conduct conferences and staff meetings . . . . Yes ? No
40. How to communicate—upwards, downwards, etc. Yes ? No
41. How to interview others . . . . Yes ? No
42. How to apply the principles of management . . . . Yes ? No
43. How to make staff studies and do staff work . . . . Yes ? No
44. How to make or write reports . . . . Yes ? No
45. How to supervise women employees . . . Yes ? No
46. How to supervise minority employees . . Yes ? No

SECTION III

Training Aids Involving Physical Facilities

The learning environment is both a psychological and a physical reality. The physical conditions of the classroom can have enormous impact on the psychological atmosphere. The following checklist, adapted from lists by numerous people who conduct meetings, will help in selecting a room or assuring that a room is ready for use.

If you are using outside resources, you'll appreciate "The Hotel/Motel User Checklist," designed by Martin M. Broadwell, experienced consultant and former training manager for Southern Bell.

The Hotel/Motel User Checklist

Needed	Done	
		1. General Features
☐	☐	Location
☐	☐	Suitability for your special function
☐	☐	Total seating capacity for required setup
		2. Setup Details
☐	☐	Type of function
☐	☐	Capacity
☐	☐	Seating arrangement—Total capacity: ☐ Minimum ☐ Maximum

	Minimum	Maximum
Auditorium	_____	_____
Schoolroom	_____	_____
Round tables	_____	_____
Conference	_____	_____
Smoking/No smoking section	_____	_____
Card tables	_____	_____
Dance	_____	_____
Other	_____	_____

Needed	Done	
☐	☐	Chairs
		Type
☐	☐	Spacing
☐	☐	Placement
		Visibility
		Obstructions
		Reflections and ambient air
		Ventilation
		Projection screen — width 1/6th distance to farthest viewer
☐	☐	Aisles
		Number
		Location
		Use
		Entrance, exit
		Accessibility of seats
		Audience contact
		Hand microphone
		Collect questions
☐	☐	Tables—special
		Service
		Supply
		Display
		Distribution of materials
		Cashier
		Projection equipment
☐	☐	Food Service
		3. Condition of room
☐	☐	Clean
☐	☐	Furnishings
☐	☐	Ventilation—control
		Cooling _____min. temperature
		Heating _____max. temperature
☐	☐	Lighting
		Control
		Adequate
		Special
		Glare
		Reflections
		Acoustics

Needed	Done	
☐	☐	Table coverings
		Clean
		Smooth
		Hanging straight
☐	☐	Pads
☐	☐	Pencils
☐	☐	Ash trays (smoking area only)
☐	☐	Matches (smoking area only)
☐	☐	Water, glasses—fresh
		Accessible
		Speaker
		Audience
		Placed for least disturbance
		_____number needed
☐	☐	Waste basket

4. Speakers table, head table

Needed	Done	
☐	☐	Location
☐	☐	Elevation
☐	☐	Number of seats
☐	☐	Cover
		Clean
		Hanging straight
		View beneath table screened
☐	☐	Name, place cards
☐	☐	Gavel
☐	☐	Pointer
		Regular
		Lighter indicator
☐	☐	Reference material

5. Safety

Needed	Done	
☐	☐	Exits
		Adequate number
		All sides of the room
		Clearly marked
		Electrically and with non-electric placards
		Unobstructed
☐	☐	Fire Prevention
		Sprinklers
		Announcements
		Extinguishers
☐	☐	Other Hazards
		Loose wires or cable
		Narrow aisles
		Loose carpet
		Litter on the tables
		Litter on the floor
		Sharp edges on the tables
		AV equipment in aisles

6. Communication cues

Needed	Done	
☐	☐	Distracting
☐	☐	Lights
		On, off, change
☐	☐	Projection
		Start, stop, change

7. Public address system

Needed	Done	
☐	☐	Microphones
		Number
		Location
		Type
		Stationary
		Portable
		Neck
		Lapel
		Hand
		Volume
		Control
		Tested
		Attendant
		Constant
		Available

8. Platforms, risers, steps

Needed	Done	
☐	☐	Location
☐	☐	Dimensions
☐	☐	Height/steps
☐	☐	Covered
		Floors
		Sides
☐	☐	Safe
		Length
		Width
		Stable, secure
		Guard rails
		Covering
		Smooth
		Fastened down
☐	☐	Wiring
		Covered
		Guarded
☐	☐	Hazards marked

9. Lights

Needed	Done	
☐	☐	Regular
☐	☐	Special
		Spot
		Colored
		Other
☐	☐	Adequacy
		No glare, reflections
		Room in general
		Behind speaker
☐	☐	Controls—separate cut-offs
		Lights only
		Individual
		Multiples
		Microphones only
		Projector only
		Signal system

10. Electricity

Needed	Done	
☐	☐	Type
		AC-DC current
		Characteristics
		Capacity of lines
☐	☐	Ground wires
☐	☐	Inlets, outlets
		Location
		Number

Needed   Done

11. Teleprompter service
☐   ☐   Operating
☐   ☐   Speed—each speaker
checked in advance
☐   ☐   Operator
On hand
Instructed
☐   ☐   Signal system

12. Blackboard, charts, display stand
☐   ☐   Size suitable to room
☐   ☐   Clean
☐   ☐   Eraser—clean
☐   ☐   Handtowels
☐   ☐   Placement timing
In place
Place on signal
☐   ☐   Standing firm, braced
☐   ☐   Location—visibility
Continuous display
Walls that will hold masking tape
☐   ☐   Chalk—visible color (yellow on
green is best)
☐   ☐   Pencils, crayons, markers, other
☐   ☐   Attachment facilities
Easy attachment
Firm hold
Easy release, flipover
☐   ☐   Supply table

13. Projection—general requirements
☐   ☐   Screen
_____
_____
☐   ☐   Projector
_____
_____
☐   ☐   Operator
_____
_____
☐   ☐   Projection materials
_____
_____
☐   ☐   Facilities
_____
_____
☐   ☐   Rules, regulations, licenses,
policies, practices
Hotel
City
Union

14. Projection screen
☐   ☐   Location
☐   ☐   Visibility
☐   ☐   Placement timing
In place
Place on signal
☐   ☐   Angled for no distortion
☐   ☐   Size suitable to room
☐   ☐   Type
Beaded
Matte

Needed   Done

15. Projector—type
☐   ☐   Use
Films
Slides
Other
☐   ☐   Suitability to room
Size
Power

16. Other projection facilities
☐   ☐   Table, stand, chair
☐   ☐   Extension wiring
Adequate
Guarded
☐   ☐   House lights control
Location
Cut-offs separate
Lights
Projector
Microphones
Attendant
Responsive
Instructed
Contributes his or her own ideas

17. Projector operator
☐   ☐   Available
☐   ☐   Instructed & rehearsed
Time schedule
Availability of projection materials
Order of projection
Signal system
Special instructions

18. Projection signal system
☐   ☐   Working
☐   ☐   Signals set
Start
Stop
Change
☐   ☐   Signals understood
Speaker
Operator

19. Projection time schedule
☐   ☐   Projection materials
available
☐   ☐   Setup
☐   ☐   Projection
☐   ☐   Operator available
Instruction conference
Setup
Projection

20. Procedures for projectionist to receive, return projection materials
☐   ☐   Where
☐   ☐   When
☐   ☐   From, to whom
☐   ☐   Receipts/to whom

Needed *Done*

21. Pre-function projection service check

☐ ☐ Projection materials
On hand
In order

☐ ☐ Operator
On hand
Instructions
Received and understood

☐ ☐ Projection equipment
Setup
Operating
Focus
Volume
Distortion
Extra bulbs, extension cords available

☐ ☐ Signal system

22. Reference materials for presiding officer

☐ ☐ Agenda
Order
Timing

☐ ☐ Speakers names (phonetic spellings)

☐ ☐ Titles of speeches

☐ ☐ Introduction and speaker biographies

☐ ☐ Special announcements

☐ ☐ Reference material
For speakers
For audience ·

☐ ☐ General instructions for audience

☐ ☐ Instructions for emergencies

23. Reference materials for speaker

☐ ☐ Name of organization
☐ ☐ Name of presiding officer
☐ ☐ Copy of speech
☐ ☐ Reference materials
☐ ☐ Films, slides, special props, other
☐ ☐ Instructions
Use of microphone
Signal systems
   Speaker timing
   Lighting
   Projection

24. Reference materials for registrants

☐ ☐ Distribute
At registration
At door
On chair or table
Handed out by attendants

☐ ☐ Supply tables, racks
☐ ☐ Pick up of filled forms
☐ ☐ Convenient
☐ ☐ No bottle-neck

Needed *Donc*

25. Admission

☐ ☐ Controlled
Badge
Ticket
Other

☐ ☐ Uncontrolled
☐ ☐ Table, chair outside door
Sale of tickets
Distribution of badges

☐ ☐ Attendants
Adequate number
Collect tickets, cards
Check badges
Distribute materials
Direct to seats
Pick up questions, take to rostrum
Carry messages

☐ ☐ Messenger service
Instructions
Restrictions

26. Post-meeting room check

☐ ☐ Organization property collected
☐ ☐ Check made for forgotten property
☐ ☐ Signs removed
☐ ☐ Films, slides, returned
☐ ☐ Switches off
☐ ☐ No smoking ashtrays or trash

27. Telephone—type of service

☐ ☐ Incoming, outgoing
Answered by
☐ ☐ Complete cutoff
Location of nearest phone
Instructions for transfer of incoming calls
☐ ☐ Outgoing only—instructions as to transfer of incoming calls

28. Photographer

☐ ☐ Instructions given
Type of picture
Titles of pictures
Time to take picture
How picture sales are to be handled
During function
Outside meeting room
At registration, other desks
Not for sale

☐ ☐ Equipment set up in advance—tested
☐ ☐ Extension wiring guarded
Disconnects
Safety

☐ ☐ Operator on hand

29. Reporting (if speakers approve)

☐ ☐ Preprinted news releases
☐ ☐ Speeches
    Off-the-record
    Release cleared
    To be edited
☐ ☐ Equipment
    Set up in advance
    Tested
☐ ☐ Operator on hand
☐ ☐ Instructions given
    Type of report
      Verbatim
      Abridged
    Number of copies—method of
    duplication
      Carbons
      Mimeo
      Other
    Time by which completed report
    is required
    Who may obtain copies from
    the reporter
      Where

30. Coffee service—meetings other than food, entertainment, social functions

☐ ☐ Time of setup
☐ ☐ Continuous
☐ ☐ Time period; specific or flexible?
☐ ☐ Type of service
    Self service
    Waiter service
      Regular
      Expedited
    Placement of service
    tables
    Accessibility
    Least disturbance
    Avoid bottlenecks
      Open area
      Several stations
☐ ☐ Menu
    Coffee
    Soft drinks
    Other

31. Signs

☐ ☐ Room identification
☐ ☐ Session title and number
☐ ☐ Speaker identification
    Inside meeting room
    Outside meeting room
☐ ☐ Speaker timing
☐ ☐ Directions to room

32. Special considerations

☐ ☐ Draperies
☐ ☐ Flowers
☐ ☐ Plants
☐ ☐ Flags, banners
☐ ☐ Special

33. Entertainment—music, other

☐ ☐ On hand
☐ ☐ Requirements known
☐ ☐ Instructed
☐ ☐ Props ready
☐ ☐ Dressing rooms
☐ ☐ Facilities, equipment,
    services ready

34. Publicity

☐ ☐ Press conferences
    Speakers
    Organization personnel
    Basis
      Individual
      Group
    Timing
    Location
☐ ☐ Admission of press
    representatives
☐ ☐ Press releases
    About organization
    About program
    Speeches
☐ ☐ Instructions, restrictions
    on release of speeches, other
    Immediate
    After editing
    Off-the-record
☐ ☐ Instructions, restrictions
    on photographs
    During functions
    Other times

35. Program information

☐ ☐ Schedule of events
☐ ☐ Final program
☐ ☐ Setup instructions
☐ ☐ Posting times of functions
☐ ☐ Hotel executive
☐ ☐ Convention bureau representative
☐ ☐ Auditorium manager
☐ ☐ Reporter
☐ ☐ Projectionist
☐ ☐ Photographer
☐ ☐ Others concerned

36. Audience care

- ☐ ☐ Meeting perks — buttons, gifts, etc.
- ☐ ☐ Participant information center
- ☐ ☐ Restrooms
- ☐ ☐ First aid facilities
- ☐ ☐ Doctor availability
- ☐ ☐ Security
- ☐ ☐ Secretarial Services
- ☐ ☐ Hospitality rooms
- ☐ ☐ Conversation lounges
- ☐ ☐ Speakers lounge
- ☐ ☐ Other_____

37. Miscellaneous

- ☐ ☐ Telephone locations
- Pay phones
- House phones
- ☐ ☐ Check room facilities
- ☐ ☐ Rest rooms
- ☐ ☐ Parking, garage facilities
- ☐ ☐ Traffic control
- ☐ ☐ Special elevator service as required—operators instructed

Our thanks to the many conference leaders who suggested one or more of these items and this format.

Hotel/Motel User Checklist

Needed *Completed*

1. CONFERENCE LOCATION CONTACTS
- ☐ ☐ Manager _____
- ☐ ☐ Maitre d'Hotel _____
- ☐ ☐ Bell Captain _____
- ☐ ☐ Service Manager _____
- ☐ ☐ Sales Manager _____
- ☐ ☐ Crisis Contact _____
- ☐ ☐ Complaint Contact _____

2. ATTENDANCE
- ☐ ☐ Total members expected
- ☐ ☐ Total guests expected
- ☐ ☐ Total wives, families
- ☐ ☐ Approximate rooms needed:
  Sing._____ Doub._____ Suites_____
- ☐ ☐ Room rates: Members_____,
  Guests_____, Wives_____,
  Child_____
- ☐ ☐ Reservation confirmation

3. TRANSPORTATION
- ☐ ☐ Arrangements for transportation
- ☐ ☐ Early/late arrivals
- ☐ ☐ Private cars
- ☐ ☐ Instructions to attendees
- ☐ ☐ Buses for tours

4. DATES
- ☐ ☐ Most of group will arrive_____
- ☐ ☐ Most of group will depart_____
- ☐ ☐ Uncommitted rooms released_____
- ☐ ☐ Registration cutoff date_____
- ☐ ☐ Arrangements for early/late arrivals
- ☐ ☐ Arrangements for "no-shows"

5. COMPLIMENTARY ACCOMMODATIONS
- ☐ ☐ Number of suits needed_____
- ☐ ☐ Room rates checked
- ☐ ☐ Bars, snacks, complimentary buffets
- ☐ ☐ Contacts for suite addresses_____
- ☐ ☐ Check rooms, gratuities
- ☐ ☐ Transportation services (reconfirming, tours, etc.)

6. GUEST SPEAKERS AND VISITORS
- ☐ ☐ Invitation to local dignitaries
- ☐ ☐ Acceptance of invitations
- ☐ ☐ Tickets provided
- ☐ ☐ Lodging provided
- ☐ ☐ Transportation arranged
- ☐ ☐ Welcome arranged
- ☐ ☐ Name tags prepared
- ☐ ☐ Honorarium required
- ☐ ☐ Honorarium prepared

Needed *Completed*

7. SPECIFIC EQUIPMENT AND FACILITIES
- ☐ ☐ Signs: Registration_____,
  Directional_____, Welcome_____
- ☐ ☐ List of equipment needed
- ☐ ☐ Price of equipment to be furnished
- ☐ ☐ List of equipment to be rented
- ☐ ☐ Lights: Spots_____, Floods _____,
  Other_____
- ☐ ☐ Lighting operator
- ☐ ☐ Staging requirements settled
- ☐ ☐ Chalkboards, easels, chart stands
- ☐ ☐ Lighted lecterns, gavel
- ☐ ☐ P.A. system:
  No. and types of microphones_____
  _____
  Location of controls for volume_____
  _____
- ☐ ☐ Recording equipment
- ☐ ☐ Recording equipment operator_____
  _____
- ☐ ☐ Projection equipment
- ☐ ☐ Projection equipment operator_____
  _____
- ☐ ☐ Location of blackout switch_____
  _____
- ☐ ☐ Phonograph
- ☐ ☐ Union clearances
- ☐ ☐ Repair kits (pliers, bulbs, wire)
- ☐ ☐ Decorations (meet fire regulations)
- ☐ ☐ Special effects (music, etc.)
- ☐ ☐ Dressing rooms required
- ☐ ☐ Reproduction equipment
- ☐ ☐ Garage and parking arrangements
- ☐ ☐ Other equipment_____
- ☐ ☐ Cost of extra equipment or services
- ☐ ☐ Telephones, number
- ☐ ☐ Flags, banners
- ☐ ☐ Photographer, stenographer
- ☐ ☐ Radio and TV broadcasting; CCTV
- ☐ ☐ Live and engineering charges for radio, TV
- ☐ ☐ Rental equipment contact_____

8. MEETINGS
- ☐ ☐ Times and dates of each
- ☐ ☐ Room assignments and rentals
- ☐ ☐ Complete floor plan furnished
- ☐ ☐ Headquarters room
- ☐ ☐ Seating plans for each meeting, seat numbering
- ☐ ☐ Speakers' tables
- ☐ ☐ Timing of meetings for speedy traffic flow
- ☐ ☐ Staging required
- ☐ ☐ Arrangements for breaks, lunches
- ☐ ☐ Other equipment

Needed
Completed

Points to Check Just Before Each Meeting
- ☐ ☐ Check room operation
- ☐ ☐ Seating plan as specified
- ☐ ☐ Location of additional seats
- ☐ ☐ Room temperature: optimum heating/cooling
- ☐ ☐ Operation of P.A. system, mikes, recording equipment
- ☐ ☐ Lectern and light, gavel, block
- ☐ ☐ Water pitcher, water and glasses at lectern, at conferees' tables
- ☐ ☐ Table ash trays, stands, matches, pencils, note pads, paper
- ☐ ☐ All audiovisual aids: charts, stands, easels, blackboards, etc.
- ☐ ☐ Projector, screen, stand, operator
- ☐ ☐ Location of restrooms
- ☐ ☐ Lighting as specified
- ☐ ☐ Signs, flags and banners placed correctly
- ☐ ☐ Special flowers and plants
- ☐ ☐ Other special facilities_____

- ☐ ☐ Signs directing members and guests to rooms
- ☐ ☐ Stenographer, photographer present

Points to Check Just After Each Meeting
- ☐ ☐ Removal of organization property
- ☐ ☐ Check for forgotten property
- ☐ ☐ Billing arrangements
- ☐ ☐ Take down signs, banners, etc.
- ☐ ☐ Recovery of films, slides, etc.

9. ORGANIZATION OF EXHIBITS
- ☐ ☐ Number of exhibits_____
- ☐ ☐ Floor plans for each exhibit furnished
- ☐ ☐ Date of setup and dismantling_____
- ☐ ☐ Room assignments and daily rentals
- ☐ ☐ Name of display company
- ☐ ☐ Directional signs/traffic flow
- ☐ ☐ Labor charges: electric and carpenter services
- ☐ ☐ Electrical power, steam, gas, water and waste lines
- ☐ ☐ Electrical charges
- ☐ ☐ Partitions, backdrops
- ☐ ☐ Storage or shipping cases
- ☐ ☐ Guard services
- ☐ ☐ Special effects
- ☐ ☐ Paging system and arrangements
- ☐ ☐ Badge arrangements
- ☐ ☐ Drawings for prizes
- ☐ ☐ Union clearances

10. REGISTRATION
- ☐ ☐ Approximate time required_____
- ☐ ☐ Registration cards: number and size_____
- ☐ ☐ Personnel to handle
- ☐ ☐ Number of tables_____, chairs_____
- ☐ ☐ Ash trays

Needed
Completed

- ☐ ☐ Typewriters: number and type_____
- ☐ ☐ Paper, pencils, pens, pins
- ☐ ☐ Signs
- ☐ ☐ Water pitchers, glasses
- ☐ ☐ Lighting
- ☐ ☐ Telephones
- ☐ ☐ Bulletin boards: number and size_____
- ☐ ☐ Cards for guest, family
- ☐ ☐ Badges, male/female
- ☐ ☐ Cash drawers: number and size_____
- ☐ ☐ File boxes: number and size_____

Points to Check Just Before Opening
- ☐ ☐ Personnel—understanding of procedure
- ☐ ☐ Necessary information on registration cards, badges
- ☐ ☐ Ticket prices, policies
- ☐ ☐ Location of programs, other material
- ☐ ☐ Policy on single ticket sales
- ☐ ☐ Policy on accepting checks
- ☐ ☐ Policy on refunds
- ☐ ☐ Hospitality desk
- ☐ ☐ Mimeograph registration lists
- ☐ ☐ Posting of instructions at convenient spots
- ☐ ☐ Location of tables
- ☐ ☐ Lighting of tables
- ☐ ☐ Waste baskets
- ☐ ☐ Cards, pencils on tables
- ☐ ☐ Adequate supply of change
- ☐ ☐ Protection of cash

Points to Check During Registration:
- ☐ ☐ Presence of administrator to make policy decisions
- ☐ ☐ Policy for registration of members after desk is closed
- ☐ ☐ Provision for checking funds at closing time
- ☐ ☐ Need for removing cash overflow

11. BANQUET FACILITIES
- ☐ ☐ Complete floor plans of banquet rooms
- ☐ ☐ Dates and times of each banquet or catered gathering_____
- ☐ ☐ Assignment and rental of banquet rooms
- ☐ ☐ Seating plan for each banquet, special menus, place cards
- ☐ ☐ Equipment for each banquet
- ☐ ☐ Other special arrangements_____

Points to Check Just Before Banquet:
- ☐ ☐ Seating style as specified
- ☐ ☐ Menus and place cards as specified
- ☐ ☐ Ash trays
- ☐ ☐ Audiovisual aids
- ☐ ☐ Special order to Maitre d'Hotel

Points to Check Just After Banquet:
- ☐ ☐ Removal of organization property
- ☐ ☐ Check for forgotten property
- ☐ ☐ Claim slides, movies, gavel, etc.

Needed
Completed

12.   **ENTERTAINMENT**

For Reception, Banquet, Special Events
☐   ☐   Entertainers and orchestra rehearsal for shows
_____
_____

☐   ☐   Recorded or live entertainment_____
_____

☐   ☐   Music stands provided by orchestra or hotel____
_____
_____

☐   ☐   Variety of entertainment program_____
_____

☐   ☐   Printed program information

Needed
Completed

13.   **MISCELLANEOUS**
☐   ☐   Baby-sitters
☐   ☐   Sightseeing trips arranged
☐   ☐   Car rentals
☐   ☐   Recreation
☐   ☐   Medical services
☐   ☐   Lost and found

14.   **PUBLICITY**
☐   ☐   Publicity committee
☐   ☐   Press room, typewriters and telephones
☐   ☐   Personal calls to city editors, radio and TV program directors
☐   ☐   Press releases
☐   ☐   Copies of speeches in advance
☐   ☐   Arrangements for photographs, publicity
☐   ☐   Notification to office of Director of Sales

SECTION IV

Instruments for Gathering Data about Students

Instructors need to know a great deal about their students. The instruments exhibited here are designed to obtain that information.

The first centers on demographic and biographical data, letting the instructor know about how much experience each participant has had in the organization and with the topic of this training. The second instrument is more concerned with the learner's feelings about being enrolled. The third, "Viewpoints About Training Tasks," is designed for a workshop for new trainers. It is a model from which other instructors could construct a similar A/DA (Agree/Disagree) questionnaire for gathering information about the opinions and feelings held by students.

Demographic and Biographical Data

Participant Information

1. _____
   　　　　　　　　Last Name　　　　　　*First Name*　　　　　*What You Like To Be Called*

2. Birthday: _____ _____
   　　　　　　Month　　*Day*

3. When did you join this organization? _____ _____
   　　　　　　　　　　　　　　　　　　　Month　　*Year*

4. What is Your present Position/Title?_____

5. When did you take on this title? _____ _____
   　　　　　　　　　　　　　　　　　Month　　*Year*

6. List other positions in which you peformed skills/duties similar to those you will study in this program?

   POSITION   SKILL

   _____   _____
   _____   _____
   _____   _____

7. About the skills/concepts you expect to acquire in this program:
   A. I perform them now.   YES   NO
   B. I expect to perform them within the next month.   YES   NO
   C. The percent of my time which is/will be spent doing this is   _____%
   D. If "NO" is your answer to A or B, what is your understanding about the reason you are attending this program?

8. Did you discuss the program objectives and the reasons for your participation with your immediate supervisor/
   manager?   YES   NO

9. What other related personal growth goals would you like to pursue during this program?

10. What two or three adjectives could you use to show that this program had been a success *for you*?

    _____   _____   _____

11. What adjectives would best describe your feeling when you learned you would attend this program?

    _____   _____   _____

12. What would you like us to know about your education and previous training?

13. List any special problems which your instructors should know about.

Feelings about Being Enrolled

How Were You Enrolled?

Take just a couple of minutes to answer these questions by check mark, short answer or YES/NO responses.
1. My organization is PROFIT-MAKING_____GOVERNMENTAL_____ACADEMIC_____NON-PROFIT ASSOCIATION_____
   My department is PRODUCTION_____SALES_____ADMINISTRATION_____PERSONNEL_____OTHER (SPECIFY)_____
2. I myself made the decision to attend this training.   YES   NO
3. If notified to attend, I was told by:
   My immediate boss_____Someone higher on my chain of command_____The Training Department_____
   If "None of the above," please specify:_____
   I was notified in writing_____By an oral message _____
   The notification reached me about_____days OR_____weeks before the first day of training.
4. If YES or NO won't quite tell the story, use the COMMENTS column at the right.
   Before I left work to attend this training, my boss:

			COMMENTS
• Explained why I was attending.	YES	NO	_____
• Explained what I was supposed to learn while I am here.	YES	NO	_____
• Explained how I'd apply the learning to my work after I return.	YES	NO	_____
• Related my attendance to a development plan, career path or personal performance problem. If you answered YES, encircle the correct reason.	YES	NO	_____

5. The way I was notified made me feel: (Check ALL applicable answers)
   Happy_____ Honored_____ Eager to Learn_____   That I was expected to work hard while here_____
   Anxious_____ Punished_____ Negative_____   That I was expected to learn something_____
                                                                            That I had earned some rest and recreation_____
   Other: (Specify)_____   That I'm supposed to do things differently in future_____
6. As I perceive it, I was ASKED TO ATTEND_____TOLD TO ATTEND_____ASKED IF I WISHED TO ATTEND_____
   I myself ASKED TO ATTEND_____, and I found it was EASY_____DIFFICULT_____to get approval.

Viewpoints about Training Tasks

Use the numbers at the left to show your estimate of the importance of the training tasks listed at the center of the page.
  Use the number 5 to indicate "Very Important."
  Let the number 4 show the task to be "Quite Important."
  Use the number 3 to indicate tasks of "Medium Significance."
  Let the number 2 indicate tasks of "Necessary but Minor" impact,
  And the number 1 indicates your opinion that tasks are of "No Importance."
Do not use the column at the right of the page until later.

IMPORTANCE   PREFERENCE

5 4 3 2 1	Analyze performance problems and counsel line and staff personnel about training activities.	5 4 3 2 1
5 4 3 2 1	Do a task analysis, outlining the detailed steps for performing a task.	5 4 3 2 1
5 4 3 2 1	Develop training programs to meet the task requirements.	5 4 3 2 1
5 4 3 2 1	Secure support for the training function and its programs.	5 4 3 2 1
5 4 3 2 1	Maintain ongoing relationships with the users of training services.	5 4 3 2 1
5 4 3 2 1	Arrange facilities, schedule programs, keep things running smoothly.	5 4 3 2 1
5 4 3 2 1	Communicate ideas in classroom or in conference settings.	5 4 3 2 1
5 4 3 2 1	Stimulate and lead group interaction in classes and conferences.	5 4 3 2 1
5 4 3 2 1	Detect and respond to hidden agendas in individuals, groups and organizations.	5 4 3 2 1
5 4 3 2 1	Apply the human resource development findings of psychologists and scholars.	5 4 3 2 1
5 4 3 2 1	Design tests which measure accomplishments of trainees.	5 4 3 2 1
5 4 3 2 1	Conduct and evaluate research on training and development.	5 4 3 2 1

Now use the column at the right to show your preferences for the twelve tasks:
  5 indicates that you enjoy doing the task enough to look forward to it;
  4 shows that you rather enjoy doing the task.
  3 indicates that you don't care much one way or the other.
  2 shows that you would just as soon not do the task.
  1 indicates that you will avoid the task when possible.

SECTION V

Training Aids Related to Visual Aids

It is difficult to overestimate the importance of visual aids in training programs!

Some studies indicate that 75% of an adult's knowledge is acquired through the sense of sight. With this in mind, you will find useful materials on the following pages:

- A matrix to help you decide on Media Choices,
- A series of lists that outline the advantages and disadvantages of the more common media.
- Some tips on how to use the most popular media wisely and well.

Media Choice Matrix

Medium	Flexibility	Visual	Color	Student control over pace of learning	Motion	"Edit-ability"
videotape reel	No, TV monitors are usually confined to a library or a classroom	Yes	Yes and no, it depends on the type of TV monitor & TV production equipment	No	Yes	No, editing requires much effort
videotape cassette	No. TV monitors and cassette players are usually confined to a library or classroom	Yes	Yes and no, it depends on the type of TV monitor & production equipment	Yes, the student can stop, rewind or fast forward the cassette; but learning pace is no faster than the speed of the cassette	Yes	No, editing requires much effort
non-illustrated workbook	Yes, it needs no electricity and can be taken almost anywhere	No	Yes and no, it depends on the production equipment	Yes, the student can read it as quickly or slowly as he likes	No	No, editing requires much effort
illustrated workbook	Yes, it needs no electricity and can be taken almost anywhere	Yes	Yes and no, it is possible but very expensive	Yes, the student can read it as quickly or slowly as he likes	No	No, editing requires much effort
16mm film	No, 16mm projectors are too heavy for a student to take home	Yes	Yes	No, unless the student is skilled at running a 16mm projector	Yes	No, editing requires much effort
slides with script audiotape optional)	Yes, a slide projector can be taken anywhere where electric current is available	Yes	Yes	Yes, the student can go through the slide script as quickly or slowly as he likes	No, but a series of slides can break a physical activity into its sequential steps; this is sometimes better than motion for study purposes	Yes and no, a series of slides can easily be altered in sequence, added to, or subtracted from; it is more difficult to edit the adjoining tape or workbook
audiotape	Yes, an audio cassette player can be taken almost anywhere but you will need a set of batteries	No	No	Yes, the student can stop, rewind or fast forward the tape but can learn only as fast as the tape runs	No	No, editing requires much effort

---

Reprinted from John T. McConnell, "If The Medium Fits, Use It" in *Select-Media For Learning*, by permission of the Association for Educational Communications and Technology. © 1974 by AECT.

Advantages and Disadvantages of Various Forms of Media

Flip Charts

Advantages
- Spontaneous
- Inexpensive
- Easy to use
- Flexibility
- Re-usable
- Normal room lighting
- Face audience
- Serves as topic outline

Rules and Techniques
- Clean pad, good pens available
- Check room for visibility
- Plan ahead, prepare in advance
- Be neat, keep information simple
- Write rapidly, legibly
- Face audience when possible
- Talk as you write
- Summarize each sheet, then cover
- Prime the audience
- Use strong transitions
- Use colors, pointer for attention control
- Outline in pencil
- Ask for assistance in turning pages or writing

Disadvantages
- Visibility factor
- Turning back is necessary
- Not good for detailed information
- Less speaker control
- Time-consuming
- More rigid sequence of materials
- Difficult to carry

Problems/Solutions
- Difficult for storage and filing
- Awkward to rearrange information
- Messy markers/chalk dust
- Easels jam or break

Best Uses
- Lists, procedural steps
- Sequencing of ideas
- New terms, definitions
- Simple sketches
- Math problems, solutions
- Assignments, guide questions for cases
- Slogans
- Group work, brainstorming

The Overhead Projector

Advantages
- Face the audience
- Normal room lighting
- Speaker control
- Flexibility in preparing, editing and revising
- Portability
- Increased visibility

Techniques
- Locate in advance
- Face audience
- On-off switch
- Revelation
- Overlay
- Chalkboard
- Pointer

Disadvantages
- Meeting location may restrict use
- Could become expensive in large quantity
- Quality may be less than in other media

Problems/Solutions
- Switch location
- Keystoning
- Burned-out bulbs
- Glare

Best Uses
- To supplement lecture or discussion
- To illustrate information for case study, demonstration
- To encourage, highlight, and review student comments
- To visually summarize group work, presentations
- To introduce and explain cognitive lessons

35 MM Slides

Advantages
- Reproduced economically and in large quantities
- Produced with ease and relatively good quality; good for novices
- Control over when and how long visual is projected
- Compact storage; portable
- Flexible presentation possible
- Instructors can back-up or advance
- Can be designed for progressive disclosure of information (revelation)
- Variety of visual techniques
- Large, still screen image permits instructor to point out critical points
- Shows realistic pictures or artwork, or both
- Equipment variety allows multimedia capabilities

Problems/Solutions
- Slide upside down or backwards
- Burned out bulb
- Difficulty in projecting image over audience
- Heat from lamp blisters film
- Slide transitions distract from continuity
- In-house slides lack quality; use good camera, right film, lens, lighting, etc.

Disadvantages
- Require more preparation time, especially for artwork
- Long lead time is necessary
- Room lights must be dimmed and controlled
- Long sequences encourage mental absenteeism
- Training needed for accessories and "professional" productions

Techniques
- Be certain vocabulary suits audience
- Rehearse entire presentation on storyboard
- Edit slides to ensure right ones used, correct sequence, correct position
- Use average of 15–20 seconds per visual
- Break presentation into short segments of 5 or 6 slides
- Use remote control or an assistant to operate
- Prepare audience for what they will learn
- Review key points at conclusion
- Prepare study questions or worksheet for review
- Set up lighted lectern for notes
- In darkened room, light yourself
- Change pace of presentation
- Never show a slide presentation after lunch
- Use as a subject preview or review
- Keep original set of slides with script or storyboard!

16 MM Films

Advantages
- Show motion; close approximation of the "real thing"
- Can use multi-sensory approach
- Communicate ideas with great penetration
- Provide exactness of detail and color
- High quality; easy to use, colorful
- Growing library of films and topics available
- Image speed control: varies speed of projection for closer analysis of details
- Good for explaining processes, operations and concepts that call for a continuous sequence

Techniques
- Prepare audience; set their mental stage
- It should make up small part of total presentation
- If long, show only portions that apply to presentation
- Have film divided into smaller segments, with blank spaces
- Composition of the whole is basic requirement
- Film editor can control, to some extent, how much and how long audience can view a subject
- Sound system should be suitable for size of audience
- Remote speakers near screen are preferable to built-in
- Relative maintenance-free

Disadvantages
- Expensive
- Difficult and time consuming to plan and produce
- Material may be obsolete by time of showing
- Some people view as only entertainment, not as learning aid
- Difficult to control attention
- Speaker is reduced to master of ceremonies when movies take up most of presentation
- More complex equipment and focal requirements may inhibit use
- In-house production requires technical equipment and expertise
- Audience is accustomed to this medium and demands high quality
- Time is a problem: learner cannot stop a frame and study

Tips on How to Use Media

Video Tape

The Newest and Fastest Growing of Our Visual Aids—Advantages and Disadvantages
1. In spite of the tremendous growth, video tape still represents the largest capital outlay of any audio visual equipment.
2. High credibility or believability which leads to acceptance by the learner.
3. Uniformity of the message—important if you're trying to communicate some complex technical information to many people on many separate occasions in different locations.
4. When you produce a video tape you can review it for acceptability instantly, as opposed to film or slides which must be sent away for processing.
5. Once you own the equipment, productions can be done in the field or office quickly and at relatively low cost using in-house personnel.

Audio-Visual Tips Too Simple To Mention
1. Always carry a 3 prong adapter.
2. Always carry an extension cord.
3. Always carry a spare piece of chalk.
4. Always carry a grease pencil or colored marking pen.
5. Always carry spare lamps for your projection equipment.
6. And-never pass out handouts until the end of your presentation, unless you want to compete with yourself.

Tips on Using Audio-Visuals Effectively

Numerous books and articles have been written on the subject of effective use of audio-visuals. The list of "how to's" that follows is intended to provide the new trainer with a few practical suggestions we have picked up from our years of conducting workshops and training programs.

A. *GENERAL*
   No matter which audio-visual technique you use, there are some general rules which apply.
   1. Don't let your audio-visuals interfere with your presentation. Thus:
      • Don't bring it out until you're ready to use it.
      • Get rid of it when you've finished with it.
   2. Don't overdo it. A picture is worth a thousand words, but 100 pictures may not be worth 100,000 words.
   3. Know your visual. Practice with it before you use it in your presentation. Make sure the visual is appropriate to the size of the room and all parts are in proper sequence.
   4. Test any equipment you may be using. Murphy's law will get you every time if you don't.
   5. Don't stand between your visual and the participants. Stand to one side. Use a pointer.
   6. Don't pass samples around while you are talking. Show them to the group as a whole or pass them around after your presentation.

B. *HANDOUTS*
   1. Vary your handouts. Use some outline handouts which require the participants to fill in information. This will stimulate interest and attention.
   2. The chart below identifies the most effective time to distribute a handout in a program:

Handout	Prior	During	After
An outline	Best	Poor	OK
Material essential to discussion	Best	OK	Poor
A summary	Poor	Poor	Best
Supplementary material	OK	Poor	Best

    3.   Don't overdo the volume. One handout that hits the nail on the head is better than five or six that loosely cover your topic.

    4.   Leave a lot of white space on each page. A crowded handout is unappealing.

C. *OVERHEAD PROJECTOR AND TRANSPARENCIES*

    1.   Try to get an overhead projector which has a built-in extra bulb.

    2.   Speak with more volume than you normally use. The listener's attention is divided, and in a darkened room, more volume is needed to hold their attention.

    3.   Transparencies can be made easily. Most duplicating machines will produce them. A little creative thinking on your part can provide some high quality overhead slides.

        a.   Don't overload your slides. A black and white reproduction of a typewritten page is one of the worst transparencies there is. The only way to make it worse is to fill the page with numbers.

        b.   Color can be used to add life to your transparencies. Pieces of colored cellophane can be taped over your transparencies to add variety.

        c.   Two-color transparencies can be used to focus participants' attention on a specified portion of a flow chart, for example. Use a bright color to highlight one section of the slide and a dark color to partially block out the rest.

    4.   Transparencies of forms are useful to demonstrate how to complete the form. You can write on the acetate sheet with water-based pens.

    5.   Mount the transparencies in cardboard frames. This protects them and makes them easy to handle.

    6.   You can write notes on the cardboard frame for reference with each transparency.

    7.   Acetate transparencies can be overlaid on one another. For example, the first transparency may be a blank worksheet and the second shows the entries on the worksheet. Or a flow chart can be developed in sequence by overlaying several transparencies. The overlays can be taped to the cardboard frame along one side so that they can be flipped on or off the main transparency.

    8.   Check the legibility of your slides from the back of the room. A rule of thumb: One inch lettering is visible at 30 feet, two inch at 60 feet, etc. The blank space between lines should be 1½ times the letter height.

    9.   Use your pencil as a pointer to emphasize detail.

  10.   Use a sheet of paper as a mask to allow you to reveal a portion of the transparency while blocking out the rest.

  11.   You may wish to distribute handouts of your transparencies to reduce the amount of note taking in the group.

D. *FLIP CHART*

    1.   Write LARGE (3 inch lettering) with a broad-tipped felt pen. Water based pens "bleed through" less than toxic types, and save paper!

    2.   Consider using two flip charts, so that you can develop ideas in tandem. (Or one chart may be pre-prepared and the second used for spontaneous comments.)

    3.   If appropriate, tear off the sheets and post them around the room. Use masking tape only. Most other tapes can damage the walls.

    4.   You can write notes lightly in hard pencil on the flip chart to aid you in your presentation. They cannot be seen even from the front row. (Don't put all your notes on the first page. When it is flipped over, your notes will be unavailable to you.)

    5.   If you pre-prepared a flip-chart presentation, write on every other page. In this way, you can flip over a page when you finish and turn to a blank sheet so that the participants will not see the next chart until you are ready for it.

    6.   Use several colors of pens for variety and to highlight specific points.

    7.   Make tabs out of masking tape. Tape them to the edges of the chart paper so that you can easily turn to a pre-prepared page. (NOTE: You'll have to put the tab on the page in front of the one you want to turn to.)

    8.   You can tape pieces of paper or cardboard over words on a pre-made chart. This allows you to reveal your points one at a time by tearing off the "reveals."

E. *TAPE RECORDERS—VIDEO AND AUDIO*

There are a number of excellent programs available on tape, however, my personal prejudice is that the best use of video or audio tape is to give immediate feedback, e.g.,

- to a person practicing a presentation
- to participants in a situation simulation
- to a team in a decision-making or problem-solving discussion
- to a class involved in an interpersonal skill exercise.

This allows participants to see themselves as others see them.

F. *FILMS, 35 mm SLIDES, FILMSTRIPS*

There are many excellent films, filmstrips, programs, and slide and tape programs available commercially.

1. Develop your program objectives first and then select the film to fit. Just because a film is well done and makes an excellent point doesn't mean it will meet your objectives.

2. If you use a film without having previewed it personally, you deserve whatever happens.

3. You don't have to show the entire film. If a ten-minute segment of a thirty-minute film is all you want, then just show that part.

4. Stopping the film for discussion at some appropriate point (e.g., after the customer challenges the sales person) is an excellent technique. After the discussion, you can view the rest of the film to compare the group's ideas with those of the author.

5. Leave some lights on (e.g., a bank in the rear of the room or recessed border lights). This allows participants to take notes if they wish.

6. Use "trigger films" to promote participation. A trigger film is a brief slice-of-life sequence which presents a problem to the participants (e.g., What would you say next to this employee if you were the boss?) The learning comes from the analysis of what the participants did in reaction to the trigger, rather than from a message in the film itself.

SECTION VI

Training Aids and Tips in Training Methods

The design of training programs should permit learners to reach desired behavioral objectives. Thus method selection and execution are important to course designers and instructors. The instruments in this section include:

1. Three charts of how different methods help with specific types of objectives, including those in the book *Taxonomy of Educational Objectives.*
2. A "Learning Continuum" based on writings and workshops by Dr. Warren Schmidt.
3. A "Checklist of Teaching Techniques," which combines media and method selection.
4. "Engineering of Training-Learning Systems," which discusses how organization realities affect method selection, and which suggests inherent measurement ideas.
5. Lists of "Tips" in using
    brainstorming,
    case studies,
    roleplays,
    nominal group process, and
    computer assisted instruction.
6. Two Items about job instruction. (Although job instruction is not truly a distinct method since it combines lecture, demonstration, and various forms of participation, it is a classic way to show people who to do a task. Thus this section includes a list of principles for JIT, and the card which is characteristically used as a training aid when teaching on-the-job instructors.)

Different Methods Accomplish Different Objectives

The techniques listed below can make contributions toward the objectives under which the bullet appears.

Techniques	Psychomotor Skills	Knowledge	Attitudes & Values	Interpersonal Skills	Managerial/ Supervisory Skills	Organizational Development
Action Maze					•	•
Assignments	•	•	•	•	•	•
Brainstorming			•	•	•	•
Buzzgroups	•		•	•	•	•
Case Method	•	•		•	•	•
Circulars (with Materials)		•				
Clinic	•	•			•	•
Colloquy		•				
Conference	•	•	•		•	•
Critical Incident			•	•	•	•
Demonstration	•	•			•	
Discussion	•	•	•	•	•	•
Displays & Exhibits (with Materials)	•	•				
Field Trips	•	•				
Films (with Materials)	•	•	•	•	•	•
Forum		•	•	•	•	•
Games	•		•	•		•
Handouts (with Materials)		•				
Human Relations Laboratories			•	•	•	•
In-Baskets			•		•	
Incident Process			•	•		
Job Instruction Training	•	•				
Learner Controlled Instruction	•	•	•	•	•	
Lecture		•	•			
Modelling					•	•
Models (with Materials)	•	•				
Newsletters (with Materials)		•				
Open Classroom	•	•	•	•	•	
Panel		•				
Programmed Instruction	•	•				
Question-Answer Sessions		•	•	•		
Related Reading		•	•	•	?	?
Roleplaying	•	•	•	•	•	•
Seminar		•				
Sensitivity Training			•	•	•	•
Simulations	•		•	•	•	•
Syllabus		•				
Symposium		•				
Syndicates	•		•	•	•	•
Tours	•	•				
Videotape (with Materials)	•	•	•	•	•	•
Workshop	•	•			•	•

Duo-Dimensional List of Methods

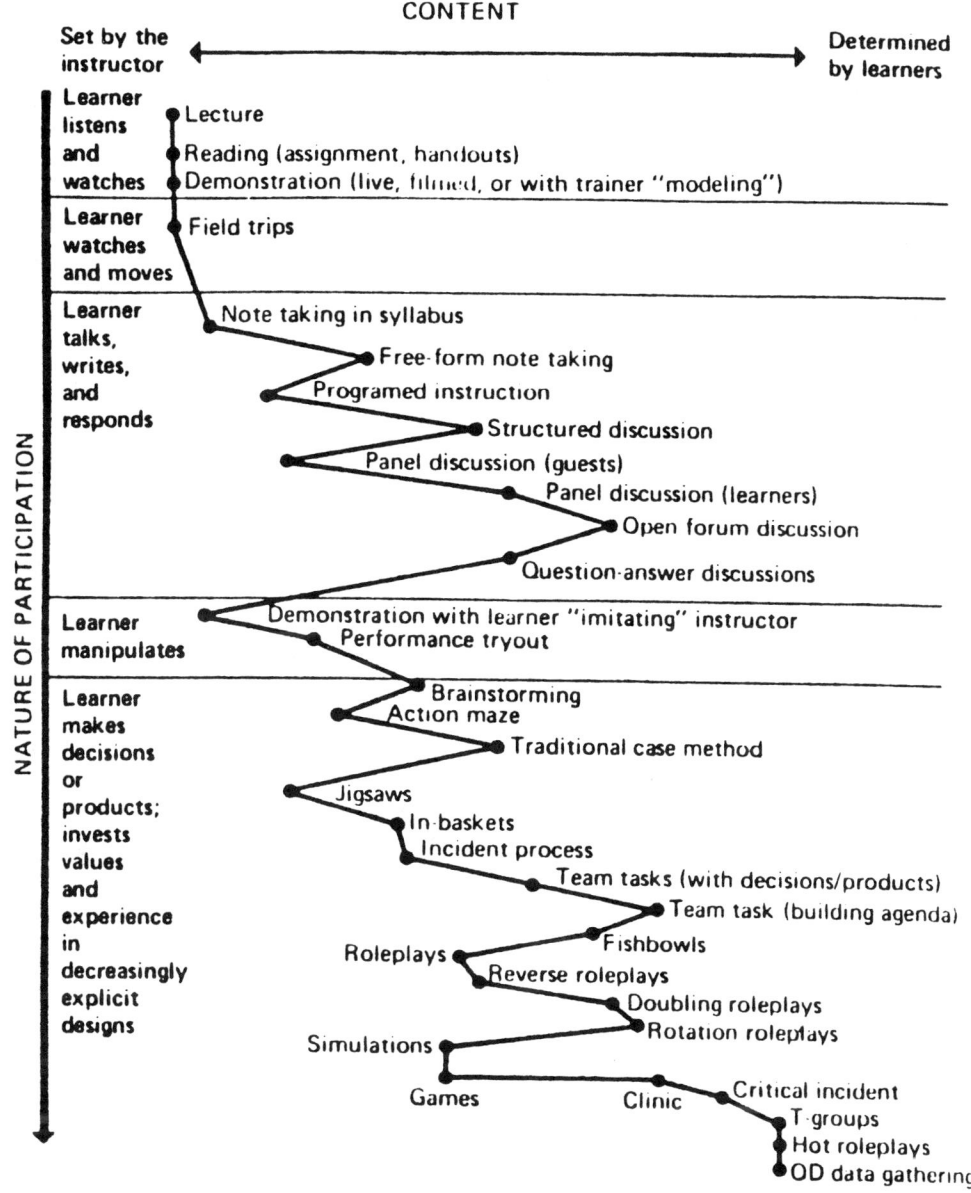

CONTENT

Set by the instructor ← → Determined by learners

NATURE OF PARTICIPATION

Learner listens and watches
- Lecture
- Reading (assignment, handouts)
- Demonstration (live, filmed, or with trainer "modeling")

Learner watches and moves
- Field trips

Learner talks, writes, and responds
- Note taking in syllabus
- Free-form note taking
- Programed instruction
- Structured discussion
- Panel discussion (guests)
- Panel discussion (learners)
- Open forum discussion
- Question-answer discussions

Learner manipulates
- Demonstration with learner "imitating" instructor
- Performance tryout

Learner makes decisions or products; invests values and experience in decreasingly explicit designs
- Brainstorming
- Action maze
- Traditional case method
- Jigsaws
- In-baskets
- Incident process
- Team tasks (with decisions/products)
- Team task (building agenda)
- Roleplays
- Fishbowls
- Reverse roleplays
- Doubling roleplays
- Rotation roleplays
- Simulations
- Games
- Clinic
- Critical incident
- T-groups
- Hot roleplays
- OD data gathering

Relating Learning *METHODS* to Learning *GOALS*

Learning Objectives

THESE METHODS become increasingly useful as learners pursue goals in THESE DOMAINS:

Lecture (with/without Visual Aids)
Panels and Symposia
Reading Assignments

Book-Based Discussions
Two-way Discussions
Self-instructional Programs
Feedback Devices
Case Problems
Laboratory Experiments
Incident Process Case Studies

Exams and Essays
Roleplays

Action Maze Case Studies
In-baskets

Dramatic Audio-Visual Stimuli
Emotional Oratory
Biographical Reading
Reverse Roleplaying
Rotation Roleplaying
Doubling Roleplays
"Hot" Roleplays (Empty Chair, Magic
   Shop/Mirror/Wand)
Permissive Discussion
Counselling & Consultation
Critical Incidents
Simulations
Games
Laboratory (T-Group) Training
Organizational Mirroring
Fishbowls
Polling/Physical Respresentations
Guided Fantasies
Reflection/Meditation/Chanting
Psychotherapy
Brain Surgery

Demonstration
Audio-Visual Programs
Field Trips
Try-out Performance
Practice Exercises & Drill

THE COGNITIVE DOMAIN: Mental Skills

KNOWLEDGE = Acquiring Data

COMPREHENSION = Generalizing from, or internalizing data

APPLICATION = Relating data to experience

ANALYSIS = Identifying parts, elements, designs or relationships

SYNTHESIS = Constructing designs, systems, communications

EVALUATION = Judgment on some identified criteria; making distinctions, discriminations

THE AFFECTIVE DOMAIN: Emotional Skills

RECEIVING = Attending, with some degree of commitment

RESPONDING = Acquiescence, Willingness, Satisfaction

VALUING = Sensing Worth

ORGANIZATION = Acquiring a Value System (Hierarchy of values)

CHARACTERIZATION = Consistently applying a value system

THE PSYCHOMOTOR DOMAIN: Physical Skills

For INTEREST (A satisfying exposure to new experience)

For SKILL (Habitual or Repeated Performance)

Learning Conditions

As analyzed by Dr. Warren Schmidt

WHEN THE PRIMARY EMPHASIS IS ON EXPANDING THE LEARNERS' EXPERIENCE, THEN		BUT WHEN THE PRIMARY EMPHASIS IS ON ORGANIZING THE LEARNERS' EXPERIENCE,
• Emphasize the kinds of problems which the learner can solve now and be willing to solve after mastering the new material • Help the learner deal with his inadequacy in confronting new material. (It's normal!)	*The preparation and orientation should:*	• Make it comfortable for the learner to make explicit his past successes and failures. • Emphasize the value of analyzing past experience to "get handles" on similar problems in the future
• Exciting, absorbing • Most strongly determined by the nature of the content	*The climate and pace of learning should be:*	• Thoughtful, not rushed • Strongly influenced by the learner's reactions and desires
• To identify real problems and concerns of the learner • To clarify learning goals and their relevance • To describe the processes by which the learner will achieve the near competence • To provide the new data and concepts or demonstrate the new behaviors	*The instructor's role is primarily:*	• To set a climate. • To create conditions for making experience explicit • To facilitate analysis of the experience • To put the learner's experience into perspective • To give "feedback" on the possible consequences of past behavior • To help the learner generalize from his past experience
• Absorb the new data & concepts • Test the new data, concepts, skills in dealing with problems • Practice until the new material is internalized • Apply new material to real situations	*The learner's role is primarily to:*	• Provide data about his own experience and assumptions • Analyze that experience • Examine alternative ways of conceptualizing his experience
• Clarity of presentation of new material • Learner's respect for presenter's competence • Learner's perception of relevance of new material	*Success depends heavily upon:*	• Extent to which climate is free of threat • Learner's feeling of need to find new approaches to old problems • Learner's willingness to risk exposure of weakness
• Learner may feel inadequate • Communications problems • Educator may under/over estimate the learner's knowledge	*Problems to anticipate*	• Learner may feel he hasn't learned anything • Learner may reject any analysis or theory which doesn't agree with his own • Learner may feel threatened in exposing his own experience

Checklist of Teaching Techniques

Technique	*Goals Potentially Achieved*
Books	Knowledge Critical Thinking?
Lecture	Knowledge Inspiration Identification with a Scholar? Critical Thinking? (By example)
Discussion	Critical Thinking Relating knowledge to student experiences Application Attitude Change
Student Panel, Student Reports	Interest & Motivation (at least for participants?)
Guest Lecturer or Resource Person	Added interest and information
Films	Makes materials more concrete Facilitates learning materials involving motion or visual detail Interest
TV	Interest (Greater involvement than film?) Motion, visual details
Slides	Permit visual materials to be greatly enlarged and held in view while explained Interest
Bulletin Boards, Mock-up	Provide opportunity for learning at student's own pace. May help student relate learning in classrooms to materials presented in mass media Provide concrete examples
Recordings	Provide concrete auditory experience, and taped recordings can be made cheaply by instructor himself to bring situations outside the classroom to the class.
Field Trips	First-hand knowledge Interest
Laboratory	First-hand experience Scientific method
Role-playing	Lifelike experience Develop human relations skills Interest
Buzz Groups	Create awareness of problems Increased involvement
Study Guides, Workbooks	Aid organization and learning of materials Promote application of knowledge
Periodicals	Bridge gap between classroom and other experiences of students
Teaching Machines and Programmed Texts	Learning knowledge and skills, particularly those requiring repetition and immediate feedback
Computer-aided Instruction	Potentially can achieve any of these goals when combined with other materials, but currently limited by availability of college-level programs

---

Engineering of Training—Learning Systems

Recognition of: Situations, Problems	Analysis	Planning	Action	Measurement of Worth
Productivity uncertain	Determine extent to which cause lies in lack of knowledge, skill	*Criteria:* Is the objective clear? a) What needs to be learned?	*Distribution of responsibilities between:* *Top executive* Department managers	*Achievement of:* a) purpose b) learning objectives
Introduction of new projects, changes in systems		b) How will this learning be productively used?	Supervisors-coaches Technical experts Personnel staff	Measurement/ evaluation against purpose
Manpower staffing needs not met	Determine feasibility of utilization of learning Estimate worth (benefits minus cost)	Is it worthwhile?	Training staff Planning staff Employees	Modification and revision
Training-learning processes ineffective		Can learning be integrated with action needed to accomplish task or solve problem?	Center for Instructional Resources	Improvement Continuity
Workers becoming obsolescent	Determine how critical the task, situation, or problem		*For the following activities:*	
Rapid technological changes outdistance human systems	Determine organizational and work environment influences	Do attributes of training-learning process help to achieve objective? Are methods such that they establish climate and conditions that spark desire to learn?	Establish priority for learning Help in understanding the meaning of learning-training within an organization	
Impact of continuous personnel changes			Advise and help managers to diagnose, plan and execute training	
Work flow characterized by backlogs, excessive error, waste, breakdowns		*Training-learning systems:* selection of most appropriate process to achieve objective and integrate with action needed to accomplish purpose	Diagnose, plan, and execute training-learning systems Review of subordinates' development of employees and recognition	
Decline of motivation		plan for environmental conditions that will provide organizational readiness and utilization: a) man at top b) framework for collaboration c) managers d) work systems e) individuals f) personnel systems g) evaluation, revision continuity	Contribute personnel, technical expertise to collaborative instruction Develop intructional skills Prepare learning-training materials Select supplementary, external programs Feedback on progress in accomplishment of results	

Rules for Brainstorming

1. Limit the topic to a single question, e.g., how to deal with absenteeism.
2. Encourage idea quantity. At this point, quality is *not* considered important. What you're seeking is as many ideas and suggestions as possible.
3. Encourage wild thinking and building an idea. Any idea, no matter how questionable, should be offered. And encourage the group to build on one another's ideas, altering them, expanding on them, and modifying them. Again, the purpose here is to get ideas, *not* pass judgment on them.
4. Discourage critical judgment and evaluation. No one is allowed to say, "That won't work because . . ." during a brainstorming session. You're looking for ways of *getting* ideas, not trying to suppress them. Someone's idea (which really won't work) just might be the thing that triggers someone else to think of one that will work.
5. Avoid side discussion and issues. During the actual brainstorming, which is of very short duration, side discussions are not to be allowed. All members of the group are required to concentrate their energies toward coming up with additional ideas.
6. Don't allow outside observers. Everyone in the room is required to participate. It may be well to require everyone to offer at least two suggestions during the session.
7. Have an idea or two in the back of your head to get the session started. This will provide a *trigger* to get the session moving. And once it begins, the ideas come fast and furious.
8. One member of the group should take notes, recording the ideas as fast as they're offered. It's a good idea to have the suggestions listed on a chart pad where everyone can see them. Previous ideas provide the *food for thought* that leads to further ideas.
9. The brainstorming session itself should not last less than 5 minutes, or more than 15. Shorter periods of time do not allow enough good ideas to surface. And after 15 minutes, a greater proportion of the ideas become clearly impractical.

© Donald Michalak. Reprinted with permission.

Effective Use of Case Studies

1. Will the case cause the learners to examine ideas related to course objectives?
2. Can the case get them talking about specific causes and action steps?

   Remember, a major reason for using case studies is to focus on specific issues and actions rather than abstract theories. If you doubt that the case you are considering will achieve this focus, select another case, or include in the write-up a set of specific questions the learners are to answer and report on at the end of their discussion.

3. Is the incident described in the case lifelike and relevant to the environment and issues that the learners face frequently in their own work?

   The issue of "verisimilitude" is important only to the degree that if there is no apparent analogy between the life and issues described in the case, the learners will see no need to discuss it. On the other hand, if the write-up includes so much detail that the learners are entrapped into extraneous "nit picking," then the real issues will be obscured. Choose a happy medium when selecting or writing up the case: reality in the environment and situation, with just enough detail to give flesh and blood—but not so much that it distracts.

4. Assign time limits based upon your sense of the value of the ideas which the learners can examine or discover in their analysis of this case.

5. Seek some form of "product" from all the cases.

   Small teams may produce a report which can be compared with the reports of other small teams. Groups may be asked to make a recommendation, a decision, a list of questions or criteria—just so the learners have a product which you can reinforce as a symptom of progress toward the learning goal that the case exemplifies.

6. Monitor the discussion to make sure that all participants are truly *participants*.

   You may want to lead the discussion yourself; in that case you can call on people who are not talking. Or you may assign certain special tasks (some who view the case from the financial position, others from the ecological standpoint and still others from the personnel perspective, *etc.*) If you divide the class into small groups, you may circulate, eavesdrop and take appropriate action to see that all the learners take an active vocal part.

7. Select only those cases that involve some ambiguity or controversy.

   Except for the most elemental problem-solving exercises, there ought to be several ways to approach the analysis, several ways to attribute the causes of the problem, and at least several ways to improve conditions. (Elementary problem-solving cases are not out-of-order; however they are useful in applying rules or rigid formulas rather than the more sophisticated cases which allow learners to apply several of the skills taught in the program.)

Tips on Using Roleplays

1. Use roleplays only when they permit the learner to practice or experiment with a new behavior that will be applied back on the job. In other words, the *roleplay must permit the learner to rehearse one of the objectives of the training program!*

2. Keep the situation as simple as possible. It need only present the chance to try out the behavior, and should not encourage "hamminess" or irrelevant behaviors on the part of the players. One or two issues with as few players as possible usually produces the most productive learning experience.

3. Give printed role descriptions which explain a motive (recognizable to the student-player) and a situation. Keep these descriptions as simple as you can, and be certain that each role contains a motive that conflicts with or differs from the motive of the other player(s.)

4. See that each roleplay involves three distinct phases: preparation, enactment, and analysis.

    The preparation should explain the objective of the roleplay, as "To practice recommended techniques for overcoming objections when selling." There should be time to read the role description twice, and then as simply as possible, begin the enactment. Keep stage settings and dramatic build-up to an absolute minimum.

    The enactment should focus on the accomplishments in practicing the desired behavior; as soon as that is done, terminate the roleplay. If learners do poorly, give them a chance to reverse the action so they can improve their performance.

    The analysis should concentrate on how well the learners applied the desired behaviors—never on how well they acted the part! During the analysis any student with ideas about other ways to play the role should be given a chance to do so. For example: "That's a great idea, Nancy. Tom, be the customer so Nancy can try it out on you. Go right ahead, Nancy."

5. To get a maximum number of learners involved, consider the "Multiple format" with several roleplays going on simultaneously and with observers completing observer sheets which focus on the learner's performance of the desired skills and behaviors.

6. If interpersonal skills are the objective of the roleplay, use reversal (in which players trade roles) during the enactment or after the analysis of one roleplay. To get maximum participation and "brainstorming" effects, use "rotation," in which the players are changed at critical moments during the enactment, or "doubling," in which several learners play the same role at the same time.

Nominal Group Process

1. (10 minutes) Individuals write their responses to question.
    E.g.—What would you like to know about the training process?
        —What obstacles prevent people from doing their jobs as well as they'd like?
2. Each person cites one response. The leader writes them on the flip chart/blackboard. (Combination and overlaps are eliminated.)
3. Continue around the group until all responses are presented.
4. Number each response. Leader calls for explanations/clarifications as needed.
5. Participants vote on "X" number, prioritizing their choices.
    E.g.—If 5 choices are made, the most important item gets 5 points, the second most important gets 4 points, and so on.
6. The data are collected, tabulated, and recorded.

© Donald Michalak

Checklist for Selection and Development of Computer Assisted Instructional Materials

Use this checklist to determine whether: your instructional program is appropriate for computer delivery, it will use the computer's capabilities effectively and the computer's relationship with the user has been considered. The last segment of the checklist outlines the steps in designing a structured instructional course for easy coding by programmers.

SELECT AN APPROPRIATE TRAINING APPLICATION
Computers may be appropriate if you can check one or more items below:
- ☐ Computers will reduce total training costs
- ☐ Improved or safer learning justifies cost of computer
- ☐ Students already use computers on the job
- ☐ Students already accept and communicate with computers
- ☐ Other; the application is appropriate because: _____

USE THE COMPUTER'S FULL TRAINING POTENTIAL
Benefits of computerized training are strengthened when the program:
- ☐ Leads students through drills
- ☐ Presents situations for student analysis and solution
- ☐ Simulates real-world situations and interprets and responds to student input
- ☐ Provides alternate instructional paths depending on student responses
- ☐ Other; this application uses the computer's potential by _____

DESIGN MATERIAL WITH POSITIVE COMPUTER—TRAINEE RELATIONSHIP
Acceptance of computerized training is improved when: (check points that apply)
- ☐ Students can proceed in program even though responses are incorrect
- ☐ Correct participant responses receive appropriate and sincere reinforcement
- ☐ Students are encouraged to feel like winners, not losers
- ☐ Techniques of pacing, color, sound, action, suspense or other devices are used to make learning compelling and challenging
- ☐ Additional media interact with computer training materials to improve learning
- ☐ Other ways that the program is "humanized": _____

DESIGN THE COURSE FOR CODING BY PROGRAMMERS
Follow these steps to write well-organized courses for coding by programmers:
- ☐ Describe everything the program and learner do to each other
- ☐ List the variables that occur when the learner provides input, information is retrieved from storage or conditions change
- ☐ Lay out general program logic and sequencing
- ☐ Develop details in program sub-routines
- ☐ Have programmer code the main program using dummy sub-routines and test it
- ☐ Have programmer code and test sub-routines, one at a time
- ☐ Run the program

Principles of Job Instruction

On Getting Ready To Instruct

HAVE AN OBJECTIVE
    Define the skill your learners are going to acquire.
    Specify the standard of performance they must attain.
    Indicate the timetable for achieving each level of proficiency.
BREAK DOWN THE JOB (TASK ANALYSIS)
    List the principal steps, in the proper sequence
    Pick out the key points:
        How each step is to be accomplished,
        How well it must be done (What makes it right?),
        Why this standard is important,
        Tips which simplify the task—or the learning process.
HAVE EVERYTHING READY: Equipment, Materials, Learning Aids
HAVE THE WORKPLACE PROPERLY ARRANGED—as the worker must maintain it on the job and with the learner facing the materials and equipment as workers face them.

And on Instructing
PREPARE THE WORKER-LEARNER
    Put the learner at ease.
    Find out what the learner already knows about the job.
    Arouse the learner's interest by:
        Relating it to what the learner already knows or can do
        Letting the learner tell how this skill will be important on-the-job

TELL   (Present the Operation Verbally)   *These steps may come concurrently for*
SHOW (Demonstrate the Proper Operation)   *experienced workers; this will enhance the*
                                            sensory activity levels.

    Stress key points.
    Question patiently; get the learner involved in the communication.
    Take up just one point at a time—at least initially.
DO   (A Try-Out Performance with the worker DOING THE JOB!)
    Have the learner explain each step while performing it.
    Patiently request repetition of omitted steps or key points.
REVIEW   (A frank appraisal of the learner's accomplishments)
    Let the worker do the appraising just as much as possible.
    Tactfully point out shortcomings not cited by the learner.
FOLLOW-UP
    Put the worker on the job; designate a source of help.
    Check often; encourage questions; encourage self-answers.
    Use positive reinforcement for all accomplishments.
    Taper off this coaching; put the worker on her/his own just as soon as possible.

Job Instruction Card

HOW TO GET READY
TO INSTRUCT

Have a Time Table—
how much skill you expect him to have, and how soon.

Break Down the Job—
list principal steps.
pick out the key points.

Have Everything Ready—
the right equipment, materials, and supplies.

Have the Work Place Properly Arranged—
just as the worker will be expected to keep it.

Job Instructor Training

WAR MANPOWER COMMISSION
BUREAU OF TRAINING
TRAINING WITHIN INDUSTRY

KEEP THIS CARD HANDY
16—26793-4   GPO

HOW TO INSTRUCT
Step 1—Prepare the Worker
Put him at ease.
Find out what he already knows about the job.
Get him interested in learning job.
Place in correct position.

Step 2—Present the Operation
Tell, Show, Illustrate, and Question carefully and patiently.
Stress key points.
Instruct clearly and completely, taking up one point at a time—but no more than he can master.

Step 3—Try Out Performance
Test him by having him perform job.
Have him *tell* and *show* you; have him explain key points.
Ask questions and correct errors.
Continue until you know *HE* knows.

Step 4—Follow Up
Put him on his own.   Designate to whom he goes for help.
Check frequently.   Encourage questions.   Get him to look for key points as he progresses.
Taper off extra coaching and close follow-up.   16—26793-3

**If Worker Hasn't Learned,
the Instructor Hasn't Taught**

SECTION VII

Training Aid for Dealing with Special Students

When people gather to learn, a number of interpersonal dynamics inevitably develop. Sometimes these dynamics involve behavior that proves troublesome to the instructor. In other words, the student participation seems inappropriate.

Donald F. Michalak has developed a guide sheet identifying some of these behaviors, suggesting their causes and some things to do when the instructor feels it necessary to take corrective action.

Getting Appropriate Participation

BEHAVIOR	WHY	WHAT TO DO
OVERLY TALKATIVE	• He may be an "eager beaver" or a showoff. • He may be well informed and is anxious to show it, or just naturally garrulous.	—Don't be embarrassing or sarcastic . . . you may need his skill later. —Slow him down with some difficult questions —Interrupt with: That's an interesting point . . . now let's see what the group thinks of it". —Let the group take care of him as much as possible.
HIGHLY ARGUMENTATIVE	• Combative personality . . . heckler. • May be normally good natured but upset by problems.	—Keep your own temper in check . . . don't let group get excited either. —Find merit in one of his points . . . express your agreement (or get the group to do so) . . . then move on. —When he makes an obvious misstatement, toss it to the group . . . let them turn it down. —Talk to him privately during a break . . . try and find out what's bothering him.
QUICK AND HELPFUL	• Really trying to help. • Makes it difficult by keeping others out.	—Cut across him tactfully by questioning others. —Thank him, suggest "we put others to work." —Use him for summarizing.
RAMBLER	• Talks about everything except subject. • Uses farfetched analogies, gets lost.	—When he stops for breath, thank him. Refocus his attention by restating the relevant points, and move on. —Grin, tell him his point is interesting, point to blackboard and in a friendly way indicate we are a bit off the subject. —Last resort, glance at watch.
PERSONALITY CLASH	• Two or more members clash. • Can divide your group into factions.	—Emphasize points of agreement. —Minimize points of disagreement (if possible). —Draw attention to the objective. —Cut across with direct question on topic. —Bring a sound member into the discussion. —Frankly ask that personalities be omitted.
OBSTINATE	• Won't budge! • Prejudiced. • Hasn't seen your point.	—Throw his view to group. Give them a chance to straighten him out. —Tell him time is short, you'll be glad to discuss it later. Suggest he accept the group viewpoint for the moment.
WRONG SUBJECT	• Not rambling, just off base.	—Take blame: "Something I said must have led you off subject, this is what we should be discussing" (restate point or use board). —Don't embarrass them.
SIDE CONVERSATION	• May be related to the subject. • May be personal. • Distracts members and you.	—Call one by name, ask him an easy question. —Call one by name, then restate the last opinion expressed made by a group member, and ask his opinion of it. —If you are in habit of moving around the room, stand casually behind members who are talking. THIS SHOULD NOT BE MADE OBVIOUS TO GROUP.
INARTICULATE	• Lacks ability to put thoughts in proper words. • Is getting idea but can't convey it. • Needs help.	—Don't say, "What you mean is this." —Say, "Let me repeat that" (then put it in better language). —Twist his ideas as little as possible, but have them make sense.
DEFINITELY WRONG	• Comes up with comment that is obviously incorrect.	—Say, "I can see how you feel." —Say, "I see your point, but can we reconcile that with the (true situation)?" HANDLE DELICATELY.

ASKS YOU FOR YOUR OPINION	• Trying to put you on spot. • Trying to have you support one view. • May be simply looking for your advice.	—Generally, avoid solving trainee problem. Help—yes. —Never takes sides. —There are times when you must—and should—give a direct answer. Before you do, try to determine the reason for your view. Say, "First, let's get some other opinions . . . Joe, how do you look upon this point?" (select a member to reply).
WON'T TALK	• Bored. • Indifferent. • Feels superior. • Timid. • Insecure.	—Your action depends on what is motivating him. —Arouse his interest by asking for his opinion. —Draw out the fellow next to him; then ask the quiet man to tell the fellow next to him what he thinks of the view expressed. —If he is seated near you, ask his opinion so that he'll feel he is talking to you, not the group. —If he is the "superior" type, ask him for his view after indicating the respect held for experience. (Don't overdo this. Group will resent it.) —Irritate him for a moment by tossing a provocative query. —The first time he does talk, compliment him. Be sincere!

© Donald Michalak

SECTION VIII

Evaluation Instruments

Evaluation forms represent an extremely wide range of format and content, depending upon what aspect of the training one wants to measure and analyze.

Form 1 is an evaluation form used by *Training* magazine.

Form 2 is employed by one branch of the armed services, courtesy of Mr. Gerald Wingate of the U.S. Marine Corps Air Station at Cherry Point, N.C.

Form 3 is probably the most typical, seeking data on content, presentation, and administration of the training program. Used by the American Society for Personnel Administration, it was supplied by Donald F. Michalak.

Form 4 is used by an observer to evaluate the extent to which training objectives were met.

Form 5 asks the participant to evaluate the course according to how well it achieved major training objectives.

Form 6 "Groupwork Evaluation Form," is used to evaluate the usefulness of groupwork done in training.

Form 7 is called "Self Development Actions," and is used at the end of training to help learners plan how they will use their new skills, what obstacles there will be to that application, and what they can do about these obstacles.

Form 1
Seminar Reaction Sheet

Please return your completed form to the door monitor as you leave the seminar room.

This reaction form is designed to collect your immediate reaction to the content and process of this session and your general feedback on the conference. The **TRAINING** staff reviews each sheet before forwarding them to the speaker(s). Your feedback is used in revising, expanding, adding or eliminating programs for future **TRAINING** conferences.

Session #_____ Session title_____

CONTENT:
1. What was your objective in attending this session?
   _____personal growth_____ideas for future action_____validate current activities_____other
2. Was this session appropriate for the accomplishment of that objective?
   _____yes_____not sure yet_____no
3. Which best describes the content of this session for you?
   _____too advanced_____O.K. for my needs_____too basic
4. Generally speaking, is the content of this session appropriate for future conferences?
   _____yes_____not sure_____no

PROCESS:
5. Circle the word in each pair that best describes the presenter(s).
   Name_____ dry/lively   organized/disorganized   interesting/dull
   Name_____ dry/lively   organized/disorganized   interesting/dull
   Name_____ dry/lively   organized/disorganized   interesting/dull
6. Please comment on one thing the speaker(s) did that you really liked.

7. What could have been done differently to make this session more worthwhile for you?

GENERAL FEEDBACK:
8. Did this session deliver what was promised?
   _____totally_____close enough_____not enough_____not at all
9. What other comments would you like to make about this session?

10. What comments would you like to make about **TRAINING MIDWEST '82** in general?

YOUR NAME (optional)_____   _____
COMPANY_____
ADDRESS _____
CITY_____STATE_____ZIP_____

Form 2
Course Evaluation

Course_____ Date_____

			YES	NO

1. Course Objectives   *YES* *NO*
   - a. Were they fully explained? ☐ ☐
   - b. Were they reviewed during the program? ☐ ☐
   - c. Were they reviewed at the conclusion of the program? ☐ ☐

   COMMENTS:

2.
   - a. Do you feel there was sufficient time and opportunity for questions and discussion by the group? ☐ ☐
   - b. Were the questions raised dealt with, either by the instructor(s) or the group? ☐ ☐

   COMMENTS:

3. What benefits do you feel you got from this session?
   - ☐ New knowledge that is pertinent.
   - ☐ Specific approaches, skills or techniques that I can apply on the job.
   - ☐ Change of attitude that will help me in my job.

   Other:

4. What do you feel are the major strengths of this course?

5. What is your evaluation of the student materials?

6. For items a through f, mark your response using these codes:

   4 Strongly Agree
   3 Agree
   2 Disagree
   1 Strongly Disagree

   _____a. The course content has been valuable for my professional or personal development.
   _____b. The course was well organized.
   _____c. The objectives set at the beginning of the course were met.
   _____d. Class time was well used.
   _____e. The amount of course work required was appropriate.
   _____f. The instruction in this class was excellent.

7. Would you recommend this course to your associates? If no, why not?

8. What significant changes can you recommend for improving future programs?

9. Please add any other comments you would like to make about any aspect of the course (instructor(s), materials, topics covered, etc.).

10. Please indicate your overall evaluation of this course.

Excellent					*Good*					*Satisfactory*					*Unsatisfactory*				
20	19	18	17	16	15	14	13	12	11	10	9	8	7	6	5	4	3	2	1

Optional: Agency_____ Name_____

Attributed to Gerald Wingate, Marine Corps Air Station, Cherry Point, NC.

Form 3
Seminar Evaluation

NAME (Optional)_____

SEMINAR TITLE _____

SEMINAR DATE/LOCATION_____

Please take a few minutes to fill out this seminar evaluation form. Your comments will be used to improve future offerings of this seminar.

1. APPRAISAL OF SEMINAR CONTENT:

		HIGH									LOW
a.	How much INTEREST did you have in the subject matter of this seminar?	10	9	8	7	6	5	4	3	2	1
b.	How much VALUE did you receive from this seminar?	10	9	8	7	6	5	4	3	2	1
c.	Would you recommend this course to others who are interested in the subject area covered by this seminar? WHY? _____	10	9	8	7	6	5	4	3	2	1

_____

d. In many cases it is difficult to find the right mix between theory and practical application. In terms of your needs, how do you evaluate this seminar?

Much Too Theoretical	Too Theoretical	Properly Balanced	Too Practical	Much Too Practical

e. Based on the stated objectives, did this seminar meet your expectations? _____

_____

2. SPEAKER EVALUATION:

Please evaluate the Speaker's effectiveness in the following areas:	EXCELLENT									POOR
a. Style and Delivery	10	9	8	7	6	5	4	3	2	1
b. Responsiveness to Participants	10	9	8	7	6	5	4	3	2	1
c. Knowledge of Subject	10	9	8	7	6	5	4	3	2	1

Other comments on Speaker's effectiveness _____

_____

d. Please comment on Speaker's use of Audio-Visuals (transparencies, slides, flip charts, etc.), group participation and role playing, seminar materials and handouts _____

_____

_____

3. SEMINAR EVALUATION:

a. What were the MOST effective segments? Why? _____

_____

b. What were the LEAST effective segments? Why? _____

_____

_____

4. ADMINISTRATIVE APPRAISAL:

Please comment on the following:
a.   HEADQUARTERS: Pre-registration service you received _____
   _____

b.   On-Site Coordination of the seminar by the local chapter representative _____
   _____

c.   Your comments on the meeting facilities _____
   _____

5.   How did you become aware of the seminar? _____
   Which of the following features were important in your decision to attend? (Rank in order of importance: 1, 2, 3, etc.)

Speaker   _____   Convenience of Date   _____
Subject Matter   _____   Recommendation of
ASPA's Reputation   _____   Employer, Co-worker, etc. _____
Convenience of Location   _____   Other   _____

6.   Any other comments you wish to make _____
   _____
   _____
   _____
   _____
   _____
   _____

THANK YOU!

Form 4
Classroom Observation Guide

A classroom observation guide must be designed to collect information about the extent to which training objectives are being met, and identify those factors in the instructional process which appear to impede or facilitate trainees' attainment of the objectives. Our sample classroom observation guide (over) has these main parts:

1. *Training objectives*. These provide a frame of reference within which the observer will base his judgments about the extent of objective attainment.
2. *Assessment*. Here the observer indicates the extent to which the objectives appear to have been attained by the trainees.
3. *Checks on attainment*. Here the observer is required to identify and judge the effectiveness of the checks made by the instructor during the session to monitor the extent to which training objectives are being attained.
4. *Factors influencing objective attainment*. The observer is required to add specificity to the general assessment which he made in 2 above.

The classroom observation approach differs from other methods in that the emphasis is on an individual *observing* the training situation and *making informed judgments* about the extent to which the objectives are being met. If the observation is to contribute significantly to the evaluation effort, the observer should have a sound background in the subject matter of the session he is monitoring, a precise knowledge of its training objectives, and an awareness of how this session ties into the entire instructional program.

The observer's presence during class should not be conspicuous. Therefore, the sample observation form has been designed to allow the observer to check the appropriate blocks during the session and fill in the required explanation later.

After the session, the observer should discuss with the instructor those factors which were believed to have facilitated or impeded the attainment of training objectives. Where appropriate, the oral critique should be followed by a written report in which effective and ineffective aspects previously discussed are noted along with recommendations for improvement. Such reports assume additional importance after the trainee performance data has been obtained, since performance data only indicates *what* has occurred while the observation reports along with opinion surveys can be used to explain *why* the trainees did or did not meet the objectives.

Classroom Observation Guide

Course _____ Session _____

Time _____ Date _____ Instructor _____

1. ***Training objectives***: _____
   _____
   _____
   _____

2. **Assessment**: To what extent did training objectives appear to be attained? (Adverse factors should be explained in item 4 below.)
   a. ☐ Fully. (Minor deficiencies, if any.)
   b. ☐ Partially. (Some factors preventing full achievement.)
   c. ☐ Hardly at all.

3. ***Checks on attainment***: What steps did the instructor take to assure himself that training objectives were being attained? _____
   _____
   _____

   How effective were they? _____
   _____

4. ***Factors influencing objective attainment***: Factors that had an adverse effect on training objective attainment as indicated in 2 above. (Check any such factors and explain on the back of this sheet.)

Factor	*Check*	*Factor*	*Check*
A. Introduction to training session	_____	I. Instructor's ability to direct discussion	_____
B. Content	_____	J. Appropriateness of material to group	_____
C. Clarity of explanations	_____	K. Time/material relationship	_____
D. Instructor's apparent knowledge of subject	_____	L. Individual trainee involvement	_____
E. Subject matter organization	_____	M. Instructional methods used	_____
F. Selection and use of training aids	_____	N. Reference materials	_____
G. Instructor's manner (tact, etc.)	_____	O. Classroom facilities	_____
G. Instructor's ability to mainain trainees' interest	_____	P. Tests and practical exercises	_____
		Q. Other (specify)	_____

_____

(Observer's Name)

_____

Modeled on materials developed by and for the U.S. Civil Service Commission.

Form 5
Workshop in Training Course Design

"This Is How It All Was"   Participant Opinion

1. Referring to your list of terminal objectives, please respond to the questions below by checking the appropriate blocks. Do elaborate or explain your opinion wherever you think it helpful to our assessment and improvement of the course.

(1) Major training objectives (refer to objective statements)	(2) As far as you are concerned, was this objective achieved?			(3) If the objective was not at all, or only partially, achieved, what factors were responsible? (Please check and explain below)										(4) Do you believe that this objective was related to the requirements of your job?			(5) Do you believe the benefits derived from pursuing this objective were worth the time and effort?		
	Definitely	To some extent	Not at all	The instructor	Lesson content	Instructional methods	Instructional level	Time allocation	Test and practical excersises	Reference materials	Training aids	Classroom facilities	Other	Definitely	To some extent (explain below)	Not at all (explain below)	Definitely	To some extent (explain below)	Not at all (explain below)
No. I																			
No. II																			
No. III																			

Objective No.	Explanations:

Modeled on materials developed by and for the U.S. Civil Service Commission.

Form 6
Group Work Evaluation Form

Please score the following questions along the scales provided: (1) represents the lowest rating and (9), the highest.

1. *Membership*: How much did you feel that you were a fully-functioning and accepted member of your group?

LOW   1   2   3   4   5   6   7   8   9   HIGH

2. *Goals*: How well-defined and clear was the purpose of your group?

LOW   1   2   3   4   5   6   7   8   9   HIGH

3. *Task*: How well did your group contribute to your understanding of the personal reactions and particular issues you presented to the group?

LOW   1   2   3   4   5   6   7   8   9   HIGH

4. *Process*: How much did you learn about group processes and how groups function?

LOW   1   2   3   4   5   6   7   8   9   HIGH

5. *Support*: How helped and/or supported did you feel in your group?

LOW   1   2   3   4   5   6   7   8   9   HIGH

6. *Value*: How valuable were your group sessions in terms of your course objectives?

LOW   1   2   3   4   5   6   7   8   9   HIGH

7. Additional Comments and Suggestions:

Name: _____
                  (optional)

Date: _____

Modeled on materials developed by and for the U.S. Civil Service Commission.

Form 7
Self-Development Actions

Name _____

Date _____
Training
Program _____

Some things to ask yourself:

Think in terms of the next 2–3 months. Turn this
sheet over for some Thought-Provoking Questions.

What am I going to do differently as a
result of this training?

_____

_____

_____

_____

_____

_____

_____

_____

_____

_____

_____

_____

How will I know if what I've done is working?
Or not working?

_____

_____

_____

_____

_____

_____

_____

_____

_____

_____

_____

_____

This is yours. Take it with you. Keep it where you will see it.

_____

Reprinted with the permission of Geoffrey Bellman. All rights reserved.

Integrating Training into Your Job

THOUGHT-PROVOKERS: To help you make your ideas work and keep them working for you.

Whom could I tell
about the changes
I plan to make?

My Boss?   My Secretary?

My Spouse?   A Subordinate?

A Friend?   Another Supervisor?

(It's best to tell someone
to whom it would make a
difference. This builds my
commitment.)

Who or what in the
organization might make it
difficult for me to
implement my actions?

What can I do to offset
their effects?

If I accomplish these
things, what will I gain?

HELP!

Where could I go for help
in making changes?

- Books?
- Films?
- College?

- The Library?
- Magazines?
- Professional
  Societies?
- Employee Relations
  Department?
- The Course Leader?
- Special Courses?

When will I take action?
When will I get results?

Should I establish
checkpoints in moving
from action to results?

If these development
actions work . . .

WHAT DO I DO NEXT?

SECTION IX

Training Aids Involving Training Budgets

Training budgets vary considerably in size and policy. The instruments exhibited here are designed to help determine the share of total budget that should be allocated to training ("Some Budgeting Policies for Training Functions") and what costs should be attributed to training ("The Cost of Doing Training").

The third instrument is actually a case study (or exercise) developed for use with the "Cost Analyzer" developed by the Praxis Corporation, which was later merged into the Kepner-Tregow organization. This exercise was developed for an institute of the American Society for Training and Development and was used in the early 1970s as a way to learn how to apply the Praxis Cost-Benefit Model.

Some Budgeting Policies for Training Functions

A. Typical training budgets are from 1% to 1.5% of the total employee salary budget.
   In my organization at this time, a realistic figure would be _____ %

B. One Training and Development Professional per 100 employees is typical.
   Right now, my organization probably needs one per _____ employees.

C. Departments in which this ratio might vary, and the number per 100 might be:

   _____ : _____ per 100
   _____ : _____ per 100

D. Should the Training Department Be a profit center, allocating its costs to client (using) departments by charging tuition?

   IT ALREADY IS   IT IS NOT BUT SHOULD BE   IT SHOULD NOT BE A "P.C."

E. Perhaps training costs should be divided between the Training Department and using departments. If so, how should the costs be Charged?

	Divided Equally	Training Dept.	Using Dept.	Other: Explain
Training Staff Salaries				
Program Production Costs				
Training Materials				
Training Facilities (Building/Rentals)				
Training Department Overhead				
Travel Costs of Trainees				
Trainee Salaries				
Tuition for Outside Programs				
Outside Resources (Trainers/Consultants)				
Production Lost While in Training				
Evaluation Datagathering & Analysis				
(Other) _____				
(Other) _____				

© Dugan Laird

The Cost of Doing Training

		DIVIDE BY # TRAINEES TO GET PER TRAINEE COST.	DIVIDE BY # HOURS IN COURSE TO GET PER HOUR COST.

PRODUCTION COSTS:

DESIGNERS _____ X MEDIAN SALARY _____ X HOURS _____   EQUALS _____

DESIGNERS _____ X TRAVEL TICKETS _____   ,,   _____ _____ _____

DESIGNERS _____ X PER DIEM _____ X DAYS _____   ,,   _____ _____ _____

DESIGNERS _____ X OVERHEAD _____ X HOURS _____   ,,   _____ _____ _____

FILM (PRODUCE: $2000/MIN.) RENTALS: _____ X DAYS _____   ,,   _____ _____ _____
AUDIO TAPE (PRODUCE: $100/MIN.) COPIES: $2.80/TAPE   ,,   _____ _____ _____
SLIDES FOR 35 MM (PRODUCE: $30/SLIDE; COPIES .75 EACH)   ,,   _____ _____ _____
ARTWORK ($1.50/SQUARE INCH)   ,,   _____ _____ _____
OVERHEAD TRANSPARENCIES (PHOTO $90; ARTWORK $10 EACH)   ,,   _____ _____ _____
MANUALS & MATERIALS (TOTAL CONTRACTS OR PRO-RATA CHARGES
    IN-HOUSE)   ,,   _____ _____ _____
OTHER (SPECIFY)   ,,   _____ _____ _____

TRAINEE COSTS:

PER PAY-GROUP _____ X MEDIAN SALARY _____ X HOURS _____   ,,   _____ _____ _____
TOTAL # TRAINEES _____ X TRAVEL & PER DIEM _____ X DAYS _____   ,,   _____ _____ _____

CONDUCTING THE COURSE:

INSTRUCTORS _____ X MEDIAN RATE _____ X HOURS _____   ,,   _____ _____ _____
INSTRUCTORS _____ X PER DIEM _____ X DAYS _____   ,,   _____ _____ _____
INSTRUCTORS _____ X TRAVEL TICKETS AVERAGE _____   ,,   _____ _____ _____
FACILITIES RENTAL/OVERHEAD _____ X DAYS _____   ,,   _____ _____ _____
EQUIPMENT PURCHASE OR RENTALS _____   ,,   _____ _____ _____

EVALUATING THE COURSE:

DESIGN HOURS _____ X MEDIAN SALARY _____   ,,   _____ _____ _____
PRINTING AND PUBLISHING AND CORRESPONDING: _____   ,,   _____ _____ _____
MEDIAN SALARY OF RESPONDENTS _____ X HOURS/FRACTIONS _____   ,,   _____ _____ _____
ANALYSIS HOURS _____ X MEDIAN SALARY _____   EQUALS _____

TOTAL COSTS OF THE COURSE: $ _____ _____ _____

© Dugan Laird

Estimating Cost of Deficiencies

	SD	1–10	%

To find the cost due to lack of skill:
1. List performance deficiencies above in order of importance.
2. Rate each deficiency from 1 to 10 (1 = not much impact and 10 = affects greatly)
3. Calculate the percentage by multiplying the *weight of each item* by 100; then divide by the *total weighting*.
4. Estimate the total cost of the problem.
5. Identify which items are attributed to skill deficiency.
6. Multiply the total percentage due to skill deficiency by the cost of the problem.

For further use of these computations, see below and the next page.

_____

Course Name

Duration ☐ Days

True Cost of Training $_____

Amount Billed to Depts. (Tuition) $_____

Estimated Cost of Problem $_____

Cost Due to Lack of Skill $_____

Request Initiated by

Name _____

Title _____

Department _____

Estimate ☐   Date of Request _____

Actual ☐   Date of Reply _____

Recommendations:

Tuition Per Student	$		True Cost of Training	$	
A) Instructor Costs			Item	Salary Factor	Cost $
_____ Days @$_____	$		Salaries of Students		
B) Course Material Costs			Organization Benefits	.33	
			Replacement Cost	1.	
	$		Lost Production	1.	
C) Cost of Classroom	$		Overhead	1.5	
D) Course Design Costs			Tuition		
			Administration	.33	
	$		Travel		
E) Number of Students			Total		

From the Praxis Corp., New York, NY

Cost-Benefit Computations:

A case study to use with the paper computer which follows

You are Training Director for Dobbs, whose entire operation is in Amos, Maine. At your training center, Staff Specialists earn median annual salaries of $24,000; operating costs run $100 per classroom-day. At the moment, you face two requests for training. Which program offers Dobbs the greater economic benefits?

Request #1 involves 40 Maintenance Engineers, who not surprisingly earn the same median salary as Staff Specialists. These people are terrible troubleshooters. They know neither good troubleshooting technique nor the 200 machines they're supposed to maintain. Hard data prove that a "down" machine costs the company $100 per hour in lost production, labor and material. Downtime last year averaged 2½ hours per machine per week; standards (based on manufacturers' warranties) are set at 90 minutes per machine per week.

Program development will be expensive. Your Specialist would need to devote one year, and would require equivalent time from Maintenance Engineers to supply technical aid. Company policy demands that all the training be accomplished during working hours. This program will probably use self-study and programmed instruction, requiring a typical 120 hours of trainee time. Elaborately illustrated books are a must—at $250 per set! Even with all this, the engineers would be able to handle only those troubles which cause 90% of the downtime.

Request #2 concerns 100 supervisors who should decide grievances—but who really give decisions only 10% of the time. These men and women earn $320 per week, and face about two grievances per month. For each they spend two hours in research, two more preparing the document which is the only form of feedback the grievant gets. Trouble is, they say "No Decision" too often, bucking it up to one of 20 Chiefs. You have determined this to be a D_K; the supervisors don't know the regulations.

Chiefs earn 50% higher salary, and fortunately they work faster. They do the research in an hour, then spend two hours writing reports. Even so, only 30% of their effort produces a decision. At this point, grievances go to a Specialist for a mandatory decision.

Analysis of objectives and content indicates a two-day program, accommodating 20 trainees per session. Material costs are negligible; you can use actual grievances and copies of the manual. Program development, including the "front end analysis" already finished, would consume a month of time from one of your specialists.

Which program offers Dobbs the greater economic payoff?

A PAPER COMPUTER

Individual Application Log #1

1. In the space provided, write the #1 critical performance problem in your organization.

2. How is poor performance hurting your organization? What is the Value Basis of the deficiency?

3. For the Value Basis you have stated, what is a single unit?

4. What is the highest value of a single unit—in dollars?

   What is the lowest value of a single unit—in dollars?

   | HIGH |
   | LOW |

5. How many units are lost or wasted by the employee in a year? (If you measure in days, or weeks, convert to one year.)

6. How many people perform the job in which the deficiency is being measured?

7. How much is the total cost of the performance deficiency to your organization each year? (Multiply 4 High × 5 × 6; then multiply 4 LOW × 5 × 6 to estimate both an upward and lower cost.)

   | HIGH |
   | LOW |

You have just computed the cost of a deficiency in performance to your organization. In other words, you have analyzed a potential training need to see whether or not it is worth pursuing. If you feel that the potential savings exceed the potential cost of training, you go on with the next steps in the training cycle. Otherwise, you invest your energies in more serious performance deficiences.

A PAPER COMPUTER*

Individual Application Log #2

1. In the space provided, write the #2 critical performance problem in your organization.

2. How is poor performance hurting your organization? What is the Value Basis of the deficiency?

3. For the Value Basis you have stated, what is a single unit?

4. What is the highest value of a single unit—in dollars?

    HIGH

    What is the lowest value of a single unit—in dollars?

    LOW

5. How many units are lost or wasted by the employee in a year? (If you measure in days, or weeks, convert to one year.)

6. How many people perform the job in which the deficiency is being measured?

7. How much is the total cost of the performance deficiency to your organization each year? (Multiply 4 High × 5 × 6; then multiply 4 LOW × 5 × 6 to estimate both an upward and lower cost.)

    HIGH

    LOW

You have just computed the cost of a deficiency in performance to your organization. In other words, you have analyzed a potential training need to see whether or not it is worth pursuing. If you feel that the potential savings exceed the potential cost of training, you go on with the next steps in the training cycle. Otherwise, you invest your energies in more serious performance deficiences.

© Dugan Laird
The Praxis Corporation, New York, NY.

SECTION X

Miscellaneous Training Aids and Instruments

The remaining instruments cover a wide array of applications. Each is labeled to reflect its intent.

1. A checklist to use on people who are leaving for training
2. A worksheet to use when designing behavioral objectives
3. A sample task analysis (job breakdown; completed)
4. A sample task analysis guide (different worksheet)
5. A list of principles for facilitative learning
6. Ten considerations *when* using consultants
7. A list of 12 mistakes made by change agents
8. A list of 13 things change agents should do
9. A checklist for apprentice training
10. A chart on developmental needs for training staff
11. A self-diagnostic instrument about learning style
12. A process chart showing how to integrate training programs with line activities

Before You Send Them Off To Training

Ask These Questions

		Yes	No
1.	Does the brochure publish learning objectives or expected outcomes which your employee will use on the job?	___	___
2.	Are those outcomes stated in behavioral terms?	___	___
3.	Are the behaviors observable, measurable & reasonable?	___	___
4.	Is a topical outline included in the announcement?	___	___
5.	Does the brochure specify who should attend? (Nature of position? Experience assumed? Level of position?)	___	___
6.	Does the schedule provide time for students to raise issues and ask questions?	___	___
7.	Does the time schedule look flexible? (Can it possibly be completed? Can it adapt to individual needs?)	___	___
8.	Is there provision for "process feedback" to let learners tell leaders how needs are/are not being met?	___	___
9.	Does the brochure mention learning methods to be used?	___	___
10.	Do these methods involve "action training" so trainees will get involved in something besides listening & watching?	___	___
11.	Is there workshop time so your employees can contemplate ways to apply their learnings back on the job?	___	___
12.	Does there seem to be a chance for your employees to access leaders in small group or one-on-one conversation?	___	___
13.	Are the leaders well known to you or managers in the field for which they are leading this training?	___	___
14.	Have the leaders published on this subject? (If so, does the course promise more than one could get by just reading their published work?)	___	___
15.	Have the leaders worked in or consulted with your type of organization (corporate, bureaucratic, association) or is their background entirely academic?	___	___

A Worksheet to Use When Determining Objectives for Training Programs

We say that we train or teach in order to produce behavior. It follows, then, that to the degree we can define the behavior we wish to produce, we increase our chance of successful instruction. Thus we try to define

PERFORMANCE OBJECTIVES

As a result of our instruction, our learners will become able to:

Do These Things (Observable Actions)	To These Standards (Measurable Statements of Criteria: How Often? How Well? How Much?)	Under These Conditions (Critical Variables Which Modify the Performance)

Adapted from Dugan Laird, *Approaches To Training and Development,* © Addison-Wesley, Reading, Massachusetts.

Job Breakdown Blueprint

JOB BREAKDOWN SHEET FOR TRAINING PURPOSES

DEPARTMENT _Lens Grinding_   JOB _Centering_

BREAKDOWN MADE BY _Joseph Nelson_   DATE _Sept. 2, 1941_

IMPORTANT STEPS
 	
(WHAT TO DO)
A logical segment of the operation,
when something happens to advance the work
	KEY POINTS
	
	(HOW TO DO IT)
	Anything that may:
	    Make or break the job
	    Injure the worker
	    Make the work easier to do

1. Place piece on plate against regulating wheel	Knack - don't catch on wheel
2. Lower level wheel	Hold at end of stroke (count 1, 2, 3, 4) Slow feed. Watch - no oval grinding
3. Raise lever - release	
4. Gauge pieces periodically	More often as approach tolerance
5. Readjust regulating wheel as required	Watch - no backlash
6. Repeat above until finished	

Task Analysis Guide

For _____
Give the name of the over-all task

STEPS Actions to take	STANDARDS How it must be done	VARIATIONS (If any) OR SPECIAL CONDITIONS	NEW KNOWLEDGE Which learners must have

Ten Considerations When Using Consultants

1. What is the consulting firm's reputation? Consultants range from the eminent authority to less than eminence. There are aggressive sales personnel, whose business is vending their various software products—and the moonlighting academicians, who range from the research-oriented lecturer-mumbler to the "circus performer." And sadly, there are outright fakers and incompetents. Don't assume that the quality of the printing in the brochures proves the quality of the consulting firm.

2. How did they happen to contact your training office? Was it done by referral? What is the reputation of the individual who made the referral? Was he trying to get rid of a pest by foisting him off onto your organization? Or, did the consulting firm make contact with you as a result of your membership in some organization? Ask the consultant, if he has made the opening contact, why he believes he is particularly qualified to serve you and your organization.

3. What are the references of the consulting firm? Have these been verified?

Answers to the following are particularly useful:

a. For whom has this consulting firm performed in the past?

b. What specific types of training activities have they presented?

c. How effective have these been?

A letter or telephone call to one or two clients may clear up any doubts and can also stir up useful ideas. In the author's experience, he has found a number of "consultants" claiming clients which they never had. The consulting firm had *talked* to the supposed clients, but had never performed a bit of work for them.

4. Who are the consultants' instructors? What are *their* professional backgrounds?

Large consulting firms often employ junior members as "trainees." Such trainees have had minimal experience. They may be cutting their teeth on your firm. Check the experiences of the particular individuals who will be working for you—and make certain that the contract, if there is one, clearly indicates the names of the personnel who will be performing the work.

5. How is the organization unique? What original, innovative work has this consulting organization created which makes it *uniquely* useful to your business and to the fulfillment of the training objectives which you set?

Training experiences in an airline may or may not be useful in a public utility. Here, the trainer must ultimately make a value judgment concerning the contribution which the outsider asserts he can provide. If an exchange of ideas (from one industry to another) is

desirable, well and good! If not, the consultant's constant reference to another field can be a bore, turning everyone off. The need for well defined objectives is again made clear.

6. How does this consulting group evaluate its own effectiveness? What attempts do they make to evaluate past performance on a *long-term basis*?

Feedback at the end of a consulting activity may be self-satisfying, particularly if the presenters were spell-binders. Yet the long-range usefulness of the consulting expenditure may be another matter.

7. What original *written* materials, manuals or other publications will be made available to your organization by the consulting firm? Are these applicable or must these be completely rewritten? Are the publications included in the total price, or is there a follow-up price based on the number of copies used?

It is vital that such publications and handouts be carefully read to check suitability. Often old bones from other cemeteries, encased in slick covers with fancy plastic bindings, are handed out. These are subsequently stored away by the trainees, rarely to be read or used.

8. Is the consulting firm using the contract with your organization as a "learning experience" for itself?

If formal classroom instruction is included, how much time will be spent by your trainees explaining exactly what they do to the outside consultants? Who is training whom? This factor can be overcome by better selection and better briefing—in depth—by the organization's trainer.

9. If formal classroom instruction is required, is the consulting firm providing a course outline and a detailed course of study?

Such materials should fit your organization's need fairly precisely and must tie in with the formal objectives which you fixed before bringing the consulting firm into the picture.

10. Finally, has the fee schedule been carefully considered and have you made an effort to determine comparable fees from other consulting firms?

Everyone is not worth the same level of reimbursement, but the consultant you need may not be the most expensive. In most instances fixed *per diem* schedules should be avoided. Written agreements or contracts are desirable when complex and long-term activities are to be fulfilled.

To sum up: A good trainer will perceive when he requires outside assistance. He develops objectives seeking help. He applies common sense rules before he hires.

My 12 Mistakes as a Change Agent

In our examination of effective performance as change agents, we will complete several tasks using this list.

1. Not realizing the client does not want to change.
2. Changing only a sub-system.
3. Attempting bottom up change.
4. Becoming trapped in one part.
5. Imposing my values.
6. Not being sufficiently candid.
7. Creating a change overload.
8. Inappropriate attachment.
9. Failing to analyze resistance with the client.
10. Losing professional detachment.
11. Not seeking help myself.
12. Unbalanced use of behavioral versus structural interventions.

Based on notes on a lecture given by W.J. Reddin (of Managerial Effectiveness, Ltd.) at The Second International Training and Development Conference, Bath, U.K., 1973

13 Rules-of-Thumb for Change Agents

1. STAY ALIVE. Beware self-sacrifice to a cause you don't want to be your last! This doesn't say never take a risk—but do so as part of a purposeful strategy, appropriately timed.
2. START WHERE THE SYSTEM IS. Systems don't necessarily like being diagnosed. Change agents must understand how the clients see themselves and their situation—must understand the culture of the system.
3. NEVER WORK UPHILL. Use organic, not mechanistic approaches to change. Use collaborative approaches, building strength—and building on strength.
4. DON'T BUILD HILLS AS YOU GO. Why work in ways which develop resistance?... with programs which are favorable to one part of the population, but which have the opposite effect on other portions?
5. WORK IN THE MOST PROMISING ARENA. You can spend years lost, shoring up weak troops, working with incompetent managers in outlying areas.
6. BUILD RESOURCES. Don't do anything alone that can be done more easily or more certainly by a team.
7. DON'T OVER-ORGANIZE. The democratic ideologies of participative management can sometimes interfere with common sense.
8. DON'T ARGUE IF YOU CAN'T WIN. Win-Lose strategies are to be avoided. They deepen conflict instead of resolving it.
9. PLAY GOD A LITTLE. If the change agent doesn't make the critical value decisions, someone else will be glad to do so.
10. INNOVATION REQUIRES A GOOD IDEA, INITIATIVE AND A FEW FRIENDS! The quality of the partner is as important as the idea—but the partners need not be numerous.
11. LOAD EXPERIMENTS FOR SUCCESS. This doesn't mean scientific immorality; it means to build an umbrella over the experiment.
12. LIGHT MANY FIRES. A large monolithic development has high visibility—and is a good target! It also prevents other subsystems from feeling ownership.
13. CAPTURE THE MOMENT. If something is possible, but not in your plan—scuttle the plan!
14. KEEP AN OPTIMISTIC BIAS. Individuals and groups locked in destructive conflict focus on their differences; the change agent's job is to help them discover and build on their commonalities!

Checklist for Apprentice Programs

Training System
☐ There is a policymaking body and it has responsibility for program development.
☐ Program objectives are written, distributed, and continuously evaluated.
☐ Training objectives are based on the skills, knowledge, and attitudes needed by journeymen in the trade; results are measured against these benchmarks.
☐ Administrative head is appointed by policymaking body and is responsible for implementation of its policy directives.
☐ Lines of authority and responsibility are clear and everyone in the administration knows how he fits in.
☐ Jobs in administration have descriptions and titles which match the job.
☐ Communication channels are established and maintained.
☐ Budget is adequate to provide continuity of training.
☐ Legal and authorized budgeting and accounting procedures are used.

Recruitment and Selection
☐ Training glossary is developed and disseminated.
☐ Trainees are recruited from all possible sources.
☐ Recruitment and selection procedures are established on a sound legal base and are made known to the public.
☐ Policy for granting advanced standing to entering trainees with applicable education or experience exists and is universally applied.
☐ Schools and other sources of trainees are provided up-to-date information on training and career opportunities in the trade.
☐ Recruitment and selection practices are studied and dropouts followed up in order to analyze retention rates.

Training Process
☐ Apprentices, journeymen, instructors, and related training personnel participate in executing a fully planned and developed curriculum.
☐ Trade analysis techniques are used to identify course content, whether for national, regional, or single-employer curriculum.
☐ Presentation of subject is in best manner to assure learning and provide for successive levels of achievement.
☐ Administrative officer controls curriculum through planning guide, and keeps record of what, when, where, and to whom content will be or was taught.
☐ National training materials are developed that can be modified according to local needs.
☐ Training materials for the instructor are also developed.
☐ Instructional material includes nontechnical subject matter, such as work planning, as well as technical subject matter.
☐ In on-the-job training, adequate job rotation is provided through jobs that provide a challenge.

☐ On-the-job training is correlated with related instruction.
☐ On-the-job training jobsites are suitable for training; production demands are not too heavy for training purposes and there is an adequate ratio of journeymen to apprentices to assure proper attention to training.
☐ Provision is made for determining achievement levels of trainees in on-the-job training.
☐ In related instruction, physical facilities are adequate and class sizes manageable.
☐ A plan for determining post-apprentice training needs and desires for journeymen is utilized.
☐ Continuation training is jointly planned and sponsored, with a view toward assuring continued job proficiency and adjustment to technological change.
☐ Journeyman training costs are shared by the employer.
☐ Records and credit for advanced training are provided.
☐ Timing of theory and skill training is coordinated in instruction.
☐ Trade materials and publications in adequate quantity are used as adjuncts to classroom training.
☐ Classroom credit is adequately appraised and recorded.
☐ If special courses are needed for groups or individuals, they are provided.
☐ Manufacturers' resources are used in training, i.e., their schools, trade literature, representatives, and the like.
☐ A competitive atmosphere is sought in training.
☐ Opportunity to contribute to trade literature is provided.
☐ Problem-solving activities are designed to develop ingenuity, leadership, and initiative.
☐ Field trips are used to acquaint trainees with new methods and modern facilities.
☐ Modern teaching tools and techniques are used in all phases of instruction.
☐ Performance standards realistically reflect industrial practice.
☐ Trainee is monitored by single individual throughout all phases of training, and adequate record of his progress and achievement is kept.
☐ Method and frequency of evaluation should meet with trainee's satisfaction.
☐ Teaching is geared to the interest and abilities of the trainees.
☐ Provision is made for adequate counseling.
☐ Instructors are selected on basis of trade competence and teaching ability.
☐ Instructor recruitment is aided by adequate recognition through economic reward and through licensing and/or certification.
☐ Training for instructors occurs both prior to and during teaching.
☐ Provision is made for periodic review of program content with view toward updating.
☐ Provision is made for forecasting technological changes and the demands they will place on the training program.

Apprentice Agreement

☐ Apprentice agreements are written and available to all parties, and special effort is made to make sure the apprentice understands his.

☐ Period of apprentice agreement is specified, whether in terms of time or competency evaluation.

☐ Apprentice agreement is comprehensive, covering terms and conditions of employment, requirements for related instruction, schedules of work processes, and responsibilities of all parties under it.

Facilities

☐ School and industry mix of facilities and equipment is adequate for training.

☐ Training stations are accessible to trainees.

☐ Space and facilities are adequate to provide for planning and implementing instruction utilizing modern techniques and technology.

☐ Safety is stressed and periodic inspections are made for hazardous conditions at training sites.

Public Relations

☐ A joint public relations program continuously presents a positive image of trade training.

☐ Trade contests, formal events, and awards help tell the apprenticeship program's story to the public.

☐ Liaison is kept and cooperation sought among labor, industry, government, and educators in advancing the common goals of trade training.

Research

☐ A research and development program provides the key to appraising the entire system on a continuing basis.

☐ Major economical, social, political, and technological forces are watched to determine their impact on trade practices and training.

On Developing the Training Specialists

Will they . . .

	Then the minimum requirements would include:	Enrichments should bring competence in:
Conduct training?	Behavioral objectives Learning theory Reinforcement theory Listening skills Questioning skills Discussion leading Lecture & demonstration Job instruction training	Case methods In-baskets Sensitivity training Use of media Open classroom and LCI Incident process cases Action mazes Roleplaying

When training staff employees who will conduct and design training/learning experiences, stress application rather than knowledge. At least 50% of staff training should go to workshops and try-out of the new skills.

Design training?	Behavioral objectives Learning theory Reinforcement theory Feedback systems Logical outlining Use of media Case methods Discussion leading Job instruction training Brainstorming	Conference design Programmed instruction Open classroom and LCI In-baskets Critical incident process Writing skills Roleplaying Reverse roleplaying Fishbowls
Administer training?	Planning skills Organizing skills Listening skills Questioning skills Speaking skills Discussion leading Budgeting skills	Sensitivity training Organization development PLUS At least 70% of the skills required of instructors and designers
Consult to the organization?	Listening skills Questioning skills Reinforcement theory Sensitivity training Performance analysis Problem-solving skills	Organization development Speaking skills Writing skills PLUS All skills listed for the instructor and designer
None of these?	Do not train any staff member in skills which will not be demanded of that member in day-to-day assignments. Such "overkill" is paralyzing to the department—but mostly to the people who must then be unfulfilled by their work!	

© Dugan Laird

A Self-Diagnosis Tool to Understand Your Learning Style
How Do You Learn?

Do all people learn in the same way? Let's find out. This experiment is based on an inventory developed by Kolb and McIntyre.

FIRST, rank the words on each line. Put "4" by the word best describing you; "3" by the next best, on down to "1"—but with no ties!

____	Involved	____	Tentative	____	Discriminating	____	Practical
____	Receptive	____	Impartial	____	Analytical	____	Relevant
____	Feeling	____	Watching	____	Thinking	____	Doing
____	Accepting	____	Aware	____	Evaluative	____	Risk-taker
____	Intuitive	____	Questioning	____	Logical	____	Productive
____	Concrete	____	Observing	____	Abstract	____	Active
____	Present-oriented	____	Reflecting	____	Future-oriented	____	Pragmatic
____	Experience	____	Observation	____	Conceptualization	____	Experimentation
____	Intense	____	Reserved	____	Rational	____	Responsible
____	Open to new experience	____	Perceptive	____	Intelligent	____	Competent

____ Total (CS)   ____ Total (AR)   ____ Total (AS)   ____ Total (CR)

Now, rank these clusters of learning methods. Again, "4" is what you like best. Put "1" by the least favored, with "2" and "3" also cited. No ties are allowed!

Workbooks; manuals; fieldtrips; lectures with drawings, models & demonstration; step-by-step instructions; drill.

RANK: ____

Movies; filmstrips with records; discussion among students; short reading assignments; lectures with discussion.

RANK: ____

NOW, total the numbers in each column at the top of the page; chart them on this wheel. Each "tick" represents 5 points from the center.

NEXT, connect the marks so you form a rough rectangle.

AFTER you have constructed your rectangle, see in which direction it "points." If you are congruent about your learning style, it will point toward the methods you like best.

Lectures; slides; audio tapes & phonograph records; oral or written reports; extensive textbook readings.

RANK: ____

Games & simulations; brief lectures; optional readings; independent study; problem solving activities.

RANK: ____

CS refers to "Concrete-Sequential" styles of learning; AS means "Abstract-Sequential; AR denotes "Abstract-Random" while CR means "Concrete Random" learning preferences.

Making Training Work

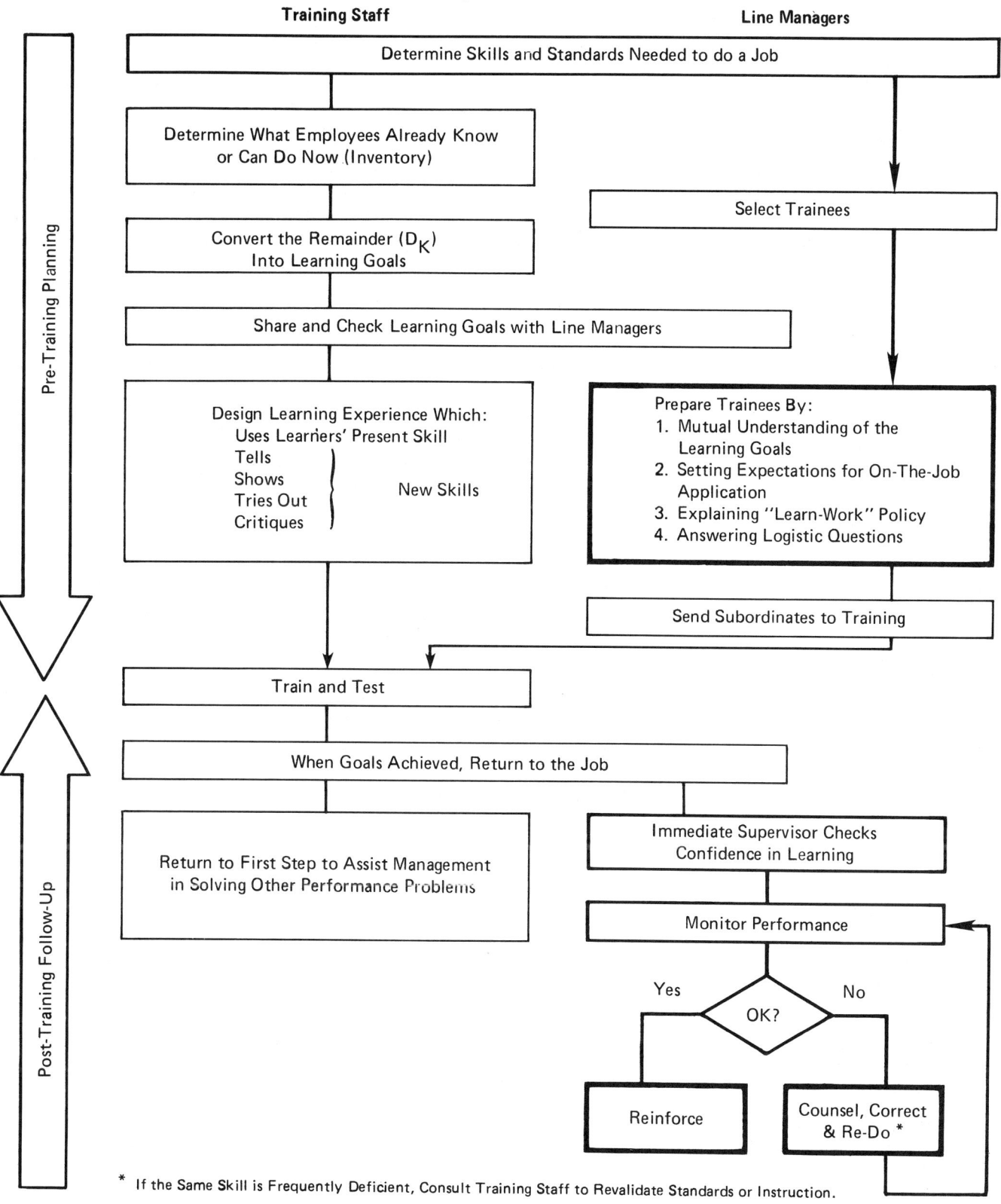

Training Staff   **Line Managers**

Pre-Training Planning

Determine Skills and Standards Needed to do a Job

Determine What Employees Already Know or Can Do Now (Inventory)

Convert the Remainder (D_K) Into Learning Goals

Share and Check Learning Goals with Line Managers

Design Learning Experience Which:
Uses Learners' Present Skill
Tells
Shows   New Skills
Tries Out
Critiques

Select Trainees

Prepare Trainees By:
1. Mutual Understanding of the Learning Goals
2. Setting Expectations for On-The-Job Application
3. Explaining "Learn-Work" Policy
4. Answering Logistic Questions

Send Subordinates to Training

Train and Test

When Goals Achieved, Return to the Job

Post-Training Follow-Up

Return to First Step to Assist Management in Solving Other Performance Problems

Immediate Supervisor Checks Confidence in Learning

Monitor Performance

OK?
Yes   No

Reinforce

Counsel, Correct & Re-Do *

* If the Same Skill is Frequently Deficient, Consult Training Staff to Revalidate Standards or Instruction.